Wissenschaftliche Untersuchungen
zum Neuen Testament · 2. Reihe

Herausgegeben von
Jörg Frey, Martin Hengel, Otfried Hofius

152

Dieter,

Sixteen years ago we met, the tangible consequence of which appears now in this book. More broadly, you taught me what it is to be a scholar. It is a pleasure to present this volume to you in gratitude.

Dale
Christmas 2002

Donald Dale Walker

Paul's Offer of Leniency (2 Cor 10:1)

Populist Ideology and Rhetoric
in a Pauline Letter Fragment

Mohr Siebeck

DONALD DALE WALKER, born 1961; 1998 Ph.D. University of Chicago; currently Associate Director of Development at the University of Chicago Library, Chicago, IL, USA.

ISBN 3-16-147891-6
ISSN 0340-9570 (Wissenschaftliche Untersuchungen zum Neuen Testament 2. Reihe)

Die Deutsche Bibliothek lists this publication in the Deutsche Nationalbibliographie; detailed bibliographic data is available in the Internet at *http://dnb.ddb.de*.

© 2002 by J.C.B. Mohr (Paul Siebeck), P.O. Box 2040, D-72010 Tübingen.

This book may not be reproduced, in whole or in part, in any form (beyond that permitted by copyright law) without the publisher's written permission. This applies particularly to reproductions, translations, microfilms and storage and processing in electronic systems.

The book was printed by Druck Partner Rübelmann GmbH in Hemsbach on non-aging paper and bound by Buchbinderei Schaumann in Darmstadt.

Printed in Germany.

Preface

This study was originally a doctoral dissertation written at the University of Chicago under the direction of Hans Dieter Betz, whose guidance I am proud to acknowledge. It was an enormous boon to have him as a resource and critic, for his insights consistently added depth to my investigation. As I reflect on this gratefully, I would add that this work is but the culmination of a larger process of education for which thanks are equally due.

Others too have shared in this enterprise, whose assistance I am pleased to recognize: Adela Yarbro Collins, Elizabeth Asmis, and Arthur Droge. They proved themselves gracious and helpful, as they asked questions, offered comments, added perspective, and insisted on clarity of both thought and expression. Looking now at the final product, I see the fingerprints of all four (untiring) professors, whom I thank.

I would like also to express my gratitude to the editors for accepting this work as part of Wissenschaftliche Untersuchungen zum Neuen Testament 2. Reihe and Dr. Georg Siebeck for publishing it. In making the transition from a 1998 dissertation to a 2002 monograph, a few minor revisions have been introduced. The staff at Mohr/Siebeck has been delightful to work with and made the task of bringing the manuscript to print enjoyable. Danke sehr.

Lastly, I wish to thank my wife, Jill. Without her this labor would never have succeeded, so with gratitude I dedicate this work to her.

Many translations of ancient and modern sources appear in this work. Unless noted otherwise, translations of ancient sources are taken from the Loeb Classical Library. I have provided my own translations of ancient and modern literature where no published translation was available.

Chicago, IL   Donald Dale Walker

Table of Contents

Preface v
Abbreviations ix

Introduction 1

I. History of Research: ἐπιείκεια and πραΰτης in 2 Corinthians 10:1 9
   1. Survey of Research 10
   2. Summary of Previous Research 33

II. Semantic Investigation πραΰτης and ἐπιείκεια 38
   1. ἐπιείκεια 38
      a. Lexicons on ἐπιείκεια 39
      b. Ancient Definitions of ἐπιείκεια 41
      c. The Nuances of ἐπιείκεια 44
      d. Defining ἐπιείκεια 51
   2. πραότης/πραΰτης 53
      a. Lexicons on πραότης/πραΰτης 53
      b. Ancient Definitions of πραότης/πραΰτης 54
      c. Nuances of πραότης/πραΰτης 56
      d. Defining πραότης/πραΰτης 61
   3. ἐπιείκεια and πραότης 62
      a. Pragmatics of ἐπιείκεια and πραότης in Conjunction 62
      b. The Semantic Field Encompassing Both ἐπιείκεια and πραότης 76
   4. 2 Corinthians 10:1a and 10:1–13:10 82
      a. Paul's Offer of Leniency 82
      b. Paul, the LXX, and Early Christian Literature 84
   5. Conclusion 89

III. Christ the Good King: The Leniency and Clemency of Christ in Paul's
    Christology 91
   1. Sources for Good King *Topoi* 92
   2. Dissemination of Good King *Topoi* 103
   3. Survey of the Good King *Topoi* 121
   4. The πραότης and/or ἐπιείκεια of a King 140
   5. Evidence of the Good King in Paul's Epistles 145
   6. The Good King in Paul's Theology 161
   7. The Christology of 2 Corinthians 10:1 183

IV. Paul's Practice of Leniency: Clemency in His Ministry
to the Corinthians and in Greco-Roman Society 189
  1. Leniency and Clemency in the Greek and Romans Worlds 191
  2. Rationales for Acting with Leniency and Clemency 231
  3. Problems Inherent to Leniency and Clemency 239
  4. Paul's Use of Leniency and Clemency 242
  5. Conclusion 257

V. Paul's Self-Presentation in 2 Corinthians 10–13:
Modest, Populist, and Antiencomiastic Rhetoric 258
  1. Ethical Argumentation in Classical Rhetoric 260
  2. Paul's Ethical Argument: Modesty and Populism 266
  3. Style: Socrates' Combination of Modesty and Irony 285
  4. Beyond Modesty: The Socratic Subversion of Encomiastic Rhetoric ... 291
  5. ἠθοποιία: The Fool's (Foolish) Rejection of Modesty 299
  6. Paul's Paradoxical Socratic Irony 312
  7. The Basis of Paul's Counterculture: Christology 318
  8. Conclusion 325

Conclusion 326

Appendix 1: Definition of ἐπιείκεια 331

Appendix 2: Definition of πραότης/πραΰτης 336

Appendix 3: Wisdom and Virtue's Counterculture
or Antiencomiastic Rhetoric 341
  1. Odysseus 341
  2. Herakles 347
  3. Socrates 351
  4. Aesop 356
  5. Odysseus, Herakles, Aesop, and Socrates as Rhetorical Figures 368
  6. Conclusion 377

Bibliography 379
  1. Ancient Authors 379
  2. Commentaries on Second Corinthians 380
  3. Modern Authors 381

Indices 419
  1. Ancient Sources 419
  2. Greek Words 434
  3. Authors 438
  4. Subjects 441

Abbreviations

1. Ancient Authors

Aes[op] *Fab[ulae]*
Am[mianus] Mar[cellinus]
App[ian]
   Bel[lum] civ[ile]
   Mith[ridatica]
   Syr[iaca]
Archy[tus of Tarentum]
   [Περὶ νόμου καὶ δικαιοσύνης]
Aristid[es, Aelius]
Aristoph[anes] *Nub[es]*
Aris[totle]
   E[thica] N[icomachea]
   Meta[physics]
   Pol[itica]
   Rhet[orica]
Arr[ian]
   Alex[andri] ana[basis]
   Cyn[egeticus]
   His[toria] suc[cessorum]
      Alex[andri]
   Parth[icorum fragmenta]
Athen[aeus] *Deip[nosophistai]*
Aug[ustus] *Res ges[tae]*
Aul[us] Gel[lius] *Noc[tes] At[ticae]*
Cae[sar]
   Bel[lo] civ[ili, De]
   Bel[lo] Gal[lico, De]
Cal[purnius] Sic[ulus] *Ec[logue]*
Cic[ero]
   Ad Att[icus, Epistulae]
   Ad Brut[um, Epistulae]
   Ad fam[iliari, Epistulae]
   Cat[ilinam, In]
   De inv[entione]
   De off[iciis]
   De or[atore]
   De part[itione] or[atoria]
   Par[adoxa] Stoi[corum]
   Phil[ippicae]
   Pro leg[e] Man[ilia]
   Pro Lig[ario]
   Pro Mar[cello]
   Pro Mur[ena]
   Pro Reg[e] Dei[otaro]
   Pro [Sex.] Ros[cio] Am[erino]
   Pro Sul[la]
   Q[uintus] fr[atrem, Epistulae]
   Top[ica]
   Tusc[ulanarum disputationum]
   Ver[rem, In]
Dem[osthenes]
   De cor[ona]
   In Med[iam]
Dio Cas[sius *Historiae Romanae*]
Dio Chrys[ostom *Orationes*]
Diod[orus] Sic[ulus]
   [*Bibliotheca historica*]
Diog[enes] L[aertius *Vitae*
   philosophorum]
Dio[nysius of] Hal[icarnassus]
   Ant[iquitates Romanae]
   Ars Rhet[orica]
Diot[ogenes] *Peri bas[ileias]*
Ecph[antus] *Peri bas[ileias]*

Epict[etus]
   Diss[ertationes]
   Ench[iridion]
   Frag[menta]
Ep[istle of] Arist[eas]
Herod[otus *Historiae*]
Hom[er]
   Il[iad]
   Od[yssey]
Hor[ace]
   Car[men] saec[ulare]
   Car[mina]
   Ep[istulae]
   Sat[irae]
Iamb[lichus] *De vit[a] Pyth[agorica]*
Isoc[rates]
   Ad Dem[onicum]
   Ad Nic[oclem]
   Ad Tim[otheum]
   Ant[idosis]
   Ep[istulae]
   Ev[agoras]
   Hel[enae encomium]
   In Cal[limachum]
   In Loch[item]
   Nic[ocles]
   Pan[athenaicus]
   Paneg[yricus]
   Phil[lippus]
Jos[eph and] Asen[eth]
Jos[ephus, Flavius]
   Ant[iquities]
   Ap[ionem, Contra]
   Bel[lum Judaicum]
   Vita [Josephi]
Lib[anius]
   Ep[istulae]
   Or[ationes]
   Decl[amationes]
Luc[ian]
   Alex[ander]
   Apol[ogia]

   Bis accus[atus sive tribunalia]
   De astr[ologia]
   De merc[ede] cond[uctis potentium familiaribus]
   De parasito [sive artem esse parasiticam]
   Dem[onax]
   Dial[ogi] meret[riui]
   Fug[itivi]
   Gal[lus]
   Hermot[imus]
   Icar[omenippus]
   Imag[ines]
   Men[nipus sive necyomantia]
   Nig[rinus]
   Per[egrini, De morte]
   Phal[aris]
   Pro lapsu [inter salutandum]
   Prom[ethus]
   Reviv[escentes] sive pisc[ator]
   Rhet[orum] prae[ceptor]
   Scy[tha]
   Som[nium sive vita Luciani]
   Ver[ae] hist[oriae]
   Vit[arum] auc[tio]
M[arcus] Aur[elius Antoninus]
   [Ta eis heauton]
Mus[onius] Ruf[us]
   Graphēn hybreōs [grapsetai tina ho philosophos, Ei]
   Phil[osophōteon k. t.] bas[ileusin]
Ovid *Pont[o, Epistulae ex]*
P[apyri] Oxy[rhynchus]
Philo [Judaeus]
   De agr[icultura]
   De con[fusione] ling[uarum]
   De dec[alogo]
   De Ios[epho]
   De leg[atio] ad Gai[um]
   De mig[ratione] Abr[ahami]
   De op[ificio] mun[di]
   De prae[miis] et poe[nis]

    De sac[rificiis] Ab[elis et Caini]
    De som[niis]
    De spec[ialibus] leg[ibus]
    De virt[utibus]
    De vita Mos[is]
    In Flac[cum]
    Leg[um] al[legoriarum]
    Quod det[erius] pot[iori] insidiari soleat]
    Quod om[nis] pr[obus] lib[er]
Philod[emus]
    Good King [according to Homer, On the]
    Rhet[oric, On]
Philos[tratus, Flavius]
    Vit[a] Apol[lonii]
    Vit[ae] soph[istarum]
Pind[ar] *Pyth[ia]*
Plato
    Apol[ogia]
    Hip[pias] mai[or]
    Leg[es]
    Men[exenus]
    Pol[iticus]
    Prot[agorus]
    Sym[posium]
    The[aetetus]
Plau[tus]
    Mil[es]
    Rud[ens]
Pliny [the Elder] *Nat[uralis] his[toria]*
Pliny [the Younger]
    Ep[istulae]
    Pan[egyricus]
Plut[arch]
    Aem[ilius Paullus]
    Alc[ibiades]
    Alex[ander]
    Ant[ony]
    Aris[tides]
    Art[axerxes]

    Cae[sar]
    C[aius] Mar[ius]
    Cato maj[or]
    Cato min[or]
    Cic[ero]
    Cor[iolanus]
    Cras[sus]
    Eum[enes]
    Fab[ius Maximus]
    Flam[ininus]
    Grac[chus, Tiberius et Gaius]
    Mar[ius, Caius]
    Mor[alia]
    Nic[ias]
    Pel[opidas]
    Phoc[ion]
    Pom[pey]
    Rom[ulus]
    Ser[torius]
    Sol[on]
    Thes[eus]
    Thes[ei] et Rom[uli, Comparatio]
Polyb[ius *Historiae*]
Ps[eudo]-Anach[arsis] *Ep[istulae]*
Ps[eudo]-Aristid[es]
    Eis bas[ilea]
    Rhod[iakos]
Ps[eudo]-Dem[osthenes] *Erot[icus]*
Ps[eudo]-Diog[enes] *Ep[istulae]*
Ps[eudo]-Her[aclitus] *Ep[istulae]*
Ps[eudo]-Plato *Def[initiones]*
Ps[eudo]-Plut[arch]
    De lib[eris] ed[ucandis]
    De vita et poe[si] Hom[eri]
Ps[eudo]-Sal[lust]
    Ad Cae[sarem senem, Epistulae]
Ps[eudo]-Sen[eca] *Oct[avia]*
Quin[tilian *Institutio Oratoria*]
Rhet[orica ad] Alex[andrum]
Rhet[orica ad] Her[ennium]
Sal[lust] *Cat[ilinae, Bellum]*

Sen[eca]
  Ad Pol[ybium] de con[solatione]
  Apoc[olocyntosis]
  De ben[eficiis]
  De clem[entia]
  De const[antia sapientis]
  De tranq[uillitate animi]
  De vit[a] b[eata]
  Ep[istulae]
  Herc[ules] fur[ens]
  Herc[ules] Oet[aeus]
  Nat[urales] qu[aestiones]
Seneca the Elder
  Con[troversiae]
  Sua[soriae]
Stat[ius] *Theb[aid]*
Sthen[idas] *Peri bas[ileias]*
Stob[aeus] *Anth[ologium]*
Suet[onius]
  Aug[ustus]
  Clau[dius]
  Dom[itian]
  Iul[ius]

Tib[erius]
Vesp[asian]
Tac[itus]
  Agr[icula]
  Ann[als]
  Hist[ories]
Ter[ence] *Adel[phoe]*
Theoph[rastus *Characteres*]
Theoc[ritus] *Id[yllia]*
Thuc[ydides *Historiae*]
Val[erius] Max[imus]
  Fact[orum] ac dic[torum
    memorabilium]
Vel[leius] Pat[erculus]
  Hist[oriae] Rom[anae]
Vir[gil] *Aen[eid]*
Xen[ophon]
  Ag[esilaus]
  Ana[basis]
  Cyr[opaedia]
  Mem[orabilia]
  Oec[onomicus]
  Sym[posium]

2. Other Sources

AB	Anchor Bible
ABD	*Anchor Bible Dictionary*
ABR	*Australian Biblical Review*
ABRL	Anchor Bible Reference Library
AJA	*American Journal of Archaeology*
AJP	*American Journal of Philology*
ANRW	*Aufstieg und Niedergang der römischen Welt*
Austin	*The Hellenistic World from Alexander to the Roman Conquest: A Selection of Ancient Sources in Translation*, M. M. Austin (Cambridge University Press, 1981).
Barrett	*The Second Epistle to the Corinthians*, C. K. Barrett, Harper New Testament Commentary (New York: Harper & Row, 1973; Peabody, MA: Hendrickson, 1987).
BBB	Bonner biblische Beiträge
Behr	*P. Aelius Aristides: The Complete Works: Translated into English*, Charles A. Behr, 2 vols. (Leiden: E. J. Brill, 1981-86); Greek text: *P. Aelii*

	Aristides: Opera quae exstant omnia, eds. Fridericus Waltharius Lenz and Carolus Allison Behr, 1 vol. in 4 pts. (Leiden: Brill, 1976-).
BETL	Bibliotheca ephemeridum theologicarum Lovaniensium
BICS	*Bulletin of the Institute of Classical Studies*
BJRL	*Bulletin of the John Rylands University Library of Manchester*
Braund	*Augustus to Nero: A Sourcebook on Roman History 31 BC-AD 68*, David C. Braund (Totowa, NJ: Barnes and Noble Books, 1985).
Bultmann	*The Second Letter to the Corinthians*, Rudolf Bultmann, trans. Roy A. Harrisville (Minneapolis: Augsburg, 1985).
Burstein	*The Hellenistic Age from the Battle of Ipsos to the Death of Kleopatra VII*, Stanley M. Burstein, Translated Documents of Greece and Rome 3 (Cambridge University Press, 1985).
BZ	*Biblische Zeitschrift*
CB	*Classical Bulletin*
CBQ	*Catholic Biblical Quarterly*
CIG	*Corpus Inscriptionum Graecarum*, ed. A. Boeckh.
CIJ	*Corpus Inscriptionum Judaicarum*, ed. J. B. Frey.
CIL	*Corpus Inscriptionum Latinarum I-XVI*, eds. Th. Mommsen, et al. (Berlin, 1862ff.).
CJ	*Classical Journal*
ClAnt	*Classical Antiquity*
CP	*Classical Philology*
CQ	*Classical Quarterly*
CR	*Classical Review*
CRAI	*Comptes rendus de l'Académie des Inscriptions et Belles-Lettres*
CREBM	*Coins of the Roman Empire in the British Museum*, eds. Harold Mattingly and R. A. Carson (London: Trustees of the British Museum).
CRR	*The Coinage of the Roman Republic*, Edward Sydenham (London: Spink & Son, 1952).
CW	*Classical World*
EDNT	*Exegetical Dictionary of the New Testament*, eds. Horst Balz and Gerhard Schneider, 3 vols. (Grand Rapids: Eerdmans, 1990-93).
EJ	*Documents Illustrating the Reigns of Augustus and Tiberius*, Victor Ehrenberg and A. H. M. Jones, rev. (Oxford University Press, 1955).
ÉTR	*Études théologiques et religieuses*
FGH	*Die Fragmente der griechischen Historiker*, ed. Felix Jacoby, 3 vols. in 15 (Leiden: Brill, 1923-58; 1954-69).
FRLANT	Forschungen zur Religion und Literatur des Alten und Neuen Testaments
Furnish	*II Corinthians*, Victor Paul Furnish, Anchor Bible 32A (Garden City, NY: Doubleday, 1984).
FVS	*Die Fragmente der Vorsokratiker*, ed. Hermann Diels, 6th ed. rev. Walther Kranz (10th ed.; Berlin, 1952).
G & R	*Greece & Rome*
Grenfell	*The Oxyrhynchus Papyri*, part 1, eds. Bernard P. Grenfell and Arthur S. Hunt (London: Egypt Exploration Fund, 1898).
HNTC	Harper New Testament Commentary
Horsley	*New Documents Illustrating Early Christiainty*, ed. G. H. R. Horsley (North Ryde, N. S. W.: Ancient History Documentary Research Centre, Macquarie University, 1981-).

HSCP	*Harvard Studies in Classical Philology*
HTR	*Harvard Theological Review*
HUCA	*Hebrew Union College Annual*
Hunt	*The Oxyrhynchus Papyri*, part 17, ed. Arthur S. Hunt (London: Egypt Exploration Society, 1927).
HUT	Hermeneutische Untersuchungen zur Theologie
ICC	International Critical Commentary
ICS	*Illinois Classical Studies*
IEph	*Die Inschriften von Ephesos*, Hermann Wankel, et al., 8 vols., Inschriften griechischer Städte aus Kleinasien 11.1-17.4 (Bonn: Rudolf Habelt, 1979-84).
IG	*Inscriptiones Graecae*
Jalabert	*Inscriptions grecques et latines de la Syria*, Louis Jalabert, René Mouterde, et al., 8 vols., Bibliothèque archéologique et historique 12, 33, 36, 61, 66, 78, 89, 104 (Paris: Librairie orientaliste Paul Geuthner, 1929-80).
JBL	*Journal of Biblical Literature*
JHS	*Journal of Hellenic Studies*
JR	*Journal of Religion*
JRA	*Journal of Roman Archaeology*
JRS	*Journal of Roman Studies*
JSNT	*Journal for the Study of the New Testament*
JSNTSS	Journal for the Study of the New Testament Supplement Series
JTC	*Journal for Theology and the Church*
JTS	*Journal of Theological Studies*
Kent	*Corinth 8.3: The Inscriptions 1926-1950*, John Harvey Kent (Princeton: American School of Classical Studies at Athens, 1966).
LCL	Loeb Classical Library
Lutz	"Musonius Rufus: 'The Roman Socrates,'" Cora E. Lutz, *Yale Classical Studies* 10 (1947): 3-147.
MAMA	*Monumenta Asiae Minoris Antiqua*
Martin	*2 Corinthians*, Ralph P. Martin, Word Biblical Commentary 40 (Waco, TX: Word Books, 1986).
Meiggs	*A Selection of Greek Historical Inscriptions*, R. Meiggs and D. M. Lewis (Oxford University Press, 1969).
Merritt	*Corinth 8.1: Greek Inscriptions, 1896-1927*, ed. Benjamin Dean Merritt (Cambridge: Harvard University Press [for the American School of Classical Studies at Athens], 1931).
NCB	New Century Bible
Neot	*Neotestamentica*
NIDNTT	*New International Dictionary of New Testament Theology*, ed. Colin Brown, 3 vols. (Grand Rapids: Zondervan, 1975-78).
NIGTC	New International Greek Testament Commentary
NovT	*Novum Testamentum*
NTS	*New Testament Studies*
OGIS	*Orientis Graeci Inscriptiones Selectae*, ed. W. Dittenberger, 2 vols. (Leipzig, 1903-5).

Oliver	*Greek Constitutions of Early Roman Emperors from Inscriptions and Papyri*, James H. Oliver (Philadelphia: American Philosophical Society, 1989).
Parsons	*The Oxyrhynchus Papyri*, vol. 42, ed. P. J. Parsons, Graeco-Roman Memoirs 58 (London: Egypt Exploration Society, 1974).
PBA	*Proceedings of the British Academy*
Plummer	*A Critical and Exegetical Commentary on the Second Epistle of St. Paul to the Corinthians*, International Critical Commentary (Edinburgh: T. & T. Clark, 1915).
QUCC	*Quaderni urbinati di cultura classica*
RAC	*Reallexikon für Antike und Christentum*
RB	*Revue biblique*
Rea	*The Oxyrhynchus Papyri*, vol. 43, eds. J. R. Rea et al., Graeco-Roman Memoirs 60 (London: Egypt Exploration Society, 1975).
Reynolds	*Aphrodisias and Rome*, Joyce Reynolds, Journal of Roman Studies Monographs 1 (London: Society for the Promotion of Roman Studies, 1982).
RhM	*Rheinisches Museum*
RHPR	*Revue d'histoire et de philosophie religieuses*
RIC	*The Roman Imperial Coinage*, eds. C. H. V. Sutherland and R. A. G. Carson, rev. (London: Spink and Son, 1984-).
SBB	Stuttgarter biblische Beiträge
SBLDS	Society of Biblical Literature Dissertation Series
SBLMS	Society of Biblical Literature Manuscript Series
SBLSS	Society of Biblical Literature Semeia Studies
SCHNT	Studia ad corpus hellenisticum novi testamenti
Schürer	*The History of the Jewish People in the Age of Jesus Christ*, Emil Schürer, rev. and ed. Geza Vermes, Fergus Millar, Martin Goodman, Matthew Black, and Pamela Vermes, 3 vols. (Edinburgh: T. & T. Clark, 1973-87).
SEG	*Supplementum epigraphicum Graecum*
Sherk 1969	*Roman Documents from the Greek East*, Robert K. Sherk (Baltimore, 1969).
Sherk 1984	*Rome and the Greek East to the Death of Augustus*, Robert K. Sherk, Translated Documents of Greece and Rome 4 (Cambridge University Press, 1984).
Sherk 1988	*The Roman Empire: Augustus to Hadrian*, Robert K. Sherk (Cambridge University Press, 1988).
SIG	*Sylloge Inscriptionum Graecarum, I-IV*, ed. Wilhelm Dittenberger, 3d ed. (Leipzig, 1915-24; Hildesheim: Georg Olms, 1960).
Small.	*Documents Illustrating the Principates of Gaius, Claudius and Nero*, Mary E. Smallwood (Cambridge: Cambridge University Press, 1967).
SNTSMS	Society for New Testament Studies Monograph Series
SVF	*Stoicorum Veterum Fragmenta*, ed. Hans Friedrich August von Arnim, 4 vols. (Leipzig: Teubner, 1903-24).
TAPA	*Transactions of the American Philological Association*
TB	*Tyndale Bulletin*

TDNT	*Theological Dictionary of the New Testament*, eds. Gerhard Kittel and Gerhard Friedrich, trans. Geoffrey W. Bromiley, 10 vols. (Grand Rapids: Eerdmans, 1964-76).
TLNT	*Theological Lexicon of the New Testament*, Ceslas Spicq, trans. James D. Ernest, 3 vols. (Peabody, MA: Hendrickson, 1994)
TNTC	Tyndale New Testament Commentary
TS	*Theological Studies*
Vermeule	*Roman Imperial Art in Greece and Asia Minor*, Cornelius C. Vermeule (Cambridge: Harvard University Press, 1968).
WBC	Word Biblical Commentary
Welles	*Royal Correspondence in the Hellenistic Period: A Study in Greek Epigraphy*, C. Bradford Welles (New Haven: Yale University Press, 1934).
West	*Corinth 8.2: Latin Inscriptions, 1896-1926*, Allen Brown West (Cambridge: Harvard University Press [for the American School of Classical Studies at Athens], 1931).
Windisch	*Der zweite Korintherbrief*, Hans Windisch, KEK 6 (Göttingen: Vandenhoeck & Ruprecht, 1924).
WUNT	Wissenschaftliche Untersuchungen zum Neuen Testament
YClS	*Yale Classical Studies*
ZNW	*Zeitschrift für neutestamentliche Wissenschaft*
ZST	*Zeitschrift für systematische Theologie*
ZTK	*Zeitschrift für Theologie und Kirche*

Introduction

This monograph investigates the opening appeal of Second Corinthians 10:1–13:10, the so-called "Four-Chapter-Letter," identified by some as the "Letter of Tears." The latter assumption provides a working hypothesis for this work, while the fragment's opening words supply the point of entry.[1] This letter fragment begins with Paul's emphatic appeal to the Corinthian church, an appeal extended through the πραΰτης and ἐπιείκεια of Christ, two nouns which have perplexed interpreters. This study seeks to resolve the questions which Christ's πραΰτης καὶ ἐπιείκεια raise, particularly in the areas of semantics, christology, and rhetoric, in order to understand Paul's self-presentation in this letter fragment and how it pervades all four chapters. To describe and correlate the phenomena that link 2 Cor 10:1 to 10:1–13:10, I have invented the label of "populist ideology and rhetoric."

As for semantics, how should Paul's appeal be translated? The history of English Bible translations tells an interesting story. Although Wycliffe translated Paul's appeal as issued "by the mildness and softness of Christ," subsequent translators as early as Tyndale altered "mildness" to "meekness," with the result that Paul "beseeches ... by the meekness and softness of Christ." Coverdale, "Thomas Matthew," the Great Bible, and

---

[1] Adolf Hausrath, *Der Vier-Capitel-Brief des Paulus an die Korinther* (Heidelberg: Bassermann, 1870); abridged in *Neutestamentliche Zeitgeschichte* (4 vols.; Heidelberg: Bassermann, 1875), 3: 302-14; J. H. Kennedy, "Are There Two Epistles in 2 Corinthians?" *The Expositor* 6 (1897): 231-38, 285-304; idem, *The Second and Third Epistles of St. Paul to the Corinthians* (London: Methuen, 1900); Günther Bornkamm, *Die Vorgeschichte des sogenannten Zweiten Korintherbriefes*, Sitzungsberichte der Heidelberger Akademie der Wissenschaften. Philosophisch-historische Klasse, 1961, 2. Abhandlung (Heidelberg: Winter, 1961); reprinted with an addendum in *Geschichte und Glaube II. Gesammelte Aufsätze IV* (Munich: Kaiser, 1971), 162-94; abridged trans. "The History of the Origin of the So-Called Second Letter to the Corinthians," *NTS* 8 (1962): 258-64; F. Watson, "2 Cor. X-XIII and Paul's Painful Letter to the Corinthians," *JTS* 35 (1984): 324-46; L. L. Welborn, "The Identification of 2 Corinthians 10–13 with the 'Letter of Tears,'" *NovT* 37 (1995): 138-53. The partition theory assumed throughout this work is as follows: 2:14–6:13 + 7:2-4 (Letter C); 10:1–13:10 (Letter D); 1:1–2:13 + 7:5-16 + 13:11-13 (Letter E); chs. 8 and 9, then, are Letters F and G (or G and F). See Hans Dieter Betz, *2 Corinthians 8 and 9: A Commentary on Two Administrative Letters of the Apostle Paul*, Hermeneia (Philadelphia: Fortress Press, 1985), 142-43; idem, "Corinthians, Second," in *ABD*, s.v.

Richard Taverner followed. In 1560, however, the Geneva Bible changed the translation to "meekness and gentleness," ending one and a half centuries of translation tradition and initiating another which prevails throughout the versions. Imitated by the Bishops' Bible, adopted by the Authorized Version (which provided modern spellings), and retained by every subsequent version except for the New American Standard Version ("meekness and kindness"), "meekness and gentleness" has become the standard translation of 2 Cor 10:1 in the versions of the English Bible, including the New Revised Standard Version.

This consistency, however, reflects the tradition's inertia, not philological insight, as the variety of Catholic translations suggests. An edition of Rheims-Douay and Challoner's first two editions translated Paul's appeal as "mildness and modesty" — a good translation actually. Challoner's third edition, alas, capitulated to the Protestant versions. More recently (1970), the New American Bible surprisingly retained "meekness," pairing it with "kindness." Its revision improved greatly to "gentleness and clemency" (though the footnote in the *Catholic Study Bible* is a step backward).[2] The Jerome Bible opted for "gentleness and patience," which the New Jerome Bible revised to "gentleness and forbearance" (a translation offered by Goodspeed decades earlier in 1931). While these are not bad, "patience" and "forbearance" may refer to how one endures circumstances, thereby connoting misfortune, hardship, endurance and persistence, rather than (as I will argue) referring to how one treats people. Considering the variety expressed in Roman Catholic translations, then, we awaken to the difficulty of translating Paul's appeal in 2 Cor 10:1.

Looking more broadly at the explosion of translations in the last half of the twentieth century reveals an enormous variety in the rendering of 2 Cor 10:1. The Good News Bible offers the cliché, "meek and mild," while the *Basic Bible* is equally bad, offering the altogether too passive "quiet and gentle behavior." The wonderful New English Bible and Revised English Bible offer the welcome antidote "gentleness and magnanimity." The *Amplified Bible* translates πραΰτης καὶ ἐπιείκεια as "gentleness and consideration," which is heir to James Moffatt (1922) and the Berkeley Version (1945). Wuest offered "meekness and sweet reasonableness" (*An*

---

[2] In the study Bible's accompanying note, "gentleness-clemency-humility" are presented as a natural group in contrast to "boldness-confidence-bravery"; moreover, "gentleness and clemency" are said to form "a striking contrast to the picture of the bold and militant Paul." Clemency and humility, however, do not have a clear and obvious connection; they have a delicately antithetical relationship and will coalesce in 2 Cor 10:1 via irony. Furthermore, this Bible's footnote misses the great degree of continuity between clemency and militancy.

Expanded Translation, 1961), while Victor Furnish proposes "gentleness and kindness" in his Anchor Bible commentary. Margaret Thrall has proposed "meekness and clemency" in her contribution to the International Critical Commentary. This diversity of translations emphasizes how little we understand Paul's words and the English language's lack of adequate glosses.

In the midst of this variety, two trends appear in twentieth century translations of 2 Cor 10:1. First, recognizing the pejorative and misleading connotations of meekness, translators now prefer to render πραΰτης as "gentleness." Second, agreement on the translation of ἐπιείκεια has vanished, giving way to at least thirteen different glosses: softness, gentleness, modesty, equity, forbearance, courtesy, consideration or considerateness, sweet reasonableness, kindness, sympathy, patience, magnanimity, and clemency. In sum, πραΰτης is the stable member of this pair, translated "meekness" in the versions and "gentleness" in the other translations, while ἐπιείκεια remains an enigma.

Faced with these difficulties, the New Revised Standard Version's retention of "meekness and gentleness" is surprising, yet perhaps to be expected. No alternative is or can be perfect — nor has any persuasive argument been advanced for one translation over another. Still, this translation is unfortunate. The most glaring problem is the word "meekness." Today this is no compliment, with the result that its emotional tone stands completely opposite that of the word it translates, πραΰτης. Secondly, "gentleness" is too vague to communicate the nuances of ἐπιείκεια. For example, if a judge were gentle, we would be more likely to describe the judge as lenient. If an American President were gentle, we would probably describe him as a man of the people, down-to-earth, or populist, but not gentle. The Greek word ἐπιείκεια applies to both contexts — and more. Gentle shepherd, indulgent father, populist orator, clement king, each of these adjectives could be ἐπιεικής, or perhaps even πρᾶος, in Greek, which would underscore the similarity among all these figures; however, English favors a different adjective for each. Having said this, and having learned still more about ἐπιείκεια, one could translate it "gentleness" and find that gloss meaningful; however, the gloss is not what communicates that meaning, but the understanding of ἐπιείκεια on which it rests. In short, "gentleness" glosses ἐπιείκεια too generically.

This investigation will clarify Paul's meaning in his use of πραΰτης καὶ ἐπιείκεια (chs. 1–2). The key is consideration of other passages which use the two nouns together. While that seems obvious, it implies the dethroning of the LXX and the idea of biblical language in the investigation of this question. If we examine the contexts in which πραΰτης καὶ ἐπιείκεια or ἐπιείκεια καὶ πραΰτης appear, noting the people, the actions, the ideas, and the associated words, we will find a pattern of connotations parallel to Paul's appeal. We will also find ourselves departing from the LXX, albeit in the company of Philo and Josephus. If we allow Paul to speak for himself, we also will not hear the Gospels, but Paul's own response to a relational crisis.

How shall we translate 2 Cor 10:1? This study will recommend translating Paul's appeal as extended "through the leniency and clemency of Christ." This rendering provides the title for this book.

This translation and the semantic study on which it rests have implications for further problems of interpretation. For example, given the understanding of πραΰτης καὶ ἐπιείκεια proposed in this study, how can Paul attribute these virtues to Christ? Previous scholarship has pointed in the correct direction, viz., his heavenly enthronement, but has failed to explain how this is so, simply placing faith in a handful of LXX examples. This study, on the other hand, will lay out the widespread, elaborate, and well-known rhetoric of good rule as a context within which the attribution of "leniency and clemency" to Christ flows clearly and obviously from his (heavenly) rule. Such ideology was commonplace in Paul's world, not at all erudite or limited to élite circles, as leniency and clemency were key components of popular rule. As the virtues of the good, ideal ruler, then, ἐπιείκεια and πραότης apply to Christ.

Chapter three will argue that Paul draws on the ideology of good rule in his christological assertion in 2 Cor 10:1. Comparing the rhetoric of rule with Paul's christology will reveal the relationship between the two, thereby demonstrating the appropriateness of Paul's formulating a christological statement by means of that ideology. When Paul, then, extends "leniency and clemency" to Christ, we witness a moment of christological innovation. Like the orators of old who took the familiar and created something new, so Paul took Christ's heavenly rule and mercy and extended it logically to the ideal of lenient and clement rule, a move not at all theoretical, but immediately relevant to his relationship with the Corinthian church.

This affects the use of 2 Cor 10:1 in the debate about Paul's knowledge of Jesus, as is discussed at the end of chapter three. At first glance, recognizing the ideology of kingship severs any connection between the earthly Jesus and the christology of Paul's appeal and should preclude use of 2 Cor 10:1 as a proof text for Paul's knowledge of Jesus. However, the christology of kingship probably influenced other early Christian thinkers, so that Paul may not be unique or independent in his formulation. Still, what Paul reflects is a matrix of ideas used to describe the significance of a heavenly figure (i.e., a christology), not the personal attributes of the historical Jesus.

Paul not only attributes πραΰτης καὶ ἐπιείκεια to Christ, but formulates his own appeal to the Corinthians through it. What, then, is the point of such an appeal, an appeal based on Christ's "leniency and clemency"? Chapter four surveys the place of leniency and/or clemency in the ancient world to illumine their stereotypical nature, motives, utility, and the problems they raise in order to bring to light their relevance to Paul's ministry. For example, the popular way leniency mitigates authority and power makes it an attractive way for Paul to present himself. Its role in moral correction further coincides with Paul's strategy of seeking the Corinthians' repentance. Its potential similarity to weakness also corresponds to Paul's debate with the Corinthians. Recognition of Paul's offer of leniency, then, connects 2 Cor 10:1 to the entire letter fragment in which it occurs, as well as to Paul's other Corinthian correspondence.

The implications of Paul's appeal for his rhetoric in the letter fragment go beyond how he wishes to interrelate with the Corinthian church and extend to how he presents himself (chapter five). Contemporary scholarship on 2 Cor 10:1 recognizes this, following the lead of Ragnar Leivestad.[3] The strength of his influential contribution is his connection of Paul's appeal to the immediately following self-description, ταπεινός.[4] The following investigation, however, disagrees with how he makes that connection, for though Paul indeed regards himself as ταπεινός, that is not the point of πραΰτης καὶ ἐπιείκεια. These things must be held apart to recognize correctly how Paul presents himself. The question to be asked is not how to turn πραΰτης καὶ ἐπιείκεια into ταπεινότης, but how one person can embody both.[5] This strangeness alerts us to irony, which plays out in Paul's reevaluation of humility and demolition of normal claims to

---

[3] "'The Meekness and Gentleness of Christ' II Cor. X. 1," *NTS* 12 (1966): 156-64.

[4] How Leivestad combines ταπεινός with the following warfare imagery is problematic. Malherbe helped out greatly in this matter, discussing the philosopher's humble appearance as in fact weapons to be unleashed in philosophical proclamation ("Antisthenes and Odysseus, and Paul at War," *HTR* 76 (1983): 143-73; reprinted in *Paul and the Popular Philosophers* [Minneapolis: Fortress Press, 1989], 91-119). To my mind, however, this suggests that the warfare imagery should not be stripped from Paul's opening offer of "leniency and clemency."

[5] Alternatively, we might ask, Does ταπεινός degrade πραότης and ἐπιείκεια or do πραότης and ἐπιείκεια elevate ταπεινός? This question emphasizes the different connotations — and social registers — of the two alternatives. The answer to the question is, however, a third option, viz., the difference between the two choices creates a dissonance which challenges the reader to think. To lay claim to Christ's leniency and clemency suggests that acceptance of ταπεινότης cannot be straightforward. As we will argue, this alerts us to a crucial, ironic element in Paul's thinking.

status. To summarize Paul's self-presentation as ταπεινός, then, misses the complexity and nuances of his rhetoric, while overlooking the place of leniency.

Subsequent to Leivestad's study, Hans Dieter Betz gave broader consideration to Paul's rhetoric.[6] Building on clues provided by Windisch in his commentary, Betz elaborated on the correlation between Paul's rhetoric and the philosophical defense speech, the seminal example being that of Socrates. In particular, Betz noted the antisophistical utility of this rhetoric and the place of parody within it. This ultimately form-critical investigation was a huge step forward in the study of 2 Corinthians 10–13, though apparently a stride too great for most to follow.

Subsequent work has, however, moved toward Windisch and Betz. Malherbe has compared Paul's ταπεινότης with the Antisthenic strain of the Socratic tradition to underscore its value for expressing positively (and powerfully) one's views rather than limiting it to the negative role of distinguishing oneself from sophists (read charlatans).[7] Though Malherbe corrects Betz in this regard, his discussion still remains inside the Socratic tradition. Fitzgerald does likewise.[8] His examination of the hardship-catalogue reveals its rhetorical use in proving the sage's mettle, with the result that Fitzgerald too has linked Paul's rhetoric with that of philosophy.[9] Moreover, the rhetoric Fitzgerald examines, as well as Malherbe and Betz, was rhetoric used by Paul to characterize himself.

The examination of Paul's self-presentation offered in chapter five will therefore build on these previous studies and seek to provide a general theory for reading 2 Corinthians 10–13 which connects and accounts for them, while simultaneously integrating Paul's offer of leniency. The key

---

[6] Hans Dieter Betz, *Der Apostel Paulus und die sokratische Tradition. Eine exegetische Untersuchung zu seiner "Apologie" 2 Korinther 10–13*, Beiträge zur historischen Theologie 45 (Tübingen: J. C. B. Mohr [Paul Siebeck], 1972).

[7] Malherbe, "Antisthenes and Odysseus, and Paul at War."

[8] John T. Fitzgerald, *Cracks in an Earthen Vessel: An Examination of the Catalogues of Hardships in the Corinthian Correspondence*, SBLDS 99 (Atlanta: Scholars Press, 1988).

[9] Subsequent work on hardship-catalogues has confirmed Fitzgerald's views: Martin Ebner, *Leidenslisten und Apostelbrief. Untersuchungen zu Form, Motivik und Funktion der Peristasenkataloge bei Paulus*, Forschung zur Bibel 66 (Würzburg: Echter, 1991); Markus Schiefer Ferrari, *Die Sprache des Leids in den paulinischen Peristasenkatalogen*, Stuttgarter biblische Beiträge 23 (Stuttgart: Katholisches Bibelwerk, 1991). Of course, Fitzgerald was not the first to investigate the hardship catalogue, as he himself gives credit to Rudolf Bultmann and Bultmann's teacher, Johannes Weiss (*Cracks in an Earthen Vessel*, 7). Betz also discusses the hardship-catalogue, connecting it with the Cynic-Stoic tradition (*Paulus und die sokratische Tradition*, 97-100).

to accomplishing this comes by approaching Paul's self-presentation in 2 Corinthians 10–13 in a new way, viz., from the rhetorical category of ἦθος, i.e., character presentation.[10]

In Hermogenes' discussion of modest oratory we find ideas and debates which parallel Paul's letter fragment. We thereby recognize in 2 Corinthians 10–13 a general level of rhetoric in which Paul shows himself to be a man of the people, which is what commonplaces of modesty seek to do. For example, such commonplaces reflect the desire to avoid imposing oneself on the public, e.g., to prefer forgiveness to public dispute. Paul's offer of leniency, in particular, is consistent with this, for leniency is a δημοτικός and κοινός trait, as well as a populist policy. Antisophistical statements are likewise expressions of modest rhetoric, for the sophist lives at court and may deceive the people, whereas the decent citizen avoids court, speaks there untrained, and appears there only as an urgent matter of justice. Was Betz wrong then to label Paul's antisophistical speech Socratic? Absolutely not, for the figure of Socrates embodied a species of modest rhetoric, the very species Paul used in 2 Corinthians 10–13.

The key to recognizing Socratic modesty in Paul's letter fragment is to see different types of irony within it. While the biting irony of the Fools' Speech is not modest, the fact that Paul speaks in another voice (ἠθοποιία) accounts for that harsh tone. In fact, his immodest, vitriolic irony and parody correspond well with the braggart's persona that Paul adopts. But beneath Paul's foolish boasting lies an irony built on philosophical paradox which subverts normal categories of encomiastic rhetoric. Such challenges lead us back to Socrates, but appear as well in the figures of Aesop, Odysseus, and Herakles (particularly as the Socratic tradition represented them). Paul uses this line of rhetoric to demolish the typical credentials of human evaluation and honor, particularly as applied to envoys of Christ, and to vindicate his own apostolic persona. While this rhetoric provides the foundation for Paul's parodies and hardship-

---

[10] My work on Paul's ἦθος in 2 Cor 10–13 was completed before Mario M. DiCicco's dissertation came to my attention: *Paul's Use of Ethos, Pathos, and Logos in 2 Corinthians 10–13*, Mellen Biblical Press Series 31 (Lewiston, NY: Mellen Biblical Press, 1995). DiCicco follows rhetorical handbooks too woodenly in his consideration of *ēthos*. As argued in chapter five, the practice of *ēthos* far outstripped anything indicated in the handbooks. For example, there were many character types used in ancient literature and rhetoric that could be used to construct identities for use in comedy, slander, encomia, psychology, exempla, defense, prosecution, or self-promotion. These provide a mechanism for integrating miscellaneous ethical observations into greater wholes. Hermogenes synthesized one of these types, the modest person, using examples from canonical orators. His work will prove helpful for the analysis presented in chapter five.

catalogues, his lowly appearance also rests on it. In Paul's contradiction of appearances and embrace of nothingness, then, lies a Socratic irony.

Lowliness and modesty then furnish Paul's self-presentation with two important motifs. By way of Socratic irony, modesty subsumes lowliness. Meanwhile, leniency and clemency interact with each, with lowliness antithetically and therefore ironically, with modesty correlatively. Paul uses these to validate himself as a true apostle of Christ and, more generically, a good leader who has the best interests of others at heart.

Chapter five, therefore, will argue that Paul's self-presentation is modest, both in a predictably populist manner, as well as in a more specifically Socratic fashion.

We turn now to the semantic portion of this investigation. The first chapter will review previous studies of πραΰτης and ἐπιείκεια in 2 Cor 10:1. The second will turn to the ancient data themselves to formulate definitions of each word, identify the words with which each associates, note the types of contexts in which various word relationships occur, and then uncover the semantic consequences of combining πραΰτης and ἐπιείκεια. This will provide a firm foundation for translating 2 Cor 10:1 as an appeal through Christ's "leniency and clemency."

Chapter 1

History of Research:
ἐπιείκεια and πραΰτης in 2 Corinthians 10:1

> St Paul thinking it fit to forbear all severity till he had by fair means reduced as many of the contrary party as he could to a full submission to his authority (vid. ver. 6) begins here his discourse by conjureing them by the meekness and gentleness of Christ as an example that might excuse his delay of exemplary punishment on the ring-leaders and cheif offenders without giveing them reason to think it was for want of power.
> John Locke[1]

The meaning of the words πραΰτης and ἐπιείκεια in 2 Cor 10:1 have engendered much discussion. Both have deep, tangled roots in the Greek language: both are old and common; both express valued ethical traits; both have multiple nuances of meaning. This semantic complexity creates a variety of options in reading 2 Cor 10:1. The following pages will survey the discussion about the meaning of these terms in 2 Cor 10:1, attempting to present each author's purpose in writing, the conclusions each drew, and the evidence and reasoning utilized, as well as evaluating each author's work — focusing specifically on comments about 2 Cor 10:1. The basic semantic issue is whether connotations of royalty and power are present in ἐπιείκεια. Some argue yes, some no. The latter assert that, on the contrary, the operative idea in 2 Cor 10:1 is weakness. Attendant issues will emerge as we immerse ourselves in this debate, such as the relation of the πραΰτης καὶ ἐπιείκεια τοῦ Χριστοῦ to the historical Jesus. In the following survey, ἐπιείκεια will receive the most attention, because the debate hinges on its meaning.

---

[1] John Locke, *A Paraphrase and Notes on the Epistles of St Paul to the Galatians, 1 and 2 Corinthians, Romans, Ephesians*, ed. Arthur W. Wainwright, 2 vols. (Oxford University Press, 1987), 1: 296 (originally printed in London, 1707).

1. Survey of Research

Adolf von Harnack wrote an essay on gentleness and humility in the early church which serves as the fundamental study for contemporary discussions of 2 Cor 10:1.[2] While his concerns extend far beyond 2 Cor 10:1, Harnack begins his analysis there. He agrees with Resch[3] that 2 Cor 10:1 is related to the early Christian use of the saying of Jesus preserved in Matt 11:29.[4] Although Paul did not explicitly quote a tradition, leaving in 2 Cor 10:1 only a hidden *Herrnwort*,[5] to Harnack's eyes ἐπιείκεια "stands as if in a formula, a formula which is not minted for the first time."[6] Accounting for this lack of originality gave rise to Harnack's paper.

> If we possess a *Herrnwort* in which Jesus characterized himself as πραΰς and ταπεινὸς τῇ καρδίᾳ, and if Paul (and also Clement) knew this self-characterization of Jesus in the form of πραΰτης (ἐπιείκεια) and ταπεινός, and if "gentleness" and "humility" describe an essential feature of ancient Christian ethics, though a notorious problem which remains to be demonstrated in its particulars —, then it seems necessary to give more precise thought to these concepts than up to now has occurred.[7]

In pursuit of this objective Harnack divides his study into five sections. The first three investigate each of the words relevant to the tradition which

---

[2] Adolf von Harnack, "'Sanftmut, Huld und Demut' in der alten Kirche," in *Festgabe für Julius Kaftan zu seinem 70. Geburtstag*, eds. A. Titius, Friedrich Niebergall, and Georg Wobbermin (Tübingen: J. C. B. Mohr [Paul Siebeck], 1920), 113-29.

[3] Alfred Resch, *Aussercanonische Paralleltexte zu den Evangelien*, vol. 1, *Textkritische und Quellenkritische Grundlegungen. Paralleltexte zu Matthäus und Marcus*, Texte und Untersuchungen zur Geschichte der altchristlichen Literatur 10 (Leipzig: J. C. Hinrichs, 1893-94); idem, *Der Paulinismus und die Logia Jesu in ihrem gegenseitigen Verhältnis untersucht*, Texte und Untersuchungen zur Geschichte der altchristlichen Literatur 27 (Leipzig: J. C. Hinrichs, 1904).

[4] Cp. *1 Clem.* 16.17; Pol. *Phil.* 10.1. "That is not to say that Polycarp knew the saying from Matthew; Paul certainly did not know it from there" (Harnack, "Sanftmut, Huld und Demut," 114: "Dabei soll nicht behauptet werden, daß Polykarp den Spruch aus Matthäus kennt; Paulus kennt ihn gewiß nicht von daher"). On the other hand, "Clement knew the traditional *Herrnspruch* in Matthew" (*Ibid*.: "... Clemens den bei Matthäus überlieferten Herrnspruch gekannt hat").

[5] *Ibid.*, 113.

[6] *Ibid.*, 115: "... es steht hier wie in einer Formel, die nicht zum erstenmal geprägt ist."

[7] *Ibid.*: "Besitzen wir aber ein Herrnwort, in welchem sich Jesus selbst als πραΰς und ταπεινὸς τῇ καρδίᾳ, charakterisiert hat, hat Paulus [und auch Clemens] diese Selbstcharakterisierung Jesu in der Form: πραΰτης [ἐπιείκεια], ταπεινός, gekannt und bezeichnen, wie notorisch ist und im Genaueren noch gezeigt werden soll, Sanftmut und Demut einen Grundzug der ältesten christlichen Ethik —, so scheint es geboten, diese Begriffe genauer ins Auge zu fassen, als bisher geschehen ist."

1.1. Survey of Research

he identifies in Matt 11:29 and 2 Cor 10:1 (ἐπιεικής, πραΰς, and ταπεινός); the fourth examines combinations of the three words, and the fifth their use in early Christian ethics.

In defining the ethical terms involved in the *Herrnwort*, Harnack begins with ἐπιείκεια/ἐπιεικής. He argues that the LXX extends this pair's basic meaning (i.e., suitable, proper, appropriate) and consistently applies them to a specific, concrete use: ἐπιείκεια and ἐπιεικής "express the proper behavior for God, i.e., the absolute king; for this 'mildness' and 'mercy' are the appropriate qualities; therefore ἐπιείκεια is the graciousness of rulers."[8] Harnack further argues that the NT does not differ from the LXX. "Thus in 2 Cor 10:1, the ἐπιείκεια τοῦ Χριστοῦ means not simply 'gentleness,' but it is the mildness of Christ as of rulers."[9] He adds that this meaning fits into Matt 11:29 as well; therefore to Jesus' disciples "the assurance that he would be a merciful Lord would be particularly apt comfort."[10] In fact, Harnack argues, this meaning appears in every occurrence of ἐπιείκεια and ἐπιεικής in the NT, with the exception of Titus 3:2.[11] While a similar use appears in early Christian literature as well, ἐπιείκεια returns to a more general meaning, which lies closer to πραΰτης and signifies the *Milde* or mildness which all people should practice (not only rulers).[12] According to Harnack, then, ἐπιείκεια has a fairly specific application in the LXX and NT which broadens in early Christian literature.

When he turns to πραΰτης and its cognates, Harnack notes that while the LXX does not apply them to God, πραΰς is applied to the messianic king. This opens the door for applying πραΰς to Christ, which both Christ himself and Paul do. Though rare in the LXX, then, πραΰς becomes common in the early church by virtue of its application to Christ.[13]

---

[8] *Ibid.*, 116: "... um das für Gott, bzw. den absoluten König, schickliche Verhalten auszudrücken; für diese sind aber Milde und Gnade die gebührenden Eigenschaften; also ist ἐπιείκεια die Huld des Herschers". LXX references are 1 Kgs 12:22; 4 Kgs 6:3; Est 3:13b (13:2); 8:12j (16:9); 2 Macc 2:22; 9:27; 10:4; 3 Macc 3:15; 7:6; Ps 85:5; Wis 2:19; 12:18; Bar 2:27; Dan 3:42; 4:24; the verb ἐπιεικεύεσθαι is used in 2 Esdr 9:8.

[9] Harnack, "Sanftmut, Huld und Demut," 116: "die Milde Christi als des Herrschers."

[10] *Ibid.*: "ein gnädiger Herr."

[11] *Ibid.* In regard to Phil 4:5 Harnack suggests that when the Philippians are "rulers — one day they will possess the earth and will even judge angels — they should demonstrate their mildness to all people" (*Ibid.*). NT references to ἐπιείκεια or ἐπιεικής are Acts 24:4; 2 Cor 10:1; Phil 4:5; 1 Tim 3:3; Titus 3:2; Jas 3:17; 1 Pet 2:18.

[12] Harnack, "Sanftmut, Huld und Demut," 117. Early Christian references are *1 Clem.* 1.2; 13.1; 21.7; 29.1; 30.8; 56.1; 58.2; 62.2; Ign. *Phil.* 1.1, 2; *Eph.* 10.3; *Herm. Mand.* 12.4.2; Aristides 15.5; Athenagoras *Supp.* 12.1; 37.1; Diognetus 7.3f.

[13] Harnack, "Sanftmut, Huld und Demut," 118.

ταπεινός on the other hand is common in the LXX. While the LXX combines it with πραΰς only twice, in early Christian literature the combination becomes common. In fact, the two become equivalents.[14] This anticipates Harnack's comments about ταπεινός in the LXX. Departing from classical usage, the LXX made ταπεινός a positive concept describing correct behavior toward God. Jesus followed the LXX and the NT followed both Jesus' teaching and example.[15] Harnack then notes a special nuance in the NT. Because love of God and love of neighbor coincide in Jesus' teaching, ταπεινός no longer indicates only one's behavior toward God, "but is profoundly social, inseparably indicating as well the correct and necessary behavior to show one's neighbor."[16]

Turning to combinations of the three word groups, Harnack emphasizes how frequently two of them appear together in Christian literature, a frequency which contrasts with the OT which pairs only πραΰτης and ταπεινοφροσύνη, and that happens only twice. Deducing from this that the three pairs — as pairs — are distinctively Christian and point to "a major ethical concept of the new religion,"[17] Harnack concludes, "The triad πραΰτης-ἐπιείκεια-ταπεινοφροσύνη characterizes the claim and the conduct of earliest Christianity in respect of its ethics just as πίστις-ἀγάπη-ἐλπίς express the basic religious attitude, insofar as one may legitimately distinguish here between religion and ethics."[18] The remaining pages of his study trace the devolution of the ethical triad — particularly humility — through the early church from its eschatologically motivated origin to its ecclesiastical-pedagogical systematization in acts of self-abasing penitence. Harnack then ends with an encomium on these virtues: by πραΰτης, ἐπιείκεια, and ταπεινοφροσύνη "Christianity won its great struggle with the world ... as the blood of martyrs was the seed of the new religion, so also was their gentleness the power of their victory."[19]

---

[14] *Ibid.*, 119.

[15] *Ibid.*

[16] *Ibid.*, 120: "Es ist von besonderer Bedeutung, daß ταπεινοφροσύνη ... bei Jesus, Paulus und im Petrusbrief keineswegs nur das Verhalten gegen Gott, bzw. die Demutsaskese bezeichnet, sondern in innigstem Verein damit und unzertrennlich auch das richtige und notwendige Verhalten gegen den Nächsten."

[17] *Ibid.*, 121.

[18] *Ibid.*, 122: "Die Trias πραΰτης, ἐπιείκεια, ταπεινοφροσύνη charakterisiert die Forderung und das Verhalten der ältesten Christenheit in Hinsicht der Ethik ebenso wie πίστις, ἀγάπη, ἐλπίς die religiöse Grundstimmung zum Ausdruck bringt, soweit man hier zwischen Religion und Ethik überhaupt scheiden darf."

[19] *Ibid.*, 129: "Den großen Kampf mit der Welt, in welche die christliche Religion einzog, und mit dem Staat, der sie nicht dulden konnte, hat sie wirklich durch Sanftmut

Though outstanding in many respects, Harnack's essay has faults. First, his correlation of 2 Cor 10:1 and Matt 11:29 cannot go uncontested, particularly his reliance on Resch for this premise.[20] While this issue will be examined later in this study,[21] for now I simply register the complaint. Second, even if it were proven that Paul was quoting a Jesus tradition, we would still have to ask how Paul understands it and how he applies it. If Jesus spoke and then the tradition, Matthew, and Paul were each to repeat him, four different meanings could potentially be expressed.[22] Third, like nearly all of his successors in this matter, Harnack privileges the role of the LXX in his study. Harnack takes the results of his study of ἐπιείκεια in the LXX and then reads it into the NT, offering no explanation why the LXX should be the exclusive semantic predecessor to the NT. Since the LXX does not put forward a new meaning for ἐπιείκεια, this reliance on the LXX is even more curious. Fourth, as Leivestad would later demonstrate, Harnack misreads Wis 2:19. As a result, ἐπιείκεια in the

---

und Demut bestanden.... Wie das Blut der Märtyrer die Aussaat der neuen Religion wurde, so wurde auch ihre «Sanftmut» die Kraft ihres Sieges ..."

[20] See note two. Resch wrote ten years after H. H. Wendt reignited widespread debate about the relationship of Paul to Jesus. Both Harnack and Resch, apparently with a majority of scholars, objected to Wendt's conclusions, stressing the continuity between Paul and Jesus. With that as his objective, Resch found 925 allusions to Jesus' sayings in (nine of) Paul's letters, 133 more in Ephesians, 100 in the Pastoral Epistles, and 64 in Paul's speeches in Acts (Resch, *Paulinismus*, xxvii). Wrede's bombshell, *Paulus*, arrived a year after Resch's *Paulinismus*. On this history see Victor Furnish, "The Jesus-Paul Debate: From Baur to Bultmann," *BJRL* 47 (1964-65): 345-50. Stephen Wilson regards such numbers as "the fantasies of Resch for whom there is scarcely a verse of Paul which does not contain such an allusion" (Stephen Wilson, "From Jesus to Paul: The Contours and Consequences of a Debate," in *From Jesus to Paul: Studies in Honor of Francis Wright Beare*, ed. Peter Richardson and John C. Hurd [Waterloo, ON: Wilfrid Laurier University Press, 1984], 7-8). Furnish comments, "Resch long ago proved that, with imagination and patience, the possibilities can be multiplied like loaves and fishes. But the really convincing instances are fewer than a dozen" (Victor Furnish, *Theology and Ethics in Paul* [Nashville: Abingdon Press, 1968], 59). The point to be made is that Harnack relies on a highly suspect authority whose work cannot adequately support Harnack's premise. Hans Dieter Betz discusses the problem of the authenticity of Matt 11:29 ("The Logion of the Easy Yoke and of Rest," *JBS* 86 [1967]: 10-24; reprinted in *Synoptische Studien. Gesammelte Aufsätze II* [Tübingen: J. C. B. Mohr (Paul Siebeck), 1992]). Davies and Allison "do not doubt that Matthew's redactional reference to Jesus' meekness is yet one more clue that in 11.25-20 Jesus is being compared and contrasted with Moses" (W. D. Davies and Dale C. Allison, *The Gospel according to Saint Matthew*, ICC, 3 vols. [Edinburgh: T & T Clark, 1988-97], 2: 290).

[21] See chapter three of this study.

[22] Jesus' self-description as humble and lowly appears in different texts with different meanings (see Betz, "Logion"). A similar phenomenon appears in the various interpretations applied to parables within the Synoptic tradition.

LXX does not have a single use; it has two. Given the excessive attention paid to the LXX, Harnack's oversight in this matter is crucial. Fifth, when Harnack discusses the relationships between ἐπιείκεια, πραΰτης, and ταπεινοφροσύνη, he claims that there is a special affinity between ἐπιείκεια and ταπεινοφροσύνη. Harnack makes this assertion because these words are combined five times in early Christian literature. Since, however, four of the five pairs appear in 1 Clement, we can say only that Clement was fond of the combination. To generalize any further courts error.[23] Last — and more significant than the previous five points — Harnack's article is not about 2 Cor 10:1; therefore, he never specifies what exactly πραΰτης means in that verse,[24] nor does he pursue an extensive, contextual exegesis of 2 Corinthians 10–13. Harnack seeks to elucidate three ethical virtues which the early church valued highly, explaining how they captured the limelight and how they contributed to the moral life of the early church. Regarded as a diachronic study of an idea, Harnack's study deserves praise. That he remains a chief spokesperson for one of the primary ways of reading 2 Cor 10:1 testifies to his importance. But his lopsided reliance on the LXX leaves room for a closer examination of ἐπιείκεια in the NT; moreover, it demands it.

Harnack's views guided Herbert Preisker when the latter wrote the article on ἐπιείκεια for the *Theologisches Wörterbuch*.[25] On the whole, Preisker followed Harnack's conclusions, contending that in the LXX ἐπιείκεια mostly refers to "God's disposition as a Ruler."[26] In order to make allowance for persons other than God who demonstrate ἐπιείκεια (viz., earthly kings, Elisha, the sons of God), Preisker formulated a more generally worded conclusion: "God in His heavenly greatness as Ruler, the king who should be His earthly reflection, all who have God's gift and commission, have this disposition of mildness just because they exercise sovereign sway."[27] Preisker added further support to this conclusion by

---

[23] Analysis of Harnack's own data actually reveals a greater relationship between ἐπιείκεια and φιλανθρωπία than ἐπιείκεια and ταπεινός (Harnack, "Sanftmut, Huld und Demut," 117-18), which is in fact the overwhelming testimony of pagan sources.

[24] Ceslas Spicq was the first to provide a statement on both ἐπιείκεια and πραΰτης in 2 Cor 10:1.

[25] Herbert Preisker, "ἐπιείκεια, ἐπιεικής," in *Theologisches Wörterbuch zum Neuen Testament*, ed. Gerhard Kittel and Gerhard Friedrich, 10 vols. (Stuttgart: W. Kohlhammer, 1933-73), 2: 585-87. English: *Theological Dictionary of the New Testament*, trans. and ed. Geoffrey W. Bromiley, 10 vols. (Grand Rapids: Eerdmans, 1964-76), 2: 588-90.

[26] *Ibid.*, 2: 589 (German ed.: "das Verhalten Gottes als Herrscher," 2: 585).

[27] *Ibid.* (German ed: "Gott in seiner himmlischen Herrschergröße und der König, der

citing references from Josephus and Philo which applied ἐπιείκεια to God, king, lawgiver, and prophet. Then he drew on Plato, Pseudo-Plato, Aristotle, and Isocrates to establish clemency or leniency as valid translations for ἐπιείκεια and noted similar uses in Plutarch and in papyri.[28]

Turning to the NT Preisker found the idea of moderated power relevant to 2 Cor 10:1; Phil 4:5; Acts 24:4; Jas 3:17; and 1 Tim 3:3. With specific regard to 2 Cor 10:1 Preisker assumed that ἐπιείκεια is once again attributed to a king. This time the king is a heavenly one, Christ, "the Revealer of divine and royal majesty."[29] As a result, ἐπιείκεια is "a complement of heavenly majesty."[30] With Christ as his example, Paul therefore sought to exercise his apostolic authority with ἐπιείκεια.[31]

While one can agree with much of what Preisker's article says, what it fails to say or what it assumes does raise objections. For example, while the history of ἐπιείκεια which he sketches does seem to validate his interpretation of ἐπιείκεια, other uses to which he gives no notice could have made his evaluation less certain. Recognizing this deficiency in his diachronic survey weakens the value of Preisker's external proof for his reading of ἐπιείκεια in 2 Cor 10:1. His remaining evidence is nothing other than the attractiveness of his commentary on 2 Cor 10:1. As a result, in choosing whether to agree or disagree with him one can only ask whether Preisker provides an acceptable reading of the texts on which he comments. Since few interpreters have found his readings of Phil 4:5 and Jas 3:17 persuasive, his view of 2 Cor 10:1 has correspondingly suffered. Furthermore, his insistence on a "distinctively Christian accent"[32] diminishes the value of his comments. Theoretically one might find this curious. More importantly, though, the data do not require it. Eschatology and heavenly majesty attach to ἐπιείκεια because of the genitive τοῦ Χριστοῦ; the Greek term itself does not require or imply them. Given these considerations, one could — at best — find Preisker correct but lacking adequate foundation.

---

sein irdisches Abbild sein soll, oder alle die, die Gottes Beauftragte und Beschenkte sind, haben diese Haltung: die Milde, weil sie Herrschergewalt haben" [5: 585]).

[28] Ibid.

[29] Ibid. (German ed: "Vorbild ist Christus als Offenbarer göttlichköniglicher Hoheit" [5: 586]).

[30] Ibid. (German ed: "... Ergänzung zur himmlischen Hoheit" [5: 586]).

[31] Ibid., 2: 590.

[32] Ibid.

The *Wörterbuch's* article on πραΰτης was begun by Friedrich Hauck and completed by Siegfried Schulz.[33] The article provides a good indication of the difficulty in interpreting πραΰτης in 2 Cor 10:1. First, Hauck and Schulz give ample and clear evidence of the word's numerous applications and nuances. Second, they give attention to an additional meaning which arose in the LXX, viz., people in "a stunted, humble, lowly position."[34] As such it can be "a social and economic term" or take the more general sense of humble, particularly in view of one's relationship before God.[35] Hauck and Schulz then add the important observation that Philo does not imitate the LXX use of πραΰτης[36] — an observation which should warn against a slavish dependence on the LXX in our semantic investigation. When they turn to the NT, the quality of their work declines. They doubt that a dominical saying lies behind 2 Cor 10:1, yet they view it as a reflection on Christ's example during his life on earth. Beyond this they do not make clear at all what exactly πραΰτης means in 2 Cor 10:1. Thus, they provide good background for thinking about 2 Cor 10:1, but fail to deliver any decisive conclusions.

Ceslas Spicq was the next scholar to examine ἐπιείκεια and πραΰτης in a lengthy study.[37] His research also surveys χρηστότης and ἠπιότης because he intends to establish the specific nuance of *bonté* (goodness) and *douceur* (gentleness) to which each of these four Greek words refers.[38] His introduction claims that each word has a precise technical meaning in the LXX and NT which diverges from secular usage. The body of his essay therefore consists of four parts (each devoted to one of the four words) which seek to specify the nuance of each word and highlight its Jewish-Christian flavor.

---

[33] Friedrich Hauck and Siegfried Schulz, "πραΰς, πραΰτης," in *Theologisches Wörterbuch zum Neuen Testament*, ed. Gerhard Kittel and Gerhard Friedrich, 10 vols. (Stuttgart: W. Kohlhammer, 1933-73), 6: 645-651. English: *Theological Dictionary of the New Testament*, trans. and ed. Geoffrey W. Bromiley, 10 vols. (Grand Rapids: Eerdmans, 1964-76), 6: 645-651.

[34] *Ibid.*, 6: 647 (German ed.: "sich in einem verkümmerten, niedrigen, geringen Zustand befinden" [6: 647]).

[35] *Ibid.* (German ed.: "ein wirtschaftlich-soziologischer Begriff" [6: 647]).

[36] *Ibid.* The article refers to Josephus only briefly, leaving unclear the extent of his alignment with the LXX. As will be seen in chapter two, Josephus, like Philo, does not imitate the LXX's use of πραΰτης.

[37] Ceslas Spicq, "Bénignité, mansuétude, douceur, clémence," *RB* 54 (1947): 321-339.

[38] *Ibid.*, 321.

1.1. Survey of Research

Spicq first discusses χρηστότης, which he translates with *bénignité* and defines as "benevolence which blossoms in beneficence."[39] A social superior demonstrates this virtue by generosity, an inferior by devotion to duty.[40] He further asserts that Paul "enriched the theological notion of χρηστός by conceiving of the entire plan of salvation as a function of divine goodness."[41] In this claim Spicq exaggerates. Since χρηστότης is only one among the many things which apostles exhibit (2 Cor 6:6), only one of the Spirit's gifts (Gal 5:22), and only one of the many expressions of ἀγάπη (1 Cor 13:4), Spicq has not identified a special theological nuance for this word.

The second and most lengthy section of Spicq's essay examines πραΰτης. Although one might expect *douceur* or gentleness as translation equivalents, Spicq argues that the LXX introduces a new nuance which requires the translation *mansuétude* (i.e., patience, longsuffering, or humility). The OT depicts a πραΰς person as weak, without defense, poor, and at the bottom of the social scale, as opposed to arrogant and violent.[42] On the positive side, the πραεῖς are approachable, affable, modest, and the object of Yahweh's special care, particularly because of the quality of their souls: they fear God and are faithful and submissive to God.[43] The result of this submission is modesty, as practiced by the poor, the wise, and the Messiah, while its opposite is ὕβρις.[44]

Turning to the NT Spicq observes that the adjective πραΰς follows the LXX (Matt 5:5; 1 Pet 3:4).[45] Similarly, in James and Peter the noun πραΰτης means modesty.[46] In Paul, however, secular Greek joins the LXX in coloring the meaning of πραΰτης, requiring the reader to determine from context which exerts the greater semantic influence. In regard to 1 Cor 4:21 ("Shall I come to you with a rod or in love and a spirit of πραΰτης?"), Spicq states that πραΰτης is "opposed to avenging anger and to severity" and is therefore "clearly Greek."[47] Curiously, references to authority, destruction, severity, punishment, and sparing in 2 Corinthians 10–13 do not factor into his analysis of 2 Cor 10:1. Instead Spicq focuses

---

[39] *Ibid.*, 323: "bienveillance qui s'épanouit en bienfaisance."
[40] *Ibid.*
[41] *Ibid.*
[42] *Ibid.*, 324-25. See Job 24:4; Pss 34:3; 110:10.
[43] Spicq, "Bénignité," 325-26. See Pss 25:9; 33:3; 45:4; 147:6; 149:4; Job 36:15; Sir 1:27.
[44] Spicq, "Bénignité," 326-27. See Sir 3:17; 10:28; 45:4; Zech 9:9.
[45] Spicq, "Bénignité," 328.
[46] *Ibid.*, 329.
[47] *Ibid.*

on ταπεινός in the second half of 2 Cor 10:1 and reads the verse in light of Zach 9:9 and Matt 11:29 as an example of the nuance of πραΰτης original to the LXX. As a result, he lumps 2 Cor 10:1 with Gal 6:1 and Jas 3:13-14 as texts which deal with the correction of offenders and teach that one must intervene with πραΰτης, which "reflects a consciousness of the weakness appropriate to Christian virtue,"[48] i.e., modesty. 2 Cor 10:1 then refers to "the discretion and humility of the Savior."[49]

The third word Spicq examines, ἤπιος, receives the briefest attention. In this word he recognizes a gentleness (*douceur*) which shades toward leniency, a gentleness void of harshness, severity, and rigidity, a gentleness which prefers to disarm rather than bully opposition.[50] Since Spicq can identify no divergence from ἤπιος in profane Greek, he distinguishes it from the other three words in his study. He therefore emphasizes that the focus of ἤπιος lies on external bearing: "it is a matter less of the manifestation of an interior sentiment, as in *bénignité* and *mansuétude*, than of comportment, of gesture, of gentle and calm speech," almost "courtesy and politeness."[51]

The final term Spicq analyzes is ἐπιείκεια, which he translates *clémence*. He mentions its base meaning ("proper, fitting, reasonable"), its quality of moderation and opposition to ὕβρις, its overlap with πραότης and χρηστότης, and its application to leaders in order to indicate their avoidance of violence, i.e., clemency.[52] Spicq observes no idiosyncratic nuance in the use of ἐπιείκεια in the LXX, where it typically indicates "a moderation that superiors bring in the exercise of their power, notably in the deployment of vindictive justice."[53] In the NT, ἐπιείκεια receives theological color, as it shades towards πραΰτης, signifying more "a gentle and humble patience."[54] But this trend is less apparent in 2 Cor 10:1, where Paul's reference to Christ's clemency points to Christ's sovereign power and implicitly to Paul's own apostolic authority. In so doing Paul

---

[48] *Ibid.*, 330.

[49] *Ibid.* We must stipulate, however, that the idea of correcting offenders with πραΰτης was in no way an innovation of Christian thinking.

[50] *Ibid.*, 332.

[51] *Ibid.*: "Il s'agit moins de la manifestation d'un sentiment intérieur, comme dans la bénignité et la mansuétude que d'un comportement, de gestes, de paroles douces et calmes ... la courtoisie et la politesse."

[52] *Ibid.*, 333.

[53] *Ibid.*, 335: "une modération que le supérieur apporte dans l'exercice de sa puissance, notamment dans le déploiement de la justice vindicative."

[54] *Ibid.*, 336: "une douce et humble patience." This development is less novel if one considers the use of ἐπιείκεια and ἐπιεικής in philosophical rather than political contexts.

emphasizes that his authority, like Christ's, is not rigid and heartless but is "tempered by gentleness and mercy."[55] Taken as a whole however ἐπιείκεια receives broader application in the NT than in 2 Cor 10:1, so that it in fact becomes a desirable virtue for all Christians, who should be "gentle and humble, following the example of the Lord Jesus."[56]

In his closing statements Spicq concludes that goodness, humility, and clemency, though distinct concepts in the OT, have merged in the NT to the surprising degree that Paul could associate clemency and humility, "the virtues of a sovereign leader and of the oppressed servant."[57] Clemency and humility both express gentleness and discretion; clemency and goodness both express mercy and affability. On the other hand humility and goodness are inner virtues, whereas clemency and gentleness are more external.[58] All are important, Spicq stresses, for Christians.

Spicq's study adds to the major alternatives in interpreting 2 Cor 10:1. Whereas Harnack did not definitely state the meaning of πραΰτης in 2 Cor 10:1, Spicq explicitly asserts that ἐπιείκεια and πραΰτης express two different ideas. While we must applaud Spicq's willingness to permit each occurrence of a word to be interpreted on its own, we must lend adequate weight to context and recognize that the most crucial factor in the interpretation of 2 Cor 10:1 is the combination of ἐπιείκεια and πραΰτης. The great problem with Spicq's study is his failure to consider the many occasions where ἐπιείκεια and πραΰτης are, as in 2 Cor 10:1, used together. As will be seen, such examples make it difficult to read two quite different meanings into each word;[59] moreover, it is precisely Spicq in his later work on these words who helps to bring this into focus.

Ragnar Leivestad wrote the only significant English language study on the phrase διὰ τῆς πραΰτητος καὶ ἐπιεικείας τοῦ Χριστοῦ.[60] He first argues that the genitive τοῦ Χριστοῦ is subjective or possessive as opposed to merely qualitative;[61] next he turns to the two nouns, investigating their individual implications and then their combined function in 2 Cor 10:1. On the meaning of ἐπιείκεια, Leivestad makes an important observation: in Wis 2:19 ἐπεικής is not applied to a person who

---

[55] Ibid., 337: "se tempèrent de douceur et de miséricorde."

[56] Ibid.: "doux et humbles, à l'exemple du Seigneur Jésus."

[57] Ibid., 338: "saint Paul associe clémence et mansuétude, c'est-à-dire les vertus du chef souverain et du serviteur opprimé."

[58] Ibid.

[59] See the following chapter.

[60] Ragnar Leivestad, "'The Meekness and Gentleness of Christ' II Cor. X. 1," NTS 13 (1966): 156-64.

[61] Ibid., 156-57.

possesses some authority but to a poor person; it therefore does not mean clemency but instead signifies "a humble, patient steadfastness, which is able to submit to injustice, disgrace and maltreatment without hatred and malice, trusting God in spite of it all."[62] Wis 2:19 therefore provides the exception which weakens Harnack's and Preisker's generalizations about the use of ἐπιείκεια in the LXX and opens the door to a new semantic nuance, which Leivestad argues is common in the NT if one looks for it. Leivestad gladly notes that this alternative understanding provides an escape from Preisker's (and by extension, Harnack's) forced reading of clemency in NT uses of ἐπιείκεια.[63]

The recognition in ἐπιείκεια of this new nuance of humility, endurance, and submission, Leivestad argues, causes its overlap with the common Christian virtue, πραΰτης (as well as ταπεινός). "In biblical terminology, πραΰτης denotes the humble and gentle attitude which expresses itself in particular in a patient submissiveness to offence, free from malice and desire for revenge."[64] Taking πραΰτης and ἐπιείκεια as a hendiadys, Leivestad suggests that the more common word, πραΰτης, should determine the sense of the pair, a priority which he claims comparison with other Christian texts verifies.[65] Together these words "describe a gentle, humble and modest attitude as a general Christian ideal, not the magnanimity and generosity to be exercised by authorities."[66] Leivestad finds particular support in the *Epistle to Diognetus* 7.4 where he thinks that the meaning of ἐν ἐπιεικείᾳ καὶ πραΰτητι is filled in by the "gospel story" or "kerygma": these words do not refer to how Christ ruled, but to the fact that, lacking any royal dignity, he came as a simple, humble human.[67] "It is the very same paradox, the kenotic revelation, Paul is alluding to, when he reminds the Corinthians of the ἐπιείκεια and πραΰτης of Christ."[68]

After raising the possibility that Christ's humble state in his self-emptying lies behind 2 Cor 10:1, Leivestad attempts to demonstrate that the context of that verse makes his interpretation probable. He finds the support he needs in the second half of verse one, where Paul quotes the accusation that he is ταπεινός. The term ταπεινός corresponds to

---

[62] *Ibid.*, 158.

[63] *Ibid.*, 158-59.

[64] *Ibid.*, 159. Comparing this with our definition of πραότης in Appendix 2 will mitigate the identification of this as "biblical terminology."

[65] Tit 3:2; 1 Clem 21:7; 30:8; Diog 7:4. But ἐπιείκεια is really too common a word to require such a move.

[66] Leivestad, "The Meekness and Gentleness of Christ," 160.

[67] *Ibid.*, 160-61.

[68] *Ibid.*, 161 (Leivestad emphasizes this sentence).

πραΰτης and ἐπιείκεια[69] and thereby establishes a correlation between apostle and Lord, albeit not a perfect one because, unlike the hendiadys, ταπεινός carries a negative connotation, as verse ten makes clear in exchanging ἀσθενής for ταπεινός. But what would normally seem bad must be reevaluated in light of the mystery of the kenotic revelation which allows Paul to make a virtue of his weakness: the apostle's ministry repeats the paradox of the incarnation, for weakness provides the platform for divine δύναμις to triumph. When therefore he appeals διὰ τῆς πραΰτητος καὶ ἐπιεικείας τοῦ Χριστοῦ, "Paul is not referring to the lenience and indulgence of the heavenly judge, nor even to his mild and gracious attitude during his earthly life; he is alluding to the fact of the kenosis, the literal weakness and lowliness of the Lord."[70]

In closing, Leivestad returns to a problem to which he alluded at the beginning of his paper. Does an appeal to Christ's "meekness and gentleness" clash with the harsh tone of argument which Paul presents in the following chapters? Leivestad answers no because the alleged conflict is a false one. When Paul appeals διὰ τῆς πραΰτητος καὶ ἐπιεικείας τοῦ Χριστοῦ, he does not appeal by kindness but by lowliness, the opposite of which is not forceful argumentation but boasting.[71] The alleged dissonance does not really exist. But is this really insightful or merely clever? Similar to kindness, lowliness seems equally incompatible with Paul's subsequent statements: words such as τολμῆσαι, στρατεύεσθαι, ὅπλα, δυνατά, καθαίρεσις, αἰχμαλωτίζειν, ὑπακοή, and ἐκδικῆσαι (10:2-6) are not the characteristics of a lowly person.

Leivestad's article has three important values. First, it is a study specifically of 2 Cor 10:1 as opposed to a study of ἐπιείκεια or πραΰτης which as a matter of course touches on 2 Cor 10:1. Second, rather than simply elaborate on 2 Cor 10:1 in view of what he thinks ἐπιείκεια and πραΰτης mean (offering exposition or flowery prose), Leivestad actually offers reasons to argue on behalf of his reading of 2 Cor 10:1. Third — and most importantly — Leivestad offers a new approach to reading 2 Cor 10:1. For these reasons this work stands out from others on 2 Cor 10:1.

Leivestad, however, limits the value of his article by limiting the scope of his research. For example, Leivestad does not enter into debate about the christology of 2 Cor 10:1, though he clearly lays out a position in the matter.[72] Given that christology serves as his thread for weaving together

---

[69] Ibid., 161-62. Leivestad states that though not entirely interchangeable, "πραΰς, in particular, is closely associated with ταπεινός in biblical language" (p. 162).
[70] Ibid., 163.
[71] Ibid., 164.
[72] See chapter three of this study.

the semantics of Wis 2:19 through 2 Cor 10:1 to *Diog.* 7.4, failure to examine the christological problems of 2 Cor 10:1 leaves his study deficient.[73] A larger problem lurks in Leivestad's restricted focus on "biblical language," which causes him to ignore semantic data outside Jewish and Christian texts. On a smaller scale, this oversight allows him to insinuate that ἐπιείκεια might be an unusual word.[74] It is not. On a larger scale, it exempts him from reflection on diachronic development. Of greatest concern, however, this allows him to neglect the many examples in which ἐπιείκεια and πραΰτης are used together. When these are considered they open a window for interpreting 2 Cor 10:1 which differs from Leivestad's reconstruction, as will be seen later in this study.[75] To date, then, Leivestad's study is the most focused attempt to understand 2 Cor 10:1, but it is nevertheless inadequate.

The contribution of Wolfgang Bauder to the *Theologisches Begriffslexikon* is of mixed value.[76] His brief reflection on secular Greek usage is exceedingly insightful on both ἐπιείκεια and πραΰς. The discussion of the latter in the OT likewise rises to that standard. When, however, he turns to the NT his comments diminish in value. In both Matt 11:29 and 2 Cor 10:1 Bauder sees reference to Christ's rule, the former stressing the Messiah's human humility and the latter characterizing the historical Jesus' attitude to people.[77] This mixing of rule and humility places Bauder's comments outside the boundaries of the debate as it now stands. If he had leisure to elaborate this position, it might prove illuminating. As is, his comments remain unsupported and odd.

Ceslas Spicq discussed ἐπιείκεια a second time in his *Notes de lexicographie néo-testamentaire*,[78] in an article organized synchronically.

---

[73] I might mention that Matt 11:29 does not figure into Leivestad's argument.

[74] "In 2 Cor 10:1 the combination πραΰτης καὶ ἐπιείκεια forms a hendiadys. It is a sound principle in such cases to assume that the sense is qualified by the more usual and familiar of the two terms. It is more reasonable to define the word ἐπιείκεια (which is relatively rare in Christian usage) in accordance with πραΰτης than the other way round" (Leivestad, "'The Meekness and Gentleness of Christ,'" 159-60).

[75] See the following chapter.

[76] Wolfgang Bauder, "Demut," in *Theologisches Begriffslexikon zum Neuen Testament*, eds. Lothar Coenen, Erich Beyreuther, and Hans Bietenhard, 3 vols. (Wuppertal: Brockhaus, 1965-71), 1: 173-75. English: "Humility," in *New International Dictionary of New Testament Theology*, ed. Colin Brown, 4 vols. (Grand Rapids: Zondervan, 1975-85), 2: 256-59.

[77] *Ibid.*, 2: 258.

[78] Ceslas Spicq, "ἐπιείκεια, ἐπιεικής," in *Notes de lexicographie néo-testamentaire*, 3 vols., Orbis biblicus et orientalis 22 (Fribourg/Suisse: Editions universitaires, 1978-

Noting the semantic complexity of the term and the consequent difficulty of translating it, he settles on a fourfold classification of ἐπιείκεια and its adjective, ἐπιεικής. First, Spicq notes the correspondence between ἐπιείκεια and clemency. In this light ἐπιείκεια expresses an equity which mollifies the strict application of written laws, "a good-naturedness which moderates the inflexible severity of anger."[79] Second, Spicq highlights the connection between ἐπιείκεια and μέτριος, yielding the nuance of moderation or balance which points to an honest or virtuous person.[80] This is a more general moral application than the first category,[81] while the third is even more so, vague to the point of being nebulous. In this third semantic class Spicq links ἐπιείκεια to πρέπον, χρηστότης and φιλανθρωπία. This wide-ranging classification of ἐπιείκεια encompasses reasonableness and propriety and describes a person who maintains "open, conciliatory and trustful"[82] relations with others. It is a "helpful obligingness,"[83] or to use Ps.-Plato's definition, "a habitual inclination of character to friendship towards people" (*Defin.* 412e).[84] Last, ἐπιείκεια shades into χάρις as "kindness, courtesy, generosity ... a proper grace."[85]

This article is a splendid model of economy. Spicq supplies a generous amount of references to ancient sources, including inscriptions and papyri, while his four categories succinctly indicate the many important relationships which ἐπιείκεια has with other Greek words. That he begins his analysis by discussing ἐπιείκεια as clemency does, however, seem at odds with the inner logic of the concept.[86] As for 2 Cor 10:1, there is nothing new here in comparison to his previous article. Thus, without argument or explanation, Spicq includes 2 Cor 10:1 in his first category,

---

82), 1: 263-67. Spicq makes similar, albeit briefer, comments in his *Théologie morale du Nouveau Testament*, 2 vols. (Paris: Librairie Lecoffre, 1965), 2: 802-4 (which is part of Appendix 9: "Le visage sans ride de l'amour dans l'Église chrétienne," 2: 781-815).

[79] *Ibid.*, 1: 264: "une débonnaireté qui modère l'inflexible sévérité du courroux."

[80] *Ibid.*, 1: 265.

[81] It seems to me that ἐπιείκεια as clemency could also be considered a specific application of the more general ἐπιείκεια as μετριότης.

[82] Spicq, "ἐπιείκεια," 1: 266: "ouvert, conciliant et confiant."

[83] *Ibid.*, 1: 267: "la complaisance serviable."

[84] *Ibid.*

[85] *Ibid.*: "bonté, courtoisie, générosité ... la bonne grâce." It seems to me that ἐπιείκεια as χάρις might also be considered as a specific application of ἐπιείκεια as φιλανθρωπία or perhaps χρηστότης.

[86] That the definition of ἐπιείκεια in Appendix 1 does not follow Spicq's underscores the rhetorical nature of semantic analysis: the analyst "invents" the connections and links between examples.

which links ἐπιείκεια to clemency; however, the correlation between ἐπιείκεια and πραΰτης he associates not with clemency but with his broadest category, the third, where he links ἐπιείκεια with humility to describe good relationships with others.[87] In 2 Cor 10:1 the apostle therefore appeals to two distinct virtues of Christ, his ἐπιείκεια or clemency and his πραΰτης. For the meaning of the latter we turn to Spicq's article on that word.

In his article on πραΰτης[88] Spicq provides a wonderful assortment of references to Greek authors. When he turns to the OT he too states that it deviates from secular usage and is applied to the humble, the abased, the ταπεινοί, expressing a "perfect submission to the divine will."[89] The NT perpetuates this understanding of πραΰτης. In regard to 2 Cor 10:1 Spicq translates πραΰτης as *mansuétude*, a humility which "disarms his opponents";[90] he adds, with little elaboration, that Paul assumes the posture of the educator in this verse.[91] How do humility and education combine? Spicq wrongly offers 2 Tim 2:25 and Dio Cas. 48.3; 55.12 and 17 as evidence, texts which display the pedagogical (or psychagogical) dimension, but in no way connote humility. Thus, Spicq is tricked by the

---

[87] The correlation of ἐπιείκεια-πραΰτης with humility is amazing given the references provided, examples which prove no such thing! This apparently mystified Spicq's English translator: "The person characterized by ἐπιείκεια is reasonable, a respecter of social norms. Sometimes the emphasis is on exactitude, loyalty, and fidelity in the accomplishment of a task; much more often on mildness; hence its connection with goodness (1 Pet 2:18), peace (Jas 3:17; *1 Enoch* 6.5, Greek frag.), and mildness-leniency (πραΰτης)" (*Theological Lexicon of the New Testament*, trans. James D. Ernest, 3 vols. [Peabody, MA: Hendrickson, 1994], 2: 36-37). In the key expression at the end, the French original reads, "la douceur-mansuétude." Given what we noted earlier in regard to Spicq's article "Bénignité, mansuétude, douceur, clémence," translating "douceur-mansuétude" as "mildness-leniency" seems inappropriate. Quoting Spicq's article on πραΰτης presses the question further (and here I will use Ernest's English translation): "Their πραΰτης is not so much mildness as indulgence (French *mansuétude*). The Latin word *mansuetudo* derives from *mansuesco*, literally, 'accustom to the hand,' hence 'tame'; so *mansuetudo*, 'taming,' came to mean serene receptiveness, as opposed to impetuosity or insolence, hostility or gruffness. It is in a way the docile and respectful attitude of a servant toward his master, always ready to submit" (*TLNT* 3: 167). Thus, leniency is not a good translation of Spicq's mansuétude, which in turn fails to represent adequately the Greek texts that Spicq cites which link ἐπιείκεια and πραΰτης.

[88] Ceslas Spicq, "Πραϋπάθεια, πραΰς, πραΰτης," in *Notes de lexicographie néo-testamentaire*, Orbis biblicus et orientalis 22, 3 vols. (Fribourg/Suisse: Éditions Universitaires, 1978-82), 3: 570-82.

[89] *Ibid.*, 3: 577-78: "une soumission parfaite à la volonté divine."

[90] *Ibid.*, 3: 580: "c'est la πραΰτης qui désarme les contradicteurs."

[91] *Ibid.*, 3: 581. Spicq applies the image of educator to 1 Cor 4:21 as well (*Ibid.*, 3: 580).

1.1. Survey of Research

LXX into seeing a nuance of πραότης where it was absent. This is unfortunate and diminishes the value of Spicq's discussion of 2 Cor 10:1 in this article.

Francesco D'Agostino has written the most significant study on ἐπιείκεια, a monograph born of interests in jurisprudence and the philosophy of law, conceived as volume one in a study of the history of equity.[92] D'Agostino traces ἐπιείκεια from Homer and Hesiod to the Church Fathers, hoping, among other things, to demonstrate "the correspondence of the theme of ἐπιείκεια to the Hellenistic mind, understanding the latter as education in the regularity of the cosmos and the former as the moment of mediation between *nomos* and pragmatic reality."[93] We will examine his diachronic work later,[94] but for now we focus on D'Agostino's sixth chapter, "L'esperienza ebraico-cristiana e l'*epieikeia*."[95] In so doing, it is important to know that his work investigates more than a word; it seeks to understand an idea and its place within a *Weltanschauung*.[96]

---

[92] Francesco D'Agostino, *Epieikeia. Il tema dell'equità nell'antichità greca*, Pubblicazioni dell'Istituto di Filosofia del Diritto dell'Università di Roma, third series, 8 (Milan: Giuffrè, 1973), xi. Jacqueline de Romilly's monograph, *La douceur dans la pensée grecque*, Collection d'études anciennes (Paris: Société d'Édition «Les Belles Lettres», 1979), is likewise a major investigation crucial to this study and will therefore be helpful in chapter two. Because it does not focus exclusively on ἐπιείκεια and offers no exegesis of specifically 2 Cor 10:1, it receives no discussion in this present survey. Romilley does, however, offer the general opinion that the profane use of πραΰτης is present in the NT (pp. 314-15).

[93] D'Agostino, *Epieikeia greca*, ix: "la corrispondenza del tema dell'*epieikeia* al genio ellenico, intendendo questo come educato alla regolarità del cosmo e quella come il momento di mediazione tra *nomos* e realtà pragmatica."

[94] See the following chapter.

[95] This chapter received separate publication as "Il tema dell' epieikeia nella S. Scrittura," *Revista di teologia morale* 5 (1973): 385-406. Only cosmetic changes were made in the independent article so as to accomodate it to its new context. In terms of substance one can read the book or the article.

[96] "In spite of its triumphal appearance in the *Nicomachaen Ethics*, ἐπιείκεια remains all the same the sign of a discrepancy in the Greek philosophical-juridical experience, namely, its impossible attempt to synthesize the universal and the particular, the infallibility of *nomos* and the fallibility of practice; or, in other words, the fallibility of man and of his doing compared to that infallibility of his duty to do what the law prescribes.... Phenomenologically, the sense of ἐπιείκεια was for the Greeks precisely that of filling up this hiatus, or resolving this disagreement. The history which will be illustrated in the following pages displays clearly the failure of this attempt, as of all the other attempts of any *Weltanschauung* which gives primacy to *nomos* or which wants to postulate an identification of *nomos*-reality." (D'Agostino, *Epieikeia greca*, ix-x: "Nonostante la sua trionfale apparizione nell'*Etica Nicomachea*, l'*epieikeia* resta nondimeno il segno della contraddizione nell'esperienza filosofico-giuridica greca, nel

D'Agostino's study of ἐπιείκεια in the LXX leads him to conclusions similar to his predecessors. In general ἐπιείκεια describes God "as a benevolent and clement sovereign."[97] Given the earlier chapters of his monograph, D'Agostino can further observe that the general LXX use corresponds with broader Hellenistic use: ἐπιείκεια is "a characteristic of moderation and refers to sovereignty as its attribute."[98] Having said this, D'Agostino adds three caveats. First, he stipulates that the correlation of the LXX and broader Hellenistic usage obscures the different foundations on which each rests. In the Wisdom of Solomon, for example, God is ἐπιείκεια not only as sovereign, but as omnipotent, which is unique to God;[99] furthermore, the combination of power, sovereignty, and ἐπιείκεια "finds its perfection only in God and in his sons" who are "nurtured by the fear of God."[100] All this is to say that in the LXX ἐπιείκεια is intertwined with Jewish religion and therefore resides in a *Weltanschauung* different from the Greek. This entrance into another *Weltanschauung* will become important in D'Agostino's later exposition. Second, it is wrong to think that the LXX attributes ἐπιείκεια "to the sovereign alone, with the unique function of moderating the use of power."[101] Third, without explanation D'Agostino warns against considering ἐπιείκεια "as something of little importance in day to day moral phenomenology."[102] These three stipulations contribute to and shape D'Agostino's reading of ἐπιείκεια in the NT.

---

suo impossibile tentativo di sintetizzare l'universale e il particolare, l'infallibilità del *nomos* e la fallibilità della prassi; o, in altre parole, la fallibilità dell'uomo e del suo fare rispetto a quell'infallibilità del suo dover fare che è il portato del diritto.... Fenomenologicamente il senso dell'*epieikeia* era per i Greci proprio quello di colmare questo *hiatus*, di risolvere questo dissidio. La storia che viene illustrata nelle pagine che seguono mostra chiaramenta il fallimento di questo tentativo, come del resto di tutti i tentativi di qualunque *Weltanschauung* che dia il primato al *nomos* o che voglia postulare una identificazione *nomos*-realtà.")

[97] *Ibid.*, 142: "... esso indica in prevalenza l'atteggiamento di Dio verso gli uomini, in quanto sovrano benevolo e clemente."

[98] *Ibid.*, 143: "caratterizzata dalla moderazione e riferita alla sovranità, quale suo attributo." Though similarity between the LXX and secular literature should startle no one, D'Agostino's observation refutes the lopsided focus Biblical studies has placed on the LXX in the study of ἐπιείκεια and situates the semantic debate in a much larger field of evidence.

[99] *Ibid.* D'Agostino callibrates ἐπιείκεια to God's power. Wisdom of Solomon equally callibrates it to God's justice (cp. the evil human rulers in 2:11, ἔστω δὲ ἡμῶν ἡ ἰσχὺς νόμος τῆς δικαιοσύνης, with God in 12:16, ἡ γὰρ ἰσχύς σου δικαιοσύνης ἀρχή).

[100] D'Agostino, *Epieikeia greca*, 144.
[101] *Ibid.*, 146.
[102] *Ibid.*

1.1. Survey of Research

D'Agostino divides his investigation of the NT into three sections. In the first he poses the problem, arguing that the study of ἐπιείκεια in the NT must begin in Matt 11:29.[103] D'Agostino follows Resch[104] in correlating 2 Cor 10:1 and other Christian texts with Matt 11:29 and thereby uncovering an "actual literary topos."[105] This topos includes πραΰτης, ταπεινοφροσύνη, ἐπιείκεια, and ἡσυχία, though not all of these words appear in any given manifestation of the topos. D'Agostino deduces therefore that

> it is entirely probable that Paul, admonishing the Corinthians in the name of Christ's *mansuetudo* and *modestia*, is not referring to a general virtue of Christ, but much more concretely to a quality of Christ's which is well known and recognizable to Paul's auditors, which very thing Jesus himself explicitly attributed to himself.[106]

The study of ἐπιείκεια in the NT is according to D'Agostino the analysis of a virtue which the earthly Jesus claimed for himself; it is the history of Matt 11:29.

One must ask in what sense Jesus can designate himself πραΰς καὶ ταπεινός (and ἐπιεικής). The remaining two sections of D'Agostino's sixth chapter explore that question. Section two reviews Harnack's study,[107] exploring his answer to that question. Section three (titled "ἐπιείκεια, νόμος, ἀγάπη") presents D'Agostino's solution, a solution which reflects his interest in the connection between ἐπιείκεια and νόμος. D'Agostino claims that the similarity of ἐπιείκεια in the LXX and NT is only superficial, because each has its own application within its individual *Weltanschauung*. Thus, in the LXX God is ἐπιεικής because God is sovereign, whereas Jesus is ἐπιεικής because he is Lord. This sounds similar until the next step is taken: God is characterized as sovereign by virtue of omnipotence, whereas in the NT Jesus is characterized as Lord by virtue of servanthood, weakness, and crucifixion. As Jesus' incarnation transforms the idea of Lord, the Lord's virtue, ἐπιείκεια, likewise changes, being colored by lowliness or

---

[103] "Ἄρατε τὸν ζυγόν μου ἐφ' ὑμᾶς καὶ μάθετε ἀπ' ἐμοῦ, ὅτι πραΰς εἰμι καὶ ταπεινὸς τῇ καρδίᾳ, καὶ εὑρήσετε ἀνάπαυσιν ταῖς ψυχαῖς ὑμῶν.

[104] Regarding Resch see above (n. 19).

[105] D'Agostino, *Epieikeia greca*, 148: "un vero e proprio *topos* letterario."

[106] *Ibid.*, 149: "Conseguentemente, è del tutto probabile che Paolo, ammonendo i Corinzi in nome della *mansuetudo* e della *modestia* del Cristo, non si sia riferito a generiche virtù di Gesù, ma molto più concretamente a delle qualità di lui ben note e conosciute al suo uditorio, quali quelle che lo stesso Gesù si era esplicitamente attribuite e tali da non rendere possibili ambiguità sul loro significato concreto e sulla loro rilevanza spirituale."

[107] Regarding Harnack see above.

ταπεινοφροσύνη.[108] In terms of worldview, Jesus has disrupted the orderly regulation of the cosmos. Jesus is now the new defining center of reality, the standard by which to structure the cosmos. In D'Agostino's terms this represents a shift from a cosmocentric to an anthropocentric *Weltanschauung*. As one of this new perspective's moral expressions, ἐπιείκεια no longer pertains exclusively to relationships of power. "Instead of the virtue of the powerful towards their subjects, [ἐπιείκεια] appears as a virtue shown towards brothers, which prefers to a moment of juridical expression that infinitely warmer and richer immediacy of the gift of itself."[109] ἐπιείκεια is no longer simply clemency but ἀγάπη.

Given that D'Agostino approaches ἐπιείκεια as a legal scholar he adds further comments concerning the connection between ἐπιείκεια and νόμος. As ἐπιείκεια has approached ἀγάπη it has taken on a new means for bridging the gap between νόμος and reality, viz. self-giving. The incarnation and its *weltanschaulich* offspring therefore signify "the primacy of spirit over matter, of the human over the cosmos, or ... of the personal *logos* over impersonal *nomos*."[110] Agent now takes the initiative in νόμος. In the victory of the personal particular over the impersonal universal, ἀγάπη has supplanted νόμος.

If therefore for a Greek the moral life was fundamentally a life of conformity to *nomos* (and sin therefore was *hybris*, a desire to place oneself outside the prescriptions of *nomos*), for the Christian the moral life can no longer consist of a conformity to the objectivity of the world, but of *fidelity to a person*, a fidelity of love.[111]

---

[108] "For the connection of omnipotence-*epieikeia* in the OT and the omnipotence-dominion-clemency of the pagan world, Christianity substitutes *tapeinophrosynē-epieikeia*" (D'Agostino, *Epieikeia greca*, 158-59: "Al nesso onnipotenza-*epieikeia* dell'Antico Testamento, a quello onnipotenza-dominio-clemenza del mondo pagano, il cristianesimo sostituisce quello di *tapeinophrosynē-epieikeia*."). Actually, Paul substitutes ταπεινοφροσύνη-κυριότης-ἐπιείκεια. Moreover, the logical extension of D'Agostino's position requires that a different *Weltanschauung* must be postulated for every type of empowerment. This implies distinct worldviews for Greek tyrants, Persian monarchs, Hellenistic kings, Roman consuls, censors, and emperors, for generals, fathers, slave-owners, and friends. Clearly each does have a different point-of-view. The amazing thing is that most of these could incorporate the same rhetoric of ἐπιείκεια into their self-identities — and usually without recognizing the differences.

[109] *Ibid.*, 167: "Invece che virtù dei potenti verso i soggetti essa appare virtù dell'incontro fraterno, che antepone al momento dell'estrinsecismo giuridico quello infinitamente più caldo e ricco di immediatezza della donazione de sé."

[110] *Ibid.*, 159: "il primato dello spirito sulla materia, dell'uomo sul cosmo o, se si vuole, del *logos* personale sul *nomos* impersonale."

[111] *Ibid.*: "Se quindi per un greco la vita morale era fondamentalmente vita di conformità al *nomos* (e il peccato quindi *hybris*, volontà di porsi al di là delle prescrizioni di quello), per il cristiano non potrà più consistere in una conformità all'oggettività del mondo, ma nella *fedeltà ad una persona*, fedeltà d'amore ..."

A Christian *Weltanschauung* has now emerged from the Greek.[112]

Although D'Agostino's approach in his sixth chapter might help to explain what ἐπιείκεια signifies generally in the NT, he inadequately addresses what ἐπιείκεια means in 2 Cor 10:1. The light D'Agostino's general picture sheds on the NT and early Christianity does not suffice to clarify a specific text, particularly the earliest one in the evolutionary scheme. In 2 Cor 10:1 ἐπιείκεια stands at a semantic threshold: on one side stands the Hellenistic world at large (e.g., the Stoa, the LXX), on the other a Christian nuance. Wis 2:19 indicates the potential for semantic evolution, while the incarnation will in fact provide an engine for it. But on which side of the threshold does Paul stand? Semantic investigation of 2 Corinthians 10–13 must answer that question, not the LXX, not Matt 11:29, not *1 Clement*. Correspondence between any of these texts and 2 Cor 10:1 cannot be assumed without question.

D'Agostino's exegesis is also open to criticism. First, reading ἐπιείκεια into Matt 11:29 is nothing more than a hunch. In my opinion D'Agostino reads Matthaean humility into Paul's psychagogy in order to serve his larger theory. Second, that 2 Cor 10:1 alludes to the words of the historical Jesus, preserved for us in Matt 11:29, is yet another issue which exegesis has yet to demonstrate and therefore cannot be uncritically assumed. Third, that Paul's audience knew the saying of Matt 11:29 is a further major assumption, one that probably defies demonstration. Fourth, given the Corinthians' attitudes as reflected in 2 Corinthians 10–13 (viz., ταπεινός and ἀσθενής are contemptible), the *Weltanschauung* which D'Agostino describes has clearly *not* taken hold in the Corinthian church. Without debating what christology was or was not present, we can say that

---

[112] "NT *epieikeia* is not therefore a way of exercising (however mild) the sovereign power which God wields and which is transmitted in the faith to his sons ... nor is NT *epieikeia* an indulgent application of *nomos* (however divine): to interpret it thus is to remain confined in the Hellenic *Weltanschauung*, in which *anankē* is really arranged by *nomos* to form the ontological horizon of understanding. On the contrary, *epieikeia* represents ... negatively the sign of the liberation which Christ has given to the world (liberation from the deification of the powers, from the idolatry of eros, from the adoration of bread) and positively the sign of the better way which with respect to *nomos* attains to *agapē*" (*Ibid.*, 164: "L'*epieikeia* neotestamentaria non è quindi un modo di esercizio [sia pur mite] del potere sovrano di cui Dio dispone e che nella fede si trasmette ai suoi figli ... non è un modo di applicazione indulgente di un *nomos* [sia pur divino]: interpretarla così sarebbe un restar confinati nella *Weltanschauung* ellenica, nella quale realmente è la *anankē* ordinata dal *nomos* a costituire l'orizzonte ontologico di comprensione. Al contrario, l'*epieikeia* rappresenta ... negativamente il segno della liberazione che Cristo ha donato al mondo, della liberazione dalla deificazione della potenza, dall'idolatria dell'eros, dall'adorazione del pane, e positivamente il segno del *prius* che rispetto al *nomos* tocca all'*agapē*.").

no approbation of ταπεινός was present among the Corinthians, let alone an entire worldview which valued it. Fifth, D'Agostino's reading of the Christian *Weltanschauung* bypasses discussion of Paul's *Weltanschauung*. D'Agostino's emphasis on Jesus' servanthood ignores the tradition according to which the humbled redeemer also conquered cosmic foes and is exalted over all the universe.[113] In short, D'Agostino does not hear the diverse voices contained in the Bible. All these facts complicate the overly simple picture D'Agostino has drawn and call for a reading of 2 Cor 10:1 based on contextual exegesis rather than the broad currents of a presumed intellectual evolution.

A final criticism rests on the christology of 2 Corinthians 10–13. If, as D'Agostino suggests, 2 Cor 10:1 evokes the image of the lowly Jesus, why does this consideration not enter into Paul's argument? The example of Jesus would have been Paul's most potent argument in his debate with the Corinthians. That the apostle was so absent-minded as to allude to Jesus' example in 10:1 only to loose sight of it in the following chapters seems unlikely. D'Agostino's reading of 2 Cor 10:1 must live with this uncomfortable silence.

Given the present interest specifically in 2 Cor 10:1, the objections just registered address D'Agostino's study at that level. At the broader level of early Christianity, D'Agostino's study may have greater value as a contribution describing a divergence of Christian thinking from its broader world. At that level his dialogue with Harnack becomes particularly important. Still, D'Agostino would do better to investigate his Christian *Weltanschauung* via ταπεινός rather than ἐπιείκεια, assuming one actually finds *Weltanschauung* a helpful (and not exaggerated) interpretive perspective.

K. Duchatelez also studied ἐπιείκεια in great detail, tracing its evolution through Greek antiquity, both pagan and Christian, but he paid particular attention to Patristic usage.[114] He traces three meanings of ἐπιείκεια, which comprise the three major sections of his paper: 1) ἐπιείκεια as *convenance* (suitability, fitness, propriety); 2) ἐπιείκεια as *équité*,

---

[113] Such selectivity is really no surprise, though, for any attempt to speak of an OT, or a Christian, or Hellenistic *Weltanschauung* will require generalization. While such abstractions often aid understanding, they crumple easily when they meet data. For example, to speak of God's omnipotence in the OT helps express the superiority of God's power, but equally suppresses the drama with which it prevails. Moreover, if one presses the philosophical meaning of omnipotence, the word becomes even less useful as an aid to understanding specific texts.

[114] K. Duchatelez, "L' 'ἐπιείκεια' dans l'Antiquité grecque, païenne et chrétienne," *Communio* 12 (1979): 203-31.

indulgence, modération, and *clémence*; and 3) ἐπιείκεια as *modestie* and *douceur* (modesty and gentleness). To these Duchatelez appends a brief section of ecumenical conclusions.

The idea of *convenance* lies closest to the etymological meaning of ἐπιείκεια, dominates Homeric usage, and is long-lived.[115] It describes the gentleman, a person who is reasonable or upright, a quality of honesty or probity — particularly in the Classical period.[116] The LXX and NT ignore this sense of ἐπιείκεια, though the Greek Fathers use it in this way, as does Philo on occasion.[117]

In the Classical period ἐπιείκεια finds widespread use to indicate *equity or moderation*, i.e., opposition to δίκαιος as strict application of the law.[118] This incites discussion. Is it appropriate to moderate law? The early Stoics regarded any such tampering as anathema; a virtuous person gives no room to clemency.[119] Meanwhile the LXX, the Letter of Aristeas, Philo, and Josephus all offer examples of ἐπιείκεια used to connote moderation of legal stipulations.[120] As for the NT, Duchatelez places 2 Cor 10:1; Matt 11:29; 1 Tim 3:3; 1 Pet 2:18; and Acts 24:4 in this category.[121] In connection to 2 Cor 10:1 Duchatelez writes,

Paul, in the exercise of his apostolic authority, appeals to the *mansuétude* and to the clemency or benevolence of Christ. If one accepts the parallelism with Matt 11:29, then clemency is particularly applied here to the royal Christ, who nevertheless remains humble and mild.[122]

This is all Duchatelez says about 2 Cor 10:1. His comments emerge from his informed opinion but nothing in the line of contextual argument appears. Basically, he echoes Spicq. Looking beyond 2 Corinthians, Duchatelez observes that in the Church Fathers the use of ἐπιείκεια for clemency persists, though sporadically.[123]

ἐπιείκεια can also signify modesty or gentleness. This meaning arises when ἐπιείκεια is influenced by other terms, such as πραΰτης or ὕβρις,

---

[115] *Ibid.*, 204.
[116] *Ibid.*, 205.
[117] *Ibid.*, 206-10.
[118] *Ibid.*, 210.
[119] *Ibid.*, 213-14.
[120] *Ibid.*, 214-16.
[121] *Ibid.*, 216-17.
[122] *Ibid.*, 216: "S. Paul, dans l'exercice de son autorité apostolique, en appelle à la mansuétude et à la clémence ou bienveillance du Christ. Surtout, si l'on accepte le parallélisme avec Mt. 11,29, la clémence s'applique ici au Christ royal, mais qui demeure pourtant humble et doux."
[123] *Ibid.*, 217.

or when reasonable moderation or gentleness (i.e., ἐπιείκεια) shade towards humility.[124] In another sense this is also a sub-category of clemency.[125] Examples of such usage are less frequent than the previous two categories, but become more common in Christian writings. Duchatelez offers Wis 2:19; Phil 4:5; Titus 3:2; Jas 3:17 and references from *1 Clement* as examples of this use,[126] as well as many more from the Fathers.[127] He then brings his study to a close, briefly stating how ἐπιείκεια could be an useful ethic in ecclesiastical ecumenism.[128]

In terms of literature on 2 Cor 10:1, Duchatelez's article plays a minor role. Its comments on Paul's appeal to the Corinthians add nothing new to the discussion and offer nothing to clarify it. On the other hand, the extensive monograph by D'Agostino mitigates Duchatelez's value as a diachronic study. The true value of this essay — which the preceding synopsis may not make clear — lies in the wealth of references Duchatelez has collected, *particularly in the Church Fathers*. While, then, Duchatelez makes a significant contribution to early church history, he is not very important for the study of 2 Cor 10:1.

H. Giesen wrote the article on ἐπιείκεια in the *Exegetisches Wörterbuch zum Neuen Testament*.[129] His article gives a good, concise statement of scholarship on ἐπιείκεια. This means that the bibliography is up to date and the content reflects the ideas of the most recent studies. It also means that he says nothing new: the structure of the article continues to pay obeisance to the LXX; the opinions follow Leivestad. Giesen accepts Leivestad's identification of a second LXX meaning for ἐπιείκεια in Wis 2:19, where, according to Giesen, ἐπιείκεια apparently means "the humble, patient firmness of the righteous."[130] The structure of Giesen's

---

[124] *Ibid.*, 222.

[125] *Ibid.*

[126] *Ibid.*, 222-23.

[127] *Ibid.*, 223-30.

[128] *Ibid.*, 230-31.

[129] H. Giesen, "ἐπιεικής, ἐπιείκεια," in *Exegetisches Wörterbuch zum Neuen Testament*, eds. Horst Balz and Gerhard Schneider, 3 vols. (Stuttgart: W. Kohlhammer, 1980-3), 2: cols. 65-67. English: *Exegetical Dictionary of the New Testament*, trans. James W. Thompson, et al., 3 vols. (Grand Rapids: Eerdmans, 1990-93), 2: 26. By the time ἐπιείκεια in the LXX reaches the English translation of this article, it has become vague: the English translations "forbearance" and "gentleness" carry no explicit connotation of the mercy which ἐπιείκεια in the LXX so conspicuously possesses. (Giesen uses *Nachsicht* and *Milde*.)

[130] *Ibid.*, 2: 26 (German ed.: "einer demütigen, geduldigen Standfestigkeit des Gerechten" [2: col. 66]).

article indicates that the meaning of ἐπιείκεια in 2 Cor 10:1 somehow reflects Wis 2:19. How the idea of "humble, patient steadfastness" fits into 2 Cor 10:1 receives no explanation. Instead Giesen defines ἐπιείκεια in Paul's letter by ταπεινός and ἀσθενής, finding in πραΰτης additional support for this. Given the derivative nature of this article, it stands or falls with its precursors, particularly Leivestad.

In the same *Wörterbuch* Hubert Frankemölle contributed the article on πραΰτης.[131] His comments reflect excellent method. Meaning, he tells us, is established by situating πραΰς/πραΰτης in a larger semantic domain of virtues and observing its synonyms and antonyms. Then one must consider the word's prehistory, particularly the LXX and virtue lists. Last, of course, is context. Frankemölle observes that Paul's meaning in 2 Cor 10:1 is governed by a christological and ethical standard; therefore, he sides with Leivestad over against Harnack. Though Frankemölle's method deserves praise, two problems remain with his study. First, to examine πραΰς/πραΰτης within the domain of virtues overlooks other words to which it is related. Second, although he is right to see πραΰτης christologically determined in 2 Cor 10:1 (as the genitive τοῦ Χριστοῦ makes clear), he does not ask what that christology is. Like Giesen, Frankemölle too relies on Leivestad.

2. Summary of Previous Research

This survey has turned up two alternative readings of 2 Cor 10:1. One, following Harnack, sees ἐπιείκεια as a royal trait of Jesus: even though he has great authority he exercises it with restraint. This position is expanded by Spicq who explicitly adds πραΰτης to his exposition: clemency combines with humility. Another view, following Leivestad, sees ἐπιείκεια as a kenotic characteristic of Jesus, emphasizing the lowly state of his incarnation and the humility he demonstrated in submitting to it; ἐπιείκεια and πραΰτης therefore are synonyms. We can summarize the opinions about ἐπιείκεια which we have analyzed as follows:

1920	Harnack	= the mildness of Christ as of rulers
1934	Preisker	= God's disposition as a ruler

---

[131] Hubert Frankemölle, "πραΰτης, πραΰς," in *Exegetisches Wörterbuch zum Neuen Testament*, 3: cols. 351-3. Whereas Frankemölle translates 2 Cor 10:1 as the "Sanftmut und Güte Christi," his English translator relies on the traditional version of the "meekness and gentleness of Christ" (*Exegetical Dictionary of the New Testament*, 3: 147).

1947	Spicq	= virtues of a sovereign ruler and an oppressed servant
1966	Leivestad	= kenotic reference: gentle, humble, and modest attitude
1973	D'Agostino	= kenotic *Weltanschauung*
1979	Duchatelez	= Spicq
1981	Giesen	= Leivestad
1983	Frankemölle	= Leivestad

Generally, these fall into two camps: 1) Harnack, Preisker, Spicq, and Duchatelez; and 2) Leivestad, D'Agostino, Giesen, and Frankemölle. To be more precise, Spicq offers a third option, something of a bridge between the two, which forces the question of whether πραΰτης and ἐπιείκεια in 2 Cor 10:1 are equivalent or not.[132]

The previous pages, as stated at the beginning, traced ἐπιείκεια in particular because it has been the focus of debate and tended to ignore πραΰτης because it has generated no real dissent. The following chapter will not only investigate ἐπιείκεια further, but will also question the generally accepted understanding of πραΰτης. The LXX has held a vice grip on πραΰτης which has not allowed its full range of meaning to be explored in 2 Cor 10:1. As the next chapter will show, πραΰτης can be used similarly to ἐπιείκεια to express the mild exercise of authority. Thus, a third option exists for reading 2 Cor 10:1, one which we will champion with the translation "leniency and clemency."[133]

---

[132] Like Spicq, Margaret Thrall's ICC commentary reaches a conclusion that bridges the two alternatives (2: 600-602). As noted earlier, she translates ἐπιείκεια as "clemency," but πραΰτης as "meekness." The latter results from reading πραΰτης as correlative with ταπεινός, which appears a line later, rather than with the following noun (ἐπιείκεια) with which it shares a definite article (2: 604). Her decision about ἐπιείκεια rests correctly on contextual observations, but how she handles the data is quite unlike the methods to be seen in the next chapter. Unlike Thrall, I think that ἐπιείκεια and πραΰτης should be interpreted as a unit. I also do not agree that where the alternatives postulated for ἐπιείκεια in 2 Cor 10:1 are concerned that "outside the NT there is as much evidence of the one sense as the other" (2: 602). While there is much evidence for many different ways to construe ἐπιείκεια, if we focus on the choices to be made in consideration of 2 Cor 10:1, we have only two to consider: one has numerous parallels, the other has a thimblefull. Finally, in looking for comparative texts, I think that similar contexts should be compared, not just appearances of a word. In addition to the context that Thrall focuses on, I will identify a semantic field. It is occurrences of this semantic field that are important to compare. When this is done, linguistic evidence is quite decisive.

[133] John Fitzgerald has correctly recognized that the synonymy of ἐπιείκεια and πραότης in political literature opens a third possibility for the reading of 2 Cor 10:1, especially as it introduces the idea of ἐξουσία ("Paul, the Ancient Epistolary Theorists,

The preceding survey also underscores the methodological problem of determining the suitable context in which to place the semantics of ἐπιείκεια and πραΰτης. All the authors studied give the LXX pride of place. All lean heavily on early Christian literature as well. Many invoke Matt 11:29 specifically. This issue is crucial. The context to which one gives priority will in large measure determine the meaning of ἐπιείκεια and πραΰτης. If Matt 11:29 receives emphasis, then Paul refers to the words of Jesus or to his earthly example. If 2 Cor 10:1 is analyzed as a component of early Christian literature, it is absorbed into "Christian" thought, an amalgamation of many varied elements, the sum of which is different than Paul. If the LXX receives priority, one loses sight of broader Hellenistic usage, the broader ideas which inform the meanings of ἐπιείκεια and πραΰτης, and must choose between only two alternatives, whose implications and associations are limited to what the LXX indicates.

A second methodological problem lies in the dependence on diachronic evidence to the frequent neglect of synchronic evidence (or pragmatics). A major omission takes place in the failure to explore the use of πραΰτης and ἐπιείκεια in combination. The two words together provide the most important linguistic evidence. Second to that I would place the use of the two words in proximity to one another, i.e., within the same context. These two categories of texts must be examined to see what words and ideas are used in conjunction with πραΰτης and ἐπιείκεια. Such examples will present significant assistance in an attempt to make specific statements about a particular text, whereas diachronic study is limited to defining semantic options and charting trends.

The final problem is the relationship of 2 Corinthians 10–13 to the semantics of 2 Cor 10:1. Surprisingly, the broader context has played too little role in the understanding of Paul's appeal. Leivestad must be congratulated for attempting this. He brought observations from the epistolary context to bear on his interpretation of 2 Cor 10:1 and was even able to resolve the problem of the seeming contradiction between an

---

and 2 Corinthians 10–13: The Purpose and Literary Genre of a Pauline Letter," in *Greeks, Romans, and Christians: Essays in Honor of Abraham J. Malherbe*, eds. David L. Balch, Everett Ferguson, and Wayne A. Meeks [Minneapolis: Fortress Press, 1990], 194, n. 26). C. K. Barrett also recognizes that πραΰτης and ἐπιείκεια are "probably a recognized pair in Hellenistic ethical thought," but his brief comments on them assign a less specific meaning than I propose. When taken together, Barrett says, the two words "suggest a tolerant attitude towards others; the man who has these virtues will not lose his temper or grow impatient" (*The Second Epistle to the Corinthians*, Harper New Testament Commentary [New York: Harper & Row, 1958; reprint, Peabody, MA: Hendrickson Publishers, 1973], 246-47). This catches the emotional bearing of such a person, but misses the connection to ἐξουσία that Fitzgerald observed.

appeal to meekness (10:1) and a threat to use powerful, destructive weapons (10:3-5). But there are other clues to which we must pay attention. As we will demonstrate in the next chapter, a larger semantic field spreads across 2 Corinthians 10–13 which points to Paul's meaning in 10:1.[134] This will clarify Paul's meaning in his opening appeal through Christ's ἐπιείκεια and πραΰτης.

In terms of methodology, we will see that a circular process is needed. On the one hand, context is the crucial semantic determinant for 2 Cor 10:1. On the other hand, the details to observe in that context become apparent only when the words in question have been examined in many other contexts. Attention to synonyms, antonyms, characters, and social contexts makes the textures and nuances of ἐπιείκεια and πραΰτης clearer. A pattern of associations emerges which we can compare with 2 Corinthians 10–13. By recognizing this pattern in Paul's letter, we can clarify his meaning.

The following study, therefore, will privilege internal semantic evidence over external christological views. Rather than formulate a christological theory to account for Paul's words, it will use a semantic domain to understand Paul's words. The semantic conclusions reached will then lead to an investigation of Paul's christology. This is necessary because Paul's appeal is based not simply on two virtues, but on two of Christ's virtues. I will argue that the evidence derived from the semantic investigation is fully compatible with a christology which posits a universal ruler, for the virtues ascribed to Christ are fully in line with the ideology of kingship. This perspective then eliminates many of the common christological issues connected to 2 Cor 10:1. Thus, it is not based on the example of the historical Jesus, is not influenced by a dominical saying, and, in short, does not draw on Jesus tradition. In fact, 2 Cor 10:1 offers as it were a window on a moment of mythological construction.

Ultimately, though, semantics and christology are prolegomena to and not the point of 2 Cor 10:1. The real questions are what Paul hopes to accomplish by his appeal and how that appeal fits into the rhetoric he addresses to the Corinthians. While every interpretation of 2 Cor 10:1 is in some way an attempt to answer such questions, the present attempt will be much more consciously directed toward them. Moreover, given the perspectives brought to bear by the semantic and christological conclusions reached in this investigation, the answers presented here will receive new and more detailed nuances. Paul's appeal reflects a tendency

---

[134] Again, as stated in the previous note, Fitzgerald already observed the link to ἐξουσία.

within his ministry at large and a rhetoric within this letter as a whole. Paul's opening appeal is no polite but quickly forgotten gesture, but profoundly integral to his objective in 2 Corinthians 10–13. Nearly three centuries ago the great philosopher John Locke grasped this: Paul's appeal to Christ's clemency explains the apostle's "delay of exemplary punishment" in such a way that his opposition has no "reason to think it was for want of power."[135] Scholarship on 2 Cor 10:1 has lost sight of this perspective.

---

[135] Recall the quotation with which this chapter opens and see note 1.

Chapter 2

Semantic Investigation of πραΰτης and ἐπιείκεια

> Here he shows both his power as well as his philosophy and forbearance. He appeals with such intensity so that he will not be forced to come and display the avenging power proper to his office, i.e., to strike and punish them and exact the strictest penalty.... He said these things, at the same time showing that even if they provided a thousand reasons to do otherwise he remains much more inclined to spare because he is gentle; moreover, it is not because he is weak that he does not prosecute the matter, since Christ acted in the same way.... [It is as if the apostle] says, "Grant me this favor: do not force me to show [my ability] ... to punish ... For this is crucial for a teacher: do not punish quickly, but correct [wrongdoers] and always prefer to move slowly in matters of punishment.
> John Chrysostom[1]

Thanks to lexicons and the works cited in the previous chapter, we have no shortage of resources to help us understand πραΰτης and ἐπιείκεια. And of course the TLG removes nearly all limitations. What these resources fail to offer are explanations of these words' nuances and their relationships, as well as ways of interpreting specific examples of them. In this chapter we will define and survey the ways these words are used and chart the semantic domain in which they participate. These investigations will provide keys for identifying these words' nuances in general and particularly in 2 Cor 10:1.

1. ἐπιείκεια

We begin with ἐπιείκεια. A quick look at Chantraine, LSJ and BAGD will orient us to this word, yet do little more. It remains to define it and to highlight the words with which it is associated. Although we will begin

---

[1] *In epist. II ad Cor. Homil.* XXI (my trans.).

our discussion in the Classical period, once we begin to map wordfields and formulate definitions, we will concentrate on the four centuries between Polybius and Dio Cassius, roughly 200 BC to 200 AD, though exceptions will appear (e.g., Diogenes Laertius).[2]

a. Lexicons on ἐπιείκεια

Chantraine's *Dictionnaire étymologique de la langue grecque* derives ἐπιεικής from ἔοικα (*s.v.*) and states that it expresses the idea of appropriateness or suitability (French: *convenance*) and carries an intellectual and moral sense. "Thus, there emerges from the ideas of image and resemblance a semantic field applicable to the intellectual and moral realm."[3] We may add that ἐπιείκεια does not lose its connection to these roots, as uses of the adjective in particular reveal.

Liddell, Scott and Jones' lexicon divides the use of ἐπιεικής into two periods, Homer and after Homer. The *Iliad* and *Odyssey* reflect the oldest meaning of the adjective, "fitting, meet, suitable."[4] With time, the adjective appears in contexts which refine the general idea of "suitable," developing for ἐπιεικής some precise applications: a suitable utterance, for example, may be more accurately characterized as "reasonable"; when contrasted with rights or justice, a suitable course of action is in fact "fair or equitable." When applied to people, the nuance of ἐπιεικής becomes more difficult to identify, due to the diversity of its uses: LSJ notes that whereas a fit person may indicate generally a person who is competent (i.e., "able or capable"), ἐπιεικής may also qualify someone morally (e.g., "reasonable, fair, good") or may connote social or political standing (i.e., "the upper or educated classes").

LSJ also shows the wide application of the adverb ἐπιεικῶς. While it resembles the adjective in meaning "fairly," it also extends to encompass "tolerable or moderately"; likewise, "reasonably" expands to "probably." Like the adjective, the adverb may have a moral quality such as

---

[2] Actually πρᾶος, φιλάνθρωπος, and ἐπιεικής (and cognate forms) did not become common until the fourth century BC, as Jacqueline de Romilly's statistics reveal (*La douceur dans la pensée grecque*, Collection d'études anciennes [Paris: Société d'édition «Les Belles Lettres», 1979], 37).

[3] *Ibid.*, 355: "Ainsi, de la notion d'image, de ressemblance est issu un groupe sémantique relatif au monde intellectuel et moral." Hjalmar Frisk sets ἐπιεικής in opposition to α-εἰκής, i.e., ἀϊκής, and connected to ἐπέοικε, even to the degree of εἰκών (*Griechisches etymologisches Wörterbuch*, 2 vols. [Heidelberg: Carl Winter Universitätsverlag, 1960-70], 1: 536).

[4] Similarly, see H. W. Nordheider, "ἐπιεικής," in *Lexikon des frühgriechischen Epos*, eds. Bruno Snell et al. (Göttingen: Vandenhoeck & Ruprecht, 1955-), *s.v.*: "*passend, angemessen.*"

"moderately, mildly, or kindly." LSJ also offers a fourth category of usage unparalleled by the adjective: ἐπιεικῶς may mean "generally or usually."

In its discussion of the noun, ἐπιείκεια, LSJ provides fewer analytic categories than it does for the adjective. That Homer did not use the noun partially explains this; moreover, the noun's absence in Homer requires LSJ to begin its discussion elsewhere, which it does by offering "reasonableness" as an equivalent for ἐπιείκεια. Like the adjective the noun can be contrasted precisely to law and therefore means "equity" or, used more generally to describe people, indicates "fairness." When describing people ἐπιείκεια may also have a general moral aspect, such as "goodness or virtuousness." Unlike the adjective, LSJ notes that the noun can be personified to represent Clemency.

While LSJ's survey of ἐπιείκεια and its cognates provides a good sense of its widespread application, a few comments may be offered. First, it seems odd that LSJ (unlike BAGD) does not refer to texts which consciously offer a definition of ἐπιείκεια. Second, LSJ does not give adequate notice that in its moral usage ἐπιείκεια frequently associates with ἡμερότης, ἠπιότης, μετριότης, συγγνώμη, φιλανθρωπία and χρηστότης. Third, LSJ does not indicate the connotation of mercy frequently present in ἐπιείκεια; therefore, the translation "clemency" should not be reserved for instances of personification. In fact, LSJ's proposals for translating ἐπιείκεια when it refers to persons, namely "reasonableness, fairness, goodness and virtuousness," lack the textures implied by other translations (e.g., "gentleness, mildness, leniency or graciousness"). Last, as numerous translators have demonstrated, many more translation equivalents exist for ἐπιείκεια and its cognates than LSJ cites (or reasonably should cite).

The discussion of this family of words in Walter Bauer's lexicon has undergone little significant alteration during its six editions.[5] For ἐπιείκεια the German editions suggest "*Nachsicht*" and "*Milde*" as translation equivalents, while the English editions offer "clemency, gentleness, graciousness, and forbearance"; for ἐπιεικής Bauer offers "*nachgiebig, mild, gütig*" and "*rechtlich denkend*," or, in the English

---

[5] What changes do occur from edition to edition involve one of the following: 1) subsequent editions add or correct references to primary sources; 2) successive editions update references to secondary sources; and 3) less commonly, later additions insert a brief comment about a specific reference. For example, the fifth edition added a reference to Appian and a statement about the use of ἐπιεικής with ἀγαθός. Of note in the sixth edition is the Alands' correction of the reference to Aristotle's *Nicomachean Ethics*, the insertion of references to the OT Pseudepigrapha, and a statement about the post-Aristotelian use of ἐπιείκεια as a legal term. Meanwhile, the English editions provide fuller references to secondary literature.

edition, "yielding, gentle, kind, right-minded and forbearing." Bauer therefore offers glosses more nuanced than LSJ and more focused on specific expressions of virtue. This combines with well chosen non-biblical references to comprise the strength of Bauer's two articles. The lack of analytic structure to the articles is a weakness, however, as the user receives no clue as to the relationships among various meanings. As in other lexicons, a definition also remains elusive.

b. Ancient Definitions of ἐπιείκεια

Many ancient texts can help us define ἐπιείκεια, for some offer a definition and others offer components of one.

Plato defines ἐπιείκεια as an infraction of strict justice (*Leg.* 6.757e).[6] Aristotle develops this in greater detail. His concern is to reconcile ἐπιείκεια with justice, which he does as follows:

> Justice and equity are neither absolutely identical nor generically different.... For equity, while superior to one sort of justice, is itself just: it is not superior to justice as being generically different from it. Justice and equity are therefore the same thing, and both are good, though equity is the better. The source of the difficulty is that equity, though just, is not legal justice, but a rectification of legal justice. The reason for this is that law is always a general statement, yet there are cases which it is not possible to cover in a general statement.... It is ... clear what the equitable man is: he is one who does not stand on his rights unduly, but is content to receive a smaller share although he has the law on his side (*E.N.* 5.10).

Like Plato, Aristotle focuses on justice and right thinking. He assumes the imperfection of law and the need for wisdom to negotiate the law's deficiencies. Those (e.g., Stoics) who assume the correspondence of law and reason will necessarily object to ἐπιείκεια. Elsewhere Aristotle offers yet another attempt to define ἐπιείκεια, again analyzing the relationship between ἐπιείκεια and law: "... equity is justice that goes beyond the written law. These omissions are sometimes involuntary, sometimes voluntary, on the part of the legislators" (*Rhet.* 1.13.13). Next, however, he illustrates situations where justice and equity diverge and where ἐπιείκεια should rule.

> Actions which should be leniently treated (συγγνώμην ἔχειν) are cases for ἐπιεική. Errors (ἁμαρτήματα) and wrong acts (ἀδικήματα) should not be considered of equal gravity, nor misfortunes.... And it is ἐπιεικές to pardon human weaknesses, and to look, not to the law but to the legislator; not to the letter of the law but to the intention of the legislator; not to the action itself, but to the moral purpose; not to the part, but to the whole; not to what a man is now, but to what he has been, always or generally; to remember good rather than ill treatment, and benefits received rather than those

---

[6] Hermogenes repeats this definition in *On Types of Style* 345. Other authors argue that to accept less than what is just or advantageous can be an even greater justice or even more advantageous.

conferred; to bear injury with patience (τὸ ἀνέχεσθαι ἀδικούμενον); to be willing to appeal to the judgment of reason rather than to violence; to prefer arbitration to the law court, for the arbitrator keeps equity in view, whereas the dicast looks only to the law, and the reason why arbitrators were appointed was that equity might prevail (*Rhet.* 1.13.15-19; Loeb trans. modified).

Aristotle then held that forgiveness and reason should guide law, not hide behind it nor allow it to be wielded like a cudgel.

While Plato and Aristotle speak eloquently of ἐπιείκεια, they fail to indicate how broadly it was actually used. Thucydides offers three texts which describe ἐπιεικής behavior and point to its broader implications. First, when the powerful refuse to act with force and instead submit to justice, their moderation exhibits ἐπιεικής behavior (1.76). This example reverses Aristotle's approach to ἐπιείκεια: whereas Aristotle sees ἐπιείκεια softening the harshness of justice, Thucydides shows ἐπιείκεια softening power and allowing justice to be implemented. Second, Thucydides offers an example in which an affront to state sovereignty fails to be ἐπιεικής; rather than resort to violence, one should engage in reasoned debate (3.66). Here the political horizon is broader than Aristotle's. This is also the case in a third example, where ἐπιεικής behavior turns from force to virtue (βία to ἀρετή), offering moderate (μέτριος) terms to a defeated enemy (4.19). The speaker argues that it is intelligent to exchange the opportunity for violence for the obligation which generosity will entail. From these examples we see that ἐπιείκεια involves an understanding of what is appropriate and a reasoned self-control which avoids severity (cf. 8.93). Though this is the essence of what Aristotle said, the applications expand beyond litigation.

But the correlation of ἐπιείκεια and reason was problematic. Thus, in Thucydides' Mytilenian Debate the advocate of leniency, Diodotus, argued his position only in terms of reasoned advantage and specifically not pity and ἐπιείκεια, dismissing both as emotions (3.48); yet the behavior which Diodotus advocated is precisely what writers throughout subsequent centuries would characterize as ἐπιείκεια. The opponent of leniency, Cleon, argued against pity and ἐπιείκεια, dismissing them because they should be reserved for people who in turn will show one pity and become one's friends. These commonplace rationales suggest that a problem surrounding ἐπιείκεια is this: How does one mesh one's intuitive (i.e., enculturated) understanding of decent behavior with the complex needs of policy and reason? Thucydides suggests that the borders of one's group circumscribe the claims of human decency. But the very context in which Thucydides discusses this argues for the recognition of leniency as a potential tool for imperial control, so that its enlarged application points to an enlarged social horizon.[7] (Philosophers also would widen the social horizon.) Still, for Thucydides, reason drives this expansion, not feelings. Correlating ἐπιείκεια with emotion and reason (or with human decency and calculation) would be an ongoing problem.[8]

Thucydides' comments lead us to the explicit definition offered by a treatise which survived in the corpus of Plato's writings. In the list of definitions extant in Ps.-Plato *Definitions*, one portion begins with ἀρετή, follows with the canonical four, φρόνησις, δικαιοσύνη, σωφροσύνη, and ἀνδρεία, then continues with four other popular virtues, ἐγκράτεια, αὐτάρκεια, ἐπιείκεια, and καρτερία. This document defines ἐπιείκεια "as an acceptance of less than what is just or advantageous, a moderation in contracts, the orderliness of a right-thinking person in regard to what is noble and shameful" (412b; my trans.). This definition reflects the breadth of uses to which ἐπιείκεια may be put much better than does Aristotle's. Moreover, its fusion of convention and reason in the last phrase, the advocacy in the middle phrase of moderation in public affairs, and the opening reference to justice and advantage as points of orientation are in fact common themes of ἐπιείκεια.

All these connections continue into the Roman empire. Qualities of convention and forbearance appear in Plutarch's statement that "it is right (ἐπιεικές) to be subservient to parents in everything else and to endure all their wrath and displeasure" (*Mor.* 483b). Connotations of reason appear in the contrast of ἐπιεικῆ and acting too hastily (προπέτεια; Jos. *Ant.* 16.263). Connections to law appear in Dio Chrysostom's description of punishments as "more severe than custom or fairness allowed" (πικρότερον τοῦ νομίμου καὶ ἐπιεικοῦς; *Or.* 1.7); likewise, Plutarch protests that a person is no "equitable (ἐπιεικής) ruler who grants favors contrary to law" (*Mor.* 807b). As Thucydides noted that the strong need not curb their violence, so Josephus contrasts the ἐπιείκεια of King Ahab with his royal authority (βασιλικὴ ἐξουσία; *Ant.* 8.356). Philo refers to the ἐπιείκεια and χρηστότης of God, whom Philo then characterizes as preferring forgiveness to punishment (συγγνώμη to τιμωρία; *De prae. et poe.* 166). Finally, Plutarch gives high praise to a person who refuses vengeance (τιμωρία) on an enemy when opportunity arises: this is ἐπιεικής (*Mor.* 90e).

Together with these continuities is a trend to recognize ἐπιείκεια in the actions of a social superior toward an inferior. The reading of 2 Cor 10:1 offered in this study rests on that trajectory. John Chrysostom's definition

---

[7] Gentleness and leniency were important components in Isocrates' panhellenic vision.

[8] Cf. the similar debate between Nicolaüs and Gylippus in Diod. Sic. 13.20-32.

of ἐπιείκεια summarizes this perspective: "This is truly ἐπιείκεια, not when someone calmly endures being wronged by people in some position of power, but when he allows himself to be abused even by those who are considered inferior."[9]

In summary, ἐπιείκεια involves reason and impulses. On the one hand, impulses to goodness are rationalized so as to allow kindness; on the other hand, rash or mean impulses are restrained, in order, again, to give room to kindness. Typically, though, self-restraint is involved, as ἐπιείκεια usually entails a renunciation of one's right to self-assertion, particularly on the part of people with power. Often these things require a negotiation among reason, law, and convention. Sometimes customs are subverted, sometimes expanded. Sometimes laws must be ignored. To be ἐπιεικής, however, many ancients would insist that reason must guide.[10]

c. The Nuances of ἐπιείκεια

We can uncover the nuances of ἐπιείκεια by highlighting three aspects of its usage. First, we will list the vocabulary with which ἐπιείκεια is associated, noting synonyms, antonyms, and other words connected with it. Afterward, we will note the kinds of contexts in which ἐπιείκεια appears, as well as the people to whom it is attributed.

First, then, the words with which ἐπιείκεια is used tell us much about its field of meaning. The following are often linked synonymously with ἐπιείκεια:[11]

ἡμερότης: Dan 4:27; Philo *De op. mun.* 103; [*De Ios.* 221]; *De virt.* 134; *De leg. ad Gai.* 119; Jos. *Ant.* 2.214; 19.333; [Philod. *Ang.* col. 44]; Diod. Sic. [32.4.3]; 32.27.3; Plut. *Cor.* 225d/ 24.4; *Cato min* 785d; [*Thes.* 6e/ 16.1]; *Mor.* 529c; [Luc. *Phal.* 1.2];

---

[9] *Hom. 52.2 in Gen.* 4.508b (my trans.). Chrysostom's definition has roots in the fourth century BC. De Romilly states, "La nouvelle douceur apparaît donc dans des rapports où aucune solidarité naturelle ne l'imposait ou ne lui frayait la voie: la *praotès* est l'invention d'un monde dans lequel la douceur est à réinventer. Par voie de conséquence, elle est souvent la vertu de ceux qui pourraient être tentés d'user de la force ou de la violence, d'est-à-dire de ceux qui détiennent une forme de pouvoir. Ainsi s'explique en partie sa place dans la réflexion politique" (*La douceur*, 42).

[10] Lucian provides an anthropological and ethical context for ἐπιεικής. For example, some people, like Icarus, fly too close to the sun and fall from the sky. Some, like Daedalus, stay closer to the ground and reach their objective safely. The latter are ἐπιεικεῖς and συνετοί (*Gal.* 23; cf. *De astr.* 15).

[11] In the following lists I have compressed cognate forms under the single heading of the noun (where one exists). Note also that references in brackets indicate appearances of the adjective ἐπιεικής rather than the noun ἐπιείκεια. Examples of ἐπιεικῶς are identified by the parenthetical statement "(adverb)".

2.1. ἐπιείκεια

ἤπιος: Add Esth 3:13b;[12]

μετριότης: [Jos. *Ant.* 15.182]; Diod. Sic. 27.16.2; Plut. [*Rom.* 26f/ 16.2; *Solon* 95a/ 19.2]; *Cato maj.* 337e; [*Galba* 1058b]; *Mor.* [250f]; 451f; [533b; 816c]; [Dio Chrys. 30.41; 41.3]; Luc. *Vit. auc.* 10; *Rhet. prae.* 15; [*Phal.* 1.2; 2.1]; Dio Cas. 21.70.9;

πραότης: to be discussed later;

φιλανθρωπία: 2 Macc 9:27; 3 Macc 3:15; *Ep. Arist.* 290; Philo *De vita Mos.* 1.198; *De spec. leg.* 2.110; Jos. *Ant.*8.213; Diod. Sic. [14.5.5]; 31.3.2; 32.2.1; 33.15.1; 33.18.1; 37.10.2; Plut. *The. et Rom.* 37f/ 2.2; *Nic.* 528f/ 9.9; *Brut.* 998c/ 30.4; *Mor.* 546e; [816d; 866f]; Dio Chrys. [21.15]; 41.9; [Luc. *Phal.* 1.2]; Dio Cas. 13.55.2; [16.57.48]; 45.21.2;

χρηστότης: [Ps 85:5]; Philo *De prae. et poe.* 166; Jos. *Ant.* 6.144; 8.213; Philod. *Rhet.* col. 16; Diod. Sic. 32.27.3; [Plut. *Aem.* 271b/ 30.1; *Mor.* 709e]; Luc. *Scytha* 6; [*Alex.* 4]; Diog. L. 7.123.

These words reveal some of the nuances which ἐπιείκεια may bear: ἡμερότης suggests an air of civility whose reasonableness and equilibrium resist passion and anger and seek alternatives to arrogance, cruelty and violence; μετριότης points to a self-aware reserve which is the key to virtue and proper conduct toward others; φιλανθρωπία reflects the gratuitous nature of ἐπιείκεια, often expressed in concrete gifts, such as respect or deliverance; χρηστότης adds the idea of kindness, whether as a general inclination to do good or more specifically to forgive. No strict hierarchy seems to exist among these words, for on occasion each may subsume the other or be used interchangeably with another.

In addition to gentleness, moderation, generosity, and kindness, we can identify still more synonyms of ἐπιείκεια. Use of these words narrows the implications of ἐπιείκεια, as well as the previous synonyms. These words identify acts of gentleness or kindness, etc., more specifically as acts of mercy, indulgence, and forgiveness:

ἔλεος: [Ps. 85:5]; Dan 3:42; 2 Esdr 9:8; Philo *De vita Mos.* 1.198; Diod. Sic. 27.16.2; [13.28.4]; Plut. *Mor.* 60e; Diog. L. 7.123;

ἵλαος: 2 Macc 2:22; [Philo *De spec. leg.* 1.97];

οἰκτιρμος: Bar 2:27

συγγνώμη: Philo *De prae. et poe.* 166; [*De spec. leg.* 4.23]; Jos. *Ant.* 6.144; 15.48; 19.334; Diod. Sic. 13.22.4; [19.86.3]; 28.7.1; 32.27.3; Aug. *Res ges.* 3 (cp. 34); [Dio Chrys. 32.18]; Diog. L. 7.123;

---

[12] Over time πραότης displaced Homer's ἤπιος (De Romilly, *La douceur*, 41).

φείδεσθαι: Wis 12:16-18; [Jos. Ant. 16.263]; Aug. Res ges. 3 (cp. 34); Plut. Cae. 733c/ 52.4; Mor. 729e; [Dio Chrys. 32.18]; Dio Cas. 65.8.4-7; Diog. L. 7.123;

χάρις: 3 Macc 7:6; [Philo De conf. ling. 116]; Jos. Ant. 6.144; Diod. Sic. [28.3.1 (= gratitude; cf. 27.15.3)]; 34/35.39.1; Plut. Cato maj. 345d/ 16.5ff.; Cato min. 761d/ 4.1; Art. 1013a/ 4.3; Mor. [468d]; 483f; [807b].

These words pair with ἐπιείκεια in relation to God, good rulers, and good laws, in order to suggest ways in which the self-restraint of ἐπιείκεια and its generous (even indulgent) regard for others may express itself.[13]

A number of antonyms for ἐπιείκεια can also be identified:

ἀγριότης: Philo De virt. 134; Plut. Mor. 60e; [Dio Chrys. 21.15; 23.36]; Luc. Vit. auc. 10;

ἀποτομία: Jos. Ant. 19.329; Diod. Sic. 1.65.3; 32.27.3;

βαρύτης: Jos. Ant. 8.213; Plut. Aris. 23.2; Flam. 17.1; [Pub. 6.1]; Mor. 69a-b;

βία: 3 Macc 3:15; Philo De cher. 37; Jos. Ant. 2.218; [15.321]; Diod. Sic. 15.1.3 (adverb); 25.11.1; [Epict. Frag. 5]; Plut. Mor. [531e]; 824d; [Luc. Phal. 1.2];

θάρσος/θράσος/θάρρος: Jos. Ant. 15.177; [20.200]; Dio Chrys. 1.6; [32.27-28]; Luc. Vit. auc. 10; Rhet. prae. 15; Dio Cas. 15.57.24;

θύμος: Jos. Ant. 19.334; Plut. Flam. 378c/ 17.1;

ὀργή: Diod. Sic. 21.21.8; Ign. Phil. 1.2;

σκαιότης: Philo De spec. leg. 2.93; [Jos. Ant. 11.216]; [Luc. Phal. 1.2];

τόλμα: [Jos. Ant. 6.264; 20.200]; Diod. Sic. 31.3.2; Luc. Rhet. prae. 15; 1 Clem. 30.8;

ὕβρις: Wis 2:19; [Epict. Frag. 5]; Plut. [Thes. 3c/ 6.4]; Mor. 80b; 259f; 259e; [Luc. Phal. 1.2];

ὑπερηφανία: Jos. Ant. 11.216; Diod. Sic. 11.70.3 (adverb); 17.66.7; [Plut. Thes. 6e/ 16.1];

χαλεπός: Philo De spec. leg. 2.93; [De Ios. 221]; Jos. Ant. 15.48; [Diod. Sic. 11.59.2; 15.1.3]; Plut. Thes. et Rom. 37f /26; [Mor. 80b; 537d]; Dio Chrys. [25.4; 32.26]; 41.9-10; [Dio Cas. 47.7.4; 65.8.5];

ὠμότης: Philo De spec. leg. 2.95; Jos. Ant. [17.342]; 19.246; Diod. Sic. 1.64.9; 27.15.1; [32.4.4]; 33.12.1; 37.19.1; Plut. [Alex. 671b/ 13.2]; Mor. 60e; [250f]; [Luc. Phal. 1.6, 10]; Dio Cas. [47.7.4]; 47.13.4.[14]

---

[13] While finding this cluster of words associated with God is a particularly Jewish phenomenon, examples of these semantic relationships in Augustus, Plutarch, Dio Chrysostom, and Diogenes Laertius show that the cluster itself is not simply Jewish.

[14] Less common antonyms include: βαρύς, [Diod. Sic. 30.23.2]; θηριώδης, Diod. Sic. 14.105.3.

2.1. ἐπιείκεια

These words suggest the parameters which we have already noted. The civility and education associated with ἐπιείκεια stand opposed to ἀγριότης. The reasonable self-understanding shuns ὕβρις. Not to insist on complete self-assertion avoids ὑπερηφανία as well as βία. Respect for others suppresses θράσος and τόλμα. All violent, forceful, overbearing, excessive, disrespectful expressions contrast with ἐπιείκεια. The ἐπιεικής person tries not to insult, diminish, or harm others.

Though neither antonyms or synonyms, other words commonly appear in conjunction with ἐπιείκεια which contribute to its semantic field. Some relate to the authority or power of those who exercise ἐπιείκεια and the nature of their actions. For example:

δεσπότης: Philo [De som. 2.295]; De leg. ad Gai. 119; [350 (adverb)]; App. Bel. civ. 2.16.106;
δύναμις: Wis 12:18; Diod. Sic. 31.3.1 (adverb); cp. 19.100.1 (ἀδυναμία); Plut. Mor. [250f] 460f (ἀδύνατος);
ἡγεμονία: Diod. Sic. 27.16.2; [Dio Chrys. 32.71];
ἐξουσία: Add Esth 3:13b; [Philo De som. 2.295]; Jos. Ant. [6.263; 8.356; 11.216; 15.321]; 19.246; Diod. Sic. 31.3.1 (adverb); 13.22.4; [Dio Chrys. 32.18]; Plut. Cic. 870b/ 19.6;
κόλασις: 3 Macc 3:26; Ep. Arist. 188; Philo [De ebr. 131]; Quod det. pot. 146 (adverb); [Jos. Ant. 13.294]; Diod. Sic. 1.65.3; 4.44.4; Plut. [Pub. 99e/ 6.1]; Art. 1013a/ 4.3; Dio Chrys. 1.7; Dio Cas. 44.21.2; [52.34.6]; [Philos. Vita soph. 2.561, 562];
τιμωρία: [Philo De som. 2.295; De Ios. 221; De spec. leg. 4.23]; Jos. Ant. [13.294]; 19.329; Diod. Sic. 1.60.3 (adverb); 4.44.4; [19.86.3]; 19.100.1; 32.4.4; 33.26.2; [Plut. Mor. 90e];
τυραννίς: Philo De leg. ad Gai. 350; [Jos. Ant. 17.342; 15.321]; Diod. Sic. 14.45.1; [28.9.1]; 33.4.4; Plut. Tim. 236c/ 1.3; Mor. 250f.

Other words suggest the effect which ἐπιείκεια seeks:

διαλλαγή: Jos. Ant. 16.367; 19.334; Plut. [Alex. 671b/ 13.2]; Cae. 733c/ 54.4;
ἐπανόρθωσις: Philo Quod det. pot. 146;
εὔνοια: Jos. Ant. 8.213; Diod. Sic. 2.28.6; 11.26.4 (adverb); 27.16.2;
καταλλαγή: Philo De prae. et poe. 166;
μετάνοια: Philo De som. 2.295; Jos. Ant. 20.178; [Jos. Asen. 15.8]; Ep. Arist. 188;

σωτηρία: [Diod. Sic. 13.28.4]; Aug. *Res ges.* 3 (cp. 34); [Dio Cas. 41.42.6; 47.7.4].

These words stipulate the results that ἐπιείκεια seeks. They reflect the value of this virtue to encourage modified behavior and restore personal or social relationships.

Finally, there remain words which have an ambiguous relationship with ἐπιείκεια. Sometimes synonyms, sometimes antonyms, or neither but related, the following words may be used to describe an ἐπιεικής person:

ἀσθένεια: Jos. *Ant.* 14.13 (cf. 13.407; one has ἐπιείκεια but is weak and withdraws from government); Diod. Sic. 27.6.2 (the wise person does not forget his or her human weaknesses); Plut. *Eum.* 595f/ 2.3 (ἐπιείκεια yields trust, ἀσθένεια flight); *Mor.* 529a (one should strive to purge ἐπιεικής of ἀσθένεια);

δειλία: Dio Cas. 13.52.1-2 (Rome did not allow ἐπιείκεια to degenerate into cowardice; cf. 8.52.2);

μαλακός: Jos. *Ant.* 6.144 (to go easy on wrongdoers to gain reputation for ἐπιείκεια is τὸ καταμαλακίζεσθαι); Plut. *Cato maj.* 345d/ 16.5 (Cato, threatening punishment, ran for office against other who promised to rule μαλακῶς); *Cic.* 870b/ 19.6 (Cicero feared going soft on the conspirators lest he look ἄνανδρος and μαλακός); *Mor.* 231b (a man renowned for ἐπιείκεια was μαλακός by nature);

ταπεινότης: [*Ep. Arist.* 263]; [Jos. *Ant.* 6.263 (private persons with no office or status may show themselves ἐπιεικής)]; Philo *De mig. Abr.* 147 (adverb; ἐπιεικῶς is the mean between ἀλαζονεία and ταπεινός); *1 Clem.* 30.8; 56.1; 58.2; 62.2 (Clement treats ταπεινοφροσύνη as a synonym of ἐπιείκεια); [Philos. *Vit. Apoll.* 8.7.475 (a young man cultivates ἐπιεικές so excessively that he is ταπεινότερος τοῦ μετρίου)]; Lib. *Ep.* 1318.2 (many people consider ἐπιείκεια to be something ταπεινός).

These references indicate an idealized antonomy to ἐπιείκεια as well as an idealized synonymy, depending on one's perspective. This conflict indicates much about the social location of the ἐπιεικής person, as well as the ambiguities inherent in ἐπιεικής behavior. For now, we simply note this. In the course of this investigation we will return to these ambiguities.

Turning to the contexts in which ἐπιείκεια appears adds flesh to the preceding semantic skeleton. A text from Philo incorporates many of the words just noted and illustrates how they fit together. In *Special Laws* Philo reflects on the law to leave land fallow every seventh year, deducing from it a commonplace theory about the effective exercise of authority. As

2.1. ἐπιείκεια 49

one goes easy on the land, so one should go easy on one's slaves, not ruining them with excessive force (βιάζεσθαι) but entertaining moderate expectations (τὰ μέτρια). This will make them more ready to work and prolong their service. He continues his lesson by turning to the problem of government, complaining about rulers who appoint heavy-handed tax-collectors.

> For they purposely choose as tax-gathers the most ruthless (ἀνηλεεστάτους) of men, brimful of inhumanity (ἀπανθρωπίας), and put into their hands resources for overreaching (πλεονεξίαν). These persons add to their natural brutality (τῇ φυσικῇ σκαιότητι) the immunity they gain from their masters' instructions, and in their determination to accommodate every action to those masters' pleasure they leave no severity (οὐδὲν ... τῶν χαλεπωτάτων) untried, however barbarous, and banish mercy (ἐπιείκειαν) and gentleness (ἡμερότητα) even from their dreams. And therefore in carrying out their collecting they create universal chaos and confusion and apply their exactions not merely to the property of their victims but also to their bodies, on which they inflict insults (ὕβρεσιν) and outrages (αἰκίαις) and forms of torture (βασάνοις) quite original in their savagery. Indeed, I have heard of persons who, actuated by abnormal frenzy (ἀγριότητα) and cruelty, have not even spared the dead, persons who become so utterly brutalized (ἐθηριώθησαν) that they venture (τολμᾶν) even to flog corpses with whips. And when anyone censured the extraordinary cruelty (τῆς ἄγαν ὠμότητος) shown in refusing to allow even death ... to procure freedom from insult (τὸ ἀνύβριστον) ... the line of defence adopted was worse than the accusation. They treated the dead, they said, with such contempt not for the useless purpose of insulting (ὑβρίζειν) the deaf and senseless dust but in order to excite the pity of those who were related to them ... and thus urge them to ransom the bodies of their friends by making a final gift in payment for them. Foolish, foolish people, I would say to them, have you not first learnt the lesson which you teach, or are you competent to induce others to shew pity (ἔλεον), even with the cruellest (ὠμοτάτον) actions before them, when you have exscinded all kindly (χρηστά) and humane (φιλάνθρωπα) feelings from your own souls? And this you have done, though you had no lack of good advisers, particularly in our laws, which have relieved even the land from its yearly tolls and provided it with a rest and respite (*De spec. leg.* 2.92-96).

As Philo continues his discussion of the fallow seventh year, he adds yet another reason: φιλανθρωπία. During the seventh year, the poor are allowed access to the land, which Philo regards as a "good and neighborly (χρηστὰ καὶ κοινωνικά)" practice (2.104). He concludes by noting that Moses added to "this first foundation" of ἐπιείκεια and φιλανθρωπία by consecrating the fiftieth year as well (2.110). This lengthy excerpt reveals many of the words and ideas with which ἐπιείκεια is associated. It stands in a domain opposite βιάζεσθαι, ἀνέλεος, ἀπανθρωπία, πλεονεξία, σκαιότης, χαλεπός, ὕβρις, αἰκία, βάσανος, ἀγριότης, θηριώδης, τόλμα and ὠμότης. It corresponds to ἡμερότης, χρηστός, ἔλεος and φιλάνθρωπος. In 4.22-24, Philo's comments add φείδεσθαι and συγγνώμη to the latter list.

Philo's single example by no means exhausts the possible uses to which ἐπιείκεια may be put. Sometimes ἐπιείκεια appears in legal contexts. On occasion it refers to the accused when accusations and charges have proven false or suspicion unfounded. In such cases ἐπιείκεια is tantamount to "innocence." More frequently in legal contexts judges are concerned with ἐπιείκεια. If a judge does not impose allowable sanctions, he is ἐπιεικής, i.e., merciful or lenient. Legal theory also applies here, inasmuch as law is intrinsically incapable of addressing all possible contingencies. As a result, judges must bring law to bear by reason so that general legal rulings address particular situations prudently. This also is ἐπιείκεια, which we gloss as "equity" or "fairness."

In the exercise of political power, ἐπιείκεια plays an important role. In such contexts it is often linked with φιλανθρωπία and connotes a generosity on the part of the ruler. When this generosity applied to matters of punishment, generosity becomes more specifically leniency or perhaps even clemency. War offers similar contexts for restrained behavior on the part of the strong; leniency or clemency again reflects the connotation of ἐπιείκεια in such contexts. Similar to these uses are attributions of ἐπιείκεια to God in Jewish scriptures. When God's people receive ἐπιείκεια from God, they receive mercy.

Other roles which assume a degree of authority also afford opportunities for ἐπιείκεια. Fathers could show ἐπιείκεια to their children, examples which reflect indulgence and (again) leniency. Moral teachers also showed ἐπιείκεια in their admonition. The only strictures which such fathers and teachers impose are words; physical beatings are refused. Attributed to such people ἐπιείκεια connotes leniency, forbearance, gentleness, or a kindly intended restraint.

When referring to the mind, ἐπιείκεια connotes a reasonableness which holds impulses or passions in check and chooses to act prudently. Accordingly, the virtue is appropriate to older, maturer people who have left impetuous youth behind and are guided by reason. Social superiors like to think of themselves in this way, as rising above the rabble and choosing better courses of action. Thus, the plural adjective, οἱ ἐπιεικεῖς, is often code for noble people, better people.[15]

---

[15] App. *Bel. civ.* 4.12.99. Reference to a social group suggests the problem of "beauty is as beauty does." Are people higher in society ἐπιεικεῖς because they are reasonable or is it their folkways which define what is reasonable? Regardless, Greeks distinguished themselves from others by their superior reason and παιδεία. Those who had this in abundance were as a class the group who conformed most closely to ἀρετή. They could naturally be regarded as ἐπιεικεῖς, whether seen from a noetic perspective ("reasonable") or a social one ("better people").

In the possible contexts just mentioned, we should emphasize the type of person exhibiting ἐπιείκεια. The person who shows ἐπιείκεια is usually a social superior. In terms of class, this is reflected in the plural adjective, οἱ ἐπιεικεῖς. In other contexts it is a ruler to subjects, a conqueror to the conquered, a judge or jury to defendant, a father to children, a teacher to students, and God to people. In showing ἐπιείκεια, then, superiors act with restraint toward inferiors, choosing not to assert themselves as befits their rights and means. Such behavior is guided by reason and seeks to elicit goodwill, cooperative (often meaning modified) behavior, or to achieve fairness.

Corresponding to such status connotations, education produces ἐπιείκεια. Thus, Education promised Lucian to adorn his soul with σωφροσύνη, δικαιοσύνη, εὐσέβεια, πραότης, ἐπιείκεια, σύνεσις, and καρτερία (*Som.* 10). This was part of Education's offer to elevate the social status of Lucian, delivering him from the servile (ταπεινός, 13) world of labor and its cruelty (3-4) and promising him honor, esteem, power, and office (11, 13). More generally, it is not surprising to see πραότης and ἐπιείκεια, together with pleasantness and wisdom, attributed to educated people (οἱ πεπαιδευμένοι; *Alex.* 61; cp. 2). Similarly, the low-born Panthea became the emperor's favorite; devoted to learning (παιδεία), her soul was adorned with ἀρετή, σωφροσύνη, ἐπιείκεια, and φιλανθρωπία (*Imag.* 11).

Yet ἐπιείκεια can filter down to a more general level. Lucian's Cynic offers the following advice to potential Cynics: "... let everything about you be bestial (θηριώδη) and savage (ἄγρια). Put off modesty (αἰδώς), decency (ἐπιείκεια) and moderation (μετριότης), and wipe away blushes from your face completely" (*Vit. auc.* 10).[16] In other words, the polite words people share and the private attending to bodily needs reflect a commonplace, everyday ἐπιείκεια (though αἰδώς remains the more normal way of expressing this).

d. Defining ἐπιείκεια

At bottom, ἐπιείκεια expresses behavior which is appropriate.[17] Concrete contexts stipulate what is appropriate and transform ἐπιείκεια into more specific forms of behavior. Greek philosophy's correlation between knowledge and correct behavior may lend ἐπιείκεια a noetic connotation, so that one's course of action is reasonable.[18] From a conventional

---

[16] Lucian offers the same advice to the aspiring orator in *Rhet. prae.* 15.

[17] In the case of ἐπιείκεια, then, etymology is no red herring.

[18] That ἐπιείκεια means only "reasonable" or "acceptable" and not both is not clear in Thuc. 3.4, 9; 5.86. The problem lies in the fact that to label something "reasonable" made a positive value judgment about it.

perspective ἐπιείκεια may point to simple human decency, the content of which is further supplied by the general (anthropological) ethic of moderation and restraint. In a legal context, reason and restraint combine to apply the law in a fair and equitable manner; also possible are mercy and leniency. In the context of (varied) human relationships, ἐπιείκεια reflects self-restraint and may suggest anything from an easy-going manner to forgiveness.

Social register also influences usage of ἐπιείκεια. Where patterns of behavior are common to all, ἐπιείκεια is open to all. When one turns to the behavioral preferences advocated by education (παιδεία), an élite social register appears. Thus, ἐπιείκεια may serve as a general reference to virtue or gentlemanly behavior. Philosophy's democratization of virtue can, however, mute the social connotations of ἐπιείκεια, perhaps even subvert them.

I offer the following as a definition of ἐπιείκεια: 1) a general compliance with good behavior: good as a) recognized conventionally, i) particularly by aristocratic folkways (typically referred to as καλοκἀγαθία and ἀρετή) ii) but also by common human decency (usually called αἰδώς, perhaps μετριότης); or, more theoretically, good as b) anthropologically appropriate: moderation; c) defined noetically: guided by reason; d) a refutation of wrongdoing in forensic contexts: innocence or a quality unworthy of conviction; e) attested by use in virtue lists; 2) *definite behavioral choices which involve declining to act with the full rights of one's person*: e.g., a) not detracting from the person of others; b) accepting slights or wrongs; c) reasonable, restrained, and temperate debate — even silence; d) kindly intended and gently administered moral correction; e) parental indulgence; f) not an overbearing busybody in public life: i) a democratic bearing towards one's lessers; ii) withdrawal from public affairs; iii) modest oratory; g) generosity which spares others; h) in particular, a ruler's (or leader's) easy, kind and generous treatment of subjects; i) more specifically, a ruler's mercy (or leniency or clemency); and 3) a technical term for a reasoned and humane application of laws and sanctions: equity.[19] These three definitions stand in a hierarchical relationship to one another, reflecting an increasingly specific context.

---

[19] This definition is repeated in Appendix 1, where references are supplied, further details are added, and Danker's most recent revision of Bauer is discussed.

2. πραότης/πραΰτης

Like ἐπιείκεια, πραΰτης is a common Greek word. Although the TLG index counts only one hundred uses of πραΰτης, its more common spelling, πραότης, registers 1,149 times.[20] The adjective is even more widely used: the nominative masculine singular form alone appears nearly seven hundred times in extant Greek literature. To understand the use of πραΰτης in 2 Cor 10:1, we will note the advice of lexicons, look at ancient definitions, then survey the word's nuances. These will allow us to construct a definition of πραΰτης. With that foundation, we will then begin to move more closely to an examination of 2 Cor 10:1.

a. Lexicons on πραότης/πραΰτης

Having nothing to say about the genesis of πραότης, Chantraine's article focuses on morphological and semantic issues. He observes the alternative spellings πρᾶος, πραΰς, and πρηΰς, but finds no semantic differences in them. Chantraine glosses πρᾶος (s.v.) as "gentle, without violence" (*doux, sans violence*), noting that the adjective is used to describe light, wind, animals, people, and acts. For the verb, πραΰνω, Chantraine suggests "to soften, to allay, to calm" (*adoucir*) and "to appease, to pacify" (*apaiser*).[21]

LSJ likewise does not differentiate semantically between πραότης (s.v.) and its later form πραΰτης. "Mildness" and "gentleness" are offered as translation equivalents. Helpfully, LSJ notes the antonyms ἀγριότης, ὀργιλότης, and ὀργή. These are important as we shall see below. Like Chantraine, LSJ notes the use of the adjective with things, animals, people, actions, and feelings, offering as glosses "mild, soft, gentle, tame." LSJ observes a second category of meaning as well: "making mild, taming."

Turning to BAGD, we find that it too equates πραΰτης and πραότης. Although the uninterrupted use of the Attic form is noted, BAGD inadequately emphasizes that the preponderance of evidence for the form πραΰτης is Jewish and Christian; even though the substitution of upsilon for omicron is a feature of Koinē, in this case literary authors shun it. As for translational equivalents, BAGD offers "gentleness, humility, courtesy, considerateness, [and] meekness." For the adjective, "gentle, humble, considerate, meek" and "unassuming" are put forward. BAGD also notes

---

[20] Apart from the LXX (9x), the form πραΰτης appears predominantly in Christian texts. The commonplace spelling is πραότης; an iota subscript appears under the alpha about one third of the time. Regardless of the spelling, this noun is rarely plural (see Isoc. *Ant.* 214; *Phil.* 116).

[21] Likewise, Hjalmar Frish, *Griechisches etymologisches Wörterbuch*, 2: 588.

the conjunction of πρᾶος with ταπεινός and ἡσύχιος, as well as the link between πραότης and ἐπιείκεια.

Together these articles alert us to four things. First, πραότης and πραΰτης are alternate spellings of the same word. Second, "gentleness" is the typical translation gloss. Third, the adjective has uses which the noun does not. Fourth, anger and savage incivility stand opposite πραότης/πραΰτης, while ἐπιείκεια overlaps with it. What we shall now seek to add to these things is a clarification of the relationship between πραότης and ὀργή (and later, ἐπιείκεια), a fuller roster of words which are associated with πραότης and, finally, a definition of πραότης. These things will help us understand more clearly the semantics of πραότης.

b. Ancient Definitions of πραότης/πραΰτης

Just as for ἐπιείκεια, Ps.-Plato also provides a succinct definition of πραότης, describing it as "a settled condition when agitated by anger (ὀργή), a well-measured mixing of the soul" (*Def.* 412d; my trans.). To paraphrase this, "πραότης is the condition of the soul which remains steady when provoked to anger, a soul well-balanced between calm and agitation."

The second half of Ps.-Plato's definition is not expendable, for it underscores that πραότης is not simply the absence of anger, but one's response to and control of it. Aristotle explains this in his definition of πραότης, where again we see it juxtaposed with ὀργή.

> πραότης is the observance of the mean in relation to anger.... Now we praise a man who feels anger on the right grounds and against the right persons, and also in the right manner and at the right moment and for the right length of time. He may then be called gentle-tempered (πρᾶος), if we take πραότης to be a praiseworthy quality (for πρᾶος really denotes a calm temper [ἀτάραχος], not led by emotion but only becoming angry [χαλεπαίνειν] in such a manner, for such causes and for such a length of time as principle [λόγος] may ordain; although the quality is thought rather to err on the side of defect, since the gentle-tempered man [ὁ πρᾶος] is not prompt to seek redress [τιμωρητικός] for injuries, but rather inclined to forgive [συγγνωμονικός] them). The defect, on the other hand, call it a sort of lack of spirit (ἀοργησία) or what not, is blamed; since those who do not get angry at things at which it is right to be angry are considered foolish, and so are those who do not get angry in the right manner, at the tight time, and with the right people. It is thought that they do not feel or resent an injury (λυπεῖσθαι), and that if a man is never angry he will not stand up for himself; and it is considered servile (ἀνδραποδῶδες) to put up with (ἀνέχεσθαι) an insult to oneself or suffer one's friends to be insulted (*E.N.* 4.5.1-6).

Aristotle also notes the opposite types of character, the irascible person (ὀργίλος), the violently quick-tempered, the simmering, slow-tempered, and the harsh-tempered (χαλεπός). The latter "lose their temper at the wrong things, and more and longer than they ought," refusing "to be reconciled (διαλλαττομένους) without obtaining redress (τιμωρίας) or retaliating (κολάσεως)" (*E.N.* 4.5.11). Aristotle also notes the ambiguity latent in these character types: "we sometimes praise those deficient in anger and call them gentle-tempered (πρᾶος), and we sometimes praise those who are harsh-tempered (χαλεπαίνοντας) as manly, and fitted to command (ἄρχειν)" (*E.N.* 4.5.13). In sum, Aristotle offers πραότης as the correct way to handle anger, namely, to curb the impulses of emotion and let reason guide, preferring forgiveness to retribution. At the same time, convention remains part of the discussion, as Aristotle notes the danger of being considered servile if one tolerates insult to one's friends as well as oneself.[22]

Not everyone agreed completely with Aristotle and Ps.-Plato. Stoics were less willing to grant a place to acting on anger; therefore, they would dispense with the second half of Ps.-Plato's definition. In *SVF* 3.632, then, πραότης is the habit of acting with kind restraint, or gently, in whatever it falls to one to do and never being carried away by anger (ὀργή). No additional statement about balancing gentleness with anger appears. In fact, Marcus Aurelius disputes that manliness requires any show of anger (θύμος) and asserts that not only humanity but manliness and strength increase with gentleness (11.18).

πραότης outgrew Aristotle's categories and the dialectic with anger. A. S. L. Farquharson observes this in connection with Marcus Aurelius, whose connection of πραότης and εὐμένεια lends the former a larger moral framework than a simple contrast with anger affords.[23] Plutarch's writings also stretch πραότης beyond Aristotle. In describing Artaxerxes, Plutarch encapsulates the various deeds of which πραότης is capable, writing that Artaxerxes was

altogether emulous of the gentleness (πραότητα) of the Artaxerxes whose name he bore, showing himself very agreeable in intercourse, and bestowing greater honors and favors than were really deserved, while from all his punishments he took away the element of insult or vindictive pleasure, and in his acceptance and bestowal of favors appeared no less gracious and kindly to the givers than to the recipients. For there was no gift so small that he did not accept it with alacrity ... (*Art*. 1013a/ 4.4).

In this description πραότης expresses itself in three ways. First, it is a democratic bearing which does not bring the full weight of one's person to bear in social and political relationships. Second, πραότης is generous (with honors, favors, and goodwill). Third, by removing their sting

---

[22] Xenophon also reflects this note of convention: "As you know, we call those creatures noble that are beautiful, great and helpful, and yet gentle (πραέα) towards men" (*Oec.* 15.4).

[23] *The Meditations of the Emperor Marcus Aurelius* (Oxford University Press, 1944), 2: 747-48.

πραότης moderates punishments and is therefore lenient. Thus, the control or absence of anger can lead to more positive behaviors which add new dimensions to πραότης. Examination of its synonyms will introduce us to these.[24]

c. Nuances of πραότης/πραΰτης

As with ἐπιείκεια so also with πραότης, the words with which the latter is associated and the contexts in which it appears help us understand it. Turning to the words, the following virtues are synonyms of πραότης:

ἀνεξικακία: Plut. *Mor.* 90e; 459c; 489c;
ἐπιείκεια: discussed below;
ἡμερότης: Philo *De op. mun.* 103; [*De vit. Mos.* 2.279]; [Polyb. 9.23.3]; [Epict. *Diss.* 2.22.36]; Plut. *Lyc.* 11.3; [*Ag.* 21.5]; Luc. *Phal.* 1.3; [*Per.* 18]; [Aristid. *Or.* 3.570]; Iamb. *De vit. Pyth.* 20.95;
ἠπιότης: Philo *De dec.* 167; [Plut. *Fab. Max.* 20.1; *Mor.* 276f];
μεγαλοψυχία: Polyb. 3.99.7; 4.27.10; 5.11.9; 30.17.4; [30.31.15]; Plut. *Cato min.* 14.4; *Tit. Flam.* 21.2; *Art.* 1.1; *Mor.* 551c;
μετριότης: [Dio. Hal. *Ant.* 4.36.2]; Plut. *Per.* 39.4; [*Mor.* 77c];
σύνεσις: Plut. *Cras.* 8.3;
φιλανθρωπία: Jos. *Bel.* 6.340; Polyb. [21.4.10]; 28.3.3; [Dio. Hal. *Ant.* 4.36.2]; Plut. [*Ag.* 20.4]; *Mor.* [464d]; 959f; App. *Cyn.* 5.2; Luc. *Phal.* 1.3; [Aristid. *Or.* 39.5];
φιλοφροσύνη: Plut. *Cras.* 30.2.
χρηστότης: [Dio. Hal. *Ars rhet.* 3.4]; Plut. *Ant.* 79.4.

Little in this list comes as a surprise.[25] More interesting is the joining of πραότης with just and lawful behavior:

δικαιοσύνη: Ps 44:5 LXX; *T. Abr.* 1.1; *T. Jud.* 24.1; Plut. *Lyc.* 28.6; *Numa* 20.3; *Comp. Lyc. et Numa* 4.7; *Per.* 2.5; *Tim.* 37.6; *Cic.* 6.1; *Tit. Flam.* 2.5; *Mor.* 543d; Dio Cas. 49.20.4; cf. Diod. Sic. 11.67.3;
νόμιμος: Plut. *Pel.* 26.2; cf. παρανόμησαι in *Ser.* 581d/ 25.6.

---

[24] In fact, the above quotation from Plutarch introduces us to one synonym, ἐπιείκεια. Had I quoted the context, the synonymous relation between ἐπιείκεια and πραότης would be clear.

[25] Idiosyncratic examples could lengthen this list. For example, Polybius connects πραότης with καλοκἀγαθία (2.60.5; 5.10.4 [cf. ἐλεύθερος in 27.12.1]) and Plutarch is fond of connecting πραότης with εὐκολία (Plut. *Cras.* 3.6; *Mor.* 462c; 461a; 608d).

2.2. πραότης

In these cases, δικαιοσύνη and πραότης are not so much interchangeable as mutually inclusive: i.e., in some cases justice requires gentleness or gentleness makes room for justice.

Turning from virtues per se, we find that πραότης overlaps synonymously with other words as well.

ἡσυχία: T. Abr. 1.1; [Jos. Ant. 6.9]; Plut. Eum. et Ser. 595f/ 2.2;
ἵλαος: Philo De spec. leg. 1.146; [De vit. Mos. 1.331]; Plut. Ant. 83.7; [Mor. 40b; 125c; 453b; 464d; 468f; 499b; 613d].

To this pair we may add a cluster of words which, as we saw earlier, stand in synonymous relation to ἐπιείκεια:

ἔλεος: Ps 89:10 LXX; Sir 36:23; [Jos. Asen. 8.8];
συγγνώμη: Jos. Ant. [6.151]; 19.333; [Epict. Diss. 2.22.36]; Plut. Mor. 458c;
φείδεσθαι: Jos. Bel. 6.340-53; App. Bel. civ. 3.11.79; Plut. Mor. 458c; 729e;
χάρις: [Jos. Bel. 6.350]; Plut. Fab. Max. 20.4; Mor. 713a; 1108b.

Here we recognize that, like ἐπιείκεια, πραότης may indicate the mercy which spares people.

πραότης often appears in contexts involving punishment and authority (which further resembles ἐπιείκεια):

βασιλικός: Polyb. 4.27.10;
δεσπότης: [Jos. Bel. 6.350];
δύναμις: Plut. Pom. 39.4;
ἐξουσία: [Jos. Ant. 11.216]; [Dio. Hal. Ant. 4.36.2]; Plut. Mor. 459c;
ἐπανόρθωσις: Plut. Mor. 459c; Grac. 9.2;
καθαίρεσις: Arr. Parth. 19;
κόλασις: Jos. Ant. 17.164 (adverb); Plut. Pom. 39.4; Mor. 459c; 550f;
κωλύειν: Plut. Pom. 39.4;
παιδεύειν: Ps 89:10 LXX;
τιμωρία: Jos. Bel. 6.338-40; [Ant. 19.330]; Plut. Mor. 550f.
τύραννος: [Dio. Hal. Ant. 4.41.4]; Plut. Sol. 15.1;

In the case of these words, of course, πραότης mitigates them. Thus, πραότης shares goals similar to those of ἐπιείκεια:

διαλλάσσειν: Jos. Ant. [6.151]; 19.333; cp. Polyb. 30.31.15 (ἀκατάλλακτης); Plut. Ant. 79.4 (ἀδιάλλακτος);

θεραπεύειν: [Jos. *Ant.* 17.204; *Bel.* 1.507];
μετάνοια: *Jos. Asen.* 15.8; Jos. *Bel.* 6.338-40; Plut. *Mor.* 550f;
νουθετεῖν: Jos. *Bel.* 6.339;
σωτηρία: Jos. *Bel.* 6.340-46; [6.350].

The similarities between these last two groups indicates the overlap of ἐπιείκεια and πραότης as virtues which treat wrongdoers kindly with a view to reforming them.

Turning to antonyms, we can supply a long list for πραότης. Not surprisingly these words describe harshness, severity, boldness, and arrogance. Some we saw in connection with ἐπιείκεια:

ἀγριότης: [Dio Chrys. 60.4]; Plut. *Pom.* 28.3; Iamb. *De vit. Pyth.* 20.95;
ἀποτομία: [Jos. *Ant.* 19.330]; Ps.-Plut. *Mor.* 13d;
βαρύτης: Polyb. 3.99.7; [Dio. Hal. *Ant.* 4.41.4]; Plut. *Fab.* 9.1;
βία: Diod. Sic. 11.67.3; Plut. *Fab. Max.* 21.3; *Cleom.* 3.1;
θάρσος/θράσος: Jos. *Bel.* 6.340; Dio Cas. 15.57.25;
σκαιότης: [Jos. *Ant.* 11.216];
τόλμα: Jos. *Bel.* 6.340; Plut. *Cim.* 5.5; [Dio. Hal. *Ant.* 4.28.2];
ὕβρις: Plut. *Alex.* 65.3;
ὑπερηφανία: [Jos. *Ant.* 11.216]; [Dio Chrys. 41.9];
χαλεπός: [Dio. Hal. *Ant.* 4.41.4]; [Epict. *Diss.* 2.22.36]; [Dio Chrys. 41.9; 60.4]; Plut. *Lyc.* 28.6; *Fab. Max.* 20.1; *Pom.* 28.3; *Cic.* 31.4; [Aristid. *Or.* 3.570];
ὠμότης: Plut. *Pel.* 26.2; *Cor.* 13.1; *Mor.* 445a.

In addition to those, πραότης has other antonyms:

αὐθάδης: Plut. *Lyc.* 11.3;
δεινότης: Polyb. 5.11.9;
θηριώδης: Plut. *Pel.* 26.2.
ὀχύτης: Aristid. *Or.* 31.5; [1.396];
σκληρός: Plut. *Lyc.* 11.3; 28.6;
τραχέως: Plut. *Alex.* 65.3; [Aristid. *Or.* 3.570];
φιλόνεικος: Plut. *Eum. et Ser.* 595f/ 2.2.
φιλοπόλεμος: Plut. *Eum. et Ser.* 595f/ 2.2.

As noted earlier, emotions also furnish πραότης with antonyms — and two of its most important:

θύμος: Ps 89:10 LXX; Add Esth 5:1e; Philo *De spec. leg.* 1.146; Plut. *Fab. Max.* 9.1; *Mor.* 449f; [453d]; 459c; 462e;

ὀργή: Ps 89:10 LXX; [Num 12:3]; *Jos. Asen.* 23.10; [Philo *De vit. Mos.* 2.279]; Jos. *Ant.* [17.212]; 19.333; [Polyb. 30.31.15]; [Dio. Hal. *Ant.* 7.2.4]; [Epict. *Diss.* 3.20.10]; [Dio Chrys. 11.127]; Plut. *Mor.* [453b]; 550f; [Dio Cas. 43.20.1]; Iamb. *De vit. Pyth.* 28.154;
πάθος: Philo *De op. mun.* 103; Plut. *Mor.* 83a.

In these lists, then, ideas of aggression, oppression, forcefulness, arrogance, overbearing self-assertion, incivility, cruelty, severity, and rage appear, helping to define what it is to be πραότης.

Still another group of related words has both synonymous and antonymous relations with πραότης. A few words with which πραότης is correlated positively are surprising:

ἀφιλότιμον: Plut. *Aris. et Cato* 5.4 (prerequisite for a statesman's πραότης);
μαλακία: [Dio. Hal. *Ant.* 7.2.4 (a person with a πρᾶος nature who is μαλακός with respect to anger)]; Plut. *Sol.* 15.1 (πρᾶος and μαλακός are alternatives to tyranny); *Grac.* 9.2.2 (a law against ἀδικία καὶ πλεονεξία is πρᾶος καὶ μαλακός); *Art.* 2.1; [*Mor.* 453b (θύμος has become πρᾶος and μαλακός)];
ταπεινός: [Ps 146:6 LXX]; [Isa 26:6]; [Zeph 3:12]; Sir 3:17; [10:14]; *T. Dan* 6.9 (the savior [var.: father] of nations is πρᾶος καὶ ταπεινός); Ps.-Dem. *Erot.* 14 (people with πραότης are often assumed to be ταπεινός); Plut. *Cor.* 21.1 (both πραότης and ταπεινός are antithetical to θύμος here, but are not synonymous).

Yet the following express opposite meanings:

ἀσθένεια: Jos. *Bel.* 6.340 (Vespasian's leniency treated as weakness); M. Aur. 11.9 (πραότης does not yield to anger or surrender to terror; each extreme is weakness);
μαλακία: Athen. *Deip.* 14.33/ 633c (μαλακία is a debasement of πραότης);
ταπεινός: Dio. Cas. 74.5.7 (Pertinax was πρᾶος without being ταπεινός).

Given the generally pejorative nature of these words, one might not expect them to correspond to a recognized virtue. They do, however, underscore the ambiguity latent within πραότης, as to whether a person restrains power or lacks power.

In sum, these words with which πραότης is associated suggest its possible relations with justice, virtue, retribution, restoration, and, possibly, softness. They signify the peace-loving and peace-making ways of the πρᾶος person, his or her civility and courtesy, as well as kindness and respect for others.

A few themes recur in the use of πραότης. First, as we have already seen in connection with its ancient definitions, πραότης stands opposite to anger (ὀργή). For philosophers in particular, this is important, since how one handles anger is a key measure of one's moral virtue. Second, πρᾶος parallels ἥμερος in referring to the domestication of animals. To make them gentle is to tame them is to bring them into the realm of civilization and reason (Xen. *Mem.* 2.3.9). Opposite this stand wildness and harshness (ἄγριος and χαλεπός; Dio Chrys. 32.69; 74.7). Third, πραότης is a way of speaking, perhaps as a way to mollify those who have been offended or upset (Theoph. 1.3), or to get someone to pay attention (Xen. *Mem.* 2.3.16), or as a way of delivering admonition. The latter case is particularly relevant for fathers (Ps.-Plut. *Mor.* 13d) and philosophers (Philos. *Vit. soph.* 1.487). Fourth, it is a way of behaving in the face of wrongdoing. Like ἐπιείκεια, πραότης does not assert its rights but restrains itself. It declines opportunities to harm others and does not react harshly to wrongs suffered. Fifth, to be πρᾶος is an act of generosity (φιλανθρωπία; Xen. *Oec.* 17).

These themes coalesce in Musonius Rufus' reflection on the philosopher's response to personal insult, injustice, or violence. Musonius makes πραότης basic to a philosopher's conduct:

I might mention many other men who have experienced insult, some wronged by word, others by violence and bodily harm, who do not appear to have defended their rights against their assailants nor to have proceeded against them in any other way, but very meekly (πράως) bore their wrong. And in this they were quite right. For to scheme how to bite back the biter and to return evil for evil is the act not of a human being but of a wild beast, which is incapable of reasoning that the majority of wrongs are done to men through ignorance and misunderstanding, from which man will cease as soon as he has been taught. But to accept injury not in a spirit of savage resentment and to show ourselves not implacable toward those who wrong us, but rather to be a source of good hope to them is characteristic of a benevolent (ἡμέρου) and civilized (φιλανθρώπου) way of life. How much better a figure does the philosopher make so conducting himself as to deem worthy of forgiveness (συγγνώμης) anyone who wrongs him, than to behave as if ready to defend himself (*Will the Philosopher Prosecute Anyone for Personal Injury?*, Lutz, p. 78).

To make his argument about philosophic behavior, Musonius drew on the *topos* of the wild, irrational beast as opposed to the rational, civilized human. He also equated reasoned civility with generosity and stated the principle that gentleness opens the door to reformed behavior and restored relations. Equally important, he states the principle of non-retaliation — here elevated to an expression of personal virtue.

In the anonymous oration Εἰς βασιλέα preserved in the corpus of Aelius Aristides, the role of πραότης is viewed from another perspective. In this encomium, the emperor's worthiness to rule appears firstly in how he became emperor, for he entered his office by popular acclaim, without bloodshed and within the laws (5-8). Once emperor, he did not swerve from the good character which παιδεία had implanted within him (9-12), an element of which was πραότης (10). This virtue appears in a summary statement praising the emperor for a quiet, peaceable realm free from imperial bloodlust. His rule required no murder, no harm to individuals, cities, or whole peoples, and no accusations of treason. Even those who really did plot against him continued to live. Thus, suppression of anger, violence, and arrogance in displays of πραότης could have consequences far beyond theoretical discussions of virtue.

Because gentleness muted self-display, and might even threaten self-preservation, gentleness required justification. We saw Musonius' attempt at this. That reason should guide one's behavior is the common rationale, but what ideas support reason's lead? In her survey of Greco-Roman attitudes toward gentleness, Jacqueline de Romilly has outlined the customary arguments advanced on behalf of πραότης (or φιλανθρωπία, ἐπιείκεια or συγγνώμη). The two most common were those of ignorance and compulsion. In each a person who suffered some wrong excused it on the assumption of mitigating circumstances: either the wrongdoer did not know any better (as above in Musonius) or some overwhelming influence made the wrongdoing inevitable (e.g., a divine will, a superior's orders, poverty, age, gender, love, anger, or drunkenness).[26] The fragility of the human condition also argued on behalf of forgiveness, as this provided a solidarity which issued in fraternity and pity.[27] In sum, then, πραότης may express basic human kindness, yet, even more, an enlightenment which exchanges impulsive responses for more gracious and productive ones.

d. Defining πραότης/πραΰτης

Like ἐπιείκεια, πραότης/πραΰτης applies to contexts of politics and philosophy; unlike the case of ἐπιείκεια, however, it is difficult to generalize about its meaning. Focusing on the individual's experience of his or her own πραότης, we find πραότης/πραΰτης used around the time of the early Empire to describe the composure which a person displays

---

[26] *La douceur*, 67-76. De Romilly observes that the intellectual component of forgiveness is reflected in the word itself, συγγνώμη, so that understanding gives birth to indulgence, whereas in Latin forgiveness rests on refusing to take note of wrongdoing (*ignosco*; pp. 65-66).

[27] *Ibid.*, 82-88.

when circumstances, other people, or emotions ought to elicit or display a harsh or violent reaction. This inner psychology is usually the issue when πραότης is used with ὀργή and θύμος or in discussions of a philosopher's virtue. Thus, πραότης/πραΰτης is, first, a calm which is not overcome by hostility, misfortune, or emotions, but responds gently and with composure: it is an imperturbable gentleness or mildness, perhaps composure, serenity, forbearance, or tolerance. Secondly, more specific social contexts lead to more precise nuances: a) a peaceable benevolence which smooths over undesirable things, especially a refusal to chide; b) the compliant response of social inferiors; c) a populist bearing, a gentle and benign exercise of government; d) showing gentleness, indulgence, and/or generosity in order to procure peace; e) mitigated retribution: forgiveness, mercy, leniency, clemency. Thirdly, πραότης/πραΰτης may be applied to things, such as a docile animal, a calm sea, or an approving glance.[28]

3. ἐπιείκεια and πραότης

We turn now to the crucial question of what ἐπιείκεια and πραότης/πραΰτης mean when they are used in combination, as they are in 2 Cor 10:1. Having examined their synonyms and antonyms, we have seen the outlines of the meanings of each word; moreover, we have defined them. Given this framework, we can now focus our attention to investigate whether the use of πραότης and ἐπιείκεια in combination has semantic significance?

a. Pragmatics of ἐπιείκεια and πραότης in Conjunction

Among the more than twenty parallels Wettstein long ago provided for ἐπιείκεια in 2 Cor 10:1, two combine ἐπιείκεια with πραότης, while a third text uses the two words in parallel.[29] All three examples come from Plutarch. Throughout this century, literature on 2 Cor 10:1 has repeated these three parallels.[30] Not always noted, though available at least since

---

[28] See Appendix 2 for references and discussion of Danker's recent revision of Bauer.

[29] Wettstein also offers an example from Philo (*De vit. Mos.* 1.198); however, his text is suspect (*Novum Testamentum Graecum* [Amsterdam, 1752; Graz, 1962], 2: 202). Cohn and Wendland read ἐπιείκειαν καὶ φιλανθρωπίαν, rather than Wettstein's ἐπιείκειαν καὶ πραότητα; nor do they even cite this as a variant (*Philonis Alexandrini opera quae supersunt* [7 vols.; Berlin: Reimer, 1896-1930; reprinted, de Gruyter, 1962], 4: 167).

[30] For example, Plummer and Barrett. Harnack and *TDNT* omit the reference to Plut. *Ser.* 25.

2.3. ἐπιείκεια and πραότης

Windisch, is an example from Philo. Even more overlooked was an example in Plutarch's *Moralia* noted by Trench.[31] We will look now at these five to see what they tell us about the semantics of the combined use of ἐπιείκεια and πραότης.[32]

1) Philo *De opificio mundi* 103. In demonstrating the perfection of the number seven, Philo outlines how a man's life breaks down into ten periods of seven years. In the sixth stage of life, "understanding reaches its bloom; in the seventh progressive improvement and development of mind and reason; in the eighth the perfecting of both these; during the ninth ἐπιείκεια and πραότης emerge, owing to the more complete taming of the passions." As this text has no specific action in view, ἐπιείκεια and πραότης should be regarded generally as an expression of equanimity, gentleness, and forbearance. What this implies is shown by the prior development of "mind and reason" and the resulting "domestication of the passions" (τῶν παθῶν ἐπὶ πλέον ἡμερωθέντων). As already observed, ἐπιείκεια and πραότης are products of the mind's triumph over emotion, the calm and forbearance which defeat impulses, a victory contingent on maturity and social status.

2) Plutarch *Pericles* 39.1. Describing the scene of Pericles' death, Plutarch relates that gathered friends were discussing Pericles' achievements, thinking that the dying man did not hear them. They were mistaken, as they learned when Pericles added to their conversation the point of pride that "no living Athenian ever put on mourning because of me." Plutarch concludes from this that Pericles deserves admiration not only for the ἐπιείκεια and πραότης "in the midst of many responsibilities and great enmities," but also for the φρόνημα which such self-evaluation reveals. Plutarch's narrative then elaborates on Pericles' virtues: he never indulged (χαρίσασθαι) his jealousy or his anger (θύμος) while exercising his enormous power (δύναμις), nor held any enemy as a foe incurable. Thus, Pericles displayed a kind and friendly character (εὐμενὲς ἦθος) and lived a life "pure and undefiled in the exercise of sovereign power (βίον ἐν ἐξουσίᾳ καθαρὸν καὶ ἀμίαντον)." In this example, references to political rule narrow the meaning of ἐπιείκεια and πραότης further than in the text from Philo. Here these virtues express themselves in the restrained and forbearing exercise of power and authority, an approach to office which relies on good opinion and goodwill. Though one might gloss this as "gentleness," the fact that no Athenian "ever put on mourning"

---

[31] Richard C. Trench, *Synonyms of the New Testament* (London, 1880[9]; reprinted, Grand Rapids: Eerdmans, 1978), 156.

[32] Philo, Plutarch, and Dio Cassius put ἐπιείκεια before πραότης, whereas Paul, Lucian, Athenaeus, and Julian place πραΰτης before ἐπιείκεια.

64 Chap. 2: Semantic Investigation

indicates that the types of possible behaviors envisioned certainly reach to leniency and clemency.

3) Plutarch *Sertorius* 25.4. An extremely competent general, Sertorius accomplished much by sound character and cleverness. As for the former, he showed himself gentle (ἥμερος) to his enemies (1.4), even sparing (φείδεσθαι) defeated foes (18.6). He did not match Cinna and Marius in ὕβρις and ὀργή, nor join in their murders (5.4). During his exile in Spain, his base of power rested on populist policies, as he avoided greed and arrogance, remitted taxes, and refused to impose the housing of his soldiers on local citizens (6.3-4; cf. 24.4). In general, he was ἥμερος, though he did not neglect to make intimidating preparations for war (6.5; cf. 22.7). In victory, he "did no wrong to those who were his suppliants ... but restored to them ... property and cities and government" (9.5). "Moreover, while he showed himself generous in rewarding deeds of valor, he used moderation in punishing transgressions" (περὶ τὰς τιμωρίας ἐμετρίαζε τῶν ἁμαρτημάτων; 10.3; cf. 25.3, κολάζοντες πικρῶς). As a result of being so πρᾶος, many people voluntarily allied themselves with him (11.1). What particularly pleased barbarian nobles was Sertorius' provision of a Greco-Roman education for their sons (14.2). This, however, led to an ugly episode later in Sertorius' life, for when the nobles arrogantly and foolishly considered themselves equal to Sertorius, he moved against their sons, "killing some, and selling others into slavery" (25.4). This turn of events perplexed Plutarch (10.3-4). How could a man change so radically as to abandon the clear path of ἐπιείκεια καὶ πραότης which he had followed his entire life? Plutarch could only surmise that relentless misfortune undermined Sertorius' moral purpose. Thus, as we reflect on Plutarch's application of ἐπιείκεια καὶ πραότης to Sertorius, what we observe is emphatic shorthand for the generous treatment Sertorius habitually showed to those under his power, whether by conquest or allurement. That the immediate context equates the lack of these virtues with murder and enslavement in turn highlights their connotations of mercy and leniency.

4) Plutarch *Caesar* 57.3. This text is not a perfect parallel to these other examples or 2 Cor 10:1, for it does not join ἐπιείκεια and πραότης with a simple καί; rather, πραότης appears nine words later justifying the attribution of ἐπιείκεια to Caesar. We nevertheless shall examine it now because it is one of the commonly invoked parallels to Paul's words. In this passage, Plutarch reflects on the temple dedicated to Caesar's clemency (ἐπιείκεια), which, Plutarch tells us, was awarded to Caesar on account of his πραότης. Plutarch then illustrates Caesar's deeds. For example, "he pardoned (ἀφῆκε) many of those who had fought against him." Not only that, but to some, like Brutus and Cassius, Caesar gave

offices and honors. "The statues of Pompey, too, which had been thrown down, he would not suffer to remain so, but set them up again." Caesar's ἐπιείκεια (i.e., clemency), then, encompassed forgiveness and generosity toward those who opposed him.

5) Plutarch *Moralia* 80b. Another example introduces the theme of education and philosophy. In Plutarch's discussion of moral progress (προκοπή), he states that one's comportment in debate reveals the extent of a person's moral development. One should not enter debate in a spirit of competition, seeking only to win rather than shed light. If, however, a person can discuss without yielding to fighting, anger, gloating, or sulking, then one is clearly growing morally. To state the test in positive terms, the virtuous person shows ἐπιείκεια καὶ πραότης in such situations (*Mor.* 80b), displaying these virtues in place of anger. Like Philo's ideal mature person, then, Plutarch also envisions people other than rulers displaying ἐπιείκεια and πραότης, in fact any and all virtuous people — who in Plutarch's mind are involved in philosophy.

These five texts — and especially those from Plutarch's *Lives* — have long supplied non-Christian parallels to Paul's phrase in 2 Cor 10:1. Unfortunately, most people have parroted them, not studied them. As we will argue soon, clues to Paul's words appear in the texts from Plutarch. For now, we may observe that of the five preceding parallels, three apply ἐπιείκεια καὶ πραότης to persons in authority, while the other two attribute the pair to moral development, Philo to the virtue gained by maturity and Plutarch to the fruit of philosophy. This difference between the exercise of authority and the process of moral development influences the semantics of the two virtues in question. Where power and authority are relevant, they narrow the connotation of ἐπιείκεια καὶ πραότης, while their absence leaves the meaning less specific. If this pattern holds up (and it does), it will assist us greatly in understanding a man who claims to have ἐξουσία, viz., the apostle Paul.

This hypothesis can be tested further in relation to four additional texts introduced by Bauer, Kittel, and Spicq during this century, taking us up to a total of nine examples.

6) Lucian *The Dream, or Lucian's Career* 10. As Education enumerates the blessings she will bring to Lucian, if he pursues her, she recites a list of virtues she will bring: σωφροσύνη, δικαιοσύνη, εὐσέβεια, πραότης, ἐπιείκεια, σύνεσις, καρτερία, etc. These qualities, then, are available not only through maturity (recall Philo), but through education as well. The context of *The Dream* further emphasizes the social register implied by the possession of these virtues. Without these virtues and without Education, Lucian would be but a laborer, a person characterized by such words as lowly (ταπεινός), worthless (εὐτελής), and, most revealingly, illiberal or

low-born (ἀγεννής). This creates a pointed comparison between what Lucian might become and how Sculpture, in the person of his uncle, acted. On Lucian's first day as an apprentice in his uncle's sculpture shop, Lucian struck a slab incorrectly, shattering it. His uncle beat him, giving him an introduction to the trade which was neither gentle or encouraging (οὐ πράως οὐδὲ προτρεπτικῶς), two behaviors which are prized in παιδεία. This beating, in fact, comes immediately before Lucian's dream, thereby juxtaposing his uncle's cruelty (ὠμότης) with Education's promise of gentleness. In this example, then, since ἐπιείκεια and πραότης appear in a virtue list, nothing immediately delimits their meaning. But they are part of a character type, the πεπαιδευμένος, drawn in contrast to another, the laborer, and thereby have a definite social location. ἐπιείκεια and πραότης belong to the educated, who typically come from the higher social classes and whose education (ideally) inculcates in them the values and folkways of the well-born. Distaste for physical abuse is one element of this.

7) Lucian *Alexander the False Prophet* 61. Lucian addressed this essay to his Epicurean friend Celsus. At the conclusion Lucian praises Celsus by reciting the latter's virtues. Celsus possesses wisdom, loves truth, leads a life characterized by πραότης καὶ ἐπιείκεια, as well as by peace (γαλήνη) and by dexterity (δεξιότης) in personal relations (61). These words contrast with the subject of Lucian's essay, Alexander, who did not love truth, gentleness, peace, or others. The comparison between Celsus (together with Lucian) and Alexander is clear at the beginning of the essay (1-2; cf. 47). Alexander is a γόης, full of "clever schemes" (ἐπίνοιαι), "bold emprises" (τολμήματα; cf. 48, 58), and "sleights of hand" (μαγγανεῖαι)" (1); he is full of "lying, trickery, perjury, and malice;" though "facile, audacious, venturesome, [and] diligent in the execution of ... schemes," he falsely impressed others as being the most χρηστὸς καὶ ἐπιεικής man in the world (4). For educated people like Celsus and Alexander to read and write about such a person is shameful — αἰδώς should deter the πεπαιδευμένοι.[33] But Lucian yields to his friend's request, offering an account of a man full of savagery (ὠμότης; 2) and an enemy of truth (25), a man who even conspired to murder Lucian (56-57)! Celsus' possession of πραότης καὶ ἐπιείκεια, therefore, contrasts with Alexander's outrageous schemes, mob agitation, and feigned graciousness; moreover, Celsus' πραότης καὶ ἐπιείκεια reflect his social identification with the literate and well-bred. When combined with his love of truth and ability to get along with others, the virtue list further idealizes Celsus as a good philosopher — and particularly a good Epicurean. Celsus is an

---

[33] Luc. *Alex.* 2; cp. 17, 20, 25, 30, 40, 45, 61.

educational success, trained in the ways of nobility, sensibility, and philosophy. His πραότης καὶ ἐπιείκεια, then, reflect his station above the mob and his restrained, easy-going manner which eschews ridicule and pursues harmonious relations with other people.[34]

8) Appian *Basilica* 1.5. In an example introduced in BAGD, Appian tells about an instance of royal intrigue in early Rome, a time when Numitor lost his throne to his younger brother, Amulius. Despite a conspiracy against his life, Numitor survived thanks to the πραότης and ἐπιείκεια of his character (ἡ τῶν ἠθῶν ... πραότης καὶ ἡ πολλὴ ἐπιείκεια).[35] In this example, the nuance of our two words is not at first clear. Perhaps they reflect specific deeds performed by Numitor. If so, was Numitor detached and withdrawn from public life, thereby preserving his life? Or did earlier acts of leniency earn him sympathy and assistance from others later? Or should we not distinguish these two options? (The difference between failure to govern and forgiveness may be unclear.) Or worse, was Numitor's submissiveness to his younger brother what spared him? We can rule out this last option, for it was generally characteristic πραότης and ἐπιείκεια which preserved Numitor, not a recent modification of behavior; moreover, characteristic submission would have eliminated any need for a conspiracy against his life. Rather, a habit of πραότης and ἐπιείκεια had surrounded Numitor with a shield of goodwill which stymied the conspiracy against him. What deeds elicited such esteem? More than withdrawal is required. Numitor's easy and gentle royal personage must have softened life for others in positive ways. Accessibility, graciousness, and forgiveness are expressions of such behavior. More to the point, Numitor's πραότης and ἐπιείκεια contrast with the ὕβρις and βία of his younger brother. This leads to the alternate way of understanding Appian's text. The point of attributing to Numitor these two virtues is to distinguish him as a good ruler from his tyrannical brother, a function these two virtues serve quite well (particularly in contrast to ὕβρις and βία).[36] What Appian then says in shorthand, Plutarch states at greater length, describing Amulius as harsh (χαλεπός) and attributing to Numitor a kind (φιλάνθρωπος) expression and gentle (πρᾶος) voice.[37] Moreover, Remus states that Numitor acts more kingly than Amulius, for the former listens and evaluates before punishing

---

[34] Lucian projects an ideal image of Celsus. If the latter were really so easy-going, why was he so anxious to have Lucian write to him about the Epicurean-bashing charlatan?

[35] That each noun has its own definite article distinguishes this example from all the others.

[36] See chapter three.

[37] Plut. *Rom.* 7.2, 4. Livy yields no insight into this matter.

(κολάζειν), whereas the latter hands people over for punishment without a trial.[38] Amulius is correspondingly a tyrant who died a tyrant's death.[39] Numitor, meanwhile, the kind king shielded by goodwill, ultimately prevailed — a perfect lesson for Greek intellectuals to read into Rome's foundation myths. Thus, by attributing πραότης and ἐπιείκεια to Numitor, Appian succinctly characterized him as an ideal ruler: not overbearing, not cruel, not lawless, but kind, generous, and forgiving.

9) Dio Cassius *Historiae Romanae* 53.6.1. Spicq also offers Dio Cassius' account of Octavian's important address to the Roman Senate in 27 B.C. (53.3-10). At that time Octavian revealed his intention to relinquish power, stepping down from office and handing over the military, laws, and provinces (53.4.3). Octavian states, "You should not be surprised at this purpose of mine, when you see my reasonableness in other respects, my mildness, and my love of quiet (τήν τε ἀλλήν ἐπιείκειάν μου καὶ πραότητα καὶ ἀπραγμοσύνην ὁρῶντες), and when you reflect, moreover, that I have never accepted any extraordinary privilege nor anything beyond what the many might gain, though you have often voted many of them to me" (53.6.1).[40] Unlike the previous texts we examined, this one is complicated by the addition of a third virtue, withdrawal from public affairs or quietude (ἀπραγμοσύνη). This third virtue is the theme of the entire speech, which suggests that the meaning of ἐπιείκεια καὶ πραότης corresponds to it. As we have already seen, withdrawal from public life is one of the meanings which both ἐπιείκεια and πραότης may have. That would seem to be the overriding idea here, so that the appendage of ἀπραγμοσύνη helps us to define ἐπιείκεια and πραότης. Our discussion would end here but for the fact that we are talking about Octavian (soon to be Augustus), who like his adoptive father Caesar was renowned for his clemency. The Senate commemorated this on the golden shield which it dedicated to Augustus, while Augustus himself enshrined it in his *Res gestae*.[41] This very speech recalls this, as Octavian reminds his audience that he brought the civil war "to an honorable conclusion and ... a humane (φιλανθρώπως) settlement, overpowering as enemies all who resisted, but sparing (περισώσαντες) as friends all who yielded" (53.7.2). Thus, Octavian's invitation to recall his "other ἐπιείκεια καὶ πραότης" must include reference to his acts of clemency. Given the close correlation with ἀπραγμοσύνη here, must we conclude that ἐπιείκεια and πραότης have two meanings? No. Instead we must

---

[38] Plut. *Rom.* 7.5.

[39] Plut. *Rom.* 8.6.

[40] Unlike the Loeb translation quoted above, I regard the definite article and adjective as governing all three nouns, not only the first. (A "hendiatrys"?)

[41] See chapter four.

look to the personality type being presented. Octavian is engaging in popular politics, ostensibly rejecting monarchy and giving the reins of government to the Senate.[42] Tyrants kill, Octavian spares. Tyrants grasp after power, Octavian lays it aside. Octavian presents himself as the kind of person who eschews personal ambition and self-aggrandizement and prefers the public good. Such an individual is a modest person who seeks goodwill, not fear. Clemency and quietude are two behaviors of such a person. The three traits in Octavian's speech, then, present Octavian as a person disinterested in domination, as evidenced by his previous acts of leniency and refusal of honors. The string of virtues then moves from an initial reference to leniency to conclude with quietude, while the combination of the three paints a picture of a Senate-oriented populist.

Bauer's, Kittel's, and Spicq's four additional texts resemble the previous five, yet add more nuances. In two we see clearly a person of authority, viz., Octavian and Numitor. The other two point to a person engaged in education or philosophy. Lucian's examples, emphasizing παιδεία, resemble the earlier example from Plutarch focusing on προκοπή. For the former, ἐπιείκεια and πραότης are the adornments of the educated person, for the latter they are the products of the developing soul. For Lucian, social register rings loudly. For Plutarch, philosophy has entered and a different key is played. But how different is this example in *Moralia* from the others? While it resembles Philo *De opificio mundi* 103 in the availability of ἐπιείκεια καὶ πραότης to all (theoretically), the behavior it sketches resembles even Pericles, Sertorius, or Octavian. For Plutarch's virtuous person, ἐπιείκεια καὶ πραότης prevent angry fighting and bitter debate. This is clemency without the element of authority. It is similar behavior, but different types of people. It is grace among equals. Two questions must, therefore, be asked of examples of ἐπιείκεια καὶ πραότης: 1) To whom are these virtues ascribed?[43] and 2) What is the nature of the behavior envisioned? These questions will guide our reading of 2 Cor 10:1.

---

[42] "Popular" or "populist politics" is ambiguous at present. What I mean is that Octavian pledged to do things which would appeal to the Senate. That is his target audience, not the masses; nevertheless, Octavian was curbing himself out of regard to his lessers. Octavian's "popular politics" were therefore colored aristocratically. Of course, to think of "Senate-oriented populism" is to herald a new political situation.

[43] De Romilly recognizes the effect of the subject's and object's identities on the nuance of πραότης or ἐπιείκεια: "Se manifestant envers les malheureux, elle devient proche de la générosité ou de la bonté; envers les coupables elle devient indulgence et compréhension; envers les inconnus, les hommes en général, elle devient humanité et presque charité. Dans la vie politique, de même, elle peut être tolérance, ou encore clémence, selon qu'il s'agit des rapports envers des citoyens, ou des sujets, ou encore des vaincus" (*La douceur*, 1).

In addition to the standard nine parallels to 2 Cor 10:1 just reviewed, still other texts present the combination ἐπιείκεια καὶ πραότης.

10) Plutarch *Caesar* 15.4. Though the later passage, 57.3, is typically listed as a parallel to 2 Cor 10:1, this text is strangely absent from such lists. In this earlier passage, Plutarch emphasizes that Caesar's accomplishments exceeded those of every other general. For example, he eclipsed one person by winning battles on more difficult terrain, another by acquiring more territory, another by defeating greater enemies, another by conciliating more savage people. Furthermore, Caesar excelled in the ἐπιείκεια καὶ πραότης which he showed to captives. Given that the subject here is Caesar and the recipients are captives, the action in view here is undoubtedly clemency. This behavior is presented as an element of his outstanding generalship.

11) Plutarch *Pericles and Fabius* 3.1. In comparing these two lives, Plutarch notes the superiority of Fabius to Pericles in regard to leniency. The ἐπιείκεια καὶ πραότης of the former contrasted with the treatment Pericles showed to Cimon and Thucydides, good men whom Pericles subjected to ostracism and exile. Clearly, Fabius is congratulated for a gentleness which spared his rival — i.e., leniency.[44]

12) Plutarch *Moralia* 729e. Continuing Plutarch's enthrallment with gentleness, in *Table-Talk* he tells a story about Pythagoras but interprets it by way of ἐπιείκεια and πραότης.[45] Legend says that Pythagoras once purchased a haul of fish and then released them back into the sea. Why? Plutarch states that Pythagoras "was not indifferent to fish ... but paid a ransom for them as for friends and relatives who had been captured" (*Mor.* 729e). More generally, Plutarch continues, the ἐπιείκεια καὶ πραότης of the Pythagoreans suggests that they "spare (ἐφείδοντο) sea-creatures out of regard for justice and a common morality" (729e).[46] This brief example is important, for it bridges the trends we have observed. On the one hand, a certain clemency is operative here, for in the behavior described, a stronger figure acted in a way contrary to custom to spare a weaker figure's life. On the other hand, ἐπιείκεια καὶ πραότης are characteristic

---

[44] That others failed to introduce this as a parallel example of ἐπιείκεια καὶ πραότης may result from the syntax of this sentence which disrupts the word order: ἡ μέντοι πρὸς Μινούκιον ἐπιείκεια τοῦ Φαβίου καὶ πρᾳότης ... However, the two nouns share the definite article and are connected by καί.

[45] In *Mor.* 582d as well Plutarch cites πραότης as a noteworthy characteristic of Pythagoras.

[46] Elsewhere Plutarch interprets Pythagoras' actions as intended "to accustom men to refrain from cruelty and rapacity in connection with dumb animals" (*Mor.* 91d). In yet another essay, Plutarch sees Pythagoras' πραότης to animals as part of a larger program designed to develop humane and merciful behavior (*Mor.* 959f).

of a school of philosophers. We see here that gentleness does not act only on the stage of politics, but trickles down to lesser venues — wherein it may still express itself as leniency.

13) Athenaeus *Deipnosophistae* 12.72/ 549d. The dinner conversation in this passage focuses on fat people. Nymphis of Heracleia says of Dionysius (the son of Clearchus, first tyrant of Heracleia) that he grew hugely obese. He died at age fifty-five, having been tyrant for thirty three years and having "excelled all tyrants before him in πραότης καὶ ἐπιείκεια." Nothing in the context specifies the deeds in view; however, that the actor is a tyrant suggests two possibilities. First, among the common distinctions between king and tyrant are goodwill and fear, lawfulness and lawlessness, and gentleness and brutality. Attributing πραότης and ἐπιείκεια here to the tyrant Dionysius succinctly characterizes him as a good ruler. To be more specific, this means that his rule is not characterized by ὕβρις or arrogance, greed, murder, or violence. While this includes judicial restraint and thus leniency, it also looks more broadly at the totality of his rule. It is easy-going, kind, and generous. Secondly, an obese tyrant further indicates an indulgence in luxury as well as indolence. These two options, however, are not mutually exclusive, for together they point to a character type, the hedonist tyrant. Gentleness accompanies luxuriousness.

14) Julian *Panegyric in Honor of the Empress Eusebia* 106a. We encounter here a virtue list which opens with the pair σωφροσύνη καὶ δικαιοσύνη and then offers πραότης καὶ ἐπιείκεια as a second pair, followed by three single items, viz., affection for her husband, generosity with her money, and liberal in the honor she shows to her family. Nothing indicates the nuance of πραότης καὶ ἐπιείκεια other than its ascription to a queen. Presumably, then, the pair indicates the easy manner in which she wore her power, which for a queen implies accessibility, graciousness, and mercy.

These five texts revive the impression first made by Plutarch, as they allude to the friendly and restrained exercise of office. The characterization of the Pythagoreans as a whole, however, suggests the wider currency of ἐπιείκεια καὶ πραότης among philosophers. This too corresponds to what we have already seen, e.g., Lucian's Epicurean friend (and patron?) Celsus.

Having surveyed these fourteen examples, we now need to analyze the group as a whole. Beyond examining the actor and the act, we may approach these data formally. (See the table on page 75.) Comparison of the word order ἐπιείκεια καὶ πραότης with πραότης καὶ ἐπιείκεια yields no difference, but the presence or absence of the definite article is significant. First, we must remove Plut. *Cae.* 57.3, which, as we noted earlier, is a commonly cited parallel but is not an example of πραότης καὶ ἐπιείκεια. Next we dismiss App. *Bas.* 1.5 because ἐπιείκεια and πραότης do not share the same definite article.[47] Of the remaining twelve, the four examples whose use of πραότης καὶ ἐπιείκεια is least precise semantically all are anarthrous, and three appear in virtue lists. Two anarthrous uses, however, can be delimited semantically. The example from Athenaeus can be understood because the actor is characterized as a tyrant. Such attribution makes πρᾶος and ἐπιεικής behavior intelligible. The remaining anarthrous example, Plut. *Cae.* 15.4, has an even more definite meaning, because person, deed, and context all converge to focus the meaning of ἐπιείκεια καὶ πραότης.[48] To talk about Caesar, to compare him to generals, and to speak of how he treated captives make the meaning of ἐπιείκεια καὶ πραότης transparent, viz., clemency. What then happens when πραότης καὶ ἐπιείκεια share a single definite article? We find the virtues mean more than "gentleness" or rather less, for they have a more narrow meaning. Six times they have leniency in view, once an absence of fighting and wrangling. The former reflect the exercise of πραότης καὶ ἐπιείκεια by a superior, the latter among equals. We conclude, unsurprised, that the use of the definite article corresponds to a context which specifies the connotation of the virtues.

Before drawing our conclusions, other evidence must be cited. Whereas we have surveyed the use of the two nouns in conjunction, the adjectives

---

[47] That each noun has its own article is probably not significant, but no parallels exist which can confirm that assumption. If, however, this example were retained, it would add further confirmation to the generalizations about to be drawn.

[48] That the article was not used corresponds to the syntax of the larger paragraph. As he praises Caesar's military prowess, Plutarch claims he eclipses Fabius, Scipio, Metellus, Sulla, Marius, the two Luculli, and even Pompey. A string of seven comparisons follows, in which Plutarch structures each clause to help communicate the comparison:

αἱ Καίσαρος ὑπερβάλλουσι πράξεις
τὸν μὲν χαλεπότητι τόπων ἐν οἷς ἐπολέμησε
τὸν δὲ μεγέθει χώρας ἣν προσεκτήσατο
τὸν δὲ πλήθει καὶ βίᾳ πολεμίων οὓς ἐνίκησε
τὸν δὲ ἀτοπίαις καὶ ἀπιστίαις ἠθῶν ἃ καθωμίλησε
τὸν δὲ ἐπιεικείᾳ καὶ πραότητι πρὸς τοὺς ἁλισκομένους
τὸν δὲ δώροις καὶ χάρισι πρὸς τοὺς συστρατευομένους
πάντας δὲ τῷ πλείστας μεμαχῆσθαι μάχας καὶ πλείστους ἀνῃρηκέναι
    τῶν ἀντιταχθέντων.

Notice that no definite articles are used for any of the nouns in the comparative phrases. This fits well with what Plutarch is attempting, for the lack of definite articles directs attention from the identity of any particular deed and emphasizes the nature or quality of the deed done.

and adverbs also appear joined together (thus, πρᾶος καὶ ἐπιεικής and πράως καὶ ἐπιεικῶς). Given that the respective adjectives have broader meanings than do their nouns, the same phenomenon in regard to the adjectives used together is not surprising. On the one hand, combinations of πρᾶος and ἐπιεικής refer to social superiors in their dealings with their lessers, e.g., kings, as well as God;[49] moreover, an inscription from Aphrodisias refers to the prominent Antonius Zosas as πρᾶος καὶ ἐπιεικής.[50] Socrates also treated his unpleasant wife ἐπιεικῶς καὶ πράως (Plut. *Cato maj.* 20.3). The adjectives also characterize God's daughter Repentance (*Jos. Asen.* 15.8). Whether this refers to her mercy toward those who repent or her solicitation of God on their behalf is unclear. The semantic connotation hinges on her social location. Toward lessers, mortals, she is merciful and kind, whereas to her superior, God, she entreats. That angels as well as God admire her virtues suggests that they encompass more than a display of solicitousness before God. I think, therefore, the pair reflects the mercy Repentance shows to sinners. Finally, Dio Chrysostom uses the two adjectives to characterize "democracy," so that a constitution may be ἐπιεικής καὶ πρᾶος.[51] While no human agent appears here, the idea of authority does.

---

[49] God: Philo *Quod det. pot.* 146. Kings: Jos. *Ant.* 11.216, Artaxerxes; Plut. *Mor.* 533b, Sparta's king, Charillus; Lib. *Decl.* 5.27: Achilles complains about Odysseus: kings accompany the latter, βασιλεῖς ἐπιεικεῖς καὶ πρᾶοι καὶ μισοῦντες φιλονεικίας, whereas the former is χαλεπός τις καὶ δύσερις. Libanius is fond of attributing ἐπιείκεια and πραότης to rulers (*Or.* 19.48-49; 30.47). Spicq also cites Diod. Sic. 19.85.3, which presents a prince full of mildness and indulgence — a predictable example (*NLNT* 1: 266 n. 2 = *TLNT* 2: 37 n. 17). Cp. the variant reading in Add Esth 3:13b which substitutes πραότητος for ἠπιότητος in a decree of Artaxerxes: "ἐπιεικέστερον δὲ καὶ μετὰ πραότητος ἀεὶ διεξάγων."

[50] *MAMA* 8: no. 524 (Spicq noted this example [*NLNT* 1: 266 n. 2 = *TLNT* 2: 37 n. 17]). Libanius wrote his patron asking how to treat a man whom Libanius describes as just and wealthy, ἐπιεικῆ καὶ πρᾶον καὶ φρόνιμον (Lib. *Ep.* 1150.2). While these traits certainly connote social status, what specific behaviors lie behind them remains unidentified. Libanius wishes only to generalize the man's virtue.

[51] Dio Chrys. 3.47. This example comes from Dio's exposition of the different types of governments, lastly turning to democracy which he describes as "possibly the most impracticable one of all (πασῶν ἀδυνατωτάτη), the one that expects by the self-control and virtue of the common people some day to find an equitable constitution based on law (κατάστασιν ἐπιεικῆ καὶ νόμιμον). Men call it 'democracy' — a specious and inoffensive name (ἐπιεικὲς ὄνομα καὶ πρᾶον), if the thing were but practicable (εἴπερ ἦν δυνατόν)." At first glance, this example looks different from the others we have observed, a result of a fascinating play on words. Further consideration reveals the consistency between this text and other examples. First, gentleness was widely considered a trait intrinsic to democracy. Second, democracy gave inadequate reward to the great and the structures they favored, while freedom gave license to the mob to indulge itself, thereby undermining order and justice. Thus, democracy proved an

Social location is not a factor in other examples. Plutarch reports a theory about how malefactors' fear of punishment after death leads to better behavior, with the consequence that filling their minds with such terrors will shock wrongdoers "into a state of greater honesty and restraint (ἐπιεικέστερον ἔχειν καὶ πραότερον)" (*Mor.* 1104b). His concern is only the prevention of greed, aggression, and violence; the nature of the perpetrator is irrelevant. Of all the examples noted, this one offers the least semantic delimitation — but also the most ambiguous actor. Next, when discussing the Gracchi, Plutarch compares their rhetorical styles. Whereas Tiberius was "gentle (πρᾶος) and sedate" (*Grac.* 824f), Caius was high-strung and vehement and would roam about the rostra while speaking, pulling his toga off of his shoulder, while his voice rose to an unseemly pitch. A servant would sound a pitch-pipe to help him regain "a decorous and gentle tone" (ἐπιεικῆ καὶ πρᾷον, *Mor.* 456a). Plutarch also compares the pair's tempers, noting that their characters corresponded to their rhetoric: "Tiberius was ἐπιεικής καὶ πρᾶος, while Caius was harsh and fiery" (*Grac.* 825b). In these examples we approach Philo's use of the words, i.e., reason's mastery of emotion. In this case self-mastery appears in the orator's demeanor and his ability or lack thereof to maintain composure in debate or censure.[52] In the Gracchi and the reformation of wrongdoers, then, we see the paired adjectives pressing on to applications broader than the nouns. As a result, only the example of Repentance (*Jos. Asen.*) comes close to matching Leivestad's reading of 2 Cor 10:1, though not in my view.

From the preceding examples we can draw the following conclusions. The presence of the definite article instructs us to seek some delimitation of πραότης καὶ ἐπιείκεια. Two ways of doing this have emerged from the examples surveyed, namely, observing the actors to whom πραότης καὶ ἐπιείκεια are attributed and the nature of the actions so designated. The latter reflects a restrained self-assertion which seeks to help others rather than harm them. The people involved are powerful, cultured (πεπαιδευμένοι), or involved in moral development, or a combination of these three things. In such people, ἐπιείκεια καὶ πραότης typically involve the mitigated use of a person's authority or, less commonly, a moderation of anger towards equals which reflects involvement in moral development. These choices then should be the options explored in the

---

impotent form of government. Similarly, rulers who were gentle might unintentionally encourage wrongdoing, lower others' estimation of their power, and so undermine their own positions. Dio cleverly makes use of these ideas to ridicule democracy here.

[52] Libanius praises a powerful orator (δύναμις λόγων) who keeps his ὀργή wrapped up under ἐπιείκεια because such discourse is the most productive kind, for πραότης fosters friendly relations (*Or.* 44.5).

Examples of ἐπιείκεια καὶ πραΰτης

Actor	Action	Form
Epicurean/ πεπαιδευμένος Luc. Alex. 61	unspecified: virtue list	ἐπί τε σοφίᾳ ... καὶ τρόπου πραότη τι καὶ ἐπιεικείᾳ
Lucian/ πεπαιδευμένος Luc. Som. 10	unspecified: virtue list	... σωφροσύνῃ, δικαιοσύνῃ, εὐσεβείᾳ, πραότητι, ἐπιεικείᾳ, συνέσει ...
Empress Eusebia Jul. Bas. enk. 106a	unspecified: virtue list	σωφροσύνης καὶ δικαιοσύνης ἢ πραότητος καὶ ἐπιεικείας
57-63 yr. old man Philo De op. mun. 103	the mind masters passions	ἐπιείκεια καὶ πραότης
Tyrant Dionysus Athen. Deip. 12.72	unspecified: a tyrant	πραότητι καὶ ἐπιεικείᾳ
Caesar Plut. Cae. 15.4	a general's action towards captives	τὸν δὲ ἐπιεικείᾳ καὶ πραότητι πρὸς οὓς ἁλισκομένους
Pericles Plut. Per. 39.1	nobody died (leniency, sparing)	τῆς ἐπιεικείας καὶ πραότητος
Sertorius Plut. Ser. 25.4	death and enslavement (mercy and leniency)	ἐκ τῆς προτέρας ἐπιεικείας καὶ πραότητος
Fabius Plut. Per. et Fab. 3.1	ostracism and exile (leniency)	ἡ μέντοι πρὸς Μινούκιον ἐπιείκεια τοῦ Φαβίου καὶ πραότης
philosopher/ προκοπή Plut. Mor. 80b	bitter words (free of anger, aggression)	ἡ γὰρ ἐν τούτοις ἐπιείκεια καὶ πραότης
Pythagoreans Plut. Mor. 729e	spared (fish) lives (mercy and leniency)	ἡ ἐπιείκεια καὶ πραότης
Octavian Dio Cas. 53.6.1	spared lives and declined offices (clemency and quietude)	τήν τε ἄλλην ἐπιείκειάν μου καὶ πραότητα καὶ ἀπραγμοσύνην ὁρῶντες
King Numitor App. Bas. 1.5	unspecified, but survived conspiracy	ἡ τῶν ἠθῶν ... πραότης καὶ ἡ πολλὴ ἐπιείκεια

interpretation of 2 Cor 10:1, not humility versus kingliness. How does Paul see himself? Is he a person holding in check his authority so as not to hurt others, but rather court their goodwill and promote good deeds, or is he a virtuous person seeking to inculcate sound character in his peers? The former alternative actually subsumes the latter; the question is one of the social location of the actor. That we have already noted Paul's claim of ἐξουσία tips our hand. Regardless, the options presented are behavioral, describing how one treats others. Humility does not fit into these uses. Thus, the usage of πραότης καὶ ἐπιείκεια or ἐπιείκεια καὶ πραότης does not support Leivestad's interpretation of 2 Cor 10:1.

b. The Semantic Field Encompassing Both *ἐπιείκεια* and *πραότης*

As we have seen in our analysis of the previous thirteen examples, three clues to meaning are the definite article, the actor(s), and the envisioned action. To identify correctly the last two factors, actor and, particularly, action, requires attention to the larger context. The only way to know what attributes πραότης and/or ἐπιείκεια possess in any use is to allow the broader passage to guide one's understanding. In the end, then, one must compare contexts rather than just two words. As we shall now see, specific words frequently cluster around πραότης and ἐπιείκεια and together convey patterns of meaning. Highlighting these words will focus our attention on the types of actions expressed by πραότης and ἐπιείκεια.

The presence of words commonly associated with πραότης and ἐπιείκεια in 2 Corinthians 10–13 reveals the meaning of Paul's opening appeal in 10:1. Turning now to look at other texts in which ἐπιείκεια and πραότης (or cognates) appear in proximity to one another will focus our eyes to read 2 Corinthians 10–13 more clearly. Adding a few examples which contain only ἐπιείκεια or πραότης will help round out this exhibition. Surveying these examples will make conspicuous the large semantic field present in 2 Corinthians 10–13, in which Paul's appeal by Christ's πραΰτης καὶ ἐπιείκεια plays a part. Identifying those related words, then, will guide our understanding of 2 Cor 10:1. While this semantic field surfaces in many texts, we will examine it in Philo, Josephus, Dio Chrysostom, Plutarch, and Lucian.

This semantic field arises in relation to faults, errors, and enmities. Such problems may be between individuals or civic bodies, between equals or inequals. How should one treat a friend? Plutarch recommends ἐπιείκεια:

For as a kind-hearted physician would prefer to relieve a sick man's ailment by sleep and diet rather than by castor and scammony, so an ἐπιεικής friend, a good (χρηστός) father, and a teacher, take pleasure in using commendation rather than blame for the correction (ἐπανόρθωσις) of character. For nothing else makes the frank person (παρρησιαζόμενος) give so little pain (λύπειν) and do so much good by his words, as to refrain (φείδεσθαι) from all show of temper (ὀργή), and to approach the erring good-humoredly and with kindliness (εὔνοια; *Mor.* 73d).

But how should one treat enemies? Rather than harm them, Plutarch sees one's response to enemies as an opportunity to demonstrate virtue.

Indeed there is nothing more dignified and noble than to maintain a calm demeanor when an enemy reviles ... In this manner, then, it is possible for us to display the qualities of πραότητα and forbearance (ἀνεξικακίαν) in connection with our enmities, and also straightforwardness (ἁπλότητα), magnanimity (μεγαλοφροσύνην), and goodness (χρηστότητα) better than in our friendships. For it is not so honorable to do a good turn to a friend as it is disgraceful not to do it when he is in need; but even to forgo taking vengeance (τιμωρίαν) on an enemy when he offers a good opportunity is a ἐπιεικές thing to do. But in case a man shows compassion for an enemy in affliction, and gives a helping hand to him when he has come to be in need, and displays some concern and zeal in behalf of his children and his household affairs when they come to want, I say that whosoever does not feel affection for such a man because of his kindliness (εὐμένειας), or does not commend his goodness (χρηστότητα), "Hath a black heart forged from adamant or else from steel" (*Mor.* 90e).

In each of these cases, the virtuous person extends ἐπιείκεια and πραότης in the face of wrongdoing, thereby refusing to indulge in anger or vengeance.

Philo fits divine chastisement into this pattern. He recommends that the guilty person beseech God, who is merciful, for punishment (κολάζειν), rather than abandoning oneself to pitiless (ἀνέλεος) nature. For

if [God] punishes (κολάζων) us, He will of His gracious goodness (χρηστός) gently and kindly (ἐπιεικῶς and πράως) correct our faults (ἐπανορθώσεται τὰ ἁμαρτήματα), by sending forth into our mind His own word, that reproves and chastens, by means of which He will upbraid it, and make it ashamed of its errors, and so will heal it (*Quod de. pot.* 146).

Here we see ἐπιείκεια and πραότης shaded by mercy and goodness in the moderation of retribution. This view of divine chastisement, moreover, parallels the ideal espoused by moral philosophers: one acts with restraint and benevolent intent in order to correct an offender.

If we turn to politics, the same ideas appear. Plutarch advises the statesman to practice ἐπιείκεια when attempting to resolve disputes. More specifically, in order to nurture concord and excise strife, the statesman must speak sympathetically with aggrieved persons (ἀδικεῖσθαι), appearing to share their sense of wrong (συναδικεῖσθαι). Then

he will try to mollify (πραΰνειν) them and teach them that those who let wrongs go unheeded are superior to those who are quarrelsome (τῶν ἐριζόντων) and try to compel (βιάζεσθαι) and overcome (νικᾶν) others, not only in ἐπιείκεια and character, but also in wisdom (φρονήματι) and greatness of spirit (μεγέθει ψυχῆς), and that by yielding in a small thing they gain their point in the best and most important matters (*Mor.* 824d).

Dio Chrysostom implemented a related strategy in his admonition to the Apameians to reach a concord with Prusa. Using Rome's clemency and benefaction as his model, Dio told to the Apameians,

> I understand how difficult it is to eradicate strife from human beings, especially when it has been nurtured for a fairly long period of time ... But still I have confidence in the character of your city, believing it to be, not rough and boorish (οὐ σκληρὸν οὐδὲ ἀμαθές), but in very truth the genuine character of those distinguished men and that blessed city [i.e., Rome] by which you were sent here as friends indeed to dwell with friends. That city, while so superior to the rest of mankind in good fortune and power (δυνάμει), has proved to be even more superior in fairness and benevolence (ἐπιεικείᾳ καὶ φιλανθρωπίᾳ), bestowing ungrudgingly both citizenship and legal rights and offices, believing no man of worth to be an alien, and at the same time safeguarding justice for all alike. In emulation of that city it is fitting that you should show yourselves gentle and magnanimous (πρᾴους καὶ μεγαλόφρονας) toward men [i.e., of Prusa] who are so close to you, virtually housemates, and not harsh and arrogant (μὴ χαλεποὺς μηδὲ ὑπερηφάνους) neighbors, since they are men with whom you have common ties ... (*Or.* 41.9-10).

Dio recognized in Rome's clemency and benefaction a way for other cities to treat one another and to treat the individual citizens of another city, so as to foster goodwill and harmony between cities. In such easy-going generosity Dio sees precluded any high-handed behavior.

Individuals in politics also latched on to ἐπιείκεια and πραότης. Josephus offers illuminating evidence for this. In *Antiquities* 19.328-34 he compares King Agrippa with Herod. Josephus praises Agrippa for being generous (εὐεργετικός) and taking pleasure in benefactions (ἡδόμενος τῷ χαρίζεσθαι) and sound reputation. Thus he departed completely from the evil (πονηρός) Herod, whose punishments were unrelenting (ἐπὶ τιμωρίαν ἀπότομος), particularly to those he did not like. And he liked Gentiles better than Jews. So he was generous to them, but cheap with the Jews. Agrippa, on the other hand, was πραΰς and showered benefactions upon all (εὐεργετικός and φιλάνθρωπος). To the Jews he showed extra goodness and compassion (χρηστός and συμπαθής) and observed their customs. In fact, when publicly accused of being ritually unclean, his accuser had nothing to prove his slander. How Agrippa handled the situation is telling. Quietly and gently (ἠρέμα τε καὶ πρᾴως) Agrippa asked his enemy to sit beside him and explain what he had done wrong (παράνομος). With nothing to say, the man begged forgiveness (συγγνώμη). Reconciliation (διαλλάττεσθαι) was immediate, for Agrippa judged πραότης more becoming to a king than ὀργή, ἐπιείκεια grander than θύμος. Agrippa then capped his indulgence by giving the man a gift. This story, then, presents πραότης and ἐπιείκεια as part of populist politics, features of the beneficent ruler who seeks his subjects' good. Our two virtues specifically come into play with matters of punishment and offence. Restrained sanctions are the expression of πραΰτης and ἐπιείκεια, and conciliation the object.

Elsewhere, as Josephus tells the story of Esther, he records a decree of Artaxerxes sent to his entire empire:

While I have ruled over many nations and have had dominion over all the habitable land which I could wish, I have not been compelled because of my power (ἐξουσίας) to wrong (ἁμαρτεῖν) my subjects by any arrogant (ὑπερήφανον) or brutal (σκαιόν) act, but have shown myself ἐπιεικῇ καὶ πρᾷον and have looked out for their peace (εἰρήνη) and good government (εὐνομίας) seeking how they might enjoy these things for ever (*Ant.* 11.216).

This decree expresses behaviors opposed to ἐπιείκεια and πραότης, viz., arrogance and violence, and evaluates the latter pair as ἁμαρτία. It also situates ἐπιείκεια and πραότης within a discussion of political ideas: they guide ἐξουσία so that it produces peace and lawful government. The broader context exposes the ideological nature of this excerpt, for the remainder of Artaxerxes' decree orders the extermination of the Jews. The outrageous combination of pogram and mildness underscores that Artaxerxes sought to present himself as playing the perfect ruler. As a result, he claimed to mix ἐξουσία with ἐπιείκεια and πραότης, not arrogance and brutality, and to defend his proposed measure as necessitated by Jewish intransigence. Thus, ἐπιείκεια and πραότης serve as a litmus test for how well one handles ἐξουσία.

Plutarch also offers examples of the words commonly connected with ἐπιείκεια and πραότης in two examples treating the actions of powerful Romans. Plutarch tells of Caesar's desire to spare Cato's life, but questions Caesar's motives, for

the treatise which Caesar afterwards wrote against Cato when he was dead, does not seem to prove that he was in a gentle (πρᾴως) or reconcilable (εὐδιαλλάκτως) mood. For how could he have spared (ἐφείσατο) Cato alive, when he poured out against him after death so great a cup of wrath (ὀργήν)? And yet from his considerate treatment (ἐπιείκεια) of Cicero and Brutus and thousands more who had fought against him, it is inferred that even this treatise was not composed out of hatred (ἀπεχθείας), but from political ambition (*Cae.* 733c/ 54.4).

This incident reflects clearly on Caesar's fabled clemency, showing its opposition to anger, its goal of reconciliation, its rejection of retribution, and its contingent application.

Elsewhere Plutarch speaks of Cicero's quandary over whether to be lenient or not (*Cic.* 870b/ 19.4; Plutarch uses only ἐπιείκεια and not πραότης). Apparently Cicero hesitated to inflict the death penalty on rebels because of his ἐπιείκεια and desire not to make a conspicuous display of his ἐξουσία nor to treat harshly (πικρῶς) men of high standing. But if he shrank from harshness and extended a milder penalty (μετριώτερον) he would only encourage the rebels' daring and rage (τόλμη and ὀργή) and make himself look weak (ἄνανδρος and μαλακός). This example, then, adds a new ingredient to our observations: in matters of authority, retribution, and severity, the person who acts with leniency runs the risk of looking weak and cowardly.

Appian offers two examples worth adding to our survey. Although the first does not contain both πραότης and ἐπιείκεια, each introduces another word into our semantic domain, the first καθαίρεσις and the second ὑπακούειν. In the first, a summary of the character of a Parthian king, Appian describes him as handsome and admired, possessed of a most royal soul and a great deal of experience in matters of war. He then adds that the king was "extremely gentle (πραότατος) to every subject (ὑπήκοον), but indefatigable in destroying (καθαίρεσιν) his opposition" (*Parth.* 19; my trans.). Here gentleness and destruction are joined within the same person; moreover, gentleness extends itself to obedient people as an alternative to destruction.

In the second example, Appian describes Brutus' strategy during Rome's civil war as one of waiting out the enemy, a strategy predicated on his being ἐπιεικής and φιλόφρων. Cassius was just the opposite, being αὐστηρός and ἀρχικός, "for which reason the army obeyed (ὑπήκουον) his orders promptly, not interfering with his authority, not inquiring the reasons for his orders, and not criticizing them when they had learned them. But in the case of Brutus they expected nothing else than to share the command with him on account of his πραΰτητα" (*Bel. civ.* 4.16.123). Brutus ignored his soldiers' discontent and refused to convene an assembly lest the unreasoning (ἀλόγιστος) mob compel a very inappropriate (ἀπρεπέστερος) course of action. In this passage ὑπακούειν enters the semantic domain and reveals the difficult relationship which it has with ἐπιείκεια.

A final example taken from Lucian of Samosata draws together ἐπιείκεια and πραότης and many words commonly associated with them. In a sophistic exercise (*Phalaris 1*), an envoy from the infamous tyrant Phalaris offers a defense of his rule to the priests at Delphi (and thus to Apollo), arguing that they have no reason to think him cruel (ὠμός). Speaking for Phalaris, the envoy opens the defense by asserting Phalaris' noble birth and good education and calling to mind his early behavior: "Never at any time did I fail to display public spirit (δημοτικόν) toward the city, and discretion (ἐπιεικῆ) and moderation (μέτριον) toward my fellow-citizens; and no one ever charged me with a single violent (βίαιον), rude (σκαιόν), insolent (ὑβριστικόν), or overbearing (αὐθέκαστον) action" (2). But at a time of factions, Phalaris took the reins of state and delivered it (σωτηρία). He then sought to rule without

2.3. ἐπιείκεια and πραότης

murder, exile, and confiscation, hoping to unify his subjects by φιλανθρωπία, πραότης, ἡμερότης and ἰσοτιμία. He then rebuilt the infrastructure and showed care (ἐπιμέλεια) for the citizens (3). As he then contemplated relinquishing his ἀρχή and δυναστεία, insurrection flared up (4). What was Phalaris to do? Treat them with φιλανθρωπία? Spare (φείδεσθαι) them? Phalaris concluded that noble and manly (ἀνδρώδη) resolve required that he respond to the wrong (ἠδικημένος) which his opponents inflicted on him (5). He therefore punished (κολάζειν) the conspirators. Why, then, Phalaris complains, has he received the reputation for being cruel (ὠμότης) when the conspirators instigated the ugly affair (6)? He blames this reputation on the fact that he bears the title of τύραννος, despite the fact that some tyrants were kind and gentle (χρηστός and ἥμερος) (7). As for the punishments he metes out, necessity drives him, for showing mercy (φείδεσθαι) would cost him his life. He is not then some animal (ἄγριος and ἀνήμερος) who enjoys hurting people, but a man who chooses to punish justly rather than die unjustly at the hand of conspirators (8-9). Phalaris then offers Pythagoras as witness that his severity (ὠμότης) was necessary and just, while presenting his φιλανθρωπία to strangers as evidence that he would not act harshly (πικρῶς) toward citizens. As for simmering people inside a metal sculpture of a bull, Phalaris claims that is a misunderstanding: the only person subjected to such horror was the evil fellow who built it (11-12). Phalaris therefore asks the priests at Delphi to accept the bull as his gift and to offer sacrifices on his behalf (13). In this argument, we again see the place of ἐπιείκεια and πραότης in popular rule, observing that they join with generosity to deter the evils which issue from violent and arrogant rule. We also see the struggle over how to respond to a wrong suffered. Does one spare or punish? While the latter was more obviously "manly," it was cruel and forever stigmatized Phalaris as a tyrant.

In these examples, the appearance of both ἐπιείκεια and πραότης in the same context typically signals wrongdoing and the need to respond to it. When such circumstances arise, ἐπιείκεια and πραότης offer courses of action which are different from and more noble and prudent than the customary ones, which typically involve brute retaliation. In many cases, the wrongdoing is merely potential: the powerful person who could harm others and escape retribution, yet chooses not to, thereby exhibits ἐπιείκεια and πραότης. Thus, when ἐπιείκεια and πραότης appear in contexts where power, punishments, offenses, and mercy are concerned, these all work together semantically. We must define or translate ἐπιείκεια and πραότης in relation to those words.

4. 2 Corinthians 10:1a and 10:1–13:10

The examples observed demonstrate the important role context plays in nuancing ἐπιείκεια and πραότης. To understand Paul requires consideration not only of 2 Cor 10:1, but of the entire letter fragment, 2 Cor 10:1–13:10. Turning now to 2 Cor 10:1 therefore means turning to 2 Corinthians 10–13.

a. Paul's Offer of Leniency

As we consider Paul's appeal through Christ's πραΰτης and ἐπιείκεια, three observations arise immediately from the preceding discussion. First, that Paul uses the definite article suggests that we seek some definite meaning, something more precise than a calm or mild disposition, something more nuanced than gentleness. While studies of 2 Cor 10:1 concur with this, biblical translation as reflected in the versions does not. Second, we note the person involved, or in this case persons: Christ to whom the virtues are attributed as a model and Paul who acts on them. That Paul claims to have ἐξουσία likens him to many of the characters we have already seen. Third, the nature of the action involved must be identified, the very problem at hand. That the texts we have already observed typically involve restraint in imposing oneself either in moral correction or legal sanction suggests the likely contours of Paul's meaning. This in fact corresponds to 2 Corinthians 10–13 but not to Leivestad's interpretation.

The key to reading Paul's appeal in 2 Cor 10:1 is its context. The opening appeal is part of a dialogue composed of the entire letter, a previous (ugly) visit to Corinth, and a subsequent letter. Together, these bring the semantics of Paul's appeal into focus.

First, then, we turn to 2 Corinthians 10–13. Paul's comments as he brings his "four-chapter-letter" to a close provide elaboration on his opening appeal. If he returns again to Corinth he will not spare those who have sinned (13:2). We have already seen that φείδεσθαι is a synonym of both πραότης and ἐπιείκεια (above, §1.c and 2.c); therefore, its presence here suggests the action involved in Paul's πραΰτης καὶ ἐπιείκεια. Moreover, Paul's display of φείδεσθαι occurs in the face of wrongdoing, which is commonplace in the texts which use ἐπιείκεια and πραότης together. As Paul continues, he notes the problem of δύναμις (13:3-4). Not to spare would demonstrate the reality of Paul's δύναμις, which his sparing has helped to call into question. In addition to enablement, Paul has authorization (13:10). He pleads therefore that he not be compelled to use his ἐξουσία in a harsh manner. In "acting harshly" we meet yet another word, ἀποτόμως, which delimits ἐπιείκεια and πραότης, in this case antithetically. This potential severity issues from a person who lays claim to δύναμις and ἐξουσία. That Paul refuses to bring his full weight to bear (βαρύτης) and restrains himself so as not to harm others is ἐπιεικής and πρᾶος.

Paul's appeal seeks moral reform on the part of the Corinthians. Paul's concern focuses on the Corinthians' repentance (μετάνοια) or lack thereof (12:21). This letter is one more attempt at this. Paul wants to see the Corinthians progress towards κατάρτισις (13:9). Though only the word μετάνοια connects with ἐπιείκεια and πραότης, the underlying idea of moral development and perfecting does as well. Like the amiable philosopher, like the clement general, like the indulgent father, and like the lenient ruler, Paul seeks to win his opposition to his side by treating them kindly, not harshly. To spare is to leave room for repentance as well as to lure people to it. It implies a consequent situation better than the present. What this means concretely varies with different contexts, but includes political harmony or even survival, as well as moral improvement. Paul certainly has the latter in view.

But what of the former, survival? The consequences of incorrigibility toward Paul are uncertain. The apostle characterizes it as destruction, καθαίρεσις (10:8; 13:10). Juxtaposed with "building up" (οἰκοδομή), the image of a razed city offers a stark contrast. Though Paul does not see destruction as his main objective, obstinate rejection of his admonitions might require it. He would then be like Appian's Parthian king who was πραότατος to his compliant subjects but relentless in καθαίρεσις toward his enemies (*Parth.* 19). Would Paul actually dissolve an ἐκκλησία? Or would he limit his sanctions to individuals? Regardless, his image is vivid and threatening.

Warfare imagery also belongs to Paul's language of πραΰτης καὶ ἐπιείκεια. That scholars have failed to understand this indicates their failure to understand Paul's appeal. Though the warfare Paul speaks of in 2 Cor 10:4-6 may contradict our concept of "meekness," it corresponds perfectly with πραότης and ἐπιείκεια. The traditionally cited parallels to 2 Cor 10:1 should have made this clear. The clemency of Pompey, Caesar, Augustus, and many other figures in Greek and Roman history illustrate the significance of sparing one's opponents. This was in fact a topic of ancient political science and historiography. Like the statesman, then, Paul stands ready to quench rebellion with harsh measures, but prefers to quell dissent with goodwill. His weapons are at the ready, but forgiveness is much sweeter. Paul, then, is ready to punish (ἐκδικῆσαι) the disobedient, but stalls, hoping such kindness will give people room and reason to realign themselves with him (10:6).

The opening paragraph and concluding appeals of Paul's letter fragment, then, have many links to πραΰτης and ἐπιείκεια. In the context of warfare and conquest, they connote clemency. To spare others in spite of their wrongdoing connotes leniency. Of course, this could simply be the reserve shown by one friend toward another in the enterprise of moral admonition, in which we would encounter simply kindness and gentleness. But Paul does not position himself as one friend to another. The entire appeal lies under the threat of punishment, issued by a person who claims authority. As such, it is leniency which Paul extends to the Corinthians.

This reading finds corroboration in the wider conduct of Paul's relationship with the Corinthian church. In the "Letter of Reconciliation" (1:1-2:13; 7:5-16; 13: 10–13), Paul reflects on what transpired previously between the Corinthians and himself. In the face of strained relations, Paul had made an emergency visit to Corinth. Failing to achieve his purposes, he left in humiliation but vowing to return and impose sanctions. Preferring that the Corinthians turn to him willingly and dreading the prospect of having to retaliate, Paul deferred his return trip, sending instead a letter, viz., the Letter of Tears (2:3-4). Paul explained this change of course as stemming from his desire to spare (φείδεσθαι, 1:23), precisely the motive he stipulated in the Letter of Tears (13:2). Paul expressed this desire at the beginning of the Letter of Tears by appealing to the Corinthians by Christ's leniency (10:1).

The results of Paul's earlier leniency appears in his further comments. Because of his or her wrongdoing (ἀδικεῖν, 7:12), the Corinthians had censured (ἐπιτιμία) someone (2:6). After this punishment (ἐκδίκησις, 7:11), forgiveness (χαρίζεσθαι) was extended, a gesture with which Paul heartily concurs (2:10). This series of events issued from repentance (μετάνοια) and produced an agreeable and happy outcome (σωτηρία, 7:9-10). Paul's call for obedience in the Letter of Tears (10:6) had been heeded (2:9; 7:15). In Paul's appeal, then, we encounter not a quickly forgotten pleasantry, but an important feature of his response to his difficulties with the Corinthian church.

b. Paul, the LXX, and Early Christian Literature

To conclude our investigation into the semantics of Paul's appeal in 2 Cor 10:1 we shall return once again to Leivestad and then summarize the preceding argument.

The fundamental problem with Leivestad's approach to the semantics of 2 Cor 10:1 is the priority he places on the LXX. There is in fact a specialized use of πραΰς and πραΰτης in the LXX, but even this observation requires qualification. First, all the evidence comes from translation Greek. Authors writing in Greek, e.g., Philo and Josephus, use πραότης as their pagan neighbors do. Second, the bulk of the evidence comes from the Psalms and Sirach, with two examples from Job and individual contributions from Zephaniah and Isaiah; other LXX examples are less clear. Third, the connotation of humility is clearest in the uses of the adjective to refer to a group of people. These people have low social status but are dear to God, thereby altering their value. To be part of that group becomes good, so that the connotation of humble (ταπεινός) changes.

These qualifications call for caution in attributing to Paul the specialized use of the LXX. First, the correlation of adjective and noun must be made more cautiously. For example, throughout Greek literature, the collective meaning of the plural adjective ἐπιεικής often points to the dominant social group, the people of good sense. As commonplace as that is, one cannot engage this use of the adjective to predict the meaning of any given use of ἐπιείκεια. What then of πραΰτης in the LXX? In Add Est 5:1 πραΰτης does not correspond to the collective adjective πραεῖς. To predicate the meaning of that use of the noun on the common use of the adjective (in the LXX) would be misleading. As for other uses of the noun, πραΰτης, in the LXX, they all occur in the Psalms and Sirach. While they tend to remain close to the meaning of the adjective, Ps 44:5 LXX; 89:10 LXX and Sir 4:8 bridge nicely the parochial and more general uses of πραΰτης. We cannot, therefore, assume that πραΰτης will express the same connotation as πραεῖς.

If we nevertheless accept that πραΰτης has an idiosyncratic meaning in the LXX, we cannot assume that Paul would comply with it. Diachronic trends do not determine meaning in a specific context, synchronic data do. The lists of synonyms and antonyms given above show that Jewish authors used the semantic field very much as their pagan contemporaries did. Even more telling, the references supplied in Appendix 2 for the definition of πραΰτης confirm that Jews contemporary with Paul used πραΰτης/πραότης in a variety of ways and did not simply imitate the LXX. These data therefore warn us to let Paul speak for himself and not insist that the LXX speak for him.

Though not necessary, the possibility remains that Paul may have imitated the LXX. This is where the semantic relations throughout 2 Corinthians 10–13 play an important role. The connections between Paul and the regular uses of πραότης and ἐπιείκεια indicate that the apostle is not working within the tight constraints of the LXX and its idiosyncratic semantics. Like other Jewish authors writing in Greek, e.g., Philo and Josephus, Paul does not follow the lead of the LXX in his use of ἐπιείκεια and πραΰτης. The privileged position given to the LXX in the semantics of 2 Cor 10:1 is therefore wrong. In fact, the LXX is relevant here only to the extent that it reflects the linguistic patterns of the larger world.

The lack of influence of the LXX on Paul's use of πραΰτης casts suspicion on recourse to Wis 2:19 in order to understand Paul's use of ἐπιείκεια. Since Paul is not thinking about πραΰτης in terms of the LXX, it is not likely that he has in mind for ἐπιείκεια an uncommon meaning predicated on the LXX.[53] This suspicion received confirmation in the preceding discussion.

To understand Paul's appeal in 2 Cor 10:1 we must look beyond the LXX. In so doing, however, we are not simply retreating to Harnack's views. Although some of our conclusions are the same, our reasons are not. The source of any agreement lies in the agreement between the LXX and its wider world. The language of royalty, power, and sparing evident in the LXX reflects the use of ἐπιείκεια at large.[54] That larger environment taught Paul how to use ἐπιείκεια and πραΰτης.

This leads to another departure from Harnack. We are not investigating early Christian history, but a single text, looking not for a trend in Christian thought, but the meaning of a specific passage. As we turn now to early Christian literature two points must be observed. First, in diachronic terms, 2 Cor 10:1 stands at the beginning of the development Harnack traces. That it already conforms to the future shape of Christian ethics may not be assumed *a priori*. Second, in synchronic terms, the differences between the apostle Paul and some Apostolic Fathers cannot be overlooked. Though they use the same words, they mean different things.

For example, *1 Clement* uses ἐπιείκεια five times and in each case connects it synonymously with ταπεινοφροσύνη (13.1; 30.8; 56.1; 58.2; 62.2). While the proximity of ἐπιείκεια to ταπεινός in 2 Cor 10:1 suggests similarity to *1 Clement*, the two are actually quite different. *1 Clement* presents ἐπιείκεια as a virtue for everyone to cultivate, whereas in 2 Corinthians 10–13 it comes to expression as a function of ἐξουσία.

The key difference between Paul and Clement is the actor not the action. Clement introduces ἐπιείκεια the first time when he advises his

---

[53] The use of ἐπιείκεια in Wis 2:19 is not unparalleled. Aesop *Proverbia* 37 promises divine assistance to the person who minds ἐπιείκεια. This use remains highly irregular.

[54] That the LXX applies ἐπιείκεια to God and kings is commonplace knowledge. What goes unnoticed is that no LXX author actually ascribes ἐπιείκεια to rulers. In 2 Macc 9:27; 3 Macc 3:15; 7:6; Add Esth 3:13b; and 8:12i, the five places where rulers have ἐπιείκεια (or a cognate) applied to them, the author is quoting a royal letter. This suggests that foreign rulers were more generous with their self-evaluation than their subjects might have been, but has no consequences semantically. (It also makes more poignant the desire for a gentle Messiah.)

readers to remember Jesus' teaching about ἐπιείκεια and μακροθυμία. Jesus said:

> Be merciful, that ye may obtain mercy. Forgive, that ye may be forgiven. As ye do, so shall it be done unto you. As ye give, so shall it be given unto you. As ye judge, so shall ye be judged. As ye are kind, so shall kindness be shewn you. With what measure you mete, it shall be measured to you (13.2; Loeb).

Christians, Clement adds, should strengthen themselves with these commands and, he repeats, be humble-minded (ταπεινοπφρονοῦντες), for Scripture says that God looks "on the πραΰν and ἡσύχιον and the one who trembles at my oracles." By extending the practice of ἐπιείκεια to all, matters of office and authority disappear. The actions envisioned, however, remain those of leaders, e.g., mercy, forgiveness, philanthropy, and judgment.[55] What transforms these typical gestures of ἐπιείκεια into those of humility is the disregarding of what they may imply. To forgive may impress others as weakness. Failure to retaliate may look like impotence. Clement's advice is to accept those consequences, which requires and results in being humble. What Clement advises, then, is patience, precisely what linking ἐπιείκεια with μακροθυμία indicates.[56] Though the temptation is great to read this sequence into 2 Cor 10:1 (thus returning to Leivestad's position), the distinction in actor must receive emphasis. As someone with ἐξουσία Paul is unlike Clement's audience.

1 Clem. 13.1 then guides our reading of 30.8. In the latter passage, Clement asserts that "frowardness and arrogance and boldness (θράσος καὶ αὐθάδεια καὶ τόλμα) belong to those that are accursed by God, gentleness and humility and meekness (ἐπιείκεια καὶ ταπεινοφροσύνη καὶ πραΰτης) are with those who are blessed by God." Here we see the combination of ἐπιείκεια and πραΰτης, but the insertion of ταπεινοφροσύνη redirects the connotation of the virtues. While by itself this would look unusual, Clement's other combinations of ἐπιείκεια and ταπεινοφροσύνη make this combination a natural part of his thinking. The example from 13.8 which we previously noted provides a foundation for this one.[57]

---

[55] This active sense differs from the Hebrew Bible. W. Bauder argues that the Hellenistic idea of lowliness influenced the Hebrew author of Sirach, exchanging "for the more passive Hebrew concept a Hellenistic active and ethical meaning. A positive lack is transformed into the praiseworthy virtue of 'gentleness' or 'humanity'" (*DNTT*, 2: 257-58).

[56] The influence of the LXX intrudes here, as πραΰς appears in a quotation from the prophet Isaiah.

[57] This text illustrates nicely Harnack's trio of virtues. A development has indeed taken place resulting in a new extension of ἐπιείκεια καὶ πραότης. Humility has been embraced as a positive good and latches onto ἐπιείκεια and πραότης.

Though the temptation is great to use *1 Clement* 13 and 30 as parallels to 2 Cor 10:1, three reasons argue against this. First, *1 Clement* is influenced by the LXX, whereas we have already seen Paul is not. Second, that Paul speaks of Christ's πραότης καὶ ἐπιείκεια and of his own ἐξουσία and the need to see δύναμις is also unlike *1 Clement*. Third, that Paul's ἐπιείκεια seeks the moral reform of the Corinthians and does not refer to his own moral condition further distinguishes him from Clement. Since these contextual issues differ from those of *1 Clement* 13, Clement's innovation does not overturn what we have already seen to be the typical use of πραότης καὶ ἐπιείκεια.

Two other texts from the Apostolic Fathers illustrate how differently Christ's ἐπιείκεια may be viewed. Ignatius uses Christ's ἐπιείκεια as an ethical example for his readers:

> Now for other men 'pray unceasingly,' for there is in them a hope of repentance (μετανοίας), that they may find God. Suffer them therefore to become your disciples, at least through your deeds. Be yourselves gentle (πραεῖς) in answer to their wrath (ὀργάς); be humble minded (ταπεινόφρονες) in answer to their proud speaking; offer prayer for their blasphemy; be steadfast in the faith for their error; be gentle (ἥμεροι) for their cruelty, and do not seek to retaliate (ἀντιμιμήσασθαι). Let us be proved their brothers by our ἐπιείκεια and let us be imitators (μιμηταί) of the Lord, and seek who may suffer the more wrong, be the more destitute, the more despised; that no plant of the devil be found in you but that you may remain in all pruity and sobriety in Jesus Christ, both in the flesh and in the Spirit (*Eph.* 10; Loeb).

Like Clement, Ignatius urges all Christians to practice ἐπιείκεια; authority is not an issue. While the goal of moral reform moves Ignatius closer to Paul, the difference is once again telling. Sanctions and punishment do not enter this picture. The ἐπιείκεια here is the behavior among equals which resists retaliation because such behavior is correct; its intrinsic rightness and beauty should win over opposition. Thus, Ignatius warns against imitating the godless and urges the imitation of Christ, which will produce correct behavior, which in turn will teach others how best to live.[58]

The *Epistle to Diognetus* also uses Christ's example of ἐπιείκεια. In extolling the superiority of Christian faith, the letter emphasizes that no human discovery produced Christianity, nor was it revealed in some predictable manner; instead the "very artificer and Creator of the universe himself" revealed it (7.2). And what was the manner of his coming? God did not send this exalted, heavenly figure, Christ, as one might suppose, as a tyrant who inspired fear (7.3).

---

[58] Ignatius can be compared to Epict. *Diss.* 3.20.9-11, where obnoxious associates train the virtuous person in the exercise of πρᾶος and ἀόργητος, as well as εὐγνώμων and ἐπιεικής.

Not so, but in gentleness and meekness (ἐπιεικείᾳ καὶ πραΰτητι), as a king sending a son, he sent him as King (βασιλέα), he sent him as God, he sent him as Man to men, he was saving (σώζων) and persuading (πείθων) when he sent him, not compelling (βιαζόμενος), for compulsion (βία) is not an attribute of God. When he sent him he was calling, not pursuing; when he sent him he was loving, not judging. For he will send him as judge, and who shall endure his coming? (7.4-6; Loeb).

In this example, ἐπιείκεια καὶ πραΰτης differs from *1 Clement* and Ignatius, but resembles what we saw above in Greek literature in general. The pair describes the mitigated expression of greatness, a self-restraint on the part of a powerful person in order to benefit others.

Both Ignatius and *Epistle to Diognetus*, then, appeal to the example of Christ's ἐπιείκεια. Side by side they demonstrate the different possibilities inherent in Christ's example. Which then is the better parallel to 2 Cor 10:1? The combinations of words and ideas in *Diognetus* parallel 2 Cor 10:1 more precisely than does Ignatius (or *1 Clement* 13).

Given these considerations of the LXX and early Christian literature, this study argues that they provide an inadequate foundation for understanding Paul's reference to πραΰτης καὶ ἐπιείκεια. Instead, by surveying many other authors and many other examples, we have uncovered synonyms and antonyms, as well as other words frequently associated with the two words. Common types of contexts, actions, and actors have also emerged. These set the stage for comparison with 2 Cor 10:1 and its wider literary context.

Beyond setting the stage, sound method requires that we focus specifically on the conjunction of the two words. Though each word has many connotations, placing them together reduces the semantic possibilities. From these we must seek the meaning of 2 Cor 10:1.

5. Conclusion

How then shall we translate Paul's phrase "τῆς πραΰτητος καὶ ἐπιεικείας τοῦ Χριστοῦ" in 2 Cor 10:1? To emphasize the connection with the warfare imagery in the following verses, I suggest the translation "clemency." Understood metaphorically, this is a fine translation. But Paul is not literally a general at the walls of a city. Nor are any laws at issue. Paul is the representative of the Lord Christ seeking to instill correct behavior in wrongdoers by a policy of deferred sanctions. Leniency seems therefore the more appropriate translation. Taking both nouns as an hendiadys, we could allow the one word "leniency" to serve as the translation of the pair. If two words are used, the complement to leniency is a difficult choice. Since Paul attributes the virtues to Christ as king (to anticipate the argument in the next chapter) "clemency" remains the best choice; moreover, next to leniency, "clemency" is the best way to express the mitigation of retribution. I hesitate to endorse "clemency" completely, however, because the meaning of that word may not be clear.[59] Gentleness" is not wrong, but only if understood with the background furnished throughout this work; without that, though, I do not think "gentleness" communicates Paul's meaning precisely (and therefore clearly) enough.[60] "Kind forbearance" or "generous indulgence" are to the point but ungainly, while "indulgence" by itself leaves room for much ambiguity. "Graciousness" would pair nicely with "leniency," but some might wish to retain that gloss for χάρις and its cognates. In the end, then, I propose the translation, "leniency and clemency of Christ."

But our investigation is not finished. A strength of Leivestad's reading is that it integrates well Paul's appeal with his weakness and lowliness: to read πραΰτης καὶ ἐπιείκεια as humility leads nicely into the rest of verse one which describes Paul as ταπεινός. Because this investigation predicates πραΰτης καὶ ἐπιείκεια on ἐξουσία and differentiates the pair from ταπεινός, some reason must be given to account for Paul's double self-description as lenient and yet humble. As we shall see in chapter five, there was in fact a personality type which encompassed these disparate qualities. Also to be investigated more carefully is the place of ἐπιείκεια and πραότης in the Greco-Roman world at large. How clear was Paul's appeal? Why did he issue it? Next, however, we will investigate how leniency and clemency fit into Paul's christology. Chapter three will argue that the ideology of good rule informs Paul's christology and gives rise to the ascription of πραΰτης καὶ ἐπιείκεια (leniency and clemency) to Christ.

---

[59] When I began this project, I thought "leniency and clemency of Christ" a good translation, not only superior to "meekness and gentleness" but also clearer. Over the years of explaining my research to people outside the academy I have discovered that the meaning of clemency is not as obvious as I thought. Most people have required an explanation of the word.

[60] Commenting on the difficulty of translating ἐπιείκεια into English, Trench suggests, "'Gentle' and 'gentleness,' on the whole, commend themselves as the best; but the fact remains, which also in a great measure excuses so much vacillation here, namely, that we have no words in English which are full equivalents of the Greek. The sense of equity and fairness which is in them so strong is more or less wanting in all which we offer in exchange" (*Synonyms of the New Testament*, 157).

Chapter 3

Christ the Good King:
The Leniency and Clemency of Christ
in Paul's Christology

> — "What does the tyrant?"
> — "Great Dunsinane he strongly fortifies:
> Some say he's mad; others, that lesser hate him,
> Do call it valiant fury; but, for certain,
> He cannot buckle his distemper'd cause
> Within the belt of rule."
> — "Now does he feel
> His secret murders sticking on his hands;
> Now minutely revolts upbraid his faith-breach;
> Those he commands move only in command,
> Nothing in love: now does he feel his title
> Hang loose about him, like a giant's robe
> Upon a dwarfish thief."
> Shakespeare, *Macbeth* 5.2

The semantic study of πραΰτης καὶ ἐπιείκεια has shown that together these words typically connote the restrained use of power in punishing offenders, as the translation "leniency and clemency" expresses (chapter 2). Since, however, Paul speaks of the "leniency and clemency *of Christ*," we must ask in what sense these virtues are appropriate to Christ. In this chapter, we will see that πραΰτης and ἐπιείκεια not only fit into a semantic field which is evident throughout 2 Corinthians 10–13, but they evidence a rhetorical *topos* for the good king in Greco-Roman literature.[1] Some of the key texts discussed in the previous chapter already point to this.[2] Now we will develop this observation more fully. In short, we contend that Paul's appeal in 2 Cor 10:1 to his recalcitrant audience by the

---

[1] New Testament scholars use the label *topos* in both a general sense and more specific form critical one. This study uses *topos* generally to describe a commonplace idea, particularly one orators could make use of.

[2] Particularly App. *Bas.* 1.5.

clemency of Christ is neither mysterious or surprising for Paul is utilizing a rhetorical commonplace.

In demonstrating this point, this chapter falls into seven parts. The first four outline the characteristics of a good king and demonstrate that this information was well-known. This survey will indicate that regarding 2 Cor 10:1 as a good king *topos* is not only feasible but very well founded. Section one provides an overview of the literature in which good king *topoi* appear. Section two demonstrates that good king *topoi* appeared outside literature as well, and were in fact widely disseminated throughout the Greco-Roman world. Section three will then survey the various good king *topoi*, while section four will focus on what it means to apply πραότης and ἐπιείκεια to a king. When taken together these first four sections will show that a good king *topos* can crop up in a letter — even in an allusive manner — and yet still be recognized as a *topos* of good rule. At that point we must turn to the second major focus of this chapter, Paul's christology. Section five looks for evidence that Paul regarded Christ as a good king and argues that kingship does form one aspect of Paul's christology. This chapter seeks then to associate "Christ's leniency and clemency" with that aspect of Paul's christology. Section six then attempts to situate Paul's regard for Christ as king within the broader context of his theology. In the seventh and concluding section, we will investigate the connection between 2 Cor 10:1 and the historical Jesus. This chapter will argue that *Paul's christology of kingship does indeed provide a context within which to understand Christ's leniency and clemency. No hypothetical connections between Paul and the historical Jesus are necessary.* To these things we now turn. First, then, if we wish to learn about the figure of the good king, where do we look?

1. Sources for Good King *Topoi*

Good king *topoi* manifest themselves in numerous places and in diverse ways.[3] For example, such *topoi* provided the building blocks for the numerous essays bearing the title Περὶ βασιλείας and informed other essays which explored related matters (e.g., Περὶ πολιτικοῦ or Περὶ πολιτείας). On a smaller scale, a single *topos* or a string of *topoi* may occur in statements or paragraphs incorporated into other genres

---

[3] See surveys in F. W. Walbank, "Monarchies and Monarchic Ideas," *Cambridge Ancient History*, eds. F. W. Walbank, A. E. Astin, et al. (Cambridge University Press, 1984), 7.1: 75-81; and Francis Cairns, *Virgil's Augustan Epic* (Cambridge University Press, 1989), 10-18.

(including letters). In fact, good king *topoi* are so well-known and widespread that they can be invoked with the briefest allusion or used as the foundation for further argumentation. We will now elaborate on these points before proceeding to explore the content of the good king tradition.

The list of people who composed essays entitled Περὶ βασιλείας is extensive and diverse. For convenience, we begin our list with Plato's Πολιτικὸς ἢ Περὶ βασιλείας. Later, Plato's student Xenocrates, eventual head of the Academy, wrote Στοιχεῖα πρὸς 'Αλέξανδρον περὶ βασιλείας in four books. Aristotle likewise wrote a Περὶ βασιλείας (Diog. L. 5.22), not to mention a Συμβουλευτικὰ πρὸς 'Αλέξανδρον.[4] Aristotle's successor, Theophrastus, continued his teacher's interest in political writings, producing three different works which bore the title Περὶ βασιλείας, one of which he dedicated to Cassander, while another filled two volumes.[5] The next head of the Lyceum, Strato, wrote a three volume Περὶ βασιλείας and a Περὶ βασιλέως φιλοσόφου.[6] Roughly contemporary, the Megarian philosopher Euphantus of Olynthus "taught King Antigonus and dedicated to him a work Περὶ βασιλείας which was very popular" (Diog. L. 2.110). The Cynic-Stoic tradition also busied itself with essays Περὶ βασιλείας. Antisthenes wrote two (6.16, 18) and afterward Persaeus, Cleanthes, and Sphaerus each wrote one.[7] And among

---

[4] Cic. *Ad Att.* 13.28; 12.40. See the testimonia and fragments collected in Marian Plezia, ed., *Aristotelis privatorum scriptorum fragmenta* (Leipzig: Teubner, 1977). Among Aristotle's corpus, Diogenes Laertius also cites five political essays filling fifteen books and a four book essay on laws. As for Aristotle's student Heraclides, Diogenes lists no Περὶ βασιλείας, but does say that Heraclides wrote Περὶ τῆς ἀρχῆς, Περὶ νόμων and other essays on similar toics, one of which was Περὶ ἐξουσίας (5.87-88). That Heraclides delivered his native city from tyranny by killing its monarch makes his thoughts about government much more than school exercises. Having noted these things, a word of caution applies to the following pages: Diogenes Laertius lists may cite spurious works. Such cases would in general still provide evidence for Hellenistic literary activity on the topic of Kingship (e.g., Goodenough, "Hellenistic Kingship," 58-59).

[5] Diog. L. 5.42, 47, 49. In addition Theophrastus wrote Περὶ παιδείας βασιλέως (Diog. L. 5.42), Περὶ τυραννίδος (5.45), Περὶ τῆς ἀρίστης πολιτειασ (5.45), five essays on laws filling thirty nine books, a two volume essay on punishments, and five works on politics requiring seventeen books (5.45), as well as Πῶς ἂν ἄριστα πόλεις οἰκοῖντο (5.49). A few fragments from his kingship writings are extant (frgs. 125-27; Dio. Hal. *Ant.* 5.73; Athen. 4.144e; POxy. 1611).

[6] Diog. L. 5.59. Strato's student Demetrius led Athens for ten years and wrote ten treatises on politics filling seventeen books (Diog. L. 5.80-81).

[7] Diog. L. 7.36, 175, and 178; see SVF 1.96 (no. 435); 1.107 (no. 481); 1.139 (no. 620), respectively. Diogenes Laertius actually lists the titles of Antisthenes' essays as Κῦρος ἢ Περὶ βασιλείας and 'Αρχέλαος ἢ Περὶ βασιλείας. These titles raise our

his hundreds of essays, Chrysippus also wrote one on kingship.[8] Περὶ βασιλείας reached a crescendo within the Cynic-Stoic tradition with Dio Chrysostom who composed six different orations on the theme of kingship.[9] The founder of the Epicurean tradition wrote a Περὶ βασιλείας; likewise, in the first century BC, Philodemus composed an essay on kingship for Caesar's father-in-law Piso entitled Περὶ τοῦ καθ' Ὅμηρον ἀγαθοῦ βασιλέως.[10] Pythagorean philosophers also showed interest in sovereignty: Stobaeus preserves Περὶ βασιλείας fragments attributed to Diotogenes, Ecphantus, and Sthenidas.[11] In

---

curiosity about Antisthenes' three additional Cyrus essays (6.16) as well as his Μενέξενος ἢ Περὶ τοῦ ἄρχειν (6.18). Walbank adds Zeno's name to the list of those who composed a Περὶ βασιλείας, see "Monarchies and Monarchic Ideas," 7.1: 77. The treatise by Zeno's student Persaeus has added interest because Persaeus had tutored Antigonus' son Halcyoneus (Diog. L. 7.36); similarly, the one by Cleanthes' student Sphaerus benefits from Sphaerus' attendance upon the court of King Ptolemy Philopator in Alexandria (6.177).

[8] See SVF 3.158ff. (nos. 617-622; 685-689; 691 and 693). Diogenes Laertius does not include a Περὶ βασιλείας in his catalogue of Chrysippus' *oeuvre*; however, only 161 of Chrysippus' 705 titles are included. Diogenes tells us that Chrysippus drew heavily on other authors (7.180); moreover, Diogenes asserts that "every subject treated by Epicurus, Chrysippus in his contentiousness must treat at equal length" (10.26). Strangely enough, Chrysippus did not dedicate any of his writings to any kings (7.185).

[9] *Orationes* 1-4, 56 (Ἀγαμέμνων ἢ Περὶ βασιλείας), and 62 (Περὶ βασιλείας καὶ τυραννίδος); see also *Oratio* 6 (Διογένης ἢ Περὶ τυραννίδος) and 49 (Παραίτησις ἀρχῆς ἐν βουλῇ) in which the idea of the philosopher-king plays an important role. Cf. 57.10-12. See John Moles, "The Kingship Orations of Dio Chrysostom," *Papers of the Leeds International Latin Seminar* 6 (1990): 297-375.

[10] See Oswyn Murray, "Philodemus on the Good King according to Homer," *JRS* 55 (1965): 161-82; Pierre Grimal, "Le 'bon roi' de Philodème et la royauté de César," *Revue des études latines* 44 (1966): 254-85; Elizabeth Asmis, "Philodemus's Poetic Theory and *On the Good King According to Homer*," *ClAnt* 10 (April 1991): 1-45; eadem, "Philodemus' Epicureanism," *ANRW* 2.36.4 (1990): 2406.

[11] Diotogenes = Stobaeus 4.7.61-62; Ecphantus = Stobaeus 4.6.22 and 4.7.64-66; and Sthenidas = Stobaeus 4.7.63, see Ioannes Stobaeus, *Anthologium*, 5 vols., eds. C. Wachsmuth and O. Hense (Berlin: Weidmann, 1884-1912). While English translations of these fragments can be culled from Erwin R. Goodenough ("The Political Philosophy of Hellenistic Kingship," *YClS* 1 [1928]: 55-102) and Jane Gardner (*Leadership and the Cult of the Personality* [Toronto: Hakkert, 1974]), Kenneth Guthrie includes them in *The Pythagorean Sourcebook and Library* (Grand Rapids, MI: Phanes Press, 1987). The most thorough discussion of these fragments (with French translation) appears in Louis Delatte, *Les traités de la Royauté d'Ecphante, Diotogène et Sthénidas*, Bibl. de la Fac. de Philos. et Lettres del'Univ. de Liège 97 (Paris-Liège, 1942). The dating of these fragments is uncertain, see Glenn Chesnut, "The Ruler and the Logos in Neopythagorean, Middle Platonic, and the Late Stoic Political Philosophy," *ANRW* 2.16.2 (1978): 1313-15. Goodenough and Holger Thesleff (*An Introduction to the*

addition to these treatises, Cicero testifies to other "Greek books containing panegyrics of Themistocles, Aristides, Agesilaus [Xenophon's?], Epaminondas, Philip, Alexander and others" (Cic. *De or.* 2.341).

Though the roster of essays on kingship is long, no examples are known from the first century AD. After Philodemus, Dio Chrysostom's essays stand alone. Or so it appears. If we consider only works which bear the specific title Περὶ βασιλείας, then we will erroneously conclude that the kingship *topos* fell out of vogue. To prevent this, we must cast our net more broadly.

The idea of the good king was taken up in a wide number of literary forms by a great number of people. Homer was regarded as a fundamental source for ideas about kingly rule. Plutarch informs us that Alexander considered Homer's *Iliad* an excellent military handbook (*Alex.* 668d; 679d-e), while Dio Chrysostom used a conversation about Homer by Alexander and Philip as the fictional setting for his second kingship essay.[12] Dio's treatise *On Homer* also offered succinct comments about what Homer thought kings should be like (53.11-12), as did Pseudo-Plutarch's *De vita et poesi Homeri* (2.178-83), while Horace drew examples of bad kings from Homer (*Ep.* 1.2). We have previously mentioned the most elaborate example, Philodemus' essay *On the Good King according to Homer*. Greek drama, especially tragedy, also presented kingship *topoi* — not surprising given the number of memorable royal figures portrayed on the stage. Stobaeus recognized this, as he lifted numerous excerpts on kingly rule from the dramatic literature.

In the fourth century BC, much was written about the good king. Pernot even asserts, "The praise of rulers is the most significant achievement of encomiastic rhetoric in the fourth century."[13] Xenophon was an influential voice, as he frequently discussed kingship. In the lengthy *Cyropaedia*, Xenophon used the life of Cyrus the Elder to offer his political views and

---

Pythagorean Writings of the Hellenistic Period, Acta Academiae Aboensis. Humaniora 24.3 [Åbo, 1961]) regard these writings as early Hellenistic, whereas Delatte argues for the second century AD.

[12] John Moles explains Dio's use of both Homer and Alexander in the kingship orations as reflecting Trajan's personal interest in both ("The Kingship Orations," 305-8 and 337-47).

[13] Laurent Pernot, *La rhétorique de l'éloge dans le monde gréco-romain*, 2 vols., Collection des Études Augustiniennes, Antiquité 137 (Paris: Institut d'Études Augustiniennes, 1993), 1: 23: "L'éloge des souverains est la conquête la plus significative de l'éloge rhétorique au IVe siècle."

in so doing treated the characteristics of a good king and general;[14] the *Hieron* presented a dialogue between the Elder Hieron of Syracuse and Simonides of Ceos in which they differentiate the tyrant from the good king; the *Agesilaus* praised the life of the famous Spartan king. Xenophon also placed an encomium for Cyrus the Younger in the *Anabasis* (1.9). Plato's *Republic* of course presented influential ideas about the philosopher-king. Isocrates' writings further develop ideas about the good king which are less utopian than Plato's and in fact prescient (albeit optimistic).[15] Aristotle criticized some typical elements of kingship theory.[16] Speusippus wrote letters to Dion, Dionysius, and Philip (Diog. L. 4.5). Given the interest of Dion and Dionysius in Plato's philosopher-king, we would expect these letters to discuss kingship. Plutarch confirms this suspicion in regard to the letter to Dion, telling us that Speusippus recommended to Dion holiness, justice, and good legislation — predictable *topoi*.[17]

In the Hellenistic period, literature reflected the new political reality. Theocritus' *Idyll* 16 and 17 both drew on royal *topoi*; the latter is in fact a royal encomium for Ptolemy II. Of *Id.* 17, Alan E. Samuel thinks that it melds third century Ptolemaic royal ideology and previous Greek thought. He says, "In this eulogy to Philadelphus, patterned on the Homeric hymns,

---

[14] See J. Joel Farber, "The *Cyropaedia* and Hellenistic Kingship," *AJP* 100 (1979): 497-514. In the introduction to his paper, Farber notes that "the odd similarity between the Athenian work of romanticized, philosophical history/biography and the later acts of Hellenistic kings is often pointed out" (p. 497); his essay then demonstrates that correspondence by comparing the *Cyropaedia* with papyri and inscriptions. Farber surmises that "we should not be surprised if the rulers of the Hellenistic kingdoms were familiar with Xenophon's work" (p. 514). Cicero knew it: "The great Cyrus was portrayed by Xenophon not in accord with historical truth, but as a model of just government, and the impressive dignity of his character is combined in that philosopher's description of him with a matchless courtesy; and indeed it was not without reason that our great Africanus did not often put those books out of his hands, for there is no duty belonging to a painstaking and fair-minded form of government that is omitted in them" (*Qfr.* 1.1.23).

[15] See especially *Evagoras, Ad Nicoclem,* and *Nicocles.* On *Ad Nic.* see S. Usher, *Isocrates: Panegyricus and To Nicocles*, Greek Orators 3 (Warminster: Aris & Phillips, 1985), 202-16. Pernot observes that Isocrates' role in encomiastic innovation is reflected in the fact that among the canonical orators, he is the only encomiast (*La rhétorique de l'éloge*, 1: 25). He later notes that encomiastic rhetoric really flowers in the imperial period, particularly within the Second Sophistic (1: 55).

[16] *Politica* 3. Aristotle's student, Phaenias of Eresus, wrote two works related to kingship: Τυραάννων ἀναίρεσις ἐκ τιμωρίας and Περὶ τῶν ἐν Σικελίᾳ τυράννων.

[17] *Mor.* 70a. Diogenes Laertius adds that Speusippus wrote a Πολίτης and Περὶ νομοθεσίας (4.4-5).

Theocritus praises Ptolemy, in Homeric language, for virtues which ... we associate with Homer's kings.... The ideology of monarchy is the same as that on which Alexander patterned his kingship: divine descent, a warrior's prowess, reverence toward the gods, and generosity toward men from his great wealth."[18] Samuel elaborates on this, adding 1) that the ideology became royal self-image and thereby motivated and guided the Ptolemaic king's behavior and 2) that the relationship between the Ptolemaic ruler and his subjects reflected the ideology.[19]

Throughout Classical antiquity, historians utilized good ruler *topoi*. Diodorus' account of the life of Sesoösis is full of kingship *topoi*, as it touches on the various aspects of his life: birth, education, prophecies, hunting, conquests, benefactions, and domestic affairs. While not at all surprising, this is noteworthy given that Diodorus' account is mediating and synthesizing the disparate views of Greek writers, Egyptian priests and poets, and the monuments extant at that time. In spite of these sources, Diodorus' narrative focuses on the *topoi* of kingship. Arrian concluded his *Alexandri anabasis* with a panegyric of his protagonist in which he piled superlative on top of superlative. "In the ninth century AD Photius noted dryly that [Arrian] praises his hero for virtually every known virtue."[20] Dio Cassius, in his version of Tiberius' funeral oration for Augustus (56.35-41), interestingly blended Greek kingship traditions with his contemporary Roman concerns.[21] Fergus Millar, in fact, lists notions about king and tyrant as one of the two dominant motifs in Dio's early speeches.[22] Examination of other Greek and Roman historians reveals similar attention being paid to royal *topoi*.[23]

---

[18] "The Ptolemies and the Ideology of Kingship," in *Hellenistic History and Culture*, ed. Peter Green, Hellenistic Culture and Society 9 (Berkeley: University of California Press, 1993), 181. Another version of this paper appears as chapter five in Samuel's *The Shifting Sands of History: Interpretations of Ptolemaic Egypt*, Publications of the Association of Ancient Historians 2 (Lanham, MD: University Press of America, 1989), 67-81.

[19] Samuel, "Ptolemies," 181-92.

[20] A. B. Bosworth, *From Arrian to Alexander: Studies in Historical Interpretation* (Oxford University Press, 1988), 135.

[21] See M. A. Giua, "Augusto nel libro 56 della storia romana di Cassio Dione," *Athenaeum* 61 (1983): 439-56.

[22] Fergus Millar, *A Study of Cassius Dio* (Oxford University Press, 1964), 79-83. In summarizing these speeches Millar states, "Dio's reasoning is banal and unoriginal" (83). Millar finds Dio's ideas lacking in historical connections and originality — precisely what makes them perfect for mining *topoi*.

[23] See, for example, Herod. 3.80-83; Polyb. *Hist.* 6; Sal. *Cat.* 9; Diodor. *Hist.* 1.69-95; Dio Cas. 52. Regarding the latter, Duncan Fishwick has highlighted the commonplaces

Besides the significant examples of *topoi* and treatises on kingship already cited, we should also take notice of the variety (and as a corollary frequency) of ways the *topoi* could appear. Sometimes the *topoi* received only brief allusion. For example, in a discussion of friendship, Aristotle introduced an analogy with the three basic forms of government (βασιλεία, ἀριστοκρατία, τιμοκρατία/πολιτεία). The relationship of a father to child, he stated, is like that of a sovereign to a subject in that both father and sovereign seek what is good for those in their charges. Drawing upon a kingship *topos*, Aristotle then concluded that royal rule is called paternal (*E. N.* 1160b). A few lines later he used another royal *topos* in noting that kings show εὐεργεσία, so that Homer rightly labels Agamemnon "shepherd of the people" (1161a). For the use of kingship *topoi* in poetry we may refer to Callimachus' *Hymn* 1.79-90 and 4.165-70, as well as to Pindar's *Pyth.* 1.94-98.[24] The latter emphasizes the value of praise by comparing the immortal glory which rises from Croesus' generosity to the infamy of the tyrant Phalaris' ruthlessness. The evils of monarchy also provided material for Statius' *Thebaid*.[25] For two epistolary examples, we may first look to Seneca, who embedded a paragraph comprised of kingship *topoi* in a letter to Lucilius (*Ep.* 90.5). These *topoi* provide a way for Seneca to describe life in the mythic golden age: all is well because the perfect ruler makes things so. An even more succinct example appears in the pseudepigraphic cover letter which introduces the *Rhetorica ad Alexandrum*. To emphasize the value of reason, the writer asserted that it is more kingly than a fine appearance (1420a). With this simple allusion to a commonplace about kingship, the author made his point.

The proliferation of kingship *topoi* which these casual allusions suggest finds documentation in the materials collected by ancient anthologists. For example, the anecdotes in Pseudo-Plutarch's *Regum et imperatorum apophthegmata* and Athenaeus' *Deipnosophistae* contain numerous kingship *topoi*. Stobaeus in particular amassed many kingship texts (which naturally include *topoi*), quoting tragedians, orators, philosophers,

---

in Maecenas' speech, yet shown how they addressed a situation contemporary to Dio ("Dio and Maecenas: The Emperor and the Ruler Cult," *Phoenix* 44 [1990]: 267-75). On Latin historians, see J. Roger Dunkle, "The Rhetorical Tyrant in Roman Historiography: Sallust, Livy and Tacitus," *CW* 65 (1971-72): 12-20.

[24] On Callimachus see Ludwig Koenen, "The Ptolemaic King as a Religious Figure," in *Images and Ideologies*, 81-113; see nn. 125, 126, and 151ff. for bibliography.

[25] William J. Dominik, "Monarchal Power and Imperial Politics in Statius' Thebaid," *Ramus* 18 (1989): 74-97; idem, *The Mythic Voice of Statius: Power and Politics in the Thebaid*, Mnemosyne Supplementum 136 (Leiden: E. J. Brill, 1994), 76-98.

historians, and statesmen, e.g., Archytas' Περὶ νόμου καὶ δικαιοσύνης, Iamblichus' *Letter to Agrippa*, and Sopatros' *Letter to His Brother Hemerion: How He Should Exercise the Office Entrusted to Him*.[26] Thus, in prose and poetry, in letters and philosophical treatises, kingship *topoi* appeared and served varied purposes.

Recognizing the diversity which expressions of the *topoi* may take, we may now turn to the more immediate neighborhood of the New Testament. First, Jewish authors reflect knowledge of the *topoi* and harness them for their own ends in apologetic writings. Royal *topoi* provide the substance of the lengthy banquet scene in Pseudo-Aristeas' *Letter to Philocrates* and furnish the conceptual matrix for Philo's *De vita Mosis*, especially book one.[27] Philo's treatise *De Iosepho*, although an essay on the good statesman, attributes to Joseph the qualities which "accord with the Hellenistic ideal of kingship."[28] In *De legatio ad Gaium*, Philo explicitly sings the praises of Tiberius and Augustus (141-42 and 143-58). Like Philo, Josephus also praises Moses as a good ruler;[29] in addition, Josephus relies on kingship *topoi* for his presentations of Saul, David, and

---

[26] Archytas = Stob. *Anth*. 4.1.132, 135-38; 4.5.61; Iamblichus = Stob. *Anth*. 4.5.76-7; Sopatros = *Anth*. Stob. 4.5.51-60. All 250 excerpts from Stob. *Anth*. 4.5-8 could also be entered as evidence of kingship *topoi*, especially 4.7, "'Υποθῆκαι περὶ βασιλείας."

[27] On Aristeas see Oswyn Murray, "Aristeas and Ptolemaic Kingship," *JTS* 18 (1967): 337-71; idem, "The Letter of Aristeas," in *Studi Ellenistici 2*, ed. Biagio Virgilio, Biblioteca di studi antichi 54 (Pisa: Giardini, 1987), 15-19; Doron Mendels, "'On Kingship' in the 'Temple Scroll' and the Ideological *Vorlage* of the Seven Banquets in the 'Letter of Aristeas to Philocrates,'" *Aegyptus* 59 (1979): 127-36. Murray balances Greek and Jewish traditions much better than Mendels, who underestimates the influence of Greek kingship thought in *Ep. Arist*. On Philo see Ray Barraclough, "Philo's Politics: Roman Rule and Hellenistic Judaism," *ANRW* 2.21.1 (1984): 417-553, especially pp. 453-61, 487-506, 518-33; see also Erwin R. Goodenough, *By Light, Light*, 181-87; idem, *The Politics of Philo Judaeus: Practice and Theory* (New Haven: Yale University Press, 1938). Wayne Meeks, "Moses as God and King," in *Religions in Antiquity: Essays in Memory of Erwin Ramsdell Goodenough*, ed. Jacob Neusner, Studies in the History of Religions 14 (Leiden: E. J. Brill, 1968), 354-71. Similar questions about the intersecting of Jewish and Greco-Roman ideas about kings arise in the reading of *T. Mos.* 6.

[28] R. Barraclough, "Philo's Politics," 499. In this opinion Barraclough agrees with Goodenough (*The Politics of Philo Judaeus*, 53-4); however, Barraclough (p. 500) disagrees with Goodenough's claim that Joseph represents the *praefectus Aegypti* (Goodenough, p. 55). See also Barraclough's conclusions about Moses and Joseph (pp. 505-6). Other examples of Philo's use of kingship *topoi* include *Leg. alleg.* 3.79-81 (about Melchizedek); *De agric.* 39-50; and *De leg. ad Gai.* 143-51.

[29] *Ap.* 2.158-60; *Ant.* 3.322. In turn, "that Moses, the greatest leader that the Israelites had ever had, chose as his successor Joshua led Josephus to the conclusion that Joshua possessed the qualities of an ideal statesman" (Louis H. Feldman, "Josephus's Portrait of Joshua," *HTR* 82 [1989]: 351).

Solomon.³⁰ Saul, in fact, provides Josephus with the opportunity to comment on the nature of the bad king and the intrinsic dangers of the monarch's position (*Ant.* 6.262-68). Less elaborately, when relaying the advice given by an Essene prophet to Herod on the right way to rule, Josephus again drew on kingship *topoi*.³¹ The figure of Joseph also attracted kingship *topoi* which ultimately influenced Byzantine iconography.³²

Second, Greek philosophers and orators gave attention to good king traditions. Cynic Epistles interact with ideas about the good king, continuing the idea of the philosopher-king, yet giving it a radical, non-utopian twist.³³ The Stoics claimed that the wise person was the true king. Musonius Rufus ("Ότι φιλοσοφωτέον καὶ τοῖς βασιλεῦσιν), Hermippus (Περὶ τῶν ἀπὸ φιλοσοφίας εἰς τυραννίδας καὶ δυναστείας μεθεστηκότων), and Plutarch (*Ad principem ineruditum*) all addressed themselves directly to matters of kingship.³⁴ So also do the anonymous orations preserved in the corpus of Pseudo-Aelius Aristides, Εἰς 'Ρώμην and Εἰς βασιλέα.³⁵ The *topoi* also surface when Philostratus reports Apollonius' advice on good kingship.³⁶ Meanwhile the figure of the tyrant was also a stock character.³⁷

---

³⁰ See Louis H. Feldman, "Josephus as an Apologist to the Greco-Roman World: His Portrait of Solomon," in *Aspects of Religious Propaganda in Judaism and Early Christianity*, ed. Elisabeth Schüssler Fiorenza (Notre Dame: University of Notre Dame Press, 1976), 69-98; idem, "Josephus' Portrait of Saul," *HUCA* 53 (1983): 45-99; and idem, "Josephus' Portrait of David," *HUCA* 60 (1989): 129-74.

³¹ *Ant.* 15.375. Cp. 10.83 and 6.262-67 for the same criteria, viz., justice, piety, and gentleness; cf. 10.155; 13.319. See also Josephus' descriptions of Herod and Agrippa (*Ant.* 19.328-334).

³² Marie-Dominique Gauthier-Walter, "Joseph, figure idéale du Roi?" *Cahiers archéologiques* 38 (1990): 25-36.

³³ See, for example, Ps.-Anach. *Ep.* 7; Ps.-Crates *Ep.* 5 and 34; and Ps.-Diog. *Ep.* 40.

³⁴ For Hermippus, see Plutarch *Mor.* 1126a. Additional sayings of Musonius Rufus on kingship can be found in Stob. *Anth.* 4.7.14-16 (= frgs. Lutz 31-33). For other examples of good king *topoi* in Plutarch, see *Mor.* 152a-b (*Septem sapientium convivium*, which, like Ep. Arist., makes kingship a sympotic topic), 776a-779b (*Maxime cum principibus philosopho esse disserendum*), and 798-825 (*Praecepta gerendae reipublicae*); and *Numa* (L. de Blois and J. A. E. Bons, "Platonic Philosophy and Isocratean Virtues in Plutarch's *Numa*," *Ancient Society* 23 [1992]: 159-88, especially pp. 183-85 and 187).

³⁵ L. de Blois, "The Εἰς βασιλέα of Ps.-Aelius Aristides," *GRBS* 27 (1986): 276-84. The latter speech presupposes the former, as well as Xen. *Ag.*, Isoc. *Ev.*, and Dio Chrys. *Or.* 1-4.

³⁶ *Vit. Apol.* 5.27 and (especially) 35-36; 6.29-34; and 8.27-28.

³⁷ D. A. Russell, *Greek Declamation* (Cambridge University Press, 1983), 32-33 and 123-28.

Third, the Romans picked up the good king traditions. In *De or.* 2.341, quoted above, Cicero reveals his familiarity with Greek royal panegyric; we can, therefore, recognize him as a conduit of Hellenistic royal thought into Rome. His *Pro lege Manilia* presented the Roman public with a sweeping image of the ideal Hellenistic ruler, while his Caesarian speeches provided the models for future panegyrists.[38] Cicero shows his knowledge of kingship *topoi* not only in his political writings, but even in his letters.[39] During the tumult at the end of the Republic, Roman political invective made scathing use of *topoi* about the king's evil twin, the tyrant.[40] Thereafter the legacy of Greek ideas about kingship in Rome is rich. Also noteworthy are Augustus' monumental *Res gestae*, Velleius Paterculus' words of praise for his former commander Tiberius (2.126), Seneca's treatise addressed to Nero, *De clementia*,[41] and Pseudo-Seneca's historical drama *Octavia*. Poets also utilized kingship *topoi*. Obvious examples are the eulogistic poems of Calpurnius Siculus and Statius. Ovid is more subtle.[42] The epic *Aeneid* is particularly remarkable, for Virgil wove kingship *topoi* throughout it in an elaborate and sophisticated manner with the result that characters and events reflect kingship motifs.[43] Virgil could, however, be blunt (*Geor.* 1.24-42). Roman political ritual also provided opportunity for the expression of kingship *topoi* in the

---

[38] Sabine MacCormack, "Latin Prose Panegyrics," in *Empire and Aftermath: Silver Latin II*, ed. T. A. Dorey (London: Routledge & Kegan, 1975), 148. Joachim Gruber comments boldly: "Wie Cicero später die griechische Philosophie in Rom heimisch machte, so hat er in der Pompeiana das xenophonteisch-hellenistische Herrscherideal übernommen und den römischen Vorstellungen und Gegebenheiten angepaßt. Die geistigen Grundlagen des Prinzipats waren gelegt und erstmals systematisch vor der römischen Öffentlichkeit dargestellt" ("Cicero und das hellenistische Herrscherideal. Überlegungen zur Rede 'De imperio Cn. Pompei,'" *Wiener Studien* 101 [1988]: 258).

[39] *Qfr.* 1.1.29; cf. Cicero's comments in *Ad Att.* 8.9.

[40] On the origins of Roman thinking about kings see Andrew Erskine, "Hellenistic Monarchy and Roman Political Invective," *CQ* 41 (1991): 106-20. On the characteristics of the bad king in Roman thought see J. Roger Dunkle, "The Greek Tyrant and Roman Political Invective of the Late Republic," *TAPA* 98 (1967): 151-71.

[41] See Miriam T. Griffin, *Seneca: A Philosopher in Politics* (Oxford: Clarendon Press, 1976), 129-71. Seneca's tragic *Thyestes* and satirical *Apocolocyntosis* also include kingship *topoi*.

[42] On Ovid's *Fasti* see J. C. McKeown, "Ovid's *Fasti* and Augustan Politics," in *Poetry and Politics in the Age of Augustus*, eds. Woodman and West (Cambridge University Press, 1984), 169ff.; Andrew Wallace-Hadrill, "Time for Augustus: Ovid, Augustus and the *Fasti*," in *Homo Victor: Classical Essays for John Bramble*, eds. Michael Whitby, Philip Hardie, and Mary Whitley (Bristol Classical Press, 1987), 221-30.

[43] See Cairns, *Virgil's Augustan Epic*, 1-84.

gratiarum actio, a custom established under Augustus whereby newly elected consuls thanked the populace for electing them.[44] When we arrive at Pliny the Younger's *gratiarum actio*, his *Panegyricus*, we find him addressing the emperor and encounter the Roman use of kingship *topoi* in full bloom.[45] The *topoi* appear repeatedly in subsequent imperial encomia and imperial biographies, as is obvious in Suetonius' *De vita Caesarum*[46] and in the later *Scriptores historiae Augustae*. These latter biographies reflect how woodenly good king *topoi* can be applied. These, in turn, point us to what may be the most explicit and analytical expressions of good king *topoi* (and it is fitting that they are written in Greek), Pseudo-Dionysios of Halicarnassus' *Ars rhetorica:* Τέχνη περὶ τῶν πανηγυρικῶν and Menandor Rhetor's Περὶ ἐπιδεικτικῶν: βασιλικὸς λόγος, which are essentially handbooks for imperial panegyric.

In sum, then, the potential sources of good king *topoi* are numerous and diverse. To be sure, some sources are more likely than others. A treatise entitled Περὶ βασιλείας is undoubtedly the best place to look. Writings which describe the lives and deeds of kings, such as histories and biographies, also depend greatly on kingship *topoi*. Still, plays, poems, hymns, encomia, philosophical essays, and letters may also do so. In these varied genres, kingship *topoi* may provide the main substance of the text

---

[44] MacCormack, "Latin Prose Panegyrics," 149; eadem, "Latin prose Panegyrics: tradition and discontinuity in the later roman Empire," *Revue des études augustiniennes* 22 (1976): 29-41.

[45] In addition to Cicero and Seneca, Josef Mesk highlights the similarities between Pliny and Tacitus, "Quellenanalyse des Plinianischen Panegyricus," *Wiener Studien* 33 (1911): 71-100. See also Lester K. Born, "The Perfect Prince According to the Latin Panegyrists," *AJP* 55 (1934): 20-35; Mark P. O. Morford, "*Iubes esse liberos*: Pliny's *Panegyricus* and Liberty," *AJP* 113 (1992): 575-93. "Pliny's *gratiarum actio* therefore had many antecedents, of which, however, none survive.... It is impossible to tell how far Pliny's *Panegyric* differs from the many earlier consular *gratiarum actiones*," MacCormack, "Latin Prose Panegyrics," 149.

[46] See K. R. Bradley, "Imperial Virtues in Suetonius' *Caesares*," *Journal of Indo-European Studies* 4 (1976): 245-53. In this connection, two studies have been done on specifically Titus: Aldo Marastoni, "La biografia suetoniana di Tito e il discorso sulla regalità," in *Atti del Congresso Internazionale de Studi Flaviani, Rieti, settembre 1981*, ed. Benedetto Riposati (Rieti: Centro de Studi Varroniani, 1983), 1: 105-23; in the same volume Maria Grazia Bajoni argues, "Tito, in ultima analisi, è come il *rex* del *De Clementia* di Seneca e la controparte positiva del *saevus tyrannus* quale appare Nerone nella *praetexta Octavia*" ("Le virtú del principe dal Seneca pedagogo a suetonio biografo di Tito," 190). On the reading of ruler *topoi* in Suetonius see Tamsyn Barton, "The *inventio* of Nero: Suetonius," in *Reflections of Nero: Culture, History, & Representation*, eds. Jaś Elsner and Jamie Masters (Chapel Hill: University of North Caroline Press, 1994), 48-63.

or receive only allusion for ancillary purposes.[47] Both situations argue for the commonplace knowledge of kingship motifs and their easy use. Therefore, we need not be surprised to find a kingship *topos* in a Pauline letter.[48]

2. Dissemination of Good King *Topoi*

The previous section traced the figure of the good king primarily through Greek and Roman literature and may have left the impression that the good king is essentially a literary phenomenon.[49] Perhaps Cicero and Seneca were influenced by literary tradition and in turn influenced subsequent authors, so that perhaps *Octavia* and Dio Cassius are not really independent witnesses to good rule, but merely echoes of Seneca limited to a tiny social circle. This section will demonstrate that the ideology of good rule is not only a literary construct known only to the literate, but in fact had wide currency. Charlesworth sought to prove this in his seminal article "The Virtues of a Roman Emperor": "What did the common people under the Empire expect of their rulers, and how were they satisfied? ... What did the farmer in Gaul, the corn-shipper in Africa, the shopkeeper in Syria, expect?" (107-8). As we shall see, evidence exists to suggest that the *topoi* were not confined to literature. To prove this, the following investigation will explore two broad categories of non-literary evidence, viz., artifacts and social contexts. Each provided opportunity and means for communication about good and bad kings in the ancient world.

---

[47] This is precisely what we saw in regard to the attribution of πραότης and ἐπιείκεια to King Numitor in App. *Bas.* 1.6 and the tyrant Dionysius in Athen. *Deip.* 12.72/ 549d. Cf. Plut. *Mor.* 537d.

[48] Given our concern to demonstrate the ubiquity of good king *topoi* we have not bothered to consider their function. Clearly, each text has its own purpose for invoking such a *topos*. In his *Panegyric*, Pliny has a transparent admonitory agenda. The mirror he holds up to Trajan is really a map. We may say the same of Dio Chrysostom's kingship orations. Encomia delivered at festivals find their justification in the competition. In the presence of the subject, flattery enters the picture. Meanwhile, philosophical literature may have a utopian purpose or analytical one. Philodemus' treatise *On the Good King according to Homer* appears to have a didactic function, using an ancient authority around which to wrap practical advice for the political person. For historians the *topoi* provide criteria for evaluation of individuals and a framework for interpreting historical causation. On the stage they may afford insight into motivation or causation, or be the topic of discussion.

[49] We ought not ignore that a centuries-old literary tradition has the power to shape reality. By providing language and enshrining positive and negative examples (as so determined by the tradition itself), literature could shape the ideas and values of a society which in turn could influence individual behavior.

The first variety, the artifactual, consists of minor objects, coins, monuments, statues, and inscriptions. By *minor objects* I mean things like housewares and jewelry. In Vermeule's discussion of imperial metalwork, two items are relevant for us. The first is a silver cup from Meroe in the Sudan, also known as the Judgment of Bocchoris cup (Vermeule, 124-28). The imagery on the cup presents a scene of judgment, whose drama is heightened by a man who bears an axe and two children cowering near the legs of a woman. While Vermeule notes that the scene awaits adequate interpretation, he suggests that the seated judge is Augustus and "whatever the specific details of the story, the king is about to pardon or spare the distraught female and the children."[50] In regard to kingship *topoi*, the cup communicates the role of the king as judge and his capacity to bring justice and pardon. Vermeule also discusses the two major cups from the Boscoreale silver.[51] One cup depicts two scenes featuring Augustus, the other offers two with Tiberius. On one side, the former shows Augustus being congratulated for victory, while on the other "barbarians come to do obeisance to Augustus" (p. 134). The cup clearly heralds the emperor's *virtus*. I think, however, that the barbarian submission suggests more than Vermeule indicates, because not only do the barbarians kneel before the emperor and present their children to him, but Augustus extends his right hand in warm welcome.[52] This suggests clemency and underscores the connection between *virtus* and *clementia*. The second cup portrays Tiberius riding in triumph and then sacrificing before the Capitol.[53] Like the other cup, the emperor's *virtus* is emphasized, only this time the

---

[50] Vermeule, 125. Although Erika Simon questions the identification of the judge with Augustus, she still agrees that the figures seek mercy from the judge (*Augustus. Kunst und Leben in Rom um die Zeitenwende* [Munich: Hirmer, 1986], 221).

[51] Vermeule, 129, 133-34, and 141. See also Simon, *Augustus*, 139-45; Ann Kuttnen, "Lost Episodes in Augustan History: The Evidence of the Boscoreale Cups and the Ara Pacis," *AJA* 91 (1987): 297-98; François Baratte, "Arts précieux et propagande impériale au début de l'Empire romain. L'Exemple des deux coupes de Boscoreale," *Revue du Louvre et des Musées de France* 41/1 (1991): 24-39.

[52] Baratte offers additional indications of clemency ("Arts précieux," 34). Hans Gabelmann, *Antike Audienz- und Tribunalszenen* (Darmstadt: Wissenschaftliche Buchgesellschaft, 1984), 132-38: "Die extreme Demütigung der Barbaren vor dem Prinzeps hatte für das römische Auge eine durchaus positive Konnotation, denn sie war ihrerseits die Voraussetzung dafür, daß in der clementia eine der typisch römischen, kaiserzeitlichen Wertvorstellungen verwirklicht werden konnte" (p. 138; cf. nos. 41, 46, 59, 61, 79, 84, 87).

[53] Vermeule suggests that the Pannonian triumph of AD 12 is in view and that the same scenes may have appeared on the Arch of Tiberius (p. 134).

relation between *virtus* and *pietas* receives notice.[54] Vermeule adds one further point of interest in regard to metalwork. Representation of the Augustan court in this medium may have been greatly influenced by Alexandrian craftsmen, who brought a long history of royal iconography from the Greek east to bear on their work, thereby providing one more bridge between Greek and Roman ideologies.[55]

Beautiful cameos also conveyed Roman imperial ideology. The Marlborough cameo which bears only the bust of Augustus with radiate crown, bespeaks his divinization.[56] A similar cameo, yet larger, actually had a bejeweled crown attached to it.[57] Another cameo presents a triumphant Augustus wearing a laurel wreath and holding a spear, while the aegis draped over his shoulder points to his deification.[58] Livia figures in yet another cameo and takes the appearance of Cybele, while holding the bust of the divine Augustus in her hand.[59] The Grand Camée portrays divine filiation, conquest, and dynastic hopes. While similarly expressing Augustus' dynastic aspirations, the relatively large Gemma Augustea also presents Augustus as the companion of gods and as the provider of victory, peace, and prosperity.[60] As stunning and eloquent as these

---

[54] T. Hölscher attempts to see all four virtues from Augustus' golden shield (which is discussed in the next chapter) on the Boscoreale cups ("Die Geschichtsauffassung in der römischen Repräsentationskunst," *Jahrbuch des deutschen archäologischen Instituts* 95 [1980]: 281-90); however, *iustitia* is not obvious to me. On the Boscoreale hoard, see now Ann L. Kuttner, *Dynasty and the Empire in the Age of Augustus: The Case of the Boscoreale Cups* (Berkeley: University of California Press, 1994).

[55] Vermeule, 136-37, and 141. Augustan gem-cutters probably received their training in the East as well (Martin Henig, "The Luxury Arts: Decorative Metalwork, Engraved Gems and Jewellery," in *A Handbook of Roman Art*, ed. Martin Henig [Ithaca, NY: Cornell University Press, 1983], 155).

[56] Inciser Gürçay Damm, "Freude an kostbarem Schmuck," in *Museum. Römisch-Germanisches Museum Köln*, eds. Andrea Kastens and Beate Schneider (Braunschweig: Westermann), 83 (illus. p. 76).

[57] Lucilla Burn, *The British Museum Book of Greek and Roman Art* (New York: Thames and Hudson, 1991), 183 (fig. 153).

[58] John P. O'Neill, et al., eds., *The Metropolitan Museum of Art: Greece and Rome* (New York: Metropolitan Museum of Art, 1987), 98.

[59] Simon, *Augustus*, 162, fig. 211.

[60] Simon, *Augustus*, 156-61 (pl. 11 offers an excellent reproduction, while fig. 208 offers a sketched reconstruction); Zanker, *Power of Images*, 230-33. For the association between the living Augustus and Jupiter, Zanker cites the so-called Sword of Tiberius as a parallel, because it also presents the emperor in the manner of Jupiter, while signifying *virtus* and *felicitas* (232-33). Simon emphasizes that the theme of the Gemma Augustea is not victory but dynastic succession (160). She also suggests that of the two pairs of barbarian captives in the gem's lower register, one entreats their captors for mercy, thus

expensive cameos were, however, they (like the silver) addressed a very exclusive audience.[61]

While silver cups and cameos were not common goods, lamps were. These bore a variety of images, including animals, love scenes, daily life, and mythological figures. An additional figure was that of the *clipeus virtutis* (an honorary, inscribed shield presented to Augustus, which is discussed in the next chapter). To dismiss this as useful evidence because on one such lamp the shield bears the message "Happy new year!" is too abrupt. It was not unusual for images on lamps to celebrate holidays, nor was it uncommon to give lamps as new year's gifts.[62] Second, the emperor's birthday was a holiday, and in fact the beginning of the new year. Connecting an imperial symbol to the new year is not silly. A lamp in the Römisch-Germanisches Museum Köln makes such a connection.[63] The shield bears the inscription: ANNVM NOVVM FAVSTVM FELICEM MIH. The entire image presents Victory holding the shield in her outstretched right hand, while cradling a cornucopia in her left; dates, nuts, and coins fill the perimeter.[64] In clever — yet not necessarily flippant — fashion, the entire image suggests a hope for prosperity in the coming year, using the vocabulary of imperial rule: a prosperous new year hinges on Victoria — and hence emperor.

Coins possibly expressed many things about rulers. I say possibly, not because the imagery of coins is uncertain, but because the process of communication is. Whereas modern scholars can derive much information from coins, debate continues as to how informative they were in their original contexts. How consciously coins were manipulated for publicizing purposes, the identities of their issuers and intended audience, and how sophisticated the audience was in interpreting them remain

---

corresponding to the Roman custom to spare subjugated peoples (157). Actually, it does not require much imagination to read all four virtues from the golden shield (discussed in the next chapter) in the Gemma Augustea.

[61] Though the audience for luxury goods was small, it would have included household slaves and guests. For additional cameos, see Zanker, *Power of Images*, figs. 77, 81, and 82; Simon, *Augustus*, figs. 205 and 210; pls. 12-13.

[62] Inciser Gürçay Damm, "Mit Öl, Talg und Kienspan," in *Museum. Römisch-Germanisches Museum Köln*, 93.

[63] See the illustration in Damm, "Mit Öl, Talg und Kienspan," 91.

[64] "In der unteren Bildhälfte sind drei Münzbilder wiedergegeben: eine Victoria, verschlungene Hände mit einem Heroldstab, ein Januskopf. Die Münzen waren beliebte Geschenke zum Neujahrstag, denn Geld an diesem Tage zu erhalten, war das beste Omen" (Damm, "Mit Öl, Talg und Kienspan," 93).

matters of dispute.[65] More concretely, scholars argue whether Roman coins were directed toward the populace, the armies, the Senate, or the Princeps, whether designs were chosen for persuasive purposes or for technical or antiquarian reasons, who designed the coins and the emperor's influence in this matter, and to what extent people even paid attention to the images and words coins bore. While these questions complicate numismatic studies, for our purposes we need not address them. Regardless of who designed coins, any image of the emperor is a vehicle for expressing ideas about his rule. As for audience, different ones existed. The expense and trouble taken to alter dies, however, suggests that someone was watching. The hesitance to issue coins with offensive images in Palestine likewise suggests that people noticed their currency. However, our question is how people learned about good king *topoi*. We can answer that coins played a role in this regard. Whether an issuer wanted to persuade the emperor to do something, or to honor him for

---

[65] On this debate see *Essays in Roman Coinage Presented to Harold Mattingly*, eds. R. A. G. Carson and C. H. V. Sutherland (Oxford University Press, 1956), particularly A. Alföldi, "The Main Aspects of Political Propaganda on the Coinage of the Roman Republic," 63-95 and A. H. M. Jones, "Numismatics and History," 13-33. Jones argues that numismatics can illumine economic history, but is less useful for political history. His influential article is reprinted in his *The Roman Economy: Studies in Ancient Economic and Administrative History*, ed. P. A. Brunt (Oxford: Basil Blackwell, 1974), 61-81. C. H. V. Sutherland responded to Jones in "The Intelligibility of Roman Coin Types," *JRS* 49 (1959): 46-55; idem, *The Emperor and the Coinage: Julio-Claudian Studies* (London: Spink and Son, 1976), especially pp. 96-121. Andrew Wallace-Hadrill championed Jones' skepticism in "Galba's Aequitas," *Numismatic Chronicle* 141 (1981): 20-39. Although some of Wallace-Hadrill's comments are less extreme than Jones' were, Sutherland nevertheless felt compelled to respond ("The Purpose of Roman Imperial Coin Types," *Revue numismatique* sixth series 25 [1983]: 73-82). In a later article, however, Andrew Wallace-Hadrill seems to have moved closer to Sutherland in granting coins a persuasive value (albeit one with an economic aspect): "Image and Authority in the Coinage of Augustus," *JRS* 76 (1986): 66-87. Although Barbara Levick has also criticized Jones, she has additionally altered the nature of numismatic persuasion by identifying the intended audience as the emperor himself ("Propaganda and the Imperial Coinage," *Antichthon* 16 [1982]: 104-16). Michael H. Crawford attempted to nuance Jones' skepticism in light of Sutherland's criticisms ("Roman Imperial Coin Types and the Formation of Public Opinion," in *Studies in Numismatic Method Presented to Philip Grierson*, eds. C. N. L. Brooke, et al. [Cambridge University Press, 1983], 47-64). Recently Robert Newman has attempted to undermine Jones' views by tracing the use of coins as vehicles for a propaganda war ("A Dialogue of Power in the Coinage of Antony and Octavian [44-30 B.C.]," *American Journal of Numismatics* second series 2 [1990]: 37-63). In the course of this debate the problems with using the word "propaganda" have been emphasized. Suggested alternates are publicity or expression. Meanwhile, the debate has not given adequate attention to a hermeneutic of deconstruction.

something already done, or whether the emperor wished to publicize himself, for our purposes the end result is the same. Some portion of the population received money which connected the emperor with a virtue perhaps or some benefaction. Such coins trade in and express the *topoi* of kingship.

Charlesworth argued that coins played a large and effective role in spreading the ideology of the good Roman emperor, a claim which Wallace-Hadrill particularly criticized.[66] Wallace-Hadrill began by raising methodological questions, but only to note the problems, for he conceded that "the types are there ... and they must in some sense reflect 'official' perceptions of the emperor" (p. 308). He then raised three issues of fact. First, after noting the difficulty of using the label 'virtues,' Wallace-Hadrill stated, "Among the forty or so personifications of the imperial coinage, only a dozen are virtues. It is also worth noting that the types which only appear once or twice are almost all virtues" (pp. 309-10). Next, he emphasized the distribution of these issues. In "the Julio-Claudian period, personifications are scarce and spasmodic" (p. 310), while the period from "the civil wars of 68/9 to Antoninus Pius ... is the heyday of the personification" (p. 311); afterward, the "repetition of types continues, more and more meaninglessly" (p. 311). Last, Wallace-Hadrill noted that it is not until Hadrian that "we have what is surely a deliberate effort to produce a gallery of *virtutes*" (p. 312). In matters of fact Wallace-Hadrill's criticisms are sound and find general support from J. Rufus Fears.[67]

In regard to the role of coins in spreading good king *topoi*, then, the following conclusions may be drawn. First, though Wallace-Hadrill is right that coins publicizing virtues were not typical, that does not mean that those which did had no impact. Second, because good king *topoi* include more than virtues, Wallace-Hadrill's criticisms address only a portion of the relevant data. Third, a coin does not require a legend to honor a virtue. For example, Augustan coins often bear the oak crown, advertising Augustus as a savior figure. Those who connected the crown to civil wars might also have seen the crown as reflecting Augustus' *clementia*. Regardless, if one were familiar with Roman culture and knew what the crown signified, reading a legend would have been superfluous. Some coins do in fact dispense altogether with any legend.[68] When

---

[66] Charlesworth, "The Virtues of a Roman Emperor," 110-11 and 114-15; Wallace-Hadrill, "The Emperor and his Virtues," 307-14.

[67] "The Cult of Virtues," *ANRW* 2.17.2 (1981): 827-948, especially 877-924.

[68] A couple of dozen coins present Augustus on the obverse wearing an oak crown. Reverses sometimes present the crown by itself (*RIC*, 1: 43ff. nos. 29a-b, 40a-b, 57, 75a-

Tiberius issued coins bearing the image of Augustus in a radiate crown, or with a star and lightening bolt, he honored his divine (step-)father.[69] This helped Tiberius to show his piety toward Augustus, while at the same time exalt the imperial dynasty, two commonplaces of royal ideology. An issue of Caligula presents the goddess Piety on the obverse with the legend PIETAS, while the reverse shows Caligula sacrificing in front of a temple.[70] This coin clearly connects the emperor with the virtue of piety. But the reverse says even more. The temple behind Caligula is carefully detailed to reveal a quadriga poised on the apex of the roof with Victories on either side. No legend is required (nor is Latin literacy) to reinforce this message of military prowess. Moreover, if the temple were in fact that of the Divine Augustus, then the advertised *pietas* is not simply a matter of the gods, but of family as well. In short, not only does this coin herald explicitly the emperor's piety, but, without the help of a legend, his *virtus* and possibly dynasty as well.[71] Nor are these last two themes unusual on imperial coins. Also common is the theme of benefaction. A Neronian coin shows two goddesses, one seated and holding an ear of corn, one standing with a cornucopia in her hand. Between these two women stands an altar on which sits a *modius* (the standard measuring cup for corn), while a ship's prow appears in the background.[72] Even if one lacks the ability to read the legends (CERES and ANNONA), the imagery suffices to connect the provision of corn with the emperor's oversight. These examples, then, illustrate how images may not require explicit legends and literate readers to be understood.

Finally, images are made further intelligible by the broader cultural context in which they exist. Although coins alone were unable to teach an ideology of good rule, coins were not the only way to communicate ideas about good rule. Coins did not speak with a solitary voice, but blended with an entire culture to express ideas about good rule.[73] In concert with

---

77b, and 278-79), other times in combination with other images (*RIC*, 1: 43ff. nos. 30a-b, 78a-79b, 285-86, 302, 549). Sometimes legends are included: OB CIVIS SERVATOS (*RIC*, 1: 43ff. nos. 29a-b, 40a-b, 75a-79b, 549) or simply OB C. S. (*RIC*, 1:62ff. nos. 278-79, 285-86, 302, and 312). Clive Foss organizes these references more succinctly than does *RIC* in his *Roman Historical Coins* (London: Seaby, 1990), 45-47.

[69] *RIC*, 1: 99 nos. 70-83.

[70] *RIC*, 1: 111 no. 36 (cf. nos. 44 and 51).

[71] Laura Breglia, *Roman Imperial Coins: Their Art and Technique* (London: Thames and Hudson, 1968), no. 9.

[72] Breglia no. 27; cf. *RIC*, 1: 161 nos. 137-42; 1: 173 no. 372. For Augustus see *RIC*, 1: 80 nos. 478, 481, and 490-91.

[73] Susan Sherwin-White and Amélie Kuhrt recognize in the Seleucid evidence that coins work with the other physical relics of ancient life in communicating a fairly

the other means to be discussed, coins made their contribution, broadcasting benefactions, virtues, accomplishments, dynastic plans, and honors. To stress this moves us past the debate between Charlesworth and Wallace-Hadrill, who argue specifically about the dissemination of ideas about imperial virtues, whereas royal *topoi* encompass more than virtues. Correspondingly, when one thinks more broadly about good rule, the evidence from coins increases significantly.

Monuments also proclaimed important ideas about kings. We discuss many of these elsewhere in this study, such as the Forum of Augustus, the Altar of Peace, the Temple of Apollo, and the Arch of Titus. Though these, of course, were all in Rome (as was Augustus' Mausoleum), monuments throughout the empire expressed similar messages.

The founding of cities reflected the power and providence of the emperor. When Galatia was organized as a Roman province, conscious steps were taken to initiate civic life.[74] The focal point of the newly created urban centers was the imperial cult.[75] Ancyra's temple of Rome and Augustus was in fact "the most notable building of all Galatia," while the imperial temple in Pisidian Antioch dominated the city and "was visible from miles away."[76] Turning to Palestine, Sebaste, Herod's Caesarea, and Tiberias were all named in honor of the builder's patron, the emperor.

Various features of cities also provided imperial imagery.[77] City gates, which easily resembled triumphal arches, became "popular vehicles of

---

consistent message. They comment as follows: "Gradually a dynastic iconography developed of which little survives except on coins, finger rings, and seals. These are interesting because they record subjects and images thought to define the greatness of the king and his royal qualities, illustrating the king's piety and status as dear to the gods, his military achievements and, in the case of Seleucus, his physical strength, symbolized by the images of Zeus and Athena Nike in a war chariot drawn by Indian elephants, Seleucus in diademed helmet draped in panther skin, [and] a charging bull" (*From Samarkhand to Sardis*, 23).

[74] Stephen Mitchell, *Anatolia: Land, Men, and Gods in Asia Minor*, 2 vols. (Oxford University Press, 1993), 1: 86-91.

[75] "Only three Roman cities in central Anatolia outside the province of Asia have yet been excavated on a substantial scale: Ancyra, Pessinus, and Pisidian Antioch. In each case the central feature of these excavations has been a temple dedicated to the imperial cult, built in the time of Augustus or Tiberius" (Stephen Mitchell, *Anatolia* 1: 100). Cf. idem, "Galatia under Tiberius," *Chiron* 16 (1986): 17-33 (especially 30-33); idem, "Imperial Building in the Eastern Provinces," *HSCP* 91 (1987): 333-65 (especially 362-63); idem and M. Waelkens, *Pisidian Antioch: The Site and its Monuments* (London: Duckworth with the Classical Press of Wales, 1998).

[76] Mitchell, *Anatolia*, 1: 103 and 105, respectively.

[77] Vermeule succinctly surveys some examples (pp. 169-70).

3.2. Dissemination of the Good King Topoi   111

imperial expression."[78] The incorporation of the emperor into the sanctuaries of other gods also provided crucial expressions about the emperor.[79] Imperial fora also placed the emperor's image and evidence of his largesse before his subjects. Less dramatically, aqueducts and fountains expressed in practical terms a ruler's care for his subjects. Altars also publicized the emperor. The altar of the *gens Augusta* from Carthage bore images of victory and prosperity on one side, piety on the other.[80] Athens may have had a smaller imitation of the Ara Pacis, perhaps honoring Claudius and his family (Vermeule, 34). In Ephesus, Augustus enlarged the temenos of Artemis. And most obvious of all, the imperial cult with its altars and sanctuaries articulated the emperor's power and care.

The remains of Aphrodisias reveal to us in dramatic form the dissemination of the imperial image.[81] The Sebasteion contained 180 reliefs which depicted "the Roman empire, the Greek world within it, and the imperial family."[82] More specifically, individual panels presented Augustus with Victory, Claudius defeating Britannia, and Nero defeating Armenia. A great series of panels represented the various territories under Roman dominion. Remains from sixteen of these are extant (e.g., Jews, Dacians, Cyprus, Crete), though the original number may have been three times that. Together, these images all expressed in overwhelming fashion the might, conquest, and dominion of Rome, while signifying the *virtus* of individual emperors. Another relief represented a naked Augustus with a circle of cloth billowing overhead, while Earth with cornucopia held his

---

[78] Vermeule, 16 (e.g., Ephesus, Aphrodisias, Pisidian Antioch).

[79] Price, *Rituals and Power*, 133-169.

[80] Zanker, *Power of Images*, figs. 283-84.

[81] Kenan T. Erim, *Aphrodisias: City of Venus Aphrodite* (London: Muller, Blond & White, 1986); Joyce M. Reynolds, "New Evidence for the Imperial Cult in Julio-Claudian Aphrodisias," *ZPE* 43 (1981): 317-27; eadem, *Aphrodisias and Rome*, Journal of Roman Studies Monographs 1 (London: Society for the Promotion of Roman Studies, 1982); eadem, "IN PROCESS," in *Studii clasiice xxiv in honore D. M. Pippidi* (Bucuresti Ed. Acad., 1986); eadem, "The Inscriptions," in *Aphrodisias de Carie. Colloque du Centre de recherches archéologiques de l'Université de Lille III*, eds. Juliette de la Genière and Kenan Erim, 81-85 (Paris: Editions Recherche sur les Civilisations, 1987); R. R. R. Smith, "The Imperial Reliefs from the Sebasteion at Aphrodisias," *JRS* 77 (1987): 88-138; idem, "*Simulacra gentium*: The *Ethne* from the Sebasteion at Aphrodisias," *JRS* 78 (1988): 50-77; idem, "Myth and Allegory in the Sebasteion," in *Aphrodisias Papers: Recent Work on Architecture and Sculpture*, eds. Charlotte Roueché and Kenan T. Erim, Journal of Roman Archaeology Supplementary Series 1 (Ann Arbor: University of Michigan, 1990), 89-100.

[82] Smith, "Imperial Reliefs," 95.

right hand and Sea with anchor held his left — a striking image of power, prosperity, and security. The intermingling of mythological and imperial imagery throughout the Sebasteion also emphasized the stature of the emperor, while explicitly publicizing the imperial family's descent from Venus Aphrodite. Elsewhere in Aphrodisias, inscriptions recorded Octavian's enormous benefactions to the city: freedom, autonomy, tax exemption, and asylum. In sum, the imagery presented in Aphrodisias made a persuasive case for Roman rule (as well as Aphrodisias' place within that realm).

The most ubiquitous objects other than coins which advertised rulers were *statues* and other forms of portraiture. Imperial figures were everywhere, lining the streets, supervising the marketplaces and theaters, and residing in temples. Vermeule summarizes the situation as follows:

> A survey ... shows that every city, however small, must have set up statues of at least a half-dozen members of the imperial families from Augustus through the fourth century to the house of Theodosius. The larger cities, of course, had statues of nearly every important emperor, and often possessed a number of statues of the same ruler, scattered throughout the city.[83]

For example, the citizens of Lydia responded to Tiberius' help by erecting a statue of him, in order to demonstrate their loyalty and gratitude. The inscription lauded Tiberius as divine, founder of the city, and benefactor of the world. Ilium, given its association with Aeneas and, therefore, his descendants, the imperial family, had numerous statues and inscriptions honoring Augustus and his family.[84]

The importance of statues and images of the emperor go beyond their accompanying inscriptions. Images themselves offered a profound message, because they were imbued with the majesty of the person they represented. As a result, they made the emperor's protection a present reality. Tacitus bemoaned the abuse of the emperor's image for asylum during the reign of Tiberius, saying,

> Bad characters were increasingly slandering and insulting respectable people and escaping punishment by grasping an effigy of the emperor. Thereby even ex-slaves and slaves had intimidated their patrons and masters with threatening words and gestures.... [I]t was the height of illegality when Annia Rufilla ... should menace and abuse ... [yet escape reprisals] because she clutched an image of the emperor (*Ann.* 3.36).

---

[83] *Ibid.*, 69. Vermeule adds that the Julio-Claudians and Hadrian figure most commonly in Greece (p. 70). As for the evidence, Vermeule quotes statistics indicating that for Claudius, the evidence for extant portraits is as follows: Italy 27, Asia 22, Achaia 16, Pisidia 4, and Macedonia 2 (p. 43). See also Vermeule's discussion of the dissemination of the imperial portrait in the East (pp. 199-201).

[84] Vermeule, 71-72; cp. Braund 67, 112.

3.2. Dissemination of the Good King Topoi

In short, the right to claim asylum at the image of the emperor automatically heralded his power, justice, mercy, and protection.[85]

Statues were also part of a dialogue. Often they were raised as an expression of gratitude, so that they pointed to some previous benefaction bestowed by the honoree. Statues of the Roman emperor were also erected after asking his permission to do so. By offering the emperor this honor, a community was positioning itself for the emperor's future consideration. The resulting statue would then represent the hope for future blessing. Statues therefore are part of the dialogue of gift, gratitude, and obligation; as such they express visually the emperor's philanthropy and care.

Inscriptions presented good king *topoi* outside the confines of literature. W. Schubart has demonstrated the epigraphical diffusion of the *topoi* in the Hellenistic period.[86] In the Roman period, Augustus' *Res gestae* provides a splendid illustration, as it broadcasted his valor, clemency, justice, piety, benefactions, offices, and accumulated honors. That copies of the *Res gestae* were posted in both Greek and Latin in Ancyra and Pisidian Antioch and Apollonia made its content available to an even larger audience. Perhaps it was inscribed elsewhere. This phenomenon of copying imperial honors throughout the empire is not unique to the *Res gestae*.[87] When Germanicus Caesar died, the Senate passed a decree proposing honors for him. In the decree the Senate also recommended that provincial leaders place copies of the decree in the most frequented places within their districts (Sherk 36a). The Senate also recommended that Tiberius' praise of the dead Germanicus be made available for public viewing (*ibid.*). Extant inscriptions show that imperial speeches, letters, and edicts also received public display. Such scattered inscriptions would have made characteristics of the good ruler, particularly the Roman emperor, available to a broad audience.

Local communities also took initiative in posting honorific inscriptions. The provincial assembly of Asia planned to draft a decree cataloging Augustus' virtues and to display it publicly, inscribed in Greek and Latin.[88] A Corinthian inscription refers to the "divine Julia Augusta" prior to her death and official deification, indicating the status of and respect for

---

[85] Tac. *Ann.* 1.73.2; 3.63; Pliny *Ep.* 10.74; Suet. *Aug.* 17.5; *Tib.* 58; Dio Cas. 47.19.2; cf. 57.24.7; Philos. *Vit. Apol.* 1.15. The power of the emperor's image paralleled that of the gods (e.g., Sen. *De clem.* 1.18.2). See Weinstock, *Divus Julius*, 242-43 and 395-57; Price, *Rituals and Power*, 191-206.

[86] "Das hellenistische Königsideal nach Inschriften und Papyri," 5-26. See also Welles 14 (care), 15 (benefactions), 52 (piety), and 54 (foresight and favor).

[87] Similarly the Ara Pacis and the *clipeus virtutis* were copied throughout the empire.

[88] EJ 98; trans. Bruand 122.

the imperial dynasty in Corinth. These two examples indicate that not all imperial recognition came from Rome. They also indicate how well local communities knew the vocabulary of good rule.

Social contexts provided a second avenue for the spread of ruler *topoi*. In general, social networks disseminated rumors, opinions, and anecdotes. This was done both naturally and with calculation, both informally and under the direction of patrons.[89] For our purposes this is important because such channels of communication provided another bridge between literate ideas and the larger population. More specific social contexts helping in the spread of kingship *topoi* were the "school"; the theater and festivals with their stage productions and encomia; public appearances; the royal court; and the ruler cult.

In rhetorical *education* students practiced making speeches about the tyrant. In the *Progymnasmata* of Aphthonios, he illustrates the commonplace by elaborating on opposition to the tyrant.[90] This example is not surprising given the trail which the tyrant leaves throughout rhetorical literature. The tyrant appears in the *controversiae* of the Elder Seneca (1.7; 2.5; 3.6; 4.7; 5.8; 7.6; 9.4) and furnishes an example in Cicero's *De inventione* (2.144). In one of his letters, Cicero recited a litany of tyrant *topoi* which he had been rehearsing (*Ad Att.* 9.4). Cicero, Seneca, and Aphthonios together indicate that the tyrant was a stock figure in rhetorical education.[91]

Reaching larger audiences than the rhetorical schools, the *stage* also disseminated ideas about kingship. Aeschylus, Sophocles, Euripides, and Seneca all portrayed kings in their plays and in so doing expressed ideas about good and bad rule. The comic stage did as well, as Stobaeus demonstrated by lifting ideas about kings from Menander. Plutarch also recognized the possibility that drama (performed or read) disseminated kingship *topoi* (*Mor.* 36f-37a). Seneca, in fact, assumed that the king was a familiar stage figure (*Ep.* 80.7). Clearly, then, the theater (whether intentionally or accidentally) was an effective medium for communicating ruler *topoi*.

Perhaps the most effective means for communicating good king *topoi* were *encomia*. Pliny's *Panegyricus* had its origins in a public expression

---

[89] Ray Laurence, "Rumor and Communication in Roman Politics," *G & R* 41 (1994): 62-74.

[90] Leonardi Spengel, *Rhetores graeci* (Leipzig: Teubner, 1854), 2.82-86.

[91] Lucian indicates that the tyrant's role in rhetorical education spilled over into subsequent rhetorical practice. In a summary of Oratory's activities, Lucian specifically includes the criticism of tyrants and the praise of nobles (*Bis accus.* 32).

of thanks. Pierre Grimal thinks that the first book of Seneca's *De clementia* originated in a similar manner as a *nuncupatio votorum* and was subsequently fashioned into a literary treatise.[92] Dio Chrysostom delivered his kingship orations publicly and to a much broader public than Seneca and Pliny. It is important to recognize that such examples were not unusual. Throughout the Roman Empire encomiastic competitions must have made good king *topoi* well-known. Such contests were in fact hosted by Corinth in its quinquennial Caesarean games.[93] Along with the athletic matches and musical competitions, orators competed in three different categories: 1) an encomiastic speech in honor of Caesar Augustus, 2) an encomium for Tiberius Caesar, and 3) a poem for the divine Julia.[94] The entries in these competitions likely drew on the good king *topoi*. While we can only conjecture what any particular orator declaimed, we can concur with Tacitus who points out the wonderful opportunity that such panegyrics afforded sycophants.[95]

Public appearances afforded rulers opportunities to shape their public image, both by their appearance and the words they spoke. When Herod Agrippa appeared before a crowd wearing a resplendent robe, his audience marvelled at the sight and hailed him as a god.[96] Such was the power of spectacle. Josephus mentions occasions on which Herod the Great addressed his subjects. For example, Herod convened the Jews in order to announce his intention to renovate the temple; this assembly obviously publicized his piety and philanthropy (*Ant.* 15.381). Another time, Herod reported to an assembled crowd in Jerusalem that through his intervention Jews in Asia could live according to their customs. He also mentioned what he had done on behalf of his audience (16.62-4). Herod convened such assemblies on other occasions as well in order to present himself to his subjects in an advantageous light and to garner popular support for his plans.[97] Such assemblies were clearly situations in which ideas of good rule could be and were promulgated.

---

[92] *Sénèque ou la conscience de l'Empire*, Collection d'Études Anciennes (Paris: Les Belles Lettres, 1979), 121-27.

[93] Many cities hosted games in honor of the emperor or his family. For example, Pergamum hosted a thirty day festival of the Romaia Sebasta (*SEG* 39 [1989]: no. 1180, line 57); cf. Sherk 1984: 109.

[94] Merritt 19; cp. West 81.

[95] Tac. *Ann.* 16.2. On speeches in general, see Laurence, "Rumor and Communication," 67-68, 71.

[96] Jos. *Ant.* 19.344-45; cf. Acts 12:21-22.

[97] Jos. *Ant.* 16.132-35 and 393; L. I. Levine, "Herod the Great," *ABD*, 3: 165.

The *royal court* itself provided opportunity for the expression of good king *topoi*. The education of princes, the maintenance of a philosophic advisor, and the utilization of educated men in the king's administration raised the possibility of introducing the literary and philosophic traditions about good rule into the royal court.[98] In this case, however, the potential dissemination of the *topoi* says little about their actual implementation.[99]

The *ruler cult* publicized the Roman emperor. Processions, hymns, prayers, sacrifices, feasts, temples, spectacles, and oaths indicated the position of the emperor at the center of civic life.[100] Like the gods, the emperor was a focal point for help, protection, and blessing. This topic has been discussed in detail by Simon Price, *Rituals and Power*.

In short, kingship *topoi* were not confined to literature. Knowledge of the *topoi* was not limited to the few souls who spent their days at leisure with scrolls. As people in antiquity looked at their money, paid their taxes, saw public monuments, drew their water, were hauled into court, participated in public rituals, watched plays, and listened to speeches, particularly encomia, they learned — and sometimes experienced — the commonplaces about good and bad rulers. Those with some education may also have learned from inscriptions or perhaps within their school curriculum.

The commonplace knowledge of the *topoi* of good rule becomes even more obvious in view of four further considerations. First, kingship *topoi* appear in literature which originated outside of elite social circles. The New Testament itself offers insight into how people perceived rulers. The Slaughter of the Innocents (Matt 2:16-18) reveals a popular perception of Herod's cruelty. The controversy over taxes indicates understanding of who stood behind the coinage (Mark 12:13-17; Matt 22:15-22; Luke 20:20-26). Paul's appeal to Caesar in Acts 25:11 indicates that people

---

[98] For the best survey of the vexed questions about what philosopher influenced what ruler, see Frank Leslie Vatai, *Intellectuals in Politics in the Greek World: From Early Times to the Hellenistic Age* (London: Croom Helm, 1984). Also, J. M. C. Toynbee, "Dictators and Philosophers in the First Century A. D.," *G & R* 13 (1944): 43-58; Miriam Griffin, "Philosophy, Politics, and Politicians at Rome," in *Philosophia Togata: Essays on Philosophy and Roman Society*, eds. Miriam Griffin and Jonathan Barnes (Oxford University Press, 1989), 1-37; Elizabeth Rawson, "Roman Rulers and the Philosophic Advisor," in *Philosophia Togata*, 233-57.

[99] Plato's failure in Syracuse in noteworthy in this regard. Herod the Great's lack of attention to leniency and (ethnic) justice is all the more remarkable given the educated men in his entourage (Schürer, 1: 310-12).

[100] On imperial festivals see Price, *Rituals and Power*, 102-14; on sacrifices, 207-33.

3.2. Dissemination of the Good King Topoi   117

associated the emperor with justice.[101] The acknowledgement that Agrippa was familiar with Jewish customs and disputes also meshes with what was expected in a (good) king. None of the examples, of course, has escaped scholarly skepticism regarding its historical authenticity, which explains my tardiness in using them as evidence. But if we adopt the most skeptical attitude possible, these examples become even more interesting, because then they show how people thought about their rulers. The less historical authenticity these examples are accorded, the greater evidence they become for the successful dissemination of good king *topoi*.

One more example from the New Testament merits our attention, namely, the execution of John the Baptist. According to the Gospels, John had incurred the king's ire because the Baptist accused Herod (Antipas) of an illicit marriage. Luke's Gospel adds that the Baptist had rebuked Herod more generally for all his evil deeds (3:19). Josephus, on the other hand, says that Herod killed John because he feared that the Baptist, with his great popularity, might foment rebellion (*Ant.* 18.116-19). These two accounts are not mutually exclusive, yet their differences are interesting. While Josephus offers a more politically sophisticated interpretation, the Gospels indicate that other people found it perfectly natural to evaluate a king by the standards of piety and justice. By those criteria Herod is a bad king, which is precisely what the conclusion of the story proves. What is relevant for our purposes is that some early Christians told a story which evaluated a king morally, or to be specific, in terms of piety and justice.[102] I take this as important evidence that the *topoi* we will survey influenced the thinking of a public much broader than the educated elite.

Second, we should recognize that good king *topoi* are essentially elements of a dialogue. The ruler who draws on them seeks honor, goodwill, legitimacy, security, or succession. But nothing can guarantee an audience's response, as Herod's wondrous temple proves. That splendid monument to his generosity and piety failed to win Jewish approbation (according to our sources). One also suspects that the Neronian coin depicting Apollo in flowing robes playing the lyre may have played

---

[101] I do not wish to imply that a naïve faith in the emperor's justice existed. The New Testament is also aware that officials had much room in which to make decisions and act. Gallio could refuse to accept jurisdiction of a case and could ignore the beating of Sosthenes (Acts 18:17-17; cp. Luke 23:7). Felix could have detained Paul in hope for a bribe (24:26). These were all perfectly believable actions and motives. Cf. also Rom 13:1-7.

[102] The story of Herod's death is similar. Both in Acts 12:23 and Jos. *Ant.* 19.347 Herod's death results directly from an act of impiety.

differently to different audiences.[103] Where an anti-neronian Senator might have recalled an emperor making a demeaning public spectacle of himself, the Athenians, enjoying the benefits of Nero's attendance at their games, might have regarded the image more highly.[104] These examples indicate that the issues involved in kingship *topoi* go beyond rhetorical invention. They are crucial ingredients in the vocabulary of political life.

Nor were the opinions of the audience irrelevant. Ziaelas, king of Bithynia, wrote to Cos, "We do in fact exercise care (ἐπιμέλειαν) for all the Greeks who come to us as we are convinced that this contributes in no small way to one's reputation" (Welles 25, c. 240 BC). This indicates the importance of well-known criteria for a good king, as opposed to the esoteric, for a standard is needed in order for a king to accumulate honor. A ruler needs the *topoi* to garner praise and the *topoi* must be known for praise to be given.

A letter written in 167/6 BC by King Eumenes II to the Ionian League thanking it for honors voted to him illustrates the dialogue of which kingship *topoi* are a part (Welles 52). This letter also reveals much about the public communication of good king *topoi*. In the first half of his letter Eumenes cited the contents of the decree which the Ionian emissaries had delivered to him. The Ionian decree praised Eumenes as benefactor, a leader in the struggles against enemies, a provider of peace and prosperity, and superior to danger; it also applauded Eumenes' zeal and foresight on behalf of the Ionian League, as well as his goodwill. All of these are kingship *topoi*, with the exception of the last one, goodwill, which is a more general commonplace used for any political relationship. Eumenes next cited the honors which the grateful Ionians conferred on him: golden crown, golden statue, and proclamation of his honors in games throughout Ionia. Eumenes then thanked the League for the honors given him and expressed his intention to continue to show his goodwill toward the League. From this letter we may draw three conclusions about the dissemination of good king *topoi*. First, the leaders of the Ionian League knew good king *topoi* and used them to address King Eumenes; moreover, this address was formal, enshrined in a decree, and consequently reflected the appropriate way of addressing a ruler. Second, King Eumenes looked favorably upon the application of the *topoi* to himself. In fact, by his repetition of them we can conclude that he found them an appealing way to present himself. Third, Eumenes' letter to the League was inscribed and displayed publicly. Anyone who could read could therefore have access to

---

[103] *RIC*, 1: 158-78 nos. 73-82, 121-23, 205-12, 380-81, 384-85, 414-17, 451-55.
[104] Suet. *Nero* 25.

the public image of Eumenes and in turn to commonplaces about the good king. Eumenes' letter would then become a vehicle for the propagation of good king *topoi, topoi* which the League's citizens themselves valued and praised.

Since kingship *topoi* are part of a dialogue, the content of that conversation provides a third observation. In short, kingship *topoi* were often simply *topoi* of good governance; therefore, many kingship *topoi* received increased dissemination by their general applicability to any type of authority or preeminence. Thus, nearly all the advice which Cicero and Pliny dispense on how to govern provinces applies to the emperor and vice versa. Elsewhere, when the legate of Pisidian Antioch controlled the price of grain and outlawed hoarding during a time of famine (Sherk 1988: 105), he acted to secure the well-being of his subjects just as the emperor might have done if he had been present. In AD 68 the prefect of Egypt sent an edict to the strategus of the Thebaid Oasis in which the prefect referred to his own πρόνοια, the πρόνοια of the strategus, and that of the emperor (Braund 600). The bulk of the edict contains merciful measures for debtors and protection from force, as well as provisions for tax relief and legal reforms.[105] The prefect also mentioned his thoughtfulness and aid (φροντίζειν and βοήθεια). Pontius Pilate provides another example.[106] He inflamed the Jews to revolt when he took funds from the Jews' sacred treasury. That he spent the money well (viz., to build an aqueduct as opposed to paying for his personal pleasures) mattered little. Had *pietas* and *iustitia* guided his policy, armed confrontation would have been unnecessary. These examples indicate that many kingship *topoi* belong to the broader vocabulary of good government.

In a similar vein, honors given to kings were often not given exclusively to kings. Much of what comprised a good (or bad) king also characterized the good (or bad) civic leader. Inscriptions from both Thasos and Lycosura praise a prominent local citizen as pious, just, and beneficent (Braund 228 and 677), while another from Egypt recognizes a strategus for his generosity, justice, and effective administration of public affairs (no. 560). An Ephesian inscription ascribes ἐπιμελεῖσθαι and προνοεῖν to the duties of provincial magistrates (no. 586). Inscriptions at Aphrodisias also honor individuals other than the princeps for deeds similar to a king's (Reynolds 28-30). In addition, the frieze honoring

---

[105] This decree resembles the Philanthropa of the Hellenistic kings, gracious gestures which we will discuss in the next chapter.

[106] Jos. *Bel.* 2.175-77; *Ant.* 18.60-62; Sherk 1988: 39. Cf. *Ant.*18.55-59 which reports Pilate's attempt to introduce images of Caesar into Jerusalem and the resulting Jewish resistance. Again, Pilate failed to respect his subjects' (legal) customs.

Zoilos, Octavian's freedman, presents Honor (Τιμή) crowning Zoilos, while Courage ('Ανδρεία) holds a shield and looks on; Roma sits nearby, leaning on a shield.[107] Honor and valor were not therefore the exclusive domain of a ruler. These examples serve to remind us that good king *topoi* were part of the broader vocabulary of honor.

Fourth, the wider applicability of many kingship *topoi* points us further to the actual experiences of real people. People whose taxes were raised or remitted formed opinions about their ruler. People whose punishments were administered with malice or commuted with kindness necessarily formed ideas about their ruler. People who suffered injustice and those who successfully obtained intervention also developed opinions about their ruler. In these situations or in others (e.g., when benefactions were doled out or asylum was claimed), good king *topoi* moved from the realm of philosophers and literature and entered (to echo Charlesworth) the world of farmers and merchants.[108]

In conclusion, then, information about kings, and particularly Roman emperors, was widespread and available to many (particularly urban) people. To be sure, some of the items we have noted had a restricted audience (silver and cameos), while some required literacy (inscriptions). But the size, location, and decoration of imperial sanctuaries required neither education nor the price of admission to be understood. Rituals also expressed the relationship between emperor and subject, while dressing it with fun and excitement. Statues conveyed numerous messages, as did coins. With just these, however, divinity, power, wealth, conquest, security, and benefaction might be the only messages which one received about good rule. Assizes and decrees, however, made the emperor's justice apparent, while access to asylum lent him the appearance of mercy. For a more articulate and detailed view of good rule we must assume that the stage offered insight and that other public assemblies did as well. Mostly, though, public encomia must have taken the ideas common to literature and presented them to the populace at large. Although I admit that we do not know for sure what was said in any particular encomiastic competition, I find it hard to believe that an orator trying to win a prize would ignore a treasure-trove of material, viz., the virtues, especially since extant orations (e.g., by Pliny and Dio Chrysostom) do dwell on them.

---

[107] Erim, *Aphrodisias: City of Venus Aphrodite*, 137-39.

[108] Lest I paint too rosy a picture, I should note that many did not find Roman domination agreeable. What came to some minds when confronted with Rome was tyranny, not justice, mercy, or peace. See, for example, Adela Yarbro Collins, *Crisis and Catharsis: The Power of Apocalypse* (Philadelphia: Westminster Press, 1984), 88-94.

3. Survey of the Good King *Topoi*

The preceding surveys of literature, artifacts, and social contexts should raise the expectation that we can identify many *topoi*. The following survey will establish that.[109] As a way of bringing order to what follows, I will follow the suggestions which the rhetorical handbooks offer for structuring epideictic rhetoric.[110] While I will do this simply for the sake of convenience, there is a rhetorical logic to the approach inasmuch as commonplaces are important building blocks for encomia.[111]

Around the first century AD, encomiasts organized their praises under a few general headings. Cicero divided praiseworthy qualities into external traits (which are fortune's gifts), virtues, and deeds, the latter two being of greater significance than the first. The *Rhetorica ad Herennium* divides

---

[109] For other discussions of the good king *topoi* see W. Schubart, "Das hellenistische Königsideal nach Inschriften und Papyri," *Archiv für Papyrusforschung* 12 (1937): 1-26; idem, "Das Königsbild des Hellenismus," *Die Antike* 13 (1937): 272-88; Lothar Wickert, "Princeps," *RE* 22.2 (1954): 1998-2296, esp. 2222-34; Pierre Hadot, "Fürstenspiegel," *RAC* 8 (1972): 555-632; G. J. D. Aalders, *Political Thought in Hellenistic Times* (Amsterdam: Adolf M. Hakkert, 1975), 17-27; Claire Préaux, "L'Image du roi de l'époque hellénistique," in *Images of Man in Ancient and Medieval Thought: Studia Gerardo Verbeke ab Amicis et Collegis Dicata*, eds. F. Bossier, et al., Symbolae Facultatis Litterarum et Philosophiae Lovaniensis A/1 (Leuven University Press, 1976), 53-75; L. De Blois, "Traditional Virtues and New Spiritual Qualities in Third Century Views of Empire, Emperorship and Practical Politics," *Mnemosyne* 47 (1994): 166-76; Farber, "The *Cyropaedia* and Hellenistic Kingship," 499-513; Walbank, "Monarchies and Monarchic Ideas," 81-84; and Cairns, *Virgil's Augustan Epic*, 18-21. Cairns offers the most comprehensive classification. For discussions of a specific dynasty see Ludwig Koenen, "Die Adaptation ägyptischer Königsideologie am Ptolemäerhof," in *Egypt and the Hellenistic World*, 143-90; and Samuel, *Shifting Sands of History*, ch. 5 ("The Ideology of Ptolemaic Monarchy"). For discussion of a particular king see Helen S. Lund, *Lysimachus: A Study in Early Hellenistic Kingship* (London: Routledge, 1992), 153-83. Leon Mooren alerts us to the distinctiveness of a particular kingdom as he distinguishes the constitutional structure of the Macedonian kingdom from the other Hellenistic kingdoms ("The Nature of the Hellenistic Monarchy," in *Egypt and the Hellenistic World: Proceedings of the International Colloquium, Leuven — 24-26 May 1982*, eds. E. Van 't Dack, P. Van Dessel, and W. Van Grucht, Studia Hellenistica 27 [Louvain, 1983], 205-40).

[110] See Cic. *De or.* 1.341-49; *Rhet. ad Her.* 3.13-15; Quin. 3.7.10-18. Menander Rhetor's *Basilikos logos* recommends a less hierarchical structure, but essentially the same topics. Pernot surveys the history of the encomium from Pericles to Cicero (*La rhétorique de l'éloge*, 19-53), then turns to the imperial period (pp. 55-111).

[111] In fact, in the progymnastic exercises, encomium and denunciation were the very next step after the commonplace. See Stanley F. Bonner, *Education in Ancient Rome: From the elder Cato to the younger Pliny* (Berkeley: University of California Press, 1977), 264-66.

praises into those concerning external circumstances, physical advantages, and virtues; this scheme divides Cicero's first category into two and combines his last two into one. Quintilian analyzes encomia into time prior to birth (country, parents, and omens), time during which one lived, and then time subsequent to life (divine honors, statues, children, laws enacted, enduring innovations or handiwork). The middle category naturally receives the greatest emphasis and is further divided into the same categories as those found in *Rhetorica ad Herennium*, viz., virtues, physical endowments and external circumstances. Quintilian explicitly agrees with Cicero, and tacitly with the *Rhetorica ad Herennium*, that virtues of character are much more important than physical or external virtues, so that these must be the focus of encomia.

One area, then, of good king *topoi* arises from the king's *physical qualities*. Though encomia tended to focus on strength, size, agility, health, and beauty, physiognomical treatises greatly expanded the repertoire.[112] Appian relates an anecdote about Seleucus in which he restrained a loose bull with his bare hands; to this story Appian adds the comment, "for which reason his statues are ornamented with horns" (*Syr.* 57). While the distinction between strength and beauty, or between health and strength is essentially artificial, it is beauty which receives the greatest emphasis among good king *topoi*.[113] Xenophon and Philo attribute this quality to their respective heroes, Cyrus and Moses. Philodemus explains that by itself beauty is worthless; nevertheless, it has the great utility of impressing common people, terrifying enemies, and extending to the king a divine quality.[114] Tacitus commented that both Germanicus and Alexander the Great were handsome (*Ann.* 2.73). In his *Panegyricus*, Pliny spoke with delight about the majesty reflected in Trajan's appearance:

His splendid bearing and tall stature, his fine head and noble countenance, to say nothing of the firm strength of his maturity and the premature signs of advancing age with which the gods have seen fit to mark his hair and so enhance his look of majesty — are these not sufficient signs to proclaim him far and wide for what he is: our prince? (4.7)

---

[112] On physiognomy see Tamsyn Barton, "The *inventio* of Nero," 56-58. On the image of the king and Plutarch's criticism of it, see W. Jeffrey Tatum, "The Regal Image in Plutarch's *Lives*," *JHS* 114 (1996): 135-51.

[113] Xen. *Cyr.* 8.1.40-42; FGH 76F 13; *Rhet. Alex.* 1420a; Plaut. *Mil.* 10; Philod. *Good King* 37-8; Cal. Sic. *Ec.* 4.55ff., 85ff. and 137; 7.6; Philo *De vita Mos.* 1.19; Sen. *Apoc.* 5.2-3; Tac. *Hist.* 1.7; Suet. *Claud.* 4.30; Am. Mar. 16.10.10; Aes. *Fab.* 126; 244; 246; Stob. *Anth.* 4.7.62 (= Diot. Περὶ βασ.).

[114] See also Jos. *Ant.* 19.344 (cf. Acts 12:21); Plut. *Pel.* 35.1.

Of course, this rhetoric cuts both ways. Suetonius mocked Nero who "never wore the same clothes twice."[115] And pity poor Claudius whose visage not only embarrassed his family, but scared even Herakles.[116]

In the Hellenistic kingdoms and in the Roman empire, relatively few people actually saw the king or emperor. Rulers therefore made their impressions on people through their imagery more than by bodily presence. On coins, reliefs, and statues appearance became more than a subject for compliments or jokes: images became powerful tools for self-presentation. Alexander apparently recognized this and

decreed that only Lysippos should make his portrait. For only Lysippos, it seems, brought out his real character in the bronze and gave form to his essential excellence. For others, in their eagerness to imitate the turn of his neck and the expressive, liquid glance of his eyes, failed to preserve his manly and leonine quality" (Plut. *De Alex. mag. fort.* 2.2.3).

Not only was care required, but choices had to be made. One might adopt an idealized youthful appearance to suggest beauty and vigor or an older visage to suggest sagacity and dignity (but not too old). One might seek associations with divinity, as many rulers did by using Herakles' imagery.[117] To cite a more specific example: after Actium, Octavian revised his public image, turning from expressive Hellenistic styles to restrained Roman ones, a conscious ploy to herald his return to Republican values.[118] Clothing too, or rather costume, was important: Augustus as togate priest or cuirassed general or half-nude hero proclaims the peace which he provided, while accentuating his piety, triumphs, or divinity.[119] Materials also made a statement. Whereas Augustus set a

---

[115] *Nero* 30. Cp. *Gaius* 52.

[116] Sen. *Apoc.* 5.2-3. Suetonius also expressed shock that Claudius went out in public all bundled up. "Unheard of!" (*Clau.* 2; cf. 30). On Caligula see Sen. *De cons. sap.* 18.1; cf. *De ira* 3.19.1.

[117] Olga Palagia, "Imitation of Herakles in Ruler Portraiture: A Survey, from Alexander to Maximinus Daza," *Boreas* 9 (1986): 137-51. For the creation of Alexander imagery see Bente Kilerich, "Physiognomics and the Iconography of Alexander," *Symbolae Osloenses* 58 (1988): 51-66; J. J. Pollitt, *Art in the Hellenistic Age* (Cambridge University Press, 1986), 19-37. Lysimachus linked his lion-killer legend to his royal imagery to stress his strength and courage and to draw connections between himself and both Alexander and Herakles (Lund, *Lysimachus*, 160-61).

[118] Paul Zanker, *The Power of Images in the Age of Augustus*, trans. Alan Shapiro, Jerome Lectures 16 (Ann Arbor: University of Michigan Press, 1988), chs. 1-3.

[119] I refer to the programmatic Ara Pacis, inspiring Prima Porta statue, and stunning Gemma Augustea cameo, respectively. For commentary and excellent reproductions see Niels Hannestad, *Roman Art and Imperial Policy* (Aarhus University Press, 1988), 62-74, 50-56, and 78-80. Cornelius Vermeule thinks that statues of the emperor in Greece

precedent of declining statues made of precious metals, Gaius Caligula, Nero, Domitian, Commodus, and Caracalla did otherwise.[120] While such visual statements were distinct from encomia per se, they shared the same concern with appearance and the same assumption that appearance said something about the ruler's qualifications for his position.[121]

A second category of encomiastic topics derive from *external circumstances*. These include such things as oracles, ancestry, education, friends, wealth, offices, powers, accomplishments, honors, and titles. *Oracles* and portents could herald the birth and career of a king. According to Callimachus, Apollo foretold the coming of Ptolemy II (*Hymn* 4.165ff.) According to Euphorion, the mother of the Seleucid ruler predicted the scope of her son's empire prior to his birth (frg. 174 Powell). Suetonius recorded a dozen portents of Augustus' career.[122]

In kingship literature, *ancestry* provided encomiastic *topoi* and moral examples.[123] Distinguished parents could add to their children's renown, whereas ignoble parentage was a cause for blame.[124] A good predecessor could function as an example to hold up to a king for emulation (Sen. *De clem.* 1.9-10). To offer a king the opposite counsel, viz., avoid the errors of a bad father, could prove dangerous to the encomiast; nevertheless, Pliny used contrasts between Trajan and his successor to magnify Trajan's merits. And, unable to resist a scandal, Suetonius introduced the life of

---

and Asia Minor "probably were divided equally between those showing the subject in cuirass, those presenting him in the toga or himation, and those representing him in the heroic nude guise of a divinity or major hero" (p. 69; cf. pp. 40-41 and 65-66).

[120] K. Scott, "The Significance of Statues in Precious Metals in Emperor Worship," *TAPA* 62 (1931): 123. See also Duncan Fishwick's comments in "Dio and Maecenas," 272-73. If the list of dissenting emperors does not reflect strict historical fact, it only serves to underscore the nature of the rhetoric used to describe good and bad emperors. Either way, the material of imperial statues became the substance of a rhetorical *topos*.

[121] On Augustan imagery see Klaus Vierneisel and Paul Zanker, eds., *Die Bildnisse des Augustus. Herrscherbild und Politik im kaiserlichen Rom* (Munich: Glyptothek, 1978); Susan Walker and Andrew Burnett, *The Image of Augustus* (London: British Musuem Publications, 1981).

[122] *Aug.* 94. Cp. *Tib.* 14.

[123] Pernot divides good birth into homeland and family. The former includes city, native country, and nation (*ethnos*), the latter parents and ancestors (*La rhétorique de l'éloge*, 1: 155).

[124] Jos. *Bel.* 2.182-83; Ps.-Plut. *Mor.* 1b; Sherk 1988: 42f. Recall the problems Herod the Great encountered because of his Idumean origins. Ancestry was also important for legitimacy (J. Gwyn Griffiths, "Apocalyptic in the Hellenistic Era," in *Apocalypticism in the Mediterranean World and the Near East: Proceedings of the International Colloquium on Apocalypticism: Uppsala, August 12-17, 1979*, ed. David Hellholm, 2d ed. (Tübingen: J. C. B. Mohr [Paul Siebeck], 1989), 273-79.

Claudius by reporting his adulterous conception and quoting the popular (and sarcastic) epigram which it inspired:

> How fortunate those parents are for whom
> Their child is only three months in the womb!

More seriously, one could sound a high note of praise by looking back beyond a ruler's parents to extol his or her divine ancestry (Theoc. *Id.* 17).

Divine ancestry also furnished an important point of royal propaganda, even more so if we look beyond literary texts.[125] For example, stories circulated reporting the divine paternity of rulers;[126] monuments and artifacts depicted the divine origins of the Julian family;[127] images presented rulers in divine guise; Roman imperial nomenclature regularly claimed divine filiation. Vespasian received acclamation as "Son of Ammon" (Sherk 1988: 81). Such associations promoted claims to personal excellence and dynastic legitimacy.

Ancestry myths also had important social and economic consequences. The Seleucids were inclined to give benefactions to Miletus because of their kinship to Apollo, who had an important sanctuary there (Welles 22). Augustus (and his successors) showered Illium with gifts out of respect for his family's reputed origins.[128] Thus, encomia, propaganda, and philanthropy all drew on a ruler's ancestry.

Given the Platonic tradition of the philosopher-king, *education* also appears among good king *topoi*.[129] How it appears in actual use depends on the speaker's views of the virtuous life; nevertheless, education is important for a king because it produces virtue, in theory the *sine qua non*

---

[125] For example, Burstein 99: "The great king, Ptolemaios (III), son of King Ptolemaios and of Queen Arsinoe, the gods Adelphoi, the children of King Ptolemaios and of Queen Berenike, the gods Soteres, descended through his father from Herakles, the son of Zeus, and through his mother from Dionysos, the son of Zeus ..."

[126] E.g., Alexander (Plut. *Alex.* 2.1-3.4; Arr. *Alex. ana.* 7.29.3; 7.30.2-3), Seleucus I (Susan Sherwin-White and Amélie Kuhrt, *From Samarkhand to Sardis: An New Approach to the Seleucid Empire*, Hellenistic Culture and Society 13 [Berkeley: University of California Press, 1993], 27-28), and Augustus (Suet. *Aug.* 94).

[127] On a large scale, the Forum Julium whose temple was dedicated to Venus Genetrix advertised the divine ancestry of the Julian *gens*; the Forum Augustum articulated Augustus' divine ancestry. Similarly the Sebasteion in Aphrodisias presented Aphrodite as the προμήτωρ of the θεοί Σεβαστοί. On a smaller scale, the dolphin beside the lower leg of the Prima Porta statue alludes to Venus. An inscription honoring Julius Caesar explicitly praised his descent from Ares and Aphrodite (SIG 760; trans. Sherk 1984: 79d).

[128] Vermeule, 71-72. Coins also reflect this imperial interest (72).

[129] E.g., Philo *De leg. ad Gai.* 142.

of good rule.[130] That literate circles were particularly interested in this *topos* comes as no surprise; however, the *topos* appeared elsewhere. A copy of an Athenian decree found in Pergamon salutes the king and queen for "having supervised the education of [their sons] well and prudently."[131] An inscription from Ephesus offers public tribute to the tutor of Attalos III.[132] We should note, though, that a prince's education involved more than virtue. At the pragmatic level, a prince needed to learn how to rule, as well as the military arts.[133] But, then, that cannot be separated from *virtus*.

In the praise of kings, their *friends* do not figure very prominently.[134] What is striking, however, is to have other kings as clients.[135] Still, the vital role which the king's friends play in his administration point to six significant considerations. First, if a king has no friends, then no doubt he is a tyrant (Cic. *Tusc.* 5.63). Second, a king opens himself to criticism if his friends are ignoble, but invites praise if he keeps good company. Third, by making friends of good people the king effectively promotes virtue within his realm. Fourth, since the king appoints his friends to administrative posts, much depends on their individual competence and integrity. Fifth, a good king needs good counselors (and should listen to them). If they offer poor advice, the ruler will run the risk of improper action. Sixth, in all these matters, in counsel, in appointments, in associations, the king must also beware of flatterers. Thus, as intimates of the king, as administrative functionaries and royal counselors, the king's friends affected significantly life within the kingdom. Their role in a good king's rule would have been greater than encomiastic rhetoric indicates.[136]

---

[130] E.g., Ps.-Aristid. Εἰς βασ. 11. See Cicero's comments on Plato's philosopher-king in Cicero's own treatise on good government (*Qfr.* 1.1.29).

[131] OGIS 248; trans. Burstein 38.

[132] Wankel, *I. Ephesos.* 202; trans. Burstein 90.

[133] Xen. *Ana.* 1.9.4-5. Hunting is a vital part of the prince's curriculum, for it teaches him courage and skills useful in war: Xen. *Ana.* 1.9.6.

[134] The king's friends do appear frequently in political theory: Arist. *Pol.* 1,287b 25.

[135] E.g., Aug. *Res ges.* 27, 32-33; Sherk 1988: 36a and 42b; Small. 401 (trans. Braund 673); *RIC* 2: no. 667 (REX PARTHIS DATUS), a senatorial issue honoring Trajan (cf. nos. 310, 668-69). In the Greek world, Cleopatra was called "queen of kings" (*CRR* no. 1210), while the Rosetta stone referred to the "lord of crowns" (Burstein 103); on Ptolemy III see Burstein 99. Cp. the common Achaemenid titulature "king of kings" and reference to the Persian ruler as "the great king" in contrast to στρατηγοί, σατράποι, and βασιλεῖς. "King of kings" remained a title for the Parthian king in a letter written in 21 AD (Welles 75).

[136] The role of the good counselor is emphasized throughout Philodemus' *Good King*. See also *Ep. Arist.* 125 and 286. The matter of friends points to the chasm between

Offices and powers likewise receive limited play. What appears to contradict this claim, viz., Roman imperial inscriptions, is rather the exception that proves the rule. The emperor's extensive list of offices originated from the attempt to cloak a *de facto* monarchy behind traditional republican terminology. Most other political contexts did not require such circumlocution. Kingship essays obviously have no problem with the office of king and therefore focus on that single, most lofty office and unparalleled power.

Kings receive a variety of *titles*. Some are idiosyncratic (e.g., Monophthalmos), while some are preferred by dynastic lines.[137] Some honorifics stress their recipients' virtues or relationship to a divinity. Of the former, two stand out, Savior (σωτήρ) and Benefactor (εὐεργήτης);[138]

---

encomiastic rhetoric and reality. Friends were crucial for successful rule, especially as the size of the territory grew larger. See Richard A. Billows, *Antigonos the One-Eyed and the Creation of the Hellenistic State*, Hellenistic Culture and Society 4 (Berkeley: University of California Press, 1990), 155-60; Lund, *Lysimachus*, 178-82; Samuel, "Ptolemies and Ideology," 185-89. Sherwin-White and Kuhrt succinctly state, "The 'Friends' of the king were appointed and deployed by him in crucial roles — as generals, governors, ambassadors — and were structurally indispensable to the functioning of the monarchy" (*From Samarkhand to Sardis,* 133). Cf. 1 Macc 10:18-20; 13:36; 14:38. Augustus' friends Agrippa and Maecenas are also illustrative. However, the Roman situation is structurally different from the Hellenistic. The Senate provided the body to which the emperor ought to turn for counsel and which should furnish government officials. As a result, how the emperor treated the Senate became one of the key criteria for his reputation. Imperial freedmen and the praetorian guard helped to confuse the picture.

[137] Eusebes was a favorite of Cappadocian rulers, e.g., Ariarathes IV, V, IX, and X, Ariobarzanes III. Ariarathes V, VI, and IX also added Philopator, while Ariarathes VII added Philometor. Five Parthian kings received the title Dikaios: Mithridates II, Orodes I, Mithridates III, Pacorus I, and Phraates IV.

[138] Savior became standard nomenclature for Ptolemy I, Antiochus I, Attalus I, Seleucid III, Demetrius I of Syria, and Ptolemy IX (see also Xen. *Ag.* 11.13; Dem. *De cor.* 43; Dion. Hal. *Ant.* 4.32.1; Dio Chrys. 3.6; Dio Cas. 52.39.3); it was even given to Verres (Cic. *Ver.* 2.2.154). A Tiberian inscription from Gytheum, Laconia refers to Augustus as the "divine Caesar Augustus Savior Liberator, son of god" (EJ 102; trans. Braund 127). The title Benefactor was added to Ptolemy III, Antigonus III Doson, Mithridates V, Ptolemy VIII, and Nicomedes III. See Norman Davis and Colin M. Kraay, *The Hellenistic Kingdoms: Portrait Coins and History* (London: Thames and Hudson, 1973), 274-75; Andrew Erskine, "The Romans as Common Benefactors," *Historia* 43 (1994): 70-87. References to emperors as "benefactor and savior" are common in inscriptions (e.g., EJ 72 and 78; Small. 134, 135, 137, 419); cp. also the letter to Antiochus IV in Jos. *Ant.* 12.261. Benefactor could be conveniently corrupted to Malefactor (Burstein 103). Dio Cassius discussed the complications of benefaction (52.11.3-12.7). Klaus Bringmann provides an interesting analysis of the phenomena of benefaction in "The King as Benefactor: Some Remarks on Ideal Kingship in the Age of

noteworthy also are Philadelphos (φιλάδελφος), Philopator (φιλοπάτωρ), and Nicator (νικήτωρ).[139] As for divine references, monarchs took the title Epiphanes (ἐπιφανής), Theos (θεός), or the name of some god,[140] while Roman emperors commonly incorporated "son of god" into their nomenclature and were described as divine.[141]

Though not technically titles, two other appellations deserve notice, namely, father and shepherd.[142] These two designations are widespread, a

---

Hellenism," in *Images and Ideologies: Self-definition in the Hellenistic World*, eds. Anthony Bulloch, et al., Hellenistic Culture and Society 12 (Berkeley: University of California Press, 1993), 7-24. V. Nutton focuses on second and third century AD Greek attitudes toward Roman benefaction, pointing out that Greeks praised peace, freedom, common laws, common fatherland, and access to help from the Romans, especially the emperor ("The Beneficial Ideology," in *Imperialism in the Ancient World*, eds. P. D. A. Garnsey and C. R. Whittaker [Cambridge University Press, 1978], 209-21).

[139] Nicator: Seleucus I and Demetrius II of Syria. Philadelphos: Ptolemy II and Attalus II. Philopater: Ptolemy IV and Seleucus IV, Mithridates IV, Ariobarzanes II (cp. Philometor: Attalus III). Ludwig Koenen demonstrates how malleable royal titles were in Egypt: Greek titles simultaneously expressed Egyptian ideas ("The Ptolemaic King as a Religious Figure," in *Images and Ideologies*, 61-66; idem, "Die Adaption ägyptischer Königsideologie am Ptolemäerhof," in *Egypt and the Hellenistic World*, 152-70).

[140] Epiphanes: Ptolemy V, Antiochus IV (cleverly ridiculed as Epimanes, Polyb. 26.1.7), Nicomedes II, and Ariarathes VI. A decree of the Asian League refers to the "epiphany" of Augustus (EJ 98); cp. also inscriptions from Ephesus calling Julius Caesar "god manifest" (Sherk 1984: 79d) and from Phrygia and Lycia describing Claudius as "god manifest" (Small. 134 and 136); likewise Nero (Small. 47). Theos: Antiochus II and Ptolemy XII. Sherk offers an example of a letter from Julius Caesar which began with the abscript [Γράμματα] Καίσαρος θεοῦ (Sherk 1969: 26, col. b). Inscriptions refer to θεός Σεβαστός (EJ 72, 88, 93, 102, etc.). EJ 134 calls Tiberius θεός! Philo labels Moses θεός καὶ βασιλεύς (*De vita Mos.* 1.158). Titular deities: Ptolemy XII Neos Dionysos and Mithradates VI Eupator Dionysos. The figure of Dionysos also played an important role in pre-Actium propaganda. After Augustus, see Sherk 1988: 42b, "... the goddess New Aphrodite, Drusilla"; 71, "Nero Zeus the Deliverer."

[141] On Alexander the Great's divinity see Plutarch *Alex.* 27.5-28.6 and specifically 27.5 and 9 for the designation "son of god." Numerous inscriptions refer to the Roman emperor as god, son of god, or divine (e.g., EJ 98, 106, 108, 115, 134, 226). Coins bearing DIVI FILIUS are too common to require annotation, as is the phenomenon of ruler cult. Among many possible inscriptions, see Jalabert 3.1: no. 718 (Octavian is θεοῦ υἱός).

[142] Father: Hom. *Od.* 2.47 and 234; Herod. 3.89; Xen. *Cyr.* 8.1.1-2, 44; 8.2.9; *Ag.* 7.3; 8.1; Arist. *E. N.* 1160b 25; Philod. *Good King* 24; Cic. *Qfr.* 1.1.31; Philo *De spec. leg.* 4.184; Sen. *Ep.* 73; Epict. 1.6.40; App. *Syr.* 61; Dio Chrys. 1.22; 53.12; Ps.-Plut. *De vita et poe. Hom.* 2.182; Ps.-Aristid. Εἰς βασ. 22; and Stob. 4.7.8 (= Hom. *Od.* 2.234); 4.7.62 (= Diot. Περὶ βασ.); 4.7.63 (= Sthen. Περὶ βασ.); and 4.7.67 (= Mus. Ruf. Φιλ. βασ.; cf. frg. 8 Lutz). Cp. Dio Chrys. 53.12. See T. R. Stevenson, "The Ideal Benefactor and the Father Analogy in Greek and Roman Thought," *CQ* 42 (1992): 421-36.

popularity based on the authority of Homeric usage as much as anything else. In fact, Philo indicates that some found the comparison of a king with a shepherd humorous; nevertheless, Philo (like so many others) argues that the work each does is similar. That similarity helps the Homeric metaphor to persist in the literary tradition. As for father, this reflects the gentleness, concern, and providential care which the good king shows to his subjects. With *Pater Patriae* the Roman Empire promoted father from metaphor to official titulature. In view of Republican tradition, the title expressed not only care but the salvation of the Roman people in time of great duress. Tiberius' receipt of the honorific designation signified its transition from personal accomplishment to dynastic nomenclature.

Kings may be praised for their *wealth*.[143] More important, though, are considerations of how one obtains wealth and what one does with it.[144] If accumulation of wealth comes through rapacity, the king deserves only criticism. Wasting money also warrants censure, which Nero's Golden Palace and other excessively grandiose projects elicited from Suetonius.[145] Hoarding money also leads to objections.[146] Tiberius' reputation suffered from this. That he built up his wealth mattered little. In the shadow of Augustus' fantastic generosity, Tiberius was regarded as cheap.[147] On the other hand, the ruler who distributes gifts generously will receive praise; moreover, a king needs to be generous, because that is precisely what people expect of the good king: he ought always to be giving gifts to his family, friends, and cities, and always to display φιλανθρωπία. Whether or not a king bore the epithet Euergetes, people expected benefactions from him. This cannot be overemphasized, as inscriptions indicate:

Shepherd: Hom. *Il.* 4.296; Xen. *Cyr.* 1.1.2; *Mem.* 3.2; Plato *Pol.* 265d; 268a; etc.; Arist. *E. N.* 1161a 12ff.; Ps.-Anach. *Ep.* 7; Ecphantus in Stob. 4.7.64; Archytas of Tarentum in Stob. 4.5.61; Philo *De agr.* 47.2; *De Ios.* 2; *De leg. ad Gai.* 44; *Quod om. pr. lib.* 31; *De vita Mos.* 1.60-64; Epict. 3.22.34-35; Dio Chrys. 1.13; 2.6; 3.41; 4.43-44; Suet. *Tib.* 32; Ps.-Aristid. Εἰς βασ. 22; Stob. *Anth.* 4.5.61 (= Archy.) and 4.7.64 (= Ecph. Περὶ βασ.).

[143] Theoc. *Id.* 17; Plaut. *Rud.* 931.

[144] Cp. the criteria for evaluating a philosopher's wealth in Sen. *De vit. b.* 23.1.

[145] *Nero* 30-32. Cp. Sal. *Cat.* 13. See, however, Jaś Elsner, "Constructing Decadence: The Representation of Nero as Imperial Builder," in *Reflections of Nero: Culture, History, & Representation*, eds. Jaś Elsner and Jamie Masters (Chapel Hill: University of North Carolina Press, 1994), 112-27.

[146] Theoc. *Id.* 17. Cp. the example of Agesilaus (Xen. *Ag.* 11.8).

[147] Cp. Lysimachus the *gaxophylax* (Lund, *Lysimachus*, 168-9) and Galba, whose reputation for simplicity and moderation looked like miserliness once he became emperor (Plut. *Gal.* 3.2). See also criticism of Vespasian in Suet. *Vesp.* 19.

εὐεργήτης and φιλάνθρωπος and their cognates may be the most common attributes of kings found in extant inscriptions. Arrian summed up this crucial kingship *topos*, writing about Alexander: "As for money, he was very sparing in using it for his own pleasures, but most liberal in employing it for the benefit of others."[148]

As previous mention of εὐεργήτης already indicates, *accomplishments and honors* play a large role in the praise of kings. Few generalizations can, however, be stated about them, because praise for such things, more than any other, depends on what things individual rulers actually do. Examples of praiseworthy deeds include the founding of cities; military successes; the elimination of bandits or pirates; establishing concord, peace, safety, law and order, and justice; opposition to false charges; legislation; relief from billeting; various asyla; respect for gods and temples; reception of supplicants; the granting of priesthoods; supplying relief for victims of earthquake and famine; establishing price controls; grants of land or special privileges; granting tax relief or exemption; allowing autonomy; the release of hostages; discharging civic services; providing entertainments; building temples, basilicas, baths, libraries, fora, porticoes, roads, harbors, aqueducts, and fountains; or any other thing which promotes the welfare of the community or state.[149] The blessings which Augustus provided find eloquent expression in Horace's poetry:

> The ox tramps safely in our fields,
> Ceres and Faustita nourish our corn,
> Sailors glide on a tranquil sea,
> Good faith shrinks from blame,
>
> Families stay chaste, undefiled,
> Law and morality prevail over sin,
> Women's children resemble their fathers,
> Punishment chases after guilt (*Ode* 4.5).

Elsewhere, Horace writes,

> As long as Augustus guards this Empire
> We'll know no civil war, no riots, no hatred
> Forging new swords, setting cities at each other's
> Throats: peace will continue, will remain (*Ode* 4.15).

---

[148] *Alex. ana.* 7.28.3; cp. Theoc. *Id.* 17.

[149] Aristophanes would interject two more of Sovereignty's benefits: public assistance officers and jury pay (*Aves* 1541)!

As Horace indicates, then, subjects look to their ruler for a wide range of blessings.[150] The high regard in which public munificence was held appears clearly in the honors which benefactors in turn received in antiquity (as recorded in inscriptions). Benefactors received citizenship, tax-exemption, crowns, statues, inscriptions, front-row seats, public proclamations, eponymous holidays, and, for the particularly outstanding, cults.

This category of accomplishments also overlaps with the ruler's virtues, for what he does indicates what quality of person he is.[151] If he brings famine relief, he is generous. If his courts are equitable, he is just. Separation of deeds and virtues is therefore too great an abstraction.[152] A good king, by definition, then possesses numerous virtues, our third subdivision of good king *topoi*.[153] Encomiasts typically enumerate the virtues

---

[150] Cp. Xen. *Cyr.* 1.6.24; Isoc. *Ev.* 45; *Hel.* 37; Plut. *Alex.* 39; Dio Chrys. 1.23-25; 2.72; Sen. *Ep.* 90.5; Welles 7, 15, 25, 30, 35, 64, and 75. Horace is more succinct in his *Letter to Augustus*, where he praises the emperor for "guarding our Italian state with arms, gracing her with morals, and reforming her with laws" (*Ep.* 2.1.1-4).

[151] *Rhetorica ad Herennium* in fact does discuss deeds and virtues together (3.14). Countless inscriptions praise kings (and many other kinds of people) for virtue; often inscriptions conclude with an unelaborated ἀρετῆς ἕνεκα or the combination ἀρετῆς καὶ εὐνοίας (or εὐεργεσίας). The simple ἀρετῆς ἕνεκα however, can be shorthand for a lot. For example, the city of Lycosura honored Nicasippus and his wife Timasistrata by placing images of them in the temple. These images bore the inscription, "The city of the Lycosurans honored Nicasippus, son of Philippus, and Timasistrata, daughter of Onasicritus, for their virtue" (Braund 677). We know this because a lengthy inscription was also displayed which related this information (*ibid.*). This inscription relates the reasons for honoring Nicasippus in greater detail. He was "a good man and descended from forefathers who were fine and illustrious and who gave their due to the city"; moreover, he was pious and just to both gods and people. The major reason, though, was that he "accepted the priesthood of the Mistress during an Olympic year when no one was willing to come forward and, when money had not accrued for the mysteries." All these things were compressed on the images into the simple ἀρετῆς ἕνεκα.

[152] Pernot states, "Les actions vertueuses restent à l'époque impériale, de l'avis unanime, le *topos* le plus important"; he adds that "dans la doctrine épidictique, les actions manifestent les vertus, et que celles-ci offrent même, le plus souvent, les rubriques sous lesquelles seront rangées les *praxeis*. L'architecture du *topos* consiste donc dans le classement des vertus" (*La rhétorique de l'éloge*, 1: 165). In n. 199 he adds, "Ce *topos* est généralement appelé *topos* des *praxis*; mais on le désigne aussi par le mot *aretai*. *Erga* est plus rare."

[153] Dio Chrysostom offers rather complete recitations of the good king's virtues: *Or.* 1.4-6; 1.39-41; 2.66-77. Josephus is succinct in listing the virtues of David: ἀνδρεῖος, σώφρων, ἐπιεικής, χρηστός, δίκαιος, φιλάνθρωπος (*Ant.* 7.391).

of good kings by describing their good deeds and by ascribing to them the canonical virtues.[154]

The good ruler can be such only by hard work. As king he assumes responsibility for the well-being of his subjects and cares for them.[155] Pseudo-Plato in fact defines ἀρχή as ἐπιμέλεια τοῦ παντός (*Def.* 415b). Dio Chrysostom summarizes the king's role as "watchful, fatherly concern."[156] Such rule involves unending toil;[157] sleepless nights are part of the job.[158] Thus Agamemnon was instructed (Hom. *Il.* 2.24-25):

> To sleep the whole night through beseemeth not a man that is a counsellor,
> to whom a host is entrusted, and upon whom rest so many cares.

These *topoi* combine in an amusing anecdote about flattery, in which a flatterer rose in the Senate and "frankly" addressed Tiberius, leveling the serious charge that Tiberius neglected himself (ἀμελεῖς σεαυτοῦ), so caught up was he in his concerns and labors (φροντίσι καὶ πόνοις) for

---

[154] On the problem with the idea of "canonical virtues" see Helen F. North, "Canons and Hierarchies of the Cardinal Virtues in Greek and Latin Literature," *The Classical Tradition: Literary and Historical Studies in Honor of Harry Caplan*, ed. Luitpold Wallach (Ithaca, NY: Cornell University Press, 1966), 165-83. See also Pernot, *La rhétorique de l'éloge*, 1: 165-69. Pernot also explores the relationships between different virtues, indicating the problems involved in trying to schematize them as one might do in organizing a speech or as we are doing in giving structure to our present chapter (1: 169-73). Philanthropy and piety are particularly problematic (1: 170-71). Despite the problems we face when generalizing, ancient orators often used a list of virtues as the outline of their speeches, and the most common virtues form a short list: ἀνδρεία, δικαιοσύνη, σωφροσύνη, and φρόνησις, followed by εὐσέβεια and later φιλανθρωπία and perhaps ἐγκράτεια.

[155] ἐπιμέλεια: Plato *Pol.* 73; Isoc. *De pace* 91; *Ep.* 7.4; *Ep. Arist.* 245; Philo *De leg. ad Gai.* 143 and 153; Dio Chrys. 1.17-21 (τῆς ἐπιμελείας καὶ τῶν φροντίδων); 2.69 (εὔνοια and κηδεμονία); 3.39; 3.55-57; 49.3 (ἐπιμελεῖσθαι καὶ φροντίζειν); *FGH* 90 §IX (Nicolaus of Damascus); Stob. 4.5.55 (= Sopatros *Letter to Hemerios*); Welles 6, 14, and 25; Jalabert 5: no. 1998.

φροντίζειν in Dio Cas. 52.10.2; Sherk 1969: 18; and Small. 384 (trans. Braund 591). Small. 33 and 380 attribute κηδεμονία to the emperors Gaius and Claudius (trans. Braund 563 and 586); the latter also attributes ἐπιμελεῖσθαι to provincial officials; cf. Oliver 23.

[156] 53.12: τὴν ἐπιμέλειαν πατρικὴν καὶ κηδεμονικήν. Cf. Tac. *Ann.* 1.11.

[157] Hom. *Il.* 10.88-89; Xen. *Cyr.* 1.2.1; 1.5.12; 1.6.25; *Ag.* 5.3; Isoc. *Evag.* 45; Philo *De vita Mos.* 1.154; Sen. *Ad Pol. de con.* 7; Plut. *Mor.* 466e; 544b (φιλόπονος); Dio Chrys. 1.21 and 34 (φιλόπονος); 3.3, 5, 56-7, 62, 83-5, 123, 136, 137; Pliny *Pan.* 7; Dio Cas. 56.41.5.

[158] Xen. *Cyr.* 1.6.42; Philod. *Good King* 23; Plut. *Alex.* 31.9; *Cae.* 69.8; *Mor.* 71d; 544c; Dio Chrys. 1.13; 3.35; Ps.-Plut. *De vita et poe. Hom.* 2.178; Stob. 4.7.5 (= Homer *Il.* 2.24-25).

his subjects that he did not bother to rest day or night (Plut. *Mor.* 60c). While we need not worry how Tiberius escaped these charges, we should note how well they articulate the well-known expectations of the good ruler.

The good ruler then faces a daunting task. But he does not shrink from this challenge because, like a good father or shepherd, he seeks what is good for his subjects. He holds counsel and formulates plans for his subjects' well-being[159] and takes the appropriate measures to bring it about. His foresight (πρόνοια) and benefactions (εὐεργεσίαι) shape his subjects' world.[160]

In the midst of such work, frivolity has no place. The good ruler should maintain a personal bearing commensurate with his office. He should not be a playful buffoon, but should recognize decorum, maintain his dignity, and exude gravity.[161] This view encountered dissent. In the Hellenistic world, some preferred a king who was accessible to diplomatic missions.[162] The Romans in particular developed their own view in this matter. To maintain the appearance of princeps rather than monarch, the emperor assumed an affable and approachable demeanor (*moderatio, comitas,* and *civilitas*). Royal magnificence had to be balanced with collegiality with the Senate.[163]

---

[159] Xen. *Ag.* 8.5; *Cyr.* 1.6.8; Isoc. *Ev.* 44; Philod. *Good King* 32-34, 41; Sen. *Ep.* 90.5; Dio Chrys. 1.12; 2.71; 3.52, 62, and 127; Ps.-Aristid. Εἰς βασ. 14; Small. 212, 391, and 418.

[160] πρόνοια/*providentia*: Dio Chrys. 3.43, 62; Luc. *Apol.* 13; Ps.-Aristid. *Eis Rh.* 36; Ps.-Aristid. Εἰς βασ. 14; Welles 52; Reynolds 12; Braund 123, 229, 571; Oliver 19. See M. P. Charlesworth, "The Virtues of a Roman Emperor: Propaganda and the Creation of Belief," *PBA* 23 (1937): 117-22; idem, "Providentia and Aeternitas," *HTR* 29 (1936): 107-32.

εὐεργεσία: see Paul Veyne, *Bread and Circuses: Historical Sociology and Political Pluralism*, abridged with intro. Oswyn Murray, trans. Brian Pearce (New York: Penguin, 1990); above, p. 132.

[161] Isoc. *Ev.* 44; Xen. *Cyr.* 8.3.1-23; *Ag.* 11.11; Philod. *Good King* 18-21; Philo *De vita Mos.* 1.20; Dio Chrys. 1.7; 2.55-56; Aes. *Fab.* 109; Athen. *Deip.* 12.510-50; Stob. 4.5.55 and 56. Cp. Herod. 2.173-74; Plato *Rep.* 388e-389a. While Isocrates described the attempt to combine dignity and courtesy as the most difficult balancing act of all (*Ad Nic.* 34), Pliny credited Trajan as having blended perfectly seriousness and humor (*Pan.* 4.6).

[162] Andrew Wallace-Hadrill, "Civilis Princeps: Between Citizen and King," *JRS* 72 (1982): 34-35.

[163] Jean Béranger, *Recherches sur l'aspect idéologique du principat*, Schweizerische Beiträge zur Altertumswissenschaft 6 (Basel, 1953); A. Wallace-Hadrill, "Civilis Princeps," 35-41.

The good king possesses the virtues which make any person good: ἀνδρεία, δικαιοσύνη, σωφροσύνη, φρόνησις and εὐσέβεια.[164] In addition to these, he also possesses two qualities related to σωφροσύνη, ἐγκράτεια and καρτερία.[165] These qualities are crucial because the essence of kingship is raw power, that is, the ability to control wealth, to control an army, to make law, and to control people.[166] Greek authors

---

[164] ἀνδρεία: Xen. *Ag.* 6.1-3; Stob. *Anth.* 4.7.3 (= Menander); Plut. *Mor.* 544b; Dio Chrys. 2.54; 3.7, 10, 58; 4.24; Ps.-Aristid. Εἰς βασ. 35-37; Sen. *Ep.* 90 (*fortitudo*). On hunting scenes and battles in Hellenistic art as expressions of bravery, see J. J. Pollitt, *Art in the Hellenistic Age* (Cambridge University Press, 1986), 38-46. In terms of virtue, courage appears as one among a few which comprise a kind of canon; however, in terms of *Realpolitik*, courage on the battlefield is the most important quality for a king — assuming he also wins. Suetonius was careful to note that Claudius was paranoid (*Clau.* 35), while Gaius crawled under his bed during thunder storms (*Gaius* 51).

ἀνδραγαθία: Herod. 1.99; Stob. *Anth.* 4.7.3 (= Diot. Περὶ βασ.).

δικαιοσύνη: Xen. *Ag.* 4; Isoc. *Ev.* 43; Philod. *Good King* 4 and 30; Philo *De vita Mos.* 154; Dio Chrys. 1.35; 2.54; 3.7, 10, 39, 60; 4.24; Ps.-Aristid. Εἰς βασ. 16-20; Stob. *Anth.* 4.7.3 (= Menander) and 4.7.62 (= Diot. Περὶ βασ.); Braund 586.

σωφροσύνη: Philo *De vita Mos.* 1.25 and 154; Plut. *Alex.* 21.11; Dio Chrys. 2.54; 3.7, 10; Ps.-Aristid. Εἰς βασ. 25-26.

φρόνησις: Xen. *Ag.* 6.4-8 (σοφία); Philod. *Good King* 32-34, 39; Philo *De vita Mos.* 1.25; Dio Chrys. 3.7, 10, 39, 58; Ps.-Aristid. Εἰς βασ. 31; Aes. *Fab.* 126.

εὐσέβεια: Xen. *Ag.* 3; Dio Chrys. 1.15-16; Ps.-Plut. *De vita et poe. Hom.* 2.184; Ps.-Aristid. Εἰς βασ. 15. Cp. Theoc. *Id.* 17; Welles 36 and 44; Burstein 2, 48, 89, 92, and 99; Sherk 1984: 79b; Jalabert 1: no. 1; 5: no. 2707 (= Agrippa II). For examples of the pragmatic advantages gained by expressions of piety to the gods (i.e., temple patronage) see Sherwin-White and Kuhrt, *From Samarkhand to Sardis,* 25-7 and 31. The important role of temples in their local economies should not be forgotten when assessing the significance of temple patronage (e.g., Burstein 2; Richard Oster, "Ephesus as a Religious Center under the Principate, I: Paganism before Constantine," *ANRW* 2.18.3 [1990]: 1661-728). Rulers also relied on the patronage which they received from the gods or a particular god.

[165] ἐγκράτεια: Xen. *Ag.* 5; Philo *De vita Mos.* 1.154; Plut. *Alex.* 21.7; 21.11; 22.7; 23.9; Dio Chrys. 3.58; Ps.-Aristid. Εἰς βασ. 27-29. καρτερία: Xen. *Ag.* 5.2; Isoc. *Ev.* 42; Philo *De vita Mos.* 1.25 and 154. Possession of these virtues enable the king to avoid two great pitfalls: rapacity and the pursuit of pleasure.

[166] Galen quoted Posidonius who was quoting Cleanthes about the soul's passionate part (*De placitis Hippocratis et Platonis* 5.6.35; my trans.):

> Reason: What do you want, Passion? Tell me.
> Passion: I? Whatever I want to do!
> Reason: Wow, a kingly [sentiment] indeed; please, say it again.
> Passion: Whatever I desire, may it be so.

This text makes explicit the association of unlimited action with kingship. Second, the genealogy of this excerpt indicates how long-lived it was, which indicates how generally and easily it elicited assent from those who heard it. Third, the casual way in which

typically express this with more delicacy: kingship is irresponsible (ἀνυπεύθυνος).[167] Cicero described what actions unfettered authority might take, when warning about the dangers of Rullus' agrarian proposal: revenues, lands, legal proceedings, laws, magistracies, and colonies are all subject to the king's discretion; moreover, the king is free from the possibility of redress (*De lege agr.* 2.32-35). The freedom of rulers in matters of law appears very clearly in the many petitions which they received asking them to continue the policies of their predecessors.[168] Tax breaks or grants of asylum were only as valid as the will of the monarch. In theory, then, the king answers to no one (not counting assassination). The only way therefore for a society to be happy is for the king to submit to its customs and to conduct himself virtuously.[169] One hopes that the king's wishes so completely merge with the law that the law is his second nature, because, for better or worse, the king (or tyrant) is νόμος ἔμψυχος.[170] This raises the most crucial issue in the evaluation of a sovereign: does he submit to the law or stand above it? The answer to that question represents the difference between king and tyrant in the Hellenistic and Roman worlds.[171]

---

kingship in introduced says much about the concensus it expressed. The point of this text is not to define kingship; rather, the common idea of what constitutes kingship is brought to bear to characterize another matter.

[167] Herod. 3.80; Demos. *De cor.* 235; Ps.-Plato *Def.* 415b; Plut. *Cae.* 57.1; *Mor.* 826e; Dio Chrys. 3.43; Diog. L. 7.122; SVF 3.167. Cp. Reynolds 28.

[168] Reynolds presents the inscriptions which record Octavian's initial grant of asylum to Aphrodisias and the decisions of subsequent emperors to maintain that privilege. Elsewhere, see Oliver 23 and 24.

[169] Xen. *Cyr.* 1.3.18; *Ag.* 7.1-2; Isoc. *Hel.* 37; *Ep.* 7.5; *Ep. Arist.* 279; Plut. *Mor.* 152a; Dio Chrys. 3.5, 39.

[170] Xen. *Cyr.* 8.1.22; Philo *De vita Mos.* 1.162; 2.4; Stob. *Anth.* 4.1.135 (= Arch); 4.7.61 (= Diot. Περὶ βασ.); and 4.7.67 (= Mus. Ruf. Φιλ. βασ.; cf. frg. 8 Lutz). See Goodenough's discussion in "Hellenistic Kingship," 59-98. Goodenough states, "... the distinctive aspect of the Hellenistic philosophy of royalty is the fact that the king's sharing in the Solar Power made him the Animate Law of his realm" (82). He elaborates on this, saying, "Animate Law ... means that the king is personally the constitution of his realm, that all the laws of localities under him must be ultimately molded by and express his will. But more, he is the savior of his subjects from their sins, by giving them what the Hellenistic world increasingly wanted more than anything else, a dynamic and personal revelation of deity" (91). Moreover, "In Plutarch ... this Animate Law conception has been fully identified with the Logos. The true king is the incarnate representation of the universal Nomos, and as such he is the incarnate representation of the Logos" (95). Goodenough concludes that the king as Animate Law is integral to "the official philosophy of kingship" in the Hellenistic period (100).

[171] Unlike the Hellenistic king, the Roman emperor had to step delicately in the matter of justice, for maintaining the appearance of the Republic required that the emperor not

136   *Chap. 3: Christ the Good King*

When the king submits to laws he is of course δίκαιος and νόμιμος. How fundamental this is to good rule appears in a saying of Agesilaüs. When comparing himself to the Persian King, the "Great," he asked, "Wherein greater than I, if not more just?" (Plut. *Mor.* 545a). As crucial as justice was for good rule, it nevertheless depended entirely on the discretion of the ruler. But why should a ruler choose a just course of action? One reason is that it benefits his realm. Justice brings prosperity and the goodwill of subjects. Both of these result in safety and well-being for the king. In theory, then, justice is in a ruler's self-interest. Encomiastic rhetoric introduces other reasons. For example, the foreign ruler can receive praise for allowing subject people to live under their traditional laws and customs.[172] More generally, the good king's justice earns praise and honor. The concrete blessings of just rule and the praise it draws is illustrated by Isocrates' report:

I hear that Cleommis, who in Methymna holds this royal power, is noble and wise in all his actions, and that so far from putting any of his subjects to death, or exiling them, or confiscating their property, or injuring them in any other respect, he provides great security for his fellow-citizens, and restores the exiles, returning to those who come back their lost possessions, and in each case recompenses the purchasers the price they had paid (*Ep.* 7.8).

Justice is perhaps the most amazing aspect of the good king: although he holds supreme power, he refrains from using it to sate his whims.[173]

Not only is the good ruler just, but of his own initiative he shows kindness to his subjects.[174] In addition to the possible benefactions which

---

interfere with the Senate; on the other hand, he had his own interests and clients to protect. Among the "arrogant" statements of Julius Caesar, Suetonius includes his shocking advice that people consider what he said to be law (77).

[172] We are familiar with Jewish desires in this matter; however, they were not unique (Burstein 23, 29, 35, and 92; Sherk 1984: 63, 81, and 108; Sherk 1988: 71; Reynolds 8 [cf. pp. 107-8 and nos. 10, 13-23, 25, and 41-43, all pertaining to Aphrodisias]; Jalabert 3.1: no. 718). Both the responsibility of the king to make law and the respect of an imperial power (Republican Rome) for local law appear in an inscription from Pergamum: the Roman Senate decreed that "whatever King Attalus and the rest of the [kings] had amended (or whatever) penalties they had imposed (or whatever) [they had taken away (or) given,] whatever of these things were done down to one [day before Att]alus died ... these things [are to be legally binding,] and [the praetors] who go to Asia ... should allow these things to remain legally binding" (Sherk 1984: 40; similarly 49).

[173] Jos. *Bel.* 5.367: "There was, in fact, an established law, as supreme among brutes as among men, 'Yield to the stronger' and 'The mastery is for those pre-eminent in arms.'"

[174] φιλανθρωπία: Isoc. *Ep.* 7.6 (μεγαλοψυχία in *Evag.* 45); *Ep. Arist.* 289-90; Plut. *Alex.* 21.3; Dio Chrys. 1.20 (with ἥμερος); 3.39; 4.24; Ps.-Aristid. Εἰς βασ. 21-24;

3.3. Survey of the Good King Topoi 137

we have already noted, the king's justice also raises the possibility of mercy. Deserved punishments are withheld because he is lenient and slow to anger (Cic. *De off.* 1.88). His enemies continue to live because he is generous. The goodwill which justice garners enables the good ruler not to exile people, for he does not fear them. His authority allows him to tailor justice so as to fashion equity. In sum, the good king stands for justice and dispenses mercy.[175]

These virtues also display themselves in war, not just in court.[176] The good ruler shows courage to fight, but does not thirst for battle.[177] When pressed to fight, he is gracious in victory. He nevertheless prefers peace, which is one of the blessings that he, as a good ruler, provides for his subjects. As a lover of peace, he promotes concord among his subjects and banishes strife.[178] In all these circumstances the king's virtues guide him and his gentleness in particular secures the goodwill of his subjects.[179]

Many *topoi* which we have surveyed appear together in a single paragraph written by Seneca. If one asks, what is a good king, this paragraph provides a fairly comprehensive answer:

FGH 90 §I, IX (Nicolaus of Damascus). In Egypt many petitions address the emperor, seeking his assistance; however, lower level administrators would have handled the cases. Such situations underscore the public perception that justice, mercy, and favor issue from the ruler.

[175] πραότης: Xen. *Ag.* 3; Isoc. *Ad Nic.* 23; *Phil.* 116; *Hel.* 37; *Ep.* 7.5; Polyb. 4.27.10; Ps.-Aristid. Εἰς βασ. 10 and 23; Dio Chrys. 1.20; 2.74; Stob. 4.5.55; Plut. *Mor.* 218b; 223e; 537d.

ἐπιείκεια: Philod. *Good King* 24; *Ep. Arist.* 188, 207; Aug. *Res ges.* 34; Philo *De leg. ad Gai.* 119.4; Jos. *Ant.* 15.375; 19.334; Dio Chrys. 3.5; Plut. *Thes. et Rom.* 2.2; Ps.-Aristid. Εἰς βασ. 24; Dio Cas. 52.34.6; cp. 52.38.1; *FGH* 90 §II.2 (Nicolaus of Damascus); Stob. 4.5.56 and 60.

ἥμερος: Plut. *Alex.* 21.3 (ἥμερος καὶ χρηστός).

χάρις: Aes. *Fab.* 155.

Clementia: Cic. *Qfr.* 1.1.25; Aug. *Res ges.* 34; Hor. *Carm.* 3; Sen. *De clem.*; *Ep.* 114.7; Suet. *Aug.* 33.1; *Nero* 10.1.

[176] It is common in encomiastic rhetoric to discuss a person's deeds by dividing them between those done during war and in a time of peace (Pernot, *La rhétorique de l'éloge*, 1: 172).

[177] Isoc. *Ad Nic.* 24; Philod. *Good King* 27; Dio Chrys. 1.27; Dio Cas. 52.37. On the distinction between φιλοπόλεμος, which is bad, and πολεμικός, which is good, see Plut. *Eum.* 595f.

[178] *Il.* 9.63-64; Xen. *Ag.* 7.4-6; Philod. *Good King* 28-9, 40, 42; Ps.-Plut. *De vita et poe. Hom.* 2.186.

[179] The ruler's gentleness and clemency will be examined more closely in the following section and in chapter four.

Accordingly, in that age which is maintained to be the golden age, Posidonius holds that the government was under the jurisdiction of the wise. They kept their hands under control, and protected the weaker from the stronger. They gave advice, both to do and not to do; they showed what was useful and what was useless. Their forethought provided that their subjects should lack nothing; their bravery warded off dangers; their kindness enriched and adorned their subjects. For them ruling was a service, not an exercise of royalty (*Ep.* 90.5).

This description of the golden age rests on qualities of the ideal king: wise, restrained, helpful, provident, brave, kind, and beneficent. Dio Cassius formulated a succinct guideline for rulers by applying the golden rule to the exercise of office: "do all that you would wish another to do if he became your ruler."[180]

So far we have examined what characterizes a good king. If we reverse the *topoi* we find a description of the bad ruler (i.e., the tyrant).[181] In Herodotus, envy and pride appear as the monarch's typical vices and these lead to violence and lawlessness (3.80). The vices which the king should particularly avoid include greed, arrogance, rage, and cruelty.[182] The worst thing which an evil ruler does is grasp after too much; πλεονεξία singularly disqualifies anyone from the lists of good ruler.[183] Insolence and arrogance also characterize the bad ruler; moreover, to behave lawlessly, to treat other people violently, or to give way to anger further tarnishes the ruler's reputation.[184] Dio Cassius summarizes the tyrant's

---

[180] 52.39.2. Dio also records an anecdote about Hadrian in which the emperor denied a woman's request to hear her petition, dismissing her because he lacked time. When she retorted, "'Cease, then, being emperor' (καὶ μὴ βασίλευε), he turned about and granted her a hearing" (69.6.3).

[181] See Plato's description of the tyrant in *Rep.* 8.566d-567c. For an example of a particular king, see Tamsyn Barton, "The *inventio* of Nero: Suetonius," in *Reflections of Nero*, 48-63. For examples in Seneca, see Anna Lydia Motto and I. R. Clark, "Exemplary Villians in Seneca's Prose," *Bollettino di studi latini* 23 (1993): 309-19. Philostratus regards tyrants and princes as stock characters of the Second Sophistic (*Vit. soph.* 481).

[182] Cp. the typical characteristics of the tyrant in Roman rhetoric: *vis, superbia, crudelitas,* and *libido,* as discussed by J. Roger Dunkle, "The Greek Tyrant and Roman Political Invective of the Late Republic," *TAPA* 98 (1967): 151-71. On the origins of this rhetoric see the better discussion of Andrew Erskine, "Hellenistic Monarchy and Roman Policital Invective," *CQ* 41 (1991): 106-20. See, e.g., Tac. *Ann.* 6.6.2.

[183] Isoc. *Ad Nic.* 24; *Ep.* 7.4; Philo *De vita Mos.* 1.152; Plut. *Cras.* 27.4; Dio Chrys. 1.65; 2.68; 3.40; Ps.-Plut. *De vita et poe. Hom.* 2.183. Diotogenes, however, justifies avarice on the grounds that it enables a king to provide εὐεργεσία (Stob. *Anth.* 4.7.62), "an astonishing rationalization" (Goodenough, "Hellenistic Kingship," 70).

[184] ὕβρις: Xen. *Oec.* 4.8; Dio Chrys. 1.13; 2.73; 3.40; Ps.-Aristid. Εἰς βασ. 25; Dio Cas. 63.22.4.

crimes as robbery, outrage, and murder.[185] Did most kings avoid such actions? Seneca tells an anecdote which suggests that unvirtuous kings were not unusual: a Roman governor in Asia beheaded three hundred people and afterward, while strolling among the carnage, shouted, "What a kingly act!"[186] In short, the bad king is harsh towards his subjects.[187] He inspires fear and engenders strife.[188] But cruelty is not the only way for a king to go bad; the opposite extreme will also be judged a poor ruler. The sovereign who indulges in luxury and pleasure and who lacks concern for his subjects will also be branded a bad king.[189]

These then are the commonplace ideals of kingship in Greco-Roman antiquity.[190] So attractive were they, that Shakespeare, as quoted at the beginning of this chapter, could use them centuries later to characterize

---

ὑπερηφανία: *Ep. Arist.* 211 and 269; Dio Chrys. 1.13 and 84. O. Murray labels this the "vice most often attributed in the LXX to kings" ("Aristeas and Ptolemaic Kingship," 356 n. 3). Polybius identifies the arrogance of rulers as the source of revolt (6.7).

παράνομος: Dio Chrys. 3.40; Ps.-Plut. *De vita et poe. Hom.* 2.183.

βιάζεσθαι: Isoc. *Ep.* 7.6; Plut. *Alex.* 7.1; 47.5; Dio Chrys. 2.68; Ps.-Plut. *De vita et poe. Hom.* 2.183; Ps.-Aristid. Εἰς βασ. 24 and 25. Cp. Cleon, who is βιάτατος (Thuc. 3.36).

ὀργή: Isoc. *Ad Nic.* 23; *Ep. Arist.* 253-54; Luc. *Dem.* 51; Ps.-Aristid. Εἰς βασ. 10. Cp. Sen. *De ira* 3.23.4-8.

ὠμότης: 3 Macc 6:24; Jos. *Bel.* 2.204-8

[185] Dio Cas. 42.27.3. Cp. Dio Chrys. *Or.* 47.24.

[186] *De ira* 2.5.5. Cato the Elder made a similar point: "the animal known as king is by nature carnivorous" (Plut. *Cato maj.* 340e).

[187] Xen. *Oec.* 4.8; Isoc. *Ad Nic.*; *Ev.* 45; *Ep.* 7.2, 4 (χαλεπός); Philod. *Good King* 3 and 24; Dio Chrys. 1.7; Ps.-Aristid. Εἰς βασ. 24 and 25; Tac. *Ann.* 6.6.2.

[188] Philod. *Good King* 24, 29, and 42; Sen. *De ira* 1.20.4; Plut. *Mor.* 152b.

[189] ἀμέλεια: Xen. *Oec.* 4.8.

ἡδονή: Isoc. *De pace* 91; *Ev.* 45; *Ep. Arist.* 245; Dio Chrys. 1.65; 3.40; Stob. *Anth.* 6.7.62 (= Diot. Περὶ βασ.).

Luxury and indulgence: Philo *De vita Mos.* 1.29; Dio Chrys. 1.3; 3.5; Suet. *Nero* 27-28. See Justin Goddard, "The Tyrant at Table," in *Reflections of Nero*, 67-82.

[190] L. de Blois identifies the good ruler *topoi* of the early imperial period as issuing from Isocrates' writings and Augustan ideology ("Third Century Views of Empire," p. 166) and identifies components of each stream (pp. 167-68). As a generalization this has value, but we should not overlook Isocrates' predecessors' views and the anachronistic reading of such sources by authors after Isocrates. De Blois argues that the Isocratean/Augustan view gave way in the third century to "divine emperorship or a monarchy by the grace of God" which became more important than rule based on goodwill (εὔνοια; p. 171). This ideological shift resembles "the *cosmos* of the Neopythagoreans and Neoplatonists" (p. 176).

his tyrant, Macbeth. In brief, people hoped that the powerful king would put his subjects' interests ahead of his own and that he would use his power and wealth for their benefit. Meanwhile, philosophers advised that the king should seek to win his subjects' loyalty by showing them goodwill. The advice was simple: the good king's authority should rest on his subjects' affection for him rather than their terror of him.[191]

4. The πραότης and/or ἐπιείκεια of a King

In light of these many *topoi*, we can recognize easily the many and transparent ways people talked about rulers. For a person who possessed ἐξουσία or ἀρχή, πραότης and/or ἐπιείκεια became measures for how benignly that authority was exercised. Since the focus of the present investigation lies on these virtues above all the other commonplaces of rule, we shall pause to examine this *topos* more closely.

When a king shows πραότης or ἐπιείκεια, he is not acting as freely as his power allows. Not overbearing, he refrains from violence and abuse, as well as oppressive policies of taxation.[192] His punishments are fair and not vindictive.[193] His subjects have greater freedom of speech.[194] Because he does not assert himself, his subjects enjoy greater lawfulness and equality.[195] Other subject peoples retain greater measures of autonomy.[196] The vanquished are spared slaughter or enslavement, while their property is not destroyed.[197]

One such ruler, according to Isocrates, was the founder of the Athenian metropolis and its national hero, Theseus (*Hel.* 18–38). Like Herakles,

---

[191] Xen. *Cyr.* 1.1.5; Plato *Pol.* 276e; Arist. *Pol.* 285a and 1315b; *Ep. Arist.* 265; Polyb. 5.11.6; Cic. *Phil.* 1.33-35; 2.112; Mus. Ruf. frg. 33 Lutz; Ps.-Sen. *Oct.* 456; Plut. *Mor.* 152b; Burstein 29. This principle applies to more than monarchy. Dr. Goebbels applied it to the Nazi party. Cicero applied it to empire: "... it is while we have preferred to be the object of fear rather than of love and affection, that all these misfortunes have fallen upon us.... [I]t is manifest that the power of goodwill is so great and that of fear is so weak ..." (*De off.* 2.29). On the other hand, Pliny pragmatically observed that Regulus' money, faction, and wide support, combined with the fear which he inspired, afforded him greater strength than he could have had simply by being liked (*Ep.* 1.5.15).

[192] Add Esth 3:13b (ἐπαίρεσθαι); Dio. Hal. 4.36.2 (ὑπερήφανος, βαρύτης and αὐθάδεια); Diod. Sic. 11.67.3 (βίαιος); Jos. *Ant.* 11.216 (ὑπερήφανος and σκαιός).

[193] *Ep. Arist.* 188; Philo *De Ios.* 221; Plut. *Art.* 4.3; Dio Chrys. 1.7.

[194] Jos. *Ant.* 19.334; Dio Cas. 43.20.1.

[195] Isoc. *Ep.* 7.5; 3 Macc 7:6; Philo *De leg. ad Gai.* 119; Dio Cass. 53.6.1; 55.12.3.

[196] Plut. *Alex.* 13.2.

[197] 3 Macc 3:15; Polyb. 5.10.4; Aug. *Res ges.* 34; Plut. *Alex.* 43.4; *Mor.* 337b.

3.4. The πραότης and/or ἐπιείκεια of a King   141

Theseus was a champion of human life (23), but his labors were even more beneficial (24). He displayed ἀνδρεία, ἐπιστήμη, εὐσέβεια, and σωφροσύνη in all his deeds, but especially in the way he ruled (31). He renounced force (βία) and chose to live among his citizens on an equal footing (32-35). He went so far as to make the δῆμος "masters of the government," though the people thought he alone should rule, "believing that his sole rule was more to be trusted and more equitable (κοινότερον) than their own democracy" (36). As Isocrates brings his discussion of Theseus to a conclusion, he expresses ideas dear to his own heart, noting that Theseus' power rested on the goodwill (εὔνοια) of his people, not a bodyguard. Theseus successfully combined a tyrant's ἐξουσία with a demagogue's benefactions (37). In fact, Theseus ruled so lawfully (νομίμως) and nobly (καλῶς) that his πραότης was etched into Athenian mores.[198]

Dionysius of Halicarnassus describes another such ruler, Servius Tullius, a man of servile origins but the adopted son of Tarquinius Priscus. By establishing himself as king, Tullius elicited the resentment of the patricians who plotted how to end Tullius' illegal rule (4.8). Tullius turned to the people for support,[199] paying off their debts, instituting graduated taxes, redistributing public lands, and giving the poor a status equal to that of the rich before the law (4.9.6-9).[200] The appreciative crowd praised Tullius as φιλάνθρωπος, μεγαλόψυχος, μέτριος, δημοτικός, νόμιμος, and δίκαιος (4.10.1), though the patricians found in Tullius' policies cause for further grievance (4.10.4-5). Tullius' justice, however, preserved his kingdom for forty years. At that time his predecessor's grandson, who was also Tullius' own ward, Tarquinius (soon to be Superbus), challenged Tullius' right to rule (4.30.4ff.). Tullius countered that kingly rule was a gift bestowed by the people and therefore submitted the decision to them. Then, however, he directed further comments to the Senate, expressing shock at being the object of conspiracy and puzzling over what he did to deserve such treatment (4.36.1-2). He had committed no tyrannical injustices: execution, exile, and dispossession were not common under his

---

[198] Plutarch says that Theseus laid aside βασιλεία and μοναρχία when establishing Athenian democracy (*Thes.* 24.1-25.2). This led to factions within the city, resulting in corruption and, for Theseus himself, contempt (*Thes.* 35). Plutarch therefore complains that Theseus went too far in the direction of ἐπιείκεια and φιλανθρωπία, thereby passing from a true king to a demagogue (*Thes. et Rom.* 2).

[199] 4.8.3, τὸ δημαγωγεῖν; cf. 4.40.1, κολακεία.

[200] Tullius did not hear all legal cases himself, only public matters, referring private cases to other judges. This cut his ἐξουσία in half — yet another δημοτικός gesture (4.25.1).

rule; nor did he assault Senators' wives and daughters. His conduct had not been arrogant (ὑπερήφανος), nor given to severity (βαρύτης) or excessive self-assertion (αὐθάδεια). Who, he wondered, was as μέτριος and φιλάνθρωπος in ἐξουσία as he? Which of his predecessors treated citizens as a πρᾶος father treats his children? Who was so just and law abiding? Given the absence of such transgressions and the presence of such virtues, Tullius believed himself justified in the exercise of his office and rightly offended at the conspiracy against him.

After his exasperated words to the Senate, Tullius reiterated his commitment to submit the issue of rule to the people: "I shall not envy the commonwealth a better ruler" (4.36.3). The crowd responded quickly and confirmed its devotion to Tullius with such enthusiasm that Tarquinius feared for his life and (seemingly) repented (μετανοεῖν), seeking reconciliation (διαλλαγή) with Tullius, whose nature was so forgiving (συγγνώμη) and conciliatory (εὐδιαλλακτός) that Tarquinius gained the reconciliation that he was seeking (4.37.5-38.2). Tarquinius then killed Tullius and installed himself as ruler.

Dionysius then summarizes the reign of Tarquinius, Rome's last king. The bloody coup which gained his throne portends what follows: Tarquinius will become an evil tyrant, guilty of every vice antithetical to good rule. And so the story unfolds. Like a ruler who gained power by force, he required a bodyguard to preserve his position (4.41.3). He abolished customs and laws, his legal decisions were capricious (4.41.4), punishments were severe and relentless, Senators experienced death, exile, and dispossession (4.43.2-3), and freedom of speech disappeared (4.42.5). Tarquinius earned the nickname Superbus, in Greek, ὑπερήφανος (4.41.4). Dionysius also says,

To none who sought an audience would [Tarquinius] grant it unless he himself had sent for them; and even to those who did gain access to him he was not gracious or mild (εὐμενὴς οὐδὲ πρᾶος), but, as is the way with tyrants, harsh and irascible (βαρύς τε καὶ χαλεπός), and his aspect was terrifying rather than genial (φοβερὸς μᾶλλον ἢ φαιδρός; 4.41.4).

And Tarquinius' evils only increased with his reign.[201]

These two figures, the demagogue Tullius and tyrant Tarquinius, embody the qualities of good and bad rule. While the evil of Tarquinius' example needs no comment, Tullius portrays both good and bad things. Although the preceding discussion of Dionysius emphasizes *topoi* of good rule, in Roman legend Tullius serves to illustrate the virtue of the Republic versus the danger of monarchy, in this case specifically that of a

---

[201] In 4.36.4 Dionysius replays succinctly Tarquinius' evil deeds.

corrupting demagogue. Tullius did not represent the interests of the patricians and did not obtain office legally; therefore, despite his sense of justice, he did not represent what was in the best interests of (patrician) Rome, but belonged to the fickle, dangerous world of monarchs. In such a world, people risked tyranny, or, equally fearsome to people of standing, democracy. Demagogues incited the rabble which was bad enough; sincere ones like Tullius posed the long range threat of excessive democratic reforms. None of these things contributed to the stability and order in which patricians flourished. From this perspective, then, Dionysius evaluates Tullius:

Tullius ... at first assumed the guise of royal guardian ... after which he gained the affections of the people by certain ingratiating acts (φιλανθρωπίαις) and was appointed king by them alone. But as he proved to be a man of mildness and moderation (ἐπιεικὴς δὲ καὶ μέτριος ἀνὴρ γενόμενος), by his subsequent actions he put an end to the complaints caused by his not having observed the laws in all respects, and gave occasion for many to believe that, if he had not been made away with too soon, he would have changed the form of government to a democracy (4.40.3).

Mixed as this review is, it contributes to the present discussion by illustrating how all of Tullius' just, merciful, and populist ways may be summarized by characterizing him as ἐπιεικής and μέτριος.[202]

These examples then lead us to five points. First, while we may identify the *topoi* individually, some or many usually work together. Justice, wisdom, generosity, moderation, and gentleness typically coalesce. The wise ruler, for example, is not likely to be unjust. This points us to a second observation. The good king is a character type. While justice may not be the same as wisdom, to posit one of a ruler implies the other. Similarly, the presence of ἐπιείκεια suggests δικαιοσύνη and φρόνησις. These suggest the absence of arrogance and violence on the one hand and the presence of goodwill and solicitousness on the other. An entire pattern of behavior then issues from the description "good king" or its opposite "tyrant." Third, the good king is a popular ruler, both in the sense of being held in affection and of pursuing policies which appeal to his subjects. We may call this populism, Greeks either called it βασιλεία versus tyranny, which means goodwill and affection as opposed to force and fear, or they contrasted good rule with demagoguery, i.e., providence versus flattery, friendly converse as opposed to servility. In the case of Tullius, then,

---

[202] Note the emphatic position of ἐπιεικής δὲ καὶ μέτριος in the quotation from 4.40.3. The importance of acts of philanthropy is described in chapter four. That "ingratiating acts" is an excellent translation in this context reveals the political ambiguity involved.

Dionysius detected a tendency toward democracy.²⁰³ Fourth, the figures we have just discussed underscore the rhetorical role of these *topoi*. Theseus, Tullius, and Tarquinius all play key roles in the founding legends of Athens and Rome. How they used power was fundamental to the way in which legends accounted for the development of their cities' political institutions. The gentleness of Athenian democracy, a national virtue, was the impress of Theseus' own character. The Republican dependence on the Senate was Rome's antidote to tyranny and demagoguery. (In fact, placing Tullius in a non-Roman context would alter the evaluation of him.) That Athens and Rome had such legends is no surprise. That the vocabulary and *topoi* we have surveyed provides the content for those legends is likewise no surprise. As our fifth and final observation, we wish only to emphasize what the last two points already expose: πραότης and ἐπιείκεια are populist and democratic themes. They incline their possessor to equality and fairness and mitigate social distance, ingratiating the ruler with the ruled.²⁰⁴

The importance of ἐπιείκεια and πραότης in good rule appears in Diodorus Siculus' political thinking also. The following passage again illustrates the commonplace nature of the rhetoric of kingship.

Gelon, the son of Deinomenes, who far excelled all other men in valor and strategy and out-generalled the Carthaginians, defeated these barbarians in a great battle, as has been told; and since he treated the peoples whom he had subdued with fairness (ἐπεικῶς) and, in general, conducted himself humanely (φιλανθρώπως) toward all his immediate neighbors, he enjoyed high favor among the Sicilian Greeks. Thus Gelon, being beloved by all because of his mild rule (πραότητα), lived in uninterrupted peace (εἰρηνικῶς) until his death. But Hieron, the next oldest among the brothers, who succeeded to the throne (βασιλείαν), did not rule over his subjects in the same manner; for he was avaricious (φιλάργυρος) and violent (βίαιος) and, speaking generally, an utter stranger to sincerity and nobility of character (τῆς ἁπλότητος καὶ καλοκἀγαθίας ἀλλοτριώτατος). Consequently there were a good many who wished to revolt, but they

---

²⁰³ That ἐπιείκεια and πραότης contribute to larger character types and contribute to populism will be pursued in chapter five when we examine Paul's self-presentation.

²⁰⁴ Xenophon's encomium for Cyrus the Younger offers suggestive contrast to the examples of Theseus and Tullius (*Ana.* 1.9). Cyrus receives praise for σωφροσύνη, hunting and horsemanship, fidelity to his word, generosity, courage, justice, treatment of friends, and the love he inspired. Xenophon offers no praise for ἐπιείκεια or πραότης. In fact, "[N]one could say that [Cyrus] permitted malefactors and wicked men to laugh at him; on the contrary, he was merciless to the last degree in punishing them (ἀφειδέστατα πάντων ἐτιμωρεῖτο), and one might often see along the travelled roads people who had lost feet or hands or eyes" (1.9.13). But rather than condemn Cyrus for brutality, Xenophon offers this as rationale for the peace and security which filled Cyrus' realm. What we wish to emphasize is that while this encomium of a good king lacks any ascription of gentleness, this king is a barbarian.

restrained their inclination because of Gelon's reputation and the goodwill (εὔνοιαν) he had shown towards all the Sicilian Greeks. After the death of Hieron, however, his brother Thrasybulus, who succeeded to the throne, surpassed in wickedness his predecessor in the kingship (βασιλεύσαντα). For being a violent man and murderous by nature (βίαιος γὰρ ὢν καὶ φονικός), he put to death many citizens unjustly (παρὰ τὸ δίκαιον) and drove not a few into exile on false charges, confiscating their possessions into the royal treasury; and since, speaking generally, he hated those he had wronged and was hated by them (μισῶν καὶ μισούμενος ὑπὸ τῶν ἀδικουμένων), he enlisted a large body of mercenaries, preparing in this way a legion with which to oppose the citizen soldiery (11.67.2-5).

Predictably, this text presents πραότης, ἐπιείκεια and φιλανθρωπία as a ruler's keys to winning εὔνοια and love, as well as preserving peace.

All the above examples display clearly the two models of tyrant and good king and the criteria which distinguish them.[205] Moderation, generosity, and indulgence guide the good ruler to preserve life and prosperity, while holding his ego in check. An act of leniency, therefore, exhibited a king's restraint, reasonableness, and moderation. We can therefore think of a ruler's πραότης and/or ἐπιείκεια as expressed in one of the specific deeds listed at the beginning of this section, or as part of a character type from which one may expect a number of typical behaviors, all of which incline toward populism.[206]

5. Evidence of the Good King in Paul's Epistles

In view of the prominent place of the king in antiquity, we now turn to investigate the role of kingship in Paul's christology. Although Paul nowhere refers to King Jesus or confesses that Jesus Christ is King, we must avoid the temptation of thinking that christology is expressed only in titles.[207] As we shall now see, Paul does speak of Christ's rule and attributes to him many features of a good ruler.

The hypothesis that kingship plays a role in Paul's christology is supported by 1 Cor 15:23-28, where Paul explicitly attributes a βασιλεία to Christ, whose work Paul also describes with the verb βασιλεύειν. Paul also describes Christ's rule as a prelude to God's βασιλεία, for Christ's

---

[205] Among other possible examples to consider are Arrian's encomium on Alexander (*Alex. ana.* 7.28.1-30.3) and Diodorus Siculus' discussion of the life of Sesoösis (1.53-58).

[206] Chapter four will examine further clement rule.

[207] Leander Keck rightly warns us against the "tyranny of titles." Focusing on them may blur the bigger picture of christology. See "Toward the Renewal of New Testament Christology," *NTS* 32 (1986): 368-69.

reign prepares for God's (15:24, 28), whose βασιλεία is the ultimate eschatological goal (1 Thess 2:12; 1 Cor 6:9-10; Gal 5:21). Christ's rule is therefore predicated on and reflects God's: the eschatological kingdom of God has begun, but is in an interim phase, in which Christ rules. Thus, Christ as king fills a divine office, serving as the agent who wields divine sovereignty.[208]

The hymn in Phil 2:6-11 describes this office. Although hazards attend the interpretation of this text, eight observations may be offered.[209] First, "the name which is greater than any name" is κύριος.[210] Second, because

---

[208] To remove ambiguity, let me specify that I am not using sovereignty as a theological term (e.g., predestination or omnipotence), but as a political term designating kingly rule.

[209] On the Christ-hymn see Ernst Lohmeyer, *Kyrios Jesus. Eine Untersuchung zu Phil. 2, 5-11*, Sitzungsberichte der Heidelberger Akademie der Wissenschaften, Philosophisch-historische Klasse, Jahrgang 1927-28, 4. Abh. (Heidelberg: Carl Winter, 1928; 1961); Ernst Käsemann, "Kritische Analyse von Phil. 2, 5-11," *ZTK* 47 (1950): 313-60; reprinted in his *Exegetische Versuche und Besinnungen*, 2 vols. (Göttingen: Vandenhoeck & Ruprecht, 1960-64), 1: 51-95; English: "A Critical Analysis of Philippians 2:5-11," *JTC* 5 (1968): 45-88; Ralph Martin, *Carmen Christi: Philippians ii, 5-11 in Recent Interpretation and in the Setting of Early Christian Worship*, SNTSMS 4 (Cambridge University Press, 1967; rev., Grand Rapids: Eerdmans, 1983); cf. idem, *Philippians*, NCB (Grand Rapids: Eerdmans, 1976), 109-16; J. A. Sanders, "Dissenting Deities and Philippians 2:1-11," *JBL* 88 (1969): 279-90; Otfried Hofius, *Der Christushymnus Philipper 2,6-11. Untersuchungen zu Gestalt und Aussage eines urchristlichen Psalms*, WUNT 17 (Tübingen: J. C. B. Mohr [Paul Siebeck], 1976); Wolfgang Schenk, "Der Philipperbrief in der neueren Forschung (1945-1985)," *ANRW* 2.25.4 (1987): 3280-313; Mathias Rissi, "Der Christushymnus in Phil 2,6-11," *ANRW* 2.25.4 (1987): 3314-26; Peter T. O'Brien, *The Epistle to the Philippians*, NIGTC (Grand Rapids: Eerdmans, 1991), 186-271; Karl-Josef Kuschel, *Born before All Time? The Dispute over Christ's Origin*, trans. John Bowden (New York: Crossroad, 1992), 243-66; and N. T. Wright, *The Climax of the Covenant: Christ and Law in Pauline Theology* (Minneapolis: Fortress, 1992), 57-98. Between the completion of this dissertation and its publication, Samuel Vollenweider has contributed two articles that have advanced the perspective presented here that ruler imagery informs Phil 2:6-11: "Die Methamorphose des Gottessohns," in *Das Urchristentum in seiner literarischen Geschichte. Festschrift für Jürgen Becker zum 65. Geburtstag*, eds. U. Mell und U. B. Müller (Beihefte zur Zeitschrift für die neutestamentliche Wissenschaft und die Kunde der älteren Kirche 100; Berlin: de Gruyter, 1999), 107-131; idem, "Der 'Raub' der Gottgleichheit: Ein religionsgeschichtlicher Vorschlag zu Phil 2.6(-11)," *NTS* 45 (1999): 413-33.

[210] C. F. D. Moule has argued that "the name above every name" is Jesus ("Further Reflexions on Philippians 2:5-11," in *Apostolic History and the Gospel: Biblical and Historical Essays Presented to F. F. Bruce on His 60th Birthday*, eds. W. Ward Gasque and Ralph P. Martin [Grand Rapids: Eerdmans, 1970], 270). This requires the absence of sequential thought in the hymn (as indeed Moule suggests). In my opinion the exaltation bestows something which was absent during the act of obedience. At his

Jesus bears this new name, every creature in the universe must bow and praise him. But, third, Jesus earned, let me repeat, earned, his new name, as new rulers, and especially new dynasts, often had to do. The greatness of the deed done and the status attained is what the acclamation of Jesus recognizes. Fourth, possession of the name κύριος, which transcends all names, suggests that Jesus has either regained or finally obtained[211] what the opening of the hymn described: as κύριος Jesus has been elevated to an equal footing with God (τὸ εἶναι ἴσα θεῷ). This requires that he (again) possesses the μορφὴ θεοῦ.[212] Fifth, since the κύριος shares the divine form and equality with God, κύριος does therefore connote divine status — though calling it "the name above every name" should make that obvious. Sixth, Christ's existence after the cross suggests the possibility of immortality, which Paul's theology as a whole confirms. Immortality further lends a divine status to Christ. Seventh, possession of the exalted name implies the possession of its authority. By sharing God's name (and thus divine status), Christ shares in God's power. Since the NT in general and Paul in particular label the exercise of God's power βασιλεία, then for Christ to share in God's power means that Christ shares God's sovereign rule (βασιλεία). κύριος expresses this and is therefore both a divine and royal epithet. Eighth, having attributed to Christ equality with God, a sharing of his name, and the reception of universal worship, the hymn's final phrase reasserts God's supremacy over Christ with father imagery. This, in turn, underscores the functional aspect of Christ's divine status: as κύριος, Christ shares God's authority (βασιλεία) in order to fulfill a role designed to enhance God's glory. Thus, by discharging dutifully a horrific labor, Christ was elevated to divine status, given divine honors, and entrusted with divine rule; he became a κύριος at the head of a βασιλεία of universal scope.

---

crucifixion, the name κύριος was lacking, not Jesus. Furthermore, the intent to build to a concluding climax inhibits the expression of the exalted name until the end of the hymn.

[211] On the debate as to whether ἁρπαγμός means the desire to attain or the refusal to relinquish see N. T. Wright, "ἁρπαγμός and the Meaning of Philippians 2:5-11," *JTS* 37 (1986): 321-52; idem, *The Climax of the Covenant*, 62-90; cp. Sanders, "Dissenting Deities," 289-90; S. Vollenweider, "Der 'Raub' der Gottgleichheit."

[212] It appears from the beginning of the hymn that Christ has two modes, the μορφὴ θεοῦ and the μορφὴ δούλου. The former would be more appropriate for sharing equality with God. It also appears that μορφὴ θεοῦ is a prerequisite (if not coterminous) to being equal to God. Scholarship has found it difficult to define μορφὴ θεοῦ. I agree with those who see in μορφή a synonym of δόξα. Why then not say δόξα? That would result in the embarrassing oxymoron δόξα δούλου. Granting the equivalence of μορφή and δόξα opens the door to εἰκών.

148   Chap. 3: Christ the Good King

In his role as κύριος Christ performs divine and royal duties. The most obvious is rule. This is underscored by the hymn itself. In his humiliation, Christ took the "form of a slave" and became obedient. While christological controversies have agonized over the meaning of μορφὴ δούλου, the contextual contrast between κύριος and δοῦλος should receive prominence: the one who traded μορφὴ θεοῦ for μορφὴ δούλου subsequently went from δοῦλος to κύριος; the obedient one now commands obedience.[213] Paul repeats this idea in Rom 14:9, where he summarizes the Christ-hymn by stating that Christ died and rose for the purpose of ruling an enormous constituency, the dead and living.

As the agent of God's rule, Christ plays a role in divine judgment. As Lord, Christ assumes the tasks associated in the OT with the "day of the Lord." Thus, Paul can speak indiscriminately of the "day of the Lord" (1 Thess 5:2; 1 Cor 5:5), the "day of the Lord Jesus" (2 Cor 1:14), the "day of the Lord Jesus Christ" (1 Cor 1:8), the "day of Christ Jesus" (Phil 1:6), and the "day of Christ" (Phil 1:10; 2:16). This is both the day of Christ's coming and the "day when God will judge humanity's secrets ... through Christ Jesus" (Rom 2:16; cf. 1 Cor 4:5), the day when Christ mounts his tribunal (2 Cor 5:10).[214]

When Paul discusses judgment in Romans, however, he does not always collapse the roles of God and Christ. In Rom 2:2-16 it is God who judges: God judges according to truth (2:2) and according to one's deeds (2:6); the unrepentant store up God's wrath for the day of wrath, the day when God reveals God's just and impartial verdicts (2:5, 11). Paul nearly ignores Christ's role in this scenario, not stipulating until verse 16 that God will judge "through Christ Jesus." And this is all that is said about Jesus in this regard. Rom 3:5-6 gives no notice of Christ's role in judgment. Rom 14:10-12 likewise refers judgment to God. In isolation from Paul's other letters, one could easily miss any connection between Christ and the judgment scene which Rom 14:10-12 describes. Comparison with other Pauline texts, however, underscores the ambiguity between the roles of God and Christ: 14:10 refers to the βῆμα of God, which 2 Cor 5:10 attributes to Christ, and 14:11 describes the scene of judgment with the words of Isaiah 45:23, the very words used in Phil 2:10

---

[213] Moule comes close to this when he suggests that the point of δοῦλος is historical-social: "slavery meant, in contemporary society, the extreme in respect of deprivation of rights" ("Further Reflexions," 268). Cp. 2 Cor 4:5 and Gal 4:1 where Paul also contrasts κύριος and δοῦλος (cf. Rom 2:11; Matt 6:24).

[214] Cf. Joost Holleman, *Resurrection and Parousia: A Tradito-Historical Study of Paul's Eschatology in 1 Corinthians 15*, Supplements to Novum Testamentum 84 (Leiden: E. J. Brill, 1996), 95-9.

to describe Christ's universal acclamation. Recognition of κύριος as Paul's essential christological confession also injects Christ's presence into the apostle's quotation of Isaiah (where κύριος also appears) and thereby draws attention to the ambiguity between θεός and κύριος. Did Paul's Roman audience detect these christological possibilities? It seems unlikely. Paul's collapsing of the roles of God and Christ leaves even contemporary readers (along with ancient scribes) guessing about how much christology to recognize in these verses. In Rom 8:31-39 Paul differentiates God and Christ as judge and advocate. No one dares accuse God's people because God is the one who pronounces acquittal. No one can condemn them because the exalted (and enthroned) Christ intercedes on their behalf. Nothing can deter the favor, goodwill, and loyalty of Christ the advocate (8:35-37), while God's regard for Christ is equally immutable, which guarantees Christ's successful advocacy. This makes the opinion of Christ determinative for the judgment.[215] Christ the advocate is, however, not merely advocate. He is described as "at God's right hand" (v. 34), which echoes one of the early church's most common OT testimonia, Ps 110:1, the introduction to a psalm of royal enthronement.[216] The Psalm as a whole enhances the royal attributes of Messiah by ascribing to him δύναμις, ἀρχή, judgment, the destruction of rival kings, and priesthood in the order of Melchizedek (who was also a king); moreover, the Synoptic tradition explicitly connected this Psalm to David. This Psalm, therefore, inspired a royal image of the church's master. By drawing on it, Paul has thereby characterized Christ the advocate as royal Messiah, or, to remain closer to Paul's vocabulary, the enthroned Lord. Christ's involvement in judgment is therefore appropriately colored as a divine and royal office. Paul's ambiguous statements in Romans about judgment, therefore, underscore the divine aspect of Christ's role as judge and hint at his participation in sovereign rule.

---

[215] The value of Christ's mediation is seen differently when viewed against the legal affairs of the Roman emperor, rather than in terms of objective atonement. When the emperor or Senate heard a trial, the emperor's interests could not be ignored. Often the Senate looked not for innocence or guilt, but for the emperor's preference. The criticism which this drew was more about whose preference prevailed than a theory of justice. The good news in Rom 8 is that God is delighted with his agent, Christ, who represents the interests of his people and pursues their acquittal. His resolve in this matter is inalienable.

[216] Mark 12:36; 14:62; 16:19; Matt 22:44; 26:64; Luke 20:42; 22:69; Acts 2:34; 1 Cor 15:25; Eph 1:20; Col 3:1; Heb 1:3, 13; 8:1; 10:12. Ps 110:4 is echoed in Rom 11:20; Heb 5:6, 10; 6:20; 7:3, 11, 15, 17, 21.

As God's divine and royal agent in judgment, Christ conducts himself in the same manner as God. As judge God is δίκαιος, yet he forbears (ἀνοξή; Rom 3:25-26). Goodness, forbearance, and patience hold God's judgment in check, kindly affording people the opportunity to repent (χρηστότης, ἀνοξή, μακροθυμία; μετάνοια; Rom 2:4). There is also the prospect that God will forgive (Rom 4:6-8). But God must not be trifled with, for not only is χρηστότης present with God, so is severity (ἀποτομία; Rom 11:21-22). Given the semantic study presented above (chapter two), we recognize easily that these words and ideas correspond to 2 Cor 10:1, where Paul indicates that Christ treats his people in the very same fashion. Like God, Christ is loathe to act with severity and prefers leniency. Thus, Paul attributes to Christ πραΰτης and ἐπιείκεια (2 Cor 10:1). This is how the divine/royal agent brings judgment to bear on people.

As the agent of God's rule and participant in judgment, Christ also delivers people. Like the good ruler, Christ prefers to save people from bad things, which in Christ's case is particularly salvation from God's wrath.[217] Christ can successfully deliver his people because he conquers his enemies (1 Cor 15:25) or reconciles them (Rom 5:10-11) and because he brings δικαιοσύνη (1 Cor 1:30), which releases his people from condemnation (Rom 5:18; 8:1). Christ has already ransomed his people from slavery (Gal 4:5) and delivered them from an evil αἰών (Gal 1:4). He guarantees their triumph. In the future he plans to transform their lowly existence into a glorious one, which he will accomplish "by the power that also enables him to make all things subject to himself" (Phil 3:21). In this verse, the phrase ὑποτάξαι αὐτῷ τὰ πάντα is drawn from Ps 8:7, as is the case in 1 Cor 15:27-28. As the latter text shows, the power in view is the rule (βασιλεία) of the exalted Lord. Thus, the transformation in Philippians 3 is based on Christ's sovereignty, the sovereignty of the κύριος who benefits his people as σωτήρ. What Christ as σωτήρ does involves the same future event as 1 Corinthians 15, the ultimate defeat of death, which is the final goal of Christ's βασιλεία. Thus, the designations Savior and Lord apply (in part at least) to the victorious triumph of Christ's royal rule, in which Christ uses his might for his people's benefit. What we wish to emphasize at present, then, is that, as God's agent and like a king, Christ is concerned with judgment, justice, and σωτηρία (victory and salvation).

Christ grants four other kingly benefactions to his people. First, he provides freedom — freedom from law (Gal 2:4; 5:1, 13), freedom from

---

[217] 1 Thess 1:10; 5:9; 2 Cor 6:2; Rom 2:5; 5:9.

superstition, and freedom from decay and corruption (Rom 8:17-23). Freedom is in fact a quality of the Lord (2 Cor 3:17). Second, he provides his own law (1 Cor 9:21; Gal 6:2; Rom 8:2) — as one concerned with righteousness should. In fact, to be a law-giver was nearly the pinnacle of royal (and human) achievement. Third, Christ brings peace: by delivering his people from God's wrath, he grants them peace with God (1 Thess 1:10; Rom 1:18; 5:1).[218] Fourth, Christ gives life (1 Cor 15:45). While I do not wish to argue that recognition of Christ as king actually generates attribution of these gifts to him, I would stress that such gifts presuppose and prove Christ's divine/royal dignity. Ordinary people do not give law and freedom or grant peace and life. Exalted figures do, and their honor is thereby further enhanced. A grandeur therefore infuses Paul's christology and allows him to make such lofty claims. From what we have so far seen, that grandeur can be called divine/royal. That Christ's freedom includes releasing nature from corruption also indicates the distinguished office in view: he is no mere king, but cosmocrator.

As a result of all Christ's benefactions, one further blessing accrues to his subjects, namely, hope. Because of Christ, his subjects can reasonably hope for righteousness (Gal 5:5). Engaged in the difficulties and struggles of the present age, they can look forward to σωτηρία (1 Thess 5:8; Rom 8:24); they can anticipate life and resurrection (1 Thess 4:13; 1 Cor 15:19; cp. Phil 1:20-21). They have joy now and await a glorious future (2 Cor 3:12; Rom 5:2; 12:12). Because of the scope of Christ's rule, all nations find hope (Rom 15:12), as does creation itself (Rom 8:20).

Christ models the behavior of a good ruler. The Philippians Christ-hymn predicates Christ's dominion on model behavior. In his disregard for ἁρπαγμός (whatever its nuance), Christ resisted πλεονεξία (as well as ὑπερηφανία and βία) and did not use his position for his own advantage; self-aggrandizement is absent from Christ. In his humiliation, Christ also showed obedience, an important experience for one who is destined to rule. The freedom from πλεονεξία and the presence of φιλανθρωπία are reinforced in 2 Cor 8:9: the divine/royal Lord enriches his subjects, and at great cost to himself (cp. 1 Cor 4:8; Phil 4:19). This is the ideal attitude of a powerful ruler toward wealth. That Christ seeks the interests of others and uses his strength to help the weak likewise characterizes him as an ideal ruler. Rom 15:3 underscores this idea, for Paul cites the example of Christ who did not please himself but made himself the object of insults in order to help others. Although in context Rom 15:3 does not reflect on this

---

[218] Cp. Klaus Wengst, *Pax Romana and the Peace of Jesus Christ* (Philadelphia: Fortress Press, 1987). Note also the challenge to human claims of "peace and security" voiced in 1 Thess 5:3.

as an expression of Christ as κύριος, this text does present Christ as an example of a strong person who helps the weak. Christ's concern for justice also intertwines with his concern for piety. Paul demonstrates this by quoting Isa 59:20: "The deliverer will come from Zion; he will remove impiety from Jacob" (Rom 11:26).[219] Here again 2 Cor 10:1 enters Paul's christology. This good king who pursues justice and piety, who helps the weak, who shows φιλανθρωπία and is free of πλεονεξία, this king also displays the qualities of πραΰτης and ἐπιείκεια: he is slow to impose judgment. Not at all surprising for one who is gracious and secures the acquittal of the undeserving.[220]

As the agent of God's rule, then, Christ rules until the End, when he hands the reins of power (i.e., βασιλεία) over to God the Father. At present, the church recognizes God's divine/royal agent as κύριος, who judges and delivers, conquers and reconciles, sacrifices and benefits, and conducts himself virtuously. He uses his power not for himself but for the good of his people and his Father's glory. In sum, the confession Jesus Christ is Lord has royal connotations.[221]

---

[219] Cranfield comments that the role of "turning back ungodlinesses from the nation of Israel ... affords a striking contrast to the Jewish expectation of a political messiah" (*Romans*, 2: 578). Both OT narratives and Greco-Roman kingship traditions expose Cranfield's dichotomy as fallacious. The kings of Israel and Judah were evaluated in terms of their promotion of God's worship, while similar piety was also desired in Greek and Roman rulers.

[220] The *fides*/πίστις of the Roman emperor is often celebrated in inscriptions and is fundamental to Roman political dialogue. Depending on how one views the questions surrounding πίστις Χριστοῦ, then Christ's loyalty might prove to be another of his virtues, and one which corresponds to ruler ideology. See Dieter Georgi, *Theocracy in Paul's Praxis and Theology*, trans. David Green (Minneapolis: Fortress Press, 1991), 36-37, 83-84, 88, and 95-100.

While I can offer no evidence of ἀγάπη being characteristic of the good ruler, the description of Christ's ἀγάπη in Rom 8:35-39 approximates loyalty and good-will, two sterling political virtues.

[221] L. Cerfaux, "Le titre Kyrios et la dignité royale de Jésus, *Revue des sciences philosophiques et théologiques* 11 (1922): 42. Oscar Cullmann comments, "The title 'King' (βασιλεύς) is ... a variant of the κύριος title, and ... the idea of the Messiah-King can be applied only to the lordship Jesus exercises after his resurrection" (*The Christology of the New Testament*, trans. Shirley C. Guthrie and Charles A. M. Hall [London: SCM Press, 1959], 220-21 [more generally see 195-237]). On κύριος see: Werner Foerster, "κύριος," *TDNT*, 3: 1039-95; H. Bietenhard, "κύριος, *NIDNTT*, 2:510-20; Joseph A. Fitzmyer, "κύριος," *EDNT*, 2: 328-31; Wilhelm Bousset, *Kyrios Christos. Geschichte des Christus-glaubens von den Anfängen des Christentums bis Irenaeus* (Göttingen: Vandenhoeck & Ruprecht, 1913; [6]1967), 75-154; English: *Kyrios Χριστός*, trans. John Steely (Nashville: Abingdon Press, 1970), 119-210; Werner Foerster, *Herr ist Jesus* (1924); Werner Kramer, *Christos Kyrios Gottessohn.*

3.5. The Good King in Paul's Epistles

This understanding highlights the imperial nature of the acclamation ritual which Christ receives in Phil 2:10-11.[222] Roueché defines acclamation as "the expression, in unison, of wish, opinion or belief, by a large gathering of people, often employing conventional rhythms and turns of phrase."[223] Acclamations were addressed to gods, kings, and noteworthy individuals. They took place in worship, legislative bodies, church councils, theater and circus, in general public assemblies, and even in riots. They could serve to honor an individual human being or god, to express public sentiment, or to voice a request. Roueché states, however, that typically "acclamations were used to honor rulers."[224] She adds that "in the Graeco-Roman world [acclamations] were in common use."[225]

Such acclamations could be simple, such as the Roman acclamation, "Imperator." A longer, yet still simple, acclamation appears in the New Testament in the protest of the Ephesian silversmiths: "Great is Artemis of the Ephesians" (Acts 19:34) — chanted for two hours! More elaborate — and literary — are the cries at the Triumphal Entry: "Hosanna. Blessed be the one who comes in the name of the Lord. Blessed be the coming kingdom of our father David. Hosanna in the highest" (Mark 11:9-10). The other Evangelists underscore the royal focus of Jesus' acclamation: "Hosanna to the son of David" (Matt 21:9); "Blessed be the one who

---

Untersuchungen zu Gebrauch und Bedeutung der christologischen Bezeichnungen bei Paulus und den vorpaulinischen Gemeinden, Abhandlungen zur Theologie des Alten und Neuen Testaments 44 (Zürich: Zwingli, 1963), 61-103, 149-81, and 215-22; English: *Christ, Lord, Son of God*, trans. Brian Hardy, Studies in Biblical Theology 50 (Naperville, IL: Alec R. Allenson, 1966), 65-107, 151-82, and 215-22; Joseph A. Fitzmyer, "Der semitische Hintergrund des neutestamentlichen Kyriostitels," in *Jesus Christus in Historie und Theologie. Festschrift für Hans Conzelmann zum 60. Geburtstag*, ed. Georg Strecker (Tübingen: J. C. B. Mohr [Paul Siebeck], 1975), 267-98; English: "The Semitic Background of the New Testament κύριος-Title," in his *A Wandering Aramean: Collected Aramaic Essays*, SBLMS 25 (Missoula, MT: Scholars Press, 1979), 115-42; Martin Hengel, *The Son of God: The Origin of Christology and the History of Jewish-Hellenistic Religion*, trans. John Bowden (Philadelphia: Fortress Press, 1976), 77-80 nn. 135-36; Larry W. Hurtado, "New Testament Christology: A Critique of Bousset's Influence," *TS* 40 (1979): 306-17.

[222] Erik Peterson argues that Phil 2:11 is an acclamation (Heis theos. *Epigraphische, formgeschichtliche und religions-geschichtliche Untersuchungen*, FRLANT 24 [Göttingen: Vandenhoeck & Ruprecht, 1926], 133-34 and 171-72 [cp. 141-45]). On acclamation see T. Klauser, "Akklamation," *RAC* 1 (1950): 213-33; Charlotte Roueché, "Acclamations in the Later Roman Empire: New Evidence from Aphrodisias," *JRS* 74 (1984): 181-99. Klauser and Roueché point to further literature.

[223] Roueché, "Acclamations in the Later Roman Empire," 181.
[224] *Ibid.*, 182.
[225] *Ibid.*, 183.

comes, the king, in the name of the Lord" (Luke 19:37); "the king of Israel" (John 12:13). Matthew and John highlight the royal nature of the event by providing OT commentary: "Look, your king is coming to you."

Labelling Phil 2:10-11 an acclamation has become common in this century. Two things have particularly led to that, viz., understanding the heavenly, earthly, and sub-terrestrial entities as beings, not things, and understanding ἐξομολογεῖσθαι generally, and not as a cultic Septuagintalism.[226] Though one might ask whether Christ receives his acclamation as a king or deity, the preceding comments have indicated that both are operative for Christ simultaneously. As κύριος Christ has divine status, which he expresses functionally by ruling. κύριος is therefore both cultic and regal, with the result that Christ receives acclamation as divine/royal Lord.

Another ritual lies behind 1 Thess 4:13-18. Though perhaps not obvious to the modern reader, the advent of Christ is described in terms of public ceremonial. The vocabulary points to this: παρουσία (v. 15) and ἀπάντησις (v. 17). In antiquity it was customary that, at the arrival (παρουσία; Latin *adventus*) of an important person, a delegation should go out to meet (ἀπάντησις) him or her.[227] This is exactly what happens in 1 Thess 4:13-18, for at the παρουσία of Christ his people, transported on clouds, go out to greet him (ἀπάντησις) in the air (v. 17). Readers of the NT should not be surprised at this method of bestowing honor.[228]

---

[226] Martin, *Carmen Christi* (Cambridge, 1967), 257-65. Martin comments on the confession, denying that it is "the personal witness of faith" (p. 263); rather, it is "the open and irrevocable admission that ... God has installed [Jesus] in the seat of uncontested authority ... [a] response to the divine epiphany which declares the sovereignty of the lordly Christ" (p. 264). This follows Peterson: "κύριος ’Ιησοῦς ist ein Ruf, eine Akklamation, eine Ehromologese im antiken Sinne ... So wenig wie «groß ist die Artemis der Epheser» ist auch «Herr ist Jesus» ein eigentliches Glaubensbekenntnis" (Heis theos, pp. 171-72 n. 3).

[227] Cic. *Phil.* 2.1-6 (Antony); Jos. *Bel.* 7.100-3 (Titus); *Ant.* 11.325-36 (Alexander); 19.340 (Marcus, president of Syria); *Vita* 90-91 and 166 (Josephus himself); 230-33 (Jonathan); Plut. *Mor.* 489e (Eumenes); Pliny *Pan.* 22-24 (Trajan); Suet. *Aug.* 53; Tac. *Ann.* 3.47 (Tiberius); Dio Cas. 51.19.2; 54.25.4; 56.41.5 (Augustus). For a Seleucid example see Sherwin-White and Kuhrt, *From Samarkland to Sardis*, 140. See Erik Peterson, "Die Einholung des κύριος," *ZST* 7 (1929-30): 682-702; idem, "ἀπάντησις," *TDNT* 1: 380-81. Gerhard Koeppel discusses monumental reliefs from II AD in his "Profectio und Adventus," *Bonner Jahrbücher* 169 (1969): 130-94.

[228] Matt 25:1, 6 (parable of the bridegroom); John 12:13 (Jesus); and Acts 28:15 (Paul). The Matthaean parable also suggests that Paul's references to a loud command, the archangel's voice, and God's trumpet are also part of the greeting ritual, serving as the heraldic activities which summon people to the ἀπάντησις. (Cp. 1 Cor 15:52, where the trumpet heralds the παρουσία.)

3.5. The Good King in Paul's Epistles

The example of a community which neglected an ἀπάντησις teaches us much about the ceremony. One night the wife of Marcus Agrippa, Julia, approached Ilium when the nearby river was running high. Since Agrippa had not notified Ilium that his wife was coming, no one planned to meet her; moreover, since she approached at night, no one saw her. Unfortunately, the high water made the river-crossing dangerous, threatening her life and those of her slaves. When Agrippa learned of the peril which Julia had encountered, he became enraged at Ilium for not having met and escorted his wife. As a result, he imposed an enormous fine on the city. Ilium obtained the intercession of Herod in the matter, who succeeded in having the fine rescinded.[229] For us, the story illustrates the practical utility of the custom, while underscoring the recognition of it as standard protocol to be shown to important people.

Another practical dimension of the greeting ritual is the opportunity it allows people to bend the ear of the approaching dignitary. One might take advantage of the situation to present a complaint to an approaching governor before the opposition did. On a larger scale, Josephus records the greeting Titus received as he approached Antioch. Moved by joy, men, women, and children went out thirty stadia to meet Titus, waving and shouting blessings. At the same time, however, "all their acclamations were accompanied by a running petition to expel the Jews from the town" (*Bel.* 7.103).[230] People therefore made use of the access to dignitaries which the ἀπάντησις provided.

The reason for citing the examples of Julia and Titus is not to suggest that at Christ's παρουσία he needs assistance or that Christians will have the first chance to seek favors. What these examples indicate is how well integrated the greeting ceremony was within its cultural context. More was involved in the ritual than obsequiousness. Utility, goodwill, and opportunity were relevant. More germane for our present purposes, though, is simply how normal and expected the practice was.

Scholars have been hesitant to recognize this honorific practice as background to 1 Thess 4:13-18. Bruce mentioned it.[231] Marshall suggested it tentatively, while Morris made only half-hearted use of the information.[232] Best thinks the overtones of the practice are present,

---

[229] Nicholaus of Damascus in *FGH* 90 F 134; trans. Sherk 1984: 98c; cf. Jos. *Ant.* 16.26.

[230] For the offering of acclamation while welcoming a dignitary, see Jos. *Ant.* 16.14, which recounts Agrippa's visit to Jerusalem.

[231] F. F. Bruce, *1 & 2 Thessalonians*, WBC 45 (Waco, TX: Word Books, 1983), 116.

[232] I. Howard Marshall, *1 and 2 Thessalonians*, NCB (Grand Rapids: Eerdmans, 1983), 131; Leon Morris, *1 and 2 Thessalonians*, TNTC., rev. (Grand Rapids:

though not intentionally.²³³ Dupont and Wanamaker doubt that the cultural dynamics of ἀπάντησις are relevant.²³⁴ Two problems obstruct the interpretation of this text.²³⁵ The first problem lies in the fact that Paul does not say where everyone goes after meeting Christ in the air, whether back to earth or to heaven. If the former, then the greeting ritual is obviously present. If, however, the heavenly body and the heavenly πολίτευμα indicate that believers return with Jesus to heaven and not to earth, then the presence of the greeting is less obvious.²³⁶ That does not mean it is absent. The vocabulary and the act of going out to meet "the Lord" point to the ceremony. That it may conclude differently than expected reflects the ontology of the people meeting and the occasion for the meeting. In other words, although the mixing of cultural practice with Christian theology may alter the normal progression of events, the underlying, commonplace public ceremony remains in sight and is applied to Jesus. The second objection to recognizing the greeting ritual in this text is the presence of apocalyptic and biblical imagery. If the eschatological drama unfolds in accord with Jewish traditions, then how can a Greco-Roman ritual interject itself? The assumed dichotomy between Jewish and Greco-Roman is objectionable. Even if it were not, the more general assumption that two traditions cannot mix is not sound. Meanwhile, the account of the Triumphal Entry in the Fourth Gospel (12:12-19) in fact illustrates the exact combination of Jewish tradition and greeting ceremony. Unlike the Synoptics, the Fourth Gospel adds the detail that people from Jerusalem went out to meet Jesus (ἐξῆλθον εἰς ὑπάντησιν, v. 13); yet the crowd's cries and the scriptural testimony

---

Eerdmans, 1984), 94; idem, *The First and Second Epistles to the Thessalonians*, NICNT, rev. (Grand Rapids: Eerdmans, 1991), 146.

[233] Ernest Best, *A Commentary on the First and Second Epistles to the Thessalonians*, HNTC (New York: Harper & Row, 1972), 199.

[234] J. Dupont, Syn Christo. *L'Union avec le Christ suivant saint Paul* (Bruges, 1952), 64-73; Joseph Plevnik, "The Taking Up of the Faithful and the Resurrection of the Dead in 1 Thessalonians 4, 13-18," *CBQ* 46 (1984): 283 n. 29; and Charles A. Wanamaker, *The Epistles to the Thessalonians*, NIGTC (Grand Rapids: Eerdmans, 1990), 175. Dupont emphasizes the apocalyptic and biblical background.

[235] Advocating the greeting protocol is Peterson, "Die Einholung des κύριος." See also L. Cerfaux, *The Christian in the Theology of St. Paul* (New York: Herder & Herder, 1967), 158; Raymond F. Collins, *Studies on the First Letter to the Thessalonians*, BETL 66 (Louvain: University Press, 1984), 385-401.

[236] If, however, the entourage returns to heaven, when and where will the world be judged? And how thoroughly integrated are the elements of Paul's eschatology at the writing of 1 Thessalonians?

preserve the aspect of Jewish tradition in the story.[237] This example undermines any objection to combining ceremonial protocol with Jewish theology. The important observation for us to draw at present is that 1 Thess 4:13-18 applies protocol for dignitaries to Christ.

Paul also connects the pageantry and ceremony of imperial rule to Christ in 2 Cor 2:14, where the apostle gives thanks to God "who always leads us in triumph in Christ" (2 Cor 2:14). The meaning of θριαμβεύειν has perplexed interpreters for a long time. Although consensus that Paul referred to a triumphal procession seemed to be gaining momentum, Egan argued that the word meant simply "to display," or "make known."[238] Marshall attempted to answer Egan and reintroduce the triumph image.[239] Furnish leaned more toward Egan, thinking that "one cannot be completely certain that Paul intends an allusion to the Roman triumph" and adding that "even if there is such an allusion here, it is secondary to the main point."[240] Hafemann, however, addressed the matter of context in his dissertation, arguing that the image of Paul the captive led in triumphal procession provides the leitmotif for 2 Cor 2:14-7:4.[241] Duff's dissertation argued that θριαμβεύειν refers to a triumphal procession, but he stipulated that Paul used this as a metaphorical way of describing an epiphany procession.[242] Such a ritual celebrated the "visitations of the

---

[237] We might also note the presence of the acclamation ritual (v. 13)!

[238] Rory B. Egan, "Lexical Evidence on Two Pauline Passages," *NovT* 19 (1977): 34-62.

[239] Peter Marshall, "A Metaphor of Social Shame: *THRIAMBEUEIN* in 2 Cor 2:14," *NovT* 25 (1983): 302-17.

[240] *II Corinthians*, 175.

[241] Scott J. Hafemann, *Suffering and the Spirit*, WUNT 2.19 (Tübingen: J. C. B. Mohr [Paul Siebeck], 1986), 18-39. The triumphal imagery presents "Paul as the conquered slave of Christ who is led to death" which "corresponds to Paul's apostolic self-conception" (pp. 38-39). To be "led in triumph" is to be "led to death" (p. 39). This study is reprinted in less technical form as *Suffering & Ministry in the Spirit: Paul's Defense of His Ministry in II Corinthians 2:14-3:3* (Grand Rapids: Eerdmans, 1990). See also Calvin J. Roetzel, "'As Dying, and Behold We Live': Death and Resurrection in Paul's Theology," *Int* 46 (1992): 5-18.

[242] Paul Brooks Duff, "Honor or Shame: The Language of Processions and Perception in 2 Cor 2:14-6:13; 7:2-4" (Ph.D. diss., University of Chicago, 1988), 115: "It is our contention therefore that being 'led in triumph' can be thought of as the same as being led in a 'triumph,' although in the case of 2 Corinthians, the triumph would not be the military victory parade but rather a cultic procession of the epiphany type and those led would not be prisoners of war but worshippers of the deity." Duff's conclusions are more carefully nuanced in "Metaphor, Motif, and Meaning: The Rhetorical Strategy behind the Image 'Led in Triumph' in 2 Corinthians 2:14," *CBQ* 53 (1991): 79-92. Cf. E. Wallisch, "Name und Herkunft des römischen Triumphes," *Philologus* 99 (1954-55):

deity" and is "often seen as a re-enactment of a beneficent act of the deity."[243] Duff further argued that the image of the procession reappears throughout Paul's subsequent discussion.[244] Breytenbach reaffirmed the presence of triumphal imagery and refined its allusion, while at the same time delivering Paul from an embarrassing mixed metaphor.[245]

While many of the arguments made about Paul's use of θριαμβεύειν are tenuous, linguistic evidence favors the view that Paul regards himself as being led in a triumphal procession. Egan's counter-argument would be more persuasive if he offered an example of θριαμβεύειν rather than of ἐξθριαμβίζειν. How Paul conceives of the triumphal procession is still another issue. Paul had never witnessed a triumphal procession, may not have seen any triumphal monuments and imagery, and certainly had not read Josephus or Dio Cassius, yet he knows enough to refer to the ceremony.[246] Perhaps he had heard stories or reports of some kind, perhaps

---

245-58. He discusses the origins of Hellenistic triumphs, suggesting that they lie in legends about Dionysos.

[243] Duff, "Honor and Shame," 41-42.

[244] Thus, 2:14-16 refers to the fragrances which allude to the deity's presence; 4:7 describes the vessal which contains the cult's sacred objects, "bearers of the deity's power" (p. 224); 4:10 reflects the role of the cult object in displaying "the beneficent or saving activity of the deity which was carried around and shown to bystanders" (p. 224); and 6:13 and 7:2 point to the role of the herald "who walked before the sacred object or image, announcing its presence, and preparing the bystanders for the epiphany" (p. 224).

[245] J. Cilliers Breytenbach, "Paul's Proclamation and God's θρίαμβος (Notes on 2 Corinthians 2:14-16b)," *Neotestamentica* 24 (1990): 257-71. He concludes that Paul refers to the procession celebrating God's earlier victory over Paul and attributes to Paul the role of incense bearer within that procession.

[246] Findlay's concern must be taken seriously ("St. Paul's Use of θριαμβεύειν," *Expositor* 10 [1879]: 403-421), viz., since Paul had not been to Rome, he would know little about a triumph. We may know more about the details of a triumph than Paul. Our monumental and literary sources give us an idea of what the triumphal procession involved: it was a grand, elaborate spectacle. (See H. S. Versnel, *Triumphus: An Inquiry into the Origin, Development and Meaning of the Roman Triumph* [Leiden: E. J. Brill, 1970]; Inez Scott Ryberg, *Rites of the State Religion in Roman Art*, Memoirs of the American Academy in Rome 22 [American Academy in Rome, 1955], 141-62, pls. L-LVII; Ernst Künzel, *Der römische Triumph. Siegesfeiern im antiken Rom*, Archäologische Bibliothek [München: Beck, 1988].) How many details of this amazing ritual would Paul have known? In Ryberg's chapter on the triumph, most of her evidence comes from Rome or Italy (Praeneste, Capua, Pompeii, Naples, and Beneventum). The exceptions are the triumph of Tiberius depicted on the Boscoreale silver (which we discussed in the previous section), two panels now in the Louvre, and the Arch of Septimius Severus from his North African hometown, Lepcis Magna. Such evidence leaves us little ground for speaking confidently about Paul's familiarity with the

he was extrapolating from the many processions common to the ancient world.[247] Though these circumstances make it difficult to state exactly what Paul means by invoking the image of a triumph, the fact remains that Paul can refer so casually to a triumph and presume to communicate intelligibly.

Although there are difficulties in reading 2 Cor 2:14a, linguistic evidence suggests that (at bottom) Paul uses θριαμβεύειν to refer to an imperial ceremony. God celebrates his triumph with a parade and Paul-in-Christ participates.[248] This verse, therefore, shows that Paul did use royal imagery in his theology.[249] Combined with the previous examples mentioned, we recognize how naturally Paul drew from the political sphere to express his ideas. That Paul could and would use political vocabulary to coin a theological idea is entirely feasible.

A christology of kingship also shapes Paul's descriptions of Christian existence because the citizens of Christ's βασιλεία share in its administration. Members of the Corinthian church thought they had already commenced reigning with Christ (1 Cor 4:8). Paul associated their self-deception with their perception that they were already living like kings, enjoying satiety and wealth (popular conceptions of rule). Paul disagreed and challenged their δύναμις, for that was the essence of

---

ceremony. The monumental arches in cities such as Ephesus may have afforded some insight into the procession.

[247] Is Paul's mixed metaphor of 2:14 actually evidence of his confusion over the ceremonial details? If Duff is correct that Paul uses the military triumph metaphorically to reflect a religious procession, the reason for this may be that Paul lacks firsthand knowledge of a triumphal procession. Thus, Paul may not simply have lost control of his metaphor, but he never really understood it clearly.

[248] But this raises one more question which discussions of this verse typically overlook: how does the phrase ἐν Χριστῷ fit into the imagery? Does it modify the participle (θριαμβεύοντι) or pronoun (ἡμᾶς)? If the latter, does Paul imply that all Christians march in God's parade of the vanquished? If the former, does Paul mean that God's triumph takes place through Christ? This question could imply one of two things, either that God obtained prisoners for a triumph via Christ or that Christ leads God's triumphal procession. This last possibility has important implications for how one reconstructs Paul's imagery in this phrase. Does God lead the parade, or does Christ? If the latter, then 2 Cor 2:14a is further evidence for the use of royal (in fact, divine and royal) imagery in Paul's christology.

[249] Duff associates 2 Cor 5:14 with 2:14 and suggests that military imagery be retained, translating συνέχειν as "take captive." Thus, "It is not the *vengeance of God* 'leading the apostle captive' before the eyes of the Corinthians ... it is the *love of Christ* which has 'taken Paul captive'" ("Metaphor, Motif, and Meaning," 87). This parallels nicely our reading of 2 Cor 10:1, where Christ shows leniency. Cf. 2 Cor 5:20 where Paul is a κῆρυξ.

βασιλεία (4:19; cp. Rom 1:4). Meanwhile, the church could experience the δύναμις of the Lord Jesus in rendering collective judgment against a sinning Christian (5:4). We may infer that such action reflects the eschatological role of the church in judging the world and angels (6:2-3).

In view of all the preceding, the royal (or imperial) connotations of εὐαγγέλιον, the technical term for the Christian message, come as no surprise.[250] This term was widely used in connection with rulers and ruler cult to indicate important events in the life of rulers which affected their subjects' lives. Often these were messages of victory or deliverance, i.e., σωτηρία, which naturally brought great joy. Likewise, Christ the king has brought σωτηρία to his subjects and filled them with joy. εὐαγγέλιον reflects this.

So far, then, we have seen that the concept of kingship provides a matrix for organizing many of Paul's christological ideas and statements. As κύριος he holds divine status and wields divine rule; Christ is not simply king, but divine cosmocrator. Like a good ruler, Christ is concerned about justice, piety, and the welfare of others, while at the same time he is free from πλεονεξία. Like a good ruler, Christ also provides

---

[250] Gerhard Friedrich, "εὐαγγέλιον," *TDNT*, 2: 721-36; Ulrich Becker, "Gospel, Evangelize, Evangelist," *NIDNTT*, 2: 107-15; Georg Strecker, "εὐαγγέλιον," *EDNT*, 2: 70-74. Hubert Frankemölle surveys the debate about the history-of-religions background of εὐαγγέλιον (*Evangelium — Begriff und Gattung. Ein Forschungsbericht*, 2d ed. [Stuttgart: Katholisches Bibelwerk, 1994], 69-99). While Strecker has emphasized the influence of royal cult on the term, Peter Stuhlmacher has argued that the term has its roots in the early Jewish church. (The references to the exchanges in this debate appear in Frankemölle.) In my opinion, Stuhlmacher's view is too heavily diachronic, sacrificing widespread connotation in order to establish historical and material continuity within the early church. That Christians in Ephesus, Philippi, Thessalonica, and Corinth were so acclimated to the LXX that it muted the influence of imperial cult is incredible. While I have larger misgivings about Stuhlmacher's optimistic approach to early Christian sources, N. T. Wright exposes the erroneous nature of this diachronic debate ("Gospel and Theology in Galatians," in *Gospel in Paul: Studies on Corinthians, Galatians, and Romans for Richard N. Longenecker*, eds. L. Ann Jervis and Peter Richardson, JSNTSS 108 [Sheffield Academic Press, 1994], 222-39). First, he observes that "the Isaianic message always was about the enthronement of YHWH and the dethronement of pagan gods ... The Scriptural message therefore pushes itself of its own accord into the world where pagan gods and rulers stake their claims and celebrate their enthronements" (p. 227). Next he adds that "the entire religious vs. secular dichotomy in this matter is fallacious because restriction of the religious to cultic matters (in regard to the emperor) is too narrow" (pp. 227-28).

σωτηρία, freedom, law, and peace, while inspiring hope.[251] The news of these things is an εὐαγγέλιον.

6. The Good King in Paul's Theology

Given the royal *topoi* in Paul's letters, how do we account for this matrix of ideas? Based on 1 Cor 15:24-25 we have license to speak of Christ's βασιλεία, and Phil 2:6-11 and Rom 14:9 reveal the universal scope of Christ's rule. How, then, do these things fit into the larger picture of Paul's theology? Royal messianism seems an obvious answer at first, but less so on reflection, for its contribution is subject to a larger story: the cosmological significance of Christ in Paul's thought elevates Christ's rule to a divine and heavenly dimension which κύριος expresses rather than βασιλεύς. Likewise, Paul's Adam typology contributes to the good king matrix. More significantly, Paul's apocalyptic outlook creates a story which involves many aspects of Christ's rule, telling of a cosmic battle in which a divine agent conquers evil. The cosmological scale of apocalyptic thought corresponds to the universal scope of Christ's office in Paul's thinking.

An even broader history-of-religions context is helpful in determining what kind of king Christ is. The king who struggles with hardship to champion the cause of good for his people (or humanity) and whose success is crowned with apotheosis, for example, Herakles, parallels the story of Christ. This indicates the nature of Christ's rule. Having struggled with death to attain his title κύριος, Christ shows himself a ruler who shares his people's sufferings, making him a populist ruler, again, like Herakles. Such rulers are precisely the kind who incline to πραότης and/or ἐπιείκεια. We turn now to examine these things.

First, then, messianism certainly does contribute to Paul's kingship christology, but stating how this is so is problematic. For one thing, semantic problems arise: what Messiah means is uncertain and what Paul means by Χριστός is also debated. Next, assuming we know what Paul means by Χριστός, what he does with messianism further complicates things. Correlating that to a christology of kingship is yet a further task. We turn now to these things.

Study of Jewish sources in this century has complicated the easy generalizations made by previous generations of Christian commentators

---

[251] In Rom 14:17 Paul attributes to God's kingdom three characteristics which we can recognize as the product of good rule: righteousness, peace, and joy. By analogy, we can probably assume that these three things equally distinguish Christ's kingdom.

about the nature of Jewish messianic expectation, particularly the easy association long made between Messiah and a davidic deliverer-king.[252] Charlesworth summarizes the situation, writing, "The complexity of messianic ideas, the lack of a coherent messianology among the documents in the Pseudepigrapha and among the Dead Sea Scrolls, and the frequently contradictory messianic predictions prohibit anything approximating coherency in early Jewish messianology."[253] Given this, it would seem that to call Jesus the Christ does not automatically ascribe to him a βασιλεία.

In another survey of messianic views at the turn of the era, however, John Collins limits the possible messianic roles. Collins identifies four types of figures: king, priest, prophet, and heavenly messiah (or Son of Man).[254] A messianic king appears in contrast to the Hasmoneans and Pompey in *Psalms of Solomon* 17 and more generally Rome in the DSS and *4 Ezra*. The priestly Messiah appears in the Qumran literature, emerging out of the political situation of the Hasmoneans and dissatisfaction with the temple cult in Jerusalem. A heavenly figure based on Daniel 7 influenced the authors of *4 Ezra* and the *Similitudes of Enoch*, both of which identify the figure as Messiah (cf. *Sibylline Oracles* 5). What I would emphasize at this point is that each of these three figures are rulers. Collins, moreover, concludes that within this limited set of choices was "a dominant notion of a Davidic messiah, as the king who would

---

[252] Morton Smith, "What is Implied by the Variety of Messianic Figures?" *JBL* 78 (1959): 66-72; Jacob Neusner, William Scott Green, and Ernest S. Fredrichs, eds., *Judaisms and Their Messiahs at the Turn of the Christian Era* (Cambridge University Press, 1987); James H. Charlesworth, ed., *The Messiah: Developments in Earliest Judaism and Christianity*, The First Princeton Symposium on Judaism and Christian Origins (Minneapolis: Fortress Press, 1992); Kenneth E. Pomykala, *The Davidic Dynasty Tradition in Early Judaism: Its History and Significance for Messianism*, SBL Early Judaism and Its Literature 7 (Atlanta: Scholars Press, 1995). Pomykala even shows that 1) a messianic king may not necessarily be a davidic king (e.g., pp. 246, 255, 263-64), whereas 2) invoking a specifically davidic king may arise from opposition to the rule of a disliked king (e.g., Hasmonean, p. 169, or Herodian, p. 214); and 3) if comparing the texts that do reflect a davidic messiah, although there may be "generic similarities," "the evidence demonstrates that no uniform conception of a davidic messiah existed in early Judaism" (p 270).

[253] James H. Charlesworth, "From Messianology to Christology: Problems and Prospects," in *The Messiah*, 28; similarly, William Scott Green, "Introduction: Messiah in Judaism: Rethinking the Question," in *Judaisms and Their Messiahs*, 1-13; Nils A. Dahl, "The Crucified Messiah," in his *Jesus the Christ: The Historical Origins of Christological Doctrine*, ed. Donald H. Juel (Minneapolis: Fortress Press, 1991), 38-39.

[254] John J. Collins, *The Scepter and the Star: Jewish Messianism in the Light of the Dead Sea Scrolls*, ABRL (New York: Doubleday, 1995), 12, 195.

3.6. The Good King in Paul's Theology

restore the kingdom of Israel."[255] In short, the denial of coherency Charlesworth asserts is true, yet an exaggeration.

While the background Collins sketches suggests that rule would enter into Paul's ideas about Christ, the foreground of other Christian texts further complicates the picture. The innovative way in which early Christians constructed a dying and rising Messiah warns us against defining Χριστός strictly against earlier Jewish usage. Paul's corresponding acceptance of Christ's death and resurrection as taking place according to the Scriptures further complicates his messianic views.

We must therefore identify what Paul does mean by calling Jesus "Christ." What Paul means by Χριστός, however, is a point of debate. A commonplace of NT scholarship is that in Paul's letters Χριστός is a name, not a title.[256] To the extent that this is true, we must be wary of basing a strand of Paul's christology on the meaning of Χριστός. But the argument that Χριστός is a name only is deficient in three ways. First, as Cullmann indicates, Paul typically avoids juxtaposing Χριστός and κύριος, indicating that Paul continued to recognize a titular aspect of Χριστός and did not see it as simply another name for Jesus.[257] Second, in listing Israel's benefits, Paul counts the Messiah as among them (Rom 9:5), revealing that the apostle recognized the titular origin of Χριστός.[258] Elsewhere in Romans (15:8), Paul states the necessity that Christ was Jewish in order to vindicate the truth of God's promises to the fathers. Third, the play on Χριστός and χρίσας in 2 Cor 1:21 further suggests that Paul recognized the generic meaning of Χριστός. These three observations make me hesitate to say that Χριστός is *only* another name for Jesus in Paul's letters; nevertheless, they do not explain what Χριστός means.

Two influential studies have investigated Paul's understanding of "Christ."[259] While both conclude that Christ is not a meaningless concept

---

[255] *Ibid.*, p. 209.

[256] Imperial nomenclature is no less confusing. We might compare the evolution of Caesar from name to title. Even more complex is the shift of Augustus from title to name — and back to title. In addition, we should note that Paul describes both Jesus and Lord as *onoma* (Phil 2:9-11).

[257] Oscar Cullmann, *The Christology of the New Testament* (1959), 134; Marinus de Jonge, "Christ," *ABD*, 1: 915.

[258] Other less convincing examples of the titular use have at one time or another been put forward, such as, Rom 10:6; 1 Cor 10:4, 5, 22; 2 Cor 4:4; 5:10.

[259] Nils A. Dahl, "Die Messianität Jesu bei Paulus," in *Studia Paulina in honorem Johannis de Zwaan* (Haarlem: Erven F. Bohn, 1953), 83-95; rev. and trans., "The Messiahship of Jesus in Paul," in his *Jesus the Christ: The Historical Origins of Christological Doctrine*, ed. Donald H. Juel (Minneapolis: Fortress Press, 1991), 15-25;

for Paul, both also argue that the meaning of the term is provided by Jesus, not a pre-existent Jewish tradition. Dahl writes, "The name 'Christ' does not receive its content through a previously fixed conception of messiahship but rather from the person and work of Jesus Christ. An *interpretatio christiana* is carried out completely" (p. 17). Later he repeats, "What provides the content of the word 'Christ' in Paul is less Paul's pre-Christian messianic concept than the pre-Pauline Christology of the church" (p. 19). Hengel reaches a similar conclusion. He reasons that Jesus was Messiah by confession, which in turn allowed Messiah to be defined by what Jesus was; as a result, "the 'nature' of the Messiah was not to be defined in the light of any traditional messianic expectations but was determined once for all through Jesus" (p. 76). Despite their agreement, Hengel and Dahl differ in how they formulate their conclusions. Since Χριστός in Paul is not defined by traditional messianic thought but by Jesus, Hengel concludes that "it makes little sense to seek to discover in Paul the use of the name as a title" (p. 76). From a similar premise Dahl infers that in Paul, Χριστός "is not a colorless proper name ... but an honorific designation, whose content is supplied by the person and work of Jesus Christ."[260] Given the contexts of each statement, however, the difference is less than it appears (though I prefer Dahl). What is important to note is that Dahl and Hengel further impede the impulse to assume that Paul's confession of Jesus as Χριστός automatically identifies him as God's royal deliverer.

Additional considerations must be raised which nuance the studies noted so far. First, as we noted already, Χριστός is not a banal term (2 Cor 1:21); nor does it lack a Jewish past (Rom 9:5; 15:7-8). Second, as also noted already, when denying the coherence of Jewish messianic ideas, one must not forget that the number of possibilities is not infinite, but one of four ideal types: king, priest, prophet, and heavenly figure.[261] (It is no accident that the NT applies each of these four categories to Jesus.) I grant that ideal types are strictly that, ideal, and that Charlesworth is correct to

---

Martin Hengel, "Erwägungen zum Sprachgebrauch von Χριστός bei Paulus und in der 'vorpaulinischen' Überlieferung," in *Paul and Paulinism: Essays in Honor of C. K. Barrett*, eds. M. D. Hooker and S. G. Wilson (London: SPCK, 1982), 135-59; English: "'Χριστός' in Paul," in his *Between Jesus and Paul*, trans. John Bowden (Philadelphia: Fortress Press, 1983), 65-77.

[260] Nils A. Dahl, "The Crucified Messiah," in his *Jesus the Christ: The Historical Origins of Christological Doctrine*, ed. Donald H. Juel (Minneapolis: Fortress Press, 1991), 37. Though it obscures a legitimate question, "honorific designation" is a better way of describing Paul's use of Χριστός than "name" or "title." Familiarity should not blind us to the respect indicated by compound appellations.

[261] John Collins, *The Scepter and the Star*, 12.

criticize the easy generalizations which generations of scholars have made about Jewish messianism. Still, ideal types do suggest possible and viable associations — particularly as they are grounded in particular and specific examples.[262] This brings us to point three. Commenting on Jewish sources in general, de Jonge says that Messiah "does not stand for a fixed concept, but rather brings with it a wealth of connotations made more or less explicit in a given context."[263] Thus, ideas interacted with specific situations to shape messianic ideas. It is no surprise that the Hasmonean period or the DSS community would envision a priestly Messiah. To say therefore that Jesus determines the meaning of Χριστός is not unlike how a specific Messiah is usually defined. Fourth, there nevertheless remains a dialectical element to the identification of Jesus as Messiah. Dahl himself recognizes this and weakens his own position by allowing that the content of Paul's messianic idea includes the fulfillment of OT promises.[264] Well, which promises? Those Jesus happened to fulfill? That is naïve. Perhaps, any and all promises? This becomes possible only when criteria for identifying promises (i.e., an ideology) are recognized. Thus, to identify promises haphazardly results in a Messiah of rhetorical accident, while screening promises according to set criteria presupposes some ideology. For example, to recognize Jesus as David's son (Rom 1:3; Matt 1:1) is a significant observation only within the context of an ideology which Jesus does not define. Furthermore, nothing obviously compels a person to label Jesus "*the* seed" of Abraham (Gal 3:16). While such a claim was certainly not obvious to Paul's Christian opponents, belief in a Gentile mission identifies it as a promise. Such a perspective can even generate a catena of OT texts to justify itself (Rom 15:7-12). And typology clearly requires

---

[262] The variety of messiahs does not render the term incomprehensible. By comparison, Americans are perfectly content to use the words clergy and minister for a variety of dissimilar figures. A Catholic priest is not a Baptist pastor is not a Pentecostal preacher; a youth pastor is not a music minister; a pastor of assimilation is not a teaching pastor; a military chaplain is not a prison chaplain. All, however, are regarded as clergy. The point is that based on the diversity of roles subsumed by the term clergy, one could argue that the term is incoherent. While religious pedants may do so, the rest of American society can and does use the word to good purpose. We can even use the term to cover rabbis. (If one wishes to counter that ordination is a common thread among the varieties of clergy, I would point to the very different kinds of ordination and would introduce the additional ambiguities raised by parachurch ministries and even *lay* ministries.) Conversely, if a person's "official" designation is priest, pastor, preacher, missionary, evangelist, or chaplain, that does not mean he or she is not a member of the clergy.

[263] "The Earliest Christian Use of Χριστός: Some Suggestions," *NTS* 32 (1986): 329-30.

[264] "The Messiahship of Jesus in Paul," 20; and "The Crucified Messiah," 39.

some underlying system of thought (1 Cor 10:4). In my opinion, then, some system of thought which views Christ as a ruler is necessary in order to attribute Ps 110:1 (1 Cor 15:25) and Ps 8:7 (1 Cor 15:27) to Christ's present situation and to attribute to him a παρουσία loaded with apocalyptic imagery (1 Thess 4:16). While experiences of Christ's power probably contributed to this belief, that it should be expressed as rule and should draw on royal imagery from the OT rests on ideas. In short, to connect OT promises to Paul's messianic idea creates a profoundly consequential dialectic. While that dialectic is too complex to yield a simple definition of Χριστός, it situates the term within a dynamic and not banal aspect of Paul's thinking.[265]

Can we, however, link Χριστός to royal rule in Paul's letters? On a theoretical level we should allow the likelihood. Again, among the four ideal types which Collins identifies, we should note that rule is intrinsic to king, likely for the heavenly figure, and possible for the priest and prophet. As for the last two, the priest was a civil authority, while the prophet too could be a ruler if defined as a prophet like Moses. In theory, then, that Χριστός would have some ἐξουσία or ἀρχή would be probable.

In actual practice, though, did Paul connect Jesus to royal messianism? Paul's use of Ps 110 seems to indicate such a connection: 1 Cor 15:25 loosely excerpts Ps 110:1, while Rom 8:34 unambiguously echoes Ps 110:1, 4. In the latter, Paul's reference to Christ's being "at God's right hand" is followed by attribution to Christ of an intercessory ministry, a combination of ideas which parallels Ps 110:1 and 4, where God's enthroned son is designated a priest. The Psalm clearly guides Paul's thoughts. In 1 Cor 15:25 ("he puts all enemies under his feet") and 27 ("he subjects all things under his feet"), Paul draws on Ps 110:1 and 8:6. The latter allusion becomes an obvious quotation when Paul subsequently offers commentary on it ("Now when it says . . ."). This suggests Paul knew his earlier statement likewise to be a scriptural allusion. That Paul in neither reference to Psalm 110 refers explicitly to it reflects its commonplace usage in Paul's Christian circles.[266] To recognize that Ps

---

[265] N. T. Wright also argues against regarding Χριστός as simply another name for Jesus in Paul's letters: "The usage of Χριστός is incorporative, that is, Paul regularly uses the word to connote, and sometimes even to *de*note, the whole people of whom the Messiah is the representative" (*The Climax of the Covenant*, 46; emphasis his). Presumably, then, how Messiah represents his people delineates his role (i.e., priest, king, etc.).

[266] See Martin Hengel, "Psalm 110 und die Erhöhung des Auferstandenen zur Rechten Gottes," in *Anfänge der Christologie. Festschrift für Ferdinand Hahn zum 65. Geburtstag*, eds. Cilliers Breytenbach and Henning Paulsen (Göttingen: Vandenhoeck &

110 contributed to Paul's christology obscures how Paul connected Christ to royal messianism. In both 1 Corinthians 15 and Romans 8, the sovereignty expressed in the testimonium has lost its explicit connections to a mundane throne and focuses on a heavenly throne. As a result, Paul does indeed use royal messianic imagery, but he extends it far beyond local, Jewish politics. Paul steps beyond even Isaiah's brand of global politics to a universalism that is cosmic in scope. This is typical of Paul's conception of Christ's messianic rule, as we will now see elsewhere.

As we seek connections between messianism and Paul's christology of kingship, two other important texts must be examined, Rom 1:3-4 and 15:12. Here again we will find royal messianic imagery, but again find it ultimately linked to a heavenly throne. Problems of sources, multiple meanings, and the understanding represented by the text of Romans likewise assert themselves. As a result, when we turn to Rom 1:3-4 we must be cautious about identifying Paul's christology, because questions surround the relationship between this pre-pauline text and Paul's theology.[267] Arguments based on vocabulary, ideas, and structure persuasively suggest that the confession which opens Paul's letter to Rome was not coined by Paul himself. This invites speculation about Pauline redaction and the pre-pauline interpretation(s) of the confession.

Four basic assumptions which scholars make in reading Rom 1:3-4 are that ἐν δυνάμει indicates a concern about adoptionism, that vv. 3 and 4 are antithetical, that σάρξ and πνεῦμα indicate some dualism, and that the prepositions are clues to the creed's structure. I wish to differ with each of these. First, that Paul was even concerned about adoptionism is a

---

Ruprecht, 1991), 43-73; Cullmann, *Christology of the New Testament*, 222-23. Cp. Paul's use of Jer 9:24: in 1 Cor 1:31, Paul introduces it as a scriptural quotation, whereas in subsequent use, 2 Cor 10:17, he does not.

[267] On Rom 1:3-4 see the commentaries. In addition, Robert Jewett surveys the issues and previous studies in his article, "The Redaction and Use of an Early Christian Confession in Romans 1:3-4," in *The Living Text: Essays in Honor of Ernest W. Saunders*, eds. D. Groh and R. Jewett (Lanhan, MD: University Press of America, 1985), 99-122. Most recently, see Georgi, *Theocracy*, 85-88; Marinus de Jonge, "Jesus, Son of David and Son of God," in *Intertextuality in Biblical Writings: Essays in Honor of Bas van Iersel*, ed. Sipke Draisma (Kampen: Kok, 1989), 95-104; Andries B. du Toit, "Romans 1,3-4 and the Gospel Tradition: A Reassessment of the Phrase κατὰ πνεῦμα ἁγιοσύνης," in *The Four Gospels 1992: Festschrift Frans Neirynck*, eds. F. Van Segbroeck, et al., 3 vols., BETL 100 (Leuven University Press/Peeters, 1992), 1: 249-56. More recently, Timo Eskola has connected Rom 1:3-4 to enthronement based on parallels in Jewish literature, and specifically as part of Jewish-Christian merkabah tradition: *Messiah and the Throne: Jewish Merkabah Mysticism and Early Christian Exaltation Discourse*, WUNT II/142 (Tübingen: J. C. B. Mohr/Paul Siebeck, 2001), 217-50.

problematic assertion. That inserting ἐν δυνάμει removes any hint of adoptionism is also not obvious. The phrase simply serves to expand on the office to which Christ was appointed at the time of his resurrection. The position of Son of God is endowed with power.

As for the relation between vv. 3 and 4, we should point out that no adversatives are present to indicate an antithetical structure. The σάρξ/πνεῦμα contrast alone suggests antithesis. Or does it? The pair may instead function to emphasize the fullness of Christ's significance, with no intent to denigrate the first member of the pair: that πνεῦμα may be of greater consequence does not mean that σάρξ is intrinsically evil. As far as Paul is concerned, this reading corresponds to the remainder of the letter, in which Paul will argue on behalf of his Gentile gospel, while not discounting the relevance of its Jewish origin. Furthermore, to the extent that Paul's audience valued the gospel's Jewish roots, criticism of Christ's Davidic origin would antagonize them — an imprudent rhetorical move. If Paul, then, saw no antagonism in the σάρξ/πνεῦμα contrast, it is possible that earlier users of the creed did not. Thus, Rom 1:3-4 seeks not to introduce discontinuity, but to assert the valid and necessary continuity between David's son and God's and to describe the progression from the one to the other.

Third, in regard to σάρξ and πνεῦμα themselves, various theories have been proposed to explain their meaning. Often the pair is identified as a Hellenistic addition to a Palestinian confession, introduced to denigrate Christ's Jewish ancestry. These theories, however, typically ignore the fact that the contrast is not between σάρξ and πνεῦμα, but between κατὰ σάρκα and κατὰ πνεῦμα ἁγιωσύνης. The latter is more precise than the former.[268] In view of this difference, we must be cautious about overloading the terms with cosmological significance.[269] We must also grant that κατὰ σάρκα is not intrinsically negative. As in Rom 4:1 and

---

[268] Unlike σάρξ, πνεῦμα ἁγιωσύνης may be an agent; alternatively, both may be agencies.

[269] Some interpreters have labelled πνεῦμα ἁγιωσύνης as a Semitism. If this is correct, then the two words are joined together even more tightly. Moreover, the resulting contrast between κατὰ σάρκα and κατὰ πνεῦμα ἁγιωσύνης combines a Hellenistic cosmology and a theological Semitism! This implies a more complex *Sitz im Leben* than is typically recognized. Who is borrowing whose ideas and how deeply have they penetrated?

That Paul added the two κατά phrases seems unlikely to me, because as Pauline as κατὰ σάρκα is, πνεῦμα ἁγιωσύνης is not. As Jewett notes, "While Paul uses the term 'holiness' in ethical contexts (1 Thess 3:17; 2 Cor 7:1), he never otherwise attaches it to 'spirit.' Also when Paul uses 'spirit' after κατά, he never otherwise affixes a qualifying noun in this instance" ("Redaction," 103).

9:3, 5, κατὰ σάρκα may qualify something which retains some value (while indicating that more remains to be said). More to the point, other NT texts suggest that while the title Son of David may be insufficient, it is nevertheless a positive affirmation.[270] Thus, while vv. 3-4 offer a contrast, they do so to express completion, and in so doing present a continuous narrative. Du Toit characterizes the structure well: "The description of the parallelism as antithetical and progressive does not imply that its first member should be understood in a pejorative sense. The second member should rather be read as climactic with regard to the preceding positive assertion."[271] The ideas of progression and climax are insightful.

Fourth, du Toit adds another observation about the structure of the creed which is likewise helpful. Refusing to see the prepositions as the key to the creed's structure, he notes that while "the phrases ἐκ σπέρματος Δαυίδ and υἱοῦ θεοῦ do not correspond lexically, they do positionally, grammatically (cf. the genitive) and semantically, referring to Jesus' relationship respectively to David and to God."[272] Building on his observation, we may organize the structure of the creed as follows:

τοῦ γενομένου
    ἐκ σπέρματος Δαυίδ
    κατὰ σάρκα

τοῦ ὁρισθέντος
    υἱοῦ θεοῦ ἐν δυνάμει
    κατὰ πνεῦμα ἁγιωσύνης
        ἐξ ἀναστάσεως νεκρῶν.

This structure emphasizes the greater amplification present in the second half of the creed and indicates the usefulness of du Toit's labels of progression and climax. "David's descendent" is paralleled not simply by "Son of God," but by "Son of God in power," while σάρξ is paralleled by the more elaborate πνεῦμα ἁγιωσύνης. In keeping with this tendency to expand, the second half then adds a concluding phrase to amplify Christ's appointment, viz., ἐξ ἀναστάσεως νεκρῶν.[273] Form therefore follows

---

[270] Not least in this regard is Rom 15:12, which we will discuss soon.

[271] A. B. du Toit, "Romans 1,3-4," 250-51.

[272] "Romans 1,3-4," 250. See also Dunn, *Romans*, 1: 5.

[273] Does the additional concluding phrase indicate Pauline redaction? I think the recognition of expansion in the previous two phrases justifies the inclusion of an additional phrase. In terms of style, the phrase is non-pauline, as many studies have noted. If Paul did add it, he was careful to conform to the style of the creed itself by

meaning: the greater honor lavished on the exalted Son is reflected in the more discursive comments made about his exaltation. If this analysis is correct, it implies that the creed did not pass through multiple versions and confirms that the second half of the hymn should be emphasized, but more as climax than antithesis.

In view of the preceding comments, we now venture to present our reading of the creed in Rom 1:3-4. The creed opens with the assertion that God's son "came from David's seed according to the flesh." To designate someone as David's heir makes him a potentially royal figure. The following phrase confirms the actual as opposed to the potential and underscores this attribution of royalty: "who was appointed God's son — with full authority — according to the spirit of cultic propriety at [his] resurrection [from] the dead." The connection of David's descendent and God's son indicates that the latter refers to the OT use of "son of God" as one of the king's designations.[274] That Paul introduces this connection as a response to Scriptural promise (Rom 1:2) also points to this conclusion. Consequently, we may observe that to appoint David's heir God's son is to elevate him to the throne and to invest him with authority and power (ἐν δυνάμει; cp. 1 Cor 4:20). In terms of OT ritual, the anointing which signified such an appointment was performed by a prophet, priest, or the people. Anointing by prophet or priest was more common and constituted "the formal expression of approval of the 'anointed' by representatives of the religious-cultic echelons of the society."[275] Jesus' appointment κατὰ πνεῦμα ἁγιωσύνης parallels that phenomenon.[276] That Jesus' resurrection marks the moment (or means) of his elevation reflects the eschatological nature of his office (and consequently its universal scope; cp. 15:12). In sum, the installation of David's heir as king brought him power and the special position of God's son; moreover, his elevation took place in his resurrection and is unimpeachable. The christological formula in Rom 1:3-4 therefore expresses Jesus' dynastic legitimacy and his installation as king.

---

stripping his normal expression of any definite article and leaving out the preposition ἐκ before νεκρῶν.

[274] 2 Sam 7:14; Ps 2:7; cp. 4Q 246 and Roman imperial nomenclature.

[275] Shemaryahu Talmon, "The Concepts of *Māšîah* and Messianism in Early Judaism," in *The Messiah*, ed. J. H. Charlesworth, 89.

[276] Alternatively, the good king champions his people's god(s), which may be demonstrated by promoting cult and upholding law; κατὰ πνεῦμα ἁγιωσύνης may therefore indicate and validate the piety of the appointed king.

3.6. The Good King in Paul's Theology

Similar ideas appear elsewhere in the New Testament.[277] Acts 13:33-35 draws on Psalm 2 to connect Jesus' resurrection to his appointment as God's son and in so doing succinctly repeats the more elaborate statements of Acts 2:29-36, a passage that explicitly connects Jesus' resurrection to his installation on the Davidic throne. Heb 1:5 also quotes Psalm 2 and connects Jesus' sonship to throne, scepter, kingdom, anointing, justice, and the defeat of his enemies (Heb 1:6-13). The rule envisioned in Hebrews is in fact cosmic rule, as the son is cosmic heir, agent of creation, and receives the worship of angels. Thus, to equate the Davidic king with God's son reflects the imagery of Psalm 2 and the OT designation of the king as God's son.[278] To identify the resurrection as the moment of Christ's royal installation parallels Luke-Acts and Hebrews. In view of such considerations, Dunn concludes that "the association between Ps. 2.7 and Jesus' resurrection/exaltation was a basic and primitive characteristic of early Christian apologetic."[279] Even so, did Paul associate the two? In 1 Cor 15:4 he quotes as part of the traditional Christian gospel that Christ "was raised on the third day according to the Scripture." Paul did not specify what texts he had in mind; however, Rom 1:3-4, in the light of Acts 2 and 13 and Hebrews 1, suggests the possibility of texts associated with Davidic promises and enthronement. That Rom 1:2 introduces vv. 3-4 with the category of promise enhances this possibility. The connections in 1 Corinthians 15 and Romans 8 to Psalms 8 and 110 also point to this conclusion. The result, however, is not a Jewish king, but a divine king in heaven, so that Paul's connection of Jesus to royal messianism leads to something different.

In terms of the present context of Rom 1:3-4, we should note its connections with Roman imperial thought.[280] In an important development with Julius Caesar, a Roman leader (tyrant/king) received apotheosis at death.[281] The emphasis on Christ's resurrection parallels the Roman emperor's *post mortem* apotheosis. As the emperor's body burned on its funeral pyre, his soul ascended to heaven. In the case of Julius Caesar, he

---

[277] Given that Rom 1:3-4 is pre-pauline, examination of passages outside of Paul's letters is all the more relevant.

[278] On the divine sonship of the OT king, see Tryggve N. D. Mettinger, *King and Messiah: The Civil and Sacral Letitimation of the Israelite Kings*, Coniectanea Biblica, Old Testament Series 8 (CWK Gleerup, 1976), 259-75; Gerald Cooke, "The Israelite King as Son of God," *ZAW* 73 (1960): 202-25 (especially 208-19).

[279] J. D. G. Dunn, *Christology in the Making*, 36.

[280] Cp. Georgi, *Theocracy*, 85-87.

[281] Suet. *Iul.* 84, 88; regarding Augustus, see Suet. *Aug.* 100; Tac. *Ann.* 13.3 (cf. 1.8-15); Dio Cas. 56.34-46 (especially 34, 42, and 46); cf. Sen. *Apoc.*

joined the stars. The parallel is not, however, perfect. Whereas Caesar's apotheosis earned him the title *divus* (θεός), Christ's resurrection and exaltation brought him υἱὸς θεοῦ — which was also the title of the deified emperor's surviving heir. Regardless, in the opening of a letter to Rome, the resonances are striking. Although these traditions may not have informed the original composition of Rom 1:3-4, they could affect the understanding of the confession in the context of Paul's letter.

Since we have been discussing a pre-pauline text, we must still consider how deeply the confession entered Paul's thinking. Did he associate "seed of David" with rule? Another text in Romans helps us to answer this question. In Rom 15:12 Paul quotes Isa 11:10, writing, "The root of Jesse shall come, the one who rises to rule (ὁ ἀνιστάμενος ἄρχειν) the Gentiles" (NRSV). In writing this Paul explicitly connected Jesus' rule to his Davidic ancestry; moreover, the Greek introduces a double-entendre (ἀνιστάμενος) which alludes to Christ's resurrection. Thus, by connecting Davidic descent, rule, and resurrection, these two lines from Isaiah provide a remarkable summary of the creed found in 1:3-4.[282]

The broad context of 15:12 further underscores its importance. In 15:7-13 Paul's spirited presentation of his gospel concludes; in 15:14 he begins to discuss his travel plans and more strictly epistolary matters. In drawing his presentation of the gospel to a conclusion, Paul exhorts his readership to follow the example of Christ who served both Jews and the nations. The apostle then elaborates on Christ's benefit to the nations by means of a catena of OT quotations. Verse 12 (Isa 11:10) is the fourth and final member of this string and with it he expresses one final, climactic time his Jew-Gentile theme. Thus, though unusual in terms of the Pauline corpus, Rom 1:3-4 and 15:13 occupy strategic places in Paul's letter to Rome and together produce an interesting effect. Whereas in 1:3-4 Paul offers a christological statement, in 15:12 his eye is no longer on christology, but ecclesiology.[283] A progression has occurred. Paul has given the historical movement of the gospel to the Jews first and then to the Greeks a

---

[282] That Rom 15:12 has not played a great role in the interpretation of Rom 1:3-4 is surprising. Some in fact have said that Paul's reference in Rom 1:3 to Jesus' Davidic ancestry is unique in his letters. On the contrary, the reference to "the root of Jesse" in Rom 15:12 is tantamount to "seed of David." Richard B. Hayes has observed the allusion to Rom 1:3 in Rom 15:12 in *Echoes of Scripture in the Letters of Paul* (Yale University Press, 1989), 72. Subsequent to my research, Christopher G. Whitsett has championed the importance of this connection in "Son of God, Seed of David: Paul's Messianic Exegesis in Romans 1:3-4," *JBL* 119/4 (2000): 661-81. His exposition of the relationship is insightful, but concluding that Paul wrote Rom 1:3-4 goes too far.

[283] Richard B. Hays, *Echoes of Scripture*, 70-73 and 160-64.

christological foundation.[284] What had been latent in the opening creed received elaborate discussion in the body of the letter, so that fifteen chapters later, when Paul expressed a similar idea, the implications for God's people of the christological affirmation were clarified. Christ's lofty rule results in the incorporation of the nations into God's people.

It would appear that Christ as God's anointed king has contributed to Paul's thinking. But Rom 15:12 cannot be extracted from the previous fourteen chapters, where Paul argued for something different than ethnic, royal messianism. It is one thing for the nations to rejoice in a ruler who sits in Jerusalem and promotes justice and piety throughout the world, while it is another to see Jewish ancestry, law, and cult as of secondary importance to the universal work of Jesus — whose throne is in heaven. Paul may share the language of other Christians (and Jews), but that should not obscure the differences. Throughout Romans, Jesus is much more than a royal messiah (e.g., ἱλαστήριον and Adam). While Paul recognizes Davidic messianism as part of the picture, his focus rests on how Jesus transcends ethnicity and has been raised by God to be much more than King of the Jews. Thus, when Paul sees the words "the one who rises to rule the Gentiles" as supporting his mission to the nations, he understands these words in a way which many other Jews and Christians would (adamantly) not have.

We may conclude then that Rom 1:3-4 penetrated Paul's thinking, but in so doing it was altered. David's seed gave way to God's son. Thus, in 1 Thess 1:10 Paul wrote that Christians "await God's son from heaven, whom [God] raised from the dead, Jesus who rescues us from the coming wrath." As in Rom 1:3-4, this text refers to Christ as God's son, associates him with heaven, and mentions his resurrection; furthermore, the act of deliverance corresponds to the regal connotations of Rom 1:3-4. But David's son has receded into the background (as does OT material in most of 1 Thessalonians). Turning to Romans itself, we can observe that, as the letter unfolds, God's son proves to be more than code for David's seed. As God's son, Christ is not simply another ruler appointed by God; he is the paradigm of Christian destiny. As the spirit was involved in Christ's installation as Son, so is the divine spirit bringing other children to God (Rom 8:14-15). We may also note that as resurrection launched Christ's sonship, so will resurrection mark the Christian's adoption (Rom 8:23). Attaining that glory, Christians will share in Christ's image and Christ

---

[284] Michael Theobald wisely draws attention to Rom 1:16 and 15:8f. in "'Dem Juden zuerst und auch dem Heiden.' Die paulinische Auslegung der Glaubensformel Röm 1,3f.," in *Kontinuität und Einheit. Für Franz Mußner*, eds. Paul-Gerhard Müller and Werner Stenger (Freiburg: Herder, 1981), 376-92, especially pp. 388-89.

will truly be the firstborn among many siblings (8:17, 29-30). In Galatians, we find that Paul describes the Christian's present existence as one lived ἐν πίστει...τῇ τοῦ υἱοῦ τοῦ θεοῦ (Gal 2:20; cf. 3:26). As for the future, we noted earlier that Christ will even share his rule with his people (1 Cor 4:8, 19; 6:2-3). In short, Rom 1:3-4 presents ideas which reappear in Paul's letters, but which receive different emphasis. To say that royal messianism appears in Rom 1:3-4 is therefore correct, but misleading, inasmuch as it tells us little about Paul.

We have looked at four texts (Rom 1:3-4; 8:34; 15:12; 1 Cor 15:25) which one could argue indicate the presence of royal messianism in Paul's writings.[285] On the surface they allow the generalization that the notion of Christ as messianic king formed one strand of Paul's christology. In their details, however, the generalization is weakened: Paul does not explicitly quote Psalm 110; Rom 15:12 focuses on ecclesiology; Rom 1:3-4 indicates that messianism is only part of Christ's royal office, for Christ's rule is exercised from heaven, not Jerusalem. We also note that Christ as Son and as Lord are equally relevant in the various texts. As a result, the data has proven as complex as our introductory comments about Χριστός indicated.

Though defining Χριστός in Paul's letters may be difficult, the texts noted in connection with it clearly do involve discussion of a figure who exercises royal office. Rom 1:3-4 presents the Davidic heir as enthroned Son of God. Rom 15:12 presents a ruler, while Rom 8:34 implies one. 1 Cor 15:25 (as already noted) explicitly attributes βασιλεία to Jesus. While the complete picture goes beyond mundane Jewish politics, adding a specifically Christian level of meaning, *we certainly can use these texts to identify a christology of kingship in Paul's letters*. But, again, this kingship is cosmic. As we have seen earlier, Christ's rule is universal, wielded from heaven, extending to heavenly and subterrestrial creatures, and present among the many ἐκκλησίαι of his people by the divine spirit. The difference is not one of politics versus religion, but local versus universal. Christ's βασιλεία blurs not only Jew and Gentile, but heaven and earth.[286]

---

[285] Here recall Rom 11:26 (Isa 59:20), which links salvation, justice, and piety to Christ, and Rom 15:13, which describes Christ using his strength on behalf of the weak.

[286] Little in this picture is unparalleled in Jewish messianic texts. How it serves Paul's Gentile mission strikes me as unique, but a heavenly Messiah is not, since the Son of Man in the *Similitudes of Enoch* is called Messiah. As for the cosmic dimension of Christ's rule in Paul's thinking, we can compare the *War Scroll* from Qumran, which speaks of the cosmic effects resulting from the victory of the Messiah of Israel. That Paul's cosmic Christ was crucified clearly distinguishes him (and other Christians) from these texts.

The worldwide scope of Christ's rule receives further elaboration in Paul's Adam-Christ typology. In 1 Cor 15:24-25, Christ exercises rule with the specific goal of conquering death, in which mission Christ parallels Adam.[287] Paul says that resurrection comes in Christ, who is the last Adam, a life-giving spirit (vv. 22, 45). As the second Adam, then, Christ brings life, while as king he defeats death. This similarity between Christ as ruler and Christ as Adam is strengthened materially in v. 27 by the phrase, "He subjects all things under his feet," a quotation from Ps 8:7. If the Adam-Christ typology also provides the conceptual rationale for applying Ps 8:7 to Christ (as is possible), then this text furthers the connection between Christ's rule and his role as second Adam.[288] Such an association would not be surprising, given that rule was one of the blessings given to Adam — a fact not overlooked by Jewish traditions, which recalled Adam's role as ruler and even identified him as a king.[289] *Ps.-Philo*, however, notes that by transgression Adam lost his dominion and brought death (13:8-9). As second Adam, Christ reverses this, banishing death and asserting rule. Thus, viewing Christ as second Adam further points to his royal office.[290]

---

[287] Besides Rom 5:12-21 and 1 Cor 15:21-28, 45, various scholars have proposed that an Adam christology is present in Rom 1:18-32; 3:23; 6:23; 7:8-9; 8:20-21; Phil 2:6-11; 3:21.

[288] J. D. G. Dunn, *Christology in the Making*, 108-9.

[289] See *2 Enoch* 30:12: "[God] assigned [Adam] to be a king, to reign on the earth"; Philo *De op. mun.* 136-50: Adam was "a king (βασιλεύς), and it befits a ruler (ἡγεμών) to bestow titles on his several subordinates." Cf. *2 Enoch* 31:3; Wis 9:2-3; 10:1-2; Sir 17:2, 4; 4 Ezra 6:53-54; *Jub.* 2:13-15. See N. T. Wright, *The Climax of the Covenant*, 21-26. That these different texts speak of Adam's dominion reflects only their common knowledge of Gen 1:28, not a common interpretation and application of that text. John R. Levison emphasizes the diversity of the way Jewish authors used the figure of Adam, *Portraits of Adam in Early Judaism: From Sircah to 2 Baruch*, JSPSS 1 (Sheffield Academic Press, 1988).

[290] N. T. Wright's analysis of Paul's Adam christology potentially tightens the association with rule. Wright first emphasizes that Adam speculation is not about humankind in general, but about God's people, Israel: given the failure of Adam and humankind, God sought a remedy in Abraham's descendants, rendering Israel a new humanity (*The Climax of the Covenant*, 20-21). In Paul's view as expressed in 1 Corinthians 15, "Israel's role is taken by her anointed king, and this Messiah has acted out her victory in himself, being raised from the dead in advance of his people" (p. 28). A similar interplay of people and representative appears in Daniel 7, "in which, within the apocalyptic imagery, the human figure, standing for the people of the saints of the most high, is exalted to a position of authority at the right hand of the Ancient of Days" (p. 28). Wright hears echoes of Daniel in 1 Corinthians 15, which corresponds to Paul's use of Psalm 8, yet another text which reflects the conjunction of ideal humanity,

Additional Pauline allusions to Adam are more controversial. Many read the Philippians hymn as contrasting Christ with Adam.[291] Created in the image of God, Adam aspired to be like God (perhaps losing sight of the distinction between Creator and creature, as in Rom 1:18ff.).[292] The result was that humankind fell victim to sin and sin brought death. Christ on the other hand was in the form of God but did not pursue equality with God, choosing rather to lower himself and in obedience go to death. As a result of his obedience, Christ was exalted to equality with God and now rules. The consequences of Adam's sin are reversed in Christ: death is overcome, and creation itself awaits release from its punishment. The glory which Adam rebelliously relinquished was obediently regained by Christ. As a result, the successful man, Christ, rules. In sum, if all these Adam parallels are genuine, then a significant portion of Christ's rule is predicated on an Adam christology — and in rather profound fashion. Although the ambiguities in this matter are numerous, 1 Corinthians 15 does connect Christ's rule and role as second Adam. Cosmogony and eschatology may therefore combine in Paul's thinking to mandate Christ's exercise of sovereignty.[293]

While Paul's Adam theology helps attribute royal rule to Christ, it does so in a manner corresponding to Paul's use of Χριστός. By identifying Christ as the second Adam, Paul interprets Christ's significance as extending beyond the Jewish race and applying to all people. Christ's βασιλεία has an anthropological significance universal in scope.

In 1 Corinthians 15 Christ's role as second Adam and the battle against death are part of a larger drama. The goal associated with Christ's rule is the defeat (καταργεῖν and ὑποτάσσειν) of all his enemies, work which is

---

Messiah, and rule (pp. 28-29). Levison criticizes Wright for ignoring passages and themes that do not fit into his reconstruction of Jewish speculation about Adam (*Portraits of Adam*, 22-23). As a result, Wright appears too eager to draw connections.

[291] Oscar Cullmann, *The Christology of the New Testament* (London: SCM Press, 1959), 181; C. K. Barrett, *From First Adam to Last: A Study in Pauline Theology* (New York: Charles Scribner's Sons, 1962), 16-17, 69-72, and more generally 1-21; Robin Scroggs, *The Last Adam* (Oxford: Blackwells, 1966); J. D. G. Dunn, *Christology in the Making*, 114-21; Seyoon Kim, *The Origin of Paul's Gospel*, WUNT 2.4 (Tübingen: J. C. B. Mohr [Paul Siebeck], 1981), 162-93, 260-67; Morna D. Hooker, *From Adam to Christ: Essays on Paul* (Cambridge University Press, 1990), 88-100; N. T. Wright, *The Climax of the Covenant*, 18-98.

[292] Morna D. Hooker has been influential in reading Rom 1:18-32 against an Adam typology. See *From Adam to Christ*, 6, 73-84, and 85-87. I am skeptical.

[293] Adam christology explicitly appears in Rom 5:12-21. Since I do not see any obvious connection to good rule, I do not discuss it here.

integral to kingship. Christ's enemies include every ἀρχή, ἐξουσία and δύναμις (15:24). Sin and death also rule in opposition to Christ (Rom 5:14, 17, 21; 6:12). Sin exercises its sovereignty in our mortal frames, holding them in its power by νόμος, using them as weapons for injustice.[294] The person under χάρις, however, has escaped sin's power and has a new κύριος (Rom 6:14, 23). Having been liberated by Christ, one's mortal frame becomes a weapon for justice (6:13, 18). Two sovereignties are therefore at war, one which rewards its subjects with death and one which offers life. The latter βασιλεία finds its culmination when it has destroyed its final enemy, death (1 Cor 15:26).

In terms of Paul's thinking, we should interpret Christ's war against these enemies in terms of Paul's apocalyptic outlook. Ernst Käsemann played an important role in situating Paul's thought within the context of apocalypticism.[295] David Way has summarized Käsemann's position as follows:

---

[294] Rom 6:12-13; 1 Cor 15:56; cf. also Rom 8:38; 1 Cor 8:4-6; 10:19; 2 Cor 4:4; 11:14; Gal 4:8; Phil 2:10. J. Christiaan Beker adds σάρξ to the list of enemies (*The Triumph of God: The Essence of Paul's Thought*, trans. Loren T. Stuckenbruck [Minneapolis, MN: Fortress Press, 1990], 80-81). Cp. W. D. Davies, *Jewish and Pauline Studies* (Philadelphia: Fortress Press, 1984), 189-99. Though problematic, I include the *stoicheia* (Gal 4:3, 9; see Hans Dieter Betz, *Galatians*, Hermeneia [Philadelphia: Fortress Press, 1979], 204-5; see however the interesting analysis of Eduard Schweizer, "Slaves of the Elements and Worshipers of Angels: Gal 4:3, 9 and Col 2:8, 18, 20," *JBL* 107 [1988]: 455-68). More difficult are the *archontai tou ai_nos toutou* (1 Cor 2:6-8). I would number them among the apocalyptic enemies of Christ's kingdom, though Fee does not (Gordon D. Fee, *The First Epistle to the Corinthians*, NICNT [Grand Rapids: Eerdmans, 1987], 103-4). W. Carr has argued at length that "the rulers of this age" are human, political leaders: "The Rulers of This Age — I Corinthians II.6-8," *NTS* 23 (1976/77): 20-35; idem, *Angels and Principalities: The Background, Meaning and Development of the Pauline Use of 'hai archai kai hai exousiai,'* SNTSMS 42 (Cambridge University Press, 1981), 118-20. The latter work removes all apocalyptic coloring from every reference to "powers and authorities" in Paul.

[295] Ernst Käsemann, "Die Anfänge christlicher Theologie," *ZTK* 57 (1960): 162-85; reprinted in *Exegetische Versuche und Besinnungen*, 2: 82-104; English: "The Beginnings of Christian Theology," in *New Testament Questions of Today*, trans. W. J. Montague (London: SCM Press; Philadelphia: Fortress Press, 1969), 82-107. This article offered the much quoted dictum, "Apocalyptic was the mother of all Christian theology" (102). Soon thereafter Käsemann wrote a follow-up essay to clarify and defend his thesis: "Zum Thema der urchristlichen Apokalyptik," *ZTK* 59 (1962): 257-84; reprinted in *Exegetische Versuche und Besinnungen*, 2: 105-31; English: "On the Subject of Primitive Christian Apocalyptic," in *New Testament Questions for Today*, 108-37. In this article Käsemann asserted that "Paul's apostolic self-consciousness is only comprehensible on the basis of his apocalyptic" (p. 131). He also says that subsequent to Christ's resurrection "the subjection of the cosmic powers has been taking place. The present eschatology of the enthusiasts is therefore picked up but apocalyptically

Käsemann's adoption of the term 'apocalyptic' is to be understood as a convenient shorthand for his understanding of primitive Christian eschatology, the main points being its cosmic scope, its expression of a theology focused on the hope of God coming into his right on earth (with the consequent defeat of powers of evil), and the theme of imminent future expectation. 'Apocalyptic' becomes a label for an interpretation of Paul's theology which is focused, not on anthropology, but on Christ's lordship and God's final triumph, and as such is a deliberate demarcation of Käsemann's own position over against Bultmann.[296]

Way's summary not only explains Käsemann's understanding of apocalypticism, but indicates its dialectic with his teacher Bultmann and the attempt to keep Paul's thought focused on righteousness.[297]

J. Christiaan Beker has pressed the importance of apocalypticism in Paul's thinking further than Käsemann. He states, "Apocalyptic is not merely a Pauline *Kampfeslehre* against Hellenistic Christian enthusiasm ... rather, it constitutes the heart of Paul's gospel, inasmuch as all that is said about Christ refers to that process of salvation which will imminently climax in the *regnum Dei*."[298] Beker argues that "the Christ-event in its

---

anchored and delimited as it is not with them. For Paul, it is not an alternative to, but a component of, a future eschatology — to express the position in terms of slogans. Its realm is called the *basileia Christi*" (p. 133). Both of Käsemann's articles also appeared in *JTC* 6 (1969): 17-46 and 99-133, trans. James W. Leitch. That entire issue was devoted to apocalypticism and contains critical responses to Käsemann's original article. Klaus Kloch surveyed the place of apocalypticism in New Testament research in *The Rediscovery of Apocalyptic: A Polemical Work on a Neglected Area of Biblical Studies and Its Damaging Effects on Theology and Philosophy*, trans. Margaret Kohl, Studies in Biblical Theology 2.22 (Naperville, IL: Alec R. Allenson, 1972), 57-97. Noteworthy among Käsemann's predecessors are J. Weiss, A. Schweitzer, D. Rössler, and U. Wilckens. Nils Dahl, with an eye on Qumran, suggests that with some exaggeration it can be said that "Bultmann's work on eschatology and history stands at the end of a period in the history of research that began when apocalyptic literature came to light" in the 1850s thanks to A. Dillmann and A. Hilgenfeld ("Eschatology and History in Light of the Qumran Texts," in *Jesus the Christ*, 50 and 61 n. 10). Will contemporary interest in Wisdom close the period of research in apocalyptic which Käsemann opened?

[296] David Way, *The Lordship of Christ: Ernst Käsemann's Interpretation of Paul's Theology* (Oxford University Press, 1991), 129.

[297] C. K. Barrett also regarded Bultmann's anthropological orientation as short-changing Paul's apocalyptic cosmology (*From First Adam to Last: A Study in Pauline Theology* [New York: Charles Scribner's Sons, 1962], 20-21).

[298] J. Christiaan Beker, *Paul the Apostle: The Triumph of God in Life and Thought* (Philadelphia: Fortress, Press, 1980), 17; idem, *The Triumph of God: The Essence of Paul's Thought*, trans. Loren T. Stuckenbruck (Minneapolis: Fortress Press, 1990); idem, "The Promise of Paul's Apocalyptic for Our Times," in *The Future of Christology: Essays in Honor of Leander E. Keck*, eds. Abraham J. Malherbe and Wayne A. Meeks (Minneapolis: Fortress Press, 1993), 152-59. The latter article argues that the

apocalyptic meaning" is the coherent center of Paul's thinking, which a "variety of symbols," such as righteousness, interpret.[299] The Protestant focus on justification by faith has been supplanted. Bultmann's demythologizing is rendered impossible. "For Paul, then, apocalyptic is the indispensable means for his interpretation of the Christ-event."

The evidence of Paul's apocalypticism appears in a variety of ways. Very important are his concerns with primordial events (Rom 5:12-20), angels, inimical spirit-beings, imminent παρουσία, resurrection, and cosmic transformation (Rom 8:19-22). Dualism is another trait: present and future age, flesh and spirit, law and grace, death and life.[300] Judgment also plays an important role in this regard. Thus, Paul can speak of God's impending wrath, yet attribute to Jesus deliverance from it (1 Thess 1:10), as well as from the present evil age (Gal 1:4).

Granted this evidence, is Beker correct to identify apocalypticism as the "heart of Paul's gospel"? Semantics are a problem, for apocalypticism is notoriously slippery. How do we move from apocalypses to apocalypticism? How much difference can exist between two apocalyptic texts before one is no longer apocalyptic? Is anything which contains a few common characteristics of apocalyptic necessarily apocalyptic or is there some competing category?[301] Also problematic is the idea of the "heart of Paul's gospel." How does one understand that label? Beker means that which lends coherence to Paul's views. But that is still ambiguous. Is the heart of Paul's gospel what drives his thinking or how he explains it? Stated in terms of apocalypticism, is Paul's apocalypticism simply a way of describing his *Weltanschauung* or is it the focus of his attention? Is Paul's apocalypticism a result of his encounter with Christ or

---

passage of time did not cause Paul to abandon apocalyptic theology, for it still appears in Romans.

[299] *Paul the Apostle*, 17.

[300] Alan F. Segal, *Paul the Convert: The Apostolate and Apostasy of Saul the Pharisee* (New Haven: Yale University Press, 1990), 160.

[301] Leander E. Keck has noted significant differences in perspective between Paul and other apocalyptic literature, in "Paul and Apocalyptic Theology," *Int* 38 (1984): 229-41. In addition, Hans Dieter Betz has pointed out that much of what we call apocalyptic is also generally Hellenistic ("On the Problem of the Religo-Historical Understanding of Apocalypticism," trans. James W. Leitch, *JTC* 6 [1969]: 134-56; similarly, cf. J. Gwyn Griffiths, "Apocalyptic in the Hellenistic Era," in *Apocalypticism in the Mediterranean World and the Near East*, 273-93; other essays in this volume are also relevant). In addition to the Uppsala conference, fundamental work on the nature of apocalyptic appears in John J. Collins, ed., *Semeia 14: Apocalypse: The Morphology of a Genre* (Missoula, MT: Scholars Press, 1979); and Adela Yarbro Collins, ed., *Semeia 36: Early Christian Apocalypticism: Genre and Social Setting* (Atlanta: Scholars Press, 1986).

did an apocalyptic worldview provide the context within which Paul interpreted his vision of Christ? Was Paul's Christian thinking built on a pre-Christian apocalyptic foundation, or was his apocalyptic narrative written in the course of Paul's attempts at Christian theology? I suspect that both are true, as Romans 5—8 seems to offer evidence of Paul elaborating his theology with the help of apocalyptic motifs. Thus, apocalypticism provided a framework for thinking and offered ideas to use in thinking. And the apostle used them. Granting that, however, does not require that apocalypticism drove Paul's thinking or was the object of his conscious reflection. The resurrection of Christ was the entry point for Paul's Christian reflection. That is a datum which could encourage an apocalyptic worldview or could be served well by a preexistent apocalyptic worldview. Either way, I regard Paul's apocalypticism more as *Weltanschauung* than the heart of his theological reflection. If I am correct, then Beker is as well, but irrelevantly so because one's worldview is precisely where the coherence of one's thinking is most likely to lie. The claim that the coherence of Paul's thinking lies in his worldview is much less dramatic than other claims about the heart of Paul's thinking.

For our present purposes, however, recognition of an apocalyptic worldview does help to place Christ's rule into context. Christ serves as the mediator of revelation, judgment and salvation for the transcendent God. Christ's resurrection indicates that the Eschaton has begun. The eschatological battle to destroy God's enemies and purge creation of the effects of sin has been joined. Christ will win that contest and will receive acclamation from every creature. Christ's people experience this power and confess Christ's authority; therefore, they confess him as κύριος and recognize his βασιλεία. Soon Christ will return as judge and God's kingdom will come. Christ will then lay down his βασιλεία and God will be all in all. In short, Paul's christology and thus Christ's rule play out their roles in a cosmological drama about God's rule.

To summarize what we have seen in this section, messianic traditions and Adam typology lend royal imagery to Paul's christology. That they are parts of a larger picture, however, mitigates the singularity of their connotations: they point not simply to Christ as a good king, but mix with other theological ideas to present Christ as the heavenly ruler. Christ's βασιλεία has a cosmic scope commensurate with Paul's apocalyptic worldview.

Paul's recognition of Christ as a good ruler is not unique to him. While our generally synchronic examination of Paul's letters has uncovered evidence of the figure of the king, a diachronic analysis alters the picture. Much was made of Phil 2:6-11. This is, by most accounts, a pre-pauline text. An equally strong consensus identifies Rom 1:3-4 as a pre-pauline text. The origin of 1 Thess 4:13-18 is less clear, but Paul is probably not its source. Similarly, Paul's vocabulary was not his own; he inherited Χριστός, κύριος, εὐαγγέλιον and βασιλεία from earlier Greek-speaking Christians. In short, much of the evidence in Paul's letters for Christ's kingship comes from pre-pauline sources.[302]

Paul shared the christology of kingship which appeared in his sources, thus recognizing Christ as king. On the one hand, even if important kingship texts are only quotes, Paul nevertheless made use of them. If he disagreed with them, he need not have used them. On the other hand, the pre-pauline materials often shaped or fell in with Paul's thinking. In particular, we can recognize the dominion of the κύριος which is presented in Phil 2:6-11 as current throughout Paul's letters. One further consideration is perhaps the most important, namely, that not all the evidence for kingship in Paul's letters can be attributed to unthoughtful repetition on Paul's part. The war against Death, the impending judgment, the lofty benefactions, the concern with justice and σωτηρία, the virtues, and in general Christ's cosmic significance present a figure for whom nothing short of divine royalty would be appropriate.

This points us to the final consideration, one from Greco-Roman religion. On a conceptual level, we might expect Paul to describe Christ as a good king because kings merged into gods in the Greco-Roman world, for rule was a path to divinization. Those who attained unprecedented power resembled gods and were treated in similar fashion. A pattern developed in which attainment of rule was followed by (potential) elevation to deity. Throughout the Hellenistic period, rulers accumulated divine honors, divine titles, and even ascriptions of deity. This trend continued into the Roman period, with the imperial cult spreading quickly and widely throughout the first century. As, however, kings could be described in divine terms, so also could gods be described in royal terms. Zeus was long regarded as a king. Isis garnered the trappings of royalty and was regarded as a queen. On a more local scale, in the territory of the Lydians, "gods [were] described as rulers or kings of villages."[303] Most noteworthy of all, though, was Herakles. Here was "the prototype of the ruler who by virtue of his divine legitimation acts in an irresistible way for the good of

---

[302] Though Phil 2:6-11 and Rom 1:3-4 are pre-pauline, this does not establish when they were composed. Whether they antedate Paul's conversion remains uncertain, likewise whether they lie behind all of Paul's missionary activity or all his letters. Despite labeling them pre-pauline, all we can really say is they antedate Philippians and Romans. We have, however, noted similarities between 1 Thess 1:10 and Rom 1:3-4.

[303] Stephen Mitchell, *Anatolia*, 1: 191.

mankind and finds his fulfillment among the gods . . ."[304] In Herakles the human benefactor attained immortality (i.e., divinity). Not surprisingly, various dynasts claimed descent from Herakles, son of Zeus. This overlap of god and king in the Greco-Roman world should sensitize us to the possibility of the same ambiguities in Paul's christology. In fact, Christ's triumph evidenced an unusual power, and by his resurrection he became immortal and took a place among heavenly beings. Together these things place Christ among kings and gods, so that to speak of his divine and royal status is perfectly natural.

In concluding this section, I wish to return to the "tyranny of titles" with which the previous section opened. As we have seen the lack of king as a title is no indication of its relevance to Paul's christology. By analogy, Χριστός ἐσταυρωμένος is an important idea in Paul's thought, though no title adequately encapsulates the idea expressed. We might also note that Paul's Adam and Wisdom christologies range more broadly than explicit appearances of those words warrant. Furthermore, Paul's christological titles do not stand independently of one another; they interconnect. 1 Cor 15:21-28 presents Christ as ruler and Christ as Adam. Phil 2:6-11 acclaims Christ as Lord, yet may also reflect Adam christology (or, depending on one's view, the suffering servant or Son of God). Rom 1:3-4 describes Christ as the enthroned king and calls him Son of God. Phil 3:20 links Savior and Lord. More generally, "Son of God" and "Adam" are both used to describe the destiny of Christ's people. More germane to this chapter, we have argued that "king" and "Lord" have much in common. As a result, the organization of the previous pages according to titles has been misleading — though convenient. The interconnections should, however, come as no surprise, for a single person is described by the various titles.

The fact that Paul has christological ideas apart from titles and that titles overlap combine to explain why Paul did not use "king" as a christological title. It would have been inadequate and potentially misleading. Anything Paul might have said with the label "king," he said with κύριος (or even Son), while avoiding the ambiguities that "king" might introduce.[305] As Lord, Christ is king, but more. κύριος points more

---

[304] Walter Burkert, *Greek Religion*, trans. John Raffan (Cambridge, MA: Harvard University Press, 1985), 211. See Dio Chrys. 1.83.

[305] For example, the nature of Christ's kingdom might be confusing (John 18:33-39), while the word itself might suggest sedition (19:15). Furthermore, Rome maintained client kings, in which case "king" is inadequate to express Christ's primacy in Paul's worldview.

directly to his divine status, a position received from God's hand. As κύριος, Christ is subject only to God. As κύριος, Christ has a heavenly throne and universal dominion. His rule reaches beyond Jews to the nations, and beyond nations to nature, and beyond nature to Death itself. κύριος is cosmocrator. To use the title King would introduce unnecessary political ambiguities. κύριος stepped past them and led more directly to Christ's cultic and universal significance. Thus, as κύριος, Christ was everything a king could hope to be, yet more. But how does one describe such a figure? Divine and royal imagery (which overlapped) were the best sources available. The early Christians, Paul included, used them.

In sum, not only did Paul share a christology of kingship in common with many others in the early church, he made additional contributions to it.

7. The Christology of 2 Corinthians 10:1

The preceding discussion was intended to provide the context for answering one question: why did Paul attribute πραΰτης and ἐπιείκεια to Christ? The first six sections of this chapter lead to the conclusion that, because Paul recognized Christ as king, leniency and clemency could be attributed to him as easily as it could to any good king. Moreover, since grace, acquittal, and reconciliation feature prominently in Christ's rule, the attribution of clemency was natural — almost predictable. Behind 2 Cor 10:1 then stands Christ the divine king.

So far this study has concluded that a semantic field present in 2 Corinthians 10–13 indicates that πραΰτης καὶ ἐπιείκεια in 2 Cor 10:1 means leniency and clemency. The people who exercise such virtues must exercise some authority and power, e.g., fathers, generals, governmental officials, and kings. Since the last is the most fitting category for Christ, we investigated Paul's writings in search of evidence that he regarded Christ as king and found such evidence. Therefore, we conclude that Christ possesses πραΰτης and ἐπιείκεια as qualities of his royal office.

A further question commonly raised in relation to this text is whether 2 Cor 10:1 refers to the historical Jesus.[306] Those who conclude that it does

---

[306] For studies which survey the Jesus-Paul problem see Victor Paul Furnish, "The Jesus-Paul Debate: From Baur to Bultmann," *BJRL* 47 (1964-65): 342-381; R. Regner, *"Paulus und Jesus" im 19. Jahrhundert. Beiträge zur Geschichte des Themas "Paulus und Jesus" in der neutestamentlichen Theologie*, Studien zur Theologie und Geistesgeschichte des Neunzehnten Jahrhunderts 30 (Göttingen: Vandenhoeck & Ruprecht, 1977); Stephen G. Wilson, "From Jesus to Paul: The Contours and

not base their argument on the infrequency of Paul's references to the historical Jesus. In support of this position this chapter has added an explanation why Paul could formulate such a description of the risen Christ.

Still, many have thought that Paul does in fact refer here to the historical Jesus.[307] Ladd argues that 2 Cor 10:1 does refer to Jesus and corresponds to Paul's other references to the historical Jesus. Among his observations is the following:

> Paul is ... familiar with traditions about the character of Jesus. He refers to his meekness and gentleness (2 Cor. 10:1), his obedience to God (Rom. 5:19), his endurance (2 Thess. 3:5), his grace (2 Cor. 8:9), his love (Rom. 8:35), his utter self-abnegation (Phil. 2:9f.), his righteousness (Rom. 5:18), even his sinlessness (2 Cor. 5:21).[308]

Though at first glance formidable, this list exaggerates the evidence. Reference to Christ's grace in 2 Cor 8:9 draws on the entire Christ story, not the "character of Jesus." The reference to 2 Thess 3:5 introduces other problems, not the least of which is the nature of the genitive τοῦ Χριστοῦ. More deceptive is the differentiation of obedience, self-abnegation, righteousness, and sinlessness. All of these reflect on Christ's

---

Consequences of a Debate," in *From Jesus to Paul: Studies in Honor of Francis Wright Beare*, eds. P. Richardson and J. C. Hurd (Waterloo, ON: Wilfrid Laurier University Press, 1984), 1-21; Stephen J. Patterson, "Paul and the Jesus Tradition: It is Time for Another Look," *HTR* 84 (1991): 23-41. More recent studies on the subject include Frans Neirynck, "Paul and the Sayings of Jesus," in *L'Apôtre Paul: Personnalité, style et conception du ministère*, ed. A. Vanhoye, BETL 73 (Leuven University Press, 1986), 265-321; M. Carrez, "Que représente la vie de Jésus pour l'apôtre Paul?" *RHPR* 68 (1988): 155-61; A. J. M. Wedderburn, ed., *Paul and Jesus: Collected Essays*, JSNTSS 37 (Sheffield Academic Press, 1989); James D. G. Dunn, "Jesus Tradition in Paul," in *Studying the Historical Jesus: Evaluations of the State of Current Research*, eds. Bruce Chilton and Craig A. Evans, New Testament Tools and Studies 19 (Leiden: E. J. Brill, 1994), 155-78. Bultmann's essays remain fundamental. Also important are Eberhard Jüngel, *Paulus und Jesus: Eine Untersuchung zur Präzisierung der Frage nach dem Ursprung der Christologie*, HUT 2 (Tübingen: J. C. B. Mohr [Paul Siebeck], 1962; ^{5}1979); Werner G. Kümmel, "Jesus und Paulus," *NTS* 10 (1963-64): 163-81; reprinted in *Heilsgeschehen und Geschichte. Gesammelte Aufsätze 1933-1965*, eds. E. Grässer et al., Marburger theologische Studien 3 (Marburg: N. G. Elwert, 1965), 439-56.

[307] Windisch, 292; Plummer, 273; Werner Georg Kümmel, "Supplemental Notes," in *An dei Korinther I, II*, by Hans Lietzmann, 165-214, Handbuch zum Neuen Testament 9 (Tübingen: J. C. B. Mohr, 1949), 208; Marinus de Jonge, *Christology in Context*, 88; G. N. Stanton, *Jesus of Nazareth in the New Testament Preaching* (Cambridge University Press, 1974), 108; Gordon D. Fee, *God's Empowering Presence: The Holy Spirit in the Letters of Paul* (Peabody, MA: Hendrickson, 1994), 451.

[308] George Eldon Ladd, *A Theology of the New Testament*, rev. Donald A. Hagner (Grand Rapids: Eerdmans, 1993), 452.

3.7. The Christology of 2 Corinthians 10:1

death and are not distinct items; moreover, they require interpretation of Christ's death. To see self-abnegation is to see more than a crucified criminal. Sinlessness is likewise not an empirical observation, but probably an inference from the resurrection. Even appeal to Christ's love looks primarily to his death (Gal 2:20). This leaves Christ's meekness and gentleness. Among Ladd's proposed examples, this is the only one which does not point to Christ's death and thus remains a potential reference to the character of Jesus.[309] Since, however, leniency and clemency are functional traits, this position must justify the application of such virtues to Jesus. Since he held no political office, what was the context for his exercise of leniency and clemency? Such things could be attributed to the historical Jesus only in conjunction with some ideology. In such a case, it is not simply memory of Jesus at work in this pair of virtues.

The strength of Leivestad's position is that it recognizes that ideas (which we usually call myth or christology) inform Paul's rhetoric in 2 Cor 10:1. Specifically, Leivestad argues that Christ's kenosis lies behind Paul's description of Christ's humility and lowliness (as he understands πραΰτης καὶ ἐπιείκεια). Again, kenosis is a story, which underscores the need to identify some pattern of ideas to lend coherence to Paul's reference to Christ in 2 Cor 10:1. This investigation, then, not only disagrees with Leivestad's semantics but offers a different story as giving meaning to Paul's words, viz., kingship.

Leivestad nevertheless has influenced subsequent views of 2 Cor 10:1. Furnish, for example, agrees with Leivestad's kenotic interpretation, but introduces problematic issues. He sees the application of the virtues to Christ originating in "Jewish Wisdom, according to which the truly wise man is always 'gentle'" (p. 460). But that persecuted wise person does not hold an ἐξουσία which he refrains from implementing. When Furnish then refers to the LXX uses of "gentleness and kindness" in relation to God and the Messiah, he has undermined Leivestad's LXX interpretation of ἐπιείκεια, for it is precisely the one time ἐπιείκεια is not applied to God or the Messiah that forms the basis for Leivestad's interpretation. While Furnish is right to look elsewhere than the historical Jesus, he invokes a christological story inappropriate to the context of 2 Cor 10:1.

Barrett seems to believe Leivestad, yet cannot resist continuing to see the historical Jesus in the background. In Barrett's opinion, Leivestad's kenotic view "would have been impossible as theology had it been known that the behavior of Jesus had been marked by arrogance and violence, and frigid if there had not been a tradition that depicted him as meek and

---

[309] Ladd does not mention Rom 15:3. Is this too a reference to Jesus' death?

gentle" (p. 246). Linking πραΰτης καὶ ἐπιείκεια to the church's experience of Christ as divine and royal Lord and Savior vitiates Barrett's comments.

The larger question of whether Paul has the historical Jesus in view must, however, be addressed. By translating πραΰτης καὶ ἐπιείκεια as leniency and clemency, Paul's meaning becomes clear: the phrase is not a reference to the meekness and gentleness of the character of the historical Jesus, but to the way in which Christ exercises authority, both now and in the future. But to attribute authority to Jesus requires understanding him in the light of some ideology, which means that some type of christology must be present in 2 Cor 10:1. We have argued that this christology is an ideology of kingship. A survey of the good ruler in antiquity revealed the appropriateness of connecting πραΰτης and ἐπιείκεια to kingly rule; nor was such knowledge the privileged domain of the educated elite. Examination of Paul's letters demonstrated the appropriateness of attributing to him a good king christology. Therefore, we conclude that *Paul's appeal in 2 Cor 10:1 arises not from the example of the earthly Jesus but from the virtue which Christ displays in the administration of his present kingdom.* The aspect of the christological story that most informs 2 Cor 10:1 is not one about Christ's past or even pre-existence, but his present.

A final question is whether the attribution of clemency to Christ the good king is original to Paul. Matthew's infancy narrative, the Triumphal Entry, the passion narratives, and the Apocalypse of John all testify to the popularity of royal christology in the early church; moreover, the evidence which we surveyed in Paul's letters revealed that when he described Christ as the good king he often drew on previously formulated material. Is 2 Cor 10:1 similar to Rom 1:3-4 and Phil 2:6-11 in that regard? Three lines of argument suggest that Paul coined the idea expressed in 2 Cor 10:1 himself. First, none of the structural or linguistic clues which elsewhere indicate pre-existent material is present in 2 Cor 10:1. Content is the only possible criterion. While the brevity of Paul's phrase makes generalizations difficult, the next two chapters will demonstrate how well it fits in with Paul's circumstances and letters. This, then, raises the second point, viz., Paul had a motive for inventing the expression (see the next chapter). Third, examples of governmental imagery from Paul's letters show that Paul himself could have generated the expression in 2 Cor 10:1. The most obvious example is Paul's reference to the sword in Rom 13:4: as God's ministers of vengeance, rulers do not "bear the sword in vain," an expression which invokes the well-known image of the sword

3.7. The Christology of 2 Corinthians 10:1

as connoting the power of life and death.[310] Elsewhere, Paul drew on the image of an emissary to describe his ministry: Christ sent Paul as his ambassador to encourage estranged creatures to be reconciled to God (2 Cor 5:20; Phlm 9?). Paul also uses political language for the church. Paul typically calls churches ἐκκλησίαι, but varies his language when he describes the Philippian church as a πολίτευμα (3:20).[311] He also uses the common political *topos* of the body to describe the church (1 Cor 12:12-27). In Gal 2:4 Paul "uses the language of political demagoguery" in describing his opponents.[312] Lastly and perhaps most elaborately, Paul relies on political language throughout 1 Corinthians.[313] Thus, it is entirely likely that Paul formulated the christological idea expressed in 2 Cor 10:1. Conversely, even if Paul did indeed shape his appeal by a pre-pauline tradition, raising the possibility of a relationship between 2 Cor 10:1 and other Jesus traditions (e.g., Matt 11:29), the need for an intervening

---

[310] Sen. *De clem.* 1.1.3; 1.11.3; Cal. Sic. 1.63; Ps.-Sen. *Oct.* 461; Tac. *Hist.* 3.68.2; Suet. *Cal.* 49.3; Dio Cas. 42.27; Acts 12:2; Heb 11:34, 37; Rev 13:10.

[311] See Peter T. O'Brien, *The Epistle to the Philippians*, NIGTC (Grand Rapids: Eerdmans, 1991), 459-61; Gerald F. Hawthorne, *Philippians*, WBC 43 (Waco, TX: Word, 1983), 170-72. Wendy Cotter proposes that Phil 3:17-21 warns against imitating the intemperate practices of other voluntary associations (particularly religious clubs), an interesting suggestion ("Our *Politeuma* is in Heaven: The Meaning of Philippians 3.17-21," in *Origins and Methods: Towards a New Understanding of Judaism and Christianity: Essays in Honor of John C. Hurd*, ed. Bradley H. McLean, JSNTSS 86 [Sheffield: JSOT Press, 1993], 92-104). However, I do not think Paul uses πολίτευμα for so specific a reason as this suggests. As Edgar Krentz illustrates, πολίτευμα fits into a group of words for military affairs which appear in Philippians ("Military Language and Metaphors in Philippians," in *Origins and Methods*, 105-27); cf. Timothy C. Geoffrion, "An Investigation of the Purpose and the Political and Military Character of Philippians" (Th.D. diss., Lutheran School of Theology at Chicago, 1992). Cotter's interpretation also hinges on how one understands Paul's references to belly and shame in 3:19. Against Cotter's view that they refer to dissipation, I take Phil 3:19 as rhetoric denigrating Jewish legal observances (as in v. 2). See Helmut Koester, "The Purpose of the Polemic of a Pauline Fragment (Philippians 3)," *NTS* 8 (1961-62): 317-32; Hawthorne, *Philippians*, 165-67; Chris Mearns, "The Identity of Paul's Opponents at Philippi," *NTS* 33 (1987): 194-204. Cotter objects that such a reading ignores the "ordinary Graeco-Roman meanings" of the terms κοιλία and αἰσχύνη. Even if this were so (but see Mearns), I would counter that the unusual twists given to Paul's words are precisely what make them so biting and forceful; furthermore, Paul is playing to a receptive audience which will indulge such slander of Jewish practices (as is also done in vv. 2-3, 8).

[312] Hans Dieter Betz, *Galatians*, Hermeneia (Philadelphia: Fortress Press, 1979), 90.

[313] Margaret M. Mitchell, *Paul and the Rhetoric of Reconciliation: An Exegetical Investigation of the Language and Composition of 1 Corinthians* (Louisville: Westminster/John Knox Press, 1991), 65-183 (180-81 summarize).

ideology, such as we have seen in regard to 2 Cor 10:1, would still be relevant and would in turn apply to other traditions as well.[314] *If therefore 2 Cor 10:1 had a relationship with Jesus traditions, it would not tie 2 Cor 10:1 closer to the historical Jesus, but would underscore the ideological foundations of the other Jesus traditions.* Given, however, that coining such an expression required little creativity and how well it corresponds to the situation in which Paul wrote 2 Corinthians 10–13, the idea is most likely Paul's own.

Since this conclusion rests on Paul's motive, it is important now to investigate why Paul formulated an appeal to the leniency and clemency of Christ. The next two chapters will do this. Chapter four will explore the place of such expressions in Paul's world and work. Chapter five will explore the consequences of Paul's particular use of the phrase in 2 Cor 10:1 in regard to his self-presentation.

---

[314] Matt 21:5 quotes Zech 9:9 to compare Jesus to a βασιλεύς who is πραΰς and mounted on a donkey. To apply an OT text to Jesus implies an ideology at work, while denotation as a king reveals the nature of the ideology. To call such a person πραΰς alters the implications of πραΰς. Applied to a king πραΰς implies accessibility and approachableness, a friendliness and warmth, peaceable in fact, perhaps dispensing forgiveness and leniency. Christ approaches like a "man-of-the-people," a populist ruler who wears his authority lightly. It should be emphasized, however, that Matt 21:5 refers to a king and how he exercises his office. Matt 11:29 describes Christ the teacher as πραΰς καὶ ταπεινός. Such a teacher is one who does not bully his students, who conducts himself in an agreeable and friendly manner. The kindness of this demeanor is subsequently emphasized, as well as the absence of its opposite, burdensomeness. Christ is implicitly compared not just to any teacher, however, but to the lawgiver, Moses, whom Philo describes further as a king; πραΰς, in fact, vividly emphasizes this comparison, for it was Moses' outstanding character trait. In this (familiar) passage as well, then, πραΰς possesses an important conceptual function.

Chapter 4

Paul's Practice of Leniency: Clemency in His Ministry to the Corinthians and in Greco-Roman Society

> [O]ne may address Anger and say, "You are able to overturn and destroy and throw down, but to raise up and preserve and spare and forbear is the work of mildness and forgiveness and moderation in passion, the work of a Camillus or a Metellus or an Aristeides or a Socrates."
> Plutarch *Moralia* 458c

Paul's appeal to "Christ's leniency and clemency" can be analyzed on different levels. We have just investigated one of those, Paul's christology. But Paul has not issued an abstract christological statement. He has applied it to himself in his interaction with the Corinthians. The appeal therefore characterizes Paul as well as Christ. We have seen the appropriateness of applying these virtues to Christ because of Christ's status as king. How is it, however, that Paul can claim that these virtues are operative in his ministry? While an examination of relevant Pauline texts could supply an answer to that question, a larger awareness is needed of the role of leniency in Paul's cultural context to see how it became relevant to his ministry. As we shall see, a policy of leniency guided Paul in his dealings with the Corinthians.

In this chapter, then, we ask this question: *what role did leniency and clemency play in Paul's ministry?* Subsidiary to that question are others which seek to know whether Paul's approach was unusual or common, what were its advantages and disadvantages, and how these pertained to his relationship with the Corinthians. To answer our opening question, then, we will formulate an answer in four steps. First, we will survey Greco-Roman antiquity to demonstrate that leniency and clemency were common ideas with widespread application. This will give us a sense of how intelligible Paul's appeal might have been. Second, we will survey the various motives for practicing leniency and clemency in the ancient world. This will provide a range of possibilities within which to understand Paul. Third, we will note the intrinsic problems and disadvantages of leniency. This will help to clarify issues surrounding Paul's appeal. Fourth, we will turn to Paul's writings to see how they correspond to what we have learned about leniency, thereby demonstrating that Paul's desire to show leniency to the Corinthians was understandable within his historical context and was consistent with his general approach to pastoral care. Accomplishing these two objectives will provide insight into how Paul attempted to structure his relationship with the Corinthians and his interaction with them. This in turn will assist in our reading of 2 Corinthians 10:1–13:10, lending clarity to the motives, expectations and actions of the different people involved.

In this chapter we shall encounter leniency throughout the literature and life of Greece and Rome. More specifically, we shall see that it was a popular practice, albeit risky, commonly discussed and at times implemented, typically applauded and sometimes criticized. Paul's offer of clemency in 2 Cor 10:1 reflects the common dynamics of leniency in his cultural world, as well as the apostle's own preference for such behavior. Thus, recognizing the popularity, motives, and dangers of clemency will help us to recognize the value of Paul's offer and the variety of responses which it might elicit.

Before we begin our analysis, two stipulations should be noted. First, I have mentioned that Paul's appeal through Christ's leniency and clemency functions on different levels; however, these different levels of meaning are intertwined and cannot be held apart easily. A variety of backgrounds are therefore relevant for illuminating Paul's leniency. Since his goal of moral and social reform parallels that of the philosophers, we shall look at their writings. In addition, Paul claims to have ἐξουσία and to command obedience, threatening the Corinthians with the imposition of punitive measures. Because of this, we will compare Paul with civil authorities. Given our previous emphasis on kings, we will examine particularly royal figures and their use of clemency. The combination of these disparate factors justifies what otherwise might appear to be a confusion of categories.

A second stipulation likewise concerns the evidence which will be presented. The following survey will focus on appearances of the words ἐπιείκεια, πραότης, and the Latin *clementia* and *lenitas*. While such semantic criteria provide helpful guidance, they do not remove all problems. For example, ἐπιείκεια and πραότης do not always refer to lenient behavior; as a result, we will concentrate on examples in which they do. We will, however, retain examples in which πραότης or ἐπιείκεια does not mean specifically clemency, but suggests a broader, related idea which subsumes clemency (e.g., kindness, generosity, or restraint). We must also recognize that sometimes the idea of leniency is present, even though our key words are not. We will not ignore such examples, although they will be used less frequently. Our semantic focus on leniency breaks down in some of the philosophic (especially Cynic) parallels. There "gentleness" does not slide as easily into "leniency"; yet, as already stipulated, the similarity in work and goals makes the philosophers relevant parallels to Paul's ministry. Thus, though our focus will be on leniency and clemency, at times we will be examining the more general trait of gentleness.[1]

Having raised these two methodological stipulations, we now turn to our present purpose of investigating the role that leniency and clemency played in Paul's ministry.

1. Leniency and Clemency in the Greek and Roman Worlds

Turning to ancient sources, we find references to clemency in varied epochs and literature. We set the stage beginning with Thucydides in the late V BC. In his "Mytilenean Debate" the Athenians argued whether or not to spare the Mytileneans (3.36-49); later the Spartans advised moderation rather than war.[2] Thucydides also recorded the great success which the Spartan Brasidas experienced by offering generous terms to Athenian allies.[3] This set the stage for the fourth century BC, during which time the Athenians debated the relationship of "force and justice, might and right."[4] Voices such as Isocrates and Xenophon, using the vocabulary of πρᾶος, ἐπεικής, and φιλάνθρωπος, recommended the value of gentleness as opposed to force and specifically cited it as characteristic of the good ruler.[5] Demosthenes recognized the need to

---

[1] As observed in chapter 2, a problem exists here in English semantics. Some may think that there is no common ground between "gentleness" and "clemency" or "leniency." I am using "gentleness," however, as a broad term which subsumes "clemency" and "leniency." This is necessary in order to encompass Greek semantics, where words can mean "gentleness" in some cases and something more specific, such as "leniency," in others.

[2] 4.17-20: important vocabulary includes τὸ ἐπεικές, μετρίως, ἀρετή, ξυναλλαγή, διαλλάσσειν, χαρίζεσθαι.

[3] 4.81, 105, 108, and 114; though Brasidas' actions are more important than the vocabulary used to describe them, key words are μέτριος (three times), πραότης, and ξυγγνώμη.

[4] Jacqueline de Romilly, "Eunoia in Isocrates or the Political Importance of Creating Good Will," *JHS* 78 (1958): 92. She draws comparisons with Thucydides, Xenophon, Demosthenes, and Isocrates.

[5] "The notion bursts out at the dawn of the 4th century and is suddenly found everywhere: it will lead to Polybian φιλανθρωπία and to Roman *clementia*" (Jacqueline

restrain reprisals (*De cor.* 96-100 and 274), while Plato advocated tailoring legal sanctions to fit their peculiar circumstances:

> Because the law could never, by laying down exactly what is noblest and most just for all at once, prescribe what is best; for the dissimilarities between men and between circumstances, and the fact that virtually nothing in human affairs is ever static, does not allow any science of any sort to put forward one simple rule to cover everything and all occasions.[6]

As we saw in chapter two, Aristotle incorporated both ἐπιείκεια and πραότης into his ethical thinking. Addressing the problem which Plato noted, ἐπιείκεια is a necessary and special type of justice, viz., equity, which corrects legal justice when the law is too general (*E.N.* 1137a-38a); it refuses to press the letter of the law — even though such action would be perfectly legal — and thereby forgives (1143a).[7] Aristotle identified πραότης as the mean between ὀργιλότης and ἀοργησία: πραότης results from reason holding emotion (viz., anger) in check, so that a person inclines to forgiveness rather than redress (1125b-26b).

Already we can observe that the ideas with which we are concerned were discussed in a variety of ways and contexts. Moderation, clemency, gentleness, leniency, equity, controlled anger were all relevant to an assortment of situations: foreign policy, battlefield strategy, good rule, law, and ethics. In addition, they appear in authors who were read and re-read throughout classical antiquity. This suggests that after IV BC clemency and leniency would appear frequently and in a variety of ways. This was in fact the case.

Turning to the philosophers, we may note first the Stoics who joined the discussion about leniency, but dissented from the majority opinion by rejecting it.[8] Chrysippus praised Justice because she "has never yielded to

---

de Romilly, "Fairness and Kindness in Thucydides," *Phoenix* 28 [1974]: 100); cp. eadem, *La douceur*, 37-38; eadem, *The Rise and Fall of States according to Greek Authors*, Jerome Lectures 11 (Ann Arbor: University of Michigan Press, 1977), 71-72, 75-80. On Isocrates see de Romilly, *La douceur*, 159-73 and her "Eunoia in Isocrates"; for Xenophon see *La douceur*, 134-44. J. Joel Farber argues that the ideas of rule in Xenophon's *Cyropaedia* reflect the ideas current throughout the fourth century, "The *Cyropaedia* and Hellenistic Kingship," *AJP* 100 (1979): 497-514.

[6] *Pol.* 294. Plato reflects belief that Athens showed clemency in its foreign affairs (*Men.* 242c-d; 243e-244b; 244e). While irony must be considered in these texts, they nevertheless indicate what encomiastic rhetoric prescribes.

[7] For a discussion of equity and secondary literature, see Hans Dieter Betz, *Sermon on the Mount*, Hermeneia (Minneapolis: Fortress Press, 1995), 167-72, 194-97, and 217.

[8] D'Agostino, *Epieikeia*, 105-14. He puts Stoic dissent into perspective: "Se dunque l'*epieikeia* appartiene principalmente alla cultura greca e solo secondariamente alle singole scuole di filosofia, sarà da tener presente che al di sotto del dissidio di queste

soothing words (ἐπιεικεῖς λόγους), to prayers and entreaties."[9] A fragment from Stobaeus elaborated on the Stoic opposition to ἐπιείκεια:

> They say that the intelligent person shows forgiveness to no one. For it is of the same person to show forgiveness and to think that the one who has acted wrongly has not done so on his own account, when everyone does [in fact] do wrong because of his own wickedness. Therefore also it is necessarily said, "Don't show forgiveness to those who behave incorrectly." Moreover, they say that the good man is not ἐπεικής, for the ἐπεικής averts the merited punishment. Also, it is of the same person to be ἐπεικής and to suppose that the punishments laid down by the law for those who act unjustly are too harsh and to consider that the lawgiver assigned excessive punishments.[10]

Diogenes Laertius described the Stoic position in very similar terms (7.123), while Horace skewered it.[11] Cicero also knew the Stoic position. In arguing against it (and Cato the Younger), Cicero used sarcasm to make Stoic teachings look absurd:

> Some wretched down-and-outs appear as suppliants; you will be a wicked criminal if pity leads you to do anything for them. A man admits that he has done wrong and asks pardon for his misdeed. "It is a crime to forgive." But it is only a trivial wrong. "All wrongs are equal" (*Pro Mur.* 62).

Cato appeared just as unyielding in Plutarch's portrait of him: influenced by a Stoic companion, Cato pursued every virtue, especially "that form of goodness which consists in rigid justice that will not bend to ἐπιείκεια or χάρις."[12] A century earlier, Sallust had characterized Cato in the same manner.[13] In looking at Cato, however, one should remember that although

---

permane un'unità fondamentale ..." (103). Though objecting to ἐπιείκεια, πραότης was acceptable, as it was part of the sage's reserve which kept him from succumbing to anger (Stob. 2.155.5-17 [= *SVF* 3.564, 632]).

[9] Fragment preserved in Aul. Gel. *Noc. Att.* 14.4.4. Gellius endorses Chrysippus' view: justice should be merciless to the guilty, despite those who think her cruel (14.4).

[10] *Anth.* 4.5.50 (my trans.). The inviolability of νόμος rests on its being λόγος ὀρθός (SVF 3.613 and 614).

[11] *Sat.* 1.3.76-142. I assume Horace had his contemporaries in view, although he does specifically name Chrysippus in his attack (127), indicating the teacher whom he held responsible for the Stoic position.

[12] Plut. *Cato min.* 761d; similarly Cic. *Pro Mur.* 60-66; cp. the anecdote in Plut. *Mor.* 534d-e. Seneca perpetuated Cato's reputation (*Ep.* 11.9-10). See D'Agostino, *Epieikeia*, 117-18. In regard to the earlier Cato, Cato the Elder, Plutarch complained that he was mean to his servants and to animals, failing to recognize that "kindness has a wider scope than justice," whereas "beneficence and charity ... flow in streams from the gentle heart" (339a).

[13] Sal. *Cat.* 54: "Caesar was esteemed for the many kind services he rendered and for his lavish generosity; Cato, for the consistent uprightness of his life. The former was renowned for his humanity and mercy; the latter had earned respect by his strict austerity. Caesar won fame by his readiness to give, to relieve, to pardon; Cato, by never offering presents. The one was a refuge for the unfortunate, and was praised for his good

his consistency in practicing virtue was exceptional, his sternness was not simply idiosyncratic, but was the embodiment of Stoic doctrine.

The Stoics were not, however, monolithic in their antipathy toward leniency. To prove this Cicero cited the examples of the former consuls Gaius Laelius, Lucius Philus, and Gaius Gallus.[14] In that same passage, Cicero also emphasized that Panaetius' teaching made Scipio (Africanus Minor) *lenissimus*. D'Agostino attributes the softening of the Middle Stoa's position to a variety of factors.

[W]e could summarize them as a choice made in favor of diversity against the coherence of doctrine, or, still better ... the necessity to create a system — sufficiently pliant — of political art.... But the decline of the early Stoa can be measured — in a manner philosophically more concrete — by the birth and by the singular development of the doctrine of καθῆκον ... to differentiate the ethics of the first Stoics, all followers of λόγος, concentrated on the singleness of virtue, in brief formula, from that which instead found its better systematization in Panaetius and which briefly has been indicated as a material ethic of duties.[15]

This evolution became most conspicuous in Seneca's writings.

Turning to Seneca's *De clementia*, one cannot fail to notice how different he sounds from the early Stoa: to write a treatise advocating

---

nature; the other was a scourge for the wicked, admired for his firmness" (S. A. Handford, Penguin).

[14] *Pro Mur.* 66. Cp. Seneca's contemporary, Thrasea Paetus, a *vir mitissimus* (Plin. *Ep.* 8.22) and an advocate of *clementia* (Tac. *Ann.* 14.48-49), who was also a biographer of Cato the Younger (Plut. *Cat. min.* 25 and 37).

[15] "Le motivazioni di questo fenomeno sono numerose e sufficentemente note: potremmo riassumerle in una scelta fatta a favore della diffusione contro la coerenza della dottrina o, ancor meglio ... la necessità di creare un sisteme — sufficientemente duttile — di arte politica.... Ma il tramonto dell'antica Stoa più concreta — dalla nascita e dal singolare sviluppo della dottrina del καθῆκον, che recepito col termine di *officium* tanta diffusione doveva avere nella cultura romana. Proprio il concetto di καθῆκον è servito ai migliori studiosi per differenziare l'etica del primo stoicismo, tutta aderente al λόγος, incentrata sull'unicità della virtù, in breve formale, da quella invece che trovò il suo miglior sistematizzatore in Panezio e che brevemente è stata indicata come un'etica materiale dei doveri." D'Agostino, *Epieikeia*, 112-13.

Further evidence of a change in the Stoa's position may appear in Stobaeus. The fragments of a treatise preserved in his *Anth.* have elements which appear Stoic, yet which also recommend πρᾶος and ἐπιεικές. See *Anth.* 4.5.51-60, in particular 60: "If the Graces overstep what is just, I do not think they should be called Graces. However, no one, unless he is made of wood or stone voluntarily denies the Friends of justice. For since the law often lays down punishments [which are] more severe than their crimes, I think that the so-called ἐπιεικές justice (which mollifies the severe voice of laws), [is] a blameless plea for [the] genuine and free Graces. Thus, a corrective measure which adheres to the contractual obligations of justice completely escapes the kind [which is characteristic] of the Graces, whereas [that] which is fixed with a view to the charges does not renounce the gentle and humanitarian face of the Graces" (my trans.).

clemency seems to be a complete reversal. To accomplish this, Seneca employed a semantic strategy.[16] First, he distinguished between *clementia* and *misericordia*: the latter "regards the plight, not the cause of it; *clementia* is combined with reason" (2.5.1). This is an important move. If clemency is associated with mercy, then it is a passion and a Stoic must regard it negatively.[17] By severing clemency and mercy and asserting that reason guides clemency, Seneca can recommend it. With that distinction in hand, Seneca next differentiated *severitas* and *crudelitas*: *severitas* is a virtue and works in harmony with *clementia*, whereas *crudelitas* is the opposite of *clementia* (2.4.1). *Crudelitas* is "harshness of mind in exacting punishment" (2.4.1). People are cruel "who have a reason for punishing, but do not have moderation in it" (2.4.3). Seneca summarizes this difference, saying, "We may define *crudelitas* to be the inclination of the mind toward the side of harshness. This quality *clementia* repels and bids it stand afar from her; with *severitas* she is in harmony" (2.4.3). Such definitions allow Seneca to esteem Cato, yet leave room for political flexibility.

Griffin, however, has argued that Seneca's treatise does indeed correspond to the ideas of traditional Stoicism. Griffin distinguishes two legal procedures, the *cognitio* and the *quaestio*, and links the former to the Emperor and Senate. In such cases the judge (i.e., emperor or Senate) had room for discretion in assigning punishments. *Clementia* was therefore not the setting aside of legally prescribed penalties, but the preference to choose from a range of possible sanctions the milder. To choose the stricter punishment based on sound reason constitutes *severitas*, which is also a Stoic virtue. To do so because of anger or animosity or some other passion is *crudelitas*, which opposes both *clementia* and *severitas*.[18] Seneca's general advice in *De vita beata*, however, suggests that *clementia* fits more broadly into his ethical thinking than Griffin's harmonization might indicate. In enumerating the principles to which he strives to adhere, Seneca writes, "I shall be agreeable to my friends, to my enemies

---

[16] D'Agostino, *Epieikeia*, 118-20.

[17] Stob. 2.91.9 (= *SVF* 3.394); Plut. *Mor.* 468d; Diog. L. 7.111; cp. Cic. *Tusc.* 3.21; 4.11; Plut. *Mor.* 1046c.

[18] Miriam T. Griffin, *Seneca: A Philosopher in Politics* (Oxford University Press, 1976), 154-70, especially 161-64. Griffin draws on the advice of Thrasea Paetus to illustrate her legal distinction. Thrasea argued that it was not necessary to hand down the harshest verdict possible when a number of different laws made available a variety of sanctions from which to choose. Legally, he implied, the emperor and Senate were free to choose exile over execution, and in so doing "would furnish a noble example of public clemency" (Tac. *Ann.* 14.48-49).

mild and indulgent (*mitis et facilis*). I shall give pardon (*exorabor*) before it is asked, and hasten to grant all honorable requests" (20.5).

Musonius Rufus' position is not clear. In one fragment he reflected the hard line position as he instructed kings "to arbitrate justice ... so that no one may have more or less than his just deserts (ἀξίαν), but may receive honor or punishment as he deserves (ἀξίους)."[19] However, about a hundred lines later he encouraged the king to be εὐεργετικός, χρηστός, and φιλάνθρωπος, the latter two being possible ways of expressing leniency. More significantly, Musonius also wrote a tract which argued that a philosopher should not pursue litigation for personal injury.[20] Instead the intelligent person would "easily (πράως) and silently bear what has happened." Musonius cites approvingly the example of "the good (χρηστός) Phocion" whose wife was insulted. When the offender asked Phocion for forgiveness (συγγνώμη), Phocion magnanimously excused him. Musonius claimed to know additional examples of people who suffered insult and assault yet took no legal action, but "meekly (πράως) bore their wrong (ἀδικίαν)." He added that "to return evil for evil is the act not of a human being but of a wild beast," whereas to accept ἁμαρτία is "a source of good (χρηστῆς) hope" and comes from "a benevolent (ἡμέρου) and civilized (φιλανθρώπου) way of life." Thus, Musonius concluded, the philosopher should "deem worthy of forgiveness (συγγνώμης ἀξιοῦν) anyone who wrongs him." These statements nuance the first fragment cited and differentiate Musonius from the Old Stoa.[21] Perhaps, however, we should introduce an argument like Griffin's about Seneca and consider that Musonius distinguished between legal contexts. Perhaps Musonius would have allowed indulgence only in matters of personal effrontery, but would have refused forgiveness in other areas of law. More likely is that the difference rests on the two different persons involved, whether king or philosopher, and the social context in which each must respond to lawlessness. What is certain is that consideration of both Seneca and Musonius smoothes the edge of the Stoa's position on leniency in the first century. What is important for this study is the evidence both provide that the dialogue continued and inclined more favorably toward leniency.

Other philosophical schools did not share the Stoics' refusal to mitigate retribution. One would assume this to be the case for the Peripatetics,

---

[19] Frg. 8 Lutz, "That Kings also Should Study Philosophy," p. 60.

[20] Frg. 10 Lutz, "Will the Philosopher Prosecute Anyone for Personal Injury?" The translated excerpts come from Lutz, pp. 78-81.

[21] Musonius' position is therefore more complicated than Griffin indicates (*Seneca*, 158), as Lutz had indicated earlier (p. 29).

given the previously noted opinions of Aristotle. Xenocrates' treatise Περὶ ἐπιεικείας continued the Peripatetic discussion (Diog. L. 4.12), while Cicero's explicit testimony confirmed the Peripatetics' approbation (*Pro Mur.* 64). Cicero also stated that the Academics differed from the Stoics and thus did not object to leniency (*ibid.*). That Plutarch endorsed ἐπιείκεια is consistent with Cicero's testimony about the Academy. Among the Cynic epistles, the twenty-ninth Socratic epistle commended ἐπιείκεια; Ps.-Anach *Ep.* 7 advised the cruel despot Tereus that a κύριος should be sparing (φείδεσθαι). Meanwhile, Epictetus characterized Diogenes as ἥμερος καὶ φιλάνθρωπος (*Diss.* 3.24.64). We will say more about the Cynics in a moment. As for the Epicureans, Philodemus included clemency among the virtues which the good king should cultivate.[22] According to Diogenes Laertius, Philodemus described the Epicurean philosopher Polyaenus as ἐπεικής (10.24). Diogenes also included ἐπιείκεια in a litany of Epicurus' personal virtues, while Iamblichus attributed πραότης to him.[23] These various examples correspond to Lucian's general assertion that philosophy is by nature ἥμερος καὶ πρᾶος.[24]

Whereas the Stoics argued about ἐπιείκεια in its relation to law, the Cynics debated the role of gentleness within their mission to reform people. The essential issue was the most effective use of παρρησία. Malherbe has outlined the different views: some Cynic misanthropes deployed unsparing verbal assaults, others showed greater understanding and gentleness.[25] This is not to say that the latter would not raise their voices and criticize. The key distinction, however, was the desire to correct; this kept admonition (νουθετεῖν) from slipping into ridicule (ὀνειδίζειν).[26] Lucian describes Demonax in the following ways:

He never was known to make an uproar or excite himself or get angry, even if he had to rebuke someone; though he assailed sins, he forgave sinners, thinking that one should

---

[22] *Good King* 24. Cp. *On Anger* 44.23-25.

[23] Diog. L. 10.10; Iambl. *De vita Pyth.* 20.95. Diogenes also tells us that some people regard πραότης as the goal of Skeptic philosophy, though others say that ἀπάθεια is (9.108).

[24] *Reviv. sive pisc.* 24. However, upon making that claim, Lucian immediately subverts it, for the speaker, Diogenes, goes on to add that if Philosophy acquits Frankness, the Cynic stick will compensate for Philosophy's gentleness/leniency.

[25] Abraham J. Malherbe, "'Gentle as a Nurse': The Cynic Background to I Thess ii," *NovT* 12 (1970): 208-14, especially 210; idem, "Self-Definition among Epicureans and Cynics," in *Self-Definition in the Greco-Roman World*, vol. 3: *Jewish and Christian Self-Definition*, eds. Ben F. Meyer and E. P. Sanders (Philadelphia: Fortress Press, 1982), 46-59, especially 50-58.

[26] Malherbe, "Gentle as a Nurse," 210-11.

pattern after doctors, who heal sicknesses but feel no anger at the sick. He considered that it is human to err, divine or all but divine to set right what has gone amiss (*Dem.* 7).

After these remarks Lucian adds that Demonax talked soberly to the happy and warmly to the unfortunate, while at other times reconciling brothers and spouses or calming crowds (8-9). Lucian then summarizes the conduct of Demonax, saying, "Such was the character of his philosophy — kind, gentle and cheerful" (πρᾶος καὶ ἥμερος καὶ φαιδρός; 9). His cheerfulness was not, however, cowardice, for when he held public office he won for himself the same animosity as had Socrates "by his freedom of speech and action" (παρρησία καὶ ἐλευθερία; 11). Demonax therefore combined παρρησία and gentleness in his words and deeds (cf. 50). In contrast to Demonax, "Heraclitus" was always glum.[27] While others therefore viewed him as a misanthrope, he regarded it as the only proper response to all the human evil which he witnessed. He noted, however, that when illness shut him in, cutting off his contact with other people, he became more gentle (*Ep.* 5.3; cf. 7.1, 3). In sum, Cynics differed among themselves as to how broadly the definition could be stretched. Was stern austerity the only possible life-style, or was a friendlier, more social manner of life possible? The difference between the Cynics and the Stoics was that the former considered gentleness (ἤπιος) in relation to freedom and bold speech as applied to moral reform, while the latter thought about the validity of leniency (ἐπιείκεια) in relation to λόγος. Both groups therefore argued about gentleness, but each in different ways.

The Romans admired clemency.[28] When Sallust recalled Rome's good old days, he envisioned a Rome which ruled by bestowing benefits and, when wronged, preferred pardon to revenge; he disparaged his decadent contemporaries because they had become harsh and acted without restraint (*Cat.* 9-10). Sallust brought the issue of clemency into sharp focus at the

---

[27] The characterization of Heraclitus as σκυθρωπός, as opposed to πρᾶος provides a parallel to the Matthean characterization of Jesus, who is πραΰς (Matt 11:29; 21:5), as opposed to the hypocrites, who are σκυθρωποί (Matt 6:16).

[28] Pierre Grimal, "La clémence et la douceur dans la vie politique romaine," *CRAI* (1984): 466-78. Grimal states, "Nous rencontrons donc la 'douceur' ... dans trois domaines de la vie publique romaine, dès l'origine, sans doute, ou du moins dès une époque très haute: d'abord dans l'application des lois ou les décisions des magistrats (rois et leurs successeurs, les consuls), puis dans la nature même des supplices, qui ne doivent pas comporter de cruauté inutile (Rome n'est pas, en ces temps anciens, la pays de la crucifixion ni du pal), enfin dans les rapports avec les étrangers, même ennemis, qui, même dans la défaite, obtenaient la vie sauve et n'étaient pas, en général, vendus comme esclaves" (p. 471). In short, Grimal calls *clementia* "une des attitudes romaines les plus instinctives, les plus radicales, l'un des fondements même de l'*imperium romanum*" (p. 473).

end of his account of the Catalinarian revolt, when Caesar and Cato debated whether or not to extend lenient sentences to the conspirators.[29] Livy portrayed various figures as using clemency as an effective military policy.[30] As an advocate, Cicero sought clemency for specific individuals in his Caesarean speeches (*Pro Marcello, Pro Ligario,* and *Pro rege Deiotaro*). *Pro Marcello*, however, points to the discomfort which *clementia* caused some Senators, for accepting clemency acknowledged inferiority on the part of the recipient.[31] Cato preferred death to Caesar's clemency, reasoning that Caesar "acts illegally saving, as if their master, those over whom he has no right at all to be the lord."[32] Later, under different circumstances, Cicero criticized Brutus for having implemented a policy of clemency (*Ad Brut.* 1.15.10). The Augustan poets regarded clemency as one of Rome's virtues.[33] Thus, Virgil could summarize Rome's unsurpassed arts of rule as seeking

> to teach the ways of peace to those you conquer,
> to spare defeated peoples, tame the proud.[34]

Valerius Maximus cited an example of clemency in which clemency led to success in battle (*Fac. et dic. mem.* 5.1.5). As already noted, Seneca wrote a treatise containing advice for Nero entitled *De clementia*;[35] moreover, his tragedies "are concerned with the slaughter of the helpless," while the "ruthlessness of absolute rulers is a central theme in *Troades,* as it is in *Thyestes* and *Agamemnon.*"[36] The historical drama *Octavia*, which shares

---

[29] *Cat.* 50-52. Cp. Ps.-Sal. *Ad Cae.* 1.1.7; 1.3.1-4; 1.4.4. Plutarch likewise pits Caesar's clement speech versus Cato's stern one (*Cic.* 871a).

[30] Hannibal, 21.48.10; Gnaeus Cornelius Scipio, 21.60.4; Philip, 36.14.7.

[31] R. R. Dyer, "Rhetoric and Intention in Cicero's *Pro Marcello*," *JRS* 80 (1990): 18, 20-26, and 30. See also C. Wirszubski, *Libertas as a Political Idea at Rome during the Late Republic and Early Principate* (Cambridge University Press, 1950).

[32] Plut. *Cato min.* 66.2. Plutarch here characterizes Caesar's clemency as σώζεσθαι χάριτι.

[33] Ovid *Fasti* 2.139-44; *Pont.* 2.1.43-48; Hor. *Car. saec.* 51-52; *Car.* 3.14.14-16.

[34] *Aen.* 6.852-53. Jasper Griffin argues that the end of the *Aeneid* undermines Rome's aspirations of clemency. As Aeneas could not spare Turnus, so is the nature of imperialism: "the conqueror finds himself destroying what he would prefer to spare" ("Virgil," in *The Roman World*, eds. J. Boardman, J. Griffin, and O. Murray [Oxford University Press, 1988], 222). See, however, Francis Cairns' mitigating comments in *Virgil's Augustan Epic* (Cambridge University Press, 1989), 80-82.

[35] In many ways, another of Seneca's treatises, *De ira,* discusses the opposite of *De clementia*. On the points of contact between the two essays, see François Préchac, *Sénèque. De la clémence*, Collection des Universités de France (Paris: Les Belles Lettres, 1921), lxxxviii-xcii. See, for example, *De ira* 1.6.3; 1.29.5-8; and 2.27.3.

[36] Denis and Elisabeth Henry, *The Mask of Power: Seneca's Tragedies and Imperial Rome* (Warminster: Aris & Phillips, 1985), 159. More specifically, they note that

numerous similarities with *De clementia* and was subsequently attributed to Seneca, examines Nero's cruelty, depicting him as a murderous tyrant.[37] Nero's chilling rejection of gentle means appears in an exchange between the emperor and his tutor, Seneca:

> Seneca: A sovereign cure for fear is clemency.
> Nero: To destroy foes is a leader's greatest virtue.
> Seneca: For the father of his country to save citizens is greater still.
> Nero: A mild old man should give schooling to boys (442-45).

Tacitus likewise knew that *clementia* played a role in imperial propaganda but preferred "either to avoid this governmental term, or to apply it ironically."[38] Thus, Tacitus wrote about the advocate who based his defense on the emperor's moderation — and lost; elsewhere, Claudius offered the *merciful* sentence that the condemned be given the *freedom* to

---

Agamemnon sought to establish *pudor, misericordia*, and *moderatio*, whereas Atreus recognized life to be a "competition of wickedness" (pp. 163 and 175, respectively). See also Sen. *Her. fur.* 731-45 and [Ps.-Sen] *Her. Oet.* 1557-63. Cp. Pierre Grimal: "Il semble donc bien que l'image que Sénèque donne du pouvoir royal dans son théâtre n'est pas restée sans influence sur la pensée politique romaine. Elle a contribué à former une véritable théologie de la monarchie qui évolua lentement, latente sous les Flaviens, affirmée et triomphante les Antonins" ("L'Image du pouvoir royal dans les tragédies de Sénèque," *Pallas* 38 [1992]: 414).

[37] "Dans le dialogue entre Néron et Sénèque comme dans la scène entre Néron et le préfet du prétoire, qui nous a fourni ces derniers rapprochements, presque tous les développements qui ne furent pas dictés par les circonstances particuliéres du drame et même quelques-und de ceux qui le furent paraissent une imitation ou une paraphrase du «premier livre» du traité de Sénèque," Préchac, *Sénèque. De la clémence*, lvi. C. J. Herington points to similarities between *Octavia* and other Senecan writings, "Octavia Praetexta: A Survey," *Classical Quarterly* n. s. 11 (1961): 28. William M. Calder, III, elaborates on the connections between Seneca's *Thyestes* and the *Octavia*, "Secreti loquimus: An Interpretation of Seneca's Thyestes," in *Seneca Tragicus: Ramus Essays on Senecan Drama*, ed. A. J. Boyle (Berwick, Victoria, Australia: Aureal Publications, 1983), 192-95. Although *Octavia* is generally considered post-Neronian (e.g., M. E. Carbone, "The Octavia: Structure, Date and Authenticity," *Phoenix* 31 [1977]: 48-67), Lucile Yow Whitman argues that Seneca himself wrote it as a defense against the charge of hypocrisy (*The Octavia: Introduction, Text, and Commentary*, Noctes romanae 16 [Bern: Paul Haupt, 1978], 5-12 and 98). Edwin S. Ramage observes that *Octavia* "fits neatly with the anti-Neroian propaganda of both Galba and Vespasian" ("Denigration of Predecessor under Claudius, Galba and Vespasian," *Historia* 32 [1983]: 210 n. 32). Patrick Kragelund elaborates on those connections and argues for a Galban *Sitz im Leben* (*Prophecy, Populism, and Propaganda in the 'Octavia,'* Opuscula Graecolatina 25 [Copenhagen: Museum Tusculanum Press, 1982], 38-54).

[38] Ronald Syme, *Tacitus* (Oxford University Press, 1958), 1: 414; similarly Martin P. Charlesworth, "The Virtues of a Roman Emperor: Propaganda and the Creation of Belief," *PBA* 23 (1937): 113 n. 14. Syme further notes Tacitus' restraint in attributing to emperors such commonplaces as *pietas, providentia, aeternitas, perpetuitas, felicitas,* and *iustitia* (1: 754-56).

choose his own means of death!³⁹ Tacitus did, however, praise Germanicus as an example of clemency, particularly in contrast to the irascible Alexander the Great (*Ann.* 2.73), while in his *Agricola* Tacitus did not hesitate to highlight his father-in-law's clement administration of Britain (20). In Suetonius' survey of Roman emperors, he used mildness and savagery as measures of an emperor's virtue.⁴⁰ Imperial panegyric did likewise.⁴¹

Leniency was not overlooked by Jewish and Greek authors. In the LXX God's leniency moves God to spare people's lives.⁴² The *Letter of Aristeas* applies that theology to human rulers and recommends that a king imitate God's eternal leniency, so that a king may preserve his kingdom and gain approval for his judicial decisions.⁴³ A letter from Ptolemy Philopator to his generals recorded in 3 Macc 3:12-29 presents the king's preference not to rule with the spear, but to treat his subjects with clemency and benevolence. It further registers Ptolemy's exasperation with the Jews who have resisted his generous overtures and forced him to resort to severe measures. Josephus makes leniency a point of distinction between the Pharisees and Sadducees, the former being "naturally lenient (ἐπεικῶς) in the matter of punishments," whereas the latter were "more heartless than any of the other Jews" (*Ant.* 13.294; 20.199). Josephus also tells of his own military success in taking the city of Tiberias with cunning and moderation (*Vita* 163-78) and of Titus' offers of leniency during the siege of Jerusalem (e.g., *Bel.* 6.414-20). Philo attributed ἐπιείκεια to God, regarded it as a basic quality of virtuous people, and used it to evaluate people who held positions of power. Although Philo generally associates ἐπιείκεια with φιλανθρωπία, he also recognizes its specific application to clemency and leniency.

---

[39] *Ann.* 3.50-51 and 11.3 (emphasis mine), respectively. See further 4.31; 14.48-49; 15.35; 16.20-34. M. Griffin notes the similarities between Tacitus' accounts of the trials of Clutorius Priscus and Antistius and, in turn, that pair's similarity to Caesar's speech in Sallust (*Seneca*, 165 n. 4).

[40] Suet. *Iul.* 75.1; *Aug.* 51.1; *Tib.* 53.2; *Nero* 10.1; *Dom.* 10.1; see K. R. Bradley, "Imperial Virtues in Suetonius' *Caesares*," *Indo-European Studies* 4 (1976): 249.

[41] Pliny *Pan.* 80; Josef Mesk highlights Pliny's dependence on Cicero, Seneca, and Tacitus in "Quellenanalyse des Plinianischen Panegyricus," *Wiener Studien* 33 (1911): 71-100. *Scriptores historiae Augustae: Had.* 5.5-6; 7.4; 13.10; 14.9-15.9; 18.4; 20.3; 23.3-9; 25.8; *Ant. Pius* 2.6; 6.3; 7.5-9.5; 9.10; 10.8; 12.2-4; *Marc. Ant.* 8.1; 13.6; 19.12; 24.1-3; 25.5-12; 26.3, 10-13. De Romilly, *La douceur*, 267.

[42] 1 Sam 12:22; Ps 85:5 LXX; Dan 3:42; 2 Esdr 9:8; 2 Macc 10:4; Wis 12:18.

[43] 187-88 and 191-92, respectively; O. Murray, "Aristeas and Ptolemaic Kingship," 355-56.

Greek authors had much to say about clemency. Polybius elaborated at length on the value of gentleness and generosity in matters of conquest (5.9-12). Posidonius recommended clemency and philanthropy as keys to governing an empire.[44] For Lucian ἐπιείκεια and πραότης were regular characteristics of a virtuous person. They also distinguished the good ruler from the tyrant, as in *Phaleris*, which was discussed in chapter two. In this sophisticated satire on tyranny (and thus the rhetoric of leniency) and religion, Phaleris' representatives argued that the tyrant preferred to exercise gentleness and generosity, but was compelled to respond to his enemies' aggressions with cruel force. Arrian indicated the importance of clemency in his panegyric on Alexander the Great (7.28.1-30.3) — by his failure to mention it! Though Arrian recited an exhaustive litany of Alexander's virtues, clemency is absent. Instead Arrian offered an apology for Alexander's volatile temper. The traditions about Alexander necessitated this, for Alexander's cruelty was too well-known to be glossed over.[45] Recognizing, then, that good rulers act clemently and that Alexander did not, Arrian defended his hero.[46] A couple of centuries earlier, however, Diodorus had attributed clemency to Alexander. He had done so in order to illustrate his thesis that hegemony is obtained by ἀνδρεία and σύνεσις, enlarged by ἐπιείκεια and φιλανθρωπία, and made secure by φόβος and κατάπληξις (32.2). To illustrate this claim, Diodorus then offered Philip, Alexander, and Rome as examples (32.4). Since omission of Alexander would have been conspicuous, Diodorus ignored contrary anecdotes and cleverly cast Alexander in a better light. This tells us little about Alexander, but much about Diodorus and his estimation of ἐπιείκεια. Diodorus is also noteworthy for recognizing the symbiotic relationship between the offer of clemency and the use of terror (32.4). Whereas these are typically viewed as mutually exclusive, Diodorus allows each a role within the same agenda. Turning to Dio Cassius, we find that he presented a gripping dialogue in which Livia

---

[44] Hermann Strasburger, "Poseidonius on Problems of the Roman Empire," *JRS* 55 (1965): 47-51.

[45] E.g., Livy 9.18; Cic. *De off.* 1.90; Sen. *De ira* 2.23.2-3; Tac. *Ann.* 2.73; Dio Chrys. 1.6-7.

[46] On Arrian's panegyric see Bosworth, *From Arrian to Alexander*, 135-56. Bosworth draws attention to the similarities between Arrian's characterization of Alexander and that of Curtius Rufus (10.5.26-36): both describe Alexander as irascible, yet neither mentions clemency (p. 136). Bosworth adds that the similarities between the two result from stock commonplaces, not literary dependence (p. 136). Arrian was, however, influenced by Xenophon's portrait of Agesilaus. Xenophon's Cyrus the Younger and Thucydides' Themistocles also influenced Arrian (pp. 138-39).

advised Augustus to rule by kindness rather than fear.[47] More generally, Dio recognized the inadvisability of "uncompromising strictness in the administration of justice" and the advisability of "φιλανθρωπία and πραότης in political behavior."[48]

Of all Greek authors, Plutarch seems to have said the most about clemency. De Romilly in fact anoints Plutarch as antiquity's most expressive author of sweetness (πραότης, ἐπιείκεια, and φιλανθρωπία).[49] While Plutarch offers many examples of such behavior, he also develops a sophisticated argument on behalf of clemency. In the paired lives of Themistocles-Camillus, Lysander-Sulla, and Pericles-Fabius, Stadter has traced Plutarch's exploration of "ambition, political strife, and power" and concludes that "πραότης, δικαιοσύνη, and μεγαλοφροσύνη replace φιλοτιμία" in order to benefit cities, and to avoid bringing them violence.[50]

Lenient behavior was therefore so much a part of Greco-Roman culture that for centuries it appeared in each type of rhetoric (encomiastic, deliberative, and forensic) and in a variety of literary forms (history, biography, drama, oration, and philosophic treatise).[51]

Literary texts do not hold a monopoly on ἐπιείκεια, πραότης, and *clementia*. Hellenistic kings did — from time to time — practice these qualities. Philip II treated Athens generously after Chaeronea (Polyb. 5.10.1-5). Antigonus I Monophthalmus "actually had a reputation for

---

[47] Dio Cas. 55.14-21. Préchac comments: "Les chapitres de Dion Cassius sur la conjuration de Cinna ont été composés soit d'après Sénèque soit d'après les sources que Sénèque avait utilisées" (*Sénèque. De la clémence*, lvi).

[48] G. J. D. Aalders, "Cassius Dio and the Greek World," *Mnemosyne* 39 (1986): 300. Fergus Millar also identifies Dio's advocacy that power should be seasoned with mercy as a dominant and recurrent motif in the early speeches (*A Study of Cassius Dio*, 78-79). Millar's comparison of Dio 36.1-5 and Livy 8.33.12-22 underscores Dio's particular reliance on commonplaces (79).

[49] De Romilly, *La douceur*, 275-308. On Plutarch, see also Hubert Martin, Jr., "The Concept of πραότης in Plutarch's *Lives*," *GRBS* 3 (1960): 65-73; D. A. Russell, *Plutarch* (London: Duckworth, 1973), 90-91, 97-99; C. P. Jones, *Plutarch and Rome* (Oxford University Press, 1971), 110-21. On Plut. *Sert.* see Luis A. García Moreno, "Paradoxography and Political Ideals in Plutarch's *Life of Sertorius*," in *Plutarch and the Historical Tradition*, ed. Philip A. Stadter (London: Routledge, 1992), 132-57.

[50] Philip A. Stadter, "Paradoxical Paradigms: Lysander and Sulla," in *Plutarch and the Historical Tradition*, ed. Philip A. Stadter (New York: Routledge, 1992), 48-50.

[51] The idea also appears in satire: in addition to Lucian, see Horace *Sat.* 1.3 and I. M. Le M. DuQuesnay, "Horace and Maecenas: The Propaganda Value of *Sermones* 1," in *Poetry and Politics in the Age of Augustus*, eds. Tony Woodman and David West (Cambridge University Press, 1984), 35-36.

being relatively mild and forgiving, especially towards the end of his life."[52] Antiochus III Doson was likewise well-known for his clemency.[53] Philip V used *clementia* and *munificentia* as a tactic in dealing with his Athamanian prisoners (Livy 36.14.8). Antiochus IV gained control of Syria "by the pretense of clemency."[54] In dealing with the Jews, Antiochus V reversed the bloodthirsty policy of his predecessor.[55] Antiochus VII, while besieging Jerusalem, granted the Jews a seven day truce, so they could celebrate the Festival of Tabernacles. This gesture helped to resolve the hostilities (Jos. *Ant.* 13.245).

To give some context to these gestures, we may look at an example from Diodorus Siculus. His account of the struggles between Alexander Balas and Demetrius II illustrates the interplay of gentle and harsh rule in the Hellenistic period:

Scorning to ingratiate himself with the populace as was customary, and waxing ever more burdensome (βαρύτερος) in his demands upon them, [Demetrius II] sank into ways of despotic brutality (ὠμότητα τυραννικήν) and lawless behavior of every sort ... In the first instance Demetrius chastened those who had been hostile to him in the war, not with mild censure (οὐ μετρίαις ἐπιτιμήσεσιν), but visited them with outlandish punishments.... Many Antiochenes, in fear and hatred [of Demetrius II], fled the city and wandered all about Syria, biding their time to attack the king. Demetrius, now their avowed enemy, never ceased to murder, banish, and rob, and even outdid his father in harshness (χαλεπότητα) and thirst for blood. For in fact his father, who had affected, not a kingly equity (ἐπιείκειαν), but a tyrant's lawlessness, had involved his subjects in irremediable misfortunes, with the consequence that the kings of this house were hated for their transgressions, and those of the other house were loved for their equity (ἐπιείκειαν). Hence at any moment there were struggles and continual wars in Syria, as the princes of each house constantly lay in wait for one another. The populace, in fact, welcomed the dynastic changes, since each king on being restored sought their favor (33.4).

Four features of this text deserve highlighting. First, the struggle went on between princes, not between the ruler and people. Second, typical evils of tyranny appear, namely, lawlessness and harshness, which manifest themselves concretely in murder, exile, and theft. Third, we see a familiar pattern: when brutal people encounter hostility, they react violently, for

---

[52] Richard A. Billows, *Antigonos the One-Eyed and the Creation of the Hellenistic State*, Hellenistic Culture and Society 4 (Berkeley: University of California Press, 1990), 12. Sven-Tage Teodorsson describes Antigonos' clemency as "proverbial" ("Theocritus the Sophist, Antigonus the One-eyed, and the Limits of Clemency," *Hermes* 118 [1990]: 381).

[53] Livy 36.12.7 (cp. 36.9.4); Jos. *Ant.* 12.138-44. Cf. Polyb. 5.9.

[54] Jacoby, *FGH* 260F 49a (Porphyry); trans. Burstein 39b. Another pretense of clemency related to Antiochus IV appears in 2 Macc 9:27.

[55] 2 Macc 11:29-32. See Sherwin-White and Kuhrt's explanation of twists in the Seleucid policy towards the Jews (*From Samarkhand to Sardis*, 226-28).

which reason those who practice it are hated and feared; meanwhile, those who show mildness are loved. Fourth, and most significant at present, changes in rulers, we are told, usually meant a period of blessing for the populace, as the new ruler wooed his subjects. Acts of clemency were a part of that courtship.

We need not rely only on Diodorus' testimony, because numerous decrees which authorize such gestures, called φιλάνθρωπα (or Philanthropa), are extant.[56] Lenger summarizes her survey of these decrees as follows:

[T]he royal privileges denoted by this term touch on every aspect of public and private law and concern every subject in the realm. They contain measures for tax relief, amnesties, jurisdictional privileges, rights of asylum, immunities, protection against high-handed actions, and claims for the protection of one's person and property. Farmers of the royal lands, soldiers (and particularly the kleruchs), priests, private citizens, all these are potential recipients of benefaction.[57]

Lenger later adds that φιλάνθρωπα can be identified with

the bulk of general interest decrees issued by the Ptolemies in the course of the second and first centuries BC: the majority of these laws, in effect, have for their theme either a penal or fiscal amnesty, or a reduction of the rates levied on the taxpayers or an increase in the rights which they enjoy, or again the condemnation of arbitrariness in government officials and, related to that, the renewal of the right to protection for victims' persons and property.[58]

---

[56] Marie-Thérèse Lenger states, "Si l'on considère l'évolution sémantique de l'adjectif φιλάνθρωπος, on constate que la signification de 'bienfait(s)' attachée au neutre singulier et pluriel de ce mot est propre à la *koinè*." Four lines later she adds, "... la correspondance des rois hellénistiques qualifie, à maintes reprises, de φιλάνθρωπα les privilèges qu'on sollicite des souverains et qu'ils accordent ou confirment à des cités grecques de leur obédience ou à des personnages importants qu'ils ont intérêt à ménager," in "La notion de 'bienfait' (philanthrôpon) royal et les ordonnances des rois Lagides," in *Studi in onore di Vincenzo Arangio-Ruiz nel XLV anno del suo insegnamento,* eds. Mario Lauria et al. (Naples: Jovene, c. 1952), 1: 487.

[57] *Ibid.*, 495: "... les privilèges royaux, désignés par ce terme, touchent à tous les aspects du droit public et du droit privé et ... concernent tous les sujets du royaume. Ce sont des allègements de charges fiscales, des amnisties, des privilèges juridictionnels, des droits d'asile, des immunités, des garanties contre les actions arbitraires, des titres de protection de la personne et des biens. Les fermiers de terre royale, les militaires et en particulier les clérouques, le clergé, les simples particuliers, tous sont susceptibles d'en bénéficier."

[58] *Ibid.*, 496-97: "... la plupart des ordonnances d'intérêt général, décrétées par les Ptolémées au cours des IIe et Ier siècles avant J.-C.: la majorité de ces lois, en effet, ont pour thème soit une amnistie pénale ou fiscale, soit une réduction des charges imposées aux contribuables ou un accroissement des droits dont ils jouissent, soit encore la condamnation de l'arbitraire dans le chef des fonctionnaires et corrélativement le renouvellement d'un titre de protection de la personne ou des biens des victimes."

Lenger's summary of these decrees reveals the broader context into which acts of clemency fit: grants of amnesty and immunity form part of a wider concern for benefiting one's subjects. This observation corresponds to Schubart's analysis of the Hellenistic data, in which he recognizes the idea of ἐπιείκεια to be subsumed by references to φιλανθρωπία.[59]

We may note two specific examples. The fabled Rosetta Stone records a decree passed on the occasion of the coronation of Ptolemaios V and includes a lengthy section listing his worthy deeds. Among these are benefactions to temples and military victory (which includes having avenged his father). We also read,

With his own resources he has assisted everyone; and of the imposts and taxes in Egypt, some he has remitted entirely and others he has lightened in order that the people and everyone else may live in prosperity during his reign; and debts owed the crown by those in Egypt and the rest of his kingdom he has canceled; and those being held in jails and those who had been detained because of accusations for a long time he has freed of charges. Likewise also he distributed justice to all (Burstein 103).

These benefactions illustrate Lenger's observations on Philanthropa and indicate the larger context in which amnesty is shown to subjects.

One of the Philanthropa of Ptolemaios VIII (118 BC) offered a fairly detailed general amnesty and now illustrates the use of favors to gain favor. It begins as follows:

King Ptolemaios and Queen Kleopatra, the sister, and Queen Kleopatra, the Wife, pardon those subject to their rule, all of them, for errors, wrongful acts, accusations, condemnations, charges of all sorts up to the 9th of Pharmouthi of the 52nd year except those guilty of willful murder and sacrilege. They have given orders also that those who have fled because of being accused of theft and other charges shall return to their own homes and resume their former occupations, and that they shall recover whatever of their property still remains unsold from that which had been seized as security because of these matters.[60]

The decree continues for many more columns forgiving debts, protecting sacred lands and revenues, prohibiting billeting and requisitions, and enjoining many other things as well. Alan Samuel argues that this decree reflects a development in the motivation behind Philanthropa: whereas an earlier decree, *P. Tebt.* 703, suggests an origin based on economic motives, "the remissions in *P. Tebt.* 5 are stated as good-will grants ... In

---

[59] "Das hellenistische Königsideal," 10: "φιλανθρωπία bildet gewissermaßen die Brücke von ἐπιείκεια zu ἔλεος, fließt aber unmittelbar aus der εὔνοια." The connection between ἐπιείκεια and justice was not yet lost, as Schubert notes: "Dem Gedanken der Gerechtigkeit steht die ἐπιείκεια nahe, die Billigkeit, freilich schon auf dem Übergange zur Nachsicht und Güte und der μακροθυμία verwandt ..." (8).

[60] *P. Tebt.* 5; trans. Burstein 107. (I have elided the textual symbols in Burstein's translation.)

fact, the document and its provisions are, I think, as much intended as φιλάνθρωπα emanating from the ideology of kingship as they are reflective of unrest in Egypt."[61] Thus, in spite of the brutalities of the Hellenistic age, acts of leniency supported an ideology of clemency — and vice versa.[62]

The history of *clementia* in the life and literature of Rome is long. Although in terms of vocabulary Roman *clementia* corresponds to Greek ἐπιείκεια, Grimal argues that the former existed long before it felt the influence of the latter.[63] He further maintains that prior to (Panaetius and) Cicero and Augustus ἐπιείκεια and *clementia* were different. The Greek concept reflected a virtue which was practiced by an individual monarch and which was useful in winning the hearts of the vanquished; the act of *clementia*, on the other hand, was the application of a transcendent principle of restraint which existed prior to conquest as the attitude of the

---

[61] "The Ideology of Ptolemaic Monarchy," 78.

[62] In "Philanthropia in the Papyri of the Roman Period" (in *Hommages à Joseph Bidez et à Franz Cumont*, Collection Latomus 2 [Brussels: Latomus, c. 1949], 31-37), H. I. Bell examined Philanthropa from the Roman period in order to evaluate Rostovtzeff's opinion that "with the advent of the Roman governors ... the voice of sympathy is dumb" (*Cambridge Ancient History*, 7: 154). Bell concluded that evidence exists "of genuine attempts on the part of the Roman government to remedy grievances and to help economic recovery ... [W]e may fairly take the frequent references to φιλανθρωπία as some evidence that it was acknowledged as an ideal to be aimed at" (36). Bell does not go so far as to vindicate Rome of charges of harshness; he only mitigates Rostovtzeff's severe characterization. As clemency is related to Philanthropa, it is also related to affairs of σύλη and ἄσυλος, about which see F. W. Walbank, *The Hellenistic World* (Cambridge, MA: Harvard University Press, 1982), 145-47.

[63] Pierre Grimal, "La clémence et la douceur dans la vie politique romaine," *CRAI* (1984): 466-73. As evidence he offers the right of appeal, the relation of *clementia* to *fides*, and the extension of *patria potestas*. Regarding the second point Grimal says, "La *clementia* est impliquée dans la *fides*, et celle-ci, d'autre part, prolonge la clémence, la garantit, fait en sorte que, à partir de ce moment, les rapports entre les deux peuples soient réglés avec une bonne volonté réciproque, qui ne devra rien aux termes d'un traité ..." (p. 472). Grimal does not refer to Cic. *De off*. 1.35, but could have: "Not only must we show consideration for those whom we have conquered by force of arms but we must also ensure protection to those who lay down their arms and throw themselves upon the mercy of our generals (note Latin: *qui armis positis ad imperatorum fidem confugient*), even though the battering-ram has hammered at their walls. And among our countrymen justice (*iustitia*) has been observed so conscientiously in this direction, that those who have given promise of protection (*in fidem recepissent*) to states or nations subdued in war become, after the custom of our forefathers (*more maiorum*), the patrons (*patroni*) of those states."

entire, collected citizenry.[64] Clemency was therefore inherent in the *disciplina romana* and the *mos maiorum*.[65]

Despite the deep roots of *clementia*, significant evidence of it does cluster in the Late Republic and, moreover, around its leading figures.[66] Livy wrote that Publius Scipio Africanus "left more conspicuous monuments of his *clementia benignitasque* than of his *virtus bellica*" (37.6.6). Cicero thought he had shown *lenitas* to the Catilinarians.[67] *Integritas, iustitia, clementia,* and *fides* were attributed to Cicero by Cato in testimony before the Senate (Cic. *Ad Att.* 7.2.7). Such virtues played an important role in Cicero's governance of Cilicia, as he attempted to exercise his authority by the principles of *abstinentia, iustitia, facilitas* and *clementia*.[68] Cicero, recognizing similar virtues in Pompey, praised him for the restraint which he showed to both ally and enemy.[69] The leniency which Pompey extended in the East to the pirates played a key role in his expeditious resolution of that problem.[70] But Pompey allowed Caesar to eclipse him in the exercise of clemency.[71] With no exaggeration, one could say that Caesar made a personal badge of honor out of *clementia*.[72]

---

[64] Grimal, pp. 473-75.

[65] *Ibid.*, 474-75. As evidence Grimal offers considerations of legal procedure and the opportunity afforded accused persons to escape capital punishment (pp. 475-76).

[66] Stefan Weinstock, *Divus Julius* (Oxford University Press, 1971), 234-37.

[67] *Cat.* 2.4, 27; *Pro Sul.* 1.92.

[68] *Ad Att.* 5.21; Plut. *Cic.* 6.1. See Manfred Fuhrmann, *Cicero and the Roman Republic*, trans. W. E. Yuill (Oxford: Blackwell, 1992), 126-29. Cic. *De off.* 1.35 and 82 refer to war, 1.88-89 to punishment.

[69] *Ver.* 2.5.153; *Pro leg. Man.* 13, 39, and 42. Cf. Vel. Pat. *Hist. rom.* 2.29.3; App. *Mith.* 117. Plutarch also attributes gentleness to Pompey (*Pom.* 636f; 640a), though he notes the exceptions as well (623c-e; cf. App. *Bel. civ.* 1.96; Val. Max. *Fac. et dic.* 6.2.8).

[70] Peter Greenhalgh, *Pompey: The Roman Alexander* (Columbia: University of Missouri Press, 1981), 95-96. Plutarch offers two examples of Pompey's clemency: he gave cities to (former) pirates and made an ally of the Armenian king Tigranes, as opposed to parading him in triumphal procession (*Pom.* 663a). Plutarch also says that Cato the Younger advised Pompey to follow two clement principles: never plunder a city subject to Rome and never kill a Roman (*Cato min.* 785d).

[71] Suet. *Iul.* 75; cf. Cic. *Ad Att.* 7.20; 8.11; 8.16; 9.7; 9.10; 10.7.

[72] *Bel. Gal.* 2.14, 31; *Bel. Civ.* 1.72, 74, 85; 3.98. Cp. Cic. *Phil.* 2.116; *Ad Att.* 9.7c; 9.16.2; 10.4.8; *Ad fam.* 6.6.8; 13.66; 15.19.4; Sal. *Cat.* 54.2; Sen. *De ira* 2.23.4; Plut. *Cae.* 714f; Dio Cas. 43.15-18. In addition to the literature which de Romilly cites (*La douceur*, 258 n. 6), see Cornelia Catlin Coulter, "Caesar's Clemency," *CJ* 26 (1931): 513-24; Stefan Weinstock, *Divus Julius* (Oxford University Press, 1971), 166-67 and 233-43 (but note the criticism in Andreas Alföldi's review of *Divus Julius* in *Gnomon* 47 [1975]: 341-42; cp. idem, review of *Die Vergottung Caesars*, by Helga Gesche, in

A key to Caesar's success was in fact his use of *clementia*. Cicero provided striking testimony to the mass appeal of such a policy:

> Upon my word, if he [Caesar] refrain from murder and rapine, he will be the darling of those who dreaded him most. The people of the country towns and the farmers talk to me a great deal. They care for nothing at all but their lands, their little homesteads and their tiny hoards. And see how public opinion has changed. They fear the man [Pompey] they once trusted, and adore the man [Caesar] they once dreaded (*Ad Att.* 8.13).

Three days later, Cicero penned the following:

> And see how they are running to meet Caesar, and selling themselves to him. The country towns are treating him as a god ... What ovations from the towns and what honor is paid him! ... They are delighted with the cunning kindness (*clementia*) of Caesar, and afraid of the anger of his rival (*Ad Att.* 8.16.2).

Cicero marvelled at this "new way of conquering," that is, "to strengthen one's position by kindness and generosity" (*Ad Att.* 9.7c.1). Cicero also lavished such praise on Caesar's clemency that Caesar himself responded by letter to Cicero, claiming that "there is nothing further from my nature than cruelty."[73] To others Caesar wrote that his greatest delight came from saving some of the people who fought against him (Plut. *Cae.* 48.4). To pay honor to this policy, Aulus Caecina wrote an entire treatise celebrating it (Cic. *Ad fam.* 6.6.8). Even more dramatic, however, was the temple decreed to Caesar's clemency.[74]

Caesar's heir followed his example.[75] When Octavian raised his army, his supporters circulated rumors and pamphlets which condemned Antony's treatment of his troops, harping on Antony's meager pay and brutal discipline.[76] After the Battle of Mutina Octavian treated his captives kindly (Cic. *Ad Att.* 10.21.4); after Philippi Octavian wrote to the Senate, promising to act according to the example of his father's clemency (πράως καὶ φιλανθρώπως; Dio Cas. 48.3.6). In summarizing Octavian's

---

Phoenix 24 [1970]: 176); Zwi Yavetz, *Julius Caesar and His Public Image* (Ithaca, NY: Cornell University Press, 1983), 174-75; Andreas Alföldi, *Caesar in 44 v. Chr*, Antiquitas, 3d ser., 16 (Bonn: Rudolf Habelt, 1985), 1: 173-388. Caesar's policy reversed Sulla's; on the latter's severity see Arthur Keaveney, *Sulla: The Last Republican* (London: Croom Helm, 1982), 148-68.

[73] *Ad Att.* 9.16. Cicero nevertheless remained suspicious of Caesar, writing to Atticus that Caesar's clemency was a calculated ploy to win popularity. Cicero speculated that once Caesar "lost popular favor, he would be cruel" (*Ad Att.* 10.4).

[74] Weinstock provides the numismatic and literary evidence and points out the uncertainty as to whether the temple was actually ever built (*Divus Julius*, 241-43 and 308-10); cf. *CRR*, 179 no. 1076.

[75] Apparently, Brutus did as well (Cic. *Ad Brut.* 5.5). He too found it an effective policy.

[76] App. *Bel. civ.* 3.43-44; cf. Dio Cas. 45.12-13.

behavior in the course of the civil war, Dio wrote that Octavian "fought to an honorable conclusion and brought ... a humane settlement, overpowering as enemies all who resisted, but sparing as friends all who yielded" (53.7.2). In that statement Dio followed the view of Augustus which the emperor himself presented, as he boasted in his *Res gestae*, "I pardoned all citizens who sought mercy. Foreign peoples who could safely be pardoned, I preferred to spare rather than put to the sword."[77] Unfortunately, Octavian's reprisals after victory at Actium clouded this picture: most of the opposing leaders were fined or killed, though some were spared.[78] Octavian's callous treatment of his defeated enemies at Philippi further eroded his claims to clemency, as did the rumored brutalities visited on the vanquished at Perusia.[79] Likewise the proscriptions.[80] However, Octavian did spare Antony's soldiers, absorbing most of them into his own legions (Dio Cas. 51.3.1), and spared all the Egyptians and Alexandrians (51.16.3). To allay the fears of Antony's followers, he claimed to have burned all of Antony's correspondence (though in fact he destroyed only a part of it).[81] He spared Lepidus and "the whole inner circle of his court he recruited from the camp of his opponents."[82] According to Cicero, Octavian gained much popularity by showing clemency in his legal rulings (*Qfr.* 1.1.19-21). Documentary sources preserve an example of Augustus' kind intervention in a murder case, in which he sided with the accused against the prosecuting Cnidians.

---

[77] *Res gestae* 3. Livy echoes this policy when he comments that one usually plunders a city which has been stormed and spares one which surrenders (37.32.12); cf. 33.12.7 and 9.

[78] Dio Cas. 51.2. Cp. 56.38: Octavian "spared the lives of most of his opponents who had survived the various battles ... to his adversaries he made defeat seem victory." See also 53.4.1; 53.6.1; 55.14-21. But Dio "betrays uneasiness that, whereas Caesar was a paragon of clemency, Augustus' record on this score was poor," John W. Rich, *Cassius Dio: The Augustan Settlement (Roman History 53-55.9)*, Classical Texts (Warminster: Aris & Phillips, 1990), 14 (cf. pp. 16-17).

[79] Suet. *Aug.* 13-15 and Sen. *De clem.* 1.11.2, respectively.

[80] Pliny *Nat. Hist.* 7.147-50 sketches the discrepancies of Augustus' life, while P. A. Brunt and J. M. Moore sketch the ugly, contradictory history glossed over by Augustus' propaganda: *Res Gestae Divi Augusti: The Achievements of the Divine Augustus* (Oxford University Press, 1967), 40-41. For a more detailed look at the proscriptions, see Ronald Syme, *The Roman Revolution* (Oxford University Press, 1939), 187-201. Cp. Ps-Sen. *Oct.* 504-32.

[81] Dio Cas. 52.42.8. Octavian was following the precedent set by Pompey who burned Sertorius' correspondence without reading it, as well as Caesar who did the same with Pompey's and Scipio's (Weinstock, *Divus Julius*, 237-38). Gaius later pretended to do likewise; Claudius actually did it (Dio Cas. 60.4.5; cf. 59.16.3)

[82] Sen. *De clem.* 1.10.1. Cp. Octavian's sparing of Herod in Jos. *Bel.* 1.386-97.

4.1. Commonplace Nature of Leniency 211

In fact, Augustus censured the Cnidians for having been too harsh (χαλεπόι) in the matter (Oliver 6). At a later point in his life, when Augustus learned that the cruel and tyrannical Archelaus "had disobeyed [Augustus'] instructions to show moderation (ἐπεικῶς) in dealing with" the Jews and Samaritans, Augustus sent Archelaus into exile.[83] Other Anecdotes recounting Augustus' leniency also circulated.[84] Which picture is then the genuine person? Seneca argued that Augustus was genuinely lenient and attributed the examples of Augustus' severity to his youth and to his having to share power with Antony and Lepidus.[85] The older, established Augustus had learned to act gently and was at that time free to do so. This explanation clearly served Seneca's purposes in admonishing his young charge Nero.[86] It does not account for Augustus' behavior, for clemency was determined by pragmatic considerations, not character. Economic factors therefore motivated the proscriptions more than the lust for vengeance.[87] As for clemency, the *Res gestae* itself admits that people "who could safely be pardoned" were spared. Thus, soldiers and subjects commonly received clemency, but not rivals. Security took priority over clemency.[88]

Despite the discrepancies surrounding Augustus' clemency, the Senate itself honored Augustus for his clemency, awarding him the so-called *clipeus virtutis*: this golden shield was displayed publicly in the Julian Senate house (near the statue and altar of Victory) and its inscription honored Augustus' *virtus, clementia, iustitia,* and *pietas*.[89] Replicas of the

---

[83] Jos. *Ant.* 17.342. Equally interesting are that Augustus cared to hear the complaint of the Jews and Samaritans, that they had access to Augustus, and that they thought to approach Augustus in the first place.

[84] Sen. *De ira* 3.24 and 40; *De clem.* 1.9.1-1.11.3; *De ben.* 3.27.1-4; Suet. *Aug.* 33; 51; 67.1; Dio Cas. 56.43.3.

[85] *De clem.* 1.9.1-2; 1.11.1. Dio Cas. also distinguishes between the periods of shared and absolute power (56.44.1). Such were the circumstances of Cicero's death (Plut. *Cic.* 46).

[86] Syme, *Roman Revolution*, 191.

[87] *Ibid.*, 194-94.

[88] Cp. *Sib. Or.* 3.652-56, where the ideal king "will stop the whole earth from evil war, killing some, imposing oaths of fidelity on others."

[89] The shield's inscription states: *Senatus populusque romanus imp. Caesari divi f. Augusto cos. VIII dedit virtutis clementiae iustitiae pietatisque erga deos patriamque.* Paul Zanker, *The Power of Images in the Age of Augustus*, trans. Alan Shapiro, Jerome Lectures 16 (Ann Arbor: University of Michigan Press, 1988), 95-98; Edwin S. Ramage, *The Nature and Purpose of Augustus' 'Res Gestae,'* Historia, Einzelschriften 54 (Stuttgart: Franz Steiner, 1987), 73-99; Pierre Grimal, "Les éléments philosophiques dans l'idée de monarchie à Rome à la fin de la République," in *Aspects de la philosophie hellénistique,* eds. Hellmut Flashar and Olof Gigon, Entretiens sur l'antiquité classique

shield were displayed elsewhere in the empire (e.g., Arles). The shield also entered into the visual imagery of the empire, appearing on coins, altars, and lamps.[90] Sometimes the shield is held by Victory, sometimes the shield bears the abbreviation CL V. Copies of the *Res gestae* (e.g., in Ancyra, Pisidian Antioch, and Pisidian Apollonia) also made the shield known, as well as specifying its virtues and interpreting its imagery.

The shield was not tangential to Augustus' imperial ideology.[91] The four virtues encapsulated much of what Augustus wished to convey in his *Res gestae* and were therefore integral to Augustan ideology. These virtues reappeared in Augustan monuments and artifacts. *Virtus* echoed in the military imagery common to coins (e.g., Victoria, the *corona civica*, and military standards), cuirassed statues, quadrigae, and triumphal arches.[92] The Temple of Apollo touted Octavian's *virtus*;[93] the Forum Augustum did so in even more dramatic and overwhelming fashion.[94] According to Dio Cassius, Augustus' military exploits were recorded "in many a book and painting, so that you can both read and behold them" (56.37.6). *Pietas* played an important role in the self-presentation of Caesar's heir, for it justified his participation in civil war. The numerous temples which he restored, the sacrifices he endowed, and the priesthoods he held also

---

32 (Geneva: Fondation Haardt, 1986), 254-59. Weinstock discusses the relevance of the four virtues for Caesar (*Divus Julius*, 228-59). As for the composition of the Senate which awarded the shield to Augustus, see Syme's comments (*Roman Revolution*, 196-201).

[90] Andreas Alföldi, *Die zwei Lorbeerbäume des Augustus*, Antiquitas, 3d ser., 14 (Bonn: Rudolf Habelt, 1973), plates 3-5, 9, and 21-22.

[91] The shield and titles Augustus and Pater Patriae form "a kind of philosophic explanation, even idealization, of Augustus' rule ... a summary of the ideology of the principate as Augustus conceives of it," Edwin S. Ramage, *Augustus 'Res Gestae,'* 73. In a similar vein, Ramage suggests that part of Sulla's rationale in comparing himself to Herakles was to underscore the virtues of *virtus, iustitia, humanitas, liberalitas, clementia,* and *pietas* ("Sulla's Propaganda," *Klio* 73 [1991]: 119).

[92] Chariots and arches in turn became the subject matter for coins. On military imagery in Augustan coinage, see C. H. V. Sutherland, *Coinage in Roman Imperial Policy* (London: Methuen & Co., 1951), 29-33.

[93] B. Kellum, "Sculptural Programs and Propaganda in Augustan Rome: The Temple of Apollo on the Palatine," in *The Age of Augustus: Interdisciplinary Conference Held at Brown University, April 30-May 2, 1982*, ed. Rolf Winkes, Archaeologia transatlantica 5/Publications d'histoire de l'art et d'archéologie de L'Université Catholique de Louvain 44 (Providence, RI: Brown University, 1985; Louvain-la-Neuve: Collège Érasme, 1985), 171 and 175-76.

[94] See, for example, T. J. Luce, "Livy, Augustus, and the Forum Augustum," in *Between Republic and Empire: Interpretations of Augustus and His Principate*, eds. Kurt A. Raaflaub and Mark Toher (Berkeley: University of California Press, 1990), 123-38; Zanker, *Power of Images,* 214; Hannestad, *Roman Art,* 83-89.

declared his piety.[95] The imagery of the Temple of Apollo, the Forum Augustum, and the Ara Pacis also emphasized Augustan piety; the latter also directs our attention to Augustus' social policies, which further expressed his concern for piety.[96] Zanker, in fact, argues that *pietas* "became the focal point of the new emperor's cultural and political program."[97] *Clementia* received allusion on coins and altars via the *corona civica* and references to the rescue of citizens.[98] The battlefield and courtroom provided numerous opportunities for offering clemency. That Augustus' jury vote counted as Athena's gave his mercy an institutional expression.[99] *Iustitia* was an important criterion in the Senate's appraisal of its *princeps*. Evidence of *iustitia*, however, existed more in the realities of legislation and legal proceedings than in images. Throughout the empire, therefore, inscribed edicts revealed the emperor's concern for justice, as did properly minted coins. And these were legion. Praise for his *iustitia* must have especially pleased Augustus, who had begun his career illegally, subsequently altered Rome's political structures, and for many years had to balance delicately his own eminence with the dignity and freedom of the Senate. The shield's four virtues also influenced imperial poetry. Horace's "Roman Odes" (*Odes* 3.1-6), Virgil's *Aeneid*, and Ovid's

---

[95] Aug. *Res ges.* 19-20, 24; Sherk 1984: 95.

[96] Diana E. E. Kleiner, "The Great Friezes of the Ara Pacis Augustae: Greek Sources, Roman Derivatives, and Augustan Social Policy," in *Roman Art in Context: An Anthology*, ed. Eve D'Ambra (Englewood Cliffs, NJ: Prentice Hall, 1993), 27-52. Much has been written about the Ara Pacis: in general see Hannestad, *Roman Art*, 62-74; for recent bibliography and on the altar's general interpretation see Richard Billows, "The Religious Procession of the Ara Pacis Augustae: Augustus' *supplicatio* in 13 B.C.," *JRA* 6 (1993): 80-92; more focused yet hermeneutically important is Karl Galinsky, "Venus, Polysemy, and the Ara Pacis Augustae," *AJA* 96 (1992): 457-75. The discussion continues in Barbette Stanley Spaeth, "The Goddess Ceres in the Ara Pacis Augustae and the Carthage Relief," *AJA* 98 (1994): 65-100.

[97] *Power of Images*, 96. On *pietas* in Augustan ideology in general, see 101-36. Cf. Sherk 1988: 36a for the concern to memorialize the piety of the deceased Drusus Caesar.

[98] Dio Cas. 53.16.4. E. Ramage, *Augustus 'Res Gestae,'* 76 n. 173. "The civic crown of oak-leaves *ob cives servatos* ... was among the most prominent of all elements in the wide range of Augustus' coin-types" (C. H. V. Sutherland, *Roman History and Coinage 44 BC - AD 69: Fifty Points of Relation from Julius Caesar to Vespasian* [Oxford University Press, 1987], 65).

[99] Dio Cas. 51.19.6-7. This passage also indicates the relevance of *tribunicia potestas* to both Augustus' *clementia* and *iustitia*. Cf. Tac. *Ann.* 14.48, where Nero used his tribunician veto to rescue a condemned man from death. Tacitus adds the comment that Nero did this to promote his own glory. See Fergus Millar, *The Emperor in the Roman World* (London: Duckworth, 1977), 509.

Fasti 2.126-44 interacted with each of the shield's four virtues.[100] These virtues also made important human connections. *Virtus* reflected Roman imperial aspiration and a key quality of Roman self-understanding, while *pietas* resonated with Roman social conservatism and, again, Roman self-understanding. *Iustitia* played well to a people proud of its ancient constitution and to people fearful of such an influential person. *Clementia* further made an august person less fearsome and also played on the sense of what it was to be Roman.[101]

Do *virtus, clementia, iustitia,* and *pietas* reflect an official, canonical ideology of the principate? M. P. Charlesworth argued that the *clipeus virtutis* publicized the four cardinal virtues essential to the legitimization

---

[100] Inez Scott Ryberg, "Clipeus Virtutis," in *The Classical Tradition: Literary and Historical Studies in Honor of Harry Caplan,* ed. Luitpold Wallach (Ithaca, NY: Cornell University Press, 1966), 232-38. Ryberg notes that *clementia* has been subsumed by *pietas* in Virgil and Propertius *El.* 3.22 (pp. 235-36). Although Andrew Wallace-Hadrill ("The Emperor and his Virtues," *Historia* 30 [1981]: 305 n. 34) rightly criticizes Ryberg for pressing the data too far, a material similarity between the shield and the noted poetry cannot be denied. Matthew Santirocco puts Horace's "Roman Odes" in perspective by indicating their additional political aspects and the literary complexity of their design (*Unity and Design in Horace's Odes* [Chapel Hill: University of North Carolina Press, 1986], 115-21). Thus, although the four virtues appear in the poetry, the poetry cannot and should not be reduced to the four virtues (p. 115). C. Joachim Classen's remarks are more forceful: "Gewiß kommen in den Versen Ovids auch die Qualitäten vor, die der *clupeus* nennt; doch treten sie nicht sehr deutlich in Erscheinung, vor allem verbinden sie sich mit zahlreichen anderen Tugenden. Davon, daß Ovid wirklich an den *clupeus* gedacht hat, fehlt jede Spur" ("Virtutes Imperatoriae," *Arctos* 25 [1991]: 35).

[101] C. Joachim Classen provides nice, succinct definitions of the four virtues: "Auf dem Augustusschild findet sich zuerst *virtus*: Das ist für den Römer die Selbstverwirklichung des Mannes, des Bürgers, durch militärischen Erfolg — stets wird *victoria* mit dem Schild verbunden; es ist die politische Leistung für die Allgemeinheit, die durch die Verleihung des Ehrenschildes anerkannt wird. *Clementia* ist die Großzügigkeit, die aus einer durch einmalige Leistung gewonnenen Position der Überlegenheit und Sicherheit dem Unterlegenen verzeiht, und zwar auch unverdientermaßen ohne Anwendung der üblichen Rechtsgrundsätze. Die Verbindung von *virtus* und *clementia* betont hier, daß der persönliche Erfolg und die individuelle Leistung den einzelnen über alle traditionellen Bindungen hinausgehoben haben. Auch die *iustitia* ist eine 'vertue essentiellement active et positive' [J. Hellegouarc'h, 265], die den Mitbürgern gibt, was sie verdienen, wie entsprechend die *pietas* den Göttern und dem Vaterland zukommen läßt, was sie beanspruchen können. Es sind alles Qualitäten eines über den anderen stehenden einzelnen, des ersten Bürgers, der sich seiner Verpflichtungen ebenso bewußt erscheint wie seiner Sonderstellung, Qualitäten, die an einem ungewöhnlichen einzelnen nach einem besonderen Erfolg herausgestellt werden" ("Virtutes Imperatoriae," 23-24). Another discussion of the four virtues appears in József Korpanty, "Römische Ideale und Werte im augusteischen Prinzipat," *Klio* 73 (1991): 432-47.

of the Principate, not only for Augustus but his successors as well.[102] This longstanding thesis was challenged by A. Wallace-Hadrill who boldly stated that "the canonical status of these virtues is a delusion."[103] He argued that the four virtues of the shield differed from the philosophical canon (which is also problematic) and that no evidence exists subsequent to the shield indicating that its virtues attained a special status — not literary, not numismatic, not inscriptional, not even the guidelines for the βασιλικὸς λόγος in the rhetorical handbooks (pp. 300-7). As for a ruler's ligitimacy, Wallace-Hadrill demonstrated that power (e.g., victory, peace, concord, rescue) was more important than character traits (p. 316).

While Wallace-Hadrill has offered sound and devastating criticism, we should pause to elaborate the problems with Charlesworth a bit further. The fundamental flaw in Charlesworth's study lay in what he ignored. For example, while correctly noting the use of the four virtues on the golden shield, he did not give adequate scope to other virtues. One problem then with identifying the shield's four virtues as cardinal is that many others consequently go unnoticed. Strangely enough, Charlesworth himself identified one of those others, namely *providentia*, and discussed it at length in the very article in question (pp. 117-22); however, he left foresight outside the "canon" because it was developing slowly, not really taking center stage until Trajan (117). The same objection could not apply to benefaction, which pervaded Hellenistic royal ideology and certainly figured in Roman imperial ideology, as Augustus' very own *Res gestae* indicates. Charlesworth also paid inadequate attention to lacunae in the evidence. While we can easily plot a trajectory from Augustus through the year-of-four-emperors to the adopted emperors, we must ask whether that adequately characterizes the gaps (AD 14-68 and 70-98). In point of fact, evidence for any canonical imperial virtues among Augustus' Julio-Claudian successors is minimal — and this is not a period which suffers a paucity of evidence. Furthermore, when comparing Augustus to AD 69 and then to Trajan and Hadrian, the evidence for a canon of imperial

---

[102] Martin P. Charlesworth, "The Virtues of a Roman Emperor: Propaganda and the Creation of Belief," *PBA* 23 (1937): 105-33, especially 114.

[103] "The Emperor and His Virtues," 300. Classen continued the attack on Charlesworth in "Virtutes Imperatoriae," 17-39. The common theme of Classen's criticisms is that attempts to trace an ideology in the virtues fails to give adequate due to the particularity of each bit of evidence and what it represents in its own context. Such criticism gives inadequate regard to the usefulness of ambiguity in slogans and propaganda and that they are drawn from a well-known pool of *topoi*. To quote from his conclusion, Classen says that the "sogenannten Kardinaltugenden ... sind vielmehr aus besonderem Anlaß zusammengestellt, um die einmalige Leistung eines einzelnen zu ehren, und so ist durch diese vier Tugenden ... kein römisches Kaiserideal fixiert worden ..." (39). I do not agree that the first half of his statement requires the second half.

virtues multiplies at each stage.[104] Reading the more ubiquitous second century data as evidence for Julio-Claudian and Flavian ideology is therefore hazardous. We must agree with Wallace-Hadrill in rejecting Charlesworth's claim that *virtus, clementia, iustitia,* and *pietas* are "cardinal virtues of a ruler" (p. 114).

Although Wallace-Hadrill has effectively refuted Charlesworth, has he offered the final word on the four virtues? To say that they were not canonical is not to deny them relevance or importance; even if they are not the "cardinal virtues of a ruler," they may nevertheless have been popular and desired virtues in a ruler. That they reappear at the moments when an ideology of the principate was needed (Augustus, AD 69, Trajan) suggests that these virtues were recognized as desirable in a ruler and had some persuasive value. The evidence from the years 14-68 (which we will soon survey) and 70-98 increases this impression. But we must keep the larger context in mind: these four virtues were only four among many which could assist royal propaganda, and virtues were only one aspect of ruler *topoi*. That the shield's virtues occasionally appear in connection with Roman rulers is no surprise given their place in Hellenistic ruler ideology and their connections with Roman values and human desires. Thus, as subsequent emperors demonstrate, the virtues displayed on Augustus' shield were among those with which rulers would associate themselves. For the purposes of this study, the shield provides evidence that at the birth of the Roman empire ideas typically associated with good kings again received concrete application. More specifically, clemency again received public commendation.

After Caesar and Augustus, the evidence for clemency diminishes. While the accident of extant evidence may contribute slightly to this, more crucial is the absence of civil war. Less evidence, however, does not mean none. For example, Tiberius issued a set of dupondii bearing the legends CLEMENTIAE and MODERATIONI;[105] meanwhile, the Senate tried to flatter Tiberius by erecting an altar to Clemency.[106] Sutherland argues that the coins call attention to the fact that, in connection with the *Lex Iuli maiestatis*, the Senate honored Tiberius with two shields, one honoring his

---

[104] J. Rufus Fears, "The Cult of the Virtues and Roman Imperial Ideology," is crucial in surveying the evidence.

[105] Sutherland, *RIC*, 1: 97 nos. 38-39 (also plate 11). Sutherland indicates that more than twenty specimens of each dupondius are extant; he dates this pair to 22 AD (1: 88-89). No. 40 is an additional coin bearing the legend MODERATIONIS. On Tiberius' *clementia* see Tac. *Ann.* 2.40; 4.31; 6.25; Suet. *Tib.* 53; on *moderatio* see Tac. *Ann.* 1.8; 1.14; 2.31; 2.36; 3.56; Suet. *Tib.* 32; 57.

[106] Tac. *Ann.* 4.74.3 (cp. 4.31). See Anthony A. Barrett, *Caligula: The Corruption of Power* (New Haven: Yale University Press, 1989), 32.

clemency and the other his moderation.[107] He then wonders whether the *ara Clementiae* might have been "a deliberate reminiscence of a conspicuous coin-type issued six years before" (p. 140).

Others have proposed different theories about the coins. Helga Gesche connects the dupondii to events of 33 AD when a sacrifice was offered to Jupiter in celebration of Tiberius' clemency.[108] The particular behavior in view was Tiberius' treatment of Agrippina and the followers of Sejanus. The honorary shields depicted are actually those awarded Germanicus and Drusus (Tac. *Ann.* 2.83 and 4.9) and help place the new heirs, Gaius Caligula and Tiberius Gemellus, in the public eye. Barbara Levick, however, thinks that *clementia* and *moderatio* were fundamental to Tiberius' reign, especially its early period, and correspondingly dates the pair of coins to the autumn of 16 AD.[109] She proposes that the coins reflect Tiberius' wish to have exercised *clementia* in the conspiracy of Libo Drusus (who committed suicide too early) and the *moderatio* shown in turning a blind eye to the supporters of Clemens.[110] Levick also offers interpretations of Tiberius' two "cardinal virtues" (p. 125), defining *clementia* as Tiberius' "forbearance to the political group that had consistently and ruthlessly opposed his elevation" (p. 130), and *moderatio* as "voluntarily circumscribing the limits of his power" (pp. 126-27). Like Gesche, Levick sees the busts on the medallions as references to the succession of the dynasty, identifying them as either Germanicus and Drusus or else Germanicus' sons.

A different suggestion about the dupondii comes from J. Rufus Fears. He returns to Sutherland's dating and suggests that the Clementia/Moderatio pair are part of an issue celebrating the fiftieth anniversary of Augustus' golden shield.[111] Support for this idea can be found in Sutherland's catalogue, which records a dupondius whose

---

[107] C. H. V. Sutherland, "Two 'Virtues' of Tiberius: A Numismatic Contribution to the History of His Reign," *JRS* 28 (1938): 137-39; cf. idem, *Roman History and Coinage*, 59-61. Niels Hannestad offers a similar interpretation of the *clementia/moderatio* dupondii: "They were perhaps given ... as a kind of defence necessitated by the increasing number of treason trials which characterized [Tiberius'] reign" (*Roman Art and Imperial Policy*, trans. P. J. Crabb, Jutland Archaeological Society Publications 19 [Aarhus: University Press, 1986], 95).

[108] Helga Gesche, "Datierung und Deutung des CLEMENTIAE-MODERATIONI-Dupondien des Tiberius," *Jahrbuch für Numismatik und Geldgeschichte* 21 (1971): 37-80. See Suet. *Tib.* 53 and Tac. *Ann.* 6.25.2.

[109] Barbara M. Levick, "Mercy and Moderation on the Coinage of Tiberius," in *The Ancient Historian and His Materials: Essays in Honor of C. E. Stevens* (Farnborough: Gregg International, 1975), 123-37.

[110] See Tac. *Ann.* 2.27-31, especially 31.4, and 2.40; cf. Suet. *Tib.* 57.

[111] "The Cult of Virtues and Roman Imperial Ideology," *ANRW* 2.17.2 (1981): 890.

obverse bears the image of the goddess Piety (as identified by the legend) and another dupondius which identifies its image as Justice.[112] As for *virtus*, Sutherland lists two dupondii from 22-23 AD whose reverses present Victoria alighting with her right hand resting on a shield inscribed SPQR.[113] Unfortunately, problems of dating plague Fears' suggestion, as does the connection of *iustitia* with Livia rather than Tiberius, and the fact that the Clementia/Moderatio dupondii look like a pair, but the others do not look like a quintet. What is interesting about the varied theories put forward is the way each highlights the relevance of clemency to varied periods of Tiberius' principate. The plausibility of each theory suggests that the golden shield's vocabulary of good rule remained viable throughout the first fifty years of the Principate.

Philo differentiated Caligula from his predecessors on the grounds that, whereas they ruled with ἐπιείκεια and laws, Gaius "exscinded all kindness from his soul and zealously practiced lawlessness" (Philo *De leg. ad Gai.* 119). Philo's meeting with Caligula confirmed this impression.

> When we were brought into his presence the moment we saw him we bowed our heads to the ground with all respect and timidity and saluted him addressing him as Emperor Augustus. The mildness and kindness (ἐπεικῶς καὶ φιλανθρώπως) with which he replied to our greeting was such that we gave up not only our case but our lives for lost!" (352).

Philo's biting irony indicates much about what was expected of the emperor and how far Gaius fell short of that expectation. That Caligula scourged and tortured senators and knights further tarnished his

---

[112] *RIC*, 1: nos. 43 and 46, respectively. Sutherland dates both to 21-22 AD, though that is disputed. No other coin celebrated *iustitia* until Vespasian. Such scarcity among Julio-Claudian issues suggests that Fears may be correct in detecting a special commemoration. However, Barbara Lichocka argues that the image of Justice is an idealized portrait of Livia, and therefore cannot be "une personnification de la vertu de l'empereur et donc ce n'était pas une propagande des qualités morales de Tibère" (*Justitia sur les monnaies imperiales romaines*, Travaux du Centre d'Archéologie Méditerranéenne de l'Académie Polonaise des Sciences 15 [Warsaw: Państwowe Wydawnictwo Naukowe — Editions scientifiques de Pologne, 1974], 107).

[113] *RIC*, 1: nos. 77-78. Military imagery is common on Tiberian coinage. Sutherland identifies a gold quinarius from nearly every year of Tiberius' principate which presents Victoria seated on a globe and holding a wreath in both hands (nos. 5-22).

reputation.[114] It was, therefore, a cowering Senate which instituted an annual festival to celebrate Gaius Caligula's clemency.[115]

At the beginning of Claudius' principate, recollection of Gaius' savagery incited the Senate to rebellion (Jos. *Bel.* 2.205). Though Claudius' (purchased) control of the military ultimately guaranteed the outcome, he promised the Senate a greater (more traditional) role in the affairs of state. In Josephus' account, Claudius

did not wonder that the Senate was not pleased at the prospect of submitting to authority because they had been oppressed by the brutality (ὠμότητι) of those who had previously held the imperial office. But he promised to behave with such propriety (ἐπιείκεια) that they would taste for themselves the savor of an era of fair (μετρίων) dealing; that only nominally would the government be his, that in reality it would be thrown open to all in common.[116]

In keeping with his promise, Claudius graciously welcomed the Senate and offered amnesty for the events surrounding his accession, both Gaius' assassination and the Senate's rebellion. Claudius took other measures to win popularity: he burned denunciations, recalled exiles, and reduced taxes.[117] In exile Seneca shamelessly flattered Claudius' clemency, "which in the list of [Claudius'] virtues holds the chief place."[118] A decade later, after the rebel Caratacus had been paraded through Rome, he entreated Claudius, saying, "Save me alive, and I shall be an everlasting memorial of your clemency."[119] Claudius did so. Such gestures advanced Claudius'

---

[114] Sen. *De ira* 18.3-19.5. Like Philo, Seneca also uses irony in relating an example of Gaius' mercy (*De ira* 3.19.5): "... he sent officers to the homes of his victims, and on that same night made away with their fathers too — that is, out of human pity he freed the fathers from their sorrow (*homo misericors luctu liberavit*)."

[115] Weinstock, *Divus Julius*, 241; Barrett, *Caligula*, 91-94. The relevant text in Dio Cassius is 59.16.10-11. As Dio tells the story, Gaius quoted approvingly the advice which Tiberius had given him (59.16.1-7): "... Therefore show no affection for any of them and spare (φείσῃ) none of them. For they all hate you ... [L]ook solely to your own pleasure (ἡδύ) and safety, since that has the most just claim (δικαιότατον).... [O]nly so long as a person is afraid (φοβεῖται), does he pay court to the man who is stronger (ἰσχυρότερον), but when he gains courage, he avenges himself (τιμωρεῖται) on the man who is weaker (ἀσθενέστερον)." This is the antithesis of good rule.

[116] *Ant.* 19.246; the translation of ἐπιείκεια in this excerpt is extremely difficult. Elsewhere Josephus described Claudius as "by nature inclined to moderation (μέτριος)" (*Bel.* 2.208).

[117] Suet. *Clau.* 11 and 14; Jos. *Bel.* 2.204-14; Dio Cas. 60.3.5-5.1; 60.6.3; 60.12.1-2.

[118] *De cons. ad Pol.* 13; cf. 6.5; 12.4.

[119] Tac. *Ann.* 12.37; however, Tacitus takes a sarcastic attitude toward Claudius' clemency elsewhere (11.2).

Caesarian platform.[120] As a judge Claudius "let himself be guided by a sense of equity" (Suet. *Claud.* 14); however, Claudius' sense of equity could lead him to severity as well as to leniency (14-15). Suetonius recorded examples of Claudius' cruelty in torture, execution, and entertainments (34). Seneca's post-mortem on Claudius provided a ghastly counterpoint to Claudius' attempts at mercy and clemency. In his *Apocolocyntosis* Seneca tallies up the bodies: "Senators killed, 35; Roman knights, 221; others as the sands and dust for multitude."[121]

When Nero began his reign, his *clementia* was advertised and even implemented.[122] He even "pledged himself to clemency in a series of speeches" (Tac. *Ann.* 13.11) and considered a sweeping tax reform only to settle on less radical relief (13.50). On the other hand, Nero acquitted two cruel proconsuls (13.52). Even worse, he conspired to kill Britannicus and then pardoned the poisoner. Nero's mother, aunt, and wife were subsequent casualties. Attempts at remarriage brought additional bloodshed.[123] Nero's counsellors fared no better, nor did strangers, nor anyone else — not even Rome itself.[124] In view of these brutalities, two items provide surprising contrast. In 66 A.D. sacrifices were offered to Clementia *ob supplicationes a senatu decretas*;[125] moreover, a judicial decree from Sardinia dated 18 March 69 reveals the emperor's clemency impinging on provincial administration. This Sardinian decree preserves the proconsul Lucius Helvius Agrippa's attempt to resolve a boundary dispute between the Patulcenses and Galillenses. In deciding in favor of the Patulcenses, the proconsul expressed consternation with the Galillenses for failing to comply and threatened punitive measures; however, "in view of the clemency (*clementiae*) of the best and greatest princeps" he instead advised them "to rest quiet and stand by the judgments reached," threatening them that "if they persist in contumacy I will take severe measures against the authors of the sedition."[126]

---

[120] Barbara Levick, *Claudius* (London: B. T. Batsford, 1990), 89-91. Levick connects Claudian clemency to his coins proclaiming OB CIVES SERVATOS, for examples of which see Sutherland, *RIC*, 1: 122-24 nos. 5, 15, 16, 40, 41, 48, 49, 50, 53, 54, 59, 60, 63, and 64.

[121] *Apoc.* 14; cp. 6.2; 9.4; 11.2; 12.2-3, 28.

[122] Cal. Sic. *Ecl.* 1.59-64; Suet. *Nero* 10.1; Tac. *Ann.* 13.11. Griffin, *Seneca*, 135-36; eadem, *Nero: The End of a Dynasty* (New Haven: Yale University Press, 1984), 64-66.

[123] Suet. *Nero* 33-7; Griffin, *Seneca*, 170-71.

[124] Suet. *Nero* 35-38; Plut. *Gal.* 4.1; Dio Cas. 63.22.2.

[125] G. Henzen, *Acta Fratrum Arvalium* (Berlin: G. Reimeri, 1874), 85.

[126] Braund 601 (cf. Small. 392 for Greek text).

4.1. Commonplace Nature of Leniency

The disturbances of the year 69 produced a variety of coins advertising the competitors' virtues.[127] Two issues presented Victoria advancing, with the *clipeus virtutis* in her hand.[128] Vitellius issued coins heralding CLEMENTIA IMP GERMAN.[129] He also spared many enemies.[130]

At the same time, Titus' campaign against Jerusalem revealed an interest in *clementia* and the horror of its absence.[131] Josephus listed casualties at (a hard-to-believe) 1,100,000 and prisoners at 97,000 (*Bel.* 6.420). In the aftermath of the war, the aged and infirm were slaughtered, while the captives were given a variety of dismal fates: those under seventeen years of age entered slavery, while those older went to mines and arenas, unless they looked good enough to garnish Titus' triumph (6.415-18). While many people might argue that such horrors militate against an image of clemency, Josephus was not one of them. The Jewish historian went to great lengths to demonstrate Titus' leniency. One indication was Titus' reaction to some disorderly troops. Though the soldiers were unquestionably guilty of a capital offence, Titus listened to supplications and was reconciled to the offenders (5.126-29). Elsewhere, Josephus complimented the leniency which Titus (and Vespasian[132]) showed to Jews by not revoking their rights as citizens in Antioch and Alexandria (*Ant.* 12.122). More to the point, though, *Jewish Wars* repeatedly emphasized Titus' reluctance to destroy Jerusalem, the temple, and the people trapped there; blame for the tragic results rests primarily on

---

[127] "The Year of the Four Emperors was a watershed in the history of the cult of Virtues within the ideological framework of the principate," J. Rufus Fears, "The Cult of Virtues," *ANRW* 2.17.2 (1981): 897. Galba in particular exploited the publicizing value of coins to proclaim VIRTVS, PIETAS, PROVIDENT, CERES, FELICITAS, AEQVITAS, PAX, CONCORDIA, OB CIVIS SERVATOS, SALVS, VICTORIA, LIBERTAS, AND ROMA RENASCENS (Sutherland, *Roman Imperial Coinage*, 1: 232-57).

[128] Sutherland, *RIC*, 1: 212 nos. 108 and 110. Two Galban issues bear an oak-wreath surrounding a small shield with SPQR on it (nos. 46-47).

[129] Sutherland, *RIC*, 1: 268-69 nos. 1, 2, and 39. Vitellius' coins advertised numerous benefits and virtues, e.g. corn, *libertas, securitas, victoria, concordia, fides,* and *pax* (1: 268-77).

[130] Suetonius' characterization of Vitellius as cruel is suspect: see Kenneth Wellesley, *The Long Year: A.D. 69* (Boulder, CO: Westview Press, 1976), 202; and Peter A. L. Greenhalgh, *The Year of the Four Emperors* (New York: Barnes & Noble, 1975), 120-23.

[131] The Judean campaign also furnished evidence of *virtus*, as seen by the Arch of Titus (both the monument as a whole and the relief on it that depicts Titus riding in a quadriga while being crowned by Victory); cp. Sherk 1988: 83c.

[132] This is the only evidence I have found in connection with Vespasian.

Jewish intransigence.[133] Other factors exculpated Titus: 1) God and fate ordained the destruction (6.250 and 267); 2) the conflagration was begun by a soldier acting on his own, not under orders (252); 3) marauding soldiers acted out of passion and greed (257 and 264); 4) meanwhile, Titus disapproved of the fire and in fact tried to extinguish it (256, 261-2, and 266). In this manner, then, Josephus attempted to save Titus from the taint of savagery and to present him as the powerful leader who preferred lenient policies. Whether or not Josephus succeeded can be debated. Nor can we say whether Josephus' emphasis on leniency reflects his knowledge of literate culture, his contact with the imperial household, or what a subject people desired in a ruler. What is certain is Josephus' sense of how Titus *should* be portrayed.[134] *Jewish Wars* demonstrates clearly the continued ideal of the emperor (or ruler) who shows *clementia*.

From Caesar to Titus, these various examples suggest that clemency became part of the vocabulary of imperial rule. On different occasions rulers and their associates regarded leniency as a noble or effective way to govern. Lenient behavior also provided a means (among many) of evaluating the quality of a ruler. The evidence surveyed also shows that emperors did not pay blind allegiance to *clementia*. With those who abused it, it was not absent, while even those who advocated it transgressed it. While one might be tempted to attribute this variation to moral failure or hypocrisy, altogether other factors account for it. First, to harm one's enemies was not considered moral failure. Second, the value

---

[133] Jewish determination to refuse peace provoked Titus to press the siege (*Bel.* 5.262). Although Titus urged repentance, he was ignored (348-75). Jews who did abandon Jerusalem, however, were usually allowed by Titus to leave (421-22). Once again Titus extended the opportunity for repentance (456). Later, Titus again sent Josephus to urge the Jews to surrender, promising to spare the temple and allow sacrifices to be resumed (6.93-110). Refusing such appeals, the Jews forced Titus — against his will — to resume hostilities (127-30). Titus made one final appeal to avert Jerusalem's doom (321-57; see especially 6.344-46, which provides a summary of events from Titus' perspective). We might add that Sulpicius Severus viewed the situation as one of clemency versus cruelty (Sherk 1988: 83b).

[134] Suet. *Tit.* 9. M. A. Levi, "La clemenza di Tito," *La parola del passato* 9 (1954): 288-93. Maria Gazia Bajoni says of Titus, "Egli conformò il suo principato al modello della *basileia* stoica in cui l'ἡγεμων o *princeps* doveva essere πατὴρ καὶ εὐεργέτης dei suoi sudditi ... Tito, in ultima analisi, è come il *rex* del *De Clementia* di Seneca e la controparte positiva del *saevus tyrannus* quale appare Nerone nella *praetexta Octavia*" ("Le virtú del principe dal Seneca pedagogo a Suetonio biografo di Tito," in *Atti del Congresso Internazionale di Studi Flaviani, Rieti, settembre 1981*, ed. Benedetto Riposati [Rieti: Centro di Studi Varroniani, 1983], 190). Titus' executions of Eprius Marcellus and Caecina Alienus in 79 raise questions. See the combination of Titus' justice and generosity as he denied the appeal of a Spanish community against its tax collector (Sherk 1988:92).

4.1. Commonplace Nature of Leniency

of leniency is proportional to the strength of the hand which wields it. By having acted forcefully at an earlier occasion, a person will elicit greater gratitude by a later display of clemency. Thus, the very real threat of violent measures makes the display of clemency a more effective tool of governance. Third, as this suggests, clemency is more than virtue: it is policy. Exigency and not simply nobility dictates its implementation. We should, therefore, expect the contradictions which we have noted.

The phenomena surrounding clemency and cruelty which we have seen associated with Hellenistic kings and Roman emperors also appear in connection with rulers in Palestine. Though cruel blood-thirst may be Herod the Great's most enduring image, this caricature rests primarily on stories about how Herod treated his rivals, particularly those with the misfortune of being related to him. But there was much more to the man than excessive cruelty. We will examine him more broadly than we did Augustus' successors.

King Herod the Great affords a parallel example with which to explore the question of cardinal virtues. Did this client of Augustus rule according to the golden shield? His successes on the battlefield indicate that attribution of *virtus* would be appropriate;[135] moreover, the battles he won were the most important ingredient of his successful rule, aside from his loyalty to Rome. He also demonstrated *pietas*, building temples and showing loyalty to his patrons and (sometimes) family (e.g., Jos. *Bel.* 1.400-18). The measures which Herod took in obtaining the woman he desired, Mariamme, revealed a concern for *iustitia* (*Ant.* 15.319-22), likewise his attempt to curtail theft (16.1). The relief he brought from bandits and robbers demonstrated both his *iustitia* and *virtus* (15.348). Herod also claimed credit for making it possible for Jews in Asia to live according to Jewish law (16.64). Examples of Herod's use of *clementia* can also be found. After defeating the Tyrians, he spared all of them; "some he even sent away with presents, to procure for himself the favor of the citizens and for the tyrant their hatred" (*Bel.* 1.238). When Herod captured Jerusalem, he tried to prevent the soldiers from butchering the people of the city, reasoning that unchecked plundering and murder would leave him with nothing to rule (1.352-56). When the Arabs spread sedition among some of Herod's soldiers, he did not react with hostility (*Ant.* 15.351-53). In fact, Herod had a reputation for being "magnanimous in pardoning foreigners" (15.356). Thus, we can conclude that the four virtues were evident in Herod's rule.

---

[135] E.g., Jos. *Bel.* 1.204f., 238, 240, 355, 366, 385, and especially 429-30.

But evidence for the occasional practice of the four virtues differs from being guided consistently by them. Two issues arise. First, Herod was inconsistent in the application of the four virtues. Although we cited examples of *clementia* and *iustitia*, Herod's eternal memory has come to grief on these two issues. He sought stability for his domain by filling his subjects with fear (*Ant.* 15.326), earning for himself the reputation that he was "the most inexorable of all men toward those of his own people who sinned" (15.356). He introduced oppressive measures and severe punishments in the name of security (15.365-69). He used torture (15.289-90). His slaughter of dissenters and rivals, including family members, even his own children, has soiled his reputation ever since. It was on matters of *iustitia*, however, that Herod's subjects particularly despised him. Herod's confiscation of citizens' property (17.307-8) and his (occasional) disregard of Jewish law and custom undermined his popularity. His setting up of images (even if on foreign soil) and his importing of alien social institutions and alien rituals (i.e., drama and games) offended (some of) his Jewish subjects.[136] Josephus underscored Herod's deficiency in *iustitia*/δικαιοσύνη and *clementia*/ἐπιείκεια by relating an anecdote in which an Essene predicted that the boy Herod would one day be king. The prophet advised that "the best attitude for you [= Herod] to take would be to love justice and piety toward God and mildness toward your citizens" (15.375). Then the Essene prophet added, "But I know that you will not be such a person ... you will forget piety and justice" (15.376). This story reflects Josephus' evaluation of Herod.[137] How deeply the issues it raises troubled Herod's subjects is reflected by the fact that his greatest benefaction, the fabulously renovated Jerusalem temple, failed to secure his subjects' esteem. Herod's shortcomings in justice and mercy then leave no room for surprise that he was denounced as a tyrant.[138]

Herod's rule also raises a second observation on the four virtues: they were not the exclusive focus of his conduct as king. As with Augustus, philanthropy and solicitousness were equally hallmarks of Herod's rule.[139]

---

[136] E.g., Jos. *Ant.* 15.268, 271, 275, 281, 328-30; 17.170.

[137] It is interesting in and of itself that Josephus selects these criteria to measure the quality of Herod's reign. This tells us more about Josephus' political theories than Herod's success or failure, though by now we should recognize that Josephus is not at all idiosyncratic.

[138] Jos. *Ant.* 15.354; cf. 319 for his inclination toward pleasure and 366 for his oppressive measures.

[139] ἐπιμέλεια: Jos. *Ant.* 15.308, 315, 316, 326, 345. While the Greek word obviously reflects Josephus' thinking, the deeds which it describes were those performed by Herod. Because the deeds can typically be described as φιλάνθρωπα, I have linked the two.

His building projects were both ambitious and amazing (palaces, temples, fortresses, and cities). He also undertook famine relief in c. 24 BC. Drawing on his own resources, Herod purchased grain from Egypt to feed his subjects, who responded to this with abundant and overwhelming goodwill.[140] A few years later in 20/19 BC, Herod also granted tax relief. Josephus says that, although it was extended in order to help the people recover from poor crops, this was only a pretext. The real reason, according to Josephus, was to recover the goodwill (εὔνοια) of disaffected subjects (*Ant.* 15.365). In 14 BC Herod remitted a fourth of the previous year's taxes because, according to Josephus, his successful meeting with Agrippa left him in a good mood. Josephus adds that this gesture elicited a favorable response.[141] Herod did not restrict his spending to the domestic front, but used his money to great effect outside Palestine, whether to ingratiate himself in imperial circles or with trading partners or neighbors.[142] His lengthy rule rested in large measure on such expenditures.

Herod then confirms what we have seen about the four virtues in regard to the emperors. The exercise of rule involves situations and issues which fall under the rubric of the various virtues; however, a ruler's tasks encompass more, making the four virtues an incomplete agenda for rule. The gifts given by both Augustus and Herod hint at their consciousness of this. Both also show that policy takes precedence over virtue: both sought survival and success, not moral rectitude. As a result, we can list examples of clemency and cruelty, justice and injustice. Moreover, it may have been the case for Herod that virtue and survival were mutually exclusive. For example, to apply consistently the ethnic conception of justice shared by his subjects to foreign affairs would have greatly complicated them — and Herod needed his foreign connections. As for clemency, Herod found it prudent to treat foreigners leniently and his own subjects harshly, perhaps because Herod knew where the origin of his crown lay. Furthermore, considering the infighting and intrigue which surrounded Herod's succession, the cruelty Herod showed to his family was in fact expedient policy. The four virtues were therefore relevant to rule, but not cardinal.

---

[140] Jos. *Ant.* 15.308, 315, and 316. The latter states: "Herod's solicitude (ἐπιμέλειαν) and the timeliness of his generosity (χάριτος) made such a powerful impression upon the Jews and were so much talked about by other nations, that the old hatreds which had been aroused by his altering some of the customs and royal practices were completely eradicated throughout the entire nation, and the munificence shown by him in helping them in their very grave difficulties was regarded as full compensation" (315).

[141] *Ant.* 16.65: οἱ δὲ καὶ τῷ λόγῳ καὶ τῇ χάριτι δεδημαγωγημένοι . . .

[142] Earlier we mentioned Herod's successful intervention on behalf of Ilium before Agrippa.

Herod's successor Archelaus (4 BC - AD 6) took a different approach to securing his rule than did Herod. When the crowds acclaimed him king, he granted their requests for tax relief and release of prisoners, thinking that his subjects' goodwill (εὔνοια) would secure his position (Jos. *Ant.* 17.204-5). Soon thereafter, however, he quenched a public disturbance by killing three thousand people in the temple (17.213-18). The latter approach apparently characterized his reign, because in the tenth year of Archelaus' rule the Jews and Samaritans joined in accusing Archelaus of cruelty (ὠμότης) before Augustus.[143] Archelaus was forced into exile.

Herod Antipas (4 BC - AD 39) killed John the Baptist. Josephus attributed this to Antipas' fears that the Baptist might use his influence with the crowds to foment rebellion (*Ant.* 18.116-19). The Gospels nuance the story differently, portraying the Baptist as the prophet who confronted the king with his lawlessness and consequently died because of it.[144] While this incident clearly does not illustrate clemency, it does underscore the serious nature of the issues we are examining. Justice and clemency were not simply jargon for political philosophers. The irresponsible exercise of power by the king could destroy people.

Judging from Josephus' summary of their rule, Philip the Tetrarch (4 BC - AD 34) and Agrippa I (37-44) were good rulers. Philip was moderate and just (*Ant.* 18.106-7), as was Agrippa. In fact, Josephus painted Agrippa as the model king, generous, just, and merciful. Agrippa was

> in no way similar in character to Herod, who was ... relentless in punishment (ἐπὶ τιμωρίαν ἀπότομον) and unsparing in action against the objects of his hatred.... Agrippa, on the contrary, had a gentle (πραΰς) disposition and he was a benefactor (εὐεργετικόν) to all alike. He was benevolent (φιλάνθρωπος) to those of other nations ... but to his compatriots he was proportionately more generous ... and he scrupulously observed the traditions of his people.[145]

As for clemency in particular, Agrippa regarded πραότης to be more kingly than ὀργή and ἐπιείκεια better than θύμος (19.334). In this description, Josephus clearly constructs a model ruler who contrasts with Herod.

Examples of leniency connected with rulers have been surveyed because they are the best documented and were probably the most conspicuous and urgent. However, the ideas of leniency, gentleness, and restraint pertain to daily life and not exclusively to a king or princeps. Two aspects of daily life commonly illustrated the interplay of gentleness and severity and

---

[143] Jos. *Ant.* 17.342-44; *Bel.* 2.111.

[144] Matt 14:3-12; Mark 6:17-29; Luke 3:19-20.

[145] Jos. *Ant.* 19.328-31. Cf. Acts 12.

made obvious the need for the former: medical care[146] and the slackening and tightening of a horse's rein.[147] More importantly, government, conquest, law-suits, debts, tax-collectors, and slavery made the threat of violence and the need for gentleness a reality for many people.[148]

The general exercise of government could be cruel or kind. Sallust reports the theory that Spanish horsemen killed Piso because they could no longer endure the "injustice, arrogance, and cruelty of his conduct as governor" (*Cat.* 18-19). In one of Cicero's letters to his brother, *clementia, mansuetudo,* and *humanitas* summarize Cicero's picture of good government.[149] The appeal of clemency to conquered peoples needs no comment; moreover, we have already cited adequate examples of it.[150] The role of gentleness and restraint in legal affairs appears in view of its opposite. Ramsay MacMullen notes that pleas for justice in Egyptian papyri indicate "the recurrence of physical outrage ... beatings, maulings, and murders."[151] Powerful people acting with arrogance and violence abused the weak. Such loathsome behavior is the antithesis of gentleness.

Perhaps other Jews shared Philo's opinion that ἐπιείκεια suffused Moses' law. Its sanctions against animals which destroy someone's fields are lenient and forgiving (*De spec. leg.* 4.23). Its provisions allowing the needy to glean in other people's fields reveal "a foundation" of ἐπιείκεια καὶ φιλανθρωπία (2.110).

Debt also created a situation ripe for violent anger or mercy. Jesus' parable of the unmerciful servant reflects these possibilities (Matt 18:23-35). A Roman edict from Egypt dated to July 68 AD records a dozen measures taken to protect citizens in the Thebaid Oasis. One measure

---

[146] Sen. *De clem.* 1.17; Dio Chrys. 32.18; Plut. *Mor.* 73d; 74d; 69b; Ps.-Plut. *Mor.* 13d; Dio Cas. 53.17.1. A more forbidding use of the analogy appears in Plut. *Cat. maj.* 345d. In general see Abraham Malherbe, "Medical Imagery in the Pastoral Epistles," in *Texts and Testaments: Critical Essays on the Bible and Early Church Fathers,* ed. W. Eugene March (San Antonio: Trinity University Press, 1980), 19-35; reprinted in *Paul and the Popular Philosophers* (Minneapolis, MN: Fortress Press, 1989), 121-36.

[147] Cic. *Ad Att.* 10.6.2; Philo *De sac. Ab. et Ca.* 9; *De som.* 2.293-95; Seneca *De clem.* 1.2.2; 1.16. (which presents additional analogies); Dio Chrys. 32.29; Ps.-Plut. *Mor.* 13d; Philos. *Vita soph.* 487.

[148] Cic. *Ad Att.* 5.21; *Ad Fam.* 15.4 and 5; *Pro leg. Man.*; *Ver.*; Fergus Millar, "State and Subject: The Impact of Monarchy," in *Caesar Augustus: Seven Aspects,* eds. Fergus Millar and Erich Segal (Oxford University Press, 1984), 37-60.

[149] *Qfr.* 1.1.25. We must add that Quintus' temper was his Achilles' heel. Cicero's letter instructs Quintus to curb his anger and be more mild and lenient (1.1.38-40).

[150] The good στρατηγός possesses the virtues of πραότης and δικαιοσύνη (Plut. *Mor.* 543d). Cf. Ter. *Eunuch* 788-89.

[151] *Roman Social Relations: 50 B.C. to A.D. 284* (New Haven: Yale University Press, 1974), 11; cp. idem, "Personal Power in the Roman Empire," 512-15.

disallows imprisonment for debtors, while another prohibits using force to extract early repayment of legally contracted loans.[152] Philo's bleak picture of tax-collectors indicates the potential for gentleness and severity in yet another context. As we saw in chapter two, tax-collectors lacked mercy, humanity, and gentleness, and were full of brutality and severity (*De spec. leg.* 2.93). Similarly, Ps.-Anacharsis criticizes a tyrant for plundering his subjects, rather than sparing (φείδεσθαι) them (*Ep.* 7). Thus, the collection of taxes as well as situations involving debt provided examples of brutality and raised opportunities for kindness.

Slavery also presented opportunities for brutality or leniency. The Romans liked to think that they had shown ἐπιείκεια to their slaves in the good old days, treating them gently and not punishing them with severity.[153] Epicurus was remembered as having been gentle to servants (Diog. L. 10.10). Philo stated that masters who inflict abuse (βιάζεσθαι) on their slaves act wrongly; masters should not begrudge slaves moderate orders (τὰ μέτρια; *De spec. leg.* 2.90-91). Seneca advised living with one's slaves "on kindly, even on affable, terms" (*clementer, comiter*; *Ep.* 47.13) and, in a variation of the golden rule, recommends that one treat inferiors in the way one wishes to be treated by one's superiors (47.11). Elsewhere, he asserts that "it is praiseworthy to use authority over slaves with moderation" (*De clem.* 1.18.1). Pliny the Younger, and Plutarch shared such views.[154] In reality, however, few "whipping posts" had such masters.[155] Romans generally behaved arrogantly and cruelly toward their slaves.[156] What is important for us is that slavery presented common situations in which people faced the choice between severity and leniency.

---

[152] Small. 391. While ἐπιείκεια is not present in this inscription, the policy on debtors certainly is lenient. Rejection of force is likewise related to gentleness.

[153] Plut. *Cor.* 225d; cf. Sen. *Ep.* 47.4.

[154] Plut. *Mor.* 53e; 59d. On Pliny see Albert A. Bell, Jr., "Pliny the Younger: The Kinder, Gentler Roman," *CB* 66 (1990): 38-39.

[155] Plut. *Cat. maj.* 349a. See M. I. Finley, *Ancient Slavery and Modern Ideology* (New York: Viking Press, 1980), 11-66; Thomas Wiedemann, *Greek and Roman Slavery* (London: Croom Helm, 1981), 167-87; K. R. Bradley, *Slaves and Masters in the Roman Empire: A Study in Social Control*, Collection Latomus 185 (Brussells: Latomus, 1984), 118-23, 134-37; Kieth Hopkins, *Conquerors and Slaves*, Sociological Studies in Roman History 1 (Cambridge University Press, 1978); and Richard Saller, "Corporal Punishment, Authority, and Obedience in the Roman Household," in *Marriage, Divorce, and Children in Ancient Rome*, ed. Beryl Rawson (Canberra: Humanities Research Centre; Oxford: Clarendon Press, 1991), 158-60. In NT literature, see J. Albert Harrill, *The Manumission of Slaves in Early Christianity*, HUT 32 (Tübingen: J. C. B. Mohr [Paul Siebeck], 1995), 9-61.

[156] Sen. *Ep.* 47.11: *superbissimi, crudelissimi, contumeliosissimi sumus.*

It was one more piece of daily life in which people had to choose between lenient, gentle behavior and its opposite.[157]

The rearing of children made the exercise of gentleness an even more familiar experience. Although the image of the stern *pater familias* terrorizing his children with his *patria potestas* might raise questions about connecting gentleness with parenting, Emiel Eyben has succinctly demonstrated that the ancient data actually show us kind, indulgent fathers.[158] Together with other historians, Eyben has undermined the caricature of the oppressive *pater familias*.[159] While funerary monuments testify to the affection between parent and child, literary texts reveal the indulgence which parents showed their children. Affection and indulgence combined with discipline and strictness to comprise the ideal father.[160] From dramatic literature, we learn that the stage portrayed the extremes of parenting. Valerius Maximus tenders the generalization that tragedy depicted the harsh father, comedy the lenient.[161] With delightful humor Terence explored the complexity of leniency in his *Adelphoe*, as he contrasted a strict father with an indulgent one and contemplated the results of each approach.[162] Similar though less developed examples appeared in Menander's *Dyscolus* and Plautus' *Mostellaria*.[163] Rhetorical writings also compare both types of father.[164] Valerius Maximus offers

---

[157] Cf. Pliny's paranoia: "No master can feel safe because he is kind and considerate (*remissus et mitis*); for it is their brutality, not their reasoning capacity, which leads slaves to murder masters" (*Ep.* 3.14). Note that liency works only if reason is respected.

[158] Emiel Eyben, "Fathers and Sons," in *Marriage, Divorce, and Children in Ancient Rome*, ed. Beryl Rawson (Canberra: Humanities Research Centre; Oxford: Clarendon Press, 1991), 114-43.

[159] Important in this regard are also Peter Garnsey and Richard Saller, *Roman Empire: Economy, Society and Culture* (Berkeley: University of California Press, 1987), 126-47; R. Saller, "*Patria potestas* and the Stereotype of the Roman Family," *Continuity and Change* 1 (1986): 7-22. See now Saller's *Patriarchy, Property and Death in the Roman Family* (Cambridge University Press, 1994).

[160] Cicero tried to combine *indulgentia, obsequium,* and *lenitas* with *severitas* in order to win his son's loyalty and affection (*Ad Att.* 10.4).

[161] *Fact. et dic.* 5.7.1; cf. the examples in 5.9.

[162] For a discussion of the ambiguity of *Adelphoe*, particularly the concluding inversion, see Nathan A. Greenberg, "Success and Failure in the *Adelphoe*," *CW* 73 (1979): 223-36.

[163] Dana F. Sutton, *Ancient Comedy: The War of the Generations*, Studies in Literary Themes and Genres (New York: Twayne Publishers, 1993), 50 and 78-86, respectively; cp. 59-60, 67-9, and 105-8. Sutton further demonstrates how Plautus' *Asinaria* subverts the easy-going father (91-2 and 95; cp. 119-21). For additional references to Plautus, see Eyben, "Fathers and Sons," 127 n. 79.

[164] Eyben, "Fathers and Sons," 127 n. 78; 128 nn. 86, 87; 129 n. 90; 130 nn. 92, 93 (Cicero, Seneca the Elder, Quintilian, and Tacitus). See also Cal. Flac. 14 and 17 (Lewis

examples of both paternal severity and moderation.[165] In Seneca's discussion of the merciful ruler, he drew explicit comparisons with a father, who "is wont to reprove his children sometimes gently (*blande*), sometimes with threats ... No one resorts to the exaction of punishment until he has exhausted all the means of correction. This is the duty of a father, and it is also the duty of a prince" (*De clem.* 1.14.1, 2). Elsewhere Seneca warned against subjecting a child to humiliation on the one hand and indulging a child on the other; both affect the child negatively (*De ira* 2.21.4-6). Quintilian in fact complained that children were treated too indulgently — a relative grievance to be sure (1.2.6-8). Ps.-Plutarch offers the following advice to fathers:

> I do not think they should be utterly harsh and austere in their nature, but they should in many cases concede some shortcomings to the younger person ... fathers should combine the abruptness of their rebukes with mildness (πραότητι), and at one time grant some license to the desires of their children, and slacken the reins a little, and then at another time draw them tight again.[166]

Plutarch repeated Cato the Elder's ideas that "the man who struck his wife or child, laid violent hands on the holiest of holy things" and that "there was nothing else to admire in Socrates of old except that he was always kind and gentle (ἐπιεικῶς καὶ πράως) in his intercourse with a shrewish wife (γυναικὶ χαλεπῇ) and stupid sons" (*Cato maj.* 20.2). Plutarch himself approved of these views, given that he labeled Cato the Elder a "good father" and "kind husband" (χρηστός ἀνήρ; 20.1). Against such a background, the simple combination "gentle father" is natural and unremarkable.[167]

A. Sussman, *The Declamations of Calpurnius Flaccus: Text, Translation, and Commentary*, Mnemosyne, Supplementum 133 [Leiden: E. J. Brill, 1994]).

[165] Richard Saller comments that "the lesson of Valerius' contrast between *severitas* and *moderatio* is that fathers should be unyielding in the interests of the state, even to the point of stepping out of their paternal role, but should display loving forgiveness toward personal injuries, even as serious as an adulterous affair between son and stepmother" (*Patriarchy, Property and Death in the Roman Family*).

[166] *De lib. ed.* 13d-e. Cp. 8f: "Children ought to be led to honorable practices by means of encouragement and reasoning, and most certainly not by blows or ill-treatment, for it surely is agreed that these are fitting rather for slaves than for freeborn." The distinction between slave and free parallels the psychology found in Terence's *Adelphoe* 64-77 and in Sen. *De ira* 2.21.3. See R. Saller, "Corporal Punishment," 144-65.

[167] *Jos. Asen.* 12.14; Jos. *Ant.* 6.92. Stob. 4.5.55 asks what name could possibly be more gentle (πραότερον) that that of "father." Cp. Plut. *Mor.* 73d. Small. 294 is an inscription to *"patri optimo et indulgenti."* When Philo speaks of repentant souls finding favor with God, he adds the encouraging simile, "as sons may with their father" (*De prae. et poe.* 167). This indicates Philo's view on how fathers behave. Cp. Matt 6:7-15; 7:7-11; Luke 15:11-32; 2 Cor 1:3. As for the marital relationship, the relevance of gentleness, leniency, and harshness can be seen in Cic. *Ad. Att.* 5.1.

The apostle Paul fits into this tradition of associating gentleness with fathers. In 1 Cor 4:14-21 Paul appealed to the Corinthians like a father to his dear children. Since some of his arrogant, misguided children needed correction, Paul hoped that his letter and Timothy's presence in Corinth would accomplish that. When he himself arrived, Paul hoped his visit would be characterized by love and gentleness (πραΰτης). Whether force would be exhibited depended on the Corinthians. Like a father, then, Paul wrestled with the issues of discipline we have surveyed. While children must be nurtured and corrected, fathers prefer to act with gentleness.[168]

The evidence surveyed leads to the conclusion that discussions and examples of lenient behavior were commonplace in Greco-Roman culture. Philosophers discussed equity and forgiveness. Politicians argued about the use and abuse of force. Rulers sometimes practiced clemency. Orators appealed to it. Various authors recorded examples of leniency and made it a criterion of character assessment. Citizens relied on leniency and restraint when they encountered the law or tax-collectors. Debtors and slaves also had need of it. Perhaps most common of all, fathers and slave owners regularly confronted the choice between severity and gentleness. Thus, when Paul appealed to the Corinthians by leniency and clemency, his point would have been clear.

2. Rationales for Acting with Leniency and Clemency

The sources surveyed so far indicate that when a person decided whether or not to be lenient, numerous factors received consideration. For the sake of convenience, I will organize the motives under six headings: theory, virtue, convention, pity, policy, and pedagogy. The last two are particularly important.

In *theory* public offices benefit the populace. Leniency is one concrete way of applying this theory. Dio Cassius stated this clearly in Livia's counsel to Augustus that he act leniently. Her advice rests on the rationale that "the office of ruler has been established for the preservation of the governed, to prevent them from being injured either by one another or by foreign peoples, and not for a moment that they may be harmed by the rulers themselves" (55.20.2). This definition of good rule makes leniency a form of behavior intrinsic to the proper excise of office.

---

[168] See Eva Maria Lassen, "The Use of the Father Image in Imperial Propaganda and 1 Corinthians 4:14-21," *TB* 42 (1991): 127-36.

By *virtue* I mean simply that lenient behavior is regarded as a praiseworthy quality, as something good.[169] This comes as no surprise, given the appearance of ἐπιείκεια and πραότης in virtue lists and in ethical treatises and the use of the plural adjective ἐπιεικεῖς as a label for noble people. Respect for leniency appears as well in its being advocated as a conduct fitting for kings and philosophers and in its being attributed to gods (Greek, Roman, Jewish, and Christian).[170] Most telling, however, are the temple dedicated to Casear's clemency and the recognition of Clementia as a goddess.[171] Thus, Isocrates could describe πραότης as being εὐδοκιμεῖν and offer this as justification for advising Philip to be benevolent, gentle, and humane (*Phil.* 116). On the other hand, Dio Cassius could describe the opposite course of action (viz., τὸ τιμωρεῖσθαί τε καὶ κολάζειν) as grievous to good men (55.15.7). Nevertheless virtue was not commonly cited as a motive for clemency.

Convention often requires clement behavior.[172] Sallust put on Caesar's lips the claim that to act otherwise is simply not Roman![173] Sallust portrayed Caesar as opposing a severe sentence for the conspirators because, Caesar argued, such reprisals would have violated law and precedent. In response, Cato regarded Caesar's position as clement (*Cat.* 51). In the Greek world, leniency was part of legal custom, as when Thucydides depicted the Plataeans arguing before the Spartans that killing suppliants violated Hellenic law (3.58, 66). If we speak more generally of gentleness, toleration, and forgiveness, we may identify ἐπιείκεια and πραότης as intrinsic to Athenian identity as well.[174] It is little wonder,

---

[169] Isoc. *Paneg.* 102; Dio Chrys. 32.37.

[170] For kings see kingship literature and, *inter al.*, 3 Macc 3:15; 7:6; Add Esth 3:13 (=13:2); Jos. *Ant.* 15.375; 19.334; 11.216; 7.391; Sen. *De clem.* 1.19.1. For philosophers see Philos. *Vita soph.* 2.561-62. For gods see Dio Chrys. 32.50; Sen. *De clem.* 1.7.2; cp. 1.26.5; *Ep. Arist.* 188; 192; 207-8; Jos. *Asen.* 11.10; 12.14; Philo *De vita Mos.* 1.198; *De spec. leg.* 1.97; *De prae. et poe.* 166; Ign. *Phil.* 1:2; cp. *Ep. to Diognetus* 7:3-6. Cp. the claims of Isis: "I ordained that suppliants be pitied.... I free those who are in bonds" (Burstein 112); also Zeus' epithets Μειλίχιος and Ἱκετήσιος.

[171] Plut. *Cae.* 57; Dio Cas. 44.6; App. *Bel. Civ.* 2.106; Pliny *Nat. His.* 2.14; Statius *Theb.* 12.481-518. *CRR*, 179 no. 1076. I should mention again the altar to Clemency intended to flatter Tiberius (Tac. *Ann.* 4.74).

[172] The difference between virtue and convention is fuzzy. Convention helps to define virtue and in so doing becomes a part of virtue. By distinguishing them I only wish to highlight two ways of arguing.

[173] Sal. *Cat.* 51. Cp. Cic. *Ad fam.* 5.1.2; *Sex. Rosc.* 154; *Verr.* 5.115; Livy 33.12.7-9; 36.27.6; 45.8.5; 45.17.7; 45.22.4; Jos. *Bel.* 5.372; 6.333.

[174] De Romilly, *La douceur* emphasizes this point in ch. 6: À la base de toute la vie athénienne, il y a donc ... la douceur et l'indulgence.... On dirait en effet que cette douceur est devenue la qualité intrinsèque d'Athènes" (p. 99).

4.2. Rationales for Leniency 233

then, that Philo apologetically (and hence retrospectively) described in detail how clemency was enshrined in Moses' law.[175]

The most common motive for leniency was *pity*, in which case lenient behavior becomes a kind, humane gesture. The frailty of the human condition in general suggests reason for pity.[176] Thus, a common motive for leniency is the understanding that it is only human to make mistakes.[177] As Pliny expresses it, "Anyone who hates faults hates mankind."[178] That "pain and punishment" comprise a common condition of human existence should also incline a person to mercy (*Ep. Arist.* 208). Clemency may also be extended to compensate someone for bad luck or injustice.[179] One may also incline to show pity out of respect for someone's age, lineage, shared social bonds, past benefits received, or merely acquaintance.[180] Those who have shown mercy may use that as a basis for seeking mercy for themselves (*Ad Her.* 2.25).[181] In short, we may point to the elaboration of the plea for pity in the rhetorical handbooks and its application in forensic speeches.[182] As we noted in chapter two, de

---

[175] Philo *De spec. leg.* 2.93; 2.110; 4.23; *De virt.* 81. Cp. Jos. *Ap.* 2.209 and 214.

[176] De Romilly, *La douceur*, 86. She observes in Sophocles' *Ajax* an important moment in the history of Greek gentleness, as human fragility provides the foundation for human solidarity and suggests the replacing of vengeance with pity (pp. 83-88). Why? "[T]ous les auterus ont lie, de le façon la plus étroite, la douceur d'Athènes avec son régime démocratique. Deuceur et démocratie seraient alors l'expression d'un unique idéal définissant le vie au sein de la cité" (p. 106).

[177] Xen. *Cyr.* 6.1.36-37; Sen. *De clem.* 2.5.3; Dio Cas. 55.16.3; 55.21.1. Thucydides rejects this motive (3.40).

[178] *Ep.* 8.22, where Pliny is actually quoting Thrasea Paetus: "Qui vitia odit, homines odit." Cp. Sen. *De ira* 1.14.2; see A. N. Sherwin-White, *The Letters of Pliny: A Historical and Social Commentary* (Oxford University Press, 1966), 474.

[179] Sen. *De clem.* 1.2.1; 2.5.3; 2.6.3. Cp. Dem. *De cor.* 274.

[180] See variously Jos. *Bel.* 1.352; *Ant.* 15.14; Plut. *C. Mar.* 225d; Dio Chrys. 41.10; Dio Cas. 55.18.2; Sen. *De clem.* 1.1.4; Tac. *Ann.* 14.40; Welles 44. On the indulgence of youth see Emiel Eyben, "Fathers and Sons," 126-27. Epictetus offers the general counsel that wrongdoing can be endured by thinking of the person, not the wrong (*Ench.* 43). Plutarch states that "the principles that govern a statesman's conduct do not force him to act with severity against the moderate errors of his friends" (*Mor.* 808b). In *P. Col.-Zen.* 102 philanthropy is requested to exempt the petitioner from an obligation. The reason given is old age and weakness (see Lenger, "La notion de 'bienfait,'" 485).

[181] Conversely, failure to be merciful is reason to be denied mercy (de Romilly, *La douceur*, 117-19).

[182] Aris. *Rhet.* 2.8; *Rhet. ad Alex.* 1445a; *Ad Her.* 2.24-25 and 50; Cic. *De inv.* 1.55.106-56.109; Quint. 6.1.7-45. Socrates' refusal to appeal for mercy is well-known (Plato *Apol.* 34b-35b). Cf. Pliny *Ep.* 2.11.3, 6, and 18. See Small. 367 (trans. Braund 568) for an example of the lengths people would go to elicit pity. Cicero's *Pro Ligario* offers a plea for mercy, though it is much more (see Holly W. Montague, "Advocacy and

Romilly emphasizes that involuntary actions (e.g., ignorance and necessity) particularly summon mercy.[183]

After pity, issues of *policy* provide the most common motive for clemency. The *Rhetorica ad Alexandrum* provides model arguments regarding expediency by using two examples in which clemency is extended because doing so is expedient (1423a). Thucydides' "Mytilenean Debate" set the stage for this, where the advocate of leniency, Diodotus, explicitly states that he bases his argument not on the goodness of clemency, but its utility:

I might prove that they are the most guilty people in the world, but it does not follow that I shall propose the death penalty, unless that is in your interests; I might argue that they deserve to be forgiven, but should not recommend forgiveness unless that seemed to me the best thing for the state (3.44).

As he later elaborates his argument on behalf of leniency, Diodotus notes that lenient policies reduce the costs of future wars and leave defeated enemies in a better position to pay richer tribute (3.46). Xenophon provides a similar example (*Cyr.* 4.4.5-8). When discussing the fate of prisoners of war, grand gestures play no role; what counts is advantage. Accordingly, the release of prisoners is proposed because of the benefits such a policy will bring. First, inhabited land can turn a profit, whereas depopulated land cannot. Second, released prisoners do not need to be guarded and fed. Third, possession of territory is tantamount to holding the people captive. Last, freeing prisoners makes for good public relations. Polybius offers an example which adds to Xenophon's list of benefits (30.17.4). When Cotys, king of the Odrysae, asked the Romans to return his son whom they held as hostage, the Romans granted his request, in order to show their leniency and to obtain Cotys' gratitude. In addition to Xenophon's four reasons, then, we see Polybius adding a fifth: the recipient of leniency, like any other favor (χάρις), incurs obligation. Livy also offers a telling example of clemency. A Roman general besieged two cities, Ceremia and Carnuns. After capturing Ceremia he did not plunder it, hoping that his display of clemency would persuade Carnuns to surrender. Carnuns refused and successfully resisted the Roman siege. The Roman general therefore returned to Ceremia and plundered it, "in order that his soldiery might not be worn out by two sieges and gain nothing" (43.1.2). The details of these examples from Thucydides, Xenophon, Polybius, and Livy show clearly that expediency guides leniency, or, as

---

Politics: The Paradox of Cicero's *Pro Ligario*," *AJP* 113 [1992]: 559-74). Cf. *Pro Mur.* 86-90. For a succinct statement of grounds of forgiveness, see Kenneth J. Dover, "Fathers, Sons and Forgiveness," *ICS* 16 (1991): 176-77.

[183] De Romilly, *La douceur*, 67.

4.2. Rationales for Leniency

D'Agostino says, "... ἐπιείκεια appears ... not as a value, but as a technique of governance, to use in a wholly amoral, concrete context."[184]

The examples from Thucydides, Xenophon, Polybius, and Livy also illustrate the calculated role of clemency in the area of foreign affairs.[185] Livy showed how conquest created opportunities for clemency and how clemency could be a tactic in military campaigns. Xenophon and Polybius described the advantages issuing from a policy of clemency. Thucydides revealed the carefully analyzed role of clemency in dealing with subjugated peoples. In short, the logistics of empire made clemency an attractive strategy: gentleness turns enemies into friends, while brutality turns friends into enemies.[186] Isocrates, however, nuanced this position when defending Athens. He argued that unwavering lenience in dealing with subject states was not possible; nevertheless, Athens deserved praise because it "acted harshly in the fewest possible cases" (*Paneg.* 102).

Clemency also promotes civic concord. The cruel ruler fills his realm with gloom, anxiety, confusion, and fear. He encourages opposition (Sen. *De clem.* 1.26.2); his violence invites violence (Sal. *Cat.* 51). Clemency, on the other hand, ushers in peace and happiness.[187] Caesar and Augustus illustrate this.[188] In their campaigns, each spared the lives of many citizens, actions which Roman tradition esteemed highly. As noted previously, this policy was wildly popular with the rural population of Italy. It also saved many patrician lives. This clemency was recognized as having helped to mend the disturbances of civil war, reconciling enemies and restoring concord.[189] Of course, civil unrest might be avoided in the first place if the ruler exercises ἐπιείκεια (Add Esth 8:12i).

---

[184] "Nei discorsi di entrambi i capipopolo, dunque, l'*epieikeia* appare ... non come un valore, ma come una tecnica di governo, da utilizzare in un contesto concreto del tutto amorale (*Epieikeia*, 40)."

[185] Other examples include Thucydides' observation (which Polybius repeated) that to overcome one's enemy with generosity obligates him to return good for the good received (4.19). Xenophon stated that Agesilaus, by φιλανθρωπία, "made himself master of fortresses impregnable to assault" (*Ag.* 1.22; cp. 1.20 for βία and πραότης). Isocrates described Timotheus as the model general who treated conquered cities πράως καὶ νομίμως in order to assure other cities that he would not wrong them (ἐξαμαρτεῖν τολμήσειεν; *Ant.* 125). Cp. Isoc. *Paneg.* 80-81; Polyb. 2.61.4; 3.99.7; 21.4.10; Plut. *Brut.* 998c; Tac. *Agr.* 20.

[186] Thuc. 3.32. For example ἐπιείκεια won for Titus Flamininus the goodwill of the Chalcidians (Plut. *Flam.* 378c; cp. *Brut.* 998c).

[187] Sal. *Cat.* 51 and Sen. *De clem.* 1.5.4, respectively. Cp. Xen. *Cyr.* 3.2.12; Cic. *Ad fam.* 5.4.2.

[188] Cic. *Phil.* 2.116; Dio Cas. 53.4.1.

[189] Vitellius and Galba later recognized these things and tried to practice them.

Clemency facilitates political relationships. In Diodorus' picture of the ideal king, Sesoösis, policies of ἐπιείκεια won the king the goodwill of his subjects (*Hist.* 1.54.2). Titus Flamininus also used ἐπιείκεια to win goodwill.[190] Elsewhere, ἐπιείκεια elicits affection and praise or inspires confidence.[191] Seneca asserts, "The more indulgent the ruler, the better he is obeyed."[192] Many others recognized that leniency encourages subjects to serve,[193] whereas fear cannot accomplish this.[194] Leniency also elicits the favor of soldiers (Plut. *Aris.* 332e). Indulgence shown to one party, can further friendly relations with yet a third party.[195] Clemency is also a way to win future friends. Thus, Pompey was kind to Tigranes and Augustus was merciful to Cinna with a view to future services.[196] Lenient behavior is also a way of showing respect, indicating trust in friends or assigning punishments which do not unnecessarily demean the recipient; it may also show itself in allowing the Senate room to operate or by avoiding any infringement on a colleague.[197] In a variety of relationships and in a variety of circumstances, clemency served useful roles in establishing or strengthening relationships between people.

A policy of leniency also yields benefits for the person offering it. A show of clemency can compensate for previous, savage behavior (Plut. *Alex.* 671b). It may also help a person avoid future retribution, as Cicero's friends hoped to prevent future censure by supporting Caesar's proposal for moderate sanctions against the Catilinarian conspirators (Plut. *Cic.* 871a). Clemency can also bring a person popularity and glory.[198] Or happiness:

True happiness consists in giving safety to many, in calling back to life from the very verge of death, and in earning the civic crown by showing mercy (*clementia*). No decoration is more worthy of the eminence of a prince or more beautiful than that crown bestowed for saving the lives of fellow-citizens; not trophies torn from a vanquished enemy, nor chariots stained with barbarian blood, nor spoils acquired in war. To save

---

[190] Plut. *Flam.* 378c. See also Xen. *Ag.* 1.20-22 and Jos. *Ant.* 8.213. Unfortunately for Nicias, goodwill proved inadequate (Thuc. 3.40 and 46).

[191] Plut. *Mor.* 90e; *Nic.* 528f.

[192] *De clem.* 1.24.1; cp. Xen. *Cyr.* 4.4.5-8; *Mem.* 2.3.16.

[193] Jos. *Ant.* 8.213 (works better than φόβος). Cp. Xen. *Cyr.* 4.4.5-8; Philo *De spec. leg.* 2.90-96; Dio Chrys. *Frag.* 5.1; Dio Cas. 55.16.5-6; 55.21.2.

[194] Isoc. *Ant.* 122 (People "who are afraid hate those who inspire this feeling in them."); Ps.-Sen. *Oct.* 442-45; Tac. *Agr.* 32.

[195] Isoc. *Ant.* 125; Jos. *Ant.* 15.48.

[196] Plut. *Pom.* 663a; Sen. *De clem.* 1.9.11.

[197] Plut. *Eum.* 595f; *Mor.* 816c-d; Philo *In Flac.* 80; Jos. *Ant.* 19.246.

[198] Popularity: Tac. *Ann.* 4.31. Glory: Sen. *De clem.* 1.17.3; 1.21.1-4; *De ira* 2.34.2; *Herc. Oet.* 1557-63; Dio Cas. 55.20.2.

4.2. Rationales for Leniency

life by crowds and universally, this is a godlike use of power; but to kill in multitudes and without distinction is the power of conflagration and of ruin.[199]

Seneca also suggested that the king who shows mercy in reality shows mercy to himself.[200] The most important benefit which accrues to a person who shows clemency, however, is personal security. The moderate use of power does not antagonize enemies and keeps subjects from contemplating revolt.[201] As we have seen earlier, rule rests more securely on love than fear. Clemency is one way of doing just that, namely, of cultivating goodwill and assuaging fears. Thus, for all kinds of reasons of policy and diplomacy, extending leniency is a smart thing to do.

Leniency also has a *pedagogical* value.[202] It provides important counterpoint to punishments, rendering them more effective. Seneca offers four reasons for this: 1) lighter punishments compel their recipients to live more carefully because they have "something left to lose"; 2) punishments lose their coercive stigma when used frequently; 3) the public's impression of a punishment's severity diminishes with frequency; and 4) "it is dangerous to show a state in how great a majority evil men are," which is what happens when every sin receives punishment.[203] In addition, preference for leniency prioritizes sanctions. Like a doctor who intervenes at first with mild measures and resorts to more drastic measures only if sickness persists, so the ruler begins with mild words and moves on to harsh words, light punishments, and severe punishments only if wrongdoers are recalcitrant.[204] All Seneca's statements rest on the assumption that punishment seeks rehabilitation not revenge;[205] only in such a context could leniency have any value. Given that assumption, then, leniency makes the punishments meted out more constructive.

---

[199] Sen. *De clem.* 1.26.5. Cp. *Herc. fur.* 731-45.

[200] The body is like a state and the king is its soul; therefore, the king who shows mercy to the state also shows mercy to himself (Sen. *De clem.* 1.5.1).

[201] Thuc. 3.46 (whereas forceful rule incites revolt, 3.103); Isoc. *Ad Tim.* 5; *Ad Nic.* 23-4; *Nic.* 32-3; Sen. *De clem.* 1.8.6-13.5; Ps.-Sen. *Oct.* 440. Cp. Isoc. *Paneg.* 80-81; Sal. *Cat.* 18-19; Sen. *Thyestes* 204-19.

[202] 2 Macc 10:4 illustrates the difficulty of classifying the uses of leniency. When the Maccabean party reinstated cultic practice, they prayed that they would never again encounter such horrible events as they had witnessed in the preceding few years. Instead, they prayed that, "if they should ever sin, they might be disciplined by [God] with forbearance (μετὰ ἐπιεικείας παιδεύεσθαι) and not be handed over to blasphemous and barbarous nations." The boundary between pedagogy and policy is not clear.

[203] Sen. *De clem.* 1.22.1; 1.22.2; 1.22.3; 1.23.1-24.1, respectively.

[204] Sen. *De ira* 1.6.2-3; 1.19.7 (cf. Plato *Leg.* 2.934a); cp. Cic. *De off.* 1.136-37.

[205] *De ira* 1.6.2-4; 1.15.3; 1.19.7. The last passage quotes Plato: "A sensible person does not punish a man because he has sinned, but in order to keep him from sin" (from *Leg.* 934a).

As a part of rehabilitation, the purpose of mildness is to encourage repentance and, ultimately, to see a person's behavior corrected.[206] This may be presented as an exchange, as when Fabius offered the Aequi clemency if they would repent (Livy 3.2.5), or when the Jews of Caesarea asked to be spared so that they might have the opportunity to repent (Jos. *Ant.* 20.178). Clemency therefore lures people back to correct behavior.[207] Dio Cassius took that one step further, suggesting that those who receive forgiveness not only will repent but will be "ashamed to wrong their benefactors again" and will in fact "repay them with many services" (55.21.3). Not surprisingly, then, Dio Chrysostom characterized the good ruler, one who is φιλάνθρωπος, as one who "forces the unrighteous to mend their ways (τοὺς ἀδίκους μετανοεῖν) and lends a helping hand to the weak" (2.77).

The goal to be kept in view in correction (ἐπανόρθωσις) is "the good of the person reproved" (Cic. *De off.* 1.137). The φίλος ἐπιεικής prefers to correct his friends by "using commendation rather than blame" (Plut. *Mor.* 73d). The good ruler patiently endures wrongdoing (as does a father), reserving punishment until all other means are exhausted, as he seeks to nurture his subjects (Sen. *De clem.* 1.14.1). From the perspective of philosophy, Dio Chrysostom adds a warning at this point: while sparing punishment is good, sparing instruction is not. With the good of the person reproved in view, Dio stipulates that "a good prince is marked by compassion, a bad philosopher by lack of severity" (32.18). Dio therefore expects that criticism will overstep sanctions.

When rehabilitation involves damaged relationships, a more specific goal is reconciliation. Philo characterized God as gentle and compassionate, preferring mercy to punishment; as a result, God's people receive reconciliation with God (*De prae. et poe.* 166). Josephus recorded an anecdote about a teacher of the law named Simon who publicly accused King Agrippa of violating the law. Agrippa summoned Simon and spoke gently to him, which moved Simon to request pardon. The king regarded gentleness as superior to anger and was therefore reconciled to Simon,

---

[206] Pliny *Pan.* 46; Tac. *Agr.* 16. Thuc. 3.46 discusses the repentance of entire cities, as does Polyb. 5.11.6.

[207] *Ep. Arist.* 187-88; Sen. *De clem.* 1.2.1. This is how God treated the Canaanites (Wis 12:8-10). Although the letters of Pliny and Trajan concerning the Christians do not specifically mention clemency, they provide a relevant illustration of actual policy (not just moral theory). Pliny noted that given the opportunity to repent, the accused Christians would reform their behavior (*Ep.* 10.96.10). In Trajan's response, the emperor stipulated that if accused Christians repent, they should be pardoned (*veniam ex paenitentia*); moreover, Trajan recognized that a general legal ruling could not adequately cover the problem of Christians (10.97.2).

which Agrippa then proved by giving Simon a gift (*Ant.* 19.332-34). In the wake of the Thirty, Isocrates reflected on the civil strife which the amnesty of 403 BC had helped to resolve: the exercise of μετριότης had brought reconciliation (*In Cal.* 29-32). When pleading before the Romans, the Rhodians appealed to their πραότης to put away their wrath and be reconciled to them (Polyb. 30.31.15).

Thus, ἐπιείκεια, πραότης, and *clementia* have a role in leading people to correct behavior. By contrast they make punishments more effective. By substitution for severity they create willing pupils. They assist the person doing out punishment to avoid rage and to focus on the good of the recipient. They may also solicit reconciliation and elicit gratitude, thereby strengthening the future relationship. In short, these virtues make corrective measures more successful tools for nurturing and rehabilitating people, as well as restoring and strengthening social relationships.

People in antiquity then showed leniency in order to align themselves with ideas of good rule (theory) or to appear praiseworthy (virtue); sometimes custom or law dictated such behavior (convention). Often they were moved by a humane impulse (pity) or recognized the advantages of such action (policy). Further, leniency could render punishments more effective and soothe strained relationships (pedagogy).

3. Problems Inherent to Leniency and Clemency

Despite the diverse advantages of clemency, at the same time it also poses dangers and disadvantages. For example, it allows subjects the opportunity to complain or to stir up trouble.[208] In a great crisis, it is too dangerous a policy to follow.[209] Some considered it a safe policy only if preceded by the spreading of fear.[210] Critics painted clemency with broad strokes, saying that it was inimical to empire, looked like a failure to govern, and reversed the principle that the weak are subject to the strong.[211] It was also

---

[208] Thuc. 1.76-77; Cic. *Ad Brut.* 1.2a.2; 8.2; Dio Cas. 49.16.7; Sherk 1984: 60.

[209] Sallust presents this as Cato's argument, *Cat.* 52; Tac. *Agr.* 8.

[210] Ps.-Sen. *Oct.* 438-592; cp. Polyb. 9.23.3; Tac. *Agr.* 20.

[211] Thuc. 3.40; Philo *De som.* 2.295 (ἀναρχία). Strong should rule weak: Thuc. 1.76-77; Isocrates, however, argues that "it is not just for the stronger to rule over the weaker" for this opposes independence and democracy, *De pace* 69; he even praises Athens for assisting weaker states as opposed to cultivating relations with stronger states, *Paneg.* 53. In a variation on the golden rule, Isocrates boasted that Athens treated weaker states as it wished to be treated by stronger ones (*Paneg.* 81). According to Seneca, Posidonius regarded the golden age as a time when wise rulers protect the weak from the stronger, *Ep.* 90.5.

denigrated as simply one more way to please the crowd.[212] Ronald Syme scathingly indicates how Caesar's and Augustus' policies of clemency perverted their armies: "Zealous to avoid the shedding of Roman blood, generals and soldiers exalted disloyalty into a solemn duty."[213] Ancient commentators offered further criticisms. The Stoics (as already noted) complained that leniency violated justice. Others suggested that it encouraged contempt, thereby undermining moral suasion and eliminating fear.[214] The removal of those deterrents produces wrongdoing, clemency's most commonly feared by-product.[215] Despite its attractions and benefits, then, offering clemency was fraught with risks.

A further problem with clemency lies in its ambiguous nature. When is an act lenient? From the perspective of the recipient, one's rulers or their punishments may not look lenient.[216] In 2 Maccabees 9, we encounter a letter from Antiochus IV encouraging loyalty to his successor and son, Antiochus V. The letter concludes by characterizing Antiochus IV's rule as ἐπιεικῶς καὶ φιλανθρώπως (v. 27). The author of 2 Maccabees immediately mocks this claim by labelling Antiochus a murderer and describing his death as horrible and similar to the kind he imposed on others (v. 28). This juxtaposition makes Antiochus' claim ring false and reveals a fundamental disagreement between the author of 2 Maccabees and Antiochus himself on the characteristics of humanitarian rule.[217]

---

[212] Cic. *Ad Att.* 10.4.8: Cicero is quoting Curio's comment.

[213] *Roman Revolution*, 159. Cf. Cic. *Ad fam.* 10.35.

[214] Plut. *Cato min.* 771e; *Rom.* 37f; cp. *Cic.* 880a. Philo specifically warns that gentleness may undermine a ruler's authority, leaving him unable to manage affairs, while his subjects will become insolent (*De agric.* 47). Although Aristotle underscores the danger of contempt ("many coups result from contempt," *Pol.* 1312a), he nevertheless recommends preserving rule by moderation (1313a). Dio Cassius, on the other hand, minimizes the threat of contempt (55.19.6).

[215] Jos. *Ant.* 6.144; Plut. *Cato maj.* 35d; *Cic.* 870b; *Mor.* 537d; Sen. *De clem.* 1.2.1. Cp. Philo *De spec. leg.* 3.96; *Ad Her.* 2.8.

[216] Thuc. 1.76-77; Philo *De Ios.* 221-22.

[217] If the letter is genuine, it reveals Antiochus' own summation of good rule and the image he wished to present, while its location in 2 Maccabees emphasizes the difference in perspective between ruler and ruled. If the author of 2 Maccabees fabricated the letter, it reveals his conception of good rule and highlights what is important in a ruler to a subject people. Either way the letter provides a splendid foil for ridiculing Antiochus. While Jonathan Goldstein is generally optimistic about the authenticity of the Roman and Seleucid documents contained in 1 and 2 Maccabees, he hedges on 2 Macc 9:19-27, which "may be a forgery" (*II Maccabees*, AB 41A [Garden City, NY: Doubleday & Co., 1983], 358; see also p. 29). Thomas Fischer thinks that authenticity of this letter "remains doubtful" ("First and Second Maccabees," *ABD*, 4: 444). See also P. S. Alexander, "Epistolary Literature," in *Jewish Writings of the Second Temple Period*, ed. Michael E. Stone (Philadelphia: Fortress Press, 1984), 586.

4.3. Problems Inherent to Leniency 241

Another ambiguity in the exercise of leniency is the degree of indulgence to be shown. How much lenience is too much? Seneca advised that it not become common because that would blur the distinction between bad and good (*De clem.* 1.2.2).

A third ambiguity requires closer scrutiny because of its relevance for the apostle Paul: what is the difference between gentleness and cowardice or weakness? The line separating the two is ambiguous yet crucial, for people who showed leniency ran the risk of being regarded as cowards or weaklings.[218] Plutarch characterized Cicero as trapped in this very ambiguity, when he feared that failure to execute the Catilinarian conspirators would make him look unmanly and soft (*Cic.* 870b). Seneca used speech and dress as the criteria for his evaluation of Maecenas' gentle behavior and thereby concluded that the man displayed not a kind and benevolent moderation, but effeminacy.[219] Diodorus reveals the stakes involved in being thought weak when he dismisses a Syrian king as being an ineffectual ruler because of his weakness.[220] Ramsay MacMullen underscores this danger in a Roman context: "If you simply accepted insulting behavior, you lost face. That was serious. You became a Nothing."[221] Thus, leniency entails a dangerous double bind: the same gentle deed issuing in the same results could bring praise or censure depending on whether others perceived it as leniency or softness.

Though a great advocate of leniency, Plutarch recognized its inherent ambiguity, as his essay *On Compliancy* (*De vitioso pudore*) reveals. When a person shows leniency, he ought not do so because of "the effeminacy and flabbiness of his spirit," or out "of timidity and apprehension at the prospect of censure" (528f), or in response to flattery (535d-536c). These betray weakness. Instead, one ought to act willingly (534a), in accord with propriety (534f) and reason (529d). Such a person successfully balances

---

[218] Cowardice: Plut. *Cras.* 566e; *Cic.* 870b; cp. Plato *Pol.* 308e-309b. Weakness: Philo *De agric.* 47; Jos. *Ant.* 14.13 (cf. 13.407; 15.165-82); Sal. *Cat.* 52; Sen. *De clem.* 1.7.3-4; *Ep.* 114.7; Pliny *Pan.* 80; cp. Isoc. *Ad Dem.* 38. ταπεινός: Jos. *Bel.* 1.312-13. This ambiguity becomes acute during times of strife, as the rhetoric of revolt twists policies of moderation, so that future-thinking becomes cowardice, temperance unmanliness, and perspective uselessness (Thuc. 3.82).

[219] *Ep.* 114.7. Cp. Plut. *Mor.* 231b.

[220] 33.3: διὰ τὴν ἀσθένειαν τῆς ψυχῆς ἄχρηστος ὢν εἰς προστάσιαν βασιλείας.

[221] "Personal Power in the Roman Empire," *AJP* 107 (1986): 518. Later MacMullen adds, "You must insist on respect — else you will be trampled on and abused. Others must see you insisting, and be warned. If you want a great deal of respect, your warnings must be dire, perhaps followed up by dire action. Which must be talked about, to yield best results" (p. 519).

"the ruthlessness of extreme severity and the infirmity of excessive courtesy."[222]

Like Plutarch, other authors also resolved the ambiguity between weakness and leniency by appraising the person involved, but used a simpler criterion. They assumed that people who showed themselves strong on other occasions were not weak when showing indulgence and forbearance. Suspicion then gathered around those whose power was in question. Dio Cassius recognized this when he commented that established nobility feels no threat if others show them inadequate attention, whereas newcomers to high standing show extreme sensitivity.

> Consequently the world is more scrupulous in the case of such persons than in the case of the emperors themselves, one might almost say; since for the latter it counts as a virtue to pardon anyone in case of an offence, but by the former such conduct is thought to argue their weakness, whereas to attack and to exact vengeance is considered to furnish proof of great power (58.5.4).

Seneca's advocacy of both *clementia* and *severitas* becomes more attractive in light of the obscure line between leniency and weakness. The former softens the latter, while *severitas* reveals the bite which makes *clementia* effective. Cicero also recognized this:

> For nothing is more commendable, nothing more becoming in a pre-eminently great man than courtesy and forbearance.... And yet gentleness of spirit and forbearance (*mansuetude atque clementia*) are to be commended only with the understanding that strictness (*severitas*) may be exercised for the good of the state; for without that, the government cannot be well administered. On the other hand, if punishment or correction must be administered, it need not be insulting; it ought to have regard to the welfare of the state, not to the personal satisfaction of the man who administers the punishment or reproof (*De off.* 1.88).

Thus, the theoretical ambiguity of *clementia* can be clarified if people see *clementia* and *severitas* working in tandem. This, in fact, summarizes Paul's predicament in Corinth. Having demonstrated *severitas* in words but not deeds, Paul gave the Corinthians no point of reference from which to appreciate leniency as anything but timidity or weakness.

4. Paul's Use of Leniency and Clemency

We are attempting to understand the rationale for Paul's appeal through the leniency and clemency of Christ and to contextualize it. The previous

---

[222] *Mor.* 529a: τοῦ ἐπιεικοῦς σφόδρα τὴν ἀσθένειαν. This essay also illustrates the interaction of leniency and justice within Greco-Roman culture. Elsewhere, Plutarch quotes the Spartan Archidamidas, asking, "How can he be a good man (χρηστός), who is not harsh (πικρός) even with rascals (πονηροῖς)?" (*Mor.* 55e and 218b).

three sections examined the workings of leniency in the Greco-Roman world, as a context in which to view Paul. In this section we will look at the role of gentleness in Paul's ministry. In so doing, we find a consistent method practiced by Paul in remedying wrongdoing: he pursues correction with gentleness, unless recalcitrance (2 Corinthians), egregiousness (1 Corinthians 5), or danger (Galatians) arises. In this, he reflects the thinking of his time. His appeal in 2 Cor 10:1 then is congruent with his culture and his habits. More particularly, his dealings with the Corinthians themselves build up to his offer of leniency. We turn now to contextualize Paul's words in his ministry to show how clearly they communicated his position and attitude toward the Corinthian church.

1 Thessalonians 2:7. In 1 Thess 2:1-12 Paul describes his ministry in comparison with the issues of his day.[223] His intent is not to defend himself against charges, but to demonstrate his sincerity and concern for the Thessalonians. Paul accomplishes this by using the criteria relevant to his social world; moreover, as Malherbe notes, even Paul's use of antithesis parallels Dio Chrysostom's self-presentation. Like an earnest and useful philosopher, then, Paul has a divine task on account of which he speaks boldly, despite the struggle, despite insult. The message is what is important for Paul. He is not content simply to hear the sound of his voice, nor is his message a mask for his own greed and ambition; correspondingly, the apostle does not flatter nor deceive. Further evidence that Paul's mission and message are genuine arises from his treatment of the Thessalonians (vv. 7-12). He points out that although he had the right to be overbearing, he treated them with gentleness. As a nurse treats her charges and a father his children, so Paul conducted himself toward the Thessalonians, sharing with them and encouraging them. His manual labor further demonstrated his intent not to use them for his own ends. By comments such as these, Paul sought to distinguish himself from the self-promoters and charlatans with whom he appeared to be in competition.

The nuance of Paul's claim to have been gentle has been uncovered by Malherbe. The need for gentleness arises from the Cynic philosopher's privilege of παρρησία: to speak freely entails the possibility of speaking harshly. One may instead choose to be gentle so as to minimize verbal

---

[223] Abraham J. Malherbe's "Gentle as a Nurse in I Thess ii" is fundamental for 1 Thess 2 (*NovT* 12 [1970]: 203-17; reprinted in his *Paul and the Popular Philosophers*, 35-48; see also his *Paul and the Thessalonians* [Philadelphia: Fortress Press, 1987], 3-4, 54-60, 73-75, and 85-87). My comments are based on these writings.

abuse.[224] To do so, however, raises the possibility of flattery: failure to say what ought to be said indicates that the speaker seeks only to please, not to correct. Such a speaker is self-interested and not concerned about the well-being of his audience. One cannot therefore say that gentleness is an unqualified good. It is ambiguous. One must therefore balance παρρησία and gentleness without lapsing into misanthropy or flattery. Paul claims to do this and thereby contextualizes his claim to gentleness, so that it appears commendable. He can therefore assert that as an apostle he had the prerogative to act forcefully, but opted for gentleness: like a good nurse, he treated the Thessalonians tenderly and preferred to share his own life with them.

A problem with Malherbe's exegesis of this passage is that he does not discuss the textual problem in 1 Thess 2:7. Papyrus 65, Codex Sinaiticus, and Codex Vaticanus agree that the text reads ἐγενήθημεν νήπιοι, rather than ἤπιοι, as Malherbe assumes, presumably following Nestle[25]. That impressive manuscript evidence persuaded the editors of UBS³/Nestle[26] and subsequently UBS⁴/Nestle[27].[225] Two committee members, however, Metzger and Wikgren, dissented, arguing that "only ἤπιοι seems to suit the context."[226] Interpreters typically side with Metzger, complaining that νήπιοι makes little sense and therefore favoring ἤπιοι.[227] If internal evidence is considered, then Malherbe's elucidation of 1 Thess 2:1-12

---

[224] "It became customary to contrast the harshness of a certain kind of παρρησία with gentle speech such as that of a nurse who knows her charges," Malherbe, "Gentle as a Nurse," 211.

[225] In their comments on the former edition, the editors state they were swayed by external evidence, but rated their determination as "C" to reflect "a considerable degree of doubt" (p. xxviii); the subsequent edition raised the level of certainty to a "B".

[226] Bruce M. Metzger, ed., *A Textual Commentary on the Greek New Testament* (corrected ed.; New York: United Bible Societies, 1975), 629-30. Metzger elaborates on his preference of ἤπιοι in his *Text of the New Testament: Its Transmission, Corruption, and Restoration* (2d ed.; New York: Oxford University Press, 1968), 231-33.

[227] For example, Helmut Koester states that νήπιοι is "clearly wrong" ("The Text of 1 Thessalonians," in *The Living Text: Essays in Honor of Ernest W. Saunders*, eds. Dennis E. Groh and Robert Jewett [Lanham, MD: University Press of America, 1985], 224-25). Other commentators have shared that opinion: Béda Rigaux, *Les Épitres aux Thessalonieiens* (Paris: Gabalda, 1956), 418-19; Raymond F. Collins, *Studies on the First Letter to the Thessalonians*, BETL 66 (Leuven University Press, 1984), 195 n. 107; Charles A. Wanamaker, *The Epistles to the Thessalonians: A Commentary on the Greek Text*, NIGTC (Grand Rapids, MI: Eerdmans, 1990), 100; and Earl J. Richard, *First and Second Thessalonians*, Sacra Pagina 11 (Collegeville, MN: Liturgical Press, 1995), 82. Translators also opt for "gentle" (e.g., NRSV, REB, NIV, NAB). In his Anchor Bible commentary, Malherbe has now discussed the textual variant, maintaining his preference for ἤπιοι (pp. 145-45).

provides sound reason for preferring ἐγενήθημεν ἤπιοι.[228] Still, the witness of the manuscripts is weighty and continues to have champions.[229] Accepting the external evidence, Gaventa tries to rationalize νήπιοι as lending dignity to Paul's mixed metaphor by calling it an "inverted" metaphor.[230] While she certainly is right that the resulting juxtaposition of images does indeed make the reader pause to scratch his or her head, this puzzlement does not change the fact that the presence of νήπιοι yields a harsh mixed metaphor. The critic must choose between well-attested bad writing and coherence. In this case, I think the more difficult reading is such because it an error, and so opt for intelligibility.

The issue is not crucial for the present study. Without ἤπιος, Malherbe's study still registers the type of person Paul presents himself as being and indicates the appropriateness of attributing gentleness to such a person. Furthermore, whatever the reading (and consequent punctuation), νήπιοι or ἤπιοι contrasts with βαρύτης. Such refusal to throw around one's weight is the essence of ἐπιείκεια, regardless of the specific vocabulary. For our purposes this is as useful as the presence of the word ἤπιος.

In Malherbe's reading of 1 Thess 2:1-12 against a Cynic background, moreover, we can hear the wider debate in which Paul's words participate. The "charges" are not peculiar to Paul or to his circumstances, but pertain to the attempts of orators to earn a living by their public speaking. 1 Thess 2:1-12 therefore provides us with a clue to Paul's conception of the social location of his ministry. We should not therefore tie Paul's words to events in Thessalonica, but see in them a reflection of Paul's ministry at large. As a result, the type of person he claims to have been among the Thessalonians was not peculiar to his ministry there. Paul's words reveal a strategy and issues relevant to his work in general. An element of this matrix of strategies and behaviors is gentleness. This is not to say that every syllable Paul uttered was gentle, but that he recognized and agreed with the general value placed on gentleness.[231]

---

[228] Internal evidence is otherwise inconclusive. Was the letter nu repeated or elided?

[229] John Gillman, "Paul's εἴσοδος: The Proclaimed and the Proclaimer (1 Thes 2,8)," in *The Thessalonian Correspondence*, ed. Raymond F. Collins, BETL 87 (Leuven University Press, 1990), 63 n. 4; more important is the focused study by Beverly R. Gaventa, "Apostles As Babes and Nurses in 1 Thessalonians 2:7," in *Faith and History: Essays in Honor of Paul W. Meyer*, eds. John T. Carroll, Charles H. Cosgrove, E. Elizabeth Johnson (Atlanta: Scholars Press, 1990), 193-207.

[230] Gaventa, "Apostles as Babes and Nurses," 203-4.

[231] Malherbe notes that some Cynics abandoned gentleness because they held a pessimistic view of other people ("Gentle as a Nurse," 212). Because the human condition was so bad, biting words were the only possible recourse. Paul would be hard

Galatians 6:1. Paul's letter to the Galatians supports this. In 6:1 he advocates treating a transgressor with gentleness, not verbal assault or full punitive sanctions. Paul advises that restoration (καταρτίζειν) be sought.[232] Like the good ruler who shows mercy to achieve reconciliation (or a father or a philosopher), so the "spiritual" Galatians were to attempt to restore transgressors and to do so with a "spirit of gentleness" (πραΰτης). With this advice Paul shares in an enlightened Greco-Roman tradition.

Paul appends to his advice a participial phrase which further stipulates that those who restore, οἱ πνευματικοί, should be careful to avoid falling into temptation themselves. What exactly this warning modifies is unclear. Does it modify gentleness? If so, then Paul would be grounding his recommendation for gentleness in the recognition of human weakness. On the other hand, if the stipulation to be wary of temptation modifies the verb (καταρτίζετε), then no rationale for a policy of gentleness is provided. Instead Paul's advice is two-fold: the spiritual who help to restore others should attend to the transgressor with gentleness and to themselves with diligence. A third option is to view the participle as having an absolute quality (which may indicate an independent use).[233] The change from plural to singular between the verb and the participle suggests a looseness in Paul's thinking such that σκοπῶν does not so much modify καρτίζετε as it does provide additional advice to the πνευματικοί. Of these three alternatives, then, I find the first least likely and the third most probable, leaving Paul's recommendation of gentleness without an explicit explanation.

Though his syntax does not link the two closely, the flow of thought and juxtaposition of πραότης and self-awareness yields a combination of ideas that is not unusual. Spicq thinks otherwise: "Meekness is a classical quality of the 'corrector,' but here the motive is new: awareness of one's own potential for failure in similar circumstance to those in which the offender fell."[234] However, that the danger is "failure in similar

---

pressed to share that view in regard to the Thessalonians. People who had turned to God from idols and were reforming their moral lives would not qualify as irremedial.

[232] The verb καταρτίζειν is ambiguous: its action can reflect either an individual or social perspective. In other words, it means reintegration within the social group (i.e., reconciliation), or, as LSJ suggests, "restore to a right mind." Of course, these two things go together, so that a distinction may be more conceptual than real.

[233] E.g., Hans Dieter Betz, *Galatians*, Hermeneia (Philadelphia: Fortress Press, 1979), 298 n. 53: "The participle σκοπῶν has an imperative meaning, parallel to καταρτίζετε."

[234] *TLNT* 3: 170 n. 39.

circumstance" is an unwarranted assumption. That "the motive is new" must be qualified on anthropological and philosophical grounds.

The anthropology of Gal 6:1-5 resembles its larger world. For example, the verb's passive voice (προλημφθῇ) seems to mitigate responsibility and extend an excuse; moreover, Paul describes the one falling into sin as ἄνθρωπος rather than τις, suggesting the nature of the sinner as human: to be human is to be weak. This assumption appears in forensic rhetoric, where the plea for mercy rests on human weakness.[235] Reversal of fortune also indicates human weakness. For example, Diodorus Siculus advises intelligent people to remember, "especially at the supreme moment of triumph, that the tables may be turned" (31.3.3). That Paul's following words stress the need to help others and warn against pride and boasting (6:2-4) develop this anthropology, as another example from Diodorus illustrates. Explaining the philanthropy of Scipio toward a defeated foe, King Syphax, Diodorus attributes to Scipio the understanding that "he himself, being but human, should do nothing amiss. For there is ... a divine Nemesis that keeps watch over the life of man and swiftly reminds those whose presumption passes mortal bounds of their own weakness" (27.6.2). What, therefore, Paul warns against are the weakness and arrogance common to humans. It is fitting anthropological advice that those who correct must be vigilant for themselves.

The philosophical background to Paul's instructions should also be noted. As Betz has noted, "to restore" is a "highly significant concept from Hellenistic philosophy, where it describes the work of the philosopher — 'psychotherapist' and educator."[236] (Malherbe calls this "psychagogy";[237] earlier we used the more general label pedagogy.) The goal of the philosopher is that of Paul and now the πνευματικοί, viz., to fix or restore souls. Paul's warning, σκοπῶν σεαυτόν, also derives from the philosophical tradition and further anchors Paul's thinking in Gal 6:1 within its Hellenistic milieu.[238] This interaction on the part of Paul with Hellenistic philosophy in regard to therapy (or pastoral ministry) corresponds to what we saw in 1 Thessalonians. We conclude, then, that Spicq exaggerates when he labels Paul's motive "new."

---

[235] The plea for mercy rests on the weakness of the offender, not the weakness of the one who corrects. While this would justify offering gentleness, it does not justify looking out for oneself. My point, though, is the anthropology of human weakness on which the plea rests reflects the anthropology which warns the corrector to look out for himself: both assume human weakness.

[236] Betz, *Galatians*, 297; see nn. 43-44 for references and literature.

[237] Malherbe, *Paul and the Thessalonians*, 81.

[238] Betz, *Galatians*, 298.

In Spicq's defense, the context does offer something new. The relevance of a gentle approach appears in 5:23, which lists πραΰτης among the "fruit of the Spirit," revealing that this quality lies within Paul's conception of ethics and is an assumed characteristic of the person controlled by the Spirit. Given this general value of πραΰτης, what we find in 6:1 is then one example of its application in the lives of πνευματικοί. In comparison with Greco-Roman sources, though we may call the context "new," the application is standard.

More important is that the entire thought of Gal 6:1 indicates not simply the spiritual and ethical value of gentleness but its strategic utility. As we saw earlier, gentleness (or leniency or clemency) was regarded as an effective pedagogical method. In Gal 6:1 Paul explicitly acknowledges this and recommends it as an appropriate course of action. In short, Paul reflects an old, widespread idea which regards gentleness as virtuous and recommends its use when attempting to redirect incorrect behavior to correct behavior.

As useful as Gal 6:1 is as evidence for Paul's advocacy of gentleness, we cannot ignore the problem of the letter as a whole. Gentleness did not grace Paul's every word. To those who preach differently than does Paul, the apostle says, "'Ανάθεμα ἔστω" (1:8-9). To the misled Galatians Paul says, "You foolish Galatians, who cast a spell over you?!" (3:1). "Are you so stupid?!" Paul asks (3:3). "Have I become your enemy because I told you the truth?" (4:16). And then there is Paul's rather indelicate hope that the circumcisors' knives might slip (5:12). He also accuses his opponents of being insincere and self-interested (4:17; 6:12-13). In short, Paul speaks bluntly and forcefully.

I do not wish to minimize the contradiction which Galatians presents. I think, however, that the examples of clemency and leniency which we traced earlier make the contradiction between the letter as a whole and 6:1 intelligible. We have seen that, although gentleness is valued as a policy, it is not followed blindly. Furthermore, given the cruelties of the clement Augustus and the clemency of the cruel Herod, we recognize the need for mixing both forms of behavior. We also noted that gentleness is usually a means to an end: one does not restrain one's reaction for the pleasure of the experience, but to accomplish something. In Gal 6:1, as in other texts we noted earlier, the goal of restraint is pedagogical, i.e., to reform someone. This points us to the larger goal which directed both philosophers and Paul, viz., the health of the soul (though Paul would understand this as doing the will of God). Paul valued gentleness as an effective means to guiding people to that end. But both Paul and the philosophers included various means in their arsenals: along with πραΰτης they used παρρησία. Both were needed to attain educational, therapeutic, or pastoral objectives.

The need to use both gentleness and frank speech was well known. Dio Chrysostom provides explicit testimony to the need for both.

> But he who in very truth is manly and high-minded would never submit to any such things, nor would he sacrifice his own liberty (ἐλευθερίαν) and his freedom of speech (παρρησίαν) ... But ... will strive to preserve his individuality in seemly fashion and with steadfastness, never deserting his post of duty, but always honoring and promoting virtue and sobriety and trying to lead all men thereto, partly by persuading and exhorting (πείθων καὶ παρακαλῶν), partly by abusing and reproaching (λοιδορούμενος καὶ ὀνειδίζων), in the hope that he may thereby rescue somebody from folly and from low desires and intemperance and soft living, taking them aside privately one by one and also admonishing them in groups every time he finds the opportunity, "With gentle words at times, at others harsh" [Hom. Il. 12.267], until, methinks, he shall have spent his life in caring for human beings ... reminding men of sobriety and righteousness and promoting concord, but as for insatiate greed and shamelessness and moral weakness, expelling them as best he can (Dio Chrys. 77/78.37-39).

Philodemus offers similar advice in his Περὶ παρρησίας, noting that different circumstances require different methods. For example, the orator must take into consideration his audience, the complexity of the problem which he addresses, and whether he speaks privately or publicly.[239] In regard to the variety of possible audiences, Malherbe summarizes Philodemus as follows: orators

> know that the young may be stiff-necked and easily irritated, that they should be treated with gentleness to make them amenable to correction, and that their capacity to endure reprimand must always be taken into consideration. The strong and forceful in nature need frankness of a harsher kind, and those of an ugly disposition must be tamed by frankness.[240]

Plutarch offers similar advice in his *Quomodo adulator ab amico internoscatur*, the second half of which focuses on παρρησία (*Mor.* 59a-74e). Frankness should be free of self-interest (*Mor.* 66e), "arrogance, ridicule, scoffing, and scurrility" (*Mor.* 67e). It should be sensitive to the occasion (68c-71d); misfortune is not the time for reproof (69a), as the following anecdote illustrates:

> It is said that when Demetrius of Phalerum had been banished from his native land and was living in obscurity and humble station near Thebes, he was not well pleased to see Crates approaching, anticipating some cynical frankness and harsh language. But Crates met him with all gentleness (πράως; 69c).

It is time to speak frankly when pleasure, anger, ὕβρις, greed, or overhastiness appear (69e), and the best place for admonishment is in

---

[239] Malherbe, *Paul and the Thessalonians*, 86.
[240] Malherbe, 86.

private (70f-71a). Plutarch also points out tactful ways of speaking frankly (71d-74c). In his conclusion, Plutarch draws (again) an analogy between the orator and physician who use both harsh and gentle measures: just as physicians soothe the pain they inflict, so those who use admonition do not "apply its bitterness and sting, and then run away; but by further converse and gentle words (λόγοις ἐπιεικέσιν) they mollify (ἐκπραΰνουσι) and assuage" (74d). Thus, sometimes the moral teacher needed to speak frankly, and sometimes gently, and in some cases he had to combine the two.

That Paul did not slavishly follow the single method of gentleness should not be surprising. The challenge of gentleness is not singleminded consistency, but knowing when and how to show it. Galatians 6:1 addresses the situation in which a Christian sins. In such a situation, Paul regards πραΰτης as an effective policy. But in the letter as a whole, Paul addressed a different situation. In Paul's eyes, the stakes in Galatia were enormous, involving the gospel itself and Paul's relationship to the Galatians. To mince his words would have been flattery; no responsible teacher would risk leaving his audience in unrecognized danger. Had Paul spoken softly, would his letter communicate the enormity of the issues (in Paul's view)? Would the Galatians understand that Paul meant every word which he had said — and had not said — earlier? Would moderate words convey clearly Paul's resolve? The contradiction between Galatians 6:1 and the rest of the letter illustrates clearly how different circumstances require different methods. While gentleness is a valuable policy, its implementation must be tailored to appropriate circumstances. In Paul's eyes, the Galatian crisis was not the right time for gentleness. We can therefore affirm the general value which Paul placed on gentleness in his ministry, while recognizing that the apostle did not follow such a policy blindly.[241]

1 Corinthians 4:21. The same pattern appears in Paul's Corinthian correspondence. In 1 Corinthians 1–4 Paul addressed problems of schism and competition within the Corinthian church. While Paul recognized the diminution of his own position in the controversy, he did not appreciate how loose his hold was on many of the Corinthian Christians. In Paul's thinking, "Christ crucified" provided a fundamental paradigm for human existence; yet many in Corinth did not regard it as such. As a result, aspects of Paul's personal example were not compelling to some (or many) Corinthians and were in fact problematic; commensurate with this,

---

[241] Similarly, Paul's rhetoric in 2 Corinthians 10–13 is sharper than the rhetoric in his first apology, 2 Cor 2:14–6:13; 7:2-4.

the Corinthians would have been unmoved by Paul's rhetoric in 1 Corinthians 4. His invocation of servile imagery (4:1) and his contrasting of the Corinthians' plentitude with his own deprivation (4:8-13) would only have increased the doubts entertained by some in Corinth. Paul, however, assumed that his personal example held persuasive value and advised the Corinthians to imitate himself (4:16). He even went so far as to send Timothy to Corinth to promulgate Pauline imitation: Timothy was Paul's dear child and a faithful Christian, which made him competent to remind the Corinthians about Paul's "ways in Christ Jesus," the very same behaviors and attitudes taught everywhere else among Christians (4:17)! As Paul viewed the situation, he assumed his personal example and emotional arguments would move the Corinthians. He then concluded his appeal with a threat. When he next came, he would confront the arrogant, and the ensuing combat would center on δύναμις not words. Then Paul asked the Corinthians' preference: "Shall I come to you with a rod or in love and a gentle S/spirit?" (4:21).

Paul's statement in 1 Cor 4:21 verifies what we saw in 1 Thessalonians 2 and Galatians 6. First, it reflects Paul's preference for gentleness. The whole point of his argument was to avoid a show of force, deflate those whom he regarded as arrogant, and reassert his paternal primacy among the Corinthians. If successful in his rhetorical pursuit, then Paul could act like the loving, gentle father he preferred to be when he next visited Corinth.[242] But (secondly), gentleness was contingent on the state of the relationship. If the Corinthians did not submit to Paul's ways, then a display of force would be necessary. In the meantime, stern rhetoric was required.[243] Thus, Paul preferred gentleness, but saw it as one of two possibilities, not an inviolable policy.[244]

2 Corinthians 10–13. One's view of what happened next in Paul's dealings with the Corinthians depends on how one reconstructs the

---

[242] Xen. *Ag.* 7.3: "Here was a man whose behavior to his political opponents was that of a father to his children: though he would chide them for their errors he honored them when they did a good deed, and stood by them when any disaster befell them, deeming no citizen an enemy, willing to praise all, counting the safety of all a gain, and reckoning the destruction even of a man of little worth as a loss. He clearly reckoned that if the citizens should continue to live in peaceful submission to the laws, the fatherland would always prosper and that she would be strong when the Greeks were prudent."

[243] Margaret M. Mitchell, *Paul and the Rhetoric of Reconciliation*, 221-25.

[244] As we shall see, however, a new criterion arose in Paul's choice between gentleness and severity: his mission was to build up, not tear down.

Corinthian correspondence and its various *Sitze im Leben*.[245] Events apparently unfolded unfavorably for Paul: the Corinthians did not respond to his offer of gentleness. The people "who were puffed up" did not change; in fact, their opinion of Paul diminished even further. Given the chance to support other, more appealing Christian ministers, influential Corinthian Christians did so. To correct that, Paul wrote a letter (the first apology); it accomplished little. Confronted with a deteriorating situation, Paul hurried to Corinth for an unscheduled visit. During this second visit, Paul did not encounter a church willing to defer to him. Many rejected Paul's identification of their behavior as sin and ignored his admonishments (12:20-13:2). Paul's hand was being forced to deal harshly with the Corinthians; but he resisted. This inaction gave rise to the devastating observation that though Paul's letters were forceful and demanding, in person he was not (10:10). The public leveling of this accusation humiliated Paul before the church (2 Cor 7:12; 12:21). He later described this as a painful experience (2:1). Stymied by this public insult, Paul left Corinth. First, however, he warned those who had sinned to repent (of their ἀκαθαρσία καὶ πορνεία καὶ ἀσέλγεια, 12:21), admonishing the Corinthians to put an end to their "quarreling, jealousy, anger, selfishness, slander, gossip, conceit, and disorder" (12:20, NRSV). Then he left them with the threat that when he returned he would not spare those who persisted in their sin (13:2).

Since the writing of 1 Corinthians, Paul's relationship with the Corinthians had changed dramatically. The gentle, paternal spirit Paul had offered in 1 Cor 4:21 had been rejected, as the Corinthians did not show Paul the esteem which he had expected. Paul, in turn, did not wield (successfully) the δύναμις he had threatened. In 1 Corinthians Paul had opposed words with power, but at his second visit showed only words. In

---

[245] As I see it, after 1 Cor came 2 Cor 2:14–6:13 + 7:2-4 (first apology), then the second visit, then 2 Cor 10:1–13:10 (letter of tears), then 2 Cor 1:1–2:13 + 7:5-16 + 13:11-13 (letter of reconciliation), then 2 Cor 8 and 9. As for the opponents encountered in 2 Corinthians, I do not think they are present in 1 Corinthians; however, 1 Corinthians does point to the circumstances and issues which would facilitate the success of Paul's rivals. Many in Corinth were happy to line up behind someone other than Paul. Paul's rivals had no need to impose themselves upon the Corinthians; they were welcomed — and even championed. This means that Paul's defense has two targets, his rivals and the Corinthians. Notice that I prefer to label the other apostles rivals instead of opponents. The battle in Corinth was not between opposing theological camps, but the quest on Paul's part to retain his status among the Corinthian Christians. I therefore read 2 Cor 10:10 as something said by a Corinthian Christian, not one of the rivals. Obviously, every sentence in this footnote is controversial; proof would require additional books. To integrate into the preceding scheme Paul's offer of leniency is the first step in such proof.

4.4. Paul's Use of Leniency

short, the Corinthians were not what Paul wished them to be and he was not what they wished him to be (12:20). A fundamental breakdown in Paul's relationship with the Corinthians had taken place.

The turn of events during Paul's second visit to Corinth left him reeling. He had been upstaged; his claims to possess δύναμις appeared fraudulent. If he genuinely had the authority which he claimed, why had he not imposed his will on the Corinthians? If he did not have it, why had he continued to threaten to use it? Paul's answer was simple: he did not want to punish anyone. But he clothed this answer in theological language: on the one hand, leniency and clemency were the manner in which Christ's authority is exercised; in addition, the apostolic mission itself discourages punitive measures, for Paul ought to be building up the church (10:8; 13:10). Expelling people was an extreme measure for extreme situations (1 Cor 5:1-5). Christology and ecclesiology therefore dictated a policy of restraint on Paul's part.

Although Paul regarded the exhibition of strength to be a policy of last resort, others did not share his opinion in this matter. When Paul describes his rivals' behavior, he draws such a shocking picture that it should raise our suspicion. That the Corinthians tolerated such behavior suggests that they interpreted it differently, even regarding it as normal. Thus, point of view may be the only difference between remuneration and exploitation. Behaving with dignity and grandeur was not intrinsically objectionable. And striking another person was a more complex social gesture than in our (egalitarian) world. Behind the extremes Paul denounces are the behaviors of people with social standing and (some) moral teachers. Though Paul objects to the superior bearing of his rivals, (some) Christians in Corinth found it appropriate. That Paul did not conduct himself as a person of social importance disappointed them. In their mind Paul should act against wrongdoers, with force if necessary. If Paul's rivals can strike blows and receive respect in return, Paul's optimistic, benevolent gentleness would elicit contempt as weakness and dilatoriness. People in Corinth wanted to see the forceful and demanding apostle in action.

We see then three potential aspects of Paul's pastoral ministry. First, he preferred gentleness, thereby giving people the opportunity to repent. Second, he was not afraid to use direct, bold speech as necessary. Third, to this he added the possibility of punitive measures; however, such measures were detrimental to the church and were to be avoided if at all possible. If pushed to the limit, though, Paul threatened to use them — albeit reluctantly. During his second visit, some were pressing Paul toward the third possibility. He did not want to go to that extreme, so he departed from Corinth, leaving a large question mark over his status and person.

The debacle in Corinth forced Paul to rethink his handling of the church in Corinth. He could not return and fail to assert his authority again. (Nor could he afford to assert his authority only to be made a fool of.) He therefore altered his travel plans, eliminating his expected quick return to Corinth. He needed some time to solidify his position and to give the Corinthians the opportunity to submit to his teaching. In place of his expected return, Paul therefore opted to write a letter and send it in care of Titus.

In 2 Corinthians 10:1–13:10 we read Paul's attempt to negotiate a resolution to the strained relationship between the Corinthians and himself. Maintaining his preferences for gentleness and παρρησία, Paul extended an olive branch to the Corinthians in an offer of "leniency and clemency." Whereas his failure to enforce his edicts in the Corinthian church looked like evidence of weakness — and not authority — Paul argued that his failure was actually restraint. His response, then, corresponded to the way in which a sage ought to act in the face of insult: wisdom shows itself in restraint, keeping anger in check, and pardoning the offender, behavior which is reasonable, civilized, and benevolent.[246] Refusal to punish therefore did not exhibit a lack of authority on his part, but a virtuous and responsible use of it. He did not wish to overstep his commission and destroy the church, but to build it up, which is what God authorized him to do. The way to accomplish that was not to punish wrongdoers, but to encourage them to repent. Corresponding to the gentleness (among equals) advised in Gal 6:1, "leniency and clemency" were the apostle's chosen means for achieving repentance and restoration (καταρτίζειν; cf. 2 Cor 13:10).

In 2 Corinthians 10–13, however, Paul had to prove that his offer of "leniency and clemency" was based on authority. His opening words did so with great force (10:1-6).[247] The fervent rhetoric which followed demonstrated the forcefulness which his opening words asserted. Paul also solemnly intoned the Mosaic law to undergird his policy (13:1). As two or three witnesses were required to convict, so his third visit would furnish the requisite evidence needed to judge wayward Corinthians. Paul's appeal to Moses removes some of the caprice from Paul's policy and lends the appearance of an official procedure. Paul's clemency also contrasts with his opponents (11:20). They enslaved and even dared to hit the Corinthians, behaviors of the tyrant. Paul, however, treats the Corinthians as free men and behaves like the good minister of the good king. In place of the insult and shame which enslavement and slapping connote, Paul

---

[246] Fitzgerald, *Cracks in an Earthen Vessel*, 103-7.

[247] Abraham J. Malherbe, "Antisthenes and Odysseus, and Paul at War."

extended friendship and goodwill. Meanwhile, if Paul's opponents can treat the Corinthians in such a manner, and if 2 Corinthians 10–13 successfully establishes Paul as their equal, then Paul too would possess analogous authority. That Paul attempts the comparison prior to invoking the Mosaic legal principle makes the latter even more effective. Having verified the substance of his claim to ἐξουσία and consequently to clemency, the appeal to proper legal procedure looks like a well-considered, rational policy. Paul's threats to pursue that policy do not bode well for the Corinthians.

The success of Paul's letter and his assistant Titus appears in the so-called "Letter of Reconciliation." There Paul explains his motivation for the way in which he has dealt with the Corinthians. In the face of their disobedience and recalcitrance, Paul preferred to show leniency. As he had not punished during his second visit in order to spare the Corinthians, so likewise he had not returned for his announced third visit in order to spare the Corinthians once again. In the face of the Corinthians' fixation on a display of force, Paul's preferred policy was to be lenient. Thus, he solemnly swears, "I summon God as my witness and stake my life on the fact that my reason for not visiting Corinth was to spare you. Don't take that to mean that we lord over your faith; no, we work together for your joy" (2 Cor 1:23-24).

Our review of Paul's lenient treatment of the Corinthian church has suggested that leniency was both part of the problem as well as part of the solution. On the one hand, Paul's insistence on "leniency and clemency" helped repair the rift in his relationship with the Corinthians. Paul's offer of a gentle S/spirit in 1 Cor 4:21 corresponds to the political morality which suffuses that letter.[248] As we have observed in section two of this chapter, leniency promotes concord and procures goodwill. In 2 Corinthians 10–13 clemency helps to lure the Corinthians to submit willingly to Paul's authority. As we have seen, clemency is in fact an effective way of making one's subjects willing subjects. We also saw that clemency turns enemies into friends. The goodwill expressed in clemency inspires trust. Given the enmity which built up between Paul and the Corinthians, he no doubt hoped that his offer of clemency would be seen as a gesture of goodwill, which would rekindle friendship (i.e., reconciliation).

But how could Paul move the Corinthians from a negative evaluation of his clemency (i.e., as weakness) to a positive one? We have noted two methods: clemency must operate in conjunction with *severitas* and with reason. Paul emphasizes that reason guides his offer of clemency. He is

---

[248] Margaret M. Mitchell, *Paul and the Rhetoric of Reconciliation*.

not guided by a fear of punishing, but by a commission. As he spells out explicitly twice, Paul has authority to build up, not tear down (10:8; 13:10; cp. 12:19). His offer of clemency is divinely mandated policy. In addition, the method by which he implements the policy has the solemn precedent of Scripture. As we noted already, when Paul states that he will punish on the weight of two or three witnesses, he adds an additional veneer of rationality to his policy of clemency. Furthermore, his policy is goal-oriented. Paul does not act on a whim, but is working for the Corinthians' κατάρτισις. He offers clemency in the hope that people will seize it as an opportunity to repent and consequently find restoration and reconciliation.[249] Office, procedure, and objective together reveal that Paul is following a rational course.

But what evidence was there of Paul's *severitas*? None. To be sure 1 Cor 5:1-5 is harsh, but that is the voice of Paul who writes letters. Could he be so stern face-to-face? Failure to do so was a major part of Paul's problem. As we have seen, clemency is recognizable as such after a few people have been abused. Clemency must work with severity, not in its absence. This underscores Paul's need to emphasize that he would indeed punish. The threats contained in 2 Cor 10:1–13:10 indicate that Paul recognizes the contingent nature of clemency and in the face of intransigence will abandon that policy.

In the meantime, while *severitas* remained lacking, clemency was part of Paul's problem in Corinth. Was he clement or weak? The apostle's failure to enforce obedience among the Corinthians during his second visit looked to many like weakness, not leniency. It raised the question as to whether Paul really had any authority. The examples which we have already examined warn us that in such a situation, suspicion gathers and contempt grows. Moral suasion withers. Paul's reluctance to punish made him look like a weak coward more fit to flatter than lead. Unfortunately, such an impression was supported by other aspects of Paul's relationship with the Corinthians. Paul therefore had to rearrange the pieces of his persona before the eyes of the Corinthians to construct a positive image. He had to turn weakness into a positive token of authority. In the next chapter we will investigate that process in more detail.

---

[249] Rom 2:4 continues the perspective that withheld judgment affords the opportunity for repentance.

5. Conclusion

As for this chapter, we conclude that Paul's offer of clemency in 2 Cor 10:1 is in no way anomalous. It summarizes how he has treated the Corinthians. It reflects how he carries out his work of nurturing Christian faith and practice. It emulates a practice known in many other quarters of human life. Furthermore, the dynamics of Paul's lenient policies unfold with the motives and difficulties common to leniency in the Greco-Roman world. Paul therefore did not seek to undermine churches by handing down destructive penalties, but preferred to be lenient, hoping to lure the disobedient into repentance and subsequent restoration. This was a well-known policy and one which he pursued consistently.

Chapter 5

Paul's Self-Presentation in 2 Corinthians 10–13: Modest, Populist, and Antiencomiastic Rhetoric

> "Behold the beginning of philosophy! — a recognition of the conflict between the opinions of men, and a search for the origin of that conflict, and a condemnation of mere opinion, coupled with skepticism regarding it, and a kind of investigation to determine whether the opinion is rightly held, together with the invention of a kind of standard of judgment."
> Epictetus *Diss.* 2.11.13

We have argued that a semantic field appears throughout 2 Corinthians 10–13 which suggests that the most helpful translation of πραΰτης καὶ ἐπιείκεια in 2 Cor 10:1 is "leniency and clemency" (ch. 2). We have also argued that the ascription of "leniency and clemency" to Christ is appropriate in view of his present βασιλεία, reflecting aspects of his gracious and philanthropic rule (ch. 3). We have also seen that these virtues touch on matters relevant to many aspects of life in the ancient world and were not esoteric. They also played a role in Paul's pastoral ministry, including his earlier dealings with the Corinthians, and were integral to his present crisis (ch. 4). His invocation of these virtues in this passage fits into the *Sitz im Leben* of 2 Corinthians 10–13, as the Corinthians must have recognized (ch. 4). We will now explore how Paul's appeal "by the leniency and clemency of Christ" corresponds to the rhetoric of 2 Corinthians 10–13 as a whole, particularly as it relates to the image of himself that the apostle projects in this letter fragment.

This chapter addresses the fundamental problem for our reading of 2 Cor 10:1. If Paul acts as a person with ἐξουσία extending πραΰτης καὶ ἐπιείκεια, how can he in the same breath describe himself as ταπεινός? That Leivestad answered this question made his analysis of πραΰτης καὶ ἐπιείκεια persuasive. To repeat, however, Paul does not present himself as the kind of person who appears in Wis 2:19; thus, that parallel is invalid. Moreover, the conjunction of the nouns πραότης and ἐπιείκεια simply never connotes humility. That 2 Cor 10:1 is not an exception to this is clear from the semantic relationships between words throughout 2 Corinthians 10–13 which parallel common usage in other Greek texts which use πραότης and ἐπιείκεια. Recognition of the typical connotation of πραότης and ἐπιείκεια, however, makes all the more perplexing the fact that a person offering leniency admits to lowliness. How can this be?

The answer to this question forces us to examine more precisely what kind of person Paul presents himself as being. In the language of ancient rhetoric, what ἦθος does Paul project in 2 Corinthians 10–13? We shall see that Paul combines elements of modest rhetoric, populist politics, and countercultural philosophy to forge a persona which integrates both ἐξουσία and ταπεινότης.

In this chapter we will argue that a rhetoric of modesty provides the foundation for Paul's self-presentation in 2 Corinthians 10–13. As a species of popular appeal, modesty relates to things we have seen about clemency and leniency. Together populism and modesty stand in contrast to Paul's caricature of his rivals. But Paul takes modesty beyond simple moderation, combining it with a positive evaluation of lowliness. Although Paul ultimately grounded his affirmation of lowliness in christology, it is also significant that there was in antiquity a rhetoric of lowliness, developed in particular among Stoics and Cynics, a rhetoric which one may label Socratic, ironic, and paradoxical. This rhetoric, moreover, was connected to that of modesty via Socrates. Paul taps into this rhetoric to exploit its antiencomiastic potential in advancing his interpretation of apostolic and, consequently, Christian existence. As a result, Paul's modesty is not a friendly way to wear his authority in the church, but the very ground of his authority. As Christ's death yielded to God's power in resurrection, so Paul's weakness gives way to Christ's power.

The argument of this chapter will unfold as follows. First, to make the subject of Paul's self-presentation (*Selbstdarstellung*) less vague, we will approach it via the rhetorical category of ἦθος (§1). This move proves itself useful because it leads us to the category of ἐπιείκεια, i.e., modesty, which provides a coherent center for Paul's persona in 2 Corinthians 10–13. It also underscores Paul's antisophistic stance (§2). The investigation of modesty will also raise a stylistic problem, which, upon examination, connects Paul's rhetoric with that of Socrates in a blending of modesty and irony (§3). Paul's modest ἦθος, in fact, follows the development of a Socratic tradition into a countercultural rhetoric that calls into question the nature of virtue and wisdom. Such rhetoric undermines the normal criteria of human status and evaluation and helps Paul to undermine his rivals' superior credentials (§4). Paul's use of aggressive, biting irony, however, points us beyond Socratic irony and provides a clue that Paul projects a second persona in 2 Corinthians 10–13. In an exercise in ἠθοποιία Paul poses as a fool. The boasting and forcefulness of his Fool's Speech reflect the pose Paul adopted (§5). His own voice, however, is modest and relies on a paradoxical, Socratic irony which interprets lowliness and weakness as valuable conditions (§6). Such rhetoric supports Paul's fundamental argument that the Corinthians misunderstand Christ: to admire his rivals is to judge in a mundane manner and not in a manner guided by the divine spirit according to the pattern of Christ's obedience (§7).

Before turning to these things, we may consider how this chapter contributes to the discussion of 2 Corinthians 10–13. First, it further connects Paul's letter fragment to the Socratic tradition. Betz launched this enterprise, but the significance of his proposal has not been appreciated. Malherbe later analyzed the role of lowliness in the warfare of the Socratic philosopher, particularly in Antisthenes' lineage, and compared that with Paul's words in 10:1-6. Recent work on hardship catalogues also exposes connections with the Stoic and Cynic traditions. This chapter will show how the hardship catalogues and Malherbe's observations connect with the larger epistolary context and, moreover, will account for the connections Betz noted between Paul and the Socratic tradition. We offer here a framework which incorporates each of these previous studies into a single explanation for Paul's rhetorical strategy in 2 Corinthians 10–13. Second, this chapter investigates Paul's rhetoric from the perspective of ἦθος. Despite the explosion of rhetorical studies since the publication of Betz's work on Galatians, the rhetoric of ἦθος has not received sufficient appreciation. This chapter remedies this. Paying explicit attention to ἦθος in fact allows us to show how the work done by Betz and Malherbe may be integrated into a comprehensive study of Paul's rhetoric in this letter fragment.

1. Ethical Argumentation in Classical Rhetoric

To speak of Paul's self-presentation is nebulous. To speak instead of ἦθος lends rhetorical focus to the topic. Since, however, study of the New Testament from the perspective of Greco-Roman rhetoric has concentrated on form critical analysis, ἦθος remains underappreciated. The use of ἦθος in this study will help correct that. Given the lacuna, however, it is appropriate to ask what ethical argumentation in Greco-Roman rhetoric was. Such discussion will lend clarity to the term and suggest what ἦθος may provide as an analytical tool. What follows, moreover, will prove to be more than a perfunctory nod to thoroughness, because the use of ethical argumentation ran far ahead of rhetorical handbooks. While convention contributed much to ἦθος, individual finesse added a vital ingredient. Reliance on handbooks will not reveal the potential for creativity in an orator's presentation of himself or his client.

Three types of proof evolved in systems of classical rhetoric. Besides the arguments (e.g., enthymemes and examples) of the speech itself, the persuasive powers of ἦθος and πάθος were recognized.[1] The latter involved persuasion which resulted from the mental state of the audience, while the former looked to what the person (or persona) of the speaker contributed to the winning over of the audience. This simple scheme, however, obscures the fact that views on ἦθος varied over time with different theoreticians and practitioners. A brief overview of ἦθος in antiquity will suggest the variety of ways it could be discussed and implemented.

Looking at Aristotle's *Rhetorica* reveals problems associated with discussion of ἦθος. On the one hand, Aristotle makes four points about ἦθος: 1) it must arise from the speech itself and not be presupposed; 2) its goal is to render the speaker worthy of belief (ἀξιόπιστος), which 3) ἦθος does by displaying wisdom, virtue and goodwill (φρόνησις, ἀρετή, εὔνοια); and 4) ἦθος is the most powerful kind of proof (1.2.4). But each of these invites comment. As for the final point, we wish to emphasize it, for it may surprise the reader of rhetorical handbooks, since comparatively

---

[1] For handbook discussion, see Arist. *De rhet.* 1.1-1.2; 2.1-17; Cic. *De or.* 2.182-84; Quint. 6.2.8-19 (cf. Eckart Schütrumpf, "Non-Logical Means of Persuasion in Aristotle's *Rhetoric* and Cicero's *De oratore*," in *Peripatetic Rhetoric after Aristotle*, eds. William W. Fortenbaugh and David C. Mirhady, Rutgers University Studies in Classical Humanities 6 [New Brunswick: Transaction Publishers, 1994], 95-110; in the same volume, William W. Fortenbaugh, "Quintilian 6.2.8-9: *Ethos* and *Pathos* and the Ancient Tradition," 183-91; D. A. Russell, "Classicizing Rhetoric and Criticism: The Pseudo-Dionysian *Exetasis* and *Mistakes in Declamation*," in *Le classicisme a Rome. Aux I[ers] siècles avant et après J.-C.*, ed. Helmut Flashar, Entretiens sur l'antiquité classique 25 [Genève: Fondation Hardt, 1979], 113-34). On ἦθος in general, see W. Süss, *Ethos. Studien zu ältern griechischen Rhetorik* (Leipzig: Teubner, 1910); Jakob Wisse, *Ethos and Pathos: From Aristotle to Cicero* (Amsterdam: Adolf M. Hakkert, 1989); cf. L. Pernot, *La rhétorique de l'éloge*; more succinctly see Christopher Carey, "Rhetorical Means of Persuasion," in *Persuasion: Greek Rhetoric in Action*, ed. Ian Worthington (London: Routledge, 1994), 26-45; and articles in *Ethos: New Essays in Rhetorical and Critical Theory*, eds. James S. Baumlin and Tita French Baumlin (Dallas: Southern Methodist University Press, 1994). For application of ἦθος in analysis see, D. A. Russell, *Greek Declamation* (Cambridge University Press, 1983), 87-105; idem, "ἦθος in Oratory and Rhetoric," *Characterization and Individuality in Greek Literature*, ed. Christopher Pelling (Oxford University Press, 1990), 197-212; Graham Anderson, *The Second Sophistic: A Cultural Phenomenon in the Roman Empire* (London: Routledge, 1993), 216-33; on a larger scale, Maud W. Gleason, *Making Men: Sophists and Self-Presentation in Ancient Rome* (Princeton University Press, 1995).

little space is devoted to ἦθος. More important at present, we must stress that the middle points are inadequate. To say that ἦθος seeks to convey trustworthiness by displaying wisdom, virtue and goodwill understates greatly the complexity and variety which ἦθος may involve, or as Carey observes concisely, "Aristotle's list is incomplete."[2] As for the first point, it was debated. Though this is transparent, Isocrates confirms this, as he sees no problem with a person's reputation influencing a court appearance and even recommends it (*Ant.* 278, καλοκἀγαθός).[3]

Like Aristotle, Dionysius of Halicarnassus recognized ἦθος as one of the key elements of a speech (Τέχνη ῥητορική 11.396). He divided ἦθος into two types, the common, which philosophy provides to lead people to virtue and away from evil, and the individual, which is rhetorical in origin, responding to the exigencies of speaker, audience, purpose, and subject matter (11.397). For examples of the former ἤθη he refers the reader to literature for it illustrates justice and injustice, self-control and its complete absence, courage and timidity, wisdom and ignorance, gentleness (πρᾶος) and fits of anger. Particular ἤθη fall under the categories of nation, family, age, choices, fate, and occupation (11.400).

One area in which practice ran ahead of ethical theory was that of dramatic characterization. Despite Antiphon's lapse in providing a young and inexperienced man with a speech imbued with Gorgianic balance and assonance, most ghostwriters matched the speech to the voice of the person who would deliver it.[4] Lysias excelled at this. He used characterization "to confirm the speaker's version of his case by presenting an implied argument from probability; the implication, sometimes reinforced elsewhere in the speech by explicit argument, is that the character before the jury is incapable of behaving in the manner alleged."[5]

---

[2] Carey, "Rhetorical Means of Persuasion," 35.

[3] Aristotle's discussion of πάθος impinges on his views of ἦθος, raising questions about the relationship between *Rhet.* 1.1 and 2.1. In his Loeb volume, Freese offers an explanation (pp. 168-69 n. b). Fortenbaugh offers a more sophisticated explanation, utilizing source and redaction criticism ("Persuasion through Character and the Composition of Aristotle's *Rhetoric*," *Rheinisches Museum* 134 [1991]: 152-56). Arguments based on Aristotle's compositional habits are proposed by Eckart Schütrumpf ("Some Observations on the Introduction to Aristotle's *Rhetoric*," in *Aristotle's "Rhetoric": Philosophical Essays*, eds. David J. Furley and Alexander Nehamas [Princeton University Press, 1994], 99-116), Jürgen Sprute (117-28), and Mary Magaret McCabe ("Arguments in Context: Aristotle's Defense of Rhetoric," 129-65).

[4] Carey, "Rhetorical Means of Persuasion," 40.

[5] Carey, "Rhetorical Means of Persuasion," 42. Dramatic characterization can also be turned against opponents. For example, Carey points to the "shameless and relentless Simon of Lysias 3, the greedy and petty Diogeiton of Lysias 32 ... [and] the arch-

In Cicero we can see Roman influence on the practice of ἦθος. Enos and Schnakenberg boil down Ciceronian ἦθος to three basic traits: *ingenium* (or *natura*), *prudentia*, and *diligentia*, which together comprise the idea of *dignitas*.[6] By exhibiting *dignitas*, one accrued *auctoritas*, which resulted in *honor* and, in turn, *gloria*.[7] James May has elaborated more concretely on the diverse ethical strategies which Cicero adopted in his speeches. Surveying Cicero's career, May identifies three stages in Cicero's self-presentation, corresponding to the growth of his *auctoritas* and subsequent fate.[8] In his early speeches Cicero contends with opponents of greater dignity and status, requiring him to position himself "as the sympathetic underdog. The persona he projects is that of the young, somewhat inexperienced, yet intelligent and capable champion of the downtrodden, fighting in the face of unscrupulous influence and power."[9] As Cicero rose through public offices, the tables turned. He became the orator with extreme *auctoritas* and *dignitas* — and he exerted them. After his exile Cicero had to develop yet another rhetorical persona. He built this around his recall and deliverance of the state: "Cicero identifies himself with the state; the Republic becomes his advocate. He is the self-sacrificing patriot who offered himself as a *devotio* for the survival of Rome."[10] Cicero's self-presentation therefore evolved with his status, as he sought the most effective manner of persuasion.[11]

---

betrayer Alcibiades in Lysias 14" all of whom are "presented with a consistency and vividness which through intrinsic plausibility invite belief, irrespective of the degree of supporting evidence" (p. 43).

[6] Richard Leo Enos and Karen Rossi Schnakenberg, "Cicero Latinizes Hellenic Ethos," in *Ethos: New Essays in Rhetorical and Critical Theory*, eds. Baumlin and Baumlin, 197-201 and 201-5, respectively.

[7] *Ibid.*, p. 203.

[8] James M. May, *Trials of Character: The Eloquence of Ciceronian Ethos* (Chapel Hill: University of North Carolina Press, 1988). Cf. Katherine A. Geffcken, *Comedy in the Pro Caelio* (Leiden, 1973); Paul Prill, "Cicero in Theory and Practice: The Securing of Good Will in the *Exordia* of Five Forensic Speeches," *Rhetorica* 2 (1986): 93-109; Ann Vasaly, *Representations: Images of the World in Ciceronian Oratory* (Berkeley: University of California Press, 1993); William W. Batstone, "Cicero's Construction of Consular *Ethos* in the *First Catilinarian*," *TAPA* 124 (1994): 211-66; James M. May, "Patron and Client, Father and Son in Cicero's *Pro Caelio*," *CJ* 90 (1995): 433-41.

[9] May, *Trials of Character*, 164; cf. pp. 47-48.

[10] *Ibid.*, 164-65. May describes the function of Ciceronian ἦθος as follows: "The thrust or purpose of Cicero's presentation of character in almost every instance is to establish mutually exclusive, radically antithetical alternatives from which the jury can choose. On Cicero's side stand justice, truth, equity, the Republic, constitutionality, Rome herself; on the other side stand their opposites, injustice, falsehood, cupidity, the anti-Republican forces that by their actions and desires deny their *Romanitas* and seek to overthrow Rome. By presenting the judges with such mutually exclusive choices in a

While Quintilian's theory is less interesting than Cicero's practice,[12] Quintilian's theory nevertheless offers more insight into the content of ἦθος than does Aristotle's. Quintilian makes πάθος and ἦθος species of *adfectus*, distinguishing them based on the emotions they incite. The former concerns "the more violent emotions," the latter "those which are calm and gentle: in the one case the passions are violent, in the other subdued, the former command and disturb, the latter persuade and induce a feeling of goodwill" (6.2.9). The gentle emotions, he continues, are not "merely calm and mild (*mite ac placidum*), but in most cases ingratiating and courteous (*blandum et humanum*) and such as to excite pleasure and affection" (6.2.13). Such emotions require art and function subtly (6.2.10, 13). Emphasizing the emotional aspect of ἦθος like this heightens its relationship with πάθος.[13]

As for application, Quintilian offers more specific advice. Character, i.e., ἦθος, appears "whenever he [an orator] speaks of what is honorable and expedient or of what ought or ought not to be done" (6.2.11); it is relevant to apologies, pardons, and admonishment (6.2.14); and it is an appropriate label for stereotypes such as the rustic, miser, coward, or superstitious person (6.2.17). As these uses suggest and as Quintilian acknowledged, ἦθος is required in nearly every speech (6.2.10).

By way of illustrating how integral ἦθος was to persuasion, we may note a story in Philostratus. When Herodes' wife died in childbirth, her brother, Braduas, prosecuted Herodes on a murder charge. Braduas

was a very illustrious man of consular rank, and the outward sign of his high birth, a crescent-shaped ivory buckle, was attached to his sandal. And when Braduas appeared before the Roman tribunal he brought no convincing proof of the charge that he was making, but delivered a long panegyric on himself dealing with his own family. Whereupon Herodes jested at his expense and said: "You have your pedigree on your

---

disjunctive mode, he in reality allows no choice but to side with him and the forces of good and the Republic" (pp. 166-67). Arthur Robinson offers further insight into Cicero's self-presentation by demonstrating how he avoided the words *exsilium, exsul,* and *exsulo* when referring to his exile ("Cicero's References to His Banishment," *CW* 87 [1994]: 475-80).

[11] On distinctions between Aristotle and Cicero, see E. Schütrumpf, "Non-Logical Means of Persuasion," especially 109-110.

[12] In fact, Cicero exhibits "a knowledge of the potentialities of rhetorical ethos far beyond those found in his Hellenistic textbooks" (May, *Trials of Character*, 14; cf. p. 47).

[13] W. Fortenbaugh, "Quintilian 6.2.8-9," compares Dionysius of Halicarnassus' treatise on Demosthenes with Quintilian and infers they depend on a tradition of the early Peripatos (p. 185). Meanwhile, in the same volume, George A. Kennedy questions the more general degree to which Quintilian depended on Aristotle, "Peripatetic Rhetoric as It Appears (and Disappears) in Quintilian," 174-82.

toe-joints." And when his accuser boasted too of his benefactions to one of the cities of Italy, Herodes said with great dignity: "I too could have recited many such actions of my own in whatever part of the earth I were now being tried" (*Vit. soph.* 555-56).

Such a prosecution is utterly unpersuasive if the issue were to hinge only on facts and arguments. But expanding the facts to include that an illustrious person is making the accusation places ἦθος at the center of the controversy. Philostratus then outlines Herodes' defense in two parts. In ten words it is noted that simple facts support Herodes' innocence. Then ἦθος returns to the spotlight, as it melds with arguments based on probabilities so that the image of the grieving husband exonerates Herodes.

> For he never would have dedicated to her memory so fine a theater nor would he have postponed for her sake the casting of lots for his second consulship, if he had not been innocent of the charge; nor again would he have made an offering of her apparel at the temple of Eleusis, if he had been polluted by a murder when he brought it, for this was more likely to turn the goddesses into avengers of the murder than to win their pardon. He also altered the appearance of his house in her honor by making the paintings and decorations of the rooms black ... (556).

These tokens of affection and grief, then, provide clinching proof. For us they raise an interesting problem: what is the difference between ἦθος, πάθος and argumentation? In theory one may be able to distinguish them, but here each merges — indispensably — with the others.

In sum, characterization, i.e., ἦθος, can be applied to anyone connected with a rhetorical situation. One might therefore flatter the audience[14] or slander the opposition.[15] As for self-presentation, the speaker adopted the persona which would undermine his opponents (e.g., a simple person would not have committed a sinisterly clever crime). The constraints of a speech also influenced ἦθος. The need to draw a quick and unambiguous portrait required orators to construct personalities which would be "normally recognized types, not individuals seen in the round."[16] Social-historical constraints also influenced the role of ἦθος in speeches. Lysias, for example, wrote speeches for his clients to deliver themselves, requiring him to write in their voices, not his own (ἠθοποιία or

---

[14] Contrast Polemo's arrogance in failing to do so (Philos. *Vit. soph.* 535) with Alexander's appropriate panegyric (572).

[15] Cicero's *Philippics* offer splendid examples.

[16] D. A. Russell, "ἦθος in Oratory and Rhetoric," 198. Cf. William W. Fortenbaugh, "Theophrastus, the *Characters* and Rhetoric," in *Peripatetic Rhetoric after Aristotle*, 15-35. Dio Chrysostom recommended that civic leaders read Menander and Euripides: among other things, the former is skilled in the "portrayal of every character and every charming trait" (μίμησις ἅπαντος ἤθους καὶ χάριτας), while the latter fills his plays with ἤθη καὶ πάθη (18.5-7). Quintilian offers similar advice (10.1.68-70).

προσοποιία). In Rome the use of advocates meant that the orator used his own voice, resulting in the need to fashion an ἦθος for both himself and his client. Dramatic impersonation (again, ἠθοποιία or προσοποιία) also allowed for ethical creativity. The development of declamation opened the door even wider to ἦθος, as speakers wrote imaginary speeches for comic figures like the miser or old grump.[17] The entire custom of imitation in rhetorical education developed the possibilities of ἦθος, while instruction in encomia furnished *topoi* for ἦθος.[18] As a result of factors such as these, the practice of ἦθος ran far ahead of handbook theory.[19]

2. Paul's Ethical Argument: Modesty and Populism

The importance of how one presents oneself in rhetoric raises the question of how Paul does so in 2 Corinthians 10–13. What does an appeal by Christ's "leniency and clemency" do for Paul? How does this appeal correspond to the persona projected throughout the letter fragment? Each of these questions will be answered in turn. The observations about to be made will raise the larger question of whether they may be subsumed by some wider ethical category. Comparison with Hermogenes will answer affirmatively, pointing to the modest persona which in turn raises connections with the populism inherent in leniency and clemency. As we shall see, then, Paul draws on a commonplace rhetorical ἦθος in his self-presentation in 2 Corinthians 10–13, a "modest" persona not recognized so far in the scholarly literature on 2 Corinthians.

a. 2 Corinthians 10:1

As we begin now to examine 2 Cor 10:1, we can first observe that all of canonical 2 Corinthians indicates the importance of ethical argumentation. Sniping about changes of itinerary (1:15-17), strained interpersonal relationships (2:5), and issues of recommendation (3:1) and financial support all indicate that the problems in Corinth are not merely theological.[20] These issues all lead to questions surrounding Paul's

---

[17] D. A. Russell, *Greek Declamation*, 87-105. Philos. *Vit. soph.* 569 offers a eunuch.

[18] See in particular W. Süss, *Ethos*. More conveniently, recall the encomiastic categories outlined in chapter 3 in our discussion of the good king.

[19] Christopher Carey's survey of actual speeches demonstrates that ἦθος and πάθος permeate them, whereas handbooks associate them with particular portions of speeches, e.g., the exordium and peroration ("Rhetorical Means of Persuasion"). Cicero differs (*De or.* 2.310).

[20] Were the problems, in fact, only incidentally theological?

character: is he fickle, a swindler, a fraud, a braggart? Is he sincere?[21] In 2 Cor 10:10 in particular the problems receive an explicit formulation which looks directly at Paul's person. His apparent inconsistency makes him look like a fawning wind-bag — a fatal conclusion. Faced with such problems (and the rivals besides), Paul will need more than theology to regain the Corinthians' trust and affection. Ethical arguments will be crucial. Paul will not ignore them.

By appealing through Christ's πραΰτης καὶ ἐπιείκεια, Paul has done five things, some obvious, some subtle. First (and most obvious), Paul has wrapped himself in two good qualities. As it has become clear throughout this monograph, πραΰτης and ἐπιείκεια are good things; they are virtues. Their attribution to Christ makes them even more obviously excellent qualities. By framing his appeal to the Corinthians with Christ's virtues, Paul presents himself as their agent and champion. Christ's good rule is, therefore, modeled by his emissary, Paul, and extended to his people. In this way Paul lays a strong claim on the audience for their respect.

Second, by admiring Christ's virtues and then emulating them, Paul implicitly indicates his own virtue — without even boasting. This is similar to one of Plutarch's acceptable methods of self-praise: he recommends that people praise "others whose aims and acts are the same as their own and whose general character is similar" (*Mor.* 542c-d). Thus, before the issues of boasting are raised later in this fragment, Paul already scores points in his favor and without any overt recourse to self-praise.

An offer of clemency tied to Christ, however, yields a third ethical advance on Paul's part: clemency is offered by superiors. Positioning himself as a broker of Christ's clemency simultaneously positions Paul as a broker of Christ's authority. Paul's opening appeal finds him occupying the position which is in dispute, yet obliquely and winsomely, as he presents an image of himself as a philanthropic agent of Christ's rule.

Fourth, Paul's appeal as an imitation of Christ sets the stage for his following argument, particularly its christophanic (12:9-10) and christological (13:4) elements. By attributing leniency and clemency to Christ Paul has expanded the possible manifestations of Christ, making

---

[21] Hans Dieter Betz discusses the problem of Paul's inconsistency in light of the apostle's historical and cultural setting (*Der Apostel Paulus und die sokratische Tradition: Eine exegetische Untersuchung zu seiner "Apologie" 2 Korinther 10–13*, Beiträge zur historischen Theologie 45 [Tübingen: J. C. B. Mohr (Paul Siebeck), 1972], 19-39; cf. also 105, 113-16, and 135). See also Christopher Forbes, "Comparison, Self-Praise and Irony: Paul's Boasting and the Conventions of Hellenistic Rhetoric," *NTS* 32 (1986): 1-30. On the braggart, see also Douglas MacDowell, "The Meaning of ἀλαζών," in *'Owls to Athens': Essays on Classical Subjects Presented to Sir Kenneth Dover*, ed. E. M. Clark (Oxford University Press, 1990), 287-92.

restraint as equally christophanic as punishment, and in fact more so. If the Corinthians come around to his way of thinking, then they will recognize that what they have wanted to see has been evident all along — just in a different form.

Fifth, "leniency and clemency" allow Paul to mend his relationship with the Corinthians from a distance. As a person who prefers leniency, Paul's words naturally are more severe than his actions; moreover, his forceful epistolary demeanor seeks to make force unnecessary when he is present. The differences observed in Paul are then the result of the Corinthians' behavior, not a flaw in Paul's character. Any problem is therefore the fault of the Corinthians themselves, while Paul acts virtuously.

In combination, these five points lend Paul's defense a compelling introduction, in which he presents himself as the virtuous broker of Christ's authority — a clement authority. In a word, these observations offer ethical proof. Such methods of persuasion tend to be overlooked: in the hunt for propositions and proofs, the ethical form of argumentation can be missed. The preceding comments, on the other hand, indicate the utility of Paul's ἦθος in 2 Cor 10:1a.[22]

b. 2 Corinthians 10–13

Other ethical arguments relate to Paul's presentation of himself as lenient. First, Paul's offer of leniency indicates his preference not to harm the Corinthians. Quintilian notes that such a preference reflects goodwill. When he discusses ἦθος he says that, in cases of toleration, pardon or admonition, the moderation which a father shows a son (or a guardian a ward, or a husband a wife) flows directly from affection and should move the recipient deeply (6.2.14). If, then, 2 Corinthians 10:1–13:10 is the "letter of tears," Paul can describe it as a demonstration of his "love" (cf. 2:4) precisely because it contained one final offer of leniency and proved that punishment and fear were options of last resort. The "letter of reconciliation" would then indicate just how moving it was.

In 10:8 Paul characterizes his ἐξουσία as given by the Lord "for building up not tearing down." Not only does this further Paul's claim to love the Corinthians, but, second, it underscores that he aims for their good. The particular term, οἰκοδομή, is Paul's equivalent of the important rhetorical term (and strategy) συμφέρειν (1 Cor 10:23) and as such emphasizes Paul's intent to work for what is best for the Corinthians. This

---

[22] The ταπεινός-θαρρεῖν contrast in 10:1b is equally ethical, but will be discussed later; see §4.

connects specifically with Paul's offer of clemency by supplying its fundamental rationale. Commissioned to build up the church, Paul hesitates to punish because that would be counter-productive. On the other hand, a church which responds to his offer of leniency and repents corresponds best to Paul's apostolic commission. In ethical terms, Paul's commission requires his policy of leniency, which in turn demonstrates his commitment to work for the good of the Corinthians.[23]

Paul's faithfulness to the terms of his commission obtains additional ethical force as his argument unfolds in the following verses (12-18), where, third, he emphasizes his moderation and piety. As Betz has shown, Greek theological and anthropological ideas underlie Paul's argument in these verses.[24] He summarizes the context in which 10:11-12 should be read with the comment, "From the Delphic teaching it follows that a person and his work cannot be the 'measure' for himself. Plato therefore contradicts the sophists when he posits that 'the measure of all things is God.'"[25] In regard to vv. 13-15, Betz argues, "With the affirmation οὐκ εἰς τὰ ἄμετρα καυχᾶσθαι Paul has noted a fundamental principle of Greco-humanistic ethics. The Delphic maxim μηδὲν ἄγαν demands that people observe the measure imposed by the deity and therefore practice σωφροσύνη in contrast to ὕβρις."[26] Paul's respect for the limitations imposed on him by the "God of measurement" (v. 13) indicates a sober and appropriate self-understanding on his part. His explanation of his authority in v. 8 reflects this as well. Together, these ideas add to the profundity of Paul's offer of leniency and clemency. Not only are they the right things to do christologically and noble politically, but now they are the expression of σωφροσύνη and piety, the right things to do anthropologically.[27]

---

[23] Paul's description of his ἐξουσία implies a threat: if his authority is antithetical to καθαίρεσις, it must be exercised actively against what appears destructive.

[24] Betz, *Paulus und die sokratische Tradition*, 118-32; further amplification appears in pp. 138-48.

[25] Betz, p. 130: "Aus der delphischen Lehre folgt, daß nicht der Mensch und sein Werk 'Maß' für ihn selber sein kann. Plato stellt deshalb der sophistischen Deutung entgegen, daß 'das Maß aller Dinge der Gott sei.'"

[26] Betz, p. 131: "Mit der Versicherung οὐκ εἰς τὰ ἄμετρα καυχᾶσθαι hat Paulus wiederum einen fundamentalen Grundsatz der griechisch-humanistischen Ethik beachtet. Die delphische Maxime μηδὲν ἄγαν gebietet dem Menschen das Einhalten des von der Gottheit gesetzten Maßes und damit die Haltung der σωφροσύνη im Gegensatz zur ὕβρις."

[27] In the midst of this restraint, Paul has made a strong claim to respect. As the one who reached Corinth with the gospel, Paul was the one who founded Christ's ἐκκλησία in Corinth. Cicero labels the foundation or preservation of new states the most divine of human accomplishments (*De re publica* 1.12; 6.13). That his opinion is clearly self-

These hints of Paul's theological and anthropological wisdom also involve a comparison. As our quotation of Betz just indicated, opposite Paul's σωφροσύνη stands ὕβρις. Marshall has elaborated on Paul's characterization of his opponents as hybrists, indicating how fruitfully the concept can be applied to Paul's debate with the Corinthians.[28] Focusing more narrowly on our present text, Marshall posits that the implication of 10:12-18 is that Paul's "enemies acted with excess. Their behavior is blameworthy."[29] Paul's rhetoric has moved with clever stealth. While denying the validity of comparison, he has indeed made one. Again, the force of his words depends on the power of ἦθος. Paul's opponents are

---

serving does not change the fact that founder figures were greatly celebrated. Thus, in the midst of his prudent speaking, Paul places himself in an honored position. In keeping with prudence, however, Paul recognizes it as the dispensation of God. One of Plutarch's principles for acceptable self-speech is thereby followed (*Mor.* 542e-543a; likewise Quintilian 11.1.23).

[28] Peter Marshall, *Enmity in Corinth: Social Conventions in Paul's Relations with the Corinthians*, Wissenschaftliche Untersuchungen zum Neuen Testament, 2. Reihe, 23 (Tübingen: J. C. B. Mohr [Paul Siebeck], 1987), 178-218, 349, 364-81. Marshall agrees with Betz that Paul paints his opponents as hybristic, but takes greater pains than Betz to describe ὕβρις, defining it more broadly than Betz (pp. 366-67). On ὕβρις see now the extensive study by N. R. E. Fisher, *Hybris: A Study in the Values of Honour and Shame in Ancient Greece* (Warminster: Aris and Phillips, 1992): "*hybris* is essentially the serious assault on the honor of another, which is likely to cause shame, and lead to anger and attempts at revenge" (p. 1); more succinctly, it is "outraged honor" (p. 1; cf. p. 148). Fisher seeks to expand the commonplace notion which restricts ὕβρις to offenses against the gods (p. 2). To think of ὕβρις as "the deliberate infliction of shame and dishonor" then is to accept Aristotle's definition as "essentially correct" (p. 493). Note, however, Douglas L. Cairns' caveats that Fisher inadequately defines the categories honor and shame; moreover, Fisher emphasizes acts of ὕβρις at the expense of dispositional ὕβρις, e.g., high-mindedness (*CR* 44 [1994]: 76-79). Arthur Adkins criticizes Fisher on semantic grounds: Fisher attempts to find a "focal meaning" for ὕβρις relevant to all its uses; as a result, he is insensitive to connotation and the interaction of ὕβρις with other words and ideas (*CJ* 90 [1995]: 451-55). Cf. Ruth Padel, *Whom Gods Destroy: Elements of Greek and Tragic Madness* (Princeton University Press, 1995), 197-209; Sir Hugh Lloyd-Jones, "Honour and Shame in Ancient Greek Culture," in *Greek Comedy, Hellenistic Literature, Greek Religion, and Miscellanea: The Academic Papers of Sir Hugh Lloyd-Jones* (Oxford University Press, 1990), 253-80.

[29] Marshall, *Enmity in Corinth*, 271. Jon D. Mikalson offers an interesting parallel to the discussions of Betz and Marshall, as he shows how piety, folly, σωφροσύνη, and ὕβρις cluster together in the tragic tradition (*Honor Thy Gods: Popular Religion in Greek Tragedy* [Chapel Hill: University of North Carolina Press, 1991], 179-83). Among Mikalson's examples are Aeschylus *Persians* 749-51; Sophocles *Antigone* 1348-53; Euripides *Hippolytus* 6; *Heraclidae* 387-88. Cf. Plut. *Mor.* 157b.

5.2. Paul's Ethical Argument 271

hybrists: theologically and anthropologically irresponsible, and socially dangerous.[30]

Fisher's research on ὕβρις amplifies its social dimension. He notes that complaints of ὕβρις typically issue from weaker people who complain about the behavior of their social superiors: "in almost all of our texts ὕβρις is seen as above all the fault of the rich and powerful."[31] Even in examples "where the litigants deploying the accusations of ὕβρις are demonstrably or probably from the wealthy and or political classes, they identify their interests with those of the poorer majority."[32] This suggests, then, with whom among the Corinthian Christians Paul wished to identify himself, namely, the same weak, ignoble, and contemptible people he championed in 1 Corinthians. At the same time, this cluster of ideas suggests part of Paul's problem. Although Paul identified with the weak and portrayed his rivals as overbearing, his opponents did at least conduct themselves with the superior bearing appropriate to their (explicit or implicit) claims to power. The typical ὕβρις shown by the rich to other people "consists of abusive language, contumely, ridicule, and often a blow"; towards Fortune they show ὑπερηφανία, βαρύτης, and μικρολογία (Dio Chrys. 65.7). Among sophists "high-handedness constituted an assertion of professional superiority."[33] Paul then positions himself in opposition to such behavior.

Juxtaposition of ὕβρις with leniency and clemency, then, allows Paul to make a fourth significant ethical statement in his favor. In an implied σύγκρισις in 11:20, Paul focuses his sight on his opponents: "someone makes slaves of you, or preys upon you, or takes advantage of you, or puts on airs, or gives you a slap in the face" (NRSV).[34] Recalling our

---

[30] While I agree with Marshall's comments on ὕβρις, I hesitate to label Paul's opponents "hybrists." To do so is to rely too heavily on Paul's rhetoric. Just because Paul wants them viewed as hybristic, does not mean that hybristic meaningfully describes them. Nevertheless, Marshall provides significant insight into Paul's rhetoric.

[31] Fisher, *Hybris*, 497; see pp. 494-98.

[32] *Ibid.*, 496.

[33] Maud Gleason, *Making Men*, 52.

[34] See Furnish, 497; Martin, 364. Noteworthy intratextual connections are 1) εἴ τις λαμβάνει in 11:20 and Paul's ironic assertion in 12:16, δόλῳ ὑμᾶς ἔλαβον; 2) εἴ τις ἐπαίρεται and the evil ὕψωμα which ἐπαιρόμενον κατὰ τῆς γνώσεως τοῦ θεοῦ, for which Paul has the remedy, καθαίρεσις (10:4-5); moreover, Paul's "thorn in the flesh" serves to keep him from being ὑπεραίρεσθαι; and 3) the broader issue of remuneration resonates in these charges. The reference to slapping the cheek is problematic. Is it to be taken literally or figuratively? On the literal side, we may refer to Philos. *Vit. soph.* 578, which reports about a sophist who interrupted his speech to slap the face of an audience member who had fallen asleep. But would a literal slap constitute a psychagogical method or simply signify the superiority of the aggressor? On the slap see Isoc. *In Loch.*

discussion of kingship in chapter three, these are the traits of the tyrant; Paul might have used just as easily the abstract nouns ὕβρις, ὑπερηφανία and πλεονεξία. Paul's use of verbs, however, is more emotive and damning. While they behave like tyrants and look out for themselves, Paul exercises his own office in imitation of the good king Christ and worries about the good of the Corinthians. Unlike their oppressive treatment of the Corinthians, Paul bears his authority gently. Paul effectively has invoked centuries of political thinking to commend himself and slander his opponents.

The contrast between Paul's good leadership and his opponents' tyranny also provides a new frame for viewing the dispute about financial support. Whereas the matter is first of all a social one and a question of friendship,[35] Paul's assertion of leniency creates a self-presentation which depicts him as exercising his ἐξουσία in noble fashion. By drawing attention to his opponents' ὕβρις, ὑπερηφανία, and πλεονεξία, he casts them in the role of people who use ἐξουσία or δύναμις selfishly. Such characters allow a different picture of the argument over money to be conducted. Paul is now the responsible leader, a father in fact, who will not be a financial burden to the Corinthians, while his rivals exploit them.

In addition to the five ethical aspects of Paul's appeal in 10:1, then, we have traced four broader connections between Paul's leniency and his self-presentation in the larger letter fragment. Paul's offer of clemency expresses (1) his love, (2) his prudent policy-making, and (3) his general σωφροσύνη and piety, while (4) contrasting him with his overly assertive, hybristic, grasping rivals. These relationships do not emerge accidentally, the mere result of proximity, but reflect a greater whole. *The data which we have just surveyed fit together as specimens of modest rhetoric which has a populist appeal.* To schematize the relationship between modesty and populism, I would say that modesty (the rhetorical technical term for which is ἐπιείκεια) is a species of populism, which provides the social rationale for the resulting rhetoric. Given the rhetorical focus of this chapter, however, the following pages will focus on modesty rather than the more general populism. We will now turn to references to ἐπιείκεια in ancient discussions of ἦθος to support our present thesis.

c. ἐπιείκεια as ἦθος: modesty and populism

Ancient discussions of ἦθος referred commonly to ἐπιείκεια, taking advantage of its wide range of meaning. Aristotle provides the first

---

3-5; Mus. Ruf. Γράφην ὕβρεως, frg. 10 Lutz; Sen. *De ira* 2.32-33; Hans Dieter Betz, *Sermon on the Mount*, Hermeneia (Minneapolis: Fortress Press, 1995), 289.

[35] Marshall, *Enmity in Corinth*, 165-258.

example, stating that "we feel confidence in a greater degree and more readily in" people who are ἐπιεικεῖς (*Rhet.* 1.2.4; cf. 2.1.6), thereby asserting the value of ethical argumentation. While Paul's offer of ἐπιείκεια appears to correspond perfectly to Aristotle's advice, we will not blur the difference between the two writers. Aristotle uses ἐπιεικές broadly as equivalent to gentleman (καλὸς κἀγαθός), whereas Paul uses ἐπιείκεια more narrowly as clemency; therefore, 2 Cor 10:1 is not a perfect echo of Aristotle. But the character of the ἐπιεικές person implied qualities which subsequent rhetoricians articulated. Paul's offer of clemency is part of a wider range of traits which he displays and which correspond to the ἐπιεικές individual.

Aristotle's use of ἐπιεικές participated in a centuries' long discussion of ἦθος.[36] This is clear in Dionysius of Halicarnassus' analysis of Lysias' powers of oratory, as he praises Lysias' skill in ἠθοποιία (*Lysias* 8).

I think he furnishes ethical proofs exceptionally well, for he endows his characters with such credibility (ἀξιόπιστα), based often on the course of their lives and natures, often on earlier deeds and moral preferences. When, however, events afford no such opportunity, he sketches their characters (ἐθοποιεῖ) himself, using speech to construct reliable and upright (πιστὰ καὶ χρηστά) figures: he attributes to them urbane dispositions, confers moderate emotions (πάθη μέτρια), attributes reasonable thoughts (λόγους ἐπιεικεῖς), introduces them as people who are mindful of their assigned places in life, makes them out to be distressed by injustice — both in words and deeds — while consciously opting for what is just, and supplies everything similar to these things, from which a person's ἦθος may appear reasonable and measured (ἐπιεικές καὶ μέτριον).[37]

In these words, we hear Dionysius echo Aristotle's use of ἀξιόπιστος and ἐπιεικές, while paralleling his close association of πάθος and ἦθος. In this passage, however, Dionysius chooses to sketch more precisely than did Aristotle how the good ἦθος may be ἐπιεικές. Thus, the characteristics which Dionysius enumerates reflect Aristotle's gentleman, but much more explicitly. This amplification is precisely what shifts the meaning of ἐπιεικές from a general ("gentleman") to a more precise referent ("reasonable"), as its combination with μέτριος indicates. Thus, the use of ἐπιείκεια in discussions of ἦθος introduced specific descriptive possibilities which unfolded in subsequent centuries.

Hermogenes illustrates this even more clearly than Dionysius. In Hermogenes' essay Περὶ ἰδεῶν (*On Types of Style*), he offers seven types

---

[36] Dieter Hagedorn, *Zur Ideenlehre des Hermogenes*, Hypomnemata 8 (Göttingen: Vandenhoeck & Ruprecht, 1964), 59-65. Though Hagedorn traces a much larger evolution than we are interested in pursuing, his argument includes this smaller observation.

[37] *Lysias* 19; my trans. These ideas add ethical force to Paul's words in 2 Cor 10:12-16, which received comment above.

of style, one of which is ἦθος.[38] As a subcategory of ἦθος we find ἐπιείκεια (345-52).[39] Hermogenes divides his discussion of ἐπιείκεια into content and form, identifying four ways to express ἐπιείκεια by one's ideas (or thoughts) and three ways by one's style. As for the former, Hermogenes writes, "A passage that reveals a modest character is produced mainly by the thought and is created whenever anyone states that of his own free will he is aiming at less than he could attain" (345). To settle for less than is one's due is for Hermogenes the essence of ἐπιείκεια. Second, he adds, "The same effect is produced whenever anyone equates himself with the average man (οἱ πολλοί) although that is not really true" (345). Third, "it is modest to grant some point to one's opponent willingly" (345). Lastly, ἐπιείκεια appears when "you say that you are going to trial against your will and that you have come to court only because you have been compelled to do so by your opponent, whereas the matter should have been settled among friends and relatives" (346). Because the examples by which Hermogenes illustrates these four points reflect their application to prosecution,[40] he then points out that they can be used in defense as well. Thus, one can argue

that he is being prosecuted although he himself could have prosecuted his opponent and that his opponent feels contempt for him because he is a good citizen and a man of the common people (οἱ πολλοί) and that he himself has never brought a charge against anyone and has even now come into court unwillingly (347).

In Hermogenes' list of typical expressions of ἐπιείκεια, then, Aristotle's recommendation of an ἐπιεικές self-presentation has gone beyond Dionysius' articulation of the ἐπιεικές person's general qualities to specific features of rhetorical content and form.

Hermogenes' identification of these ethical *topoi* is not original, but parrots rhetorical tradition. Dionysius of Halicarnassus analyzes a speech of Lysias in which the speaker opens with what Hermogenes would call a modest ἦθος. Dionysius comments that the prooemium "has all the virtues that an introduction ought to have, as a comparison with the rules in the handbooks will show" (*Lysias* 24). Dionysius then recites a litany of *topoi* which appear in Lysias' speech. These parallel the *topoi* which Hermogenes attributes to ἐπιείκεια/modesty. At the end of Dionysius' list of *topoi* he concludes, "These are the themes recommended by the

---

[38] Greek text: Hugo Rabe, ed., *Hermogenis Opera* (Leipzig: Teubner, 1913; Stuttgart: Teubner, 1985); Eng. trans.: Cecil W. Wooten, *Hermogenes' On Types of Style* (Chapel Hill: University of North Carolina Press, 1987). Reference numbers indicate Rabe's page numbers.

[39] Wooten translates ἐπιείκεια as Modesty; we will defer to him in our discussion of Hermogenes. (In Wooten's translation he capitalizes rhetorical technical terms.)

[40] Hermogenes' examples of ἐπιείκεια typically come from Demosthenes.

rhetorical theorists in order to make the litigant appear more fair-minded (ἐπιεικέστερον) than his opponent; for this can secure the goodwill (εὔνοιαν) of the jury, which is the most important function of the argument here" (*Lysias* 24). What we encounter in Hermogenes is, then, a typical constellation of ideas relevant to rhetorical self-presentation which takes the label of ἐπιείκεια.

Turning to Paul, we can observe that on the whole his strategy has remarkable similarities to Hermogenes' suggestions. That Paul "is aiming at less than he could attain" is the very essence of his argument about clemency, which he predicates precisely on the threat that he could act more forcefully than he has, but chooses to restrain himself. That his reference to his ταπεινότης encompasses his refusal to act on his right to financial support further shows that he accepts less than is his due. Paul emphasizes this when he characterizes his practice as refusing to burden them (11:9). "Aiming at less than he could attain" also summarizes the restraint shown by Paul's actions in contrast to his rivals who exert themselves fully (11:20). Paul's rhetoric also parallels Hermogenes' second means of expressing ἐπιείκεια, as he identifies himself with the common person. His self-reference as ταπεινός (10:1) suggests this, while 11:6 reinforces it: accused of contemptible speech, Paul aligns himself with the masses as an ἰδιώτης (11:6). Paul is explicit about this identification in 11:29: "Who is weak and I am not weak?" Third, Paul concedes his opponents' accusations. Perhaps he did boast a bit too much about his ἐξουσία (10:8). Perhaps his letters and presence have not matched. He embraces ταπεινότης. And, yes, as an orator he is an ἰδιώτης, a concession which is indeed a commonplace of modesty.[41] Paul does not deny these charges. As for denying the desire to appear in court,

---

[41] The posturing of such an admission must not be ignored. Dio Chrysostom also called himself a rhetorical ἰδιώτης, precisely to align himself with the οἱ πολλοί (*Or.* 12.16; 32.39; 47.8; cf. 35.1). Socrates made a similar move (Plato *Apol.* 17) as had Gorgias before him (*Palamedes* = Diels-Kranz frg. 11a) and Isocrates afterward (*Ant.* 26-27); also Demosthenes *Or.* 44.1-4; 55.2; Isaeus *Or.* 10.1; above we noted Cicero; Quin. 11.1.19-20. The opposite move is to label the opposition eloquent and warn of the danger that poses (e.g., Demosthenes *Or.* 27.1-2; 46.1; 52.1). What therefore 2 Cor 11:6 tells us about the quality of Paul's rhetoric cannot be stated precisely. Betz rightly traces the place of this *topos* in the debates between philosophy and sophistic (*Paulus und die sokratische Tradition*, 59-67) and concludes that Paul's concession was recognizable as a *topos* from the Socratic tradition (p. 66). We should add, however, that the *topos* is not simply Socratic, but is more generally a commonplace of rhetoric — which Betz himself notes (p. 64). Pogoloff offers a helpful, nuanced discussion of ἰδιώτης (*Logos and Sophia*, 148-52), though I wonder whether in some ways he has fallen victim to the *topos*. His observations serve as reminder, however, that to label ἰδιώτης a *topos* does not mean that everyone uses it in the same manner.

this *topos* does not apply precisely to Paul's situation. We see some similarity, however, when he stresses his distaste for the whole enterprise of self-recommendation and self-defense and thinks that these should be unnecessary.[42] His offer of clemency also parallels the disuse of court *topos* for it rests on the preference to forgive.[43] His disavowal of rivalry and jealousy toward his opponents (e.g., 10:12-13; 11:2-4) also reflects another application of modesty *topoi*;[44] similarly, one might point to the necessity which compels one to speak,[45] or more particularly, the opponent's τόλμη.[46] Paul's attitudes, then, reflect those of a person who does not frequent the courts and so does not have a litigious disposition.[47] As for Hermogenes' quick suggestion for how one applies these approaches to a defense speech, Paul's self-characterization as lenient transforms his enemies' scorn into contempt for virtue. His acceptance of ἰδιώτης and ταπεινότης makes the accusations against him a matter of contempt for the common man. And, as the subsequent actions of the Corinthians toward the offender (ὁ ἀδίκησας) revealed, Paul could have "prosecuted" his slanderer rather than pass over him in (relative) silence. It would appear then that in ethical matters Paul's self-presentation

---

[42] Paul is explicit about this in his earlier letter at 3:1-2 and implicit in 11:6 and 12:19 (reading these latter two texts in line with Betz, *Paulus und die sokratische Tradition*): Socrates' whole life demonstrated the falsity of the charges against him, whereas rhetorical histrionics could not get at truth.

[43] Lysias *Or*. 10.1-3; 32.1.

[44] Lysias *Or*. 31; cp. 3.40. In Demosthenes *Exordia* 13 he presents himself as an ἰδιώτης and one of the οἱ πολλοί and notes how his opposition to eminent speakers might seem to some to be ἐπίφθανον. Cf. Cicero's disavowal of motives of rivalry in his first speech against Catilina (1.5).

[45] Lysias *Or*. 3.3; 12.3.

[46] Lysias *Or*. 3.1, 20, 40; 16.8 (here, though, the speaker is not modest); 31.1; Isaeus *Or*. 8.1-5. Cf. Isocrates' similar uses of τόλμη: *In Cal*. 7, 16, 22, 23, 24, 26, 29, 38, 56; *In Loch*. 4, 8, 21. These passages raise the question of what exactly Isocrates means when he cites an inadequate voice and lack of τόλμη as his reasons for avoiding public speaking (*Pan*. 10; *Phil*. 81; *Ep*. 1.9; 8.7). Does he refer to poise and self-confidence or does τόλμη have a pejorative connotation? Although *Pan*. 9 points to the former, Isocrates' subsequent comments suggest the latter: "the majority of the orators have the audacity to harangue the people (δημηγορεῖν τολμῶντας), not for the good of the state, but for what they themselves expect to gain" (12). In *Phil*. 81, τόλμη is needed to deal with the mob and trade insults. This pejorative connotation helps to mitigate Isocrates' inadequacy.

[47] At a general level, Paul's instructions in 1 Cor 6:1-8 correspond to the rhetorical *topos* of unfamiliarity with the courts, for he regards it as shameful for Christians to settle their disputes in a public, civil forum. (Matters of ethnic identity and philosophical considerations about virtue also impinge on Paul's ideas in 1 Corinthians 6.)

throughout 2 Corinthians 10–13 corresponds well to Hermogenes' description of ἐπιείκεια.

That Paul presents a persona with so many points of contact with Hermogenes' handbook is not as surprising as it may at first appear for he is defending himself. In general, such rhetoric required discussion of events which featured the speaker and in formulating arguments based on probabilities which hinged on the speaker's character; appealing for pity likewise required speaking about oneself. In narration, proof, and peroration, then, speakers had to present themselves as good people. Such self-speech, however, could annoy people or, even worse, arouse jealousy. This dilemma was exacerbated by the broader cultural patterns of competitive self-display, for, despite its odium, self-praise was common.

This need to speak about oneself inoffensively inspired "how-to" treatises. Plutarch wrote an essay on the topic, while Quintilian and Hermogenes treated the subject in their rhetorical handbooks.[48] Plutarch offered nearly a dozen suggestions about how to praise oneself inoffensively. For example, victims of slander, accusations, or injustice are free to speak out in their defense, as may the unfortunate (540c-541e). He also suggests that a speaker can avert jealousy by mentioning the labors and dangers involved in one's accomplishments (544c-d). Quintilian agreed that mounting a defense could require self-praise, but suggested mitigating its effrontery by emphasizing the necessity which compelled it in order "to throw the odium attaching to such a proceeding on the man who had forced [the speaker] to it" (11.1.22). Sharing credit for one's success with others or with the gods also makes self-praise more palatable. Both Plutarch and Quintilian, then, recognize the necessity which one faces in self-defense, as well as methods of maintaining some decorum while boasting. These latter indicate that modesty and boasting are not mutually exclusive. Modesty does preclude the possibility of boasting, but may help to make self-praise acceptable. That Paul feels compelled to boast, then, motivates a modest self-presentation, for it offsets the offense which boasting entails. That Paul more broadly presents himself as moderate, the ταπεινός vessel of divine power, and the clement possessor of Christ's ἐξουσία corresponds nicely with the constraints of modesty and the mitigation of self-praise. In fact, we should expect a modest persona.

Two matters, however, complicate congratulating Paul for anticipating Hermogenes' advice. First, we must address the semantic problem. Is

---

[48] On Plutarch and Quintilian, see Betz, *Paulus und die sokratische Tradition*, 75-78; idem, "De laude ipsius (Moralia 539A-547F)," in *Plutarch's Ethical Writings and Early Christian Literature*, ed. idem, SCHNT 4 (Leiden: E. J. Brill, 1978), 367-93; Christopher Forbes, "Comparison, Self-Praise and Irony," 8-10.

"leniency and clemency" the same thing as "modesty," that is to say, do Paul and Hermogenes use ἐπιείκεια in the same way? Before answering this question, however, we must raise a methodological problem: although we attempt to avoid semantic overload, Hermogenes was less careful. This appears clearly in his discussion of δεινότης, where his use of the word slides back and forth between noetic facility ("clever") and rhetorical effect ("forceful").[49] As for his discussion of ἐπιείκεια, Hermogenes invokes Plato's definition. The latter, however, discusses ἐπιείκεια in a legal sense, i.e., ἐπιείκεια as equity, the fair and kindhearted application of the law. This is different from a rhetorical persona. Thus, Hermogenes sees a kernel of stable meaning in words and ignores differing connotations. We therefore face the problem of working with precision on material which is not precise. If we follow Hermogenes' example, all we need is the use of ἐπιείκεια to suggest the relevance of an attendant (perhaps intrinsic) ἦθος.

If we attempt to be more precise semantically, however, we must raise the question whether Paul and Hermogenes use ἐπιείκεια in mutually exclusive ways. In Hermogenes' examples ἐπιείκεια describes the person who does not rashly flood the courts with frivolous litigation, nor is vindictive and mean-spirited in prosecution. What such a person prosecutes must (presumably) be important and worthy of the jury's attention; moreover, such a person can be trusted not to exaggerate, but to be fair. This forensic focus is also apparent in Hermogenes' (previously quoted) advice on demonstrating ἐπιείκεια in defense speeches. Paul's use of ἐπιείκεια, however, appears not in his non-use of courts, but in his non-use of ἐξουσία. Paul, therefore, demonstrates his ἐπιείκεια from a different point of reference than Hermogenes. Still, Hermogenes' definition that a person "of his own free will" aims "at less than he could attain" can apply equally to each situation. The question is this: How different is hesitance to prosecute from hesitance to extend sanctions? Both involve forbearance and foregoing one's rights. Both may involve forgiveness. Again, they differ primarily with respect to point of reference. Looking beyond Hermogenes to examples of the non-use of courts in speeches confirms this view. We can find many claims in the speeches of Lysias and Demosthenes that the speaker would prefer to avoid appearing in court, for to air one's infelicities in public is shameful.[50] The alternative

---

[49] This imprecision occurs despite Hermogenes' lengthy argument about the meaning of δεινότης as a rhetorical term! In fact, Hermogenes argues for a minority position (372).

[50] Lysias 3.1-3, 9, 20, 30, 40; 7.1; 10.1-3; 12.3; 17.1; 31.1-2; 32.1; Demosthenes 26.1-3; 27.1-2; 29.1-3; 48.1-4; 54.1-2. In Aeschines Κατὰ Τιμάρχου he is concerned to be μέτριος (1 and 3), which he proves by his refusal to bring indictments against any one

course of action would have been to forgive the wrongdoing, preferring perhaps a financial loss to the loss of public esteem.[51] This attitude reflects various nuances of ἐπιείκεια nicely: it reflects the modesty which shuns litigiousness, while also expressing the leniency which indulges and forgives. Thus, while Paul's use of ἐπιείκεια has a more precise meaning than does Hermogenes', many of the word's associations overlap in the two authors.

Ultimately, though, comparison of Hermogenes and Paul rests on the content of what each says, not the potentially accidental use by each of ἐπιείκεια. In my opinion, the ideas we have just surveyed warrant the comparison made and justify the identification of Paul's ἦθος as modest.

Turning to the second issue, style, we encounter both correspondence and dissimilarity. As for the former, Hermogenes recommends minimizing one's advantages and accomplishments (347-48); Paul's protestations against boasting align him with this inclination. Similarly, Hermogenes also lists παράλειψις as appropriate to ἐπιείκεια, i.e., purposely omitting a relevant fact, with or without mentioning it.[52] The teasing mention of signs and wonders in 12:12 seems to function in this manner, as Paul suggests he could meet his opponents' credentials head-on but refrains — although, as 10:1–12:11 indicates, he finds such arguments inappropriate and irrelevant. Paul's reticence about the offender (ὁ ἀδικήσας) may also be an example of παράλειψις.[53]

"The third approach that is typical of Modesty" relates to diction: one "must speak in a style that gives the impression of being very simple, the sort of style that someone who is quite unskilled in the rules of rhetoric would understand" (352). This matter of style is extremely complex. Without analyzing 2 Corinthians 10–13, we can note the verdict already passed on Paul's rhetoric in 10:10: it is contemptible. Paul's concession that he is an ἰδιώτης allows this verdict to stand. The rejection of rhetorical apology together with Paul's implied oath in 12:19 add to the picture of simplicity. Should Paul's style contradict his claims, this would

---

prior to this case. Thus, the overlap of ἐπιείκεια and μετριότης extends to the connotation of modesty as well as forbearance and forgiveness. Cp. Demosthenes 48.1-4: prior to coming to court, the accuser had offered "reasonable (μέτρια) and fitting terms."

[51] Again, cf. 1 Cor 6:1-8.

[52] To mention that one is not mentioning something is actually classified as irony in *Rhet. Alex.* 1434a/21; cf. the example offered in 1436b/29.

[53] I refer to 2 Cor 2:5-11; 7:12 and, again, assume that those verses were written after 2 Cor 10:1–13:10.

not alter the explicit claims to simplicity.[54] Meanwhile, aspects of simple style do appear in 2 Corinthians 10–13.[55]

Against these parallels between Hermogenes and Paul stands Hermogenes' comment on irony: "Ironic passages ... are not modest. Such passages do reveal Character, but they are indignant rather than modest" (348). In other words, irony is too vehement for ἐπιείκεια. Paul's use of irony therefore seems to contradict stylistically Hermogenes' notion of an ethical presentation of ἐπιείκεια. But this does not necessarily negate our previous observations.

The goal of a speech is not to present an ἦθος, but to persuade. Thus, "Modesty" is subservient to "Forcefulness" (δεινότης, a clever and effective rhetoric). Hermogenes opens his discussion of δεινότης, saying,

> In my opinion Force in a speech is nothing other than the proper use of all the kinds of style previously discussed and of their opposites and of whatever other elements are used to create the body of a speech. To know what technique must be used and when and how it should be used, and to be able to employ all the kinds of style and their opposites and to know what kinds of proofs and thoughts are suitable ... seems to me to be the essence of true Force (368).

The aspect of Force, therefore, changes the question from whether Paul followed slavishly a handbook idea to whether his rhetoric was successful. It reminds us that important as ἐπιείκεια is in Paul's self-presentation, it is only one aspect of his argument.[56]

---

[54] Dionysius of Halicarnassus criticizes a speech by Isaeus because he makes claims to simplicity but uses too artful a style (*Isaeus* 10-11). The function of Hermogenes' criterion can be filled in by Dionysius of Halicarnassus, when he compares Lysias and Isaeus. The former writes so naturally that what he says seems transparently true, whereas Isaeus uses such obvious art that one becomes suspicious that perhaps he hides the truth (*Isaeus* 16; cp. 4). This aspect of simplicity links our observations on Paul's rhetoric with Betz's analysis of Paul's rhetoric as antisophistic (*Paulus und die sokratische Tradition*).

[55] Hermogenes' examples of simple style include the expression of obvious thoughts (322; cp. 227), use of definite details as opposed to general abstractions (326), the use of oaths (326), and loose word order (329).

[56] Cicero illustrates this. In private speech, Cicero advises avoiding anger in reproof in favor of a clement approach combined with earnestness. What harshness is necessary must accompany a transparent concern for the good of the one criticized (*De off.* 1.137). Looking to the courts, Cicero recommends that an advocate show a mild tone and gentle language, modesty, uprightness, and piety; moreover, he should not be grasping, hasty, stubborn, harsh, or contentious (*De or.* 2.182-84). Such a self-presentation conciliates people, winning over their goodwill. Like Hermogenes, Cicero sees a key ethical strategy in "the faculty of seeming to be dealing reluctantly and under compulsion" (2.182). While these things parallel 2 Corinthians 10–13 nicely, the tone and bearing which Cicero expects to accompany modesty is unlike the charged tone of Paul's rhetoric. Yet Cicero recognizes that mild and emotional speech "have something in

Turning from this theoretical consideration to specific examples further contradicts Hermogenes' view. In his speech against Eratosthenes, Lysias presented himself modestly as someone unaccustomed with law courts (*Or.* 12.2), whose inexperience might prove no match for his opponents' skill (12.86). In his presentation he contradicts our attitudes toward modesty and recounts his benefactions in order to underscore his undeserved fate (12.20-22); in the process, he contradicts Hermogenes' view of modesty by resorting to sarcasm (12.20). In another (spurious) oration, the speaker likewise opens with a modesty *topos*, as he complains about how grievous it is to speak publicly of his affairs (*Or.* 8.2). He feels justified in so doing, however, because he met with treatment which contradicted his expectations, being cheated by people whom he thought were his friends (8.3). This complaint and its subsequent repetition and elaboration appears to be indignation.[57] In *Pro Publio Quinctio*, Cicero opens with elaborate ethical portraits. He and his client are modest and restrained, while his opponents are grasping and arrogant. Of himself Cicero states, I "have little natural ability and insufficient experience" (2; cf. 77). This modest Cicero shortly afterward uses irony to describe the opponent Naevius as a "good man" (*vir bonus*; 11). Later Cicero twice refers to Naevius as a *vir optimus* (16 and 19), on the second occasion explicitly noting the irony intended — denying it of course! Later Cicero draws an incredibly sarcastic portrait of Naevius (39). Given Cicero's rhetoric in this speech (and we might mention as well his speech on behalf of Sextus Roscius), Cicero would have no problem with Paul's combination of modesty and irony. In the real world of rhetoric, then, Hermogenes' borders were not respected.

How Paul blends modesty and irony in 2 Corinthians 10–13 will be discussed later in this chapter (§5). What we must consider now is what Paul does with the modesty *topoi*. First, as Betz argued in *Der Apostel Paulus und die sokratische Tradition*, Paul's modesty is antisophistical. Thus, modesty *topoi* functioned to distinguish the speaker from (presumably prevaricating) sophists, to distinguish truth from error (or

---

common, making them hard to keep apart" (2.212). The best speech blends the two, in order to secure goodwill yet also to incite the audience to action.

[57] Antiphon *Or.* 1 opens with a modesty *topos*, as the speaker immediately notes his youth and inexperience; in the peroration πάθος (no surprise) comes to the fore, as the speaker expresses amazement (θαυμάζειν) at his opponent's τόλμη. (Cp. *Or.* 3.2.) Antiphon's combination of strong emotion and modesty is common, but differs from Paul in that the outrage is directed only against the speaker's opponent, not audience (the jury).

deception) so as to lay claim to the truth.[58] Antiphon testifies to this when his speaker opens modestly, saying, "I now see that sheer misfortune and necessity can force those who hate litigation to appear in court and those who love peace to show boldness (τόλμη) and generally belie their nature in word and deed" (*Second Tetralogy* 2.1). Moments later this speaker takes refuge in the claim that "apparent fact puts the advantage with the clever speaker (ἡ δόξα τῶν πραχθέντων πρὸς τῶν λέγειν δυναμένων ἐστίν), but truth (ἀλήθεια) with the man who lives in justice and righteousness" (2.2).[59] Betz then was correct to emphasize the antisophistical aspects of Paul's rhetoric (which we now recognize more generically as modesty) in 2 Corinthians 10–13.[60]

---

[58] Even sophists tried to distinguish themselves from sophists. For example, Aelius Aristides, imitating Isocrates, attempts to distinguish himself from sophists, though by means other than modesty (Behr 2: 23.1-7).

[59] Actually, this example is a bit more complicated. The speaker knows he is about to embark on a sophisticated argument and has apologized ahead of time for that. What we have just quoted is his inversion of the antisophistical *topos* to justify his impending sophistry — while still maintaining a modest façade! Cp. Cicero *Pro Publio Quinctio*, which opposes two ways of life, one "supported by overwhelming eloquence and influence and marked by avarice, audacity, and wickedness, has unjustly assailed the other, characterized by modesty, helplessness, and a rustic and simple frugality and supported only — but most importantly — by the truth" (May, *Trials of Character*, 14).

[60] Does recognition of Paul's modest rhetoric eliminate the Socratic element from the antisophistical? That we have already noted enough examples from the canon of orators to indicate that modesty was not simply Socratic suggests yes. (Note also Kenneth Seeskin, who traces the similarities between Gorgias and Socrates and argues that the modesty of Plato's *Apology* is part of a parody of Gorgias' *Palamedes* ["Is the *Apology* of Socrates a Parody?" *Philosophy and Literature* 6 (1982): 94-105; cf. James Coulter, "The Relation of the Apology of Socrates to Gorgias' Defense of Palamedes and Plato's Critique of Gorgianic Rhetoric," in *Plato: True and Sophistic Rhetoric*, ed. Keith Erickson (Amsterdam: Rodopi, 1979), 31-67]). But, to say that modesty was not Socratic in the fifth and fourth centuries B.C. does not mean the same thing for rhetoric at the turn of the era. Readers were acquainted with Plato, and Socrates was legendary. Discussions of irony and modesty orbited around the figure of Socrates (see below, §3). The modesty *topoi*, thus, developed Socratic associations. Third, history of religions considerations which Betz introduces make the antisophistical dimensions of the Socratic tradition even more relevant to 2 Corinthians 10–13. Fourth, other aspects of 2 Corinthians 10–13 suggest the propriety of drawing specifically Socratic connections within the broader category of modesty *topoi*. The strange conjunction of modesty and high-mindedness, the disavowal of rhetorical means while in fact using them, particularly the use of irony, parody, and paradox, and the turning of his own self-defense into a trial of his auditors suggest links between Paul's rhetoric and Socrates'. (Aelius Aristides also turns his self-defense into criticism of his auditors, *Behr* 2: 33.34). Important similarities between Paul's rhetoric and that of philosophy more generally argue for comparing Paul's modesty particularly with the Socratic tradition (as we will see in §3-5).

5.2. Paul's Ethical Argument

Second, using modesty to distinguish oneself from sophistic falsehood may be pressed further to distinguish oneself from sophistic culture. Paul does this. Lacking the social distinction which thorough education affords, Paul's modesty therefore helps to associate himself more solidly with the οἱ πολλοί over against the socially advantaged and ambitious. Given this rhetorical situation, Paul's modesty then slides into populist rhetoric.

Third, Paul's modest, populist self-presentation coincides with how he bears power and authority. This is consistent with his rhetoric in 1 Corinthians. Laurence Welborn has emphasized the political language (and connected social dynamics) which Paul uses in 1 Corinthians 1–4. In a struggle among powerful people for prominence in the Corinthian Christian ἐκκλησία, Paul identifies himself with the poor (albeit as well with Stephanus, Fortunatus, Gaius, and Chloe). Observing this, Welborn concludes, "Paul sought, like a Greek politician of old, to 'bring the δῆμος into his faction' (Herodotus 5.66)."[61]

Paul's populist self-presentation received further elaboration by Dale Martin, who has indicated the usefulness of labeling Paul's leadership style demagogic.[62] He identifies five commonplaces about the demagogue: first, the popular leader is enslaved to those whom he leads;[63] then, "the leader is said to be a chameleon, changing himself to suit his audience; he lowers himself socially; he is said to do so for gain," as his opponents allege, whereas he himself "claims to be working not for selfish gain but for the salvation of the people."[64] Martin also uses the word populist to describe this type of leadership, a word which I prefer.[65] Martin

---

[61] L. L. Welborn, "On the Discord in Corinth: 1 Corinthians 1-4 and Ancient Politics," *JBL* 106 (1987): 101. Paul's siding with the poor as well as Stephanus, et al., warns us to be suspicious about his rhetoric.

[62] *Slavery as Salvation: The Metaphor of Slavery in Pauline Christianity* (New Haven, CT: Yale University Press, 1990), 86-116.

[63] J. Albert Harrill disputes this in *The Manumission of Slaves in Early Christianity*, HUT 32 (Tübingen: J. C. B. Mohr [Paul Siebeck], 1995), p. 9 n. 11; see also Harrill's review of Martin in *JR* 72 (1992): 246-27. Harrill contends that Martin never actually proves this point — and it is important to Martin's argument.

[64] Martin, *Slavery as Salvation*, 87; cf. p. 100. Though Martin discusses ways in which the adaptability of the demagogue differs from other forms of leadership, I think it is wrong to conclude that adaptability pertains only to demagogic leadership; moreover, that the demagogue works for the salvation of the people does not differ significantly from the rhetoric of ideal monarchy. I also think that Martin's models of benevolent patriarch and populist leader are too easily disentangled. For example, to hold out Cato as the illustration of the benevolent patriarch is to use an extremely austere model (p. 96). And what does it mean for a demagogue to be sincerely motivated (p. 95)?

[65] Demagogue strikes my ear as pejorative, whereas populist is more flexible (and to my ear tends to bear positive connotations). As for the twists and turns of demagogue,

emphasizes that the populist leader shared life with the οἱ πολλοί and represented their interests. Paul's identification with the weak and arguing on their behalf against the strong identifies him as a populist leader, as does his endurance of humility and lowliness. Paul's modest acceptance of ταπεινότης, then, according to Martin, identifies his leadership style as that of a demagogue or populist.[66]

Paul's modest self-presentation in 2 Corinthians 10–13 contributes to and corresponds with his populism. We have already seen how the ἦθος of ἐπιείκεια appears in one's identification with the οἱ πολλοί. We may therefore label Paul's concessions that he is ταπεινός, οὐδέν, and an ἰδιώτης as populist. Similarly, we may point to Paul's offer of clemency as populist. In the preceding chapter we noted the role of royal Philanthropa in popular politics. We also observed the wildly popular policy of *clementia* which Julius Caesar used to win the Italian countryside to himself. Plutarch provides another example, when he describes a woman whose mind was πολιτικός and whose ἦθος was φιλάνθρωπον. She influenced her father greatly; as a result, his government was πραότερος and δημοτικώτερος. His nickname for his daughter was Εὔμητις (*Mor.* 148d). Paul's offer of clemency functions similarly, seeking to attract the Corinthians to his beneficent leadership.

Paul's populist self-presentation then accounts for other connections which we have already traced between 10:1 and the remainder of the letter fragment. Not only does he hesitate to impose sanctions, he disclaims interest in taking people's money.[67] He insists on his love and goodwill for the Corinthians. He is guided by a policy of doing what is best for them (οἰκοδομή). Moreover, the contrast between his self-assertive rivals and himself becomes clearer. From Paul's perspective, their superior bearing (11:20) reflects their interests in their own station, not concern for

---

Ian Worthington notes, "By the fourth century δημαγωγός has lost its odious fifth-century connotation and meant simply a popular leader, one actively involved in politics. The nature of citizens who participated in political life had also changed from the dominating στρατηγοί of the fifth century, and their numbers had increased to include men outside the aristocratic families." He further notes that such a person was most commonly called a ῥήτωρ. (*A Historical Commentary on Dinarchus: Rhetoric and Conspiracy in Late Fourth-Century Athens* [Ann Arbor: University of Michigan Press, 1992], 122.) This reminds us of the disparate connotations of being a demagogue.

[66] The *topoi* connected with the demagogue issue from sources which typically reflect an aristocratic perspective. This complicates any reconstruction of demagogue *topoi*. Although more needs to be done on the figure of the demagogue and Paul's relationship to it, I think Martin is right to point us in this direction.

[67] Martin notes that evaluations of demagogues hinge on their personal gain or lack thereof (*Slavery as Salvation*, 99). Cf. Dinarchus *In Demosthenem* 1, which indicates that (in that time and place) taking bribes violated what was expected of a δημαγωγός.

the ἐκκλησία, while their sense of rivalry, guile, and masquerading (11:12-15) contrast with Paul's antisophistic simplicity and modesty. Thus, Paul's offer of leniency and clemency fits into a broader modest and populist self-presentation.[68]

For now let us summarize what we have seen. Hermogenes identifies a rhetorical style of ἐπιείκεια as relevant to the person who pursues less than what is his due. One's attitude to litigation is one standard for this. So also is one's attitude toward other people: superiority or identity. While still claiming ἐξουσία, Paul concedes his opponents' charges and affirms his manual labor in order to connect himself with the οἱ πολλοί. This contrasts with Paul's opponents who display their superiority. Paul's sense of measure heightens the distinction between his rivals and himself, while his ταπεινότης makes it quite concrete. In this context, then, Paul's offer of ἐπιείκεια and πραΰτης reflects a larger attempt on his part at populist rhetoric.

Paul's self-presentation in 2 Corinthians 10–13 therefore rests on a foundation of modesty (rhetorical perspective) and populism (political perspective). But there is more to what Paul is doing. We observed Hermogenes' opinion that irony contradicts stylistically a modest ἦθος. Though we argued that in practice orators did not follow Hermogenes' view, thereby allowing our recognition of modesty in Paul to stand, it remains to ask why Paul did in fact use irony in 2 Corinthians 10–13. This will point us to a Socratic debate that will further clarify Paul's embrace of both ἐξουσία and ταπεινότης.

3. Style: Socrates' Combination of Modesty and Irony

Although Paul's use of irony does not undermine our recognition of modesty in his ἦθος, accounting for it reveals much about his argument. As a matter of fact, a precedent existed for the combination of irony and rhetoric-eschewing modesty, viz., (Plato's) Socrates. His embodiment of both probably accounts for Hermogenes' discussing the two together — ultimately, if not consciously. That Hermogenes decides the two lack

---

[68] We might compare James May's summary of Cicero's defense of Publius Quinctius: "Unable to grapple eye to eye with his adversary, Cicero adopts a strategy of lament, openly and repeatedly complaining about his disadvantage, a method that accounts for a major motif of the speech and the defense. Cast in the role of the defender of the disadvantaged and the advocate of equity and truth, Cicero can appeal to the hearts of the judges and the human predilection to support the honest, innocent, but downtrodden victim in the face of influential, unscrupulous, and dastardly oppressors" (*Trials of Character*, 21).

compatibility reflects an understanding of irony which moves away from the example of Socrates. In Socrates, however, modesty and irony came together.

In the ancient world, irony (εἰρωνεία/*dissimulatio*) took two forms. The simpler is that of word play, the wry double meaning which we still associate with irony. Cicero considered ironic repartee a refined form of humor, as had Aristotle before him.[69] A more complex form of irony involved one's behavior. Theophrastus, for example, discussed the ironic person (the εἴρων) in his treatise on various kinds of human characters, defining εἰρωνεία as "an affectation of the worse in word and deed." He characterized the εἴρων as a person who reacts to people and circumstances in a manner opposite to what one would expect; the dissembler is not forthright and direct, but full of pretense. In general, Theophrastus viewed the εἴρων negatively.

Quintilian thought more systematically about irony and further refined its categories. He divided irony into two types, labeling one a trope, the other a figure. He wrote that "in the *trope* the conflict is purely verbal, while in the *figure* the meaning, and sometimes the whole aspect of our case, conflicts with the language and the tone of voice adopted; nay, a man's whole life may be colored with *irony*, as was the case with Socrates" (9.2.46). This suggests that the figure can be constructed in one of two ways, either through the piling up of tropes or independently of them, which is precisely what Quintilian concludes. Helpfully, he describes some of the ways one may develop the figure. For example, if one issues a command which clearly violates what one really wishes, it is an ironic figure. Or, if one concedes to opponents qualities which one clearly does not want them to possess, it is an ironic figure. Similarly, one may pretend to faults which one does not have in order to suggest that the opponent does. These last two examples ironically undermine the opposition while subtly commending the speaker. As Quintilian's attempt to illustrate irony grew more complicated, he had to point to yet other figures

which have a strong family resemblance: *confession* of a kind that can do our case no harm ... secondly, *concession*, when we pretend to admit something actually unfavorable to ourselves by way of showing our confidence in our cause ... thirdly, *agreement* ... This last form of *figure* becomes more striking when we agree to something which is really likely to tell in our favor ... Sometimes we may even praise some action of our opponent ... At times we may exaggerate charges against ourselves which we can easily refute or deny ... At other times we may by this same method make the charges brought against us seem incredible just because of their gravity (9.2.47-53).

---

[69] Cic. *Brutus* 292; Aris. *Rhet.* 3.18.7; *E. N.* 4.7.16. Cf. Plut. *Mor.* 632d-633a.

5.3. Socrates' Modesty and Irony

Quintilian thus recognizes a variety of ways in which irony can be expressed and suggests three levels of irony to look for: 1) verbal irony, i.e., a contradiction of words; 2) a contradiction with the rhetorical context; and 3) the entire nature of one's life.

Quintilian's mention of Socrates points to the most famous example of irony in the ancient world. Quintilian elaborates on how it was that Socrates acted ironically: "he assumed the role of an ignorant man lost in wonder at the wisdom of others" (9.2.46). Prior to Quintilian, Cicero tells us that Socrates "far surpassed all others for accomplished wit in this strain of irony or assumed simplicity (*in hac ironia dissimulantiaque*)."[70] In an aside in his *Brutus*, Cicero records that the

> irony, which they say was found in Socrates, and which he uses in the dialogues of Plato, Xenophon, and Aeschines, is a choice and clever way of speaking. It marks a man as free from conceit, and at the same time witty, when discussing wisdom, to deny it to himself and to attribute it playfully to those who make pretensions to it. Thus Socrates in the pages of Plato praises to the skies Protagoras, Hippias, Prodicus, Gorgias, and the rest, while representing himself as without knowledge of anything and a mere ignoramus (292).

The irony of Socrates, then, was legendary and encompassed both words and behavior. We must also emphasize that it was viewed positively.

In our particular concern with ἦθος, however, we encounter a problem with the εἴρων. While Socrates was respected, the εἴρων in general was not. In his survey of irony in classical antiquity, Zoja Pavlovskis has noted the conflicting views of the εἴρων.[71] While Aristophanes and (later) Theophrastus have negative views of the ironic person, Plato and Aristotle, presumably influenced by the figure of Socrates, offer a more positive view.

> Irony ... is not as bad as the qualities which Aristotle contrasts with it, βομολοχία and ἀλαζονεία. For while boastfulness is sometimes assumed for the sake of some advantage, irony has no such purpose. At its best, it is the mark of the superior man who is modest in order not to overawe others. Occasionally, such modesty may serve a specific purpose, namely, facilitate the teaching process: people are more willing to accept lessons from a humanly fallible man than from an aloof teacher of majestic grandeur.[72]

Ideas about irony were, however, largely negative following Aristotle's student and successor, Theophrastus. The εἴρων was "a perennial flatterer, an unreliable man who always puts on a false front"; neither Peripatetics, Epicureans, Stoics, or Cynics approved of the εἴρων.[73] In

---

[70] *De or.* 2.270. Cf. *De off.* 1.30.108.
[71] Zoja Pavlovskis, "Aristotle, Horace, and the Ironic Man," *CP* 63 (1968): 22-41.
[72] *Ibid.*, 25.
[73] *Ibid.*, 26.

rhetorical theory, however, irony became an artifice for ambiguity and less a character type, "a stylistic concept ... a subtle way of ridiculing others, not of abasing oneself."[74]

As the previous quotes from Cicero and Quintilian show,[75] however, the example of Socrates did not disappear. In fact, the main point of Pavlovskis' article is to demonstrate that Horace presented himself as an ironic person, taking up the "self-depreciation and self-disparagement" of the εἴρων.[76] Vlastos argues that Latin evidence reveals that Socrates came to define irony, displacing the reprehensible, deceitful εἴρων of the fifth and fourth centuries.[77] W. Büchner meanwhile argues that the figure of Socrates caused an evolution in rhetorical thought: "Aristotle understands Socrates' εἰρωνεία as a behavior which rhetoric later described as ἐπιείκεια (an appropriate forbearance) and clearly distinguished from irony because it is free from any ridicule."[78] These observations lead us

---

[74] Ibid., 27.

[75] On the Roman use of irony, see M. LeGuern, "Elements pour une histoire de la notion d'ironie," in L'Ironie, Linguistique et Semiologie 2 (Lyon: Presses Universitaires de Lyon, 1978), 47-60.

[76] "Aristotle, Horace, and the Ironic Man," 28. Pavlovskis offers Callimachus as a precursor of Horace. Callimachus "discovered a way of annihilating hostile criticism by an ironic pretense of either external limitations, such as poverty, illness, danger, madness, proximity of death, or of disparaging statements about his art as a forgivable weakness" (p. 28).

[77] Gregory Vlastos, Socrates: Ironist and Moral Philosopher (Ithaca, NY: Cornell University Press, 1991): Although Vlastos cannot account lexically for the change, he avers that we know "*who* made it happen: Socrates.... He changes the word not by theorizing about it but by creating something new for it to mean: a new form of life realized in himself which was the very incarnation of εἰρωνεία in that second of its contemporary uses [i.e., mockery innocent of deceit, rather than simply deceit], as innocent of intentional deceit as is a child's feigning that the play chips are money, as free from shamming as are honest games, though, unlike games, serious in its mockery (*cum gravitate salsum*), dead earnest in its playfulness (*severe ludens*), a previously unknown, unimagined type of personality ... The image of Socrates as the paradigmatic εἴρων effected a change in the previous connotation of the word" (p. 29). See Alexander Nehamas' review article in Arion (3d ser., 2 [1992]: 157-86).

[78] "Über den Begriff der Eironeia," Hermes 76 (1941): 344: "Aristoteles versteht also unter der εἰρωνεία des Sokrates ein Verhalten, das die Rhetorik später als ἐπιείκεια (billige Nachsicht) bezeichnete und von der Ironie scharf trennte, weil es frei von jedem Spott ist." Pavlovskis also observes that the "attributes of an εἴρων include a certain degree of gentleness and softness" (p. 36). Cf. Leon Guilhamet, "Socrates and Post-Socratic Satire," Journal of the History of Ideas 46 (1985): 3-12: "Never from Plato's Socrates, and certainly not from Xenophon's, do we hear vituperative satire usually associated with moral outrage. Socrates is gentle with his antagonists even as he utterly demolishes them. Interlocutors more acute than Hippias and Ion may recognize the irony

5.3. Socrates' Modesty and Irony

back to our earlier examination of Hermogenes' modest ἦθος, his persona of ἐπιείκεια. Hermogenes does in fact permit examples of Socrates' self-speech as acceptable to modest rhetoric. Apparently, then, Hermogenes distinguishes Socratic irony from biting, verbal irony, and applies the label εἰρωνεία only to the latter. As a result, what we identified initially as two forms of irony are really three. To begin with, the figure of the εἴρων is twofold: in general its timidity and insincerity are objectionable, yet the dissimulation of Socrates forced what had to be regarded as a positive example on subsequent thinkers.[79] Socrates' irony, however, lacked the biting ridicule which many found intrinsic to witty irony. These three things then made for a complicated picture of irony in the ancient world. Büchner's identification of the Socratic influence on rhetorical modesty complicates our understanding of 2 Corinthians 10–13. Whereas modesty stylistically precludes biting irony, modesty incorporates Socratic irony.[80]

Why then in a discussion of ἐπιείκεια did Hermogenes think to stipulate that irony violates that ἦθος stylistically? One reason is that these topics were debated. As already suggested, there was a problem of definition. The εἴρων could be bad, like a flatterer, or good, like Socrates; moreover, irony could be modest or vicious — and even modest irony could be both pleasing and offensive. For example, a rich and powerful person had to play the role of populist carefully, for the transparency of his ploy could easily provoke his audience. Quintilian in fact complained about modesty:

I am not sure that open boasting is not more tolerable, owing to its sheer straightforwardness, than that perverted form of self-praise, which makes the millionaire say that he is not a poor man, the man of mark describe himself as obscure, the powerful pose as weak, and the eloquent as unskilled and even inarticulate. But the most ostentatious kind of boasting takes the form of actual self-derision (11.1.21).

While Quintilian indicates that such rhetoric is a *topos*, he does not reflect the typical evaluation of the *topos*. His comments attempt to exculpate his hero, Cicero, from blame for bragging. Quintilian's comments about modesty, thus, seek to make Cicero's boasts reasonable and palatable, yet

---

... but in most cases the opponent does not grasp the extent of his own humiliation" (p. 7).

[79] According to Aristotle, irony is the opposite of boasting (*E. N.* 2.7.12; 4.7.2). Such a definition of irony encompasses both Socratic irony and that of a weak character. The usefulness of modesty to combat its opposite is apparent.

[80] On Socratic irony see Betz, *Paulus und die sokratische Tradition*, 87-88 (which relies on Paul Friedländer's important three volume work *Plato* [Eng. trans. H. Meyerhoff (London, 1964-69)]); Vlastos, *Socrates*, 20-44; cf. Paula Gottlieb, "The Complexity of Socratic Irony: A Note on Professor Vlastos' Account," *CQ* n.s. 42 (1992): 278-79.

in so doing take a position at odds with centuries of rhetorical practice. Hermogenes, meanwhile, marked out his own position within the debate. That we can see him making distinctions indicates his awareness of the debate. For example, Hermogenes allows examples of Socrates' self-speech (which we would consider as ironic) as acceptable to modest rhetoric.[81] But ironic modesty may become unacceptable. Although modest speakers pretend to be less than they are, by speaking ironically they suggest opposite meanings; therefore, what may at first seem modest actually may imply just the opposite. Such rhetoric is no longer simple, but acquires a more vigorous tone, perhaps even a bite. In Hermogenes' view, this tone shifts irony from an ἦθος of modesty to one of indignation (βαρύτης). Thus, self-irony is materially modest, but functionally something more. Recognizing this divergent function, Hermogenes writes,

Indignant thoughts are created even out of those that seem to be modest,[82] whenever they are approached in such a way that the speaker willingly gives up some of his own advantages or agrees to yield an advantage to his opponent or, from what he says in his speech, obviously deems himself or his opponent worthy of deeds or words that are the opposite of those stated (365).

Thus, Hermogenes criticizes ironic modesty because it is mock-modesty and as such expresses indignation, which is vehement. What we see in Quintilian and Hermogenes, then, is a debate about the proper roles of modesty and irony in rhetoric. Hermogenes inserts explicit commentary on irony in his discussion of modesty precisely because of their common link and the confusion about that link which the figure of Socrates introduced. The rhetoric of modesty could easily turn into the trio of modesty, Socrates, and irony.

In 2 Corinthians 10–13 Paul takes up that trio (replacing "Socrates" with "Socratic tradition"). Though the modest ἦθος will require the first half of the letter fragment to establish, the opening verse begins that process. As we have already observed, the appeal by "leniency and clemency" points to the forgiveness which modesty prefers (as well as the common, populist gesture of political figures). The immediately succeeding confession of ταπεινότης furthers Paul's identification with others. But the juxtaposition of lowliness with leniency is contradictory. To be ταπεινός undermines leniency and exposes a person as weak, soft, or dilatory. How can Paul be both? This contradiction alerts us to the

---

[81] That general Socratic dissimulation does not seem to be part of Hermogenes' concept of irony is a weakness in Hermogenes' theory of irony.

[82] I am quoting Wooten's translation of this passage, whereas Forbes' translation fails to make explicit the connection between indignation and the ἦθος of ἐπιείκεια: "instances of indignation also arise from the manipulation of what may seem to be *reasonable* 'forms of thought'" ("Comparison, Self-Praise and Irony," 12; italics mine).

presence of irony. Some idea is being stretched and twisted. To affirm both leniency and lowliness requires a radical adjustment of ἐξουσία, or more particularly, apostolic ἐξουσία. Whom does Christ send? The person extending Christ's clemency acknowledges that he is himself ταπεινός.

Such affirmation contradicts the Corinthians' expectations about Christ's envoys. In place of signs and wonders, Paul offers his nothingness. Like the wise Socrates whose wisdom rested on his recognition that he knew nothing, Paul avers that his ἐξουσία rests on his being nothing. Paul's view of his Christian existence, then, contradicts common religious notions and involves a complete reevaluation of values. This process resembles the rhetoric of the Socratic tradition.

4. Beyond Modesty:
The Socratic Subversion of Encomiastic Rhetoric

In his fourth oration, Περὶ βασιλείας d, Dio Chrysostom tells a popular story about the encounter between Alexander and Diogenes. Years later, Dio relates, people continued to praise Alexander for his conduct toward Diogenes because even though he was a great king with great power he showed respect to a poor man who was smart and had great powers of endurance. To see a strong man honor a wise one naturally pleases people. Little wonder that over time, as people embellished this story, they stripped Diogenes of everything like money, honor, or strength in order to emphasize his intelligence.

Alexander's interview of Diogenes encapsulates an awareness within Hellenistic society that what is truly honorable is not always what one might expect, nor is the dishonorable always so. In Alexander, all that humans admire confronts the status-renouncing Diogenes whose wisdom compensates for all that he otherwise lacks and makes him Alexander's match. In fact, Diogenes' renunciation of convention is the wellspring of his wisdom and virtue, so that by embracing lowliness, Diogenes attains a certain eminence. Nor is Diogenes unique. Similar figures were prominent in Hellenistic culture, e.g., Odysseus, Herakles, Aesop, and Socrates, the last of whom inspired Diogenes and other Cynic successors. In each example, wisdom and virtue are the wildcards which subvert normal standards of evaluation. In each we see either that wisdom and virtue reside in an unlikely place, a place which challenges social respectability, or that they lead to actions which contradict social mores and values. While these figures were, to be sure, ambiguous, controversial, and as dissimilar as they were similar, they nevertheless overlapped in challenging people to reappraise cultural norms, or more specifically, encomiastic norms. Wisdom and virtue compensate for shortcomings and question the worth of things commonly perceived as good.

The story Dio told about Diogenes and Alexander therefore illuminates Paul's strategy in defending himself to the Corinthians. To confront the Corinthians, who were impressed by status and culture, Paul stripped himself of everything except his moderation and intelligence, and then even those. Rejecting the accepted tokens of educated culture, as well as divine familiarity, Paul portrayed himself as a humble fool. His foolishness, however, turned out to be clever and intelligent, his humility the threshold of divine empowerment. His wisdom and weakness therefore became tokens of his legitimacy and commendation (i.e., honor), challenging the credentials of his rivals and undermining the criteria upon which they were based. Paul's strategy was therefore not unusual and in fact well-known.

That Paul does not refer to Socrates, then, is not surprising because the apostle has tapped into more than just the figure of Socrates. An entire philosophical tradition flowing from Socrates developed a whole system of rhetoric on which Paul drew in 2 Corinthians 10–13. Paul's use of that rhetoric accounts for the parallels that Betz noted with Plato's Socrates.

In particular, Paul used two aspects of the rhetorical tradition of Socratic philosophy. One is its antisophistic potential, a common element of forensic rhetoric (in fact the modest rhetoric discussed above), but most famously embodied in Plato's Socrates. Betz emphasized this in his monograph. The second, which we wish now to emphasize is its "antiencomiastic" potential.[83]

A basic premise of the Cynic and Stoic traditions was that things were not what they seemed. Attitudes toward pleasure, hardship, and death were challenged. Virtue was not the possession of the well-born, the rich, or the beautiful. Happiness was not a factor of wealth. True dominion was exercised over the soul, not a people. What people normally equated with happiness, wisdom, or virtue was in error. The philosopher knew better for he could look past the surface of things. Philosophers therefore questioned the value of such things as noble birth, athletic prowess, and even παιδεία. Paul's rhetoric follows a similar line of argument.

Legendary figures in Greek culture embodied these challenges to traditional values. Aesop, a slave, proved wiser than his master, a great philosopher. Odysseus demonstrated the value of ignoring status and propriety in conquest and survival. The humiliations Herakles suffered in

---

[83] The evidence for this rhetoric, particularly as it found expression in the figures of Aesop, Herakles, Odysseus, and Socrates, appears in Appendix 3.

5.4. Subversion of Encomiastic Rhetoric

route to benefiting humankind and attaining apotheosis further confuses nobility and ignobility. And Socrates, the ugly and the odd, incarnated the rebuke of custom.

Paul's rhetoric in 2 Corinthians 10–13 shares this countercultural perspective. Like the antiencomiastic traditions, Paul reevaluates what is good, and therefore can view suffering and lowliness positively. For example, Paul's recitation of a hardship catalogue reflects this countercultural rhetoric. Though the evidence which Paul presents to vindicate his ministry, e.g., deprivation, travel hardships, or persecution by authorities, may sound strange to modern ears, it did not to ancient ones, as Fitzgerald has shown.[84] He documented the "intimate connection between virtue and adversity,"[85] showing how hardships participate in a person's παιδεία, either revealing what he is becoming or showing what he has already become.[86] "His serene endurance of the greatest possible calamities is the definitive proof of his virtue and serves to distinguish him from every charlatan who merely claims to be 'wise.'"[87] Thus, hardship served to validate wisdom, virtue, and sincerity. Paul's litany of ills in 2 Cor 11:23-29 was not an original line of argument, but drew on widespread cultural precedent for its persuasive value. In Fitzgerald's language, endurance of hardship proved who was a "sage."[88] When Paul

---

[84] John T. Fitzgerald, *Cracks in an Earthen Vessel: An Examination of the Catalogues of Hardships in the Corinthian Correspondence*, SBLDS 99 (Atlanta: Scholars Press, 1988). We may now refer as well to Martin Ebner, *Leidenslisten und Apostelbrief. Untersuchungen zu Form, Motivik und Funktion der Peristasenkataloge bei Paulus*, Forschung zur Bibel 66 (Würzburg: Echter, 1991); Markus Schiefer Ferrari, *Die Sprache des Leids in den paulinischen Peristasenkatalogen*, SBB 23 (Stuttgart: Katholisches Bibelwerk, 1991).

[85] *Cracks*, 114.

[86] Cf. *Cracks*, 97: "Training for adversity is what philosophy essentially concerns."

[87] *Ibid.*, 115. Fitzgerald notes that Herakles, Odysseus, Socrates, Diogenes the Cynic, Epicurus, and Cato the Younger all exemplify the sage in this regard (p. 116).

[88] *Ibid.*, esp. pp. 47-116. Suffering hunger, thirst, sleeplessness, cold, and nakedness in particular connect Paul with the Socratic image. Fitzgerald also notes a connection between Paul's wandering and that of Odysseus (p. 134; cf. p. 49). In an earlier article, Robert Hodgson drew connections between Paul and Herakles ("Paul the Apostle and First Century Tribulation Lists," *ZNW* 74 [1983]: 59-80). Though stimulating, Hodgson's article inadequately considers the longstanding association of Alexander with Herakles and how that affects the rhetoric of Plutarch and Arrian. He has also given inadequate attention to the connections between Herakles and the sage. More recently, Martin Ebner connected Herakles to hardship catalogues, linking Paul's self-reference in 1 Cor 4:11 about his nakedness (γυμνιτεύειν) not to nudity or merely tattered clothing, but the wearing of clothing similar to the Cynic, attire modeled after Socrates, the Spartans, and Herakles (*Leidenslisten und Apostelbrief*, 40-47, 161-72, and 289-98).

draws on the rhetoric of hardship catalogues he therefore positions himself within the counterculture of wisdom and virtue.[89]

But was Paul the only Christian using hardship catalogues as a credential? Anitra Bingham Kolenkow champions the opinion of previous (yet out of fashion) scholars and argues that he was not.[90] She offers the persuasive observation that using suffering as an apostolic credential corresponds to widespread Christian paraenesis about enduring persecution. Moreover, the logic of 2 Cor 11:21b-12:10 suggests that Paul's rivals had endured hardships, for the comparative element in 11:23 assumes the connection between suffering and being a διάκονος. That the Corinthians accept the other criteria (viz., ancestry, visions, healings) noted in Paul's argument further implies congruence on the matter of hardships.[91]

But what does Paul do with this affinity? Despite the recent attention to the hardship catalogues, Scott Andrews notes that the function of 2 Cor 11:23-29 has received inadequate consideration.[92] While Andrews argues that Paul's "being overcome by hardships results in his low status,"[93] the list is more complex than that. First, the sheer number of difficulties cited is amazing, while, second, the specific enumeration of Paul's brushes with death parodies lists which offer exact tallies of a great leader's amazing accomplishments:[94] the social capital accumulated by the great man's great deeds has been reduced to a servile person's brushes with death. The humiliating, physical abuses endured cast a shadow of ambiguity over Paul's lowliness, for they suggest his great endurance; however, the stipulated frequencies indicate that his is no noble condescension, but the very condition of his life. Paul's lowliness is indeed habitual and endemic. Does the list, then, point to his ὑπομονή or emphasize his ταπεινότης? Or both? The elaboration on his toils in 11:27 ties Paul into the traditions about Herakles and Socrates, so that endurance of cold and hunger become badges of honor; yet the following verse obliterates any suggestion of

---

[89] Fitzgerald also notes the antiencomiastic nature of ἀδιάφορα catalogues (*Cracks*, 53-54).

[90] "Paul and Opponents in 2 Cor 10–13 — *Theioi Andres* and Spiritual Guides," in *Religious Propaganda and Missionary Competition in the New Testament World: Essays Honoring Dieter Georgi*, eds. Lukas Bormann, Kelly del Tredici, and Angela Standhartinger, Supplements to Novum Testamentum 74 (Leiden: E. J. Brill, 1994), 351-74.

[91] My reading of 12:12 offers support for Kolenkow's thesis; see below, n. 128.

[92] "Too Weak Not To Lead: The Form and Function of 2 Cor 11.23b-33," *NTS* 41 (1995): 263-76.

[93] *Ibid.*, 272.

[94] Martin Ebner, *Leidenslisten und Apostelbrief*, 130.

5.4. Subversion of Encomiastic Rhetoric 295

ἀπάθεια on Paul's part and hints at the fragility of his ὑπομονή and ἀνδρεία, for he suffers anxiety about his churches, identifying with others' weaknesses and failures. The function of this hardship catalogue is, then, unclear. Some agreement between Paul and his opponents seems to exist that Christ's servant should experience some difficulties. The philosophic tradition provides a rhetoric which dignifies apparent misfortune — in fact many of Paul's hardships correspond to circumstances which the philosophic tradition reappraises. But the volume of Paul's sufferings and what he reveals of his interior life affirm his ταπεινότης and ἀσθένεια, while omitting commentary about his virtue. Paul then takes up the rhetoric of philosophers and Christian ministers but redirects it to underscore his weakness. Moreover, Andrews is correct that Paul's embrace of hardship, lowliness and weakness work together to identify him with people in general and correspond to his populist rhetoric.

As scholars have previously noted, Paul's admission of ταπεινότης in 10:1 also challenges cultural norms. Hans Dieter Betz recognized the connection between Paul's lowliness and debates about the philosopher's appearance (σχῆμα), connecting Paul's ταπεινότης with the "struggle which existed since Socrates and was particularly developed by the Cynic diatribe, namely, the debate over the σχῆμα of the true philosopher in contrast to the imposter."[95] The figure of Socrates stands at the center of that debate, as his repulsive appearance exposes the emptiness of the splendid: a philosopher's true beauty is proportional to his lowly and mean outward appearance.[96] Similarly, Betz recognizes in Paul's concession that he is nothing (οὐδέν εἰμι, 12:11c) a self-reference which "belongs to the longstanding debate between philosophy and rhetoric,"[97] as seen in Plato, Epictetus and Lucian: the sophist criticizes and dismisses the philosopher as useless and of no value, whereas the philosopher views nothingness as the path to mastery.[98]

---

[95] *Paulus und die sokratische Tradition*, 47: "Die von Paulus als 'ταπεινότης' wiedergegebene Anklage der Gegner stellt in der hellenistischen Welt keineswegs etwas Neues oder Ausgefallenes dar. Der ganze Komplex gehört vielmehr hinein in den seit Sokrates anhaltenden und durch die kynische Diatribe zu besonderer Entfaltung gelangten Kampf um das 'σχῆμα' des wahren Philosophen im Unterschied zu dem des Scheinphilosophen."

[96] *Ibid.*, 51.

[97] *Ibid.*, 122: "Das Zugeständnis des Paulus in 12,11c 'εἰ καὶ οὐδέν εἰμι' ist aber nun nicht einfach ein Trick. Vielmehr gehört diese Selbstaussage hinein in die uns längst bekannte Auseinandersetzung zwischen Philosophie und Rhetorik."

[98] *Ibid.*, 123-27. Betz further discusses how the philosopher's insight stands in continuity with Delphic anthropology, i.e. "the nothingness of humanity in the face of

With the philosopher's σχῆμα Betz discusses also his λόγος. Regarding 2 Cor 11:6, Betz takes up Windisch's suggestion that Paul draws on the contrast between the sophists and the truly wise, a *topos* with roots in Socrates:[99] though a rhetorical ἰδιώτης, Socrates knows truth and wisdom, unlike the eloquent orators who do not. This contest between philosophy and rhetoric pervades subsequent thought, e.g., Cicero, Quintilian, and Cynics. Thus, by taking up the *topos* of the ἰδιώτης, Paul not only presents himself as modest but places himself on the side of truth, while ranging his opponents on the side of the sophists.

Beyond commenting on Paul's ταπεινότης, in 2 Corinthians 10–13 as a whole Betz recognizes the rhetoric which criticizes sophisticated culture.[100] Analyzing 2 Corinthians 10–13 form-critically, Betz argues that these chapters are part of "a very deliberately and artfully composed 'apology' in letter form,"[101] as 12:19 both suggests and denies. To account for this discrepancy, Betz adopts Windisch's recognition of antisophistic rhetoric and proposes that "Paul stands in a tradition which goes back to Socrates."[102] More precisely, "The renunciation of apology, i.e., in a rhetorical sense, goes back to the representation of Socrates in the Socratic literature and from there perhaps back to the historical Socrates himself."[103] Paul "rejects the idea of ἀπολογεῖσθαι because in his mind it is associated with the concept of rhetorical-sophistic persuasiveness. Truth ... prohibits Paul from defending himself by rhetorical means."[104] In short, 2 Corinthians 10–13 offers the kind of apology which would be appropriate for a philosopher. This means that Paul, like Socrates, chose to rely on truth and innocence rather than verbal sleight of hand. For example, Socrates refused to wail and cry his way to acquittal, or to flatter

---

divine power ... expressed above all in the Delphic maxim 'γνῶθι σαυτόν'" (p. 127; see pp. 127-31).

[99] *Ibid.*, 59-66.

[100] *Ibid.*, particularly ch. 2.

[101] *Ibid.*, 14.

[102] *Ibid.*

[103] *Ibid.*, 15: "Der Verzicht auf die Apologie, d. h. auf die rhetorische, geht auf die Darstellung des Sokrates bei den Sokratikern und darüber hinaus wohl auf den historischen Sokrates selbst zurück."

[104] *Ibid.*, 18: "Er weist den Gedanken an das ἀπολογεῖσθαι deshalb zurück, weil sich für ihn mit diesem Begriff die rhetorisch-sophistische Überredungskunst verbindet. Die 'Wahrheit,' um die es in seiner Verkündigung geht, ist natürlich die christliche Botschaft, aber es ist eben die Wahrheit, die sich nicht mit den Mitteln der Rhetorik verteidigen läßt — ebensowenig, wie sie sich mit diesen Mitteln 'empfehlen' und 'propagieren' läßt."

his audience.[105] In addition, the philosopher's focus on truth distinguishes him fundamentally from the orator whose goal is victory; the philosopher thereby assures his audience that sincerity motivates him, not self-promotion or deceit.[106] Paul's use of rhetoric in 2 Corinthians 10–13, then, accepts the pose of an ἰδιώτης with respect to speech in order to distance himself from deceit as well as the proponents of sophistic culture.

Abraham Malherbe takes Betz's discussion of the philosopher's σχῆμα further in his article "Antisthenes and Odysseus, and Paul at War,"[107] in which he notes how 2 Cor 10:3-6 interacts with Cynic-Stoic traditions originating in Antisthenes. Malherbe argues (against Windisch and Betz) that the philosophical background to Paul's warfare imagery encompasses more than antisophistic debate, for it appears also in discussions about the moral life.[108] The figure of Odysseus provides a focal point for such discussions. Not simply one among many illustrations, Odysseus is relevant to the investigation of 2 Corinthians 10–13 because of criticism which challenged his inconsistency and adaptability, charges levied against Paul as well. Paul then fought in a manner similar to that of Odysseus. That the latter could exercise wisdom and virtue in (and by means of) a beggar's clothes provides a precedent for Paul's self-presentation. The figure of Odysseus points also to the similar figures of (some) Cynics who regarded their humble appearance as a moral weapon.

---

[105] Cf. Quintilian who regards appeals to emotions, rare words, and rhythmic structure as inappropriate to philosophical rhetoric (11.1.33-34).

[106] The pursuit of truth has another effect which Betz mentions: it raises forensic rhetoric to the level of philosophical dialogue. This happens because a focus on truth makes for a two-edged sword which not only defends but convicts: as the speaker exonerates himself, suspicion accrues to his accusers (as in 2 Cor 10–13).

[107] Originally published in *HTR* 76 (1983): 143-73 and subsequently reprinted in his *Paul and the Popular Philosophers* (Philadelphia: Fortress, 1989), 91-119. My references are to the latter edition.

[108] The distinction between antisophistic and philosophical may shrink in a debate about truth because the manner in which one may seek to prevail may involve the characterization of one's opponents as sophists. The distinction does, however, help to underscore the wider use of the warfare imagery than might be evident by calling it only antisophistic; furthermore, the distinction is also necessary for demonstrating the different uses to which the imagery can be put. Thus Malherbe notes, "Military imagery to describe the sage's life became popular especially among Stoics, and particularly in the early Empire" ("Antisthenes and Odysseus," 101). He also observes that the Cynics differed from the Stoics, as the former "do not use the image of the fortified city to describe the intellectual exercises by which the sage attains security, as the Stoics did, but in conscious rejection of the need or desirability of intellectual sophistication, they stress the practical life which is lived by willing it" (p. 105). The Cynics, therefore, pick up a second Antisthenic tradition and apply military imagery instead to their garb as the armaments with which they conduct their warfare.

Like them, then, Paul can in 2 Cor 10:1-6 turn his ταπεινότης into a weapon. Malherbe's discussion of this aspect of the Antisthenic legacy makes explicit the connection between lowliness and a morally compelling self-presentation.

The investigations of Betz, Malherbe, and Fitzgerald have situated Paul's rhetoric within its historical context. Betz has shown numerous parallels between Paul's rhetoric and that used against sophists. Though Betz is correct as far as he goes, Malherbe rightly expands our view of Paul's rhetoric to recognize it as more broadly that of philosophy. Fitzgerald's work supports this, expanding our thinking to the figure of the sage.

We are left to ponder why Paul takes up the rhetoric of the philosophers. I argue that the need for antiencomiastic rhetoric in his self-defense motivated Paul — though in so doing he merely continued a trend which runs throughout his letters. In his study of 1 Thess 2, Malherbe has shown how Paul drew on philosophical *topoi* to validate his conduct and ministry. Controversies about and competition among philosophers created a rhetoric for propaganda and legitimacy which furnished Paul with a vocabulary and concepts with which to articulate his sincerity and goodwill as a teacher. That Paul would rely on such rhetoric in his dealings with the Corinthians comes as no surprise. However, additional factors make philosophic rhetoric even more germane to 2 Corinthians 10–13. Chief among these are rivals with superior status and the caricature which mocked Paul's speech, distancing him from educated culture. In response to these circumstances, Paul does not attempt to parade other status markers to offset the impression that he is a socially insignificant person, but accepts his lack of typical status indicators, acknowledging that he is an ἰδιώτης in matters of speech and broadly characterizing himself as ταπεινός.[109] But the tradition of Socratic rhetoric redeems these shortcomings. As exemplified by Odysseus, Herakles, Socrates, Aesop, and Socratic philosophers, the ἰδιώτης and the ταπεινός may be in fact the wise and the virtuous. Thus, in a war of self-promotion with the status-minded Corinthians and their champions, the antiencomiastic dimension of philosophical rhetoric was particularly useful for Paul.[110]

---

[109] By way of contrast, note Apuleius who presents himself as an educated person (πεπαιδευμένος) in his defense speech, using his παιδεία to run circles around his ignorant accuser while gaining the sympathy of his educated judge. See Graham Anderson, *The Second Sophistic*, 223-27.

[110] One wonders how deeply the rhetoric penetrated Paul's thought. Does he use the subversive rhetoric of wisdom and virtue only for reasons of expedience or are those ideas which he fundamentally believes? His experience as a practitioner of a dissenting religion/culture (Judaism) and as a preacher of a crucified Lord incline me to the latter.

We have seen then that Paul presented a modest ἦθος, which corresponded to his populist rhetoric. Though the modest persona was common to rhetoric, one example towered over all others, viz., Socrates. The connections between modesty and Socrates led Betz to connect Paul and Socrates, though the similarity was no mere accident, for both had antisophistic motives — and modesty is fundamentally an antisophistic ἦθος.[111] The motive reaches wider than Betz proposed, for Paul shares a philosophical perspective. Malherbe demonstrated this in regard to Paul's σχῆμα: like some Cynic philosophers Paul's appearance served as a pedagogical lesson and weapon. But Paul also presents an antiencomiastic rhetoric (applied to religious phenomena) which parallels philosophical rhetoric, particularly within the Socratic tradition. This is what allows Paul to claim ἐξουσία while affirming ταπεινότης, for his ἐξουσία does not issue from social status, but defies normal categories of value.

5. ἠθοποιία: The Fool's (Foolish) Rejection of Modesty

So far we have seen that Paul's explicit ἦθος reflects Hermogenes' persona of ἐπιείκεια. For example, Paul hesitates to impose sanctions, avoids asserting himself in an authoritarian manner, and refuses financial support. Furthermore, Paul concedes that he may have spoken excessively of his authority, acknowledges that he is an unskilled speaker, and dislikes the game of recommendation and boasting. Moreover, Paul goes beyond modesty to Socratic irony, embracing lowliness, weakness, and nothingness, qualities which prove to be the very foundation of his ἐξουσία. He further makes use of the rhetoric of the Socratic tradition to overturn the conventional criteria of wisdom and virtue.

How Paul accomplishes those things, though, involves forceful, vitriolic rhetoric, in fact the type of irony to which Hermogenes objects.[112]

Meanwhile, the slippery nature of rhetoric should be observed: while taking advantage of the subversive side of wisdom and virtue, Paul simultaneously makes nice use of traditional Delphic anthropology (Betz, *Paulus und die sokratische Tradition*, 118-48).

[111] Modesty kept someone from litigating, precisely the opposite of a sophist.

[112] What do I mean by irony? Irony relies on the possibility of seeing and interpreting things in multiple and divergent ways and takes advantage of overstatement, understatement, innocence, and contradiction. Irony plays with expectations, thriving on negation and reversal. Related to irony are parody and paradox. Parody utilizes the alternate meanings and perspectives of irony, but adds an element of imitation. As for paradox, it thrives on the conjunction of opposites, the contradiction of the obvious, or the affirmation of the unexpected (all of which invite irony). Later in this chapter, we will use the word "countercultural" as a substitute for one ancient use of paradox, that is, an idea which contradicts common opinion. See Søren Kierkegaard, *The Concept of*

How does Paul combine this with his modesty? In this section we shall argue that when Paul uses biting irony, he takes up a second persona, one which imitates his rivals. Paul calls this one the fool. This method of rhetorical imitation was a standard feature of ancient rhetoric and a basic component of rhetorical education. By recognizing Paul's role-playing we can distinguish the voices he projects. One, his own, leans to Socratic irony, the other to aggressive, biting irony. Modesty has room for the former, not the latter. Thus, Paul's exercise in ἠθοποιία opens the door to the assertive irony encountered in the Fool's Speech.

Next to Paul's modest traits, then, stands his biting stylistic irony, as the following ten examples demonstrate.[113]

1) 11:1 — "my foolishness" (ὄφελον ἀνείχεσθέ μου μικρόν τι ἀφροσύνης): Foolishness is a bad thing. No one claims to be a fool. To do so signals some kind of ironic dissimulation or understatement. Since, however, Paul has defined competitive self-comparisons as ignorance (10:12; cf. 11:17-18), his admission of foolishness refers to something specific, viz., boasting. To put up with his foolishness is to indulge him in some boasting, the inappropriateness of which is underscored by labeling it foolishness. Paul therefore is imitating his rivals. To become a fool in order to imitate his rivals is clearly to ridicule them. Paul takes on a bad characteristic which he lacks in order to attribute it to his opponents. Quintilian identified such rhetoric as a figure of speech related to irony. Although as of 11:1 it is not yet obvious what Paul will do with the foolishness motif, the combination of irony and imitation does hint at the parody to follow. (Other ironic aspects of this verse are discussed below.)

2) 11:5 — "super-apostles" (οἱ ὑπερλίαν ἀπόστολοι): Paul's reference to his rivals as "super-apostles" contradicts Paul's own opinion of them

---

Irony with Continual Reference to Socrates, eds. and trans. Howard V. Hong and Edna H. Hong (Princeton University Press, 1989); Wayne Booth, *The Rhetoric of Irony* (University of Chicago Press, 1974); Alba Claudia Romano, *Irony in Juvenal*, Altertumswissenschaftliche Texte und Studien 7 (New York: Georg Olms, 1979), 36-7; C. Muecke, *Irony and the Ironic* (New York: Methuen, 1982); Candace D. Lang, *Irony/Humor: Critical Paradigms* (Baltimore, MD: The Johns Hopkins University Press, 1988).

[113] Aida Besançon Spencer, "The Wise Fool (and the Foolish Wise): A Study of Irony in Paul," *NovT* 23 (1981): 349-360; J. A. Loubser, "A New Look at Paradox and Irony in 2 Corinthians 10–13," *Neot* 26 (1992): 507-21; Glenn S. Holland, "Speaking Like a Fool: Irony in 2 Corinthians 10–13," in *Rhetoric and the New Testament: Essays from the 1992 Heidelberg Conference*, eds. Stanley E. Porter and Thomas H. Olbricht, JSNTSS 90 (Sheffield Academic Press, 1993), 250-64. Spencer identifies nine examples of irony in 11:16-12:13, viz., 11:16, 17, 19-20, 21, 29; 12:5, 11, 13 (p. 351 n. 4). She does not differentiate the ways irony functions in these examples, nor explain how 11:29 is ironic.

and exaggerates their personae.[114] That Paul would not endorse this view indicates his ironical perspective, while the exaggeration indicates a mocking tone. Like the previous example, this also corresponds to the ironic method noted by Quintilian in which one concedes qualities to opponents which one does not want them to possess.

3) 11:7 — "sin" (ἁμαρτία): To preach the gospel free of charge clearly is not a sin, while condemning a person for working in order to make such proclamation possible is patently ridiculous;[115] thus, Paul erroneously labels his actions as sin, thereby making obvious his irony.[116] This again matches Quintilian's discussion of ironic methods. (Paul's use of ταπεινός may also be ironic, a concession to his accuser which ultimately will play out to Paul's advantage, another ironic ploy noted by Quintilian.[117])

4) 11:8 — "robbed" (συλᾶν): Paul exaggerates his circumstances to make the criticism against him even more ridiculous: like an impious devil he plundered other religious communities to serve the Corinthian Christian cult. Such overstatement indicates the presence of irony.[118]

5) 11:11 — "Do I not love you?" (διὰ τί; ὅτι οὐκ ἀγαπῶ ὑμᾶς;): Here we encounter a *reductio ad absurdum*: does Paul suffer deprivation because he does not like the Corinthians? Of course not, he goes without precisely because of his goodwill toward them. The suggestion that Paul does not love the Corinthians therefore asserts just the opposite, viz., that he does.

6-7) 11:19-21 — Paul contrasts speaking κατὰ κύριον with ἐν ἀφροσύνῃ and then identifies the latter with boasting (v. 17). He then

---

[114] I follow Furnish (pp. 502-5) in regarding the "super-apostles" as Paul's rivals rather than a third party such as the Jerusalem apostles.

[115] It is possible that ἁμαρτία sounds more forceful to ears tuned to Christendom than to Paul's audience. I think, though, that the word has sufficient negative moral connotation in Paul's letters to validate our seeing its use hear as ironic exaggeration. The emphatic placement of the word right after the conjunction and its subsequent contrast with δωρεάν heighten the irony.

[116] Although Marshall (*Enmity in Corinth*) has nicely sketched the social historical context in which Paul's failure to accept money became problematic, what we are commenting on now is Paul's rhetoric, how he shapes his side of the debate. He suppresses the social issues to make the matter look ridiculous. Similarly, one might note that manual labor was demeaning for a man of standing, so that it might indeed be wrong for Paul to engage in it. Again, Paul's rhetoric seeks to exclude such considerations and focus on the sacrifice which he made on behalf of the Corinthians.

[117] If ταπεινός is an ironic concession to Paul's opponents' slander, then it serves to map their social location, not Paul's.

[118] On 11:7 and 8 recall the words quoted above from Quintilian to the effect that exaggerating charges makes it easier to refute them.

labels such boasting κατὰ σάρκα (v. 18). Since this fleshly, foolish type of boasting is what his rivals practice and what the Corinthians admire, both groups must then be fools. To label the latter φρόνιμοι ὄντες is clearly erroneous and indicates that the opposite is intended. Paul is therefore ironic — and in fact sarcastic. The result of the Corinthians' foolishness is spelled out in the following verse (v. 20), where Paul describes how his rivals conduct themselves among the Corinthians: the rivals enslave the Corinthians, they eat them alive, they take advantage of them, they put on airs, they slap their faces! Paul piles up these exaggerated terms to expose the opponents' leadership as excessively self-assertive. Whereas to some eyes such actions might seem to validate the opponents' social position, Paul's contextualization of these actions under the rubrics of foolishness and κατὰ σάρκα impart a different interpretation, making the actions appear pretentious, presumptuous, and dangerous. If Paul's interpretation is correct, the Corinthians have suffered shame at the hands of his rivals and should be embarrassed at having tolerated their conduct. Thus, his opening words in v. 21 ("For shame!") appear at first to accuse the Corinthians of wrongly suffering insult at the hands of the rivals. But that is not how Paul finishes the thought. Instead he twists the thought back to himself: how shameful that we were too weak to act like them! Paul's ironic sarcasm is clear. He actually feels no shame in the matter, whereas the opponents were shameless in their pretension and the Corinthians were made shameful by enduring it. Paul is the prudent one, for he recognizes foolish boasting for what it is and does not act according to its dictates. Such prudence frees him from any charge of shame and proves his weakness to be something much more. This recognition encourages the reader to see in Paul's "weakness" a responsible style of leadership beneficial to the Corinthians.[119]

---

[119] Although the irony of 11:19, φρόνιμοι ὄντες, is generally recognized, Holland argues differently: "when the Corinthians 'suffer fools gladly' they are in fact exhibiting what was widely recognized as the behavior of the wise person in the face of the tribulation caused by 'fools' ("Speaking Like a Fool," 256-57). This observation does not change the fact that φρόνιμοι ὄντες is ironic. We must consider the context. Because Paul defined wrong boasting as foolishness (11:16-18), all who participate in it are fools. The Corinthians' acceptance of wrong boasting then makes them fools. Thus, to call them wise must be ironic sarcasm. The philosophic background Holland points to, however, may account for the logic of Paul's thinking: since the wise person endures fools, Paul thinks to label their toleration of foolishness 'wise.' But since the Corinthians did not regard boasting as foolish, they would not regard their acceptance of it as toleration or endurance nor consider those who engage in it as fools. Paul has redefined terms and construed the situation in completely different fashion. Furthermore, the way his terms map the social positions of the parties involved reverses the Corinthians' perspectives. Identifying the Corinthians as wise and the opponents as fools switches the

8) 12:11 — "super-apostles" (οἱ ὑπερλίαν ἀπότολοι): The irony of the phrase "super-apostles" was noted in connection with 11:5.

9) 12:13 — "forgive me this injustice" (χαρίσασθέ μοι τὴν ἀδικίαν ταύτεν): Some people in Corinth may have construed Paul's refusal of money as a social transgression, e.g., ingratitude.[120] Paul's stubborn refusal to alter his policy in this matter indicates that he sees no ἀδικία involved whatsoever; moreover, he views his policy as honorable (11:7-10; 12:14-18). By either ironic concession or exaggeration, then, Paul labels his actions ἀδικία precisely to demonstrate their inherent nobility. In fact, if ingratitude is the connotation, he will turn the tables by positioning himself as their benefactor (12:14-15). Removing the possibility of ἀδικία in turn precludes the need for forgiveness, which is likewise ironic.

10) 12:16 — "being unprincipled, I tricked you" (ὑπάρχων πανοῦργος δόλῳ ὑμᾶς ἔλαβον): The forcefulness of Paul's words leads many to conclude that Paul repeats what some in Corinth say about him. The New Revised Standard Version and Revised English Bible both reflect this by inserting "you say" into the translation of this verse. While that may be a correct historical judgment, it is an intrusion into Paul's rhetoric. Such a gloss dulls the point of Paul's irony — and in fact eliminates it. Paul does not put what he says on the lips of the Corinthians, but on his own.[121] That it is so obviously not the kind of thing anyone would admit makes clear that Paul only agrees ironically with what he says: by making this statement he intends to deny it. His following comments do precisely that. But the irony is more pointed than simply noting that Paul's words are generally not what someone would lay claim

---

status of the latter from superior to inferior. That this contradicts the facts indicates that Paul's words must be construed ironically. The background Holland introduces, however, does create another level of meaning in Paul's words (whether intended or unintended I do not know). The behavior which the Corinthians tolerated on the part of Paul's rivals as appropriate self-assertion Paul transforms into the ambitious grasping of fools. One cannot put up with such bad behavior out of an appropriate deference but only as wiser people who wisely put up with fools' foolishness. Holland, then, points to a way for the Corinthians' to save face in the matter. But it was not the road they traveled when Paul wrote, further increasing the Corinthians' culpability (from the perspective of Paul's rhetoric). φρόνιμοι ὄντες only amplifies how foolish they were. Cf. Spencer, who notes the stylistic aesthetics of Paul's irony here in placing ἀφρόνων and φρόνιμοι side by side ("The Wise Fool," 358).

[120] Marshall describes the social dynamics which might lead to such a conclusion (*Enmity in Corinth*, 15).

[121] Actually the identity of the voice in 12:16 is more complex than our present comments suggest, as will become clear below. Our subsequent comments, however, do not change the essence of our present reading.

to. Paul uses the word πανουργία, which Betz connected to antisophistic polemic, and thereby indicates that he is making important ethical moves in these words.[122] Throughout 2 Corinthians 10–13 Paul seeks to present himself as restrained, sincere and truthful, while showing his opponents to be deluded, overbearing, sophistic impostors. By the time we reach 12:16 the terms of both Paul's ἦθος and that of his opponents have been laid. In 12:16, then, Paul is not simply taking up an undesirable self-characterization, but takes up his characterization of his opponents! This is furthered by Paul's verb λαμβάνειν, which is precisely how he described his rivals in 11:20, while δόλος echoes Paul's description of his rivals in 11:13 as δόλιοι; likewise, Paul attributed the Corinthians' move away from allegiance to him to the effects of πανουργία. That Paul then elaborates on his ironic denial by disavowing πλεονεξία (12:17-18) further connects his words in 12:16-18 with the ἦθος of his opponents as he outlined it in 10:13; 11:12, 20. The force of Paul's irony in 12:16, therefore, rests on how successfully he sketched his own and his rivals' characters. If successful, his words in 12:16 are transparently ironic because they characterize his opponents' behavior and have no part in his own ἦθος.

Beyond these ten examples, Paul also ironically plays with rhetorical forms, i.e., he indulges in parody. In 11:23-29 he plays with the hardship catalogue (which we have already examined). In 11:32-33 Paul plays with his escape from Damascus (as I plan to discuss in another study). In 12:1-6 Paul mocks visions, while in 12:7-10 he parodies healing stories and oracles.[123] In these examples Paul's irony is even more elaborate and strikingly profound.

Similar to the preceding examples, Paul parodies the noble birth *topos*, turning status language upside down as he undermines noble birth (11:22). The connection of his rivals with Jewish antiquity helped further their cause. Whether they did this by means of the good-birth *topos* or implicitly through their preaching cannot be determined. Paul's response, however, frames the issue as a good-birth *topos*, asking, "Are they Hebrews? ... Are they Israelites? ... Are they Abraham's offspring?" (11:22). Dieter Georgi has shown how "Hebrew" or "Israelite" or "Abrahamic" could conjure up associations of antiquity and mystery, thereby lending them some persuasive value.[124] But do they work as a

---

[122] Betz, *Paulus und die sokratische Tradition*, 104-6.

[123] Hans Dieter Betz, "Eine Christus-Aretalogie bei Paulus (2Kor 12, 7-10)," *ZTK* 55 (1969): 288-305; reprinted in his *Paulinische Studien*, 1-19; see also idem, *Paulus und die sokratische Tradition*, 84-94.

[124] *The Opponents of Paul in Second Corinthians*, 40-60. Perhaps the use of Hebrew words in magical incantations (or Gospel miracle stories) is comparable.

good-birth *topos*? Is being a Hebrew, an Israelite, and a child of Abraham laudable? Compared to locating one's ancestors among the imperial household or among ancient worthies such as prominent office holders or benefactors — or even gods — boasting that one is a Hebrew looks ridiculous. To place value on being a Jew assumed a minority religious-cultural perspective, so that the status as Paul claimed it stood at odds with the social values of the larger world and lacked the eminence usually sought in talk of ancestry. This is Paul's purpose in stringing the three claims together. Baldly repeating the boast three times emphasizes the insignificance of the claim.[125] By parodying speech about noble birth, Paul joins the chorus of countercultural voices which criticize conventional values.

This reading of 2 Cor 11:22 reflects Paul's attitudes elsewhere. Although he himself clearly recognized the privileges connected to being Jewish (Rom 9:4-5) and the reasons it afforded for pride (Phil 3:5), these advantages rest only on the faithfulness of God and are mitigated by the surpassing righteousness of Christ (cf. Rom 2:17-3:26; 5:17; Phil 3:9). In fact, Paul disowns the advantage of his status as a Jew. While different rhetorical contexts may account for the strident tone of Philippians 3, Paul's attitude there suggests that he does not endorse the value of the criteria championed in 2 Corinthians 11. That he speaks as a fool in 2 Corinthians 11 further suggests that he does not agree with the value of Jewish origins in the present debate. Meanwhile, Paul's ability to co-opt his rivals' identity in the face of his indifference toward it relativizes and undermines its evidentiary value.

The effects of Paul's parodies reverberate widely. Though he targets his rivals, his parodies victimize himself as well, for each argument which Paul denies to his opponents becomes useless to him as well. If sufferings prove nothing about his rivals, they prove nothing about Paul. If visions and revelations do not qualify as valid criteria for others, then not for him as well. Yet, sufferings and revelations clearly are part of his Christian existence. Paul, therefore, has not simply parodied his opponents, but apostleship. How, then, can he assert his superiority over his rivals? One way is the imitation of Christ, which we will discuss later (§6). Meanwhile, Paul's parodies recommend him in two ways. They allow Paul to crush a witty caricature (2 Cor 10:10) with even more deadly wit, thereby turning the tables on his accuser.[126] They also portray him as

---

[125] Cp. Horace *Satire* 2.4 which ridicules gastronomy simply by describing it in detail and with enthusiasm.

[126] Centuries earlier Gorgias observed that it was effective to "confound the opponents' earnest (σπουδήν) with jest and their jest with earnest," an opinion with which Aristotle agreed (Aris. *Rhet.* 3.18.7). Aristotle noted, though, that people become

possessing greater insight and a clearer vision of truth, for he sees the shortcomings of what others prized. In short, Paul shows that he is the voice of wisdom and virtue.[127]

This allows us to recognize how Paul parodies himself in 12:12. If signs are as useful as the Corinthians believe, then they should recognize Paul as an apostle, because what the Corinthians regard as signs have been associated with his ministry. But as Paul just argued, such signs prove little, so he himself places little faith in such evaluations. The previous fool's speech, then, undermines the claim made in 12:12. The Corinthians' present response to Paul in fact proves how ambiguous such criteria can be. By citing this evidence here in 12:12, then, Paul shows how empty it is and drains his own ministry of such credentials.

Paul does, however, offer a positive credential. In 12:11 he asserts that he lacks nothing in comparison with the super apostles and then adds εἰ καὶ οὐδέν εἰμι. This statement distinguishes him from his rivals and, for Paul, makes all the difference between him and them. That he is nothing and that signs accompanied his ministry reflect what he learned in the oracle reported in 12:9: Christ's power comes to perfection in Paul's weakness. Thus, reading 12:12 in light of 11:16–12:10 mitigates its apparent evidentiary value. To see Paul parodying himself in 12:12 throws his emphasis back on his concession at the end of 12:11: he is οὐδέν.[128]

Recognizing parody and biting verbal irony in 2 Corinthians 10–13, as well as modest self-irony, takes us back to the problem noted earlier in this chapter. In Hermogenes' opinion, Paul's biting verbal irony conflicts stylistically with his modest ἦθος and Socratic irony. Although we saw above that ethical practice is oriented to results, not handbooks, it is worth investigating how Paul combined the two. In our view, *the mixture of modesty and irony in 2 Corinthians 10–13 results from Paul's projection of two different personae.* While he projects a modest persona for himself, in the middle of his presentation he puts on a mask and acts out another part, that of the fool. He does so quite self-consciously and repeatedly

---

angry "with those who employ irony, when they themselves are in earnest; for irony shows contempt" (Aris. *Rhet.* 2.2.24). Though neither of these texts parallels 2 Cor 10:10 precisely, together they suggest the dynamics of such speech.

[127] As discussed in §4 and Appendix 3, this is a countercultural, antiencomiastic rhetoric.

[128] The translation of 12:12 is difficult. The function of the particle μέν is mysterious, perhaps simply emphasizing τὰ σεμεῖα. More significantly, the reason for placing σημεῖον, τέρας, and δύναμις in the dative case is unclear. In my opinion, they answer to the preposition ἐν and thus are correlative to πᾶσα ὑπομονή. In 12:12, then, Paul provides a shorthand recapitulation of the preceding fool's speech: endurance of sufferings and the performance of superhuman deeds are the Corinthians' main expectations of an apostle.

reminds the audience of that mask. Paul's movement between modesty and irony in 2 Corinthians 10–13 then reflects the presence of two personae which purposely oppose each other.

Paul prepares the fool's mask in 10:12-16, where he discusses the problem of recommendation. When he introduces the subject he states his antipathy toward comparisons and then makes two significant moves: he characterizes the process as people "measuring themselves by themselves" and labels such people as lacking understanding (10:12).[129] By introducing the idea of measure, Paul can draw on theological, anthropological, and political ideas to present a picture of his rivals as overweening usurpers, while he himself is the pious, legitimate servant of God. By classifying comparisons between individuals as evidence for a lack of understanding, Paul prepares a persona which he can employ in the heart of his argument. He will play this fool. If he must compare himself to his rivals in terms of their credentials, Paul will make the comparison, but only as one of them, as one who "does not understand" and who oversteps his God-given borders.

Paul takes up the mask of the fool in order to engage in σύγκρισις (11:1–12:13). His opponents who practice σύγκρισις lack understanding, so by joining in comparisons Paul imitates them and acts the role of the fool. We should not lose sight of the basis of that identity: he is a fool because he boasts. The comic stage was filled with blowhards and windbags whose boasts were shown repeatedly to be empty and ridiculous. To imitate braggarts, then, and expose their bragging as empty, even to parody the nature of their boasts, was commonplace comedy (and satire as well).

That Paul speaks as a fool to imitate his rivals also suggests reasons for Paul's use of irony. Since it is boasting that is being emulated, modesty is not to be expected. Stylistically, then, biting irony corresponds to the change from modesty to boasting. Irony also corresponds in stylistic terms to the caricature of Paul recalled in 10:10. Since ancient theoreticians regarded irony as a display of grace and wit, we can see in Paul's use of irony a retaliatory volley intended to deflect the earlier display of wit

---

[129] In his discussion of aspects of forceful speech (Περὶ μεθόδου δεινότητος), Hermogenes devotes a little attention to inoffensive self-praise (see Rabe, pp. 441-42). He offers three tips: first, express commonplace ideas about what is good but which specifically apply to oneself; second, attribute self-praise to necessity; third, alternate characters (προσώπου ὑπαλλαγή). Illustrating the latter, Hermogenes draws from Demosthenes *De corona* 299 and 112 to show Demosthenes addressing moderate comments to the Athenians and offensively arrogant words to Aeschines. Demosthenes' opposition of ὑπερήφανος and τι μέτριον λέγειν parallels Paul's rhetoric suggestively.

directed against him. Of course, Paul seeks to show that this remains a battle of wits fought by fools.

The fool also figures in countercultural rhetoric. Like the foolish braggart who lacks wisdom, so also the person who fails to see through appearances is foolish. Paul's language of foolishness, thus, corresponds to philosophical rhetoric about wisdom and virtue. Each school offered its version of what is good and each version criticized common opinion. The philosopher therefore delivered people from their foolishness. In the case of the lowly Cynic, he sought to deliver people from their mistaken ideas (δόξα) by his exhibition of lowliness. He therefore confronted human foolishness by embracing behavior which those enthralled by δόξα could only regard as foolish.

The nature of foolishness and the identity of the fool then belong to philosophical rhetoric. The philosopher who denies interest in offices and wealth and who endures hunger and cold looks foolish in the eyes of others.[130] He claims, however, to have arrived at correct judgments, while the majority are deceived and foolishly pursue what is of no consequence. Who then is wise and who is foolish? Epictetus asserts the common Socratic sentiment that the recognition of truth "frees from madness (μανίας) those who use only opinion (δοκεῖν) as the measure of all things" (*Diss.* 2.11.18).[131]

Another category of fool enters with those who pretend to be philosophers. Such people misapply philosophy and become a fool among fools (Epict. *Diss.* 4.8.30). To seek acclaim as a great philosopher is ridiculous, for such a person seeks the adulation of those whom he labels mad. "What then? do you wish to be admired by the mad (μαινομένων)?" Epictetus asks (*Diss.* 1.21.4). For the philosopher, then, popular appeal may be cause for suspicion.

Paul reflects both sides of the debate about foolishness in 2 Corinthians 10–13. In 10:12 he uses a subtle word-play which lays the foundation for his fool's speech by equating self-recommendation and ignorance: the opening clause denounces self-recommendation and concludes with

---

[130] E.g., Hor. *Sat.* 2.3; Sen. *Ep.* 71.7.

[131] Cf. Ruth Padel, who offers excellent insight into the development of ideas about madness. She observes, "The *Phaedrus* slid into Greek imagination a hieroglyph of seductive new thoughts about madness. These could work two ways. First, the way things are put overtly in the *Phaedrus*: that true madness may engender privileged, truer seeing. Second, a more elitist idea, implied in the dialogue's playful somersault over loving and nonloving, madness and sanity: that privileged seeing may *look*, to noninitiates, *like* madness. There may be superior ways of seeing that other people wrongly call madness" (*Whom Gods Destroy: Elements of Greek and Tragic Madness* [Princeton University Press, 1995], 90).

5.5. Fool's Rejection of Modesty

συνίστημι (in the participial form συνιστανόντων), while the second half defines his opponents' practice as stupid, concluding with συνίημι (in the verbal form συνιᾶσιν). When he later turns to his fool's speech, Paul resumes the Cynic-like use of foolishness. Though he wishes to stand apart from his rivals, he asks to take up their mask of foolishness to imitate their boasting (11:16b). His preceding request not to be taken as a fool (11:16a), however, reflects the ambiguity of the term (ἄφρων). Others might regard the lowly Paul as a fool, but like the Cynic he wishes to alter the perspective of the term: the fool is not the person who lacks the signs of status and accomplishment, but the one who mistakenly values them and boasts about them.[132]

The fool which Paul plays, then, has varied roots. From a religious perspective, foolishness may be theological and anthropological, characterizing a person's hybristic stance toward deity. In terms of comedy, the person who boasts is a fool, expressing overblown and exaggerated claims or perspectives. In philosophical terms, the fool lacks the wisdom to see what is genuinely good and important. Paul plays on each of these aspects of foolishness for he views his rivals as guilty of ὕβρις, boasting, and ignorant superficiality.

Paul takes the fool's mask in his hand and initially notifies his readers of his intent to put it on in 11:1. In 11:5 he makes his first foolish pronouncement as he compares himself to his opponents. He quickly follows this assertion with modest qualification that he is unskilled in speech[133] and then asserts that he possesses γνῶσις (11:6). This reminds the audience that the image of the fool is only a façade. Paul then continues to indulge in foolish comparisons, contrasting the financial aspect of his ministry to that of his opponents, ironically exaggerating the terms of the debate to make it look foolish. In 11:16 Paul begins to play his role in earnest, describing it more explicitly than before. First, however, he reminds the Corinthians that he is not a fool, but asks to be taken as one so that he can join in the boasting. Paul's reasoning has trapped his opponents. By Paul's definition braggarts are fools; therefore, his opponents are fools. Since Paul is about to boast, is he then a fool? No, because he has distanced himself from this foolishness. Paul has made it clear that in boasting he only plays a role. For Paul, the fool is only a mask. His previous reticence to boast verifies this. His opponents can

---

[132] Cp. Isocrates' advice: "Be not fond of violent mirth, nor harbor presumption of speech (λόγον μετὰ θράσους); for the one is folly (ἀνόητον), the other madness (μανικόν)" (*Ad Dem.* 15).

[133] Of course, using this *topos* indicates some familiarity with rhetoric, while the popularity of the *topos* reminds the reader of the fearsome power of the eloquent and the greater reliability of the unskilled. (That this is a *topos* was noted in §1.)

make no such claims.[134] To these disclaimers about foolishness Paul quickly appends an artful comparison of his demeanor and bearing as a minister with that of his rivals.

In 11:21 Paul reiterates that what he does is only a façade and then begins the comparison of credentials. After a quick exchange of the standard encomiastic topics on noble origins, Paul raises the serious question, "Are they διάκονοι of Christ?" (11:23). Before answering that question, the foolish persona reasserts its presence and only then brazenly states, "I more." But (as we have already discussed) the evidence presented is disarming, for it overwhelmingly details Paul's sufferings, dangers, hardships, and concerns, concluding with Paul's solidarity with the weak. It would appear that this brazen fool is subverting his argument.

The boasting fool indicates that he cannot play the game straight in 11:30: "If boasting is mandatory, I will boast about the evidence of my weakness." The fool then swears an oath to that effect, which is in keeping with the both foolish and modest simplicity.[135] Paul then tells the embarrassing story of his flight from Damascus. Unlike the heroic soldier who first scales the enemy's wall, Paul flees his enemies by being lowered down the city wall.[136] Why boast of such a thing? To give evidence of ἀσθένεια. From this Paul wryly concludes that "boasting is necessary" (12:1) and continues to a key credential, visions.

Turning his attention to visions, even the fool becomes uncomfortable. He indicates this with the preface οὐ συμφέρον (12:1).[137] Then, to put discreet distance between himself and the boast, the fool — yes, even the fool — switches to the third person[138] and maintains that additional guise until 12:5: "About such a person I will boast, but about myself I will boast only in examples of weakness." But even here the fool boasts subversively. His prefatory οὐ συμφέρον criticized the game even as he played it. Moreover, the fool's boast itself proves the critique, because the

---

[134] The reference to boasting κατὰ σάρκα in 11:18 is probably polemical as well: whereas the weak, lowly Paul is accused of living κατὰ σάρκα, it is his opponents teaching and boasting that really operates in that manner (cp. 5:16).

[135] See Hermogenes' comments on oaths in Περὶ ἰδεῶν 327.

[136] Edwin A. Judge, "The Conflict of Educational Aims in New Testament Thought," *Journal of Christian Education* 9 (1966): 44-45; idem, "Paul's Boasting in Relation to Contemporary Professional Practice," *AusBR* 16 (1968): 47; Furnish, 541-42.

[137] Only a fool would pursue what is οὐ συμφέρον. Deliberative rhetoric seeks τὸ συμφέρον; the opposite quest would violate common sense. Gorgias therefore connected the desire for οὐ συμφέρον with μανία (Padel, *Whom Gods Destroy*, 207).

[138] The use of the third person is a standard autobiographical device, cp. Xenophon, Isocrates, Caesar, and Nicolaus of Damascus. Paul states his reason for using it in 12:6b: he does not want any one to appraise him "beyond what he sees in me or hears from me."

fool's boast itself introduces ambiguities. First, he does not know whether it happened in or out of the body. Second, what he heard is impious to repeat. These ambiguities are underscored, the first by repetition, the second by redundancy (ἄρρετα...ἃ οὐκ ἐξὸν ἀνθρώπῳ λαλῆσαι). What then is the public value of the heavenly journey? If it is reduced simply to an event about which one can take pride and brag, then it has been significantly debased. But God disallows even that. God gave Paul the "thorn in the flesh" to prevent him from pride in his heavenly journey. The boasts of the fool have then destroyed the value of this credential.

And the foolishness continues. What happened to Paul's "thorn in the flesh"? The fool boasts of a non-healing, of a healing which does not come. Ridiculous? In view of Hellenistic propaganda, absolutely. But the fool has an important lesson to pass on. In place of healing, the fool received an oracle. In another context the oracle might have splendid value as a credential in itself. Here it does not, for the content of the oracle destroys the entire competitive enterprise. The oracle refutes personal power and nobility, claiming, "My grace is sufficient for you, for my power is made perfect in weakness" (12:9). The fool has learned the lesson that his boasting was foolish, so he confesses, "Gladly will I rather boast in my weaknesses ... for when I am weak, then am I strong" (12:9-10).

After this Paul begins to put down the fool's mask. Any further boasting (except in weakness) would violate the oracle. Any further boasting would be guilty of foolishness. Paul knew this when he took up the fool's guise and so offers the plaintive "you made me do it" (12:11).[139] He then offers censorious remarks that confirm the injustice which the constraint to boast placed upon him.[140]

Paul has pretended to be like his opponents in order to assert his concept of Christian ministry and existence. Because those two characters are antithetical, Paul distinguished two personae throughout his argument. The person voicing the comparisons was a fool, a persona distinct from Paul himself, who has γνῶσις. The fool who spoke represented values opposed to Paul, but similar to his rivals. But when Paul's fool boasted he

---

[139] Appeal to necessity is yet another autobiographical commonplace.

[140] The nature of 12:12-13 is ambiguous: is the fool still speaking, or do we hear Paul's own voice? Or both? The concession that Paul is nothing sounds like the modest voice again, but the self-parodying reference to signs (12:12) and the ironic exaggeration (12:13, 16) sound like the fool. The combination of elements here may signal a move from boasting to reproach. What Paul projects is an ἦθος for destroying λογισμοί, opening the door to self-assertion. What is in evidence here then is the persona which Paul specifically does not want to project and which leniency and clemency seeks to make unnecessary.

made boasting look like a foolish enterprise. His boasts devolve into evidence that the braggart's criteria are inadequate: what they brag about proves to be insignificant. That Paul trumps their boasts with parodies indicates that his fool has wisdom the other fools lack. His self-consciousness in regard to foolishness further differentiates Paul's foolishness from that of his rivals. Although Paul's opponents' boasting had appeared impressive, Paul has made them doubly foolish, once for boasting and secondly for failing to recognize its inherent foolishness.

Is it fair, then, to attribute Paul's biting irony to the fool's persona? His use of irony and sarcasm elsewhere (e.g., 1 Corinthians 4 and Galatians) reveals that a mask is not necessary. That he uses the mask here, though, corresponds to the case he is arguing. As he wears the mask he proves that he does indeed have divinely empowered weapons for destroying pretension, though his preference not to wear the mask corresponds to his desire not to tear down but to build up. The Corinthians therefore hold the wrong expectation of apostolic ἐξουσία, for Paul's ἐξουσία requires ταπεινότης which mandates ἐπιείκεια. Those who diverge from this pattern compel Paul to unleash a barrage of divinely empowered weapons to bring them into line. Paul's persona, then, has two sides to it, one which he prefers and one which is compelled; 2 Corinthians 10–13 seeks to extend the former and render the latter unnecessary. As part of Paul's rhetoric, then, he advocates ἐπιείκεια but wields irony and parody to signify the vehemence of the alternative.

We can, therefore, account for the apparent discrepancy which Hermogenes would identify in Paul's ἦθος. Paul's irony, in fact, helps to indicate the presence of a persona distinct from his own preferred persona, one which corresponds to his boastful opponents. The location of Paul's biting irony indicates this. The examples of verbal conflicts appear in the verses leading up to and away from his fool's speech, specifically 11:1-21a and 12:11-13. Within the fool's speech proper, the irony conflicts with forms and expectation and not just words, so that parody comes to the forefront. Paul's style in these verses, then, helps to show that he speaks not as himself, modestly, but, in imitation of his rivals, as a boastful fool. But even then Paul is modest, for his foolishness is actually wise, as Paul's parodies "demolish the obstacles obscuring knowledge of God," as he promised in 10:5.

6. Paul's Paradoxical Socratic Irony

Although we have noted Paul's use of ἠθοποιία to distance himself from what he writes in his fool's speech, the question remains as to what really is his voice. This leads us back to our problem of Paul's lowliness and weakness and the presence of (Socratic) irony.

Behind Paul's verbal irony and parody, a more broadly conceived irony informs 2 Corinthians 10–13. The value of Loubser's essay "A New Look at Paradox and Irony in 2 Corinthians 10–13" lies in his recognition that different types of irony operate in these chapters. He regards the broader irony informing 2 Corinthians 10–13 as paradoxical irony. Much of what he refers to is what we earlier labeled antiencomiastic rhetoric and identified as being the language of philosophers who challenge the normal values of everyday life. It is in fact a mode of Socratic irony. Loubser describes this paradoxical irony as distinct from dissimulative irony in the following manner.

> Since ancient times the focus of irony has been upon the notion of dissimulation, first defined by Quintilian.... Dissimulative irony mostly depends upon exaggeration, overstatement or understatement to establish its code.... By paradoxical irony the sender leads his audience to view certain contraries as *necessary*, thus creating the sense of an open-ended reality.... Whereas dissimulative irony presupposes a stable view of reality, paradoxical irony riddles the observer's perceptions of reality."[141]

Loubser's categories of dissimulative and paradoxical irony come from Karl Plank's investigation of irony, in which he contrasts the two, writing, "Where the irony of dissimulation suggests that the expressed meaning appears to be other than it is, the irony of paradox notes that the expressed meaning *is* what it appears to be, but what appears to be is not all that it is."[142] By way of illustration, he then draws on Socrates: "in this perspective, Socrates' ignorance is not a clever disguise, but the real awareness of not knowing which expresses at once the only genuine knowledge."[143] Such knowledge proves to be dialectical as it only raises further questions; it "does not lead to any security of what is known, but to an openness to what is not known."[144] Such is the irony which underlies Paul's foolishness and nothingness and makes his parodies so forceful. This becomes particularly clear at the climax of the fool's speech when the voice of the Lord reveals the sufficiency of grace in the face of weakness and Paul consequently confesses the paradox that when he is weak he is strong (12:9-10).

To label Paul's self-confession a paradox is common enough. What needs to be emphasized, however, is not simply the presence of the figure,

---

[141] "A New Look at Paradox and Irony in 2 Corinthians 10–13," *Neot* 26 (1992): 511.

[142] Karl A. Plank, *Paul and the Irony of Affliction*, SBLSS (Atlanta: Scholars Press, 1987), 40.

[143] *Ibid.*

[144] *Ibid.*, 66.

but its pedagogical function. While paradox is ubiquitous in the ancient world, I wish to emphasize that the use of paradox was central to philosophic expression.[145] Not only did paradoxes pose logical problems and exercises (such as Zeno's puzzle about Achilles and the tortoise), but they afforded striking and economical expression of important philosophical ideas in the area of ethics and politics, particularly in the Socratic tradition.[146] For example, Socrates was the wise man who knew nothing. He did not fear death. He was the ugly man who was beautiful. He regarded virtue as knowledge and postulated that one does not do wrong knowingly. Cynics and Stoics challenged the happiness of the rich; happiness resides in virtue. Virtue, moreover, can be learned. The sage was regarded as a king. Friendship existed only among the good and wise. Pain was not evil. All wrong-doing was equally wrong. The wise alone were free, as well as free from distress. Central to these themes was the reversal of common opinion: for example, whereas most people feared death and pain and regularly felt distress, the sage did not.[147] As for the form of these paradoxes, we should note that philosophic paradoxes need not express both sides of the contradiction. Because they so obviously conflict with typical life and common sense, only one half needs to be expressed. The simple expression of the philosophical idea within the context of human life generates a paradox. The form of Paul's self-

---

[145] Eckard Lefèvre, "Die Bedeutung des Paradoxen in der römischen Literatur," in *Das Paradox. Eine Herausforderung des abendländischen Denkens*, eds. Paul Geyer and Roland Hagenbüchle, Stauffenburg Colloquium 21 (Tübingen: Stauffenburg, 1992), 209-46: "Wie die vorstehenden Andeutungen lehren, kann das Paradoxon zu allen Zeiten und in allen Literaturgattungen begegnen" (p. 213).

[146] Cic. *Par. Stoi.* 4. Cf. Lefèvre, "Die Bedeutung des Paradoxen," 231: "Es war bereits von den Paradoxa der Stoiker die Rede. Sie liebten es, ihre Lehrsätze pointiert zuzuspitzen." His comments on Seneca's use of paradox are suggestive with regard to 2 Cor 12:9-10: "So wird man sagen dürfen, daß wie in den Tragödien auch in Senecas philosophischen Schriften das Paradoxon einerseits der stilistischen Pointierung dient, andererseits als Ausdruck wesentlicher Spannungen des menschlichen Daseins empfunden wird" (p. 233).

[147] See, e.g., Cic. *Tusc.*; *Par. Stoi.*; Hor. *Sat.* 1.3; Sen. *Ep.* 9; Diog. L. 7.119-28; Johanna Schmidt, "Paradoxa," *RE* 18.3 (1949): 1134-37; Kazimierz Kumaniecki, "Ciceros Paradoxa Stoicorum und die römische Wirklichkeit," *Philologus* 101 (1957): 113-34; Alessandro Giannini, "Studi sulla Paradossografia Greca," *Rendiconti dell'Istituto Lombardo* 97 (1963): 247-66; Michael J. O'Brien, *The Socratic Paradoxes and the Greek Mind* (Chapel Hill: University of North Carolina Press, 1967); Jürgen Blänsdorf and Eberhard Breckel, *Das Paradoxon der Zeit. Zeitbesitz und Zeitverlust in Senecas Epistulae morales und De brevitate vitae. Probleme und unterrichtliche Behandlung* (Freiburg: Plötz, 1983).

revelation then suggests that it is of no incidental nature, but delivers concise summary of an important theoretical position.[148]

Paul's paradox, then, that when he is weak he is strong, encapsulates a paradoxical view of Christian ministry and existence. Other ironical statements in 2 Corinthians 10–13 reflect such paradoxical irony.

1) 11:1 — "foolishness": Paul equates foolishness with his rivals' competitive self-comparisons. When he joins in this foolishness, he is a fool. But he knows this. What, then, happens when a fool recognizes his foolishness? This suggests that Paul really is wise and that through a pretense of foolishness he will in fact produce wisdom. This is what unfolds in Paul's argument. When Paul boasts he makes boasting look foolish because his boasts are phrased in such a way as to drain them of boasting value (i.e., parody). When therefore Paul joins in on the foolishness he does not really act foolishly. With each claim to foolishness, then, he proclaims his wisdom and condemns his rivals. In this way Paul is like Socrates: as the latter's ignorance led to a dialogue which exposed his conversation partner's ignorance, so Paul's foolishness appears in a monologue which exposes his rivals' (and readers') ignorance. In both cases, the exposure of ignorance and pretense leads to a better understanding of truth. The difference between Socrates and Paul is that Paul attributes foolishness to his opponents' position from the beginning and takes up foolishness as an imitation of his opponents and not as the expression of his own mental state. Paul in fact disavows any ignorance of his own (11:6).

2) 11:5 — "I fall short in no way": We may compare this statement to Diogenes' boast during the Olympic games that he was the true athlete. The context of the boast suggests that either the speaker is an absurd fool or the audience requires a different perspective than they at first adopt. Since Paul's problem is that he certainly does appear to fall short of his rivals, his claim not to do so suggests either vanity or redefinition. Which

---

[148] Paradox also played a role in religion. See Ian T. Ramsey, "Paradox in Religion I," *The Aristotelian Society*, Suppl. 33 (London, 1959), 195-218; in the same volume, see Ninian Smart, "Paradox in Religion II," 219-32; elsewhere, Wilfried Joest, "Zur Frage des Paradoxon in der Theologie," in *Dogma und Denkstrukturen*, eds. Wilfried Joest and Wolfhard Pannenberg, 116-51 (Göttingen: Vandenhoeck & Ruprecht, 1963); Burkhard Gladigow, "'Das Paradox macht Sinn': Sinnkonstitution durch Paradoxien in der griechischen Antike," in *Das Paradox*, eds. Geyer and Hagenbüchler, 195-208; in the same volume, Heinrich Kraft, "Die Paradoxie in der Bibel und bei den Griechen als Voraussetzung für die Entfaltung der Glaubenslehren," 247-72. Cp. H.-J. Klimkeit, "Der leidende Gerechte in der Religionsgeschichte," in *Religionswissenschaft. Eine Einführung*, ed. Hartmut Zinser, 164-84 (Berlin: Dietrich Reimer, 1988). We should also note the sayings, "The last shall be first and the first last," and, "Whoever loses his/her life will find it."

interpretation applies to Paul's words appears in view of Paul's entire argument, though his opening embrace of ταπεινός (10:1) suggests a similar irony at work here. Like Diogenes, Paul's statement necessitates a redefinition, one which subverts expectations and establishes new criteria. Although the details become apparent only as Paul's argument unfolds, he ultimately proves that he does not fall short; rather, they have veered from the mark.

3) 12:11 — "I am nothing": Like 11:5, here as well Paul's self-description reflects ironic understatement. It reflects modesty and suggests that Paul is more than he lets on. This alone would be ironic. But the irony goes deeper. Paul really does consider himself ουδέν (or ταπεινός), but his entire point is that being nothing is in fact to be something (specifically, in Paul's case, an apostle). Thus, the paradox that he does not fall short of the super-apostles even though he is nothing is transformed into a statement of why in fact he is not less than his rivals. This example then straddles the border between verbal irony and that which depends on Paul's life and view of the world.

Whereas we have identified irony and paradox throughout 2 Corinthians 10–13 in general, they are operative specifically in 2 Cor 10:1 as well. The irony which appears there, however, is not the biting irony to which Hermogenes objects, but the modest and paradoxical irony which Socrates modeled. As we observed earlier, an appeal through leniency followed by the description ταπεινός suggests altered meanings. The offer of clemency suggests modesty on Paul's part. The embrace of lowliness suggests that more than modesty is at work.[149] The combination of ταπεινός and θαρρεῖν points to the Cynic's self-presentation, wherein his lowly appearance visually heralds his message while his tongue explicitly bludgeons people about their vices. It is, however, the Cynic's lowliness which leads to his railing, as the former represents the virtue which provides the insight to identify vice and the integrity to criticize it. Paul's use of ταπεινός-θαρρεῖν, then, softens the contradiction intended in the accusation levied against him. Paul counters that his presence does not undermine his letters, but models the teaching which leads to his moral criticism. This is ironic because Paul has altered the value of the language used against him. To call him weak and lowly is in fact correct; ironically, however, that is a good thing. How? Through an oracle (12:9) and by the example of Christ (13:4), Paul formulates a paradox which guides his ministry: "when I am weak, then am I powerful" (12:10). The fact that divine power operates precisely in Paul's weakness resolves the

---

[149] Only later do we learn that when Paul is weak, he is strong, indicating how in fact an offer of clemency may issue from one who is ταπεινός.

5.6. Paul's Paradoxical Socratic Irony 317

puzzle of how an offer of clemency may issue from one who is ταπεινός; moreover, it alters the nature of his failure to punish: ironically, Paul demonstrates Christ's leniency and clemency, tokens of the modesty Paul regards as appropriate to Christian ministry.[150]

The irony in 10:1b is obvious. The contrast between lowly presence and bold absence takes up and appears to affirm the accusation lodged against Paul. If Paul concedes the charge then there is little left for him to say. He must therefore mean something different. Such a situation indicates the likelihood of irony. That Paul recasts the accusation also indicates that he is playing with its meaning. That his choice of words, ταπεινός-θαρρεῖν, points to a useful figure confirms that he wishes to redirect the meaning of the criticism directed against him.[151]

The irony in 10:1a is more subtle, yet as effective. Whereas in ταπεινός Paul takes a bad personal characteristic and treats it as good (which alerts us to irony), in leniency Paul takes an alleged personal shortcoming and makes it good. In the latter case, a course of events outside the text is referred to in a way which subverts the way in which those events were described previously. Paul's positive spin is twofold in character: first, he redefines his behavior as virtuous, for it is leniency and clemency; second, it imitates Christ. Both are ironic. The former indicates a person who accepts less than is his due. Rhetorically, this points to modesty, an ἦθος of ἐπιείκεια, and raises the likelihood of (Socratic) dissimulation or irony. The extent to which Paul will develop the potential of the modest ἦθος cannot be determined in 10:1, but awaits the unfolding of the entire letter fragment. The second element of Paul's irony in 10:1a is more immediately recognizable as ironic. To validate apostolic ministry one requires evidence of the voice and hand of Christ. To attach clemency to Christ brings a surprise to Paul's interpretation of events which changes their nature from bad to good: where Christ was alarmingly absent Paul now shows him surprisingly present. The evidence brought against Paul now stands for his defense.

As Paul's defense unfolds, it does in fact draw further on irony. In distinction to his boastful rivals, Paul plays down his own qualifications. His understatement in "visions and revelations" as well as wearing a fool's mask and standing as an ἰδιώτης, combined with his non-hybristic leadership and antiencomiastic rhetoric mark him as the modest man who

---

[150] Furnish sees irony in 10:1, but in a different way than presented here, for he understands πραΰτης and ἐπιείκεια differently. Thus, Furnish suggests that to label Paul weak and servile is to miss the fact that he acts with the gentleness and kindness of Christ (p. 460). It is ironic, then, that the accuser fails to see just how important Paul's ταπεινός is.

[151] Recall Quintilian's ironic figures of confession, concession, and agreement.

disclaims his praiseworthiness in addressing common people. The modesty reflected in 2 Cor 10:1 therefore points to Paul's stance as a modest and thus Socratic-ironic figure. Paul's ironic modesty, however, is not simply a gracious demeanor, but the expression of paradoxical reality.

7. The Basis of Paul's Counterculture: Christology

Although we have been comparing Paul's rhetoric with his contemporaries, particularly the philosophers, the question in Corinth was not whether Paul was a good philosopher. The question involved identifying the true servants of Christ. What Paul had to do was fashion a persuasive model of apostolic ministry. More precisely, Paul had to champion his conception of Christian existence and ministry over against an alternative and more appealing model. Wisdom and virtue's counterculture and correlative issues of self-presentation allowed Paul to articulate a coherent and morally persuasive ἦθος, to expose his rivals as pretentious, and to destroy the criteria which supported their status. It remained, however, to provide a positive view of the true servant of Christ. Who is such a person?

Paul's conception of apostleship spans his letters and resists heroic imagination. An important aspect of apostleship is to model Christ. Actually, Paul considers this normal for a Christian (Rom 8:28-29; Gal 2:20). An apostle, however, must provide a more immediate model for imitation. Thus, Paul can reflect on his own call as happening when "God revealed his son in me" (Gal 1:16)[152] and can regard the task of founding a church as seeing "Christ formed" (μορφωθῇ Χριστός, Gal 4:19). For the person who heralded Χριστὸς ἐσταυρωμένος, a key element of being like Christ was the experience of suffering (Rom 8:16-18; Phil 3:10). For Paul, then, to embody Christ entails suffering persecution and hardship, and daily dying, yet experiencing Christ's indwelling life, a foretaste of eventual glory (Rom 8:29-30). By embodying these experiences the apostle provides an example for his churches to follow. Like him, they can recognize their sufferings as ordained by God and a normal part of the path of God's children.

The Thessalonian and Philippian churches witnessed Paul's struggles and in turn experienced similar difficulties. Paul congratulated them for this and encouraged them to endure (1 Thess 3:3-4; Phil 1:27-30). Given

---

[152] Translating ἐν ἐμοί as "to me" harmonizes this phrase with the stories of Paul's conversion in Acts, but fails to appreciate Paul's own conception of himself, his "conversion," and his ministry.

Paul's extant letters to those churches and their (generous) participation in the Jerusalem collection, it would appear that Christians in Thessalonica and Philippi persevered through affliction and did indeed follow Paul's (and thus Christ's) example. Perhaps, like Paul, the Macedonians had learned to take pride in afflictions, "knowing that affliction (θλῖψις) produces steadfastness (ὑπομονήν), and steadfastness proof (δοκιμήν), and proof hope" (Rom 5:3-4).

The value of θλῖψις and ὑπομονή for δοκιμή was lost on the Corinthians. Paul's incarnation of Christ's death was likewise unappreciated. They focused on their experiences of Christ's indwelling which reflected Paul's original proclamation. Their tastes went to "demonstrations of the divine spirit and power," such as λόγοι, γνῶσις, and δυνάμεις, each of which received particular manifestation in the Corinthians' various χαρίσματα or πνευματικά. These things, not suffering, defined the Corinthians' Christian existence. The Corinthians therefore disdained Paul's ministry as weak and menial.

How then was Paul to persuade the Corinthians of his view of Christian existence? As already stated, Paul regarded weakness and authority as combined in his role as apostle. Since that connection corresponds to Paul's christology, one might expect Paul to draft a christological argument. As the person who heralded Χριστὸς ἐσταυρωμένος and who listed as his ambition "to know Christ and the fellowship of his sufferings," he could have explained his conduct as the proper response to Christ. It comes as a surprise then that Paul's argument in 2 Corinthians 10–13 does not focus on christology. But the christological differences probably were not clear to all the partners in the debate. Thus, for example, what Paul asserts in 11:4 may have reached the Corinthians' ears as news: that they heed another Jesus, another spirit, and another gospel may reflect Paul's rhetorical shaping of the debate, not the self-evident terms of the debate.[153] It is in fact possible that Paul's christology is being clarified precisely within the context of his problems with the Corinthians.

---

[153] What Paul does then in 11:2-4 is to clear the stage of all ignoble motivation and stress the urgent need for him to speak out. Whereas some might draw the (obvious) conclusion that Paul tilted with his opponents out of a desperate and petulant need for recognition, he counters that the jealousy which motivates him is commendable, for the issues are urgent. (We should not underestimate the profound role of jealousy in ancient psychology. It was regarded as one of the most fundamental motives of human behavior. The author of Luke-Acts in fact could treat it as a heuristic device of historiography.) He rescues the Corinthians from deception in order to preserve their pure devotion to Christ. A similar observation may pertain to 2 Cor 5:16. If κατὰ σάρκα refers to evaluating Christ by the standards of the world (as opposed to referring to the earthly Jesus), then Paul is placing *his* perspective on the christological issues involved in his dispute with

Though christology contributed greatly to Paul's thinking, his argument required other means to be made persuasive. This does not mean that christology is absent (10:1, 5, 7; 11:2-4; 12:9, 19; 13:3-4), only that other means of persuasion had to be pursued.

Paul therefore drew upon Hellenistic propaganda.[154] As we have seen already, one set of criteria came from philosophical schools. On the one hand, it was easy to imitate a philosopher. One could impersonate Diogenes by wearing only a τρίβων (and not a ἱμάτιον) and carrying a begging-bag (πήρα) and staff (βακτερία or βάκτρον). This σχῆμα could be furthered by growing a beard, and going barefoot. Some aspiring philosophers impersonated Herakles, wearing the lion's skin and carrying the club, bow, and quiver. The superficiality of this σχῆμα required, on the other hand, that a person give more substantial evidence of philosophy. Dio Chrysostom (70.7-8) demanded that the philosopher differ from the world in general in regard to study, regimen, frugality (εὐτέλεια), temperance (σωφροσύνη), dress, table manners, gymnasia, and baths (cp. 77/8.41), thereby directing himself toward ἀλήθεια, φρόνησις, and piety towards the gods, rather than ἀλαζονεία, ἀπάτη, τρυφή, and ἄνοια. Elsewhere Dio characterizes the philosopher as possessing ἐλευθερία and παρρησία and contrasts him with the so-called philosopher who is a parasite, a κόλαξ and ταπεινός (77/8.34-37).

Paul made a furtive attempt to argue along these lines in his first apology (2 Cor 2:14–6:13; 7:2-4).[155] Faced with rivals whose apostolic σχῆμα met the Corinthians' expectations, Paul attempted to move past the superficial to more substantive concerns. In attempting this, Paul used criteria and argumentative strategies common to Hellenistic

---

the Corinthians. They certainly would not regard their understanding of Christ as κατὰ σάρκα.

[154] Like Josephus' *Vita*, Paul could have characterized his deeds as a prophetic mission. This would not have been difficult for Paul, particularly given the points of contact between Paul and Jeremiah: 1) Paul's reflection on his call and commission in Gal 1:15-16 parallels Jeremiah; 2) grief over and intercession for Israel is a prophetic trait found in both Paul and Jeremiah; 3) suffering was the common experience of both Paul and Jeremiah; 4) both were stoned; 5) repentance was another prophetic theme common to both; 6) Jeremiah claimed to be unskilled in speaking (Jer 1:6); 7) Paul's approach to boasting is drawn from Jeremiah ("boast in the Lord," 9:22-23 [LXX]); 8) Jeremiah presented the concept of the new covenant; and 9) Paul's description of his apostolic ἐξουσία ("build up not tear down") reflects Jeremiah's commission ("to pluck up and to pull down, to destroy and to overthrow, to build and to plant," 1:10; cp. 31:28). Of these items, numbers three through nine appear in the Corinthian correspondence. With some imagination, Paul might have parlayed these things into a self-presentation as a prophet of God. But Paul did not do so.

[155] See Betz, "The Problem of Rhetoric and Theology," 40.

(philosophical) culture. For example, Paul stressed his sincerity, his pursuit of truth, his role as God's agent, his risks, the benefits which he brought others, his boldness, and his open, public speech (2:17; 4:1, 7, 11; 5:12; 6:4-5, 10).[156] In these arguments Paul sought to stress his integrity, to underscore the impossibility of human adequacy, and to deflect all credit for success to God.[157] These proposals failed to persuade the Corinthians.

After his humiliating second visit to Corinth Paul realized that to win over the Corinthians he had to cater to their expectations, entering more deeply into the competitive world of Hellenistic propaganda. Paul hesitated to do this for two reasons. First, it required boasting and he had repeatedly told the Corinthians that this was improper. Second, to argue within the parameters of Hellenistic propaganda represented (to Paul) a fundamental misunderstanding and misrepresentation of Paul's gospel. To surmount these obstacles Paul fashioned a populist and modest persona which drew on traditional countercultural rhetoric. But ultimately Paul had to fashion an image of Christian existence, not philosophical. His countercultural rhetoric therefore needed christological rationale. He offered this in 10:1, 5, 7; 11:2-4; 12:9; and 13:3-4.

In 10:7 Paul begins his defense with a simple fact: no one in Corinth may claim to be Χριστοῦ without admitting that Paul shares that status. Paul's interpretation of this fact (presumably) rests upon the assumption that he founded the church in Corinth.[158] If then the Corinthians do experience Christ's presence among them, they have Paul to thank for that. As a result, regardless of how he compares to other apostles, he cannot be ignored. For the Corinthians to claim Christian existence is to concede it to Paul.[159]

---

[156] Betz, "The Problem of Rhetoric and Theology," 21-23; cp. 1 Thess 2:1-13, on which see Malherbe, "Gentle as a Nurse."

[157] Jeffrey Crofton draws on Burkean rhetoric to distinguish Paul's rhetoric in these chapters from his rhetoric in chs. 10–13. In these earlier chapters "Paul rarely and only vaguely mentions his opponents, for his argument is about different *modes* of apostleship. Here the primary contrast is between a ministry characterized by openness and faithfulness (agency), and one that creates obstacles which hinder God's activity (agent)" (*The Agency of the Apostle: A Dramatistic Analysis of Paul's Responses to Conflict in 2 Corinthians*, JSNTSS 51 [Sheffield Academic Press, 1991], 102).

[158] Are Paul's words in 10:7 merely a bald assertion, or an argument of some kind? I assume the former.

[159] The meaning of Χριστοῦ is problematic. Perhaps it is an ablatival genitive indicating source or origin, indicating one's commission from Christ and thus functioning as a technical term for apostle. If that is the case, Paul's logic suffers. If his rivals are commissioned by the Jerusalem church, then Paul certainly may not assert that as they are Χριστοῦ so also is he. The nature of their commissions in fact would be

Paul also adjusts the concepts of κατὰ σάρκα and κατὰ κύριον. He first notes the inescapable reality that existence is factually sarkic (10:3a). Then he holds out the possibility that it can be experienced in another manner (10:3b). In Paul's language, life is ἐν σαρκί but not κατὰ σάρκα. This distinction raises the problem of identifying genuine Christian existence. This intellectual problem is reflected in Paul's attempts to destroy λογισμοί and obstacles to true knowledge of God (10:5). If one acknowledges the hand of Providence, which Paul recognizes as God Who Measures (10:13), then competition and comparisons among apostles become moot questions. Based on the theological idea of God's allotment, Paul refocuses the problem at hand to one concerning his living up to what God assigned to him, as opposed to measuring himself by what others accomplish. The idea of measurement also introduces that of ministerial province. By claiming what God allotted him as his own and focusing strictly on that, Paul characterizes his rivals as interlopers and usurpers. He also sets up an appropriate standard for boasting, viz., fulfillment of assigned tasks. To boast in such things is to boast "in the Lord." The appropriateness of this is clinched with the words of Scripture: "Let the one who boasts do so in the Lord" (10:17). A partitio then applies this insight to δοκιμή. By virtue of having delivered the gospel to Corinth Paul fulfilled the obligations of his God-allotted province and therefore is δόκιμος. Those who do not recognize these principles Paul labels as lacking understanding (10:12). The boasts typical of human competition are foolishness; they are not κατὰ κύριον but κατὰ σάρκα (11:17-18). With these moves then Paul recalibrates the ideas of what is σαρκικός, so that competitive boasting stands in conflict with the Lord.

He also emphasizes the moral aspect of existence which is κατὰ κύριον. In stressing his sincere concern for the Corinthians, Paul characterizes his mission as having betrothed the Corinthian church to one man to present her as a pure virgin to Christ (11:2). Paul then frets that they might betray the simplicity and purity which are for Christ (11:3).

---

quite different. To consider another scenario, if Paul's rivals were not emissaries from Jerusalem, but were sent out by a vision of Christ, Paul's argument then begs the question. He can claim to have a similar commission, but that proves nothing. The validity of their experience would not hang on the recognition of his own. A further problem is the identification of the referent of the pronoun τις. Does it point to any reader in the Corinthian church or a specific person? Does the singular in fact reflect one individual or does it generalize? If a specific referent is in view, is the person or persons Corinthian? I understand Paul to be referring to a specific individual within the Corinthian congregation who antagonizes Paul and champions the cause of his rivals. In such a case, being Χριστοῦ is a matter of Christian existence, not apostleship. As the founder of the Corinthian Christian community, Paul can assert that no one there may claim to be Χριστοῦ to the exclusion of himself. They can be Χριστοῦ only if he is.

5.7. Paul's Counterculture and Christology

This could happen if they fall victim to a false perspective of Jesus (or a different spirit or gospel message, 11:4).[160] In Paul's eyes, this is the case. Enchanted by the wrong Jesus, spirit, and gospel, the Corinthians are alienated from Paul and failing to repent. Factions, slander, and other shameful behavior exists among the Corinthian Christians (12:20-21). Paul's vision of Christian existence offers the antidote for such problems.

The goal of Paul's current dealings with the Corinthians is to capture every thought for "the obedience of Christ" (10:5). In this statement Paul reflects his typical conjunction of noetic and moral existence. The question to ask is whether τοῦ Χριστοῦ is an objective or subjunctive genitive. The answer to that question determines the specificity of Paul's reference. If Paul points his readers to obedience to Christ, then what constitutes that obedience remains open and must be defined elsewhere. If Paul directs his readers to Christ's obedience, then he provides a more specific goal, one which 2 Corinthians 10–13 then describes. Comparing Paul's uses of the noun ὑπακοή throughout his letters suggests that when he modifies it with a genitive referring to a person, he describes the subject of the implied action.[161] Thus, as Paul models his behavior on Christ in 10:1 (i.e., Christ's leniency and clemency), so he calls the

---

[160] This raises the question of Paul's rivals' position on moral failure. Do they tolerate wrongdoing? Do they condone πορνεία (12:21)? That Hebrews tolerate πορνεία seems unlikely. Alternatively, then, they do not. That moral failings persist among the Corinthian Christians indicates that Paul's rivals have failed to motivate some in Corinth to repent. Why this failure? Methods and/or social groups might provide answers. As for the former, Paul's caricature of his rivals suggests that they have asserted themselves — and perhaps precisely in the area of moral reform. Their heavy-handed approach lent them an impressive self-presentation, but did not elicit repentance from erring Christians. Perhaps the forceful approach alienated some offenders. On the other hand, perhaps divergent house-churches account for competing social groups within Corinth. Perhaps one church champions the rivals over Paul, allowing the rivals to assert themselves, the result being that the moral problems plaguing Paul's group do not exist. Among Paul's house-churches, however, Paul does not wish to alienate anyone and holds out the opportunity for repentance. Where the rivals would act quickly and perhaps severely, Paul opts to act less destructively. He prefers not to excommunicate or humiliate publicly. In such a scenario, methods of moral guidance and correction would have been a bone of contention.

[161] ὑπακοή takes a genitive in Rom 1:5; 5:19; 15:18; 16:19, [26]; 2 Cor 7:15; 10:6; Phlm 21. Surveying this data, the genitive in Rom 1:5 (ὑπακοὴν πίστεως) could be many things, e.g., apposition, source, object or subject; Rom 16:26 offers the same phrase with similar possibilities. However, Rom 5:19; 15:18; 16:19; 2 Cor 7:15; 10:6; and Phlm 21 are clearly subjective or possessive genitives. Note also that in these six latter examples the genitive refers to persons, whereas the ambiguous examples in Romans involve an abstract noun (cf. 1 Pet 1:22, ἐν τῇ ὑπακοῇ τῆς ἀλεθείας). The ambiguities of the noun with genitive do not exist in the case of the verb, as the verb's subject and dative object provide clarification.

Corinthians likewise to model Christ and specifically Christ's obedience. How that is done is then the point of debate. While it requires a moral dimension, which apparently is germane to the Corinthians' situation, it also reinforces Paul's insistence on the importance of embracing Jesus' death (cf. 2 Cor 4:7-15), as submission to death was the defining character of Jesus' obedience (Phil 2:8). If the Corinthians do in fact respond to Christ's death, then the way is cleared to legitimize Paul's apostolate and to implement moral reform.[162]

Christ's obedience returns to the fore in the explicit christological statement in 13:3-4. In these verses Paul concedes the Corinthians' experience of Christ as one of power not weakness. But this experience must be seen in the proper light. Paul therefore elaborates on the nature of this experience to note its two proper aspects: Christ's power (1) issues from God as (2) a consequence of his acceptance of death. Paul then claims to recapitulate that process in his ministry, sharing Christ's weakness and subsequent life through God's power. That he does this for the Corinthians positions him as a mediator of God's power in Christ, while dignifying his weakness as the appropriate channel for encountering God's power.

Earlier, though, Paul made an important observation about how Christ's power comes to expression in his servants. Christ's power comes to perfection in weakness (12:9); moreover, this further expresses his χάρις.[163] This revelation blankets Paul's entire Christian existence with Christ's grace and establishes a paradigm for how Christ's grace responds to weakness: it becomes a stage for Christ's power. Weakness leading to power, then, is not simply christological (13:3-4), but christophanic. Paul, therefore, points directly to evidence of his ταπεινότης and rejoices in the stage it sets for revelation of Christ's empowerment.

Christ's χάρις, then, sets an example for the use of power. It comes in kindness to help the weak. This suggests the important role of "the

---

[162] Does the christology of "Christ's obedience" (10:5) conflict with kingship christology (10:1)? I regard both as part of Paul's christology, the former leading to the latter. As we will see, 13:3-4 states as much. That Paul combines the two aspects in a single paragraph does not trouble me. The combination is interesting, though, in that Paul regards the obedience as prelude to the rule, while the Corinthians sidestep the former. Paul, therefore, ascribes to the christology which the Corinthians prefer, but predicates it on the aspects which they do not.

[163] Does the oracle view χάρις as a historical fact or an ongoing experience? On the one hand, χάρις may refer to Paul's apostolic call and office, such that Paul should be content with simply having been called and must live within ongoing weaknesses through which Christ shows his power; alternatively, the ongoing manifestation of Christ's power compensating for Paul's weakness reveals Christ's kindness. More likely, these two things are inseparable.

leniency and clemency of Christ." By stressing how lightly the exalted Christ imposes his authority, Paul establishes a paradigm for wielding Christ's authority within the ἐκκλησία. The modesty suggested by Christ's ἐπιείκεια is clinched in 13:4 by Paul's reference to Christ's career path: the power of the resurrected one rests on his weakness. Paul argues that weakness-then-strength is an indissoluble pair locked in an unalterable sequence. The representative of Christ must embody that sequence. Christ's leniency and clemency therefore guide Paul's ministry while confirming the legitimacy of his claims to be Christ's apostle.

8. Conclusion

To recapitulate, when Paul defends himself in 2 Corinthians 10–13 he wishes to be seen as a man of the people. To accomplish this he takes up the conventional ἦθος of modesty. This corresponds nicely to his antipathy to boasting, as well as his desire to show how he uses his ἐξουσία for the good of others: Paul offers leniency, his rivals tyranny. Paul's need to subvert the arguments upon which his rivals' eminence is based makes the modest ἦθος even more useful, for its association with Socrates opens the door to irony and a rhetoric which contradicts conventional norms. Thus, Paul's admission of ταπεινότης is part of his Socratic rhetoric, an ironic and paradoxical concession which assaults conventional status markers, serving as a polemical weapon and pedagogical tool. The Socratic demolition of typical encomiastic categories, then, creates a persuasive context for Paul's christology of death-resurrection to assert itself.

Conclusion

This investigation has attempted to understand Paul's appeal by Christ's πραΰτης καὶ ἐπιείκεια in 2 Corinthians 10:1. First, I argued that the nuance of these words has escaped every translation of the English Bible. By discovering a semantic field present in 2 Corinthians 10–13 to which Paul's appeal belongs we have evidence which reveals the connotation of πραΰτης and ἐπιείκεια, suggesting the translation "leniency and clemency." The associations revealed by the semantic field also reveal the many connections between Christ's πραΰτης καὶ ἐπιείκεια and the remainder of the letter fragment. In addition, this translation connects 10:1 directly to the warfare imagery which follows in 10:4-6, so that the long tradition of scholars who thought those verses contradicted Paul's opening appeal are wrong.

At a more general level, the semantic investigation in chapter two advances the enterprise of New Testament lexicography. We have provided definitions for both ἐπιείκεια and πραότης/πραΰτης, as well as identifying the words with which they typically appear. Beyond simply listing their synonyms and antonyms, we have tried to illustrate how they interact with those words; moreover, we have looked beyond synonyms and antonyms to identify other common members of their semantic fields and observe what relations ἐπιείκεια and πραότης/πραΰτης have with those words. Whereas current reference works offer some clues on these matters, the data in chapter two go far beyond anything previously available in lexical works.

Next, given the results of the semantic investigation, how the idea of Christ's "leniency and clemency" fits into Paul's christology was examined. Having outlined the ideology of good rule in the Greco-Roman world, we recognized the commonplace, popular appeal of a ruler's leniency to which Christ's clemency corresponds. Examination of Paul's christology then revealed his conception of Christ as a king and the variety of ways that idea contributed to Paul's christological thinking. Seeing Christ's βασιλεία behind his πραΰτης καὶ ἐπιείκεια then undermines the attempt to see any reference to the historical Jesus in Paul's words.

Why Paul formulated such an expression as Christ's "leniency and clemency" was the next point we investigated. While this formulation grew out of his typical pattern of ministry, the particular circumstances of Paul's relationship with the Corinthians gave rise to it. His attempt to bring about Christian formation among the Corinthians required Paul to admonish them; yet they challenged his right to do so. In the face of their disobedience, his customary gentle approach became one of leniency, as he offered to overlook their wrongdoing in the hope that they would repent. Their prolonged recalcitrance pressed Paul into one last desperate attempt to secure their cooperation, which came to expression in Paul's appeal by Christ's clemency and the threat that the time for sparing would soon expire.

This investigation also disclosed that the connections between Paul's appeal in 2 Cor 10:1 and the rest of the letter fragment go beyond semantics, extending to the way he presents himself. On one level, by basing his appeal on Christ's pattern Paul positioned himself as an agent of Christ's authority who exercised it in the same manner as Christ (like a local official extending the emperor's clemency). This was important in presenting himself as an apostle. An offer of leniency also portrays Paul as a person who bears authority lightly, using it for the good of others and not self-aggrandizement. This populist program corresponds to his general treatment of the Corinthians.

At a broader level, though, we have discovered that Paul's self-presentation follows a pattern of modest rhetoric, or in Hermogenes' terms, an ἦθος of ἐπιείκεια. This appears in Paul's hesitation to impose sanctions and assert himself in an authoritarian manner, his refusal to accept money and affirmation of his manual labor, his concessions that he is an unskilled speaker and that he may have spoken excessively of his authority, his distaste for the entire enterprise of boasting, and his ready identification with the weak and lowly.

A (controversial) stylistic element of the modest ἦθος was irony. Though dissimulation resembles modesty, the connection between irony and modesty actually came into being through the example of Socrates. Paul taps into the irony common in the Socratic tradition which distinguishes truth from appearance so as to challenge what most people mistakenly regard as good. I called this both countercultural and antiencomiastic rhetoric. More precisely, it is philosophy's redefinition of wisdom and virtue. It is the challenge embodied in the figure of Socrates (and in varying degrees in Aesop, Odysseus, and Herakles). This rhetoric helped Paul to challenge the status markers of his rivals and reappraise the value of his own lowliness, weakness, and nothingness. As God's power intervened in the death-resurrection of Christ, so Christ's power finds expression in Paul's weakness. It is precisely the ταπεινός Paul who astonishingly therefore extends "leniency and clemency."

Biting irony oversteps Hermogenes' definition of the modest ἦθος. Paul's Fool's Speech, therefore, with its forceful irony and parody conflicts in terms of style with the persona projected in the remainder of the letter fragment. This further distinguishes Paul's own voice from that presented in the Fool's Speech, where Paul presents an exercise in ἠθοποιία.

In light of Hermogenes' discussion of ἦθος, then, we were able to provide a theory about Paul's rhetoric which connects and accounts for previous studies of 2 Corinthians 10–13. By thinking in terms of ἦθος, ἐπιείκεια and ἠθοποιία, as well as irony, paradox and counterculture, we now have a general theory to account for Paul's rhetoric in this letter fragment.

The conclusions which we have reached have further implications. First, we now see in 2 Cor 10:1-6 all the elements of Paul's argument in 2 Corinthians 10–13. His appeal through Christ's "leniency and clemency" resurfaces near the end of the letter when Paul again appeals to the Corinthians to repent, warning them that he will not spare when he returns. Paul's admission of ταπεινότης anticipates his concession of (and boasting in!) his weakness and nothingness. That Paul's lowliness is the credential which validates his ministry against conventional standards of status is a paradoxical (Socratic) irony whose truth emerges in the Fool's Speech. Paul's lowliness in fact embodies his message. These key points in Paul's argument arise in 10:1-6.

Such content suggests that 2 Cor 10:1-6 followed immediately upon the epistolary prescript in the letter's pre-canonical form. We say this based on Paul's habit of encapsulating an entire epistle in its opening paragraph. Though Paul prefers to open his letters with a thanksgiving period, Galatians provides the best analogy for 2 Corinthians 10–13, for both struggle forcefully to rescue their readers from great dangers. As in Galatians, so also in 2 Corinthians 10–13, then, the situation precludes thanksgiving and demands that Paul open with strong words.

The case can be made that 10:1-6 was in fact Paul's exordium. For example, the confidence Paul expresses in these verses is appropriate to a situation in which he seems to lack advantage. As Cicero observes, when an audience sees "that he whom they think is shaken by the opponent's speech is ready to speak in reply with confidence and with assurance, they generally think that they have assented too readily rather than that he is confident without good cause" (*De inv.* 1.25).[1] The reference to the charge levied against Paul in 10:1b corresponds to Cicero's advice to "begin by a

---

[1] For speeches which open with expressions of confidence, see for example Lysias *Contra Simonem* 1; Aeschines *De falsa legatione* 1-11.

reference to what has been said by your opponent" (1.25). Though Paul's typical expressions of goodwill are absent, viz., prayer and thanksgiving, clemency expresses goodwill (as we have seen), as does entreaty (Quint. 4.1.33). In 10:1-6 we also see a strategy recommended for "scandalous cases": Paul substitutes something good (leniency) for something bad (inconsistency), shifting the audience's attention from what is hated to what is favored (Cic. *De inv.* 1.24). These things, then, further intimate that 2 Cor 10:1-6 opened the body of the original letter.

In view of these possibilities, we conclude that the letter fragment preserved for us in canonical 2 Corinthians preserves the bulk of the original letter. Perhaps only the epistolary prescript and postscript were excised by the editor. That being the case, Paul's offer of leniency sounds the opening note of his urgent and desperate communication with his estranged church.

Lastly, the research presented here continues the trend of historical biblical criticism to ignore the boundaries of the canon when interpreting biblical texts. In semantics, we have seen the error produced by privileging the Septuagint. In christology, we have eliminated the need to assume a connection between Paul's remarks and the historical Jesus. As for 2 Corinthians, the validity of interpreting an individual letter fragment on its own terms rather than on its redactor's has proven fruitful. Identifying the connections between Paul's opening offer of leniency and the following references to lowliness, warfare, and punishment has exposed the thematic unity of 2 Corinthians 10–13. This integration of the last four chapters emphatically distinguishes them as a literary unit discrete from their canonical home in 2 Corinthians. Finally, exposing Paul's rhetoric further reveals how tenuous his position was within the Corinthian church. As we observe Paul characterizing his rivals unfavorably, forcing matters into more amenable categories, manipulating status markers, and simply pleading, we are forced to see beyond the apostolic legend to a man who desperately claimed to be nothing, in order that he might appear to be something.

Appendix 1

Definition of ἐπιείκεια

Chapter One provided a definition of ἐπιείκεια, but did not cite references. That definition is repeated here in greater detail and with references furnished. A definition of ἐπιείκεια during the early Roman Empire is as follows:[1]

1) a general compliance with good behavior, Jos. *Ap.* 2.43; Diod. Sic. 1.93.2; Dio Chrys. 79.1; Luc. *Scy.* 6; Dio Cas. [41.29.2; 57.24.2, 8; 64.5.1]; 78.11.2; [Philos. *Vit. Apol.* 2.39.39]; [Phil 4:5]: good as:
   a) recognized conventionally,
      i) particularly by aristocratic folkways (typically called καλοκἀγαθία and ἀρετή), [Philo *De conf. ling.* 116]; Diod. Sic. [9.10.2]; 14.4.1; 34/35.35.1 (παιδεία); [Plut. *Thes.* 3c/ 6.4; *Pom.* 633e/ 28.3 (civilized); *Mor.* 489e; 533b; 709e; 842f]; Dio Chrys. [7.33, 60, 111; 13.13; 30.41; 31.28, 41, 58; 40.29; 43.3; 49.1 (with πεπαιδευμένος); 65.5]; 79.1; Luc. *Alex.* 4; [Dio Cas. 38.3.1; 46.20.3]; Diog. L. 3.89 (ἐλεύθερος or μέτριος appear in many of the preceding references); but cp. Aristid. [1.390] and 1.392; Spicq notes the attribution to "functionaries and servants" who "acquit themselves of their duties 'appropriately'" (*TLNT* 2: 37 n. 16); the result is an "emphasis on exactitude, loyalty, and fidelity in the accomplishment of a task" (2: 36-37); yet such uses still reflect the perspective of social superiors;
      ii) but also by common human decency (linked with αἰδώς and μετριότης), Plut. *Mor.* 529c; Luc. *Vit. auc.* 10; *Rhet. prae.* 15;

   b) anthropologically appropriate: moderation, [Luc. *Gal.* 23 (cf. *De astr.* 15)];

---

[1] Again, references enclosed within brackets indicate the appearance of a form of the adjective ἐπιεικής, rather than the noun ἐπιείκεια. A definition of the adjective would differ from this because its range of meaning is more broad. We also should emphasize that this definition is constructed to elucidate a mid-first century text, viz., 2 Cor 10:1, and not a millennium of usage.

c) defined noetically: guided by reason, Plut. *Mor.* 451f (which combines noetic and anthropological uses); Dio Chrys. 30.20, 24; Aristid. 1.257;
d) (in forensic contexts general compliance may serve as) a refutation of wrongdoing: innocence, or not worthy of conviction, Dem. *In Med.* 207; App. *Bel. civ.* 4.6.50; Lib. *Ep.* 664.1;
e) as attested by use in virtue lists, Aug. *Res ges.* 34; Luc. *Alex.* 61; *Som.* 10; *Vit. auc.* 26; *Imag.* 11; [1 Tim 3:3]; [Titus 3:2]; [Jas 3:17];

2) definite behavioral choices which involve declining to act with the full rights of one's person, Plut. *Mor.* 231b; 483f: e.g.,
a) not detracting from the person of others, [Plut. *Mor.* 816c-d]; [*1 Clem.* 21.7];
b) accepting slights or wrongs, Plut. *Mor.* 460f (because of friendship); 824d; Dio Cas. 22.76.2;
  i) this reflects more general philosophic teaching about not acting on anger, passions, or bad impulses, [Epict. *Diss.* 3.20.12]; Philo *De op. mun.* 103; cf. Ign. *Phld.* 1.1-2;
  ii) in Wis 2:19 (used with ἀνεξικακία) ἐπιείκεια comes from a weak person and is exercised in the face of ὕβρις rather than being a powerful person's behavioral alternative to ὕβρις; this parallels the potential practice of this virtue by all people as envisioned by philosophy; the weak person's ἐπιείκεια, however, rests on God's power, which is expected to intervene and protect, so that the weak person models God's response to wrongdoing; the behavior is therefore grounded theologically, not philosophically; cf. Aesop *Proverbia* 37, which identifies God as the avenger of the silent mouth, i.e., "The person who consciously respects ἐπιείκεια will have help against his/her enemies from God" (my trans.); cp. Diod. Sic. 18.28.6;
  iii) Christian theology further developed this in view of Jesus' teaching and example, Ign. *Eph.* 10.3; *1 Clem.* 13.1;

c) a friendly or democratic bearing towards one's lessers, Diod. Sic. 1.54.2 (with ὁμιλία); 8.30.1 (adverb); Plut. *The. et Rom.* 37f/ 2.2; *Cor.* 225d/ 24.4; *Cato maj.* 337e/ 3.1; Dio Chrys. 41.9; [Luc. *Phal.* 1.2]; Dio Cas. 21.70.9; [60.12.1]; 68.7.3; (cf. Dio Cas. 57.11);
d) withdrawal from public affairs, Jos. *Ant.* 15.165, 177, 182; [Dio Cas. 38.36.1-2]; Diog. L. 10.10; (cf. Dio Cas. 53.6.1);

Definition of ἐπιείκεια 333

e) modest oratory, Hermogenes *On Types of Style* 345-352; [Philos. *Vit. Apol.* 8.7.475];
f) generosity which spares others, Jos. *Ant.* 14.13; Diod. Sic. 4.57.4; Polyb. 1.14.4 (an historian's partiality); Plut. *Flam.* 378c/ 17.1; *Cato min.* 785d/ 53.4; *Mor.* 729e; Dio Cas. 13.55.2; 50.27.7; 57.11.2; [Philos. *Vit. soph.* 2.562.32];
- i) especially enemies, Jos. *Ant.* 12.122; 13.245; Diod. Sic. 37.19.1; Plut. [*Sol.* 95a]; *Fab.* 191b/ 3.1; *Aris.* 334e/ 25.7; *Mor.* [90e]; 295c;
- ii) and defeated foes, 3 Macc 3:15; Diod. Sic. 1.55.10 (adverb); 4.44.4; [14.105.3]; 15.88.1, 3; 17.38.4; 17.76.2; 17.91.8; 27.6.2; 29.10.1 (= Roman tradition, as also [31.9.4] and 40.2.1); 32.4.2; Plut. *Ser.* 595f/ 2.3; *Pom.* 663a/ 3.2; *Alex.* 690b/ 43.4; *Cae.* 733c/ 54.4; *Brut.* 998c/ 30.4; [Dio Cas. 41.42.6; 41.63.4];

g) the easy, kind and generous treatment shown to subjects or inferiors:
- i) of God or gods: 2 Macc 2:22; Diod. Sic. 4.12.7 (= Herakles);
- ii) of rulers and leaders: 2 Macc 9:27 (adverb); Add Esth 3:13b; *Ep. Arist.* 207; 290; Philo *De vita Mos.* 1.198; *De spec. leg.* 2.110; *De leg. ad Gai.* 119; Jos. *Ant.* 8.213; 15.375; 19.246; Diod. Sic. 14.45.1; 16.20.6 (adverb); 17.69.9; 18.14.2; 33.18.1; Plut. *Aris.* 332/ 23.2; *Cato maj.* 345d/ 16.5; *Art.* 1013a/ 4.3; *Mor.* 60e; Dio Chrys. 1.6; Dio Cas. 26.88.1; 43.17.2; *Diogn.* 7.3-6;
- iii) of slaveholders: Diod. Sic. 34/35.2.39; [1 Pet 2:18 (slaveholder)];

h) a ruler's mercy (or leniency or clemency), 3 Macc 7:6; [*Ep. Arist.* 188]; Philo *De prae. et poe.* 166; [*De Ios.* 221]; Jos. *Ant.* 15.48; 19.334; Diod. Sic. 1.65.3; 2.28.6; Dio Cas. 44.8.1; [Philos. *Vit. soph.* 2.561.30 (philosopher-like behavior; cp. above 2.b.i.)]; 2 Cor 10:1;
- i) this may be personified as Clemency, Plut. *Cae.*734d/ 57.4; App. *Bel. civ.* 2.16.106; Dio Cass. 44.6.4;
- ii) as the Roman Empire aged, ἐπιείκεια became a commonplace attribute of rulers and all those in positions of authority, leading to appeals to "your clemency" (Grenfell no. lxvii; Hunt no. 2133; Parsons no. 3126); Acts 24:4;
- iii) applied to God, Ps 85:5 LXX; Dan 3:42; 4:27 (variant); Bar 2:27; Wis 12:18; *Ep. Arist.* [188]; 192; 207; [211]; [*Pss. Sol.* 5.12]; [*Jos. Asen.* 11.10; 12.14]; Philo *De prae. et poe.*

166; [*1 Clem.* 29.1]; but cf. Diod. Sic. 3.65.1, 7 where Dionysus treates all people ἐπιεικής; 4.12.7 of Herakles;

i) parental indulgence, [*Jos. Asen.* 12.14]; App. *Bel. civ.* 2.20.144; Ps.-Aristid. *Eis bas.* 22; [cf. Diod. Sic. 3.61.4];
j) kindly intended and gently administered moral correction, 2 Macc 10:4 (God); [*Ep. Arist.* 188 (ruler)]; Philo *Quod det. pot.* 146 (adverb); Plut. *Mor.* 69b; [73d; 74d]; [Dio Cas. 55.17.3]; [Philos. *Vit. Apol.* 4.16.31];
k) reasonable, restrained, and temperate speech — even silence, [Philo *De conf. ling.* 37]; Plut. *Mor.* 80b; [Dio Cas. 41.15.2]; Ign. *Phld.* 1.1-2 (?); [*Herm. Man.* 12.4.2];

3) a technical term for a reasoned and humane application of laws and sanctions: viz., equity, Aris. *E. N.* 5.10; *Rhet.* 1.13.13; [Dio Cas. 4.17.7]; Diog. L. 7.123;[2]

To the preceding we may compare the definition supplied by Danker in his recent revision of Bauer.[3] I should say that comparison is unfair, as the preceding does not labor under the constraints of space that the lexcion must; furthermore, the introduction of definitions into the standard lexicon is a wonderful advance for which all in the field of New Testament are grateful.

Danker defines ἐπιείκεια as "the quality of making allowances despite facts that might suggest reason for a different reaction." Users of this definition should understand that typically "making allowances" involves behavior, not simply a mental exercise like rationalization. Through deeds one "makes allowances," i.e., acts with restraint, undue generosity, or (as I propose above) declines to act with the full rights of one's person. I would also underscore what Danker's proposed glosses suggest: the "different reaction" is one which is generous or courteous.

What my more lengthy definition provides beyond Danker is a sense of the social register implied by ἐπιείκεια and the social contexts in which it

---

[2] When Dio Cassius uses the adjective in 52.34.6, he reflects three of the usages distinguished here: 2.h, 2.j, and 3, i.e., a ruler's mercy which applies laws humanely in order to achieve moral rectitude. Such overlap is not unusual.

[3] Frederick William Danker, *A Greek-English Lexicon of the New Testament and other Early Christian Literature*, 3rd ed., based on Walter Bauer's *Griechisch-deutsches Wörterbuch zu den Schriften des Neuen Testaments und der frühchristlichen Literatur*, 6th ed., eds. Kurt Aland and Barbara Aland, with Viktor Reichmann, based also on previous English editions by W. F. Arndt, F. W. Gingrich, and F. W. Danker (University of Chicago Press, 2000), p. 371.

appears. The former reflects the respect placed on the exercise of the virtue and its cultural connotations. An important example of the latter is its association with reason as a trait that distinguishes a cultured person from a brutal, uncultured one. The line between cultured and uncultured could be that between Greek and Barbarian or between educated and uneducated. Other connotations are aristocracy and populism. On the one hand it is the behavior of society's better people, on the other it helps blur the line between those who are better and the masses. By refusing to enforce one's personal rights, a person can stoop to blend in with the crowd — hence, for example, modest rhetoric.

The contexts in which ἐπιείκεια appears also influence its translation. As indicated in this investigation and reflected in my definition, these include the battlefield, the palace, the household, the court and any public office, as well as in moral reflection and oratory. Other times no specific context appears to be in view. Danker does not have the leisure to outline these different contexts.

Semantic contexts are equally important. Danker notes a few of these, but again cannot reasonably present them all. I have attempted to provide this information in this investigation. Danker also notes correctly the connection between ἐπιείκεια and πραΰτης, while this investigation has detailed the consequences of their collocation and the clues that point to their meaning when used together.

The glosses that Danker proposes are fine, though a sensitive translator might want to invent others to suit the particulars of varied contexts. In selecting among Danker's recommended glosses, I would suggest that a translator ask who is the person acting with ἐπιείκεια, what is the relative social standing between the actor and recipient(s), is there any differential in power between them, what is the setting of the action (court, battlefield, household), what would the expected behavior be and what might it, and more generally, what type of action does the context suggest is in view. The more concrete the context, the people involved, and the nature of the behavior, then the more precise the gloss used to translate ἐπιείκεια.

Appendix 2

Definition of πραότης/πραΰτης

As for ἐπιείκεια, a definition was provided earlier in the body of this work, but references were not furnished. Those are provided here. Moreover, this definition seeks to outline the meaning of πραΰτης at the time when Paul wrote his letters.[1] A definition of πραΰτης/πραότης follows, organized around two basic perspectives:

1) πραότης from the subject's perspective with reference to the subject's psychology: a calm which is not overcome by sundry disturbances but responds with measure and composure: an imperturbable gentleness or mildness; composure, serenity, forbearance, tolerance, Plut. *Per.* 5.1; *Mor.* 100d; 608d; Athen. *Deip.* 14.24/ 627f; [Diog. L. 2.136];
   a) a patient calm in the face of hostility or confrontation, Plut. *Themis.* 11.4; *Mor.* 90c (with ἀνεξικακία); of criticism or dejection, Plut. *Mor.* 78b; 1 Peter 3:16 (or 2.a.ii).
   b) ability to endure misfortune, Plut. *Mar. Cor.* 21.1; folly, Plut. *Per.* 2.5; slander, Plut. *Ages.* 21.5;
   c) contrast to anger (ὀργή, θύμος), Add Esth 5:1e; *Jos. Asen.* 23.10; Philo *De vit. Mos.* 2.279; cf. *De spec. leg.* 1.146; [Dio Chrys. 11.127]; Plut. *Mor.* 445a; 457d; 458c; 462c; 489c; [M. Aur. 11.9 and 18]; James 1:21.
   d) a lessening of the power of emotions, Plut. *Mor.* 83a;
   e) half-hearted, Sir 10:28 (boasting), Plut. *Alex.* 4.8 (indulgence in the pleasures of the flesh);
   f) general recognition as a virtue, [*FVS* 10.3.b.19 (1: 63); 64.C.2 (2: 67); 68.B.46 (2: 156, adverb)]; [Xen. *Oec.* 15.4]; Diod. Sic. 11.67.3; [Epict. *Diss.* 4.5.22]; Athen. *Deip.* 14.24/ 627f;
      i) a philosopher has πραότης, Plut. *Brut.* 2.4; *Mor.* 37a; 457d; 582d (Pythagoras); 1108b (Socrates); Diog. L. 9.108 (identifies πραότης or ἀπάθεια as the Skeptic τέλος);

---

[1] Again, the brackets indicate references to the adjective, πρᾶος. Moreover, while I have supported uses of the noun with examples of the adjective, I have not provided a survey of all the uses and meanings of the adjective.

Definition of πραότης/πραΰτης 337

ii) use in virtue lists, Philo *De sac. Ab.* 27; Dio Chrys. 32.37; Luc. *Som.* 10; *Alex.* 61; Aristid. 3.212; cf. Arr. *His. suc. Alex.* 26; Galatians 5:23; Colossians 3:12 (par. Ephesians 4:2)

2) πραότης as expressed and experienced in a social context:
   a) a peaceable benevolence which smoothes over undesirable things, especially a refusal to chide, [Plut. *Mor.* 81d]; [Aristid. 28.147]; [M. Aur. 7.63]; Galatians 6:1
      i) extending a generous reception to a pagan, [*Jos. Asen.* 8.8]; to a former tyrant, Polyb. 2.60.5; to a failure, Plut. *Fab. max.* 18.4; to the poor, Sir 4:8; to visitors and neighbors, Aristid. 1.8;
      ii) desired bearing in debate, Plut. *Mor.* 80b; cf. 394f; [468a]; Aristid. 4.11 (cf. [4.16]); or in admonition, M. Aur. 11.18 (adverb); Philos. *Vit. soph.* 1.487; 2 Timothy 2:25; 1 Peter 3:16 (or 1.a)
      iii) a father's indulgence, [Dio. Hal. *Ant.* 4.36.2]; Ps.-Plut. *Mor.* 13d; 1 Corinthians 4:21

   b) the compliant response of social inferiors, Plut. *Ages.* 2.1; *Cras.* 13.1; *Mor.* 144c; M. Aur. 9.42;
      i) submissive: Aristid. 3.491; to God (πίστις), Sir 1:27; 45:4 (cf. 2.c); of political allies, [Polyb. 3.52.6]; Jews to Roman rule, Jos. *Bel.* 2.340; an admonished crowd, [Dio Chrys. 18.2]; women, Sir 36:23; Plut. *Comp. Lyc. et Numa* 4.7; a son to his father's admonitions, Philo *De vit. Mos.* 1.328 (adverb); of a younger brother to his elder, Plut. *Mor.* 487c; of slaves (docile), Plut. *Cato maj.* 21.2;
      ii) cooperative, yielding: of opposition, [Aristid. 12.41]; App. *Bel. civ.* 1.6.49.
      iii) humility (ταπεινός): expands to be a characteristic of God's people, whether great or small, Sir 3:17 (cf. 2.c.iii); cf. 4:8; cf. 10:28; plural adjective as a collective for God's typically troubled people, [Job 24:4; 36:15; Ps 24:9 LXX; 33:3 LXX; 36:11 LXX; 75:10 LXX; 146:6 LXX; 149:4; Isa 26:6; Sir 3:19 variant; 10:14]; singular but collective, Zeph 3:12 (λαὸν πραΰν καὶ ταπεινόν); of individuals, Moses, [Num 12:3], but cp. 1.i and 1.iii; of promised king, [Zech 9:9], but cp. 2.c; Joel 4:11 LXX ("let the πραΰς be a fighter");
      iv) meek (pejorative use), of a teacher loyal to a rich but cheap student, Plut. *Cras.* 3.6;

c) a populist bearing, a gentle and benign exercise of government, Ps 44:5; [Zech 9:9]; Add Esth 3:13b variant; [Dio Hal. *Ant.* 10.19.1]; Plut. *Cic.* 6.1; *Numa* 20.3; [*Mor.* 86b; 148c]; Philos. *Vit. soph.* 2.621;
  i) non-tyrannical, *T. Jud.* 24.1 (Messianic); Dio. Hal. *Ant.* 1.83.1; [4.41.4]; Diod. Sic. 11.67.3; Plut. *Sol.* 15.1; *Pel.* 26.2; *Dion* 13.3; *Dion et Brut.* 3.2; 3.10; Luc. *Phal.* 1.3; Athen. *Deip.* 12.72/ 549d; [Dio Cas. 55.12.3];
  ii) bears or exercises power lightly, [*T. Dan* 6.9 (humble savior)]; Polyb. 3.99.7 (Rome's gentle imperial rule); 4.27.10 (royal rule); Plut. *Per.* 39.4; *Sulla* 6.5 (an obliging colleague); Aristid. *Pan.* 149; [Athen. *Deip.* 10.61/ 444a (democratic leaders allow many liberties)]; Aristid. 1.137, 149 (a compliant ally; cf. 3.240); cp. Dio Cas. 15.57.25; [43.20.1];
  iii) equalizes inequality, Philo *De dec.* 167;
  iv) attractive to common people, Diod. Sic. 19.81.3; Plut. *Cim.* 5.5; (cf. *Aris.* 23.2; *Cato min.* 23.1); Dio Cas. 49.20.4;
  v) freedom from ambition is required for πραότης, Plut. *Aris. et Cato* 5.4 (cp. *Fab. max.* 1.4; 22.8; *Cras.* 3.6; *Eum. et Ser.* 595f/ 2.2; [*Mor.* 468f]); Dio Cas. 53.6.1 (ἀπραγμοσύνη);

d) showing gentleness, indulgence, and/or generosity in order to procure peace (Titus 3:2; James 3:13):
  i) preferred way to treat cities in revolt and agitations of allies, Jos. *Bel.* 6.340; Plut. *Fab. Max.* 20.1-4;
  ii) to use persuasion rather than force of arms, Plut. *Lys. et Sul.* 2.1; Aristid. *Lak.* 11;
  iii) the friendly motive which pursues peace talks with one's enemy, Plut. *Cras.* 30.2;
  iv) to offer generous, just terms in peace talks, Plut. *Tit. Flam.* 2.5 (cp. 21.2);
  v) to place trust in foes, [Plut. *Ag.* 21.5; cf. 20.4];

e) mitigated retribution: forgiveness, mercy, leniency, clemency; M. Aur. 9.42; 2 Corinthians 10:1;
  i) soft-peddling sins, Plut. *Alc.* 16.4; (cp. *Mar. Cor.* 13.1; *Dion et Brut.* 3.10);
  ii) go easy in court, reticent prosecution, Plut. *Cim.* 14.5; *Per.* 10.6;
  iii) slow to punish, Plut. *Fab. Max.* 9.1; *Mor.* 550f and 551c (God);
  iv) mild punishment, [Jos. *Ant.* 17.164]; Plut. *Pel.* 35.12; [*Cato min.* 23.1]; [*Ant.* 83.7];

v) take no retribution, lack severity, [*Sib. Or.* 4.159]; Jos. *Bel.* [1.507]; 7.451; Plut. *Lyc.* 11.3; *Pom.* 39.4; *Cae.* 54.2; *Mor.* 459c (toward slaves); 489d; Luc. *Per.* 18; [Dio Cas. 43.20.1]; [Aristid. 13.26];

vi) clemency to defeated foes, Jos. *Bel.* [2.54]; 6.383; Polyb. 5.10.4 (releasing captives without ransom); [21.4.10]; 30.17.4; [30.31.15]; Plut. *Cae.* 15.4; 57.4; *Tit. Flam.* 21.2; *Fab. Max.* 22.8; *Mor.* 337b; 543d; App. *Bel. civ.* 3.11.79;

f) the graciousness of gods: Plut. *Mor.* [413c]; 550f and 551c (an example to be emulated); Luc. *Pod.* 134 (the goddess Gout!); Aristid. 38.24 (Asklepios' sons); [39.5 (Asklepios)]; cf. 30.17;

3) of things: Plut. *Mor.* 45b (a glance, thus expressing approbation or friendliness); 590d (sound); Aristid. 17.22 (bosom and harbor); 44.10 (Aegean Sea); Aes. *Fab.* 178 (sea); [210 (camel)]; [Athen. *Deip.* 7.32/ 288e].

Again it seems appropriate to comment on Danker's definition, which is "the quality of not being overly impressed by a sense of one's self-importance."[2] Unlike with ἐπιείκεια, Danker and I are far apart in our proposals concerning πραΰτης/πραότης. I think the term "self-importance" is entirely out of place and the perspective of Danker's definition is too greatly internalized rather than focused on behavior.

As the first part of my definition indicates, an internal perspective is not inappropriate. One use of πραΰτης/πραότης does correlate to an individual's inner psychology. The issue, however, is the individual's ability to remain composed in response to external stimuli, whether hostility or misfortune, and the alternative is anger, not self-delusion or arrogance.

The definition I have proposed also reveals that the meaning of πραΰτης/πραότης must be calibrated to the social standing of the individual expressing it. Personal identity was typically derived from social factors, thus self-importance is a problematic term. To release captives without demanding ransom, which expresses πραΰτης/πραότης, does not hinge on whether or not one is impressed with one's self-importance. To be in that position is to have a great deal of importance, which is evident in a corpse-strewn field, a clutch of captives, and an array of soldiers. Whether one decides to press that hard-won importance to a

---

[2] *A Greek-English Lexicon of the New Testament and other Early Christian Literature*, 3rd ed., p. 861.

brutal extreme can hinge on a variety of factors, generosity and policy are two. The language of not being impressed by one's self-importance is not a plausible explanation to me.

I think that Danker's definition has mistakenly moved from describing behavior to accounting for it. This move is not intrinsic to πραΰτης/πραότης, so his definition suffers accordingly. That Danker's definition implies a critique present in πραΰτης/πραότης I find equally unnecessary. Although one might argue for the historical validity of Danker's definition based on the philosophical critique of "seeming," the definition of πραΰτης/πραότης is not related to that doctrine.

What ultimately separates Danker's definition from my own is the corpus each of us has in view. Danker is accounting for early Christian literature, while this investigation focuses on 2 Cor 10:1, which lies at the beginning of the Christian tradition. There are theological considerations that enter the picture as defined by Danker's project that are not relevant to the present one. Since each has different targets, it is not surprising that they differ, especially since πραΰτης/πραότης would enter the orbit of the Christian vocabulary for humility. Even within Danker's project, however, one should not collapse πραΰτης/πραότης into the Christian virtue of humility.

The final destination of πραΰτης/πραότης within Christian discourse is what makes me most suspicious of Danker's definition. I think he has accommodated to a fault the Christian connection between πραΰτης/πραότης and humility. The connection is decidedly Christian and not relevant to all Christian texts;[3] moreover, the manner in which Danker's definition accounts for their connection is too psychological and insufficiently social.

---

[3] James 1:21 is a good illustration. Based on its juxtaposition with ὀργή, I would place it above under definition 1.c. Psychological and social disturbances, which yield evil, must be replaced with a calm demeanor. Such a reasonable person can then hear and receive the word and implement it. James 3:13 continues this line of thinking. The "tongue is a fire" (3:6); it blesses and curses (3:9). Wise persons prove themselves wise with deeds that have a quality of restrained gentleness, which comes from wisdom. They do not give into rivalry and strife, but tend to peace. It is telling that not only is πραΰτης related to wisdom, so are peace reasonableness, and mercy (εἰρηνική, ἐπιεικής, εὐπειθής, μεστή ἐλέους, 3:17). No Christian theology needs to be introduced in these texts to account for the meaning of πραΰτης. I most certainly would not translate πραΰτης in James 1:21 and 3:13 as "with humility."

Appendix 3

Wisdom and Virtue's Counterculture or Antiencomiastic Rhetoric

When accused of being nobody Paul answered yes, but used contemporary rhetorical resources to show how that could in fact be a good thing. On one level, Paul's acceptance of his lack of status markers continued his modest, populist self-presentation; however, on another level, he subverted the conventions of status. Paul's acknowledgement that he is ταπεινός, an ἰδιώτης, and in fact οὐδέν not only link him with the οἱ πολλοί, but, together with what he accomplishes in his fool's speech, destroys the pretension of those who place faith in the conventions of prestige. Once again, Paul accepts the facts of the charge, but reinterprets them. The rhetoric which enabled Paul to offer an alternate perspective provides the topic of this appendix. The following survey will focus first on the figures who contributed to wisdom and virtue's counterculture and then look more generally at the source of that rhetoric.

1. Odysseus

The figure of Odysseus is multiform.[1] Some praise him as eloquent and wise, even a (wandering) philosopher with endurance and self-mastery; yet others criticize his deceit and lies, his tears, greed and appetite. Sophocles,

---

[1] William B. Stanford offers the basic study in *The Ulysses Theme: A Study in the Adaptability of a Traditional Hero* (Oxford: Basil Blackwell, 1954). Also important is Félix Buffière, *Les mythes d'Homère et la pensée grecque* (Paris: Les Belles Lettres, 1956), especially pp. 365-91. A revisionist view of Odysseus set within a Marxist agenda appears in Fidel Fajardo-Acosta, *The Hero's Failure in the Tragedy of Odysseus: A Revisionist Analysis*, Studies in Epic and Romance Literature 3 (Lewiston, NY: The Edwin Mellen Press, 1990); nevertheless, he too sees in Odysseus a paradigmatic hero of alternative form. Brief and to the point is Norman Austin, "Odysseus/ Ulysses: The Protean Myth," in *The Odyssey and Ancient Art*, eds. D. Buitron and B. Cohen (Annandale-on-Hudson, NY: The Edith C. Blum Art Institute, Bard College, 1992), pp. 201-7. For more on Odysseus in art see Frank Brommer, *Odysseus. Die Taten und Leiden des Helden in antiker Kunst und Literatur* (Darmstadt: Wissenschaftliche Buchgesellschaft, 1983). Also, Cedric H. Whitman, *The Heroic Paradox* (Ithaca, NY: Cornell University Press, 1982).

in fact, did both.[2] In his *Ajax*, Odysseus is a generous peacemaker,[3] while in *Philoctetes* Sophocles presents Odysseus as a contemptible sophist.[4] Meanwhile, both sides of Odysseus appear in the *Odyssey*. R. B. Rutherford argues that in the course of the *Odyssey*, Odysseus' character develops in such a way that, while the "wily Odysseus" is not displaced, the "philosophic Odysseus" gains greater control.[5] Rainer Friedrich likewise argues for development in Odysseus' character, describing how his heroic, intellectual and moral qualities sought to balance each other. Thus, the "boasting and presumptuous Sacker of Cities, whom we see in the finale of the *Cyclopeia*, will become the just ruler who, executing the will of Zeus, restores the order of justice in Ithaca, while his heroic qualities are made to serve this cause."[6] These developmental views announce the ambiguities and contradictions inherent in Odysseus even if one looks only at the *Odyssey*. Without that restriction and method the problems multiply.

In the *Iliad* and *Odyssey* Odysseus stands in contrast to Achilles, who is strong, courageous and hates dishonesty, while Odysseus is clever and the master of subterfuge.[7] Griffin describes the pair as creating

a tension between two types of heroism: the dashing Iliadic fighter like Achilles, pitted against other heroes in equal battle, and the wily opponent of giants and witches, who must use guile against overwhelming force and impossible odds. Achilles chooses a glorious death at Troy rather than long life without fame, but Odysseus ... must show

---

[2] Stanford, *The Ulysseus Theme*, pp. 104-11.

[3] Helen Gasti, "Sophocles' *Ajax*: The Military *Hybris*," *QUCC* 40 (1992): 81-83; Graham Zanker, "Sophocles' *Ajax* and the Heroic Values of the Iliad," *CQ* 42 (1992): 20-25.

[4] The latter, negative image prevailed in tragedy (Cic. *De off.* 3.97), though Euripides' *Cyclops* offers another exception (Scott Goins, "The Heroism of Odysseus in Euripides' *Cyclops*," *Eos* 79 [1991]: 187-94).

[5] "The Philosophy of the *Odyssey*," *JHS* 106 (1986): 145-62, esp. pp. 150 and 160.

[6] "The Hybris of Odysseus," *JHS* 111 (1991): 27-28.

[7] This contrast exists more in ancient commentators than in the *Iliad* itself (Katherine Callen King, *Achilles: Paradigm of the War Hero from Homer to the Middle Ages* [Berkeley: University of California Press, 1987], p. 69). The existence of the *Odyssey*, however, necessitated the subsequent comparisons (Gregory Nagy, *The Best of the Achaeans: Concepts of the Hero in Ancient Greek Poetry* [Baltimore, MD: Johns Hopkins University Press, 1979], pp. 45-49). Nagy's study has been influential. Among others, Sheila Murnaghan follows Nagy's characterization of Odysseus in relation to Achilles in *Disguise and Recognition in the Odyssey* (Princeton University Press, 1987), pp. 9-10; likewise, Margalit Finkelberg ("Odysseus and the Genus 'Hero,'" *G&R* 42 [1995]: 1-14); Finkelberg also argues that "the *Odyssey* not only is aware of the fact that the situation of its hero differs essentially from that of the heroes of the *Iliad*, but that this poem proceeds from a different idea of hero than that found in the *Iliad*" (p. 2).

himself a survivor, prepared to beg, to use guile, to accept humiliations, to conceal his feelings.[8]

Odysseus' attitude to food, possessions, and truth also move him away from Achilles and closer to common attitudes.[9] The distinction between Achilles and Odysseus can be described in various ways. Nagy describes it as a conflict between dependence on force (βία) and cleverness (μῆτις),[10] much as Philodemus compared Achilles' superiority with the spear to Odysseus' superior ability to formulate plans (*Good King* 39). Sophocles and Euripides made use of Odysseus to contrast honesty and duplicity.[11] Plato and Eustathius made the comparison of Achilles and Odysseus one of courage and wisdom (*Hipp. min.* 366a). In broader terms, Achilles and Odysseus served as "antithetical exemplars of honest deeds and deceitful words, the naturally powerful aristocrat versus the swayer of the masses."[12]

In some comparisons, Ajax replaced Achilles. The results are similar, however, as the bravehearted warrior and champion takes bold, aggressive action, while Odysseus is more ambiguous, getting by on his wits. For example, the *Little Iliad* emphasized Ajax's crimes and by way of contrast made Odysseus look better.[13] Antisthenes highlighted the contrast between the atypical Odysseus and more typically heroic figures in his version of

---

[8] Jasper Griffin, *Homer: The Odyssey*, Landmarks of World Literature (Cambridge University Press, 1987), p. 93. Everett L. Wheeler describes an entire ethos which grew up around Odysseus and which encouraged a military leader to embrace guile. In this ethos "unseen, often non-violent and/or psychological means were not only superior to direct brute force for achieving goals, but also could accomplish feats when weapons proved to be failures." He adds, "The connotation of στρατήγημα was entirely positive: a form of cunning free from reproach and whose associations lay with wisdom, cleverness, good fortune, and success" (*Stratagem and the Vocabulary of Military Trickery*, Mnemosyne, Supplementum 108 [Leiden: E. J. Brill, 1988], p. 21). P. Walcot, in fact, defends Odysseus' lies ("Odysseus and the Art of Lying," *Ancient Society* 8 [1977]: 1-19). Based on anthropological parallels, Walcot states that Odysseus does nothing "unusual or outrageous ... What is significant is the skill with which he concocts his lies, and this is a measure of his ability and not of his moral failings" (p. 9).

[9] Griffin, *Homer*, Pp. 93-95; cf. Finkelberg, "Odysseus and the Genus 'Hero,'" p. 2.

[10] Nagy, *The Best of the Achaeans*, pp. 45-49.

[11] King, *Achilles*, pp. 69-77 and 91-94 (e.g., Sophocles' *Philoctetes* and Euripides' *Telephos* and *Hecabe*).

[12] King, *Achilles*, p. 223.

[13] Philip Holt, "Ajax's Burial in Early Greek Epic," *AJP* 113 (1992): 319-31. Cf. also Ovid *Meta.* 13.362 and Sal. *Cat.* 1.7-2.2.

the contest between Odysseus and Ajax for Achilles' arms.[14] According to Giannantoni, Odysseus represents intelligence (φρόνησις) to Ajax's strength (ἰσχύς), that is λόγος to ἔργον.[15] Cicero recognized the wide gulf between the two figures:

> How much Ulysses endured on those long wanderings, when he submitted to the service even of women ... and strove to be courteous and complaisant to all! And, arrived home, he brooked even the insults of his men-servants and maid-servants, in order to attain in the end the object of his desire. But Ajax, with the temper he is represented as having, would have chosen to meet death a thousand times rather than suffer such indignities![16]

To suffer indignity, that is the sticking point. Can a noble person do this? Can a person who does this actually be noble? Odysseus, one of the Homeric kings, did. His intelligence led him to do otherwise unacceptable deeds.

Two incidents in particular in the life of Odysseus highlight the odd things that clever epic hero would do: Odysseus put on beggar's clothes to sneak into Troy (*Od.* 4.244-58), while upon returning to Ithaka he wore a similar disguise to move among the members of his household and the suitors.[17] For an aristocratic person like Odysseus such comportment is shocking and incongruous, yet was a clever and necessary means for accomplishing his objectives.[18] Odysseus' unlikely behavior received a surprising amount of attention in ancient sources. Both Aristophanes and Euripides refer to it.[19] During the Empire, Epictetus alludes to it (frg. 11 Loeb), while *P. Köln* VI 245 preserves a fragment of what may have been an original production from II/III A.D. whose plot centered on Odysseus' espionage at Troy.[20] Plutarch puts the incident to humorous use by describing the pseudo-philosopher's removal of his guise to join in the

---

[14] See G. Giannantoni, *Socratis et Socraticorum reliquiae*, 2: 157-61; cf. 4: 257-64; Stanford, *The Ulysses Theme*, pp. 96-100; H. D. Rankin, *Antisthenes Sokratikos* (Amsterdam: Hakkert, 1986), 155-71.

[15] Giannantoni, *Socratis et Socraticorum reliquiae*, 4: 260.

[16] *De off.* 1.113 (cf. Cicero's remarks in *Tusc.* 1.98; 4.52). See also Theon *Progymnasmata* 9 (Walz, *Rhetores Graeci*, 1: 231; also Spengel, *Rhetores Graeci* 2: 112).

[17] See Beth Cohen, "Slaughter of the Suitors," in *The Odyssey and Ancient Art*, pp. 168-75; Elizabeth Block, "Clothing Makes the Man: A Pattern in the *Odyssey*," *TAPA* 115 (1985): 1-11.

[18] Cp. Cic. *De off.* 1.108: "Especially crafty and shrewd was the device of Solon, who, to make his own life safer and at the same time to do a considerably larger service for his country, feigned insanity."

[19] *Wasps* 350-51 and *Hecuba* 239-41, respectively. Dio Chrysostom comments on how Aeschylus and Euripides handled Odysseus' disguise when he returned home (52.5-6).

[20] Maryline Parca, *Ptocheia or Odysseus in Disguise at Troy (P. Köln VI 245)*, American Studies in Papyrology 31 (Atlanta: Scholars Press, 1991).

wine and laughter of some wealthy person.[21] Dio Chrysostom saw in Odysseus' rags a striking confutation of normal human thought: Odysseus, "for all his being a beggar and begging of the suitors, was none the less a king and the owner of the house, while Antinous and Eurymachus, whom Homer named 'kings' were miserable and unfortunate wretches."[22] Aelius Aristides compares Odysseus' sneaking into Troy with the Persian Zopyrus as two men who exhibited enormous endurance, so that they even sacrificed their bodies to defeat their enemies (Behr 2: 34.15-17). Favorinus describes Odysseus' behavior as that of a pious wise man (Περὶ φυγῆς). In Ps.-Diog. *Ep.* 34, the author reflects on Odysseus' rags and concludes that Cynic attire is not shameful after all, for while Odysseus wore dirty rags for a limited goal, the Cynic seeks a long term one, viz., happiness; if Odysseus was justified, then even more so the Cynic. In Odysseus, then, we encounter a figure who humbled himself, but in so doing displayed true wisdom. The Cynic epistle just referred to, however, presses Odysseus' example even further, reaching the conclusion that the Cynic's beggarly appearance is beautiful and noble, as well as weapons in the fight against what only seems to be good (δόξα). This tradition of interpretation, however, encounters opposition in Lucian, who observes that Odysseus did not take the occasion of his rags to promulgate Stoicism: "when he entered Troy after flogging himself and putting on wretched Stoic rags ... he did not call that a more delightful end!" (*De parasito* 10).

In these examples, Odysseus symbolized not only wisdom but endurance in the face of hardship and misfortune. Homer's epithets bear this out, as he called Odysseus not only wily (πολύμητις), but also much-enduring (πολύτλας). This tradition appears in Horace, who sees Odysseus as an example of courage (*virtus*) and wisdom since he endured hardships and triumphed over adversity (*Ep.* 1.2.1-26). Seneca observes that Stoics in general regard Odysseus and Herakles as examples of the wise person, "because they were unconquered by struggles, were despisers of pleasure, and victors over all terrors."[23] Stanford identifies Antisthenes

---

[21] *Mor.* 52c. Cf. Luc. *De parasito* 10.

[22] 14.22. See also Dio Chrys. 7.83-86. Philostratus records an incident in which Dio dramatically reenacted Odysseus' removal of his rags in order to quell a mutiny in a military camp (*Vit. soph.* 488). Lucian makes a self-reference which takes advantage of Odysseus' rags in *Herakles* 8. Cf. Heliodorus *Aethiopica* 7.6-7, where Kalasiris, after ten years of wandering, throws off his rags to reveal his royal personage in order to stop his sons from fighting.

[23] Sen. *De const.* 2.1; cf. *Ep.* 88.5; *De tranq.* 16.4. Anna Lydia Motto and John R. Clark examine references to Odysseus in Sen. *Ep.* 31, 56, and 123 where Odysseus' voyages provide an analogy for the vicissitudes of human existence ("Seneca and

as the origin of this tradition[24] in which Odysseus and Herakles serve as examples which defy "conventional heroic standards of conduct" for they can "endure toil and suffering in lonely enterprises to serve humanity."[25]

In "Odysseus and the Genus 'Hero,'" however, Finkelberg attempts to read the connection between Herakles and Odysseus in the *Odyssey* itself. She notes that Odysseus' concern with food, carrying of a bow, humiliations, labors (ἄεθλοι) and endurance combine with his intelligence to place him among the heroes, among whom Herakles provides the best parallel (pp. 2-5). This connection is not merely an Odysseus-Herakles parallelism, but lies in the nature of heroism. She points out that Herakles "is only the most prominent representative of an entire category of such heroes of Greek tradition who, like Perseus, Bellerophon, Jason, Theseus, and others, are mostly conspicuous by the labors they performed; some of them, as, for example, Theseus, also underwent the ultimate experience of a κατάβασις. None of the heroes of this group died on the battlefield" (p. 5). Finkelberg draws together texts from Diodorus Siculus and Pindar to show the association of Herakles, Jason, and Perseus with the fame arising from ἄεθλοι, an idea which recurs in Herodotus, Sophocles, and Socrates (p. 6). This leads to the conclusion that a "popular notion of heroism" existed which the *Odyssey* recognized and used to model its hero (p. 8). Finkelberg goes on to suggest that this idea of heroism issues from the human condition ("human life is nothing but a long series of ups and downs," p. 9) and portrays how some not only endured it but transformed their "toil and suffering into a supreme achievement" (p. 10). "As distinct from the Iliadic hero, who sets an example of how one ought to die, all Odysseus' life-experience demonstrates how one ought to live" (p. 10). Thus, Finkelberg argues, the *Iliad* and *Odyssey* offer two models of heroism. "According to the *Odyssey* a hero is one who is prepared to go through life enduring toil and suffering," a view which "conforms to the popular Greek attitude to the phenomenon of hero-worship" (p. 12). While Finkelberg is proposing important theses about the *Odyssey* in particular and the nature of hero-worship in general (i.e., more than cult is pertinent), of present interest is her situating of Odysseus among a larger group of figures who suffered but in so doing benefited others and earned great reward for themselves. This advances our argument that Odysseus is

---

Ulysses," *CB* 67 [1991]: 27-32). The overlap of Herakles and Odysseus appears in literary fashion in the similiarity between the songs and dances for Odysseus at the Phaeacean court (Hom. *Od.* 8) and Virgil's hymn of the Salii in honor of Herakles in *Aen.* 8 (Steven Lonsdale, "Simile and Ecphrasis in Homer and Virgil: The Poet as Craftsman and Choreographer," *Vergilius* 36 [1990]: 7-30).

[24] Stanford, *The Ulysses Theme*, p. 96.
[25] Stanford, p. 99.

a maleable figure from Greek culture whose virtue appeared in nonconformity to aristocratic tastes. What we wish to emphasize now are the wit, humiliation, and endurance which characterize Odysseus, while the connections between Odysseus and Herakles lead us to the next point of our survey.

2. Herakles

Over a century ago Emmanuel Des Essarts surveyed the development of the image of Herakles, from his unflattering appearance in Old Comedy to the high regard paid by the Stoics.[26] More recently, G. Karl Galinsky devoted the first two hundred pages of his book *The Herakles Theme* to the literary life of Herakles from Homer to Seneca.[27] He notes the many roles Herakles could play: tragic sufferer, "paragon of superhuman physical prowess and bravado," the perfect nobleman, the epitome of virtue, "incarnation of rhetoric and intelligence and wisdom," a divine mediator and example of apotheosis, yet also "a comic, lecherous, gluttonous monster or ... romantic lover."[28] These disparate images are usually linked by the trait of "more than human strength and endurance" (p. 7). In broader terms, the positive evolution of Herakles' image

---

[26] *Type d'Hercule dans la littérature grecque depuis les origines jusqu'au siècle des Antonins* (Paris: Ernest Thorin, 1871). See also Abraham Malherbe, "Herakles," *RAC* 14 (1988): 559-83; cf. idem, "Pseudo-Heraclitus, Epistle 4: The Divinization of the Wise Man," *JAC* 21 (1978): 54-58, which discusses Herakles' apotheosis. The popularity of Herakles is evident in representational artifacts: see Frank Brommer, *Herakles. The Twelve Labors of the Hero in Ancient Art and Literature*, trans. Shirley J. Schwarz (New Rochelle, NY: Aristide D. Caratzas, 1986); idem, *Herakles 2. Die unkanonischen Taten des Helden* (1984); idem, *Vasenlisten zur griechischen Heldensage*, 3d ed. (Marburg: N. G. Elwert, 1973); Jaimee Pugliese Uhlenbrock, ed., *Herakles: Passage of the Hero through 1000 Years of Classical Art*, Edith C. Blum Art Institute, Bard College, March-May 1986 (New Rochelle, NY: Aristide D. Caratzas, 1986); Rainer Vollkommer, *Herakles in the Art of Classical Greece*, Oxford Committee for Archaeology Monograph 25 (Oxford University Committee for Archaeology, 1988); K. Schefold and F. Jung, *Die Urkönige, Perseus, Bellerophon, Herakles und Theseus in der klassischen und hellenistischen Kunst* (Munich: Hirmer, 1988).

[27] G. Karl Galinsky, *The Herakles Theme: The Adaptations of the Hero in Literature from Homer to the Twentieth Century* (Totowa, NJ: Rowman and Littlefield, 1972).

[28] Galinsky, pp. 1-2. He later emphasizes that despite scholarship's preoccupation with tragedy, Herakles appeared much more frequently on the comedic stage than the tragic (p. 81).

presented him in four important ways, which Des Essarts summarizes as the dispenser of justice, the warrior, the liberator, and the benefactor.[29]

The strength of Galinsky's work is its attention to the rhetorical evolution of Herakles. His life's story did not exist in a single, polished canonical form or text, a fact which made it easy to embellish the story or emphasize a single aspect of it. Thus, Galinsky can identify and describe important developments in the use of Herakles by the sophists (e.g., Prodicus and Isocrates), Euripides (particularly his *Herakles*) and Euhemerus.[30] He draws on a statement by Isocrates which underscores this phenomenon:

Coming now to Heracles, all others who praise him harp endlessly on his valor or recount his labors; and not one, either of the poets or of the historians, will be found to have commemorated his other excellences — I mean those which pertain to the spirit. I, on the other hand, see here a field set apart and entirely unworked — a field not small nor barren, but teeming with many a theme for praise and with glorious deeds, yet demanding a speaker with ability to do them justice.[31]

A few paragraphs later Isocrates specifies two of Herakles' underappreciated excellences of the spirit, viz., his φιλανθρωπία and εὔνοια (*Phil.* 114), two qualities dear to Isocrates' own heart — and agenda. Here we see myth as a rhetorical enterprise generated by and dependent on the ingenuity of the speaker.[32]

---

[29] *Type d'Hercule*, pp. 231-32. "Il est *le Guerrier* plus encore qu'Arés, le guerrier intraitable dans les combats mais humain après la victoire, enterrant le premier ses annemis morts, épargnant ceux qui survivent à la bataille. Il combat pour punir; mais ensuite il sait pardonner" (p. 231).

[30] Galinsky, *The Herakles Theme*: Prodicus, pp. 101-3; Isocrates, pp. 104-6; Euripides, pp. 57-66; Euhemerus, pp. 129-31. Cf. G. J. Fitzgerald, "The Euripidean Heracles: An Intellectual and a Coward?" *Mnemosyne* 44 (1991): 85-95.

[31] *Phil.* 109; see Galinsky, *The Herakles Theme*, pp. 104-5.

[32] Four studies underscore the rhetorical maleability of the Herakles myth. Clara Auvray-Assayas examines Seneca's *Oetaeus* in light of Cicero's use of Herakles in *Tusc.* 2.17-22, thereby reconstructing a debate about pain and the role of Herakles in the arguments of each side ("La douleur d'Hercule dans l'*Hercule sur l'Oeta* de Sénèque et la tradition romaine des Tusculanes," in *Présence de Sénèque*, eds. Raymond Chevallier and Rémy Poignault, Caesarodunum 24 [Paris: Touzot, 1991], pp. 31-44). Werner Schubert shows how two authors can use the figure of Herakles in both similar yet distinct ways ("Zur Sage von Hercules und Cacus bei Vergil [*Aen.* 8, 184-279] und Ovid [*Fast.* 1, 543-586]," *JAC* 6 [1991]: 37-60). Virgil exhibits the constructive value of the Herakles myth as he used it to shape his epic portrait of Aeneas, repeatedly using *labor* to describe Aeneas as a sufferer who struggled to achieve success (Scott Goins, "Two Aspects of Virgil's Use of *labor* in the *Aeneid*," *CJ* 88 [1993]: 375-84). Galinsky discusses the Herakles-Aeneas parallels at length (*The Herakles Theme*, pp. 131-38 and 141-49).

Our primary concern is the use of Herakles to portray the reversal of human conventions and values.[33] Such use appears among the Cynics and Stoics. While Cleanthes was a "second Herakles," the Stoics in general regarded Herakles as the "mythological ideal of virtue" and in essence were his disciples.[34] Similarly, Herakles "became a veritable patron saint to the Cynic movement."[35] The high estimate which Cynics placed on hardship (πόνος) found a shining precedent in Herakles, which both Antisthenes and Diogenes invoked.[36] His appearance and habits also provided a model for Cynics, as he paid no attention to the weather or food, had no need for a bed, and wore a dirty skin (Dio Chrys. 8.30). Herakles further served Diogenes the Cynic as a model for regarding freedom as a guiding principle of life (Diog. L. 6.71); yet we must recall that the Cynic idea of freedom suggested a rigorous way of life which most people would not covet. A common story told about Herakles underscored this.[37] At an early stage of his life Herakles had a vision in which he saw two roads, an easy one leading to Pleasure/Vice, a steep one to Virtue. Confronted with this choice, Herakles opted for the more difficult. This story set a precedent for Stoics and Cynics who likewise took the difficult road to Virtue/Happiness.[38]

Seneca wrote a great deal about Herakles. Galinsky observes that in addition to Seneca's *Hercules furens* and *Hercules Oetaeus*, "There is enough evidence in Seneca's philosophical writings for his admiration for Herakles and his Stoic conception of the hero. Contemner of pleasures, Fortune, and circumstance, selfless benefactor *pro bono publico*, victor over all terrors, and exemplar of aspiration for the highest virtue — none of the important qualities are missing."[39] This, however, is only one of

---

[33] Like Odysseus, Herakles' image can be used in many ways, not only to contradict conventional values, but also to support them; see Mark Padilla, "The Heraclean Dionysus: Theatrical and Social Renewal in Aristophanes's *Frogs*," *Arethusa* 25 (1992): 359-84.

[34] Des Essarts, *Type d'Hercule*, pp. 219-20. Recall Sen. *De const.* 2.1.

[35] Dudley, *History of Cynicism*, p. 13; Galinsky, *The Herakles Theme*, pp. 106-7.

[36] Dudley, *History of Cynicism*, p. 1 (cf. Diog. L. 6.71).

[37] Xen. *Mem.* 2.1.21-34, quoting Prodicus' Περὶ Ἡρακλέους; Cicero notes Xenophon's use of Prodicus in *De off.* 1.118; in Dio Chrys. *Or.* 1.64-84 Herakles chooses between βασιλεία and Tyranny. Cp. Theseus' choice of roads in Plut. *Thes.* 6-7. Mary Kuntz thinks that Prodicus created this story by reshaping myth — and not simply adding Herakles' name to the story ("The Prodikean 'Choice of Herakles': A Reshaping of Myth," *CJ* 89 [1994]: 163-81). Cf. Galinsky, *The Herakles Theme*, pp. 101-3.

[38] Lucian puts the *topos* to humorous use in *Ver. hist.* 2.18.

[39] *The Herakles Theme*, pp. 167-68. Victoria Tietze elaborates on Seneca's picture of Herakles as the Stoic wise man ("The *Hercules Oetaeus* and the Picture of the *sapiens* in

two traditions influencing Latin literature; not only was Herakles regarded as the Stoic sage, Alexander the Great had also given him a prominent role in ruler imagery. Seneca merges these two traditions, so that Herakles represents the just king.[40]

Dio offers another angle on Herakles. In response to criticism from the citizens of his hometown, Dio responded that (to paraphrase another) no philosopher is without honor except in his hometown. Homer, for example, "in his way a philosopher," preferred to be a wanderer, beggar, and madman than live at home (47.5). Herakles, on the other hand, did go home, but what did that get him? Although he

> made himself master of Egypt and Libya, and ... both Thracians and Scythians, and ... captured Ilium ... and ... actually set himself up as king; still when he arrived in Argos he busied himself with removing the dung from the stables of Augeas or hunting serpents or chasing birds, to keep them from troubling the farmers in Stymphalus, or with performing other such menial and humble tasks at the bidding of another; and finally, they say, he was sent to Hades, with such exceeding fairness did his fellow townsman treat him!"[41]

Though Dio's point is that like Herakles he encounters his worst reception at home, his comparison introduces (and assumes knowledge of) Herakles' example of enduring hardship and insult to benefit others. Elsewhere, Dio argues that Herakles' performance of demeaning labors proves that applause did not motivate him (8.35). Enduring humiliation in fact teaches an important lesson about appearances and their deceptive nature. Herakles' submission to degrading tasks therefore illustrates the value of ignoring conventional values.

One of the most important aspects of philosophy was teaching about death. Here Herakles offered a bold example which Peregrinus imitated in extreme fashion. Keeping to his public proclamation, Peregrinus mounted a pyre and burned to death, thinking that a person who lives like Herakles, should also die like him (Luc. *Per.* 33); moreover, he wished "to benefit mankind by showing them the way in which one should despise death." Maintaining his Heraklean persona, Peregrinus concluded that everyone "ought to play Philoctetes to me" (*ibid.*). In this example, then, we see

---

Senecan Prose," *Phoenix* 45 [1991]: 39-49). Matías López López describes how Ovid uses Herakles and Odysseus to illustrate a Greco-Roman, yet particularly Stoic, theme, viz., the transition from original chaos to a better world thanks to human effort ("Mito y filosofía en las Metamorfosis de Ovidio: Ulises, Hércules, Níobe, Licaón," *Cuadernos de filología clásica* 22 [1989]: 167-74).

[40] Carmen Codoñer, "Hércules romano," *Euphrosyne* 19 (1991): 27-46.

[41] *Or.* 47.4. An indication of how horrible such service may be appears in Hom. *Od.* 11.620-22 where Herakles' shade complains to Odysseus about having had to serve a man inferior to himself (cf. *Il.* 15.639-40).

how completely Peregrinus conceived of his life as a Cynic as one which followed in the footsteps of Herakles.[42]

In sum, Herakles and Odysseus served as key examples for the Cynics and Stoics. "The reasons why these two were chosen as a philosopher's ideal lie in their self-restraint, endurance of hardships, disregard for indignities and humiliation, and in their readiness to serve the common good."[43]

3. Socrates

Socrates (and then especially Diogenes) became the paradigm for philosophic subversion of cultural — and human — norms. "It was Socrates who gave currency to the notion of a 'wise man,' whose life is an extraordinary challenge to conventional views on human needs and priorities and yet a paradigm of excellence and happiness."[44] Exchanging the comfort of shoes and heavy clothing for self-mastery and exercising it as well in food and sex reveals only the surface. He also filled his discussions with sailors, cobblers, and potters, ignoble characters all. His ugliness cloaked a beautiful soul.[45] Though of poor origins, he declined payment for teaching.[46] This, combined with a hesitation to set himself up as a teacher, distinguished him from the sophists. His ideas rested on paradoxes, e.g., "ἀρετή is knowledge" and "no one does wrong willingly." Even more strange, Socrates was the wise man who knew nothing. This resulted from carefully analyzing conventional notions (e.g., justice, piety, etc.) and finding them inadequate. Though this focus on truth landed him in trouble, he remained the champion of truth, so much so that he resisted the temptation to defend himself with rhetorical theatrics and tricks, but relied on truth. He approached his resultant execution with equal

---

[42] See also Lucian *Dem.* 1.

[43] Finkelberg, "Odysseus and the Genus 'Hero,'" p. 13 n. 52.

[44] A. A. Long, "Hellenistic Ethics and Philosophical Power," in *Hellenistic History and Culture*, ed. Peter Green, Hellenistic Culture and Society 9 (Berkeley: University of California Press, 1993), p. 141. Long places Socrates at the root of Hellenistic philosophy "as a new kind of hero, a living embodiment of philosophical power, a figure whose appeal to the Hellenistic world consisted in self-mastery" (p. 142), as expressed in σωφροσύνη and particularly ἐγκράτεια (pp. 143-44).

[45] Socrates recommended virtue to compensate for a lack of beauty (Plut. *Mor.* 141d; Diog. L. 2.33).

[46] See David L. Blank, "Socratics Versus Sophists on Payment for Teaching," *ClAnt* 4 (1985): 1-49. See Plato *Hip. mai.* 283a-b which contrasts the poverty of wise men in the past with the then popular sentiment which expected wisdom to prove itself by financial gain.

resolution. Not wavering from his ideas about death, his calm embrace of it became legendary. Thus, Socrates shed the typical human dread of death, while challenging the values of Athenians and in particular the pretentions and methods of sophists.[47]

Socrates' examples were not forgotten, but founded a lasting legacy. Beyond the philosophical schools which traced their lineage back to him and valued his example,[48] we have the writings of individuals which reflect their various interests in Socrates. In his monograph *Exemplum Socratis*, K. Döring opens with the observation that "interest in the person of Socrates experienced a remarkable surge within popular Cynic-Stoic philosophy."[49] Döring later adds that within popular philosophy, Socrates was always one of the most popular figures. If someone had an expression or idea to support, Socrates was invoked; if someone needed a concrete example, Socrates was a likely source. To prove this, Döring notes, one need only glance at Teles' fragments and Cicero's *Tusculananrum disputationum*, or Seneca, Musonius, Epictetus, Plutarch, Favorinus, or Maximus of Tyre. In collections of *chreia* as well, Socrates occupied an important position, while in the Socratic Epistles he became an ever-present moral authority.[50] Döring accounts for Socrates' popularity in the first two centuries by noting the general influence of Atticism, i.e., the idealization of the Classical period and its emulation. More specifically, he suggests that the persecution of philosophers (by Nero, Vespasian and Domitian) would have made Socrates' example relevant, particularly his defiance of the Thirty and his conduct in court and prison. Socrates' simplicity also provided a model for later philosophers to draw on (which is important to note for our present purposes). Lastly, the complexity of Socrates' image allowed it to be used by many people in different situations in varied ways. At the same time, because the tradition

---

[47] Robert Eisner draws many comparisons between Socrates and Odysseus, as well as Socrates and Herakles, in "Socrates as Hero," *Philosophy and Literature* 6 (1982): 106-18.

[48] Klaus Döring, *Exemplum Socratis. Studien zur Sokratensnachwirkung in der kynisch-stoischen Popularphilosophie der frühen Kaiserzeit und im frühen Christentum*, Hermes Einzelschrift 42 (Wiesbaden: Franz Steiner, 1979), pp. 3-12. (In his review of Döring, A. A. Long complains that Döring merely catalogues common knowledge [*CR* 31 (1981): 298-99]). The Stoics, Cynics, Cyrenaics, and Academic Skeptics valued Socrates. The Lyceum was less enamored and at times hostile. The Epicureans did not like Socrates (see Knut Kleve, "Scurra Atticus: The Epicurean View of Socrates," in *Suzetesis. Studi sull'Epicureismo Greco e Romano offerti a Marcello Gigante*, ed. G. P. Carratelli [Naples, 1983], 1: 227-53).

[49] *Exemplum Socratis*, p. 1: "... das Interesse an der Person des Sokrates in der kynisch-stoischen Popularphilosophie einen bemerkenswerten Aufschwung erlebte."

[50] Döring, pp. 12-13.

contained an assortment of traits, Socratic traditions were not violated by diverse usage.[51] With these observations, then, Döring launches his examination into the abundant references to Socrates in Seneca, Epictetus, Dio Chrysostom, and epistolary literature.[52] We will now survey some of this evidence in order to highlight the use of Socrates' image to countermine typical human values.

Epictetus "reveals as deep a perception or utilisation of Socrates' philosophy as we find in any ancient thinker after Plato."[53] Like many other philosophers, Epictetus looked to Socrates as exemplifying the proper (i.e., unconventional) approach to money (*Diss.* 2.2.15; frg. 11 LCL) and death (*Diss.* 1.4.23-25; 1.29.16-19), even illness and hunger (3.5.18). Socrates also set an example of cosmopolitanism as against normal civic allegiance (1.9.1) and stood as a challenge to teachers of grammar and speech (3.23.17-32) and to philosophers (3.5.14-18), as well as conventional wisdom and methods of argument (4.1.167-69). His restraint towards Alcibiades revealed his superiority to pleasure (2.18.20-22). More generally, Socrates represented a contradiction of the way people typically pursue peace and happiness (3.22.26) and offered a model of the life of virtue, i.e., a life which subjects all else to moral purpose (4.4.19-23).

Some of Dio Chrysostom's references to Socrates reflect the latter's poverty and indifference to the norms of human status. He identifies Socrates as a man of the people, but ignored by most of the powerful people and professional speakers (54.3). Like other wise men, he did not know whether a particular king was happy, for he predicated happiness on one's inner life, not extraneous matters (3.1-2). Socrates was not boastful,

---

[51] Döring, pp. 16-17. Though Socrates was a canonical figure, not all philosophers agreed on how to interpret him. A. A. Long demonstrates well not only how schools viewed Socrates differently but also how even members within the same school could diverge — a major purpose of Long's paper, "Socrates in Hellenistic Philosophy," *CQ* 38 (1988): 150-71.

[52] Jackson P. Hershbell surveys Plutarch's references to Socrates in "Plutarch's Portrait of Socrates," *ICS* 13 (1988): 365-81, a project he took up precisely because Döring did not.

[53] A. A. Long, "Socrates in Hellenistic Philosophy," p. 150. (Döring likewise observes Epictetus' special affinity for Socrates [*Exemplum Socratis*, p. 44].) Long further notes that despite Epictetus' deep reflection on Plato's and Xenophon's texts, the Socrates he draws from them constitutes the ideal form of the philosophical life as Epictetus himself conceives it (p. 151). Hershbell reaches a similar conclusion about Plutarch's appropriation of Socrates: Plutarch "considered Socrates a model or paradigm for the best human life. Socrates followed his *daimon*, and led a busy life while maintaining self-control and the capacity for quiet reflection. Plutarch's own life was not wholly different" ("Plutarch's Portrait of Socrates," pp. 380-81).

but restrained and prudent (55.7-8). He also took no interest in wealth (55.9). In these things, then, the wise Socrates stood juxtaposed to those who pretended to be wise and lived by conventional human standards. Beyond these things, Dio also presents himself as imitating Socrates, so that Dio borrows the claim to know nothing (12.14) and repeats the Athenian's message.[54] When confronted with an indictment, Dio again compared himself to Socrates, whose charges were likewise contrary to justice and gratitude (43.8-12). These examples from Dio are particularly interesting given the public performances of his speeches. We are not reading esoteric school rhetoric, but ideas presented to public assemblies.

Socrates' countervention of forensic rhetoric also influenced subsequent philosophers. A certain Heracleitus took Socrates' example too literally. In a lawsuit about some property he stated in his conclusion, "But neither will I entreat you, nor do I care what your decision is going to be, and it is you who are on trial rather than I" (Epict. *Diss.* 2.2.17). Though Epictetus criticizes his friend Heracleitus for going too far (it is not necessary to provoke one's judge, 2.2.18), he generally approves of Socrates' philosophic rhetoric, albeit within the terms of Epictetus' own philosophy:

When therefore desire and aversion are under your own control, what more do you care for? This is your introduction (προοίμιον), this the setting forth of your case (διήγησις), this your proof (πίστις), this your victory, this your peroration, this your approbation. That is why Socrates, in reply to the man who was reminding him to make preparation for his trial, said 'Do you not feel, then, that with my whole life I am making preparation for this?' ... But if you wish to maintain also what is external, your paltry body and your petty estate and your small reputation, I have this to say to you: Begin this very moment to make all possible preparation, and furthermore study the character of your judge and your antagonist. If you must clasp men's knees, clasp them; if you must wail, then wail; if you must groan, then groan.[55]

Socrates' rhetoric is noted in the *Socratic Epistles* as well, which state that Socrates could have won his case, but disdained flattery and entreaty and relied on the presentation of truth and justice.[56] He could not go wrong by

---

[54] 3.26-41; 13.14-28. For example, "Socrates" says that "he who cannot check a fit of anger, which is often caused by mere trifles; who cannot conquer a lust for the basest things; who cannot thrust pain aside, imaginary as it often is; who cannot endure toil, even to gain pleasure; who cannot drive fear from his soul, though it avails naught in the midst of alarms but works the greatest mischief — must not such a man be greatly lacking in strength, be weaker than a woman, weaker than a eunuch" (3.34).

[55] *Diss.* 2.2.6-10. Epictetus offers further commentary on Socrates' rhetoric in 2.5.18-21, 27-29; 3.23.17-32; 4.1.161-66 (cf. 3.18.4-8; 4.1.123). Are Epictetus' remarks close to Musonius Rufus' views on this subject?

[56] Quin. 11.1.33 suggests that philosophers avoid all ornaments of oratory, especially the appeal to passions.

3.3. Socrates

such a procedure, though he left room for injustice on the part of the jury (14.4). Dio Chrysostom also reflected familiarity with Socrates' rhetoric (or more precisely anti-rhetoric) in his Olympic discourse (12.14-16). None of this is surprising, however, given the wide readership of Plato's *Apology*.[57]

In general, as the figure of Socrates challenged Athenian norms, so in Hellenistic philosophy he opposed general human norms. Fear of death and love of money stood condemned by his example. He was the standard by which to measure philosophers and to recognize pretenders. As a symbol for right thinking, he opposed all behaviors issuing from misunderstanding. For those who regarded Diogenes as the true interpreter of Socrates, the challenge to human norms was pushed to extreme lengths

---

[57] Dio Chrysostom strongly urges aspiring orators to read Socratic authors, though in particular he recommends Xenophon as his personal favorite (18.13 and 16); cp. Cicero's similar advice in *Tusc.* 2.8; and the example in *Luc. Prom.* 4. We should note that Plato's Socrates also subverts encomiastic rhetoric as well as forensic, though not as dramatically and explicitly. See Andrea Wilson Nightingale, "The Folly of Praise: Plato's Critique of Encomiastic Discourse in the *Lysis* and *Symposium*," *CQ* 43 (1993): 112-30: "Socrates' elenctic method is diametrically opposed to the language of the encomium. It does not aim at gratification or glory, nor does it promulgate falsehoods that instill in the auditor a proud and stubborn ignorance. On the contrary, it encourages self-knowledge ... [by removing] false conceits" (p. 115). Nightingale later argues that Socrates' dissimulation shifts his rhetoric from the competitive realm of praise and censure to a "co-operative dialectical quest" (p. 123). Ultimately, she contends that because "Socrates insists on the existence of absolute goodness and on the impossibility of the perfect instantiation of this goodness in the human world," he therefore holds "an ontology which challenges the binary logic of the rhetoric of praise and blame" (p. 130). Cp. Plato *The.* 174a-175e where he contrasts the philosopher whose mind ponders large questions with an uneducated person whose mind concentrates on small, petty affairs. Encomiastic topics cater to and impress the latter, while the former laughs. Plato's *Menexenus* also subverts encomiastic rhetoric, on which see Nicole Loraux, *The Invention of Athens: The Funeral Oration in the Classical City*, trans. Alan Sheridan (Cambridge, MA: Harvard University Press, 1986), esp. pp. 304-27; Lucinda Coventry, "Philosophy and Rhetoric in the *Menexenus*," *JHS* 109 (1989): 1-15; Bruce Rosenstock, "Socrates as Revenant: A Reading of the *Menexenus*," *Phoenix* 48 (1994): 331-47; Lesley Dean-Jones, "Menexenus — Son of Socrates," *CQ* 45 (1995): 51-57. For an alternative (and less persuasive) reading of *Menexenus*, see Bernard K. Duffy, "The Platonic Functions of Epideictic Rhetoric," *Philosophy and Rhetoric* 16 (1983): 79-93. On the funeral oration see Takis Poulakos, "Continuities and Discontinuities in the History of Rhetoric: A Brief History of Classical Funeral Orations," *Western Journal of Speech* 54 (1990): 172-88. On Plato's stance against sophistic rhetoric, see John Poulakos, *Sophistical Rhetoric in Classical Greece*, Studies in Rhetoric/Communication (Columbia, SC: University of South Carolina Press, 1995), pp. 74-112, esp. 104-6. On Cicero's critique of Socrates see Raymond Di Lorenzo, "The Critique of Socrates in Cicero's *De oratore: Ornatus* and the Nature of Wisdom," *Philosophy and Rhetoric* 11 (1978): 247-61.

(e.g., public defecation and masturbation). Together, Socrates and Diogenes were responsible for the philosopher's uniform (σχῆμα) as well, which challenged norms visually and not just with words. We see in Socrates, then, a figure who is not well-born, who is not beautiful, who is not wealthy, but who attains to great eminence based on his wisdom and virtue and, as a result, stands as a challenge to those whose prominence rests on the traditional pillars of birth, physique, wealth, office, and education.[58]

4. Aesop

Discussing Aesop in regard to a cultural type is appropriate to the traditions about Aesop, for they do the same. For example, the Delphians' belief that their ancestors had killed Aesop (Herod. 2.134) was encased in scapegoat mythology.[59] As for Aesop's place of origin, this too was intertwined with mythology. Perry comments:

> Aesop became a Phrygian instead of a Thracian because he was conceived on the analogy of the Phrygian Marsyas, to whom he is likened explicitly in the *Life*, as the spokesman of a homely rural culture characteristic of Phrygia and the satyrs coming into rivalry and conflict with the Apolline culture, and on that account, like Marsyas and like the Phrygian Midas in consequence of his preference for Pan's music, having become the victim of Apollo's anger. The analogy between Aesop and Marsyas, in respect to what each stood for culturally and what they suffered in consequence of rivaling Apollo, was much closer than that between Aesop and any Thracian known to mythology. For that reason, and because he was a slave, which the word 'Phrygian' almost implies, it was natural to imagine that Aesop, like the famous Marsyas, was a Phrygian.[60]

Traditions also compare Aesop with the Seven Sages, Socrates, and

---

[58] Plato *Sym.* 216d-e: "I tell you, all the beauty a man may have is nothing to him; he despises it more than any of you can believe; nor does wealth attract him, nor any sort of honor that is the envied prize of the crowd. All these possessions he counts as nothing worth, and all of us as nothing, I assure you; he spends his whole life in chaffing (εἰρωνευόμενος) and making game (παίζων) of his fellow-men."

[59] Todd Compton, "The Trial of the Satirist: Poetic *Vitae* (Aesop, Archilochus, Homer) as Background for Plato's *Apology*," *AJP* 111 (1990): 342-44; p. 343 n. 45 offers further bibliography. On the ritual see Walter Burkert, *Structure and History in Greek Mythology* (Berkeley: University of California Press, 1979), pp. 59-77; idem, *Greek Religion*, trans. John Raffan (Cambridge, MA: Harvard University Press, 1985), pp. 82-84 (and note the language Burkert associates with φαρμακός: καθάρσιον, καθαρμός, περίψημα); Jan Bremmer, "Scapegoat Rituals in Ancient Greece," *HSCP* 87 (1983): 299-320.

[60] Ben E. Perry, *Babrius and Phaedrus*, LCL (Cambridge, MA: Harvard University Press, 1965), pp. xl-xli.

Diogenes,[61] while associating him with King Croesus and the Babylonian legend of Ahiqar.

The *Vitae Aesopi* present an entertaining account of Aesop, characterizing him as horribly ugly and amazingly witty.[62] In the process it subverts educated culture and its encomiastic rhetoric. The opening words herald these themes, introducing Aesop as a great benefactor, yet immediately characterizing him as ill-starred and low-born, not merely servile but a worthless servant, and grotesquely ugly.[63] On top of all that, he was mute. How Aesop can be all these things and yet "benefactor" emerges as the narrative unfolds.

The story's first three incidents answer this question implicitly and explicitly. As for the former, the quality of Aesop's character is revealed, showing that he is clever, pious, and just. When other slaves conspire to blame Aesop for their wrongdoing, the mute Aesop finds a way to convey his innocence and prove the true perpetrators' guilt. Later, when a lost priestess of Isis seeks guidance, Aesop not only assisted but fed her and gave her drink. Afterward, when Aesop could speak, he defended another slave against a brutal overseer. Aesop, then, has qualities that commend him. More important, though, are the gifts of Isis and the Muses. Because of his kindness to her priestess, Isis healed Aesop's tongue (as he slept near a stream) and encouraged the Muses to give Aesop gifts, which they did. "They conferred on him the power to devise stories and the ability to conceive and elaborate tales in Greek" (7). Isis then added a prayer that Aesop might become famous. Here then is the secret to Aesop's success: the direct intervention of the gods to bless him. Though lacking wealth, office, high birth, beauty,[64] or education, this repulsive creature

---

[61] Cp. Dio Chrys. 72.13, which offers a list of wisdom teachers: Socrates-Diogenes-Seven Sages-Aesop.

[62] For Greek text see Ben E. Perry, *Aesopica: A Series of Texts Relating to Aesop or Ascribed to Him or Closely Connected with the Literary Tradition that Bears His Name*, vol. 1: *Greek and Latin Texts* (Urbana: University of Illinois Press, 1952), pp. 35-77 (codex G) and 81-107 (codex W). For English translation see Lloyd W. Daly, *Aesop Without Morals* (New York: Thomas Yoseloff, 1961), pp. 31-90.

[63] Aesop is so ugly that a dozen words are needed in the *Vita's* (G) opening period to describe him. Subsequent comments about Aesop's ugliness occur throughout the *Vitae* (11, 14 [περικάθαρμα, turnip, pot, jar, goose egg], 15, 16, 21, 23, 24, 26, 30, 31 [κυνοκέφαλός], 33, 75, 87, 98 [αἴνιγμα, τέρας]). On the apotropaic value of Aesop's ugliness (to thwart envy, βασκανία, in 16), see Matthew Dickie, "A Joke in Old Comedy: Aristophanes Fragment 607 *PCG*," *CP* 90 (1995): 241-43.

[64] §26: "Don't look at my appearance, but examine my soul." §88: "You shouldn't consider my appearance but examine my wits. It's ridiculous to find fault with a man's intelligence because of the way he looks." §99: "Have pity on me, for I have no power to injure an army, nor am I so handsome that I might give false evidence against someone

nevertheless receives a divine power of clever speech, which he will use for the public good.

As seen already in the quotation of Perry, in his clever speech Aesop represents rural wisdom against Apollonian, educated culture. Theologically, this theme begins with the gift of the Muses and reappears when Aesop builds a shrine for them and at the consequent inflaming of Apollo's envy, Aesop's alleged desecration of Apollo's temple, the Delphians' disregard for Aesop's sanctuary in the Muses' shrine, and Aesop's condemnation and death in Delphi.[65] On a social level, Aesop's intelligence repeatedly trumps that of his master, Xanthus, a renowned and respected philosopher. This begins at their first encounter, when Xanthus looks at Aesop's appearance, not his soul, while Aesop runs circles around Xanthus' sloppy questions. Such word games set the tone for their subsequent conversations. When Xanthus asks how many men are at the bath, Aesop answers only one (66). (Many people, but only one genuine man.) When Xanthus sends food home to the one who loves him, Aesop delivers it to Xanthus' dog (and not his wife; 44-49). These wearisome word games provide much of the interaction between Aesop and Xanthus. To this reader these incidents parody philosophic investigation with its concern for careful definition.[66] Regardless, such examples enhance

---

and get away with it. Poor as my body is, I utter words of commonsense and thereby benefit the life of mortals." Commensurate to these claims are the fable of the fox and leopard (Plut. *Mor.* 155b; 500c) and Dio Chrysostom's interpretation of the owl (12.1-8).

[65] Aesop's mistress dreamed that her husband would bring home a slave as handsome as Apollo (29). Instead she received the ugly but eloquent Aesop, who explained the source of her false dream. Zeus apparently sends false dreams in order to punish Apollo for the pride he took in his oracular skill and his excessive boasting (33).

[66] In defending Logic, Epictetus draws on Chrysippus, Zeno, Cleanthes, and Antisthenes, affirming the notion that "the beginning of education is the examination of terms." He adds that even (Xenophon's) Socrates began his examinations by asking, "What does it mean?" (*Diss.* 1.17.10-12). Aristotle compares the desire for exactitude with popular impatience toward it: "Thus some people will not accept the statements of a speaker unless he gives a mathematical proof; others will not unless he makes use of illustrations; others expect to have a poet as witness. Again, some require exactness (ἀκριβές) in everything, while others are annoyed by it, either because they cannot follow the reasoning or because of its pettiness (μικρολογία); for there is something about exactness which seems to some people to be mean (ἀνελεύθερον), no less in an argument than in a business transaction" (*Meta.* 2.3.995a). Dio Chrys. 12.43: "Now I am aware that to most men strict exactness (τὴν ἀκρίβειαν) in any exposition is on every occasion irksome (κοπωδές)." Dio then argues for precision, concluding that educated people (οἱ πεπαιδευμένοι) will accept and follow careful analysis. Cf. Plato *The.* 172d; Isoc. *Helen* 4-5; Philodemus *On Music* 4, col. 37-38 (on which see Elizabeth Asmis, "Epicurean Poetics," in *Proceedings of the Boston Area Colloquium in Ancient*

Aesop's image at the expense of his educated master. Other incidents add to the philosopher-master's image as a fool. For example, Xanthus is henpecked by his wife (32) and too dull to recognize when he is cuckolded (75-76). Furthermore, when drunk he makes an ill-advised wager which requires Aesop's superior wit to win (69-73).

Xanthus looks even worse when he turns to philosophy. When a gardener poses a question about why weeds grow so well in his garden, Xanthus is stumped (35-37). Aesop's laughter at his master's feeble response stings Xanthus. Aesop assures him, however, that he is not laughing at him but "at the professor you studied under." Offended, Xanthus responds with venom: "You blackguard, this is blasphemy against the Hellenic world, for I studied at Athens under philosophers, rhetoricians, and philologists. And do you have the effrontery to set foot on the Muses' Helicon?" (36). The reader, of course, knows that Aesop does in fact represent the voice of the Muses, so that Aesop's retort (viz., talking nonsense invites jeering) throws suspicion over Hellenic παιδεία.[67] Xanthus' other specimens of reasoning make him look even more ridiculous: he offers wisdom about the best way to urinate on a hot day (28)[68] and later asks the precious question, "Why do people look at their feces?"[69] Perhaps most devastating is the passage where the assembly of Samos calls upon Xanthus to interpret omens. This invitation comes from an old man who observes that "it is no easy matter to tell the significance of a portent. If a man is not thoroughly educated, he will not properly analyze a portent. But we have Xanthus, the philosopher who is known to all of Greece, in our midst" (81). This confidence proves to be misplaced. Unable to unravel the portents, Xanthus verges on suicide when Aesop intervenes, asking, "Master, where is your philosophy? Where is your boasted education? Where is your doctrine of self-control?" (85). Aesop then promises to interpret the omens and later does so. Afterward, Aesop's wisdom guides the people of Samos in their response to the omens; not only dispensing advice, Aesop also serves as emissary

---

Philosophy 7, ed. John J. Cleary [Lanham, MD: University Press of America, 1991], pp. 89-90).

[67] Philostratus mentions some orators who regarded their talents as the gift of the Muses. Given the acclamation which sophistic talent could garner, Aesop represents a startling countertype.

[68] This discussion takes place on the way to Xanthus' house just after he had purchased Aesop. At the end of this "philosophic" conversation, Aesop congratulates Xanthus' wisdom in this matter. Xanthus responds, "Well, I didn't realize I had bought myself a master." What Xanthus intends as sarcasm directed at Aesop, the reader recognizes as ironic confession: Xanthus had in fact just purchased his superior.

[69] *Vit. Aes.* 67. Cf. Phil. *Vit. soph.* 483.

and does so successfully, as his efforts deliver Samos from oppression. Xanthus, on the other hand, plays no role in Samos' salvation. Thus, in the *Vitae Aesopi* the slave's conquest of his master and his vaunted education is complete. The Muses cause a hideous looking slave to win the battle of words and intelligence. Where then does one turn to find wisdom? Not to a person with praiseworthy qualities, not to a person of high status and educated culture, but to its antitype, Aesop.

We must, however, consider how idiosyncratic the picture of Aesop in the *Vitae* may be. While the telling of fables and Aesop's death in Delphi clearly are not innovations, what of the rest of the story, particularly the image of the ugly slave who outsmarts his master, the famous philosopher? Because this image very much depends on its narrative form, the question is difficult to answer. Nevertheless, Martin L. West is optimistic about the antiquity of many of the elements of the Aesop biography:

In the fifth century, probably in Samos, the legend of a repulsively ugly and worthless-looking slave, who was unjustly put to death by the Delphians in circumstances like those of the pharmakos rite, was developed into a fully-fledged novella in which the slave was a shrewd and witty fellow, given to impressing points on his superiors by means of apt parables. Once given this starting-point, the Greek instinct to attach anonymous compositions or achievements to any appropriate individual ensured that Aesop would attract fables.... By Aristophanes' time ... there is apparently a book in which the inquisitive may read about Aesop's life and death, and his wit and wisdom.[70]

Francisco Rodríguez Adrados is also optimistic, but less specific:

The Greek tradition of the fable teller is not essentially different than certain iambic poets, although of a mythical character, and more or less parallels the oriental tradition, being founded on the Thracian or Phrygian Aesop, a slave and a wise man who tells fables, solves riddles, is protected by Apollo, and yet was unjustly killed.[71]

Rodríguez Adrados accounts for this unity by his view that our *Vitae Aesopi* has a Hellenistic prototype, distinct from Demetrius of Phalerum and arising within Cynicism (1.2: 664-65). Like West, then, he thinks an early text existed, though the two have different origins in mind. If we

---

[70] "The Ascription of Fables to Aesop in Archaic and Classical Greece," in *La Fable*, ed. Francisco Rodríguez Adrados, Entretiens sur l'antiquité classique 30 (Genève: Fondation Hardt, 1984), p. 128.

[71] Francisco Rodríguez Adrados, *Historia de la fábula greco-latina*, 3 vols. (Madrid: Editorial de la Universidad Complutense, n.d. [1979-1987]), 1.2: 661-62: "La tradición griega del narrador de fábulas, no esencialmente diferente de ciertos poetas yámbicos, pero de carácter mítico ya, y la tradición oriental más o menos paralela, se fundieron en el Esopo tracio o frigio, esclavo y sabio, narrador de fábulas, solucionador de enigmas, protegido por Apolo y, sin embargo, muerto injustamente." Connections between *Vitae Aesopi* and Cynicism are discussed below.

follow these two scholars, we would conclude that the basic elements of the *Vitae Aesopi* have old precedents and are not innovations of the Imperial period.

Two approaches can be taken in thinking about the portrait in the *Vitae*. We can compare Aesop's image in other texts and look at the themes within the *Vitae Aesopi* itself. The first approach does offer some help, indicating some consistency in the figure of Aesop. Diogenes Laertius says that Chilon asked Aesop what Zeus was doing and was told, "He is humbling the proud and exalting the humble" (1.69). While that is one of the most common of commonplaces in antiquity, it certainly corresponds to how Aesop appears in the *Vitae*. The anecdote, therefore, either relies on the *Vitae* or (more likely) suggests that the persona presented in the *Vitae* corresponds with what is expected of Aesop.

One place we can find a more extended picture of Aesop is Plutarch's *Dinner of the Seven Wise Men*, a story about a symposium at which the legendary wise men of Greece gathered.[72] Others also attended, including Aesop. In this essay, Plutarch corresponds to the *Vitae* in his presentation of Aesop as a fabulist (no surprise), a punster (155e), and an expert in riddles.[73] Aesop also relates a fable which indicates his lowliness (150a-b) and contrasts with Alexidemus who stormed off when his ego was bruised (148e-149b). Aesop's low status agrees with the *Vitae*. More important are Aesop's roles in the symposium. At the end (164b-c), he serves as an interpreter of Delphic maxims, a role which corresponds to the legends of his death at Delphi. In the earlier portions of Plutarch's essay, however, Aesop plays the part of an under-appreciated gadfly. After the Seven offered opinions on how to increase a ruler's reputation, Aesop offered a mocking retort (152b-e). Solon responded with condescension, for which Aesop had yet another ready answer. A third exchange followed in similar fashion which concluded with Solon's laughter. Moments later Aesop made fun of an earlier comment by Thales, at which Periander erupted in laughter and said, "We are fittingly punished, Aesop ..." (152e). Later, Aesop trumped Cleodorus, making him laugh (154b-c). Soon thereafter Aesop interrupted Pitticus and Anacharsis to tell a fable which Chilon correctly recognized as a rebuke which at the same time vindicated Aesop

---

[72] Though the number seven is canonical, its membership varies. Plutarch offers Thales, Bias, Pittacus, Solon, Chilon, Cleobulus, and Anacharsis. For commentary see David Aune, "Septem sapientium convivium (Moralia 146B-164D)," in *Plutarch's Ethical Writings and Early Christian Literature*, ed. Hans Dieter Betz, Studia ad Corpus Hellenisticum Novi Testamenti 4 (Leiden: E. J. Brill, 1978), pp. 51-105.

[73] 150e-f. In 150a a messenger from the king of Egypt presents to Bias a riddle about drinking the sea dry. This same riddle appears in *Vitae Aesopi* and requires Aesop's wisdom to solve.

himself (155f-156a). Elsewhere, when Diocles proposed household management as a new subject of conversation, Aesop laughed and teased Anacharsis who had no house (154f-155c). Anacharsis offered a pained response based on philosophic considerations and including one of Aesop's own fables. That Aesop is here portrayed as ridiculing a philosophical position is of immediate interest, as it matches nicely the portrait in the *Vitae*. On the whole, then, while much of this is simply the banter appropriate to a banquet, the specific comments and particular emphasis on Aesop as the one who disagrees seems to emphasize Aesop's role as a gadfly.[74] His lower esteem appears as well in statements of disrespect for his fables.[75] There is then a general correspondence between Plutarch's Aesop and the *Vitae Aesopi*.

What then of the details of Aesop's life? Although specific points lack precise corroboration, many of them belong to larger themes and patterns on which we can comment and which suggest associations appropriate to Aesop. They make the composition of the *Vitae* transparent and perhaps predictable. To be more explicit, the *Vitae Aesopi* present a figure which corresponds to traditional fables, the comedic stage, the figure of Socrates, and the ideas of Cynicism. We will now examine these.

The image of Aesop presented by the *Vitae* corresponds to what one might expect of a fabulist. For example, two other ancient fabulists, Phaedrus and Babrius, were ex-slaves. More to the point, though, fable scholarship identifies fables as rhetoric of the οἱ πολλοί.[76] This appears

---

[74] Some teasing must be allowed as the normal course of sympotic banter (and competition). Aesop is therefore not the only one to criticize others. Thales teases Bias (150b-c), while Anacharsis and Pittacus exchange digs (155f). Aesop, however, does this with greater frequency. Periander's criticisms, like Aesop's, fit his character (152b; 154f).

[75] 150b; 152b-e; 162b; 164b-c. These statements indicate that Aesop's fables are viewed as a lesser kind of wisdom, though Cleobulus' use of a fable inserts some ambiguity into the picture (157b). Patrizia Puppini argues that Plutarch does not denigrate Aesop's wisdom, as he does not present it as simply comic or popular ("Esopo a Simposio," *Sileno* 17 [1991]: 185-206). The alignment of Aesop with Homer and Hesiod clearly grants Aesop a measure of respect. That is not the same thing, however, as equating fables with philosophical discourse. By way of contrast, in *Vitae Aesopi* fables provide guidance for policy decisions (as also Aris. *Rhet.* 2.20.6), whereas in Plutarch's symposium Solon suggests that fables are inadequate for political thinking. Plutarch explicitly places fables below philosophy in *Mor.* 14e and 16b-c. (Cf. Quin. 5.11.19-20: fables "are specially attractive to rude and uneducated minds.") We might also note that not only are fables slighted, so are riddles, requiring Aesop to rise to their defense (154b-c).

[76] Kenneth S. Rothwell, Jr., "Aristophanes' *Wasps* and the Sociopolitics of Aesop's Fables," *CJ* 90 (1995): 233-54 (especially pp. 233-39). Previous research on this matter includes the following: Antonio La Penna, "La morale della favola esopica come morale

in the perspective of many fables, which "reflect the viewpoint of the downtrodden," such as those which depict the lowly outwitting the mighty.[77] Charting the use of fables also indicates this, because, as Rothwell generalizes, in "the more serious genres no Greek of the respectable classes tells a complete animal fable; instead, fables were relegated more to comedy and iambos than to epic and tragedy."[78] Cross-cultural comparisons likewise suggest that fables belong to lower levels of society, among the poor and weak.[79] In terms of rhetoric, then, the telling of a fable is a good way to hold an audience's attention and gain its goodwill, as it makes a person look like a common man.[80]

The themes of specific fables associated with Aesop reflect the stance of the *Vitae* and undermine encomiastic standards. For example, a fox and leopard argued about who was prettier. The fox challenged the "obvious" answer by arguing that his ψυχή was superior to the leopard's.[81] Whereas encomia praise intelligence and physique, another fable presents them as mutually exclusive (*Fab.* 110). Another fable describes Herakles' friendly interaction with all the gods except Plutus, to whom he gave the cold shoulder because W/wealth usually kept company with scoundrels (*Fab.* 113).

The figure of Aesop in the *Vitae Aesopi* also corresponds to a broad cultural type, the clever slave of New Comedy.[82] Taken into Roman drama, Plautus used this figure effectively in *Pseudolus*, which preserves for us the most elaborate example of the clever slave.[83] Reflecting on the

---

delle classi subalterne nell'antichità," *Società* 17 (1961): 459-537; M. T. W. Arnheim, "The World of the Fable," *Studies in Antiquity* 1 (1979-80): 1-11; Francisco Rodríguez Adrados, "Sociolingüistica y griego antiguo," *Revista española de lingüistica* 11 (1981): 311-29; idem, ed., *La fable*, Entretiens sur l'Antiquité Classique 30 (Vandoeuvres-Genève: Fondation Hardt, 1984).

[77] Rothwell, "Aristophanes' *Wasps* and the Sociopolitics of Aesop's Fables," p. 235.

[78] Rothwell, p. 237.

[79] Pp. 237-38.

[80] P. 253.

[81] *Fab.* 12; see also 159. Cf. Plut. *Mor.* 155b; 500c.

[82] The mocking of philosophy is yet another *topos* which the *Vitae Aesopi* shares with comedy (e.g. Menander *Dyskolos* 713-14; *Aspis* 336-40; 599).

[83] See also Tranio in *Mostellaria*, Chalinus in *Casina*, Libanus and Leonida in *Asinaria*. Cf. *Bacchides* and *Captivi*. See W. T. MacCary, "Menander's Slaves: Their Names, Roles and Masks," *TAPA* 100 (1969): 277-94; W. G. Arnott, *Menander, Plautus and Terence* (Oxford University Press, 1975). On the slave in plastic art see Margarete Bieber, *The History of The Greek and Roman Theater* (Princeton University Press, 1961), pp. 150, 245; T. B. L. Webster, *Monuments Illustrating New Comedy*, 2d ed., Bulletin of the Institute for Classical Studies, Suppl. 24 (London 1969); R. L. Hunter, *The New Comedy of Greece and Rome* (Cambridge Univeristy Press, 1985).

role of slaves in Plautus' comedy, William Anderson notes that "resourcefulness, sheer energy, and what we call 'street smarts' inevitably win out over established authority and self-satisfied, self-serving softness ..."[84] Philostratus offers a sobering example of life imitating art in his account of Scopelian, whose father disinherited him after falling victim to the conniving of his slave (*Vit. soph.* 517). As a slave, then, Aesop's quick mind linked him to a stereotype. While this alone provides sufficient connection, we must also recall ancient costuming. With a mask and dangling phallus, the image of the comedic slave further corresponds to the "hero" of the *Vitae Aesopi*. That this combination of outrageous ugliness and cleverness clearly echoes comedy then raises questions of origins and influences. Did the comedic stage influence Aesop traditions which the *Vitae* incorporate, or did the author(s) of the *Vitae* use the comedic figure to flesh out the figure of Aesop? Or did both possibilities occur? Or did Aesop and the stage both reflect a social idea about the ugliness of slaves relative to the beauty of the rich?

The picture of Aesop in the *Vitae* also draws on the image of Socrates.[85] "For a long time people have observed that the image of Aesop in the *Vita Aesopi* shares numerous traits in common with Plato's Socrates and that in the *Phaedo* (60b-c) Plato as well relates the two figures to one another by placing on the lips of Socrates a *mythos* told in the manner of Aesop."[86] The similarities are as follows: 1) both spring from humble origins; 2) both are ugly,[87] but 3) have inner beauty;[88] 4) both gain fame by their intellectual gifts, although 5) both "know nothing"; 6) as Aesop is cheeky toward the renowned philosopher Xanthus, Socrates defies established sophists; 7) both press their conversation partners to define

---

[84] "The Roman Transformation of Greek Domestic Comedy," *CW* 88 (1995): 178. Andreson links clever women to the clever slave as a destroyer of pretension to power (e.g., Phronesium [note name] in Plautus' *Truculentus*).

[85] M. J. Luzzatto, "Plutarco, Socrate e l'Esopo di Delfi," *ICS* 13 (1988): 427-45; Stefano Jedrkiewicz, *Sapere e paradosso nell'antichità. Esops e la favola* (Roma: Edizioni dell'Ateneo, 1989); Todd Compton, "The Trial of the Satirist," pp. 330-47; Markus Schauer and Stefan Merkle, "Äsop und Sokrates," in *Äsop-Roman. Motivesgeschichte und Erzählstruktur*, ed. Niklas Holzberg, Classica Monacensia 6 (Tübingen: Gunter Narr, 1992), pp. 85-96.

[86] Schauer and Merkle, "Äsop und Sokrates," p. 85: "Man hat längst beobachtet, daß die Gestalt Äsops in der *Vita Aesopi* zahlreiche Züge des platonischen Sokratesbildes aufweist und daß auch Platon die beiden Männer zueinander in Beziehung setzt, indem er Sokrates im *Phaidon* (60 b3-c7) einen *mythos* in äsopischer Manier erzählen läßt."

[87] Both have snub-noses (Xen. *Sym.* 5.6) and are potbellied (*Sym.* 2.19). See also Plato *The.* 143e.

[88] Plato *Sym.* 215b; 216d-e.

3.4. Aesop

concepts precisely;[89] 8) both have a funny way (γέλοιος) of discourse;[90] 9) Aesop has a close relationship with the Muses, while the Delphic oracle identifies Socrates as the wisest person; 9) both are accused of religious crimes and condemned unjustly; 10) while in jail both receive visits from friends; 11) both prophesy what will happen after their deaths; and 12) statues are erected for each after their deaths. All these parallels leave no room for doubt that the figure of Aesop in the *Vitae* is composed with Socrates in mind.

In the face of the similarities, the point of Schauer and Merkle's article is to emphasize the dissimilarity between the deaths of Aesop and Socrates. Whereas the latter quietly and serenely accepted death, the former resisted it energetically. While Socrates consoled his sad friends before he died, Aesop refused to accept any consolation. What Aesop regarded as the greatest misfortune, (Plato's) Socrates saw as a step in the soul's immortality and an opportunity to greater knowledge. These differences then suggest Plato's reason for introducing a fable at the beginning of the *Phaedo*.

At the beginning of his dialogue about the immortality of the soul Plato has called to mind the legendary death of a wise man who sought to escape his imminent execution by his eloquence. The Aesop legend serves therefore as a foil by which Plato portrays Socrates as a truly wise person who does not fear death and, because of his knowledge, is ready to die.[91]

These remarks certainly assist one's reading of the *Phaedo*, but not of Aesop. Since Aesop was not a citizen of Delphi, he lacked the moral ties to Delphi which Socrates had to Athens, leaving him no reason to tolerate Delphi's injustice. Within the context of the *Vitae*, however, the differences between Socrates and Aesop probably are relevant. As Aesop makes philosophy look ridiculous, his death affords one final criticism. Aesop recognizes death as death and nothing more. The only appropriate response is dread and avoidance. Aesop's behavior in the face of death is then not simply un-Socratic, but anti-philosophical, which corresponds to the rest of the *Vitae*.[92] With this in mind, the parallels between Socrates

---

[89] Socrates, however, takes this enterprise more seriously than does Aesop.

[90] Plato *Sym.* 221e.

[91] Schauer and Merkle, "Äsop und Sokrates," p. 90: "Platon hat also zu Beginn seines Dialogs von der Unsterblichkeit der Seele an den legendären Tod eines weisen Mannes erinnert, der durch sein Redetalent der drohenden Hinrichtung entkommen wollte. Die Äsop-Legende wird damit zu einer Folie, vor der Platon Sokrates als einen wahren Weisen darstellt, der den Tod nicht fürchtet und aus Einsicht zu sterben bereit ist."

[92] Cp. Lucian's subversion of Homer in *Ver. hist.* 2.35, where Odysseus writes a letter to Calypso from the Isle of the Blessed in which he repents having left her and the

and Aesop point to an interesting dialogue. The figure of Aesop influenced Plato in his writings, while later the image of Socrates influenced an anonymous author who wrote a life of Aesop.

As many have noted, the *Vitae* also have Cynic features. H. Zeitz noted many parallels between Aesop and Diogenes.[93] Both were auctioned as slaves. To both are attributed anecdotes about encountering only one man at the bath; they share other anecdotes as well. Both figures also advise kings and raise questions about φύσις and νόμος. Lastly, the word "dog" characterizes both.[94] In addition to these parallels from Zeitz, Francisco Rodríguez Adrados identifies more general Cynic parallels in his *Historia de la fábula greco-latina*. Important in this regard is the polemic between Aesop and philosophy, which Rodríguez Adrados compares to Cynic (/Mennipian) satire of their rivals, particularly Stoics (1.2: 673). Hand-in-hand with this is satire of women and "the powerful, etc., and the same forms of speech based on the diatribe, *chreiai*, anecdotes, similies, etc."[95] Adrados, however, emphasizes six other important Cynic themes in the *Life of Aesop*.[96] First, Aesop is a living paradox, for his two outstanding features are his "ugliness and intelligence." He embodies the paradox "of the mute person who ... is wiser than anyone," of a slave who is genuinely free, of a person who is ugly but beautiful. Second, Aesop lives the frugal and temperate life of a Cynic. Third, he stands in opposition to wealth, παιδεία, and might. Fourth, Aesop stands for nature over against νόμος (as Zeitz observed). Fifth, he exercises freedom of speech (παρρησία) and shamelessness (ἀναίδεια). Last, sexual practices and misogyny mark Aesop as a Cynic.[97] According to Rodríguez Adrados, the importance of

---

immortality she offered. Also, Tac. *Ann.* 16.17-20, where the hedonist Petronius binds his slit wrists to prolong death, so that he may listen to frivolous songs and verses.

[93] H. Zeitz, "Der Aesoproman und seine Geschichte," *Aegyptus* 16 (1936): 225-55.

[94] *Vitae Aesopi* refers to Aesop's "dog's head" (30), and labels him "a dog in a basket" (87).

[95] 1.2: 673-74: "... poderosos, etc., y la misma forma de hacerla, a base de diatriba, *chreiai*, anécdotas, símiles, etc." Cf. p. 691.

[96] *Historia de la fábula greco-latina*, 1.2: 692-96.

[97] The sex scene between Aesop and his master's wife (75-76 W) is difficult to pigeonhole. S. E. Goins notes the sexual proclivities of slaves in Old Comedy, which suggests that Aesop's being a slave is motive enough for the scene ("The Influence of Old Comedy on the *Vita Aesopi*," *CW* 83 [1989]: 28-30). Yet Aesop's masturbation also corresponds to Cynicism. But would a Cynic be motivated to do something he thought was wrong in order to receive a new shirt? Perhaps the scene is, like the Delphi scene, anti-Socratic and anti-philosophical: i.e., as Aesop rejects a philosophical approach to death, so also to sexual pleasure and material goods. Rodríguez Adrados bases his judgment on comparable scenes in *Satyricon* and *Ass*.

these motives lies in their totality as well as the particularity, for together they contribute to a larger picture of literary origins, viz., Cynic satire.

Our focus so far on the life of Aesop may raise the question whether he is in fact parallel to Odysseus, Herakles, and Socrates. While the latter three not only critique encomiastic values, they also model virtue. Does Aesop as well, or is he only a caustic wit? Our focus on Aesop's life should not blind us to his greatest significance, viz., as a fabulist. He is, then, more than a critic. While he may not model virtue in as particular a way as do Odysseus, Herakles, and Socrates, he does possess wisdom, teaching how to navigate life well. To compare Aesop to the other three, then, invites a value judgment on folk wisdom as an alternate form of wisdom and positive instruction. While I grant that fables are not ethics, they communicate quite useful messages about living prudently and successfully.

A *topos* which suggests this is that of the wise rustic who showed up the sophisticated urban elite. Maximus of Tyre tells of an incident related to Anacharsis, who arrived at Athens from Scythia with a wisdom short on words but containing an exact summary of life, a sound understanding, and concise, witty speech. Because he met no one who measured up to his expectations, he wandered about Greece looking for wisdom. In an insignificant town he at last found a good man (ἀνὴρ ἀγαθός). This man managed his house and fields well, was prudent in matters of marriage, and was an excellent father. Meeting this person ended Anacharsis' quest and convinced him not to seek "wordy" wisdom (*Diss.* 25.1). Dio Chrysostom presents a similar figure in *Or.* 7. A simple, kind hunter is summoned to court, charged with misappropriation of public lands. At his hearing, he is prosecuted vehemently, but prevails with his simplicity and honesty. In the end, his virtue carries the day and not only does he escape penalties, rewards are decreed on his behalf.[98] This image of the virtuous rural person was in fact a stereotype which appeared frequently in Greco-Roman rhetoric and provided rhetorical ammunition with which to fight against urban pretension.[99]

To summarize our discussion of the *Vitae Aesopi*, we have encountered a figure who overturns the pretensions of nobility and παιδεία. Like

---

[98] This sounds like Socrates' trial only with a happy ending.

[99] Ann Vasaly, *Representations*, pp. 156-90; eadem, "The Masks of Power: Cicero's *Pro Roscio Amerino*," *Rhetorica* 3 (1985): 1-20. Vasaly shows how Cicero could play this *topos* in the opposite direction. Similar rhetoric appears in comedy. Aristophanes favors the virtuous peasant, while Plautus prefers hedonistic urbanites to rustic boors. Menander seems to go both ways (R. L. Hunter, *The New Comedy of Greece and Rome*, 109-13; Dana Sutton, *Ancient Comedy*, pp. 35-36 and 52-53). Cf. Theophrastus' portrait of the rustic.

slaves from the comic stage, Aesop is more clever than everyone else and grotesquely ugly. Yet he also has many points of contact with Socrates — plus the important, anti-philosophical difference that he abhors death. He also shares similarities with Diogenes, while Cynic themes infuse the work as a whole. All these streams converge in a clever figure who subverts standard expectations of wisdom and virtue.

5. Odysseus, Herakles, Aesop, and Socrates as Rhetorical Figures

Having surveyed the four preceding figures and their roles in wisdom and virtue's counterculture, we must note the equivocal and (hence) rhetorical nature of much of our evidence. As many footnotes have indicated, legendary figures may illustrate polar opposites. Odysseus can portray convention as well as subversion, while Herakles can serve as a moral exemplar or the object of derision. Even Socrates could inspire diverse opinions. The perspective taken on these figures depended on the views and rhetorical exigencies of our sources. The thematic unity which we have traced therefore resides more in an attitude of social and cultural criticism than in the figures themselves. The rhetoric of social and cultural criticism (subversive or otherwise) therefore takes up well-known figures and shapes them to serve its own purposes. This was, however, done often enough that the rhetorical images (of Odysseus, Herakles, Aesop, and Socrates) became widespread and well-known *topoi*.

Noting the rhetorical use which social critics made of legendary figures, we can return to Dio Chrysostom for a final example. In the introduction of his *Olympic Discourse*, Dio picks up Aesop's language of fables to contrast the wisdom of the owl with the beauty of the peacock (12.1-8). The fable eases Dio into his speech in a disarming and pleasant manner, setting up Dio's own self-presentation, in which he emphasizes his lack of outward attraction (like the owl) and the consequent hope such an appearance affords that he dispenses wisdom. Dio, however, comments that as the other birds gather about the owl despite the fact the owl has grown silent, so his audience had gathered about him even though he had not yet said anything of note. Dio's next words parallel him with Socrates: "...I have no knowledge superior to your own. But there are other men who are wise and altogether blessed; and if you wish, I shall make them known to you" (12.10). The (obviously enough) Socratic nature of those words becomes explicit a few paragraphs later (12.14). These words combine with their context to present Dio as a man of the people with simple ideas to express, a populist image indicating that despite appearances Dio is a social critic worth hearing.[100]

Not only can we observe the rhetorical function of Odysseus, Herakles, Socrates, and Aesop, we can note its location. The majority of evidence cited stems from the Stoic and Cynic traditions. The use of these figures, and particularly the canonical status of Socrates within many circles of Hellenistic philosophy, suggests the direction of Hellenistic philosophy. The Cynic-Stoic tradition did in fact reject common societal values, viewing them as false assumptions based on unanalyzed appearances (δόξα) — in other words, foolishness. This was the heart of Dio Chrysostom's philosophic message.[101] While reflecting on the origins of his philosophic ministry, he summarizes his message as follows:

> And the opinion I had was that pretty well all men are fools, and that no one does any of the things he should do, or considers how to rid himself of the evils that beset him and of his great ignorance and confusion of mind, so as to live a more virtuous and a better life; but that they all are being thrown into confusion and are swept round and round in the same place and about practically the same objects, to wit, money and reputation and certain pleasures of the body, while no one is able to rid himself of these and set his own soul free (13.13).

A similar view appears in Epictetus, who regarded the reappraisal of commonplace values as the threshold of philosophy, and therefore wrote:

> Behold the beginning of philosophy! — a recognition of the conflict between the opinions of men, and a search for the origin of that conflict, and a condemnation of mere opinion, coupled with skepticism regarding it, and a kind of investigation to determine whether the opinion is rightly held, together with the invention of a kind of standard of judgment (*Diss.* 2.11.13).

Earlier he described the beginning of philosophy as "a consciousness of a man's own weakness and impotence with reference to the things of real

---

[100] In antiquity the rhetoric of social and cultural criticism is better known as the rhetoric of comedy, philosophy and/or satire. The data which we have surveyed suggest the connection between social critique and philosophy. We have not discussed comedy much because it contributes little to the specific contours which we have traced; moreover, when comedy does make use of Socrates and Herakles, rather different purposes are at work, as these two become objects of derision. In general, however, comedy played an important role in social criticism. While this is emphatically true of Old Comedy, even comedies of manners imply some social commentary (though it is less politically charged than Old Comedy). Though the conjunction of comedy and philosophy may sound strange, we must bear in mind that Cynic hybrid of "serious humor" (σπουδαιογέλοιον: see Lawrence Giangrande, *The Use of Spoudaiogeloion in Greek and Roman Literature* [The Hauge: Mouton, 1972]).

[101] At the beginning and end of his Ninth Oration, Dio Chrys. makes foolishness (ἄνοια) the basic human condition from which Diogenes delivers people (9.1, 21).

consequence" (2.11.1). Not to philosophize is to remain satisfied with δόξα "as the measure of all things," which is madness (μανία; 2.11.18). Later, he specified two examples of mistaken δόξα, poverty and the holding of office (*Diss.* 4.6.23-24).

Epictetus' views follow those of his teacher, Musonius Rufus. In discussing the training (ἄσκησις) necessary for living virtuously (frg. 6 Lutz), Musonius (in good Socratic fashion) rejects creature comforts: one should grow accustomed to heat and cold, hunger and thirst, and hard beds. Endurance of hardship and abstinence from pleasure are also necessary, for they train the soul for courage and temperance. The mind should also be stocked with proofs which demonstrate that what seems good is not necessarily so. He then reflects on the consequences of his views, noting that "all of us who have participated in philosophic discussion have heard and apprehended that neither pain nor death nor poverty nor anything else which is free from wrong is an evil, and again that wealth, life, pleasure, or anything else which does not partake of virtue is not a good." As a result, the person "who is in training" must grow accustomed to avoid loving pleasure and money, loathing difficulty and death, and preferring receiving to giving.

These views go back to Socrates by way of Diogenes, whose example and teaching challenged numerous conventions. This appeared in his frank speech (παρρησία) and shameless indifference to public tastes (ἀναίδεια), and was summarized by the idea of "changing the currency." This suggests a νόμος-φύσις dichotomy and points to the Cynic attempt to live according to nature (κατὰ φύσιν), which was accomplished by removing "all the accretions of convention, tradition, and social existence." At the heart of this teaching was an asceticism[102] which challenged normal lifestyles and promoted simplicity and independence (even self-sufficiency, αὐτάρκεια), all of which removed Diogenes and his followers from the competitive world of encomiastic values. Thus, Dudley can summarize Diogenes' mission as a "thoroughgoing onslaught on convention, custom, and tradition in all respects."[103]

---

[102] M.-O. Goulet-Cazé, *L'Ascèse cynique. Un commentarire de Diogène Laërce VI.70-71*, Histoire des doctrines de l'antiquité classique 10 (Paris: J. Vrin, 1986), pp. 17-92.

[103] Dudley, *A History of Cynicism*, p. 28. As for other Cynics, Dudley comments on Crates' essay which offered "an ironic picture of a wealthy man's account book" (p. 47). Menippus portrayed the absurd "trappings of wealth, the pedantry of learning, the vanity of beauty" (p. 74). Teles wrote about exile, self-sufficiency, poverty, wealth, hardships, and appearance vs. reality (p. 85). During the last two centuries B.C. Cynic ideas like self-sufficiency, simplicity, and appearance vs. reality were common, but were absorbed into Stoicism (pp. 118-20).

The reevaluation of pleasure, hardship, death, and money was widespread among philosophers. Money was a key litmus test. Dio Chrysostom's *Euboean Discourse* offers an elaborate recommendation of poverty. At one point Dio mixes philosophy and pragmatism and asserts that poverty is more likely than wealth to lead people to act in accordance with nature (κατὰ φύσιν; *Or.* 7.103). Seneca offers the example of the Cynic philosopher Demetrius of Sunium, asserting, "I have found that he lacks nothing. It is in the power of any man to despise all things, but of no man to possess all things. The shortest cut to riches is to despise riches. Our friend Demetrius, however, lives not merely as if he has learned to despise all things, but as if he has handed them over for others to possess" (*Ep.* 62.3). Lucian records Nigrinus' persuasiveness in this matter. Prior to conversation with Nigrinus, an interlocutor valued money and honors; afterward his priorities changed so dramatically that he prefered ταπεινὰ καὶ καταγέλαστα (Luc. *Nig.* 4). As mad as this sounds, Nigrinus argues that the position is in fact reasonable (6). Phoenicides' humorous use of a philosopher's attitude toward money indicates how well-known this *topos* was. One of his characters, a prostitute, complained about her former lovers: the soldier talked endlessly of wars; the doctor actually killed people; the philosopher insisted that money was not a Good. Phoenicides adds that despite the prostitute's arguments with the philosopher that he should therefore throw his money away, to her of course, "he was not persuaded" (frg. 4.4-21). In this example, the *topos* has taken a further step and become a satirical caricature.[104]

Good birth was also challenged.[105] [Ps.-] Heraclitus *Ep.* 4 defends Hermodorus whom the Ephesians exiled because he wrote "civil rights legislation for freedmen and equal rights laws for their children." Among the arguments put forward, virtue and nature are regarded as true tests of people, not fate. Thus, the centuries-old respect paid to birth is rejected.[106]

---

[104] Isocrates seems to argue against a Cynic attitude in *Helen* 7-10, as he complains that they "have the effrontery to write that the life of beggars and exiles is more enviable than that of the rest of mankind ..." (8). Later he asks "what sensible man would undertake to praise misfortunes?" and answers that "it is obvious that they take refuge in such topics because of weakness" (ἀσθένεια; 10). Cf. Appian *Mithr.* 28.

[105] Recall that Socrates' father was a stone-mason, his mother a midwife.

[106] Given the good-birth *topos*, rhetorical theory developed means both for exploiting it and for negating it. Thus, the argument in [Ps.-] Heraclitus is common. Looking elsewhere, in Philostratus' eyes Isocrates' rhetorical accomplishments elevated him above his blue collar family origin (*Vit. soph.* 506; cf. 544). Praising a man from a prominent family, Philostratus prefers instead to overlook the man's origins and to register his greatness on the basis of his eloquence and intelligence (597). Philostratus also offers a rhetorical dodge for the low-born in his discussion of Dionysius of Miletus:

Antisthenes likewise repudiated noble birth — which he lacked (Sen. *De const.* 18.5). Diogenes Laertius notes that Cynics in general despise high birth (6.104), and specifically mentions Diogenes and Hipparchia in this regard (6.72 and 96).[107]

Athletic prowess was also subverted. The genuine strong man is not the wrestling champion, but the one who conquers even greater enemies, like hardship and pleasure. The struggle which takes place within a person presents a far greater challenge than any external opponent. As a result, the Cynic is the real Olympian and deserving of the victor's crown.[108]

Even education was challenged. While Cicero (*De oratore*) and Quintilian thought comprehensively about the perfect curriculum, others launched spirited attacks on education. Plato and Epicurus disliked the inclusion of poetry in the educational curriculum.[109] "Plutarch shows that Epicurus' opposition to poetry is part of a larger issue, education. Like Plato in the *Republic*, Epicurus believed that the whole traditional educational system, with its teaching of Homer and other poets, was a corrupting influence ... [Epicurus] assured his students that it was an advantage not to be educated."[110] From an Epicurean perspective, the "so-called liberal studies is παιδεία only in the etymological sense of being the occupation of children, παῖδες; it is not παιδεία in the proper sense in which education is a training for happiness."[111]

Cynic views further undermined παιδεία. In his Fourth Oration Dio Chrysostom overviews two contrasting kinds of education, divine and human (26-45). The former is great, forceful, and easy, while the latter is

---

"to have recourse to one's ancestors is the mark of those who despair of applause for themselves" (522).

[107] Reality also made the value of good-birth problematic. What if someone rose from obscurity to high office? Amasis did just that in Egypt (Herod. 2.172; Plut. *Mor.* 151e). What if someone rose from poverty to great wealth? This was a problem in the Roman Empire, so that we read of wealthy freedmen and can view the large funerary monuments of successful business people who lacked noteworthy social connection. Social and economic reality in Corinth probably affirmed and contradicted the value of family connections.

[108] Dio Chrys. argues this winsomely in *Or.* 8 and 9, telling the story of Diogenes at the Isthmian games. Cp. Diog. L. 6.43, 49, and 61.

[109] Plato *Rep.* 10 (especially 605c; 607b); *Laws* 967c-d. Stanley Rosen, *The Quarrel Between Philosophy and Poetry: Studies in Ancient Thought* (NY: Routledge, 1988); Thomas Gould, *The Ancient Quarrel between Poetry and Philosophy* (Princeton University Press, 1990).

[110] Elizabeth Asmis, "Epicurean Poetics," in *Proceedings of the Boston Area Colloquium in Ancient Philosophy* 7, ed. John J. Cleary (Lanahm, MD: University Press of America, 1991), p. 69.

[111] Asmis, p. 76.

the opposite, i.e., small, weak, and dangerous — not to mention full of lies. Human παιδεία is really παιδιά, while the divine is ἀνδρεία (or μεγαλοφροσύνη). The one curriculum is based on literature, listening, and talking and includes scoundrels among its alumni, the other is patterned after Herakles and produces stout souls acquainted with justice.[112] This two-part scheme did not originate with Dio, but was presented by Antisthenes.[113]

The challenge to education points to the fundamental challenge of Cynicism. The Cynic offered a short-cut to virtue (Julian 188c-d). They jettisoned physics, logic, literature and rhetoric (Diog. L. 6.103); imitating Cynic simplicity was an express lane to wisdom and virtue. This not only undermined encomiastic standards, but philosophy itself. Though the Stoics retained physics and logic, they too emphasized virtue and recognized how it could contradict conventions, as we have seen in Musonius and Epictetus. Thus, Cynic-Stoic tradition cast a suspicious eye on the commonplaces of encomiastic rhetoric.[114]

The Socratic philosopher's countercultural rhetoric went far beyond words and permeated his dress and demeanor as well. Fernanda Decleva Caizzi notes that "the philosopher clearly appears as somebody different from other people in his external features and, what is more interesting, as somebody whose external features and behavior are related to the contents of his philosophical thought."[115] Dio Chrysostom offers much insight into how a philosopher presented himself. In *Or.* 72 (Περὶ τοῦ σχήματος), Dio discusses the matter of personal appearance. Just as sailors, farmers, shepherds and tavern-keepers wear distinctive clothing, so does the

---

[112] Cp. Dio Chrys. 13.14-28 for further criticism of education. Cf. Musonius Rufus frg. 6 Lutz: the soul is trained for ἀνδρεία by ὑπομονὴ τῶν ἐπιπόνων.

[113] See J. Gildemeister and F. Bücheler, "Themistios Περὶ ἀρετῆς," *RhM* 27 (1872): 438-62: they present a German translation of a Syriac fragment in which Themistius refers to Antisthenes' views (pp. 450-51).

[114] Stobaeus *Eclog.* p. 3 aligns Pythagoras with what we have seen of Cynics and Stoics: "Pythagoras says that one must choose the best [manner of] life, for habit will make it sweet. Wealth is a weak anchor, reputation (δόξα) weaker still, likewise the body, offices, honors. All these things are weak and impotent. What anchors hold? Intelligence, spirit, and courage (φρόνησις, μεγαλοψυχία, ἀνδρεία). No storm will move these. This is God's law: virtue is the only strong thing, all others are frivolous" (my trans.).

[115] "The Porch and the Garden: Early Hellenistic Images of the Philosophic Life," in *Images and Ideologies: Self-Definition in the Hellenistic World*, eds. Anthony Bulloch, et al., Hellenistic Culture and Society 12 (Berkeley: University of California Press, 1993), p. 304.

philosopher: he wears a ἱμάτιον but no χιτών.[116] He also sports a beard and lets his hair grow long.[117] Other texts add that philosophers tend to affect a gloomy (σκυθρωπός) or overly serious expression.[118] Cynics, in particular, also wore a pouch (πήρα) and carried a staff (βάκτρον).[119] Dio further notes in *Or.* 72 that the philosopher's costume corresponds to the statues of gods, kings, and generals; more precisely it is the garb of Socrates and Diogenes. Unfortunately, Dio wryly observes, the world is overrun with people so clothed. When Dio himself went into exile, he too took up this garb: "after exhorting myself in this way neither to fear or be ashamed of my action, and putting on the lowly clothing (στολὴν ταπεινήν) and otherwise chastening (κόλασας) myself, I proceeded to roam everywhere" (*Or.* 13.10). People who saw him called him a tramp, beggar, or philosopher; that this appearance (σχῆμα) was recognized by others as philosophic is also attested at *Or.* 12.9.

In *Or.* 70 Dio adds to his picture of the philosopher. A philosopher must be such in deed, not simply in name. Together with his dress, the philosopher should be distinguished by his behavior at the table, gymnasium, and baths — and at life in general. He should dislike what is αἰσχρόν or φαῦλον, including laziness, gluttony, and drunkenness.[120] He should embody truth, wisdom, piety, frugality, and sobriety. Dio asserts that failure in these matters disqualifies anyone from being a philosopher. In fact, to banish common human appetites and "to lead the soul to hate and condemn them is the essence of philosophy" (10).

Dio offers further commentary on the philosopher in *Or.* 77/78 (Περὶ φθόνου).[121] In arguing that the wise man does not envy, Dio characterizes

---

[116] Alternatively, he wears a τρίβων (Ps.-Dog. *Ep.* 34; Epic. *Diss.* 3.1.24) or τρίβων διπλοῦς (Ps.-Diog. *Ep.* 7; 19).

[117] If nature gives men beards, then men should grow them. The philosopher's beard then graphically presents him as living according to nature (κατὰ φύσιν). Depilation is horrific. We should take note of Paul's position on this matter. Like the philosophers he formulates an argument about personal appearance on the basis of what accords with nature (1 Cor 11:14); however, he draws the opposite conclusion, arguing against a man's wearing long hair. This provides an important warning about what follows. I am not arguing that Paul is a philosopher, but that his rhetoric fits into pre-existing patterns which we can trace in philosophic literature.

[118] See below.

[119] Or ῥάβδος (Ps.-Diog. *Ep.* 7). Dudley discusses the origin of the Cynic outfit: Philosophy borrowed the rags, staff, and pouch of the wandering beggar; according to Dudley, however, ancient tradition errs in attributing this innovation to Antisthenes (*A History of Cynicism*, pp. 6-7).

[120] This attitude leads very quickly to the philosopher as σκυθρωπός.

[121] Actually Dio is reticent about labeling his ideal person a philosopher, choosing instead only to describe him: φρόνιμος καὶ σοφός ἀνήρ (14); μεγαλόφρων καὶ

him as unconcerned with reputation (17-27) and pleasure (28-33) and clinches each argument with a comparison (or σύγκρισις). Afterward he offers a refutation with an even more elaborate σύγκρισις, in which he distinguishes the so-called philosopher from the genuine article. Surveying the three comparisons, we find in the first σύγκρισις (26-27) that Dio presents the wise man as disinterested in riches, praise or external ostentation; instead he is ταπεινός and self-chastened. Opposite this Dio offers the cowardly, bragging soldier, as well as demagogues and sophists. Dio therefore offers two contrasting images: ταπεινότης vs. ἀλαζονεία. Two observations should be made. First, the character that usually stands opposite the ἀλαζών is the εἴρων, so the figure of Socrates remains an important unspoken example. Second, to be ταπεινός is here presented as something good. In the second σύγκρισις (33), the philosopher makes no effort to flatter or be merely agreeable, but remains truthful and austere, so that he looks more inglorious than beggars, more destitute than street-people, and worthy of no consideration; he will not become a flatterer and charlatan (κόλαξ καὶ γόης), but remains noble (γενναῖος) and true (ἀληθές). The third σύγκρισις continues the image of the κόλαξ καὶ γόης. Sham philosophers turn up at the doors of the rich, debasing and dishonoring themselves (ταπεινοὶ καὶ ἄτιμοι); wretched and ἀνόητοι, corrupted by luxury and idleness, they are "fawning and groveling" (σαίνων καὶ ταπεινός).[122] Dio labels such a person κόλαξ. In contrast, the true philosopher is ἀνδρεῖος καὶ μεγαλόφρων and never sacrifices his ἐλευθερία and παρρησία for money or power; nor does he envy those who do. He steadfastly promotes ἀρετή and σωφροσύνη, while defending ἐλευθερία from lusts, opinions and all humankind, training his body to endure πόνοι. Two observations should be made. First, the κόλαξ and γόης join the ἀλαζών as contrasting images to the wise person. Second, ταπεινός has now become something bad. Why? The difference is ἐλευθερία. If ἐλευθερία leads to ταπεινότης, such ταπεινότης is commendable; on the other hand, the ταπεινότης which results from relinquishing one's ἐλευθερία is contemptible. In Dio's view, then, correctly understanding the nature of wealth and praise should diminish one's interest in them. If this attitude runs its course, a person is left ταπεινός but has also obtained genuine ἐλευθερία. The ταπεινότης which results from and leads to ἐλευθερία is good. Thus, lowly and free is

---

ἄλυπος, ὁ νοῦν ἔχων καὶ φιλάνθρωπος, who knows that ἀρετή is συμφέρον (15); ὁ γενναῖος καὶ τέλειος ἀνήρ (17); τῷ ὄντι φρόνιμος (25); ὁ γενναῖος καὶ σώφρων καὶ κεκολασμένος ἀνήρ (26); τὸν γενναῖον ἄνδρα καὶ μεγαλόφρονα (29); τοῦ μετρίου καὶ πεπαιδευμένου ἀνδός (30); ἀνδρεῖος καὶ μεγαλόφρων (37).

[122] Cf. Diog. L. 7.15 re Zeno: Antigonus admired Zeno because the many gifts which he gave the philosopher never made him conceited or ταπεινός.

better than selling-out to avoid being lowly; moreover, the lowliness which supplies freedom is commendable.

The interplay of lowliness and freedom is fundamental to Cynic thought. The person who sees past appearances has found the path out of enslavement. Thus, Nigrinus praised philosophy and the ἐλευθερία it provides, while ridiculing "the things that are popularly considered blessings — wealth and reputation, dominion and honor, yes and purple and gold" (Luc. *Nig.* 4). When Nigrinus' words were taken to heart, what people commonly regarded as blessings became ταπεινὰ καὶ καταγέλαστα.[123] This means that a Cynic can use lowliness in two different ways. From his own perspective, he can regard what normal people consider to be honorable as enslaving and therefore ταπεινός; he can also adopt the common perspective when referring to himself and thus regard himself as ταπεινός. Because of these different perspectives, different meanings surround references to lowliness. This is the perfect playground for irony.

Looking again at Dio, he described his entering exile and adoption of philosophic garb as "putting on στολὴν ταπεινήν" (13.10).[124] From the view of most people, Dio's appearance was indeed ταπεινός. But was it really? Dio offers the description of his clothing while discussing whether or not exile is bad. Drawing on an oracle from Delphi and the example of Odysseus, Dio determined that exile was not as bad as commonly thought. As a result, he would not be ashamed of it, but would adopt the humble clothing and head out. Dio's revised opinion about exile raises doubts as to what he really thought about his attire.

Evidence from the Cynic epistles is unambiguous. The humiliating garb was not humiliating.[125] A certain pride was taken in the dishonorable uniform, a pride which elevated the apparel's value in the eyes of its wearer. Ps.-Diogenes is clear about this matter:

Do not be upset, Father, that I am called a dog and put on a double, coarse cloak, carry a wallet over my shoulders, and have a staff in my hand. It is not worthwhile getting distressed over such matters, but you should rather be glad that your son is satisfied with little, while being free (ἐλεύθερος) from popular opinion (δόξης), to which all, Greeks

---

[123] Luc. *Nig.* 4. Cp. *Icar.* 4; Epic. *Diss.* 2.14.22: people's attempts to avoid things which appear bad (a mistaken opinion) are ταπεινός (i.e., evidence of foolishness and consequent lack of freedom; cf. 3.26.33-35).

[124] The following comments rely on Abraham Malherbe, "Antisthenes and Odysseus, and Paul at War."

[125] Other people had reasons for resorting to humble garb. For example, Esther did not consider it dishonorable to put on humble clothing in order to save her people (Jos. *Ant.* 11.225). Josephus himself used a humble self-presentation as part of a stratagem (*Bel.* 2.604). Again, recall the above discussion of Odysseus.

and barbarians alike, are subservient (δουλεύουσιν). Now the name, besides not being in accord with my deeds, is a sign that is notable as it is. For I am called heaven's dog, not earth's, since I liken myself to it, living as I do, not in conformity with popular opinion (κατὰ δόξαν) but according to nature (κατὰ φύσιν), free (ἐλεύθερος) under Zeus (*Ep.* 7.1).

These claims are bolstered by the example of Odysseus and by attributing the origin of the uniform to the gods.[126] Similar claims appear in *Ep.* 34, where we read that the τρίβων and begging are not disgraceful (αἰσχρά) for free men. "Rather, it is noble and can be armament against the appearances which war against life." Thus, not only does the humble clothing reflect one's freedom from servile (false) opinions, it serves as a weapon in the fight against them. Not only are they not disreputable, they are not weak. This deepens their irony.

The power of the humble uniform is a common motif. In the fight against appearances,[127] it provides effective weapons.[128] It is also royal raiment (Ps.-Diog. *Ep.* 19) or the uniform of Herakles, who was "mightier than every turn of fortune" (Ps.-Diog. *Ep.* 26). These divine weapons enable their bearer to fight on behalf of truth.[129]

We should recapitulate the philosopher's σχῆμα. Socrates and later Diogenes established a model which subsequent philosophers emulated. Not simply ideas, doctrines, or behaviors, but actual physical appearance indicated one's allegiance to philosophy. The outfit adopted ran counter to social norms and placed the philosopher in dialogue with those norms. While that appearance (σχῆμα) suggested lowliness, the philosopher argued that appearances (δόξαι) were quite deceiving. While the Socratic philosopher did not look like a free man, he in fact claimed true possession of that status. Some even went so far as to argue that their σχῆμα helped to assert that claim, for the rejection of conventional attitudes reflected by the philosopher's "uniform" brought freedom and placed the philosopher on the road to wisdom. Lowliness criticized the mistaken commonplace notions which people held about what is important in life and indicated the philosopher's superior insight into such matters.

6. Conclusion

The figures we have surveyed punctured aristocratic culture and its entrenched rhetoric, contradicting the value of good birth, wealth, athletic

---

[126] The "clothing is god's invention" (7.2).

[127] Ps.-Diog. *Ep.* 5; 10.2; 37.3.

[128] Ps.-Diog. *Ep.* 34; Ps.-Crates *Ep.* 16; 23; 33.

[129] Ps.-Crates *Ep.* 16; Ps.-Diog. *Ep.* 10.

prowess, and education. Tradition attributed delightful and insightful fables to a slave, whose biography went further and humiliated the slave's philosophic master. This particular aspect of Aesop's life in turn paralleled what appeared regularly on the comedic stage: the clever slave who outwits his master. Not only may wisdom be found outside the ranks of the cultured, it may dictate acting against the values of that culture. Although Odysseus' stratagems clashed with heroic values, he nevertheless prevailed by them. Socrates further demonstrates the reaction of those in power to wisdom and the challenge of recognizing it in an unlikely place. His ugly body was a strange receptacle for such intelligence and, together with his birth and attitude toward money, impeded conventional criteria of evaluation. Cynic philosophers particularly embodied the entire problem of proper thinking and evaluation. Appearances are very deceiving and must be seen through if one is to find wisdom (a theoretical position shared by Stoics).

Countercultural rhetoric provided precisely the opening Paul needed to enter into debate with the Corinthians. As early as 1 Corinthians 1–4 we can see that the Corinthians were under the spell of status and higher culture. Lineage, wealth, power, education were the criteria by which they evaluated people. (And they did so in conformity with their culture.) But educated culture itself contained subversive figures who challenged those very values. Paul's rhetoric in 2 Cor 10:1–13:10 situates him among such figures. Like philosophers, Paul disputed the value of the a "good" birth. He contradicted the value placed on wealth and power. He defied the status of educational accomplishment. His demolition of his rivals' credentials unveils a wisdom issuing from an unlikely source, a triumph of lower status over greater status. His conscious acceptance and explicit assertion of lowliness further place him within the countercultural debate we have surveyed. His Cynic-like clothes[130] and his manual labor convey essential information about what he believes and teaches. Precisely this rescues and commends his ταπεινότης. His identification with the οἱ πολλοί is no mere pose, but an essential embodiment of his teaching, which is to say of Christ. Paul's rhetoric therefore challenges the status-oriented Corinthians to look past conventional thinking in order to recognize the voice and hand of Christ in an unlikely place.

---

[130] See above, p. 293 n. 88.

Bibliography

1. Ancient Authors

All English translations of Greek and Latin texts in this monograph were taken from the Loeb Classical Library, unless otherwise noted. All references to ἐπιείκεια and πραότης/πραΰτης were derived from the Thesaurus Linguae Graecae. The texts to which TLG referred at the time of investigation are listed in Luci Berkowitz and Karl A. Squitier, with technical assistance from William A. Johnson, *Thesaurus Linguae Graecae: Canon of Greek Authors and Works* (3rd edition; Oxford University Press, 1990).

Arnim, ed. Hans Friedrich August von. *Stoicorum Veterum Fragmenta*. 4 vols. Leipzig: Teubner, 1903-24.
Behr, Charles A. *The Complete Works of P. Aelius Aristides*. 2 vols. Brill: Leiden: 1981-86.
Burnett, John, ed. *Platonis Opera*. 5 vols. Oxford: Clarendon Press, 1900-1907.
Daly, Lloyd W. *Aesop Without Morals*. New York: Thomas Yoseloff, 1961.
Diels, Hermann, ed. *Die Fragmente der Vorsokratiker*. 6th ed. rev. Walther Kranz. 10th ed. Berlin, 1952.
Dorandi, Tiziano. *Filodemo. Il buon re secondo Omero*. Istituto Italiano per gli Studi Filosofici. La Scuola di Epicuro 4. Naples 1982.
Giannantoni, Gabriele. *Socratis et Socraticorum reliquiae*. 4 vols. Elenchos 18. Napoli: Bibliopolis, 1990.
Gildemeister, J., and F. Bücheler. "Themistios Περὶ ἀρετῆς." *RhM* 27 (1872): 438-62.
Jacoby, Felix, ed. *Die Fragmente der griechischen Historiker*. 3 vols. in 15. Leiden: Brill, 1923-58; 1954-69.
Keil, Bruno. *Aelii Aristidis Smyrnaei quae supersunt omnia*. Berlin: Weidmann, 1898.
Lenz, Friedrich Walther, and Charles A. Behr. *P. Aelii Aristidis: Opera quae exstant omnia*. 2 vols. Leiden: Brill, 1976-.
Lutz, Cora E. *Musonius Rufus: 'The Roman Socrates.'* Yale Classical Studies. New Haven: Yale University Press, 1947.
Malherbe, Abraham J. *The Cynic Epistles: A Study Edition*. SBL Sources for Biblical Study 12. Atlanta, GA: Scholars Press, 1977.
Perry, Ben E. *Aesopica: A Series of Texts Relating to Aesop or Ascribed to Him or Closely Connected with the Literary Tradition that Bears His Name*. Vol. 1: *Greek and Latin Texts*. Urbana: University of Illinois Press, 1952.

Préchac, François. *Sénèque. De la clémence.* Collection des Universités de France. Paris: Les Belles Lettres, 1921.

Rabe, Hugo, ed. *Hermogenis Opera.* Leipzig: Teubner, 1913; Stuttgart: Teubner, 1985.

Rankin, H. D. *Antisthenes Sokratikos.* Amsterdam: Hakkert, 1986.

Spengel, Leonhard von. *Rhetores Graeci.* Ed. C. Hammer. 16 vols. Bibliotheca scriptorum graecorum et romanorum Teubneriana. Supplement auctorum graecorum. Leipzig: Teubner, 1894.

Stobaeus, Ioannes. *Anthologium.* Eds. C. Wachsmuth and O. Hense. 5 vols. Berlin: Weidmann, 1884-1912.

Sussman, Lewis A. *The Declamations of Calpurnius Flaccus: Text, Translation, and Commentary.* Mnemosyne, Supplementum 133. Leiden: E. J. Brill, 1994.

Usener, H., and L. Radermacher, eds. *Dionysii Halicarnasei quae exstant.* 5 vols. Leipzig: Teubner, 1899; Stuttgart, 1965.

Walz, Christian. *Rhetores graeci, ex codicibus florentinis, mediolanensibus, monacensibus, neapolitanis, parisiensibus, romanis, venetis, taurinensibus et vindobonensibus.* 9 vols. Stuttgart: J. G. Cottae, 1832-36.

Whitman, Lucile Yow. *The Octavia: Introduction, Text, and Commentary.* Noctes romanae 16. Bern: Paul Haupt, 1978.

Wooten, Cecil W. *Hermogenes' On Types of Style.* Chapel Hill: University of North Carolina Press, 1987.

2. Commentaries on 2 Corinthians

Allo, Ernest Bernard. *Saint Paul. Seconde épître aux Corinthiens.* 2d ed. Études bibliques. Paris: J. Gabalda, 1956.

Bachmann, Philip. *Der zweite Brief des Paulus an die Korinther.* Kommentar zum Neuen Testament 8. Leipzig: Deichert, 1909.

Baird, William. *1 Corinthians, 2 Corinthians.* Atlanta: John Knox, 1980.

Barrett, Charles Kingsley. *A Commentary on the Second Epistle to the Corinthians.* HNTC. New York: Harper & Row, 1973; Peabody, MA: Hendrickson, 1987.

Best, Ernest. *Second Corinthians.* Interpretation. Atlanta: John Knox Press, 1987.

Betz, Hans Dieter. *2 Corinthians 8 and 9: A Commentary on Two Administrative Letters of the Apostle Paul.* Hermeneia. Philadelphia: Fortress Press, 1985.

Bruce, F. F. *1 and 2 Corinthians.* NCB. Grand Rapids: Eerdmans, 1971.

Bultmann, Rudolf. *The Second Letter to the Corinthians.* German ed. Erich Dinkler. Trans. Roy A. Harrisville. Minneapolis: Augsburg, 1985.

Carrez, M. *La deuxième épître de saint Paul aux Corinthiens.* Geneva, 1986.

Danker, Frederick W. *II Corinthians.* Augsburg Commentary on the New Testament. Minneapolis: Augsburg, 1989.

Fallon, Francis T. *2 Corinthians.* New Testament Message 11. Wilmington, DE: Michael Glazier, 1980.

Furnish, Victor Paul. *II Corinthians.* AB 32A. Garden City, NJ: Doubleday & Company, Inc., 1984.

Harris, Murray J. "2 Corinthians." In *The Expositor's Bible Commentary*, ed. F. E. Gaebelein, 10: 299-406. Grand Rapids: Zondervan, 1976.

Heinrici, Carl Friedrich Georg. *Der zweite Brief an die Korinther*. Kritisch-exegetischer Kommentar über das Neue Testament 6. 8th ed. Göttingen: Vandenhoeck & Ruprecht, 1900.

Héring, J. *The Second Epistle of Saint Paul to the Corinthians*. Trans. A. W. Heathcote and P. J. Allcock. London: Epworth Publishing Company, 1967.

Hughes, Philip Edgcumbe. *Paul's Second Epistle to the Corinthians*. New International Commentary on the New Testament. Grand Rapids: Eerdmans, 1962.

Klauck, Hans-Josef. *2. Korintherbrief*. Die Neue Echter Bibel 8 Würzburg: Echter, 1986.

Kruse, Colin. *The Second Epistle of Paul to the Corinthians*. TNTC. Grand Rapids: Eerdmans, 1987.

Lang, F. *Die Briefe an die Korinther*. Göttingen: Vandenhoeck & Ruprecht, 1986.

Lietzmann, H. *An die Korinther 1/2*. Handbuch zum Neuen Testament 9. Tübingen: J. C. B. Mohr (Paul Siebeck), 1969.

Martin, Ralph P. *2 Corinthians*. WBC 40. Waco, TX: Word Books, Publisher, 1986.

Menzies, Allan. *The Second Epistle of the Apostle Paul to the Corinthians*. London: Macmillan, 1912.

Plummer, Alfred. *A Critical and Exegetical Commentary on the Second Epistle of St. Paul to the Corinthians*. ICC. Edinburgh: T. & T. Clark, 1915.

Prümm, Karl. *Diakonia Pneumatos. Der zweite Korintherbrief als Zugang zur apostolischen Botschaft*. Auslegung und Theologie. 2 vols. in 3. Freiburg: Herder, 1960-67.

Strachan, Robert Harvey. *The Second Epistle of Paul to the Corinthians*. Moffatt New Testament Commentary. New York: Harper, 1935.

Talbert, Charles H. *Reading Corinthians: A Literary and Theological Commentary on 1 and 2 Corinthians*. New York: Crossroad, 1987.

Thrall, Margaret E. *The First and Second Letters of Paul to the Corinthians*. Cambridge Bible Commentary. Cambridge University Press, 1965.

_____. *Critical and Exegetical Commentary on the Second Epistle to the Corinthians*. 2 vols. ICC. Edinburgh: T. & T. Clark, 1994-2000.

Wendland, Heinz-Dietrich. *Der Briefe an die Korinther*. Das Neue Testament Deutsch 8. Göttingen: Vandenhoeck & Ruprecht, 1964.

Windisch, Hans. *Der zweite Korintherbrief*. Kritisch-exegetischer Kommentar über das Neue Testament 6. 9th ed. Göttingen: Vandenhoeck & Ruprecht, 1924.

Young, Frances, and David F. Ford. *Meaning and Truth in 2 Corinthians*. Grand Rapids: Eerdmans, 1987.

3. Modern Authors

Aalders, G. J. D. *Political Thought in Hellenistic Times*. Amsterdam: Adolf M. Hakkert, 1975.

_____. "Cassius Dio and the Greek World." *Mnemosyne*, 4th ser., 39 (1986): 282-304.

Adam, Traute. *Clementia Principis. Der Einfluss hellenistischer Fürstenspiegel auf den Versuch einer rechtlichen Fundierung des Principats durch Seneca*. Kieler historische Studien 11. Stuttgart: Ernst Klett, 1970.

Adkins, Arthur. "Review of N. R. E. Fisher, *Hybris: A Study in the Values of Honour and Shame in Ancient Greece*." *CJ* 90 (1995): 451-55.

Adloff, K. *Predigt als Plädoyer. Versuch einer homiletischen Ortsbestimmung erarbeitet am zweiten Korintherbrief*. Hamburg: Furche, 1971.

Alexander, P. S. "Epistolary Literature," in *Jewish Writings of the Second Temple Period*, ed. Michael E. Stone, 579-96. Compendia Rerum Iudaicarum ad Novum Testamentum 2.2. Philadelphia: Fortress Press, 1984.

Alföldi, Andreas. "The Main Aspects of Political Propaganda on the Coinage of the Roman Republic." In *Essays in Roman Coinage Presented to Harold Mattingly*, eds. R. A. G. Carson and C. H. V. Sutherland, 63-95. Oxford University Press, 1956.

———. *Die zwei Lorbeerbäume des Augustus*. Antiquitas, 3d ser., 14. Bonn: Rudolf Habelt, 1973.

———. *Caesar in 44 v. Chr. Antiquitas*, 3d ser., 16. 2 vols. Bonn: Rudolf Habelt, 1985.

Allison, Dale C., Jr. "The Pauline Epistles and the Synoptic Gospels: The Pattern of the Parallels." *NTS* 28 (1982): 1-32.

Anderson, Graham. *The Second Sophistic: A Cultural Phenomenon in the Roman Empire*. London: Routledge, 1993.

Anderson, William. "The Roman Transformation of Greek Domestic Comedy." *CW* 88 (1995): 171-80.

Andrews, Scott B. "Too Weak Not to Lead: The Form and Function of 2 Cor 11.23b-33." *NTS* 41 (1995): 263-76.

Arnheim, M. T. W. "The World of the Fable." *Studies in Antiquity* 1 (1979-80): 1-11.

Arnott, W. G. *Menander, Plautus and Terence*. Oxford University Press, 1975.

Asmis, Elizabeth. "Philodemus' Epicureanism." *ANRW* 2.36.4 (1990): 2369-406.

———. "Philodemus's Poetic Theory and *On the Good King According to Homer*." *ClAnt* 10 (April 1991): 1-45.

———. "Epicurean Poetics." In *Proceedings of the Boston Area Colloquium in Ancient Philosophy* 7, ed. John J. Cleary. Lanham, MD: University Press of America, 1991.

Aune, David. "Septem sapientium convivium (Moralia 146B-164D)." In *Plutarch's Ethical Writings and Early Christian Literature*, ed. Hans Dieter Betz, 51-105. Studia ad Corpus Hellenisticum Novi Testamenti 4. Leiden: E. J. Brill, 1978.

Austin, M. M. *The Hellenistic World from Alexander to the Roman Conquest: A Selection of Ancient Sources in Translation*. Cambridge University Press, 1981.

Auvray-Assayas, Clara. "La douleur d'Hercule dans l'*Hercule sur l'Oeta* de Sénèque et la tradition romaine des Tusculanes." In *Présence de Sénèque*, eds. Raymond Chevallier and Rémy Poignault, 31-44. Caesarodunum 24. Paris: Touzot, 1991.

Bajoni, Maria Grazia. "Le virtú del principe dal Seneca pedagogo a Suetonio biografo di Tito." In *Atti del Congresso Internazionale di Studi Flaviani, Rieti, settembre 1981*, ed. Benedetto Riposati, 2: 189-94. 2 vols. Rieti: Centro di Studi Varroniani, 1983.

Barnett, P. W. "Opposition in Corinth." *JSNT* 22 (1984): 3-17.

Barraclough, Ray. "Philo's Politics: Roman Rule and Hellenistic Judaism." *ANRW* 2.21.1 (1984): 417-553.

Barré, M. L. "Paul as 'Eschatologic Person': A New Look at 2 Cor 11:29." *CBQ* 37 (1975): 500-526.

Barrett, Anthony A. *Caligula: The Corruption of Power*. New Haven: Yale University Press, 1989.

Barrett, Charles Kingsley. *From First Adam to Last: A Study in Pauline Theology*. New York: Charles Scribner's Sons, 1962.

_____. "Paul's Opponents in II Corinthians." *NTS* 17 (1971): 233-254. Reprinted in *Essays on Paul*, 60-86. Philadelphia: Westminster Press, 1982

_____. *Essays on Paul*. Philadelphia: Westminster Press, 1982.

Barton, Tamsyn. "The inventio of Nero." In *Reflections of Nero: Cutlure, History & Representation*, eds. Jaś Elsner and Jamie Masters, 48-63. Chapel Hill, NC: University of North Carolina Press, 1994.

Batstone, William W. "Cicero's Construction of Consular Ethos in the First Catilinarian." *TAPA* 124 (1994): 211-66.

Bauder, Wolfgang. "Demut." In *Theologisches Begriffslexikon zum Neuen Testament*, eds. Lothar Coenen, Erich Beyreuther, and Hans Bietenhard, 1: 173-75. 3 vols. Wuppertal: Brockhaus, 1965-71. English: "Humility." In *NIDNTT*, ed. Colin Brown, 2: 256-59. 4 vols. Grand Rapids: Zondervan, 1975-85.

Bauer, Walter. *A Greek-English Lexicon of the New Testament and Other Early Christian Literature*. Translated and adapted by William F. Arndt and F. Wilbur Gingrich. 2d ed., revised and augmented by F. Wilbur Gingrich and Frederick W. Danker. Chicago: University of Chicago Press, 1979.

_____. *Griechisch-deutsches Wörterbuch zu den Schriften des Neuen Testaments und der frühchristlichen Literatur*. 6th ed, completely revised by Kurt Aland and Barbara Aland. Berlin: Walter de Gruyter, 1988.

Baumlin, James S., and Tita French Baumlin, eds. *Ethos: New Essays in Rhetorical and Critical Theory*. Dallas: Southern Methodist University Press, 1994.

Becker, Ulrich. "Gospel, Evangelize, Evangelist." In *NIDNTT*, ed. Colin Brown, 2: 107-15. 4 vols. Grand Rapids: Zondervan, 1975-85.

Beker, J. Christiaan. *Paul the Apostle: The Triumph of God in Life and Thought*. Philadelphia: Fortress, Press, 1980.

_____. *The Triumph of God: The Essence of Paul's Thought*. Trans. Loren T. Stuckenbruck. Minneapolis: Fortress Press, 1990

_____. "The Promise of Paul's Apocalyptic for Our Times." In *The Future of Christology: Essays in Honor of Leander E. Keck*, eds. Abraham J. Malherbe and Wayne A. Meeks, 152-59. Minneapolis: Fortress Press, 1993.

Bell, Albert A., Jr., "Pliny the Younger: The Kinder, Gentler Roman." *CB* 66 (1990): 38-39.

Bell, H. I. "Philanthropia in the Papyri of the Roman Period." In *Hommages à Joseph Bidez et à Franz Cumont*, 31-37. Collection Latomus 2. Brussels: Latomus, c. 1949.

Belleville, Linda L. "Gospel and Kerygma in 2 Corinthians." In *Gospel in Paul: Studies on Corinthians, Galatians and Romans for Richard N. Longenecker*, eds. L. Ann Jervis and Peter Richardson, 134-64. JSNTSS 108. Sheffield Academic Press, 1994.

Béranger, Jean. *Recherches sur l'aspect idéologique du principat.* Schweizerische Beiträge zur Altertumswissenschaft 6. Basel, 1953.

Berger, K. "Die impliziten Gegner." In *Kirche. Festschrift für Günther Bornkomm zum 75. Geburtstag*, eds. D. Lührmann and G. Strecker, 373-400. Tübingen: J. C. B. Mohr (Paul Siebeck), 1980.

Best, Ernest. *A Commentary on the First and Second Epistles to the Thessalonians.* HNTC. New York: Harper & Row, 1972.

Betz, Hans Dieter. "On the Problem of the Religo-Historical Understanding of Apocalypticism." Trans. James W. Leitch. *JTC* 6 (1969): 134-56.

_____. *Der Apostel Paulus und die sokratische Tradition. Eine exegetische Untersuchung zu seiner "Apologie" 2 Korinther 10–13.* Beiträge zur historischen Theologie 45. Tübingen: J. C. B. Mohr (Paul Siebeck), 1972.

_____. *Paul's Apology: II Corinthians 10–13 and the Socratic Tradition.* Ed. Wilhelm Wuellner. Protocol of the 2d Colloquy. Berkeley: Center for Hermeneutical Studies in Hellenistic and Modern Culture, 1975.

_____. "De laude ipsius (Moralia 539A-547F)." In *Plutarch's Ethical Writings and Early Christian Literature*, ed. idem, 367-93. SCHNT 4. Leiden: E. J. Brill, 1978.

_____. *Galatians.* Hermeneia. Philadelphia: Fortress Press, 1979.

_____. "Corinthians, Second." *ABD*, ed. David N. Freedman, s.v. 6 vols. Garden City: Doubleday, 1991.

_____. "Eine Christus-Aretalogie bei Paulus (2 Cor 12, 7-10)." *ZTK* 55 (1969): 288-305. Reprinted in *Paulinische Studien. Gesammelte Aufsätze III*, 1-19. Tübingen: J. C. B. Mohr (Paul Siebeck), 1994.

_____. "The Problem of Rhetoric and Theology according to the Apostle Paul." In *L'Apôtre Paul. Personnalité, style et conception du ministère*, ed. A. Vanhoye, 16-48. BETL 73. Leuven University Press, 1986. Reprinted in *Paulinische Studien. Gesammelte Aufsätze III*, 126-67. Tübingen: J. C. B. Mohr (Paul Siebeck), 1994.

_____. *A Commentary on the Sermon on the Mount, Including the Sermon on the Plain (Matthew 5:3-7:27 and Luke 6:20-49).* Hermeneia. Minneapolis: Fortress Press, 1995.

Bieber, Margarete. *The History of The Greek and Roman Theater.* Princeton University Press, 1961.

Bieringer, Reimund. "Paul's Divine Jealousy: The Apostle and his Communities in Relationship." In *Sharper than a Two-edged Sword: Festschrift for Jan Lambrecht*, eds. V. Koperski and Reimund Bieringer, 197-231. Louvain Studies 17. Leuven University Press, 1992. Reprinted in *Studies on 2 Corinthians*, eds. Reimund Bieringer and Jan Lambrecht, BETL 112. Leuven University Press, 1994.

_____, and Jan Lambrecht. *Studies on 2 Corinthians.* BETL 112. Leuven University Press, 1994.

Billows, Richard A. *Antigonos the One-Eyed and the Creation of the Hellenistic State.* Hellenistic Culture and Society 4. Berkeley: University of California Press, 1990.

_____. "The Religious Procession of the Ara Pacis Augustae: Augustus' supplicatio in 13 B.C." *JRA* 6 (1993): 80-92.

Binder, H. "Die angebliche Krankheit des Paulus." *Theologische Zeitschrift* 32 (1976): 1-13.

Blank, David L. "Socratics Versus Sophists on Payment for Teaching." *ClAnt* 4 (1985): 1-49.

Blänsdorf, Jürgen, and Eberhard Breckel. *Das Paradoxon der Zeit. Zeitbesitz und Zeitverlust in Senecas Epistulae morales und De brevitate vitae. Probleme und unterrichtliche Behandlung.* Freiburg: Plötz, 1983.

Block, Elizabeth. "Clothing Makes the Man: A Pattern in the *Odyssey*." *TAPA* 115 (1985): 1-11.

Blois, Lukas de. "The Εἰς βασιλέα of Ps.-Aelius Aristides." *GRBS* 27 (1986): 276-88.

_____. "Traditional Virtues and New Spiritual Qualities in Third Century Views of Empire, Emperorship and Practical Politics." *Mnemosyne* 47 (1994): 166-76.

Bonner, Stanley F. *Education in Ancient Rome: From the elder Cato to the younger Pliny.* Berkeley: University of California Press, 1977.

Booth, Wayne. *The Rhetoric of Irony.* University of Chicago Press, 1974.

Born, Lester K. "The Perfect Prince According to the Latin Panegyrists." *AJP* 55 (1934): 20-35.

Bornkamm, Günther. *Die Vorgeschichte des sogenannten Zweiten Korintherbriefes.* Sitzungsberichte der Heidelberger Akademie der Wissenschaften. Philosophisch-historische Klasse, 1961, 2. Abhandlung. Heidelberg: Winter, 1961. Reprinted with an addendum in *Geschichte und Glaube II, Gesammelte Aufsätze IV.* Munich: Kaiser, 1971. Abridged English translation in "The History of the Origin of the So-Called Second Letter to the Corinthians." *NTS* 8 (1962): 258-64.

_____. *Early Christian Experience.* Translated by Paul L. Hammer. New York: Harper & Row, 1969.

Bosworth, A. B. *From Arrian to Alexander: Studies in Historical Interpretation.* Oxford University Press, 1988.

Bousset, W. *Kyrios Christos: A History of the Belief in Christ from the Beginning of Christianity to Ireneaus.* Translated by J. E. Steely. Nashville: Abingdon, 1970.

Bradley, K. R. "Imperial Virtues in Suetonius' *Caesares*." *Journal of Indo-European Studies* 4 (1976): 245-53.

_____. *Slaves and Masters in the Roman Empire: A Study in Social Control.* Collection Latomus 185. Brussells: Latomus, 1984.

Braun, Herbert. "Der Sinn der neutestamentliche Christologie." *ZTK* 54 (1957): 341-377. English: "The Meaning of New Testament Christology." *Journal for Theology and the Church* 5 (1968): 89-127.

Braund, David C. *Augustus to Nero: A Sourcebook on Roman History 31 BC-AD 68.* Totowa, NJ: Barnes and Noble Books, 1985.

Breglia, Laura. *Roman Imperial Coins: Their Art and Technique.* London: Thames and Hudson, 1968.

Bremmer, Jan. "Scapegoat Rituals in Ancient Greece." *HSCP* 87 (1983): 299-320.

Breytenbach, J. Cilliers. "Paul's Proclamation and God's θρίαμβος (Notes on 2 Corinthians 2:14-16b)." *Neotestamentica* 24 (1990): 257-71.

Bringmann, Klaus. "The King as Benefactor: Some Remarks on Ideal Kingship in the Age of Hellenism." In *Images and Ideologies: Self-definition in the Hellenistic*

World, eds. Anthony Bulloch et al., 7-24. Hellenistic Culture and Society 12. Berkeley: University of California Press, 1993.

Brink, C. O., and F. Walbank. "The Construction of the Sixth Book of Polybius." *CQ*, new series, 4 (1954): 97-122.

Brommer, Frank. *Vasenlisten zur griechischen Heldensage*. 3d ed. Marburg: N. G. Elwert, 1973.

——. *Odysseus. Die Taten und Leiden des Helden in antiker Kunst und Literatur*. Darmstadt: Wissenschaftliche Buchgesellschaft, 1983.

——. *Herakles. The Twelve Labors of the Hero in Ancient Art and Literature*. Trans. Shirley J. Schwarz. New Rochelle, NY: Aristide D. Caratzas, 1986.

Bruce, F. F. *1 & 2 Thessalonians*. WBC 45 Waco, TX: Word Books, 1983.

Brunt, P. A. and J. M. Moore. *Res Gestae Divi Augusti: The Achievements of the Divine Augustus*. Oxford University Press, 1967.

Büchner, W. "Über den Begriff der Eironeia." *Hermes* 76 (1941): 339-58.

Buffière, Félix. *Les mythes d'Homère et la pensée grecque*. Paris: Les Belles Lettres, 1956.

Bultmann, Rudolf. "Die Bedeutung des geschichtlichen Jesus für die Theologie des Paulus." Theologische Blätter 8 (1929): 137-151. Reprinted in *Glauben und Verstehen*, 1: 188-213. Tübingen: J. C. B. Mohr (Paul Siebeck), 1933, [6]1966. English: "The Significance of the Historical Jesus for the Theology of Paul." In *Faith and Understanding*, ed. Robert W. Funk, trans. Louise Pettibone Smith, 220-246. New York: Harper & Row, 1969.

——. "Jesus und Paulus." In *Jesus Christus im Zeugnis der Heiligen Schrift und der Kirche*, 68-90. Beiheft zu Evangelische Theologie 2. Munich: Christian Kaiser, 1936. English: "Jesus and Paul." In *Existence and Faith: Shorter Writings of Rudolf Bultmann*, trans. Schubert M. Ogden, 183-201. New York: Living Age Books, 1960.

——. "Das Verhältnis der urchristlichen Christusbotschaft zum historischen Jesus." In *Sitzungsberichte der Heidelberger Akademie der Wissenschaften*, Philosophisch-historische Klasse, Jahrgang 1960. 3. Abhandlung. Heidelberg: Carl Winter Universitätsverlag, 1960. English: "The Primitive Christian Kerygma and the Historical Jesus." In *The Historical Jesus and the Kerygmatic Christ: Essays on the New Quest of the Historical Jesus*, ed. Carl E. Braaten and Roy A. Harrisville, 15-42. Nashville: Abingdon Press, 1964.

——. *Theology of the New Testament*. Translated by Kendrick Grobel. 2 vols. New York: Charles Scribner's Sons, 1951-1955.

——. *Exegetica. Aufsätze zur Erforschung des Neuen Testaments*. Ed. Erich Dinkler. Tübingen: J. C. B. Mohr (Paul Siebeck), 1967.

Burdeau, François. "L'Empereur d'après les panégyriques latin." In *Aspects de l'Empire Romain*, eds. idem, Nicole Charbonnel, and Michel Humbert. Paris: Presses universitaires de France, 1964.

Burkert, Walter. *Structure and History in Greek Mythology*. Berkeley: University of California Press, 1979.

——. *Greek Religion*. Trans. John Raffan. Cambridge, MA: Harvard University Press, 1985.

Burstein, Stanley M. *The Hellenistic Age from the Battle of Ipsos to the Death of Kleopatra VII*. Translated Documents of Greece and Rome 3. Cambridge University Press, 1985.

Cairns, Douglas L. "Review of N. R. E. Fisher, *Hybris: A Study in the Values of Honour and Shame in Ancient Greece*." *CR* 44 (1994): 76-79.
Cairns, Francis. *Virgil's Augustan Epic*. Cambridge University Press, 1989.
Caizzi, Fernanda Decleva. "The Porch and the Garden: Early Hellenistic Images of the Philosophic Life." In *Images and Ideologies: Self-Definition in the Hellenistic World*, eds. Anthony Bulloch, et al. Hellenistic Culture and Society 12. Berkeley: University of California Press, 1993.
Calder, William M. "Secreti loquimus: An Interpretation of Seneca's *Thyestes*." In *Seneca Tragicus: Ramus Essays on Senecan Drama*, ed. A. J. Boyle, 192-95. Berwick, Victoria, Australia: Aureal Publications, 1983.
Carbone, M. E. "The Octavia: Structure, Date and Authenticity." *Phoenix* 31 (1977): 48-67.
Carey, Christopher. "Rhetorical Means of Persuasion." In *Persuasion: Greek Rhetoric in Action*, ed. Ian Worthington, 26-45. London: Routledge, 1994.
Carr, W. "The Rulers of This Age–I Corinthians II.6-8." *NTS* 23 (1976/77): 20-35.
_____. *Angels and Principalities: The Background, Meaning and Development of the Pauline Use of 'αἱ ἀρχαὶ καὶ αἱ ἐξουσίαι.'* SNTSMS 42. Cambridge University Press, 1981.
Carrez, Maurice. "Le 'Nous' en 2 Corinthiens. Contribution à l'étude de l'apostolicité dans 2 Corinthiens." *NTS* 26 (1980): 474-486.
_____. "Que représente la vie de Jésus pour l'apôtre Paul?" *RHPR* 68 (1988): 155-61.
Carson, Donald A. *From Triumphalism to Maturity: An Exposition of 2 Corinthians 10–13*. Grand Rapids: Baker Bookhouse, 1984.
Cerfaux, L. *The Christian in the Theology of St. Paul*. New York: Herder & Herder, 1967.
Chantraine, Pierre, ed. *Dictionnaire étymologique de la langue grecque. Histoire des mots*. 5 vols. Paris: Klincksieck, 1968-1980.
Charlesworth, James H., ed. *The Messiah: Developments in Earliest Judaism and Christianity*. The First Princeton Symposium on Judaism and Christian Origins. Minneapolis: Fortress Press, 1992.
Charlesworth, Martin Percival. "The Virtues of a Roman Emperor: Propaganda and the Creation of Belief." *PBA* 23 (1937): 105-33.
Chesnut, Glenn F. "The Ruler and the Logos in Neo-Pythagorean, Middle Platonic and Late Stoic Political Philosophy." *ANRW* 2.16.2 (1978): 1310-32.
Chevallier, Max-Alain. "L'argumentation de Paul dans II Corinthiens 10 à 13." *RHPR* 70 (1990): 3-15.
Chow, John Kin-Man. *Patronage and Power*. JSNTSS 75. Sheffield Academic Press, 1992.
Classen, C. Joachim. "Virtutes Imperatoriae." *Arctos* 25 (1991): 17-39.
Codoñer, Carmen. "Hércules romano." *Euphrosyne* 19 (1991): 27-46.

Cohen, Beth. "Slaughter of the Suitors." In *The Odyssey and Ancient Art*, eds. D. Buitron and B. Cohen, 168-75. Annandale-on-Hudson, NY: The Edith C. Blum Art Institute, Bard College, 1992.

Collins, Adela Yarbro. *Crisis and Catharsis: The Power of Apocalypse*. Philadelphia: Westminster Press, 1984.

———, ed. *Semeia 36: Early Christian Apocalypticism: Genre and Social Setting*. Atlanta: Scholars Press, 1986.

Collins, John J., ed. *Semeia 14: Apocalypse: The Morphology of a Genre*. Missoula, MT: Scholars Press, 1979.

———. *The Scepter and the Star: Jewish Messianism in the Light of the Dead Sea Scrolls*. ABRL. New York: Doubleday, 1995.

Collins, John N. "Georgi's 'Envoys' in 2 Cor 11:23." *JBL* 93 (1974): 88-96.

Collins, Raymond F. *Studies on the First Letter to the Thessalonians*. BETL 66. Leuven University Press, 1984.

Compton, Todd. "The Trial of the Satirist: Poetic *Vitae* (Aesop, Archilochus, Homer) as Background for Plato's *Apology*." *AJP* 111 (1990): 342-44.

Conzelmann, Hans. *Grundriß der Theologie des Neuen Testaments*. 4th ed., rev. Andreas Lindemann. Tübingen: J. C. B. Mohr (Paul Siebeck), 1987. English: *An Outline of the Theology of the New Testament*, trans. J. Bowden. New York: Harper & Row, 1969.

Cotter, Wendy. "Our πολίτευμα is in Heaven: The Meaning of Philippians 3.17-21." In *Origins and Methods: Towards a New Understanding of Judaism and Christianity: Essays in Honor of John C. Hurd*, ed. Bradley H. McLean, 92-104. JSNTSS 86. Sheffield: JSOT Press, 1993.

Coulter, Cornelia Catlin. "Caesar's Clemency." *CJ* 26 (1931): 513-24.

Coulter, James. "The Relation of the Apology of Socrates to Gorgias' *Defense of Palamedes* and Plato's Critique of Gorgianic Rhetoric." In *Plato: True and Sophistic Rhetoric*, ed. Keith Erickson, 31-67. Amsterdam: Rodopi, 1979.

Coventry, Lucinda. "Philosophy and Rhetoric in the *Menexenus*." *JHS* 109 (1989): 1-15.

Crawford, Michael. "Greek Intellectuals and the Roman Aristocracy in the First Century B.C." In *Imperialism in the Ancient World*, eds. P. Garnsey and C. R. Whittaker, 193-207. Cambridge University Press, 1978.

———. "Roman Imperial Coin Types and the Formation of Public Opinion." In *Studies in Numismatic Method Presented to Philip Grierson*, eds. C. N. L. Brooke et al., 47-64. Cambridge University Press, 1983.

Crafton, Jeffrey A. *The Agency of the Apostle: A Dramatistic Analysis of Paul's Responses to Conflict in 2 Corinthians*. JSNTSS 51. Sheffield Academic Press, 1991.

Cruz, H. *Christological Motives and Motivated Actions in Pauline Paraenesis*. European University Studies, Series 23: Theology 396. Frankfurt: Lang, 1990.

Cullman, Oscar. *The Christology of the New Testament*. Trans. S. C. Guthrie and C. A. M. Hall. Rev. Philadelphia: Westminster Press, 1963.

D'Agostino, Francesco. *Epieikeia. Il tema dell'equità nell'antichità greca*. Pubblicazioni dell'Istituto di Filosofia del Diritto dell'Università di Roma, 3d series, 8. Milan: Giuffrè, 1973.

———. "Il tema dell' epieikeia nella S. Scrittura." *Revista di teologia morale* 5 (1973): 385-406.

Dahl, Nils A. "Die Messianität Jesu bei Paulus." In *Studia Paulina in honorem Johannis de Zwaan*, 83-95. Haarlem: Erven F. Bohn, 1953. Rev. and trans., "The Messiahship of Jesus in Paul." In his *Jesus the Christ: The Historical Origins of Christological Doctrine*, ed. Donald H. Juel, 15-25. Minneapolis: Fortress Press, 1991.

———. "The Crucified Messiah." In his *Jesus the Christ: The Historical Origins of Christological Doctrine*, ed. Donald H. Juel, 27-48. Minneapolis: Fortress Press, 1991.

Danker, Frederick William. "Paul's Debt to the *De Corona* of Demosthenes: A Study of Rhetorical Techniques in Second Corinthians." In *Persuasive Artistry: Studies in New Testament Rhetoric in Honor of George A. Kennedy*, ed. Duane F. Watson, 262-80. JSNTSS 50. Sheffield: JSOT Press, 1991.

———. *A Greek-English Lexicon of the New Testament and other Early Christian Literature*. 3rd ed. Based on Walter Bauer's *Griechisch-deutsches Wörterbuch zu den Schriften des Neuen Testaments und der frühchristlichen Literatur*, 6th ed., eds. Kurt Aland and Barbara Aland, with Viktor Reichmann, based also on previous English editions by W. F. Arndt, F. W. Gingrich, and F. W. Danker. University of Chicago Press, 2000.

Davies, W. D. *Jewish and Pauline Studies*. Philadelphia: Fortress Press, 1984.

———, and Dale C. Allison. *The Gospel according to Saint Matthew*. ICC. 3 vols. Edingurgh: T & T Clark, 1988-97.

Davis, Norman, and Colin M. Kraay. *The Hellenistic Kingdoms: Portrait Coins and History*. London: Thames and Hudson, 1973.

Dean-Jones, Lesley. "Menexenus — Son of Socrates." *CQ* 45 (1995): 51-57.

Delatte, Louis. *Les traités de la royauté d'Ecphante, Diotogène et Sthénidas*. Bibliothèque de la Faculté de Philosophie et Lettres del'Université de Liège 97. Paris: Droz, 1942.

Des Essarts, Emmanuel. *Type d'Hercule dans la littérature grecque depuis les origines jusqu'au siècle des Antonins*. Paris: Ernest Thorin, 1871.

DeSilva, David A. "Measuring Penultimate against Ultimate Reality: An Investigation of the Integrity and Argumentation of 2 Corinthians." *JSNT* 52 (1993): 41-70.

Dewey, Arthur J. "A Matter of Honor: A Social-Historical Analysis of 2 Corinthians 10." *HTR* 78 (January/April 1985): 209-217.

Dickie, Matthew. "A Joke in Old Comedy: Aristophanes Fragment 607 *PCG.*" *CP* 90 (1995): 241-43.

DiCicco, Mario M. *Paul's Use of Ethos, Pathos, and Logos in 2 Corinthians 10–13*. Mellen Biblical Press Series 31. Lewiston, NY: Mellen Biblical Press, 1995.

Di Lorenzo, Raymond. "The Critique of Socrates in Cicero's *De oratore: Ornatus* and the Nature of Wisdom." *Philosophy and Rhetoric* 11 (1978): 247-61.

Di Marco, Angelino-Salvatore. "Koinōnia Pneumatos (2 Cor 13,13; Flp 2,1) — Pneuma Koinōnias. Circolarità e ambivalenza linguistica e filologica." *Filologia Neotestamentaria* 1 (1988): 63-75.

Dittenberger, Wilhelm, ed. *Orientis Graeci Inscriptiones Selectae*. 2 vols. Leipzig, 1903-5.

_____. *Sylloge Inscriptionum Graecarum, I-IV.* 3d ed. Leipzig, 1915-24; Hildesheim: Georg Olms, 1960.

Dominik, William J. "Monarchal Power and Imperial Politics in Statius' *Thebaid*." *Ramus* 18 (1989): 74-97.

_____. *The Mythic Voice of Statius: Power and Politics in the Thebaid.* Mnemosyne Supplementum 136. Leiden: E. J. Brill, 1994.

Dorandi, T. "Der 'gut König' bei Philodem und die Rede des Maecenas vor Octavian (Cassius Dio LII 14-40)." *Klio* 66 (1985): 158-67.

Döring, Klaus. *Exemplum Socratis. Studien zur Sokratensnachwirkung in der kynisch-stoischen Popularphilosophie der frühen Kaiserzeit und im frühen Christentum.* Hermes Einzelschrift 42. Wiesbaden: Franz Steiner, 1979.

Dover, Kenneth J. "Fathers, Sons and Forgiveness." *ICS* 16 (1991): 171-81.

Duchatelez, K. "L' 'epieikeia' dans l'Antiquité grecque, païenne et chrétienne." *Communio* 12 (1979): 203-231.

Duff, Paul Brooks. "Honor or Shame: The Language of Processions and Perception in 2 Cor 2:14–6:13; 7:2-4." Ph.D. diss., University of Chicago, 1988.

_____. "Metaphor, Motif, and Meaning: The Rhetorical Strategy behind the Image 'Led in Triumph' in 2 Corinthians 2:14." *CBQ* 53 (1991): 79-92.

Duffy, Bernard K. "The Platonic Functions of Epideictic Rhetoric." *Philosophy and Rhetoric* 16 (1983): 79-93.

Dungan, D. *The Sayings of Jesus in the Churches of Paul.* Philadelphia: Fortress Press, 1971.

Dunkle, J. Roger. "The Rhetorical Tyrant in Roman Historiography: Sallust, Livy and Tacitus." *CW* 65 (1971-72): 12-20.

_____. "The Greek Tyrant and Roman Political Invective of the Late Republic." *TAPA* 98 (1967): 151-71.

Dunn, James D. G. *Christology in the Making: A New Testament Inquiry into the Origins of the Doctrine of the Incarnation.* Philadelphia: Westminster Press, 1980.

_____. "Jesus Tradition in Paul." In *Studying the Historical Jesus: Evaluations of the State of Current Research*, eds. Bruce Chilton and Craig A. Evans, 155-78. New Testament Tools and Studies 19. Leiden: E. J. Brill, 1994.

DuQuesnay, I. M. Le M. "Horace and Maecenas: The Propaganda Value of *Sermones* 1." In *Poetry and Politics in the Age of Augustus*, eds. Tony Woodman and David West. Cambridge University Press, 1984.

Dyer, R. R. "Rhetoric and Intention in Cicero's *Pro Marcello*." *JRS* 80 (1990): 18-30.

Ebner, Martin. *Leidenslisten und Apostelbrief. Untersuchungen zu Form, Motivik und Funktion der Peristasenkataloge bei Paulus.* Forschung zur Bibel 66. Würzburg: Echter, 1991.

Egan, Rory B. "Lexical Evidence on Two Pauline Passages." *NovT* 19 (1977): 34-62.

Ehrenberg, Victor, and A. H. M. Jones. *Documents Illustrating the Reigns of Augustus and Tiberius.* 2d ed. Oxford University Press, 1955.

Eisenhut, Werner. "Clementia." In *Der Kleine Pauly. Lexikon der Antike auf der Grundlage von Pauly's Realencyclopädie der classischen Altertumswissenschaft unter*

Mitwirkung zahlreicher Fachgelehrter, rev. and ed. Konrat Zielger and Walther Sontheimer, 1223. 5 vols. Stuttgart: Druckenmüller, 1962-75.

Eisner, Robert. "Socrates as Hero." *Philosophy and Literature* 6 (1982): 106-18.

Ellingworth, Paul. "Grammar, Meaning, and Verse Divisions in 2 Cor 11:16-29." *Bible Translator* 43 (1992): 245-46.

Enos, Richard Leo, and Karen Rossi Schnakenberg. "Cicero Latinizes Hellenic Ethos." In *Ethos: New Essays in Rhetorical and Critical Theory*, eds. Baumlin and Baumlin, 197-205. Dallas, TX: Southern Methodist University Press, 1994.

Erim, Kenan T. *Aphrodisias: City of Venus Aphrodite*. London: Muller, Blond & White, 1986.

Ernesti, I.C.T. *Lexicon technologiae graecorum rhetoricae*. Second edition. Hildesheim, 1962.

Erskine, Andrew. *The Hellenistic Stoa: Political Thougth and Action*. Ithaca, NY: Cornell University Press, 1990.

_____. "Hellenistic Monarchy and Roman Policital Invective." *CQ* 41 (1991): 106-20.

_____. "The Romans as Common Benefactors." *Historia* 43 (1994): 70-87.

Eskola, Timo. *Messiah and the Throne: Jewish Merkabah Mysticism and Early Christian Exaltation Discourse*. WUNT II/142. Tübingen: J. C. B. Mohr (Paul Siebeck), 2001.

Eyben, Emiel. "Fathers and Sons." In *Marriage, Divorce, and Children in Ancient Rome*, ed. Beryl Rawson, 114-43. Canberra: Humanities Research Centre. Oxford: Clarendon Press, 1991.

Fajardo-Acosta, Fidel. *The Hero's Failure in the Tragedy of Odysseus: A Revisionist Analysis*. Studies in Epic and Romance Literature 3. Lewiston, NY: The Edwin Mellen Press, 1990.

Farber, J. Joel. "The Cyropaedia and Hellenistic Kingship." *AJP* 100 (1979): 497-514.

Fears, J. Rufus. "Nero as the Viceregent of the Gods in Seneca's 'De Clementia.'" *Hermes* 103 (1975): 486-96.

_____. "Solar Monarchy of Nero and the Imperial Panegyric of Q. Curtius Rufus." *Historia* 25 (1976): 494-96.

_____. "Cult of Virtues and Roman Imperial Ideology." *ANRW* 2.17.2 (1981): 827-948.

Fee, Gordon D. *The First Epistle to the Corinthians*. NICNT. Grand Rapids: Eerdmans, 1987.

_____. *God's Empowering Presence: The Holy Spirit in the Letters of Paul*. Peabody, MA: Hendrickson, 1994.

_____. "'Another Gospel Which you did not Embrace': 2 Corinthians 11.4 and the Theology of 1 and 2 Corinthians." In *Gospel in Paul: Studies on Corinthians, Galatians and Romans for Richard N. Longenecker*, eds. L. Ann Jervis and Peter Richardson, 111-33. JSNTSS 108. Sheffield Academic Press, 1994.

Feldman, Louis H. "Josephus as an Apologist to the Greco-Roman World: His Portrait of Solomon." In *Aspects of Religious Propaganda in Judaism and Early Christianity*, ed. Elisabeth Schüssler Fiorenza, 69-98. University of Notre Dame Press, 1976.

_____. "Josephus' Portrait of Saul." *HUCA* 53 (1983): 45-99.

_____. "Josephus's Portrait of Joshua." *HTR* 82 (1989): 351-76.

_____. "Josephus' Portrait of David." *HUCA* 60 (1989): 129-74.
Ferrari, Markus Schiefer. *Die Sprache des Leids in den paulinischen Peristasenkatalogen.* SBB 23. Stuttgart: Katholisches Bibelwerk, 1991.
Findlay. "St. Paul's Use of θριαμβεύω." *Expositor* 10 (1879): 403-421.
Finkelberg, Margalit. "Odysseus and the Genus 'Hero.'" *G&R* 42 (1995): 1-14.
Finley, M. I. *Ancient Slavery and Modern Ideology.* New York: Viking Press, 1980.
Fischer, Thomas. "First and Second Maccabees." In *ABD*, ed. David Noel Freedman, 4: 444. Garden City, NJ: Doubleday &. Co., 1991.
Fisher, N. R. E. *Hybris: A Study in the Values of Honour and Shame in Ancient Greece.* Warminster: Aris and Phillips, 1992.
Fishwick, Duncan. "The Development of Provincial Ruler Worship in the Western Roman Empire." *ANRW* 2.16.2 (1978): 1201-1253.

_____. *The Imperial Cult in the Latin West: Studies in the Ruler Cult of the Western Provinces of the Roman Empire.* 2 vols. in 4. Leiden: E.J. Brill, 1987-92.

_____. "Dio and Maecenas: The Emperor and the Ruler Cult." *Phoenix* 44 (1990): 267-75.
Fitzgerald, G. J. "The Euripidean Heracles: An Intellectual and a Coward?" *Mnemosyne* 44 (1991): 85-95.
Fitzgerald, John T. *Cracks in an Earthen Vessel: An Examination of the Catalogues of Hardships in the Corinthian Correspondence.* SBLDS 99. Atlanta: Scholars Press, 1988.

_____. "Paul, the Ancient Epistolary Theorists, and 2 Corinthians 10–13: The Purpose and Literary Genre of a Pauline Letter." In *Greeks, Romans, and Christians: Essays in Honor of Abraham J. Malherbe*, eds. David L. Balch, Everett Ferguson, and Wayne A. Meeks, 190-200. Minneapolis: Fortress Press, 1990.
Forbes, Christopher. "Comparison, Self-Praise and Irony, Paul's Boasting and the Conventions of Hellenistic Rhetoric." *NTS* 32 (1986): 1-30.
Fortenbaugh, William W. "Persuasion through Character and the Composition of Aristotle's Rhetoric." *RhM* 134 (1991): 152-56.

_____. "Theophrastus, the Characters and Rhetoric." In *Peripatetic Rhetoric after Aristotle*, eds. idem and David Mirhady, 15-35. Rutgers University Studies in Classical Humanities 6. New Brunswick, NJ: Transaction Publishers, 1994.

_____. "Quintilian 6.2.8-9: Ethos and Pathos and the Ancient Tradition." In *Peripatetic Rhetoric after Aristotle*, eds. idem and David C. Mirhady, 183-91. Rutgers University Studies in Classical Humanities 6. New Brunswick: Transaction Publishers, 1994.
Fowl, S. E. *The Story of Christ in the Ethics of Paul: An Analysis of the Function of the Hymnic Material in the Pauline Corpus.* JSNTSS 36. Sheffield: JSOT Press, 1990.
Frankemölle, Hubert. "πραΰτης, πραΰς." In *Exegetisches Wörterbuch zum Neuen Testament*, eds. Horst Balz and Gerhard Schneider, 3: 351-53. 3 vols. Stuttgart: W. Kohlhammer, 1980-83. English: In *EDNT*, trans. James W. Thompson et al., 3: 146-47. 3 vols. Grand Rapids: Eerdmans, 1990-93.

_____. *Evangelium — Begriff and Gattung.* Ein Forschungsbericht. 2d ed. SBB 15. Stuttgart: Katholisches Bibelwerk, 1994.

Freedman, David Noel, ed. *Anchor Bible Dictionary*. 6 vols. Garden City: Doubleday, 1991.
Fridrichsen, A. "Peristasenkatalog und res gestae. Nachtrag zu 2 Cor. 11.23ff." *Symbolae osloenses* 8 (1929): 78-82.
Friedrich, Gerhard. "εὐαγγέλιον." *TDNT*, 2: 721-36.
_____. "Die Gegner des Paulus im 2. Korintherbrief." In *Abraham unser Vater. Festschrift für Otto Michel*, eds. O. Betz, M. Hengel, and P. Schmidt, 181-215. Arbeiten zur Geschichte des antiken Judentums und des Urchristentums 5. Leiden: Brill, 1963.
Friedrich, Rainer. "The Hybris of Odysseus." *JHS* 111 (1991): 27-28.
Frisk, H. *Griechisches etymologisches Wörterbuch*. 2d ed. Heidelberg, 1973.
Fuchs, Eric. "La faiblesse, gloire de l'apostolat selon Paul: Étude sur 2 Corinthians 10-12." *ÉTR* 55 (1980): 231-252.
Fuhrmann, Manfred. *Cicero and the Roman Republic*. Trans. W. E. Yuill. Oxford: Blackwell, 1992.
Fuller, Reginald H. *The Foundations of New Testament Christology*. New York: Charles Scribner's Sons, 1965.
Furnish, Victor Paul. "The Jesus-Paul Debate: From Baur to Bultmann." *BJRL* 47 (1964-65): 342-381.
_____. "Corinth in Paul's Time: What can Archaeology tell Us?" *Biblical Archaeology Review* 14 (1988): 14-27.

Gabelmann, Hans. *Antike Audienz- und Tribunalszenen*. Darmstadt: Wissenschaftliche Buchgesellschaft, 1984.
Galinsky, G. Karl. *The Herakles Theme: The Adaptations of the Hero in Literature from Homer to the Twentieth Century*. Totowa, NJ: Rowman and Littlefield, 1972.
_____. "Venus, Polysemy, and the Ara Pacis Augustae." *AJA* 96 (1992): 457-75.
García Moreno, Luis A. "Paradoxography and Political Ideals in Plutarch's Life of Sertorius." In *Plutarch and the Historical Tradition*, ed. Philip A. Stadter, 132-57. London: Routledge, 1992.
Garnsey, P., and C. Whittaker, eds. *Imperialism in the Ancient World*. Cambridge University Press, 1978.
_____, and Richard Saller. *Roman Empire: Economy, Society and Culture*. Berkeley: University of California Press, 1987.
Gasti, Helen. "Sophocles' *Ajax*: The Military *Hybris*." *QUCC* 40 (1992): 81-83.
Gaventa, Beverly R. "Apostles As Babes and Nurses in 1 Thessalonians 2:7." In *Faith and History: Essays in Honor of Paul W. Meyer*, eds. John T. Carroll, Charles H. Cosgrove, and E. Elizabeth Johnson, 193-207. Atlanta: Scholars Press, 1990.
Gauthier-Walter, Marie-Dominique. "Joseph, figure idéale du Roi?" *Cahiers archéologiques* 38 (1990): 25-36.
Geffcken, Katherine A. *Comedy in the Pro Caelio*. Leiden:Brill, 1973.
Geoffrion, Timothy C. "An Investigation of the Purpose and the Political and Military Character of Philippians." Th.D. diss., Lutheran School of Theology at Chicago, 1992.
Georgi, Dieter. *The Opponents of Paul in 2 Corinthians*. English translation with Epilogue. Philadelphia: Fortress Press, 1986.

———. *Theocracy in Paul's Praxis and Theology*. Trans. David Green. Minneapolis: Fortress Press, 1991.

Gesche, Helga. "Datierung und Deutung des CLEMENTIAE-MODERATIONI-Dupondien des Tiberius." *Jahrbuch für Numismatik und Geldgeschichte* 21 (1971): 37-80.

Giangrande, Lawrence. *The Use of Spoudaiogeloion in Greek and Roman Literature*. The Hauge: Mouton, 1972.

Giannini, Alessandro. "Studi sulla Paradossografia Greca." *Rendiconti dell'Istituto Lombardo* 97 (1963): 247-66.

Giesen, H. "ἐπιεικής, ἐπιείκεια." In *Exegetisches Wörterbuch zum Neuen Testament*, eds. Horst Balz and Gerhard Schneider, 2: 65-67. 3 vols. Stuttgart: W. Kohlhammer, 1980-83. English: *EDNT*, trans. James W. Thompson et al., 2: 26. 3 vols. Grand Rapids: Eerdmans, 1990-93.

Gilchrist, J. M. "Paul and the Corinthians — the Sequence of Letters and Visits." *JSNT* 34 (1988): 47-69.

Gillman, John. "Paul's εἴσοδος: The Proclaimed and the Proclaimer (1 Thes 2,8)." In *The Thessalonian Correspondence*, ed. Raymond F. Collins, 62-70. BETL 87. Leuven University Press, 1990.

Ginami, Corrado. "Gli 'pseudo-apostoli' in 2 Cor 11,13." In *Antipaolinismo. Reazioni a Paulo tra il I e il II secolo. Atti del II Convegno Nazionale di Studi Neotestamentari (Bressanone, 10-12 settembre 1987)*, ed. Romano Penna, 55-64. Bologna: Centro editoriale dehoniano, 1989.

Giua, M. A. "Augusto nel libro 56 della storia romana di Cassio Dione." *Athenaeum* 61 (1983): 439-56.

Gladigow, Burkhard. "'Das Paradox macht Sinn': Sinnkonstitution durch Paradoxien in der griechischen Antike." In *Das Paradox. Eine Herausforderung des abendländischen Denkens*, eds. Paul Geyer and Roland Hagenbüchle, 195-208. Tübingen: Stauffenburg, 1992.

Gleason, Maud W. *Making Men: Sophists and Self-Presentation in Ancient Rome*. Princeton University Press, 1995.

Goins, Scott. "The Influence of Old Comedy on the *Vita Aesopi*." *CW* 83 (1989): 28-30.

———. "The Heroism of Odysseus in Euripides' *Cyclops*." *Eos* 79 (1991): 187-94.

———. "Two Aspects of Virgil's Use of *labor* in the *Aeneid*." *CJ* 88 (1993): 375-84.

Goldstein, Jonathan. *II Maccabees*. AB 41A. Garden City, NY: Doubleday & Co., 1983.

Goodenough, Erwin R. "The Political Philosophy of Hellenistic Kingship." *YClS* 1 (1928): 55-102.

———. *The Politics of Philo Judaeus: Practice and Theory*. New Haven: Yale University Press, 1938.

Gottlieb, Paula. "The Complexity of Socratic Irony: A Note on Professor Vlastos' Account." *CQ* n.s. 42 (1992): 278-79.

Gould, Thomas. *The Ancient Quarrel between Poetry and Philosophy*. Princeton University Press, 1990.

Goulet-Cazé, M.-O. *L'Ascèse cynique. Un commentarire de Diogène Laërce VI.70-71*. Histoire des doctrines de l'antiquité classique 10. Paris: J. Vrin, 1986.

Green, William Scott. "Introduction: Messiah in Judaism: Rethinking the Question." In *Judaisms and Their Messiahs at the Turn of the Christian Era*, eds. Jacob Neusner et al., 1-13. Cambridge University Press, 1987.
Greenberg, Nathan A. "Success and Failure in the *Adelphoe*." *CW* 73 (1979): 223-36.
Greenhalgh, Peter A. L. *The Year of the Four Emperors*. New York: Barnes & Noble, 1975.
_____. *Pompey: The Roman Alexander*. Columbia: University of Missouri Press, 1981.
Grenfell, Bernard P., and Arthur S. Hunt, eds. *The Oxyrhynchus Papyri*, part 1. London: Egypt Exploration Fund, 1898.
Griffin, Jasper. *Homer: The Odyssey*. Landmarks of World Literature. Cambridge University Press, 1987.
_____. "Virgil." In *The Roman World*, eds. J. Boardman, J. Griffin, and O. Murray, 206-25. Oxford University Press, 1988.
Griffin, Miriam T. *Seneca: A Philosopher in Politics*. Oxford University Press, 1976.
_____. *Nero: The End of a Dynasty*. New Haven: Yale University Press, 1984.
_____. "Philosophy, Politics, and Politicians at Rome." In *Philosophia Togata: Essays on Philosophy and Roman Society*, eds. Miriam T. Griffin and Jonathan Barnes, 1-37. Oxford University Press, 1989.
Griffiths, J. Gwyn. "Apocalyptic in the Hellenistic Era." In *Apocalypticism in the Mediterranean World and the Near East: Proceedings of the International Colloquium on Apocalypticism, Uppsala, August 12-17, 1979*, ed. David Hellholm, 273-93. Tübingen: J. C. B. Mohr (Paul Siebeck), 1983.
Grimal, Pierre. "Le 'bon roi' de Philodème et la royauté de César." *Revue des études latines* 44 (1966): 254-85.
_____. "Le De Clementia et la royauté solaire de Néron." *Revue des études latines* 49 (1971): 205-17.
_____. *Sénèque ou la conscience de l'Empire*. Collection d'Études Anciennes. Paris: Les Belles Lettres, 1979.
_____. "La clémence et la douceur dans la vie politique romaine." *CRAI* (1984): 466-78.
_____. "Les éléments philosophiques dans l'idée de monarchie à Rome à la fin de la République." In *Aspects de la philosophie hellénistique*, eds. Helmut Flashar and Olof Gigon, 233-73. Entretiens sur l'antiquité classique 32. Geneva: Fondation Hardt, 1986.
_____. "L'Image du pouvoir royal dans les tragédies de Sénèque." *Pallas* 38 (1992): 409-16.
Gruber, Jaochim. "Cicero und das hellenistische Herrscherideal. Überlegungen zur Rede 'De imperio Cn. Pompei.'" *Wiener Studien* 101 (1988): 243-58.
Guilhamet, Leon. "Socrates and Post-Socratic Satire." *Journal of the History of Ideas* 46 (1985): 3-12.
Gunther, J. J. *St. Paul's Opponents and Their Background: A Study of Apocalyptic and Jewish Sectarian Teachings*. Novum Testamentum, Supplements 35. Leiden: Brill, 1973.
Guthrie, Kenneth. *The Pythagorean Sourcebook and Library*. Grand Rapids, MI: Phanes Press, 1987.

Güttgemans, Erhardt. *Der leidende Apostel und sein Herr: Studien zur paulinischen Christologie.* Religion und Literatur des Alten und Neuen Testaments 90. Göttingen: Vandenhoeck & Ruprecht, 1966.

Hadley, R. A. "Royal Propaganda of Seleucus I and Lysimachus." *JHS* 94 (1974): 50-65.

Hadot, Pierre. "Fürstenspiegel." *RAC* 8 (1972): 555-632.

Hafemann, Scott J. *Suffering and the Spirit.* WUNT 2.19. Tübingen: J. C. B. Mohr (Paul Siebeck), 1986.

_____. *Suffering & Ministry in the Spirit: Paul's Defense of His Ministry in II Corinthians 2:14–3:3.* Grand Rapids: Eerdmans, 1990.

_____. "'Self-Commendation' and Apostolic Legitimacy in 2 Corinthians: A Pauline Dialectic?" *NTS* 36 (1990): 66-88.

Hagedorn, Dieter. *Zur Ideenlehre des Hermogenes.* Hypomnemata 8. Göttingen: Vandenhoeck & Ruprecht, 1964.

Hamel, E. "La vertu d'épikie." *Sciences ecclésiastiques* 13 (1961): 35-56.

Hannestad, Niels. *Roman Art and Imperial Policy.* Trans. P. J. Crabb. Jutland Archaeological Society Publications 19. Aarhus: University Press, 1986.

Harding, Mark. "On the Historicity of Acts: Comparing Acts 9.23-5 with 2 Corinthians 11.32-3 [C. J. Hemer's Argument]." *NTS* 39 (1993): 518-38.

Harnack, Adolf von. "'Sanftmut, Huld und Demut' in der alten Kirche." In *Festgabe für Julius Kaftan zu seinem 70. Geburtstag,* eds. A. Titius, Friedrich Niebergall, and Georg Wobbermin, 113-29. Tübingen: J. C. B. Mohr (Paul Siebeck), 1920.

Harrill, J. Albert. *The Manumission of Slaves in Early Christianity.* HUT 32. Tübingen: J. C. B. Mohr (Paul Siebeck), 1995.

Hasler, Victor. "Das Evangelium des Paulus in Korinth, Erwägungen zur Hermeneutik." *NTS* 30 (1984): 109-129.

Hauck, Friedrich, and Siegfried Schulz. "πραΰς, πραΰτης." In *Theologisches Wörterbuch zum Neuen Testament,* ed. Gerhard Kittel and Gerhard Friedrich, 6: 645-651. 10 vols. Stuttgart: W. Kohlhammer, 1933-73. English: *Theological Dictionary of the New Testament,* trans. and ed. Geoffrey W. Bromiley, 6: 645-651. 10 vols. Grand Rapids: Eerdmans, 1964-76.

Hausrath, Adolf. *Der Vier-Capitel-Brief des Paulus an die Korinther.* Heidelberg: Bassermann, 1870.

Hawthorne, Gerald. F. *Philippians.* WBC 43. Waco, TX: Word, 1983.

Hays, Richard B. *Echoes of Scripture in the Letters of Paul.* New Haven: Yale University Press, 1989.

Heckel, Ulrich. *Kraft in Schwachheit. Untersuchungen zu 2. Kor 10–13.* WUNT 2.56. Tübingen: J. C. B. Mohr (Paul Siebeck), 1993.

_____. "Der Dorn im Fleisch. Die Krankheit des Paulus in 2 Kor 12,7 und Gal 4,13f." *ZNW* 84 (1993): 65-92.

Hengel, Martin. "Erwägungen zum Sprachgebrauch von Christos bei Paulus und in der 'vorpaulinischen' Überlieferung." In *Paul and Paulinism: Essays in Honor of C. K. Barrett,* eds. M. D. Hooker and S. G. Wilson, 135-59. London: SPCK, 1982. English: "'Christos' in Paul." In his *Between Jesus and Paul,* trans. John Bowden, 65-77. Philadelphia: Fortress Press, 1983.

———. "Psalm 110 und die Erhöhung des Auferstandenen zur Rechten Gottes." In *Anfänge der Christologie. Festschrift für Ferdinand Hahn zum 65. Geburtstag*, eds. Cilliers Breytenbach and Henning Paulsen, 43-73. Göttingen: Vandenhoeck & Ruprecht, 1991.

Herington, C. J. "Octavia Praetexta: A Survey." *Classical Quarterly* n. s. 11 (1961): 18-30.

Henry, Denis and Elisabeth. *The Mask of Power: Seneca's Tragedies and Imperial Rome*. Warminster: Aris & Phillips, 1985.

Henzen, G. *Acta Fratrum Arvalium*. Berlin: G. Reimeri, 1874.

Heuss, A. "La monarchie hellénistique." In *Relazioni del X congresso internazionale di scienze storiche II*, 201-213. 7 vols. Florence: Sansoni, 1955.

Hodgson, Roger. "Paul the Apostle and First Century Tribulation Lists." *ZNW* 74 (1983): 59-80.

Höistadt, R. *Cynic Hero and Cynic King*. Uppsala, 1948.

Holland, Glenn S. "Speaking Like a Fool: Irony in 2 Corinthians 10-13." In *Rhetoric and the New Testament: Essays from the 1992 Heidelberg Conference*, eds. Stanley E. Porter and Thomas H. Olbricht, 250-64. JSNTSS 90. Sheffield Academic Press, 1993.

Holleman, Joost. *Resurrection and Parousia: A Traditio-Historical Study of Paul's Eschatology in 1 Corinthians 15*. Supplements to Novum Testamentum. Leiden: E. J. Brill, 1996.

Hölscher, T. "Die Geschichtsauffassung in der römischen Repräsentationskunst." *Jahrbuch des deutschen archäologischen Instituts* 95 (1980): 281-90.

Holt, Philip. "Ajax's Burial in Early Greek Epic." *AJP* 113 (1992): 319-31.

Hooker, Morna D. *From Adam to Christ: Essays on Paul*. Cambridge University Press, 1990.

Hopkins, Kieth. *Conquerors and Slaves*. Sociological Studies in Roman History 1. Cambridge University Press, 1978.

Horsley, G. H. R. *New Documents Illustrating Early Christiainty*. North Ryde, N. S. W.: Ancient History Documentary Research Centre, Macquarie University, 1981–.

Hultgren, Arland J. *New Testament Christology: A Critical Assessment and Annotated Bibliography*. Advisory editor, G. E. Gorman. New York: Greenwood Press, 1988.

Hunt, Arthur S., ed. *The Oxyrhynchus Papyri*, part 17. London: Egypt Exploration Society, 1927.

Hunter, R. L. *The New Comedy of Greece and Rome*. Cambridge University Press, 1985.

Jackson, Bernard S. "Legalism." *Journal of Jewish Studies* 30 (1979): 1-22.

Jalabert, Louis, René Mouterde, et al. *Inscriptions grecques et latines de la Syria*. 8 vols. Bibliothèque archéologique et historique 12, 33, 36, 61, 66, 78, 89, 104. Paris: Librairie orientaliste Paul Geuthner, 1929-80.

Jedrkiewicz, Stefano. *Sapere e paradosso nell'antichità. Esops e la favola*. Roma: Edizioni dell'Ateneo, 1989.

Jervell, J. "Der schwache Charismatiker." In *Rechtfertigung. Festschrift für E. Käsemann*, eds. J. Friedrich, W. Pöhlmann, and P. Stuhlmacher, 185-98.

Tübingen: J. C. B. Mohr (Paul Siebeck); Göttingen: Vandenhoeck & Ruprecht, 1976.

Jewett, Robert. "The Redaction and Use of an Early Christian Confession in Romans 1:3-4." In *The Living Text: Essays in Honor of Ernest W. Saunders*, eds. D. Groh and R. Jewett, 92-122. Lanham, MD: University Press of America, 1985.

Jocelyn, H. D. "The Ruling Class of the Roman Republic and Greek Philosophers." *BJRL* 59 (1976/7): 323-66.

Joest, Wilfried. "Zur Frage des Paradoxon in der Theologie." In *Dogma und Denkstrukturen*, eds. Wilfried Joest and Wolfhard Pannenberg, 116-51. Göttingen: Vandenhoeck & Ruprecht, 1963.

Johnson, Sherman E. "A New Analysis of Second Corinthians." *Anglican Theological Review* 47 (1965): 436-443.

Jones, A. H. M. "Numismatics and History." In *Essays in Roman Coinage Presented to Harold Mattingly*, eds. R. A. G. Carson and C. H. V. Sutherland, 13-33. Oxford University Press, 1956. Reprinted in *The Roman Economy: Studies in Ancient Economic and Administrative History*, ed. P. A. Brunt, 61-81. Oxford: Basil Blackwell, 1974.

Jones, C. P. *Plutarch and Rome*. Oxford University Press, 1971.

Jonge, Marinus de. "The Earliest Christian Use of Christos: Some Suggestions." *NTS* 32 (1986): 329-30.

_____. *Christology in Context: The Earliest Christian Response to Jesus*. Philadelphia: Westminster Press, 1988.

_____. "Jesus, Son of David and Son of God." In *Intertextuality in Biblical Writings: Essays in Honor of Bas van Iersel*, ed. Sipke Draisma, 95-104. Kampen: Kok, 1989.

Judge, E. A. "The Conflict of Educational Aims in New Testament Thought." *Journal of Christian Education* 9 (1966): 32-45.

_____. "Paul's Boasting in Relation to Contemporary Professional Practice." *ABR* 16 (October 1968): 37-50.

Jüngel, Eberhard. *Paulus und Jesus. Eine Untersuchung zur Präzisierung der Frage nach dem Ursprung der Christologie*. HUT 2. Tübingen: J. C. B. Mohr (Paul Siebeck), 1962; ^{5}1979.

Kagan, Donald. *The Great Dialogue: History of Greek Political Thought from Homer to Polybius*. History of Western Political Thought. Ithaca, NY: Cornell University Press, 1965.

Käsemann, Ernst. "Die Legitimität des Apostels: Eine Untersuchung zu II Korinther 10–13." *ZNW* 41 (1942): 33-71. Reprinted, *Die Legitimität des Apostels: Eine Untersuchung zu II Korinther 10–13*. Darmstadt: Wissenschaftliche Buchgesellschaft, 1956. Reprinted in *Das Paulusbild in der neueren deutschen Forschung*, ed. Karl Heinrich Rengstorf, 475-521. Wege der Forschung 2. Darmstadt: Wissenschaftliche Buchgesellschaft, 1964.

_____. "Die Anfänge christlicher Theologie." *ZTK* 57 (1960): 162-85. Reprinted in *Exegetische Versuche und Besinnungen*, 2: 82-104. Göttingen: Vandenhoeck & Ruprecht, 1965. English: "The Beginnings of Christian Theology." In *New Testament Questions of Today*, trans. W. J. Montague, 82-107. London: SCM Press; Philadelphia: Fortress Press, 1969.

_____. "Zum Thema der urchristlichen Apokalyptik." *ZTK* 59 (1962): 257-84. Reprinted in *Exegetische Versuche und Besinnungen*, 2: 105-31. Göttingen: Vandenhoeck & Ruprecht, 1965. English: "On the Subject of Primitive Christian Apocalyptic." In *New Testament Questions for Today*, trans. W. J. Montague, 108-37. London: SCM Press; Philadelphia: Fortress Press, 1969.

Keaveney, Arthur. *Sulla: The Last Republican*. London: Croom Helm, 1982.

Keck, Leander E. "Paul and Apocalyptic Theology." *Int* 38 (1984): 229-41.

_____. "Toward the Renewal of New Testament Christology." *NTS* 32 (1986): 368-69.

Kellum, B. "Sculptural Programs and Propaganda in Augustan Rome: The Temple of Apollo on the Palatine." In *The Age of Augustus: Interdisciplinary Conference Held at Brown University, April 30-May 2, 1982*, ed. Rolf Winkes, 169-76. Archaeologia transatlantica 5/Publications d'histoire de l'art et d'archéologie de L'Université Catholique de Louvain 44. Providence, RI: Brown University; Louvain-la-Neuve: Collège Érasme, 1985.

Kennedy, George A. "Peripatetic Rhetoric as It Appears (and Disappears) in Quintilian." In *Peripatetic Rhetoric after Aristotle*, eds. William W. Fortenbaugh and David C. Mirhady, 174-82. Rutgers University Studies in Classical Humanities 6. New Brunswick: Transaction Publishers, 1994.

Kennedy, James Houghton. "Are There Two Epistles in 2 Corinthians?" *The Expositor* 6 (1897): 231-8, 285-304.

_____. *The Second and Third Epistles of St. Paul to the Corinthians*. London: Methuen, 1900.

Kent, John Harvey. *Corinth 8.3: The Inscriptions 1926-1950*. Princeton: American School of Classical Studies at Athens, 1966.

Keoppel, Gerhard. "Profectio und Adventus." *Bonner Jahrbücher* 169 (1969): 130-94.

Kierkegaard, Søren. *The Concept of Irony with Continual Reference to Socrates*. Eds. and trans. Howard V. Hong and Edna H. Hong. Princeton University Press, 1989.

Kim, Seyoon. *The Origin of Paul's Gospel*. WUNT 2.4. Tübingen: J. C. B. Mohr (Paul Siebeck), 1981.

King, Katherine Callen. *Achilles: Paradigm of the War Hero from Homer to the Middle Ages*. Berkeley: University of California Press, 1987.

Klauser, T. "Akklamation." *RAC* 1 (1950): 213-33.

Kleiner, Diana E. E. "The Great Friezes of the Ara Pacis Augustae: Greek Sources, Roman Derivatives, and Augustan Social Policy." In *Roman Art in Context: An Anthology*, ed. Eve D'Ambra, 27-52. Englewood Cliffs, NJ: Prentice Hall, 1993.

Kleinknecht, Karl Theodor. *Der leidende Gerechtfertigte. Die alttestamentlich-jüdische Tradition vom 'leidenden Gerechten' und ihre Rezeption bei Paulus*. Tübingen: J. C. B. Mohr (Paul Siebeck), 1984.

Kleve, Knut. "Scurra Atticus: The Epicurean View of Socrates." In *Suzetesis. Studi sull'Epicureismo Greco e Romano offerti a Marcello Gigante*, ed. Giovanni Pugliese Carratelli, 1: 227-53. Naples, 1983.

Klimkeit, H.-J. "Der leidende Gerechte in der Religionsgeschichte." In *Religionswissenschaft. Eine Einführung*, ed. Hartmut Zinser, 164-84. Berlin: Dietrich Reimer, 1988.

Kloft, Hans. *Liberalitas principis. Herkunft und Bedeutung. Studien zur Prinzipatsideologie*. Kölner historische Abhandlungen 18. Köln-Wien: Böhlau, 1970.

Knauf, Ernst Axel. "Zum Ethnachen des Aretas, 2 Kor 11,32." *ZNW* 74 (1983): 145-147.
Koenen, Ludwig. "Die Adaptation ägyptischer Königsideologie am Ptolemäerhof." In *Egypt and the Hellenistic World: Proceedings of the International Colloquium, Leuven — 24-26 May 1982*, eds. E. Van 't Dack, P. Van Dessel, and W. Van Grucht, 143-90. Studia Hellenistica 27. Louvain, 1983.

——. "The Ptolemaic King as a Religious Figure." In *Images and Ideologies: Self-definition in the Hellenistic World*, eds. Anthony Bulloch et al., 81-113. Hellenistic Culture and Society 12. Berkeley: University of California Press, 1993.

Kolenkow, Anitra Bingham. "Paul and Opponents in 2 Cor 10–13 — Theioi Andres and Spiritual Guides." In *Religious Propaganda and Missionary Competition in the New Testament World: Essays Honoring Dieter Georgi*, eds. Lukas Bormann, Kelly del Tredici, and Angela Standhartinger, 351-74. Supplements to Novum Testamentum 74. Leiden: E. J. Brill, 1994.

Koester, Helmut. "The Purpose of the Polemic of a Pauline Fragment (Philippians 3)." *NTS* 8 (1961-62): 317-32.

——. "The Text of 1 Thessalonians." *In The Living Text: Essays in Honor of Ernest W. Saunders*, eds. Dennis E. Groh and Robert Jewett. Lanham, MD: University Press of America, 1985.

Korpanty, Józef. "Römische Ideale und Werte im augusteischen Prinzipat." *Klio* 73 (1991): 432-47.

Kraft, Heinrich, "Die Paradoxie in der Bibel und bei den Griechen als Voraussetzung für die Entfaltung der Glaubenslehren." In *Das Paradox. Eine Herausforderung des abendländischen Denkens*, eds. Paul Geyer and Roland Hagenbüchle, 247-72. Tübingen: Stauffenburg, 1992.

Kragelund, Patrick. *Prophecy, Populism, and Propaganda in the 'Octavia.'* Opuscula Graecolatina 25. Copenhagen: Museum Tusculanum Press, 1982.

Krentz, Edgar. "Military Language and Metaphors in Philippians." In *Origins and Method: Towards a New Understanding of Judaism and Christianity: Essays in Honour of John C. Hurd*, ed. Bradley H. McLean, 105-27. JSNTSS 86. Sheffield: JSOT Press, 1993.

Kruse, Colin G. "The Offender and the Offence in 2 Corinthians 2:5 and 7:12." *Evangelical Quarterly* 88 (1988): 129-39.

——. "The Relationship between the Opposition to Paul Reflected in 2 Corinthians 1–7 and 10–13." *Evangelical Quarterly* 61 (1989): 195-202.

Kumaniecki, Kazimierz. "Ciceros Paradoxa Stoicorum und die römische Wirklichkeit." *Philologus* 101 (1957): 113-34.

Kümmel, Werner Georg. "Supplemental Notes." In *An dei Korinther I, II*, by Hans Lietzmann, 165-214. Handbuch zum Neuen Testament 9. Tübingen: J. C. B. Mohr, 1949.

——. "Jesus und Paulus." *NTS* 10 (1963-64): 163-81. Reprinted in *Heilsgeschehen und Geschichte. Gesammelte Aufsätze 1933-1965*, eds. E. Grässer, et al., 439-56. Marburger theologische Studien 3. Marburg: N. G. Elwert, 1965.

——. *The Theology of the New Testament according to Its Main Witnesses Jesus — Paul — John*. Translated by John E. Steely. Nashville: Abingdon Press, 1973.

——. *Dreißig Jahre Jesusforschung (1950-1980)*. Bonner biblische Beiträge, 60. Bonn: Peter Hanstein, 1985.

Kuntz, Mary. "The Prodikean 'Choice of Herakles': A Reshaping of Myth." *CJ* 89 (1994): 163-81.
Künzel, Ernst. *Der römische Triumph. Siegesfeiern im antiken Rom.* Archäologische Bibliothek. München: Beck, 1988.
Kuttner, Ann L. *Dynasty and the Empire in the Age of Augustus: The Case of the Boscoreale Cups.* Berkeley: University of California Press, 1994.

Ladd, George Eldon. *A Theology of the New Testament.* Rev. Donald A. Hagner. Grand Rapids: Eerdmans, 1993.
Lampe, G. W. H., ed. *A Patristic Greek Lexicon.* Oxford University Press, 1961-1968.
Lane, William L. "Covenant: The Key to Paul's Conflict with Corinth." *TB* 33 (1982): 3-29.
Lang, Candace D. *Irony/Humor: Critical Paradigms.* Baltimore, MD: Johns Hopkins University Press, 1988.
La Penna, Antonio. "La morale della favola esopica come morale delle classi subalterne nell'antichità." *Società* 17 (1961): 459-537.
Lassen, Eva Maria. "The Use of the Father Image in Imperial Propaganda and 1 Corinthians 4:14-21." *TB* 42 (1991): 127-36.
Leary, T. J. "'A Thorn in the Flesh' — 2 Corinthians 12:7." *JTS* 43 (1992): 520-22.
Lefèvre, Eckard. "Die Bedeutung des Paradoxen in der römischen Literatur." In *Das Paradox. Eine Herausforderung des abendländischen Denkens*, eds. Paul Geyer and Roland Hagenbüchle. Stauffenburg Colloquium 21. Tübingen: Stauffenburg, 1992.
LeGuern, M. "Elements pour une histoire de la notion d'ironie." In *L'Ironie*, eds. C. Kerbrat-Orecchioni, M. Le Guern, P. Bange and A. Bony, 47-60. Linguistique et Sémiologie 2. Lyon: Presses Universitaires de Lyon, 1978.
Lenger, Marie-Thérèse. "La notion de 'bienfait' (φιλάνθρωπον) royal et les ordonnances des rois Lagides." In *Studi in onore di Vincenzo Arangio-Ruiz nel XLV anno del suo insegnamento*, eds. Mario Lauria et al., 483-99. Naples: Jovene, c. 1952.
Levi, M. A. "La clemenza di Tito." *La parola del passato* 9 (1954): 288-93.
Levick, Barbara M. "Mercy and Moderation on the Coinage of Tiberius." In *The Ancient Historian and His Materials: Essays in Honor of C. E. Stevens.* Farnborough: Gregg International, 1975.
_____. "Propaganda and the Imperial Coinage." *Antichthon* 16 (1982): 104-16.
_____. *Claudius.* London: B. T. Batsford, 1990.
Levison, John R. *Portraits of Adam in Early Judaism: From Sircah to 2 Baruch.* JSPSS 1. Sheffield Academic Press, 1988.
Leivestad, Ragnar. "'The Meekness and Gentleness of Christ' II Cor. X. 1." *NTS* 13 (1966): 156-164.
Lichocka, Barbara. *Justitia sur les monnaies imperiales romaines.* Trans. Zsolt Kiss. Travaux du Centre d'Archéologie Méditerranéenne de l'Académie Polonaise des Sciences 15. Warsaw: PWN — Editions scientifiques de Pologne, 1974.
Liddell, Henry George, and Robert Scott, eds. *A Greek-English Lexicon.* 9th edition, revised and augmented by Henry Stuart Jones. Supplement edited by E. A. Barber. Oxford University Press, 1968.

Lisco, Heinrich. *Judaismus triumphatus. Ein Beitrag zur Auslegung der vier letzten Kapitel de zweiten Korintherbriefes.* Berlin: F. Schneider (H. Klinsmann), 1896.

Lloyd-Jones, Hugh. "Honour and Shame in Ancient Greek Culture." In *Greek Comedy, Hellenistic Literature, Greek Religion, and Miscellanea: The Academic Papers of Sir Hugh Lloyd-Jones.* Oxford University Press, 1990.

Locke, John. *A Paraphrase and Notes on the Epistles of St Paul to the Galatians, 1 and 2 Corinthians, Romans, Ephesians.* Ed. Arthur W. Wainwright. 2 vols. Oxford University Press, 1987 (originally printed in London, 1707).

Lohse, Eduard. *Verteidigung und Begründung des apostolischen Amtes (2 Kor 10–13).* Biblisch-ökumenische Abteilung 11. Rome: Abtei St. Paul vor den Mauern, 1992.

Long, A. A. "Review of *Exemplum Socratis* by Klaus Döring." *CR* 31 (1981): 298-99.

_____. "Socrates in Hellenistic Philosophy." *CQ* 38 (1988): 150-71.

_____. "Hellenistic Ethics and Philosophical Power." In *Hellenistic History and Culture*, ed. Peter Green. Hellenistic Culture and Society 9. Berkeley: University of California Press, 1993.

Lonsdale, Steven. "Simile and Ecphrasis in Homer and Virgil: The Poet as Craftsman and Choreographer." *Vergilius* 36 (1990): 7-30.

López López, Matías. "Mito y filosofía en las Metamorfosis de Ovidio: Ulises, Hércules, Níobe, Licaón." *Cuadernos de filología clásica* 22 (1989): 167-74.

Loraux, Nicole. *The Invention of Athens: The Funeral Oration in the Classical City.* Trans. Alan Sheridan. Cambridge, MA: Harvard University Press, 1986.

Loubser, J. A. "Winning the Struggle (or: How to Treat Heretics)." *Journal of Theology for Southern Africa* 75 (1991): 75-83.

_____. "A New Look at Paradox and Irony in 2 Corinthians 10–13." *Neot* 26 (1992): 507-21.

Luce, T. J. "Livy, Augustus, and the Forum Augustum." In *Between Republic and Empire: Interpretations of Augustus and His Principate*, eds. Kurt A. Raaflaub and Mark Toher, 123-38. Berkeley: University of California Press, 1990.

Lund, Helen S. *Lysimachus: A Study in Early Hellenistic Kingship.* London: Routledge, 1992.

Lutz, Cora E. "Musonius Rufus: 'The Roman Socrates.'" *Yale Classical Studies* 10 (1947): 3-147.

Luzzatto, M. J. "Plutarco, Socrate e l'Esopo di Delfi." *ICS* 13 (1988): 427-45.

Lyons, George. *Pauline Autobiography: Toward a New Understanding.* SBLDS 73. Atlanta: Scholars Press, 1985.

MacCary, W. T. "Menander's Slaves: Their Names, Roles and Masks." *TAPA* 100 (1969): 277-94.

MacCormack, Sabine. "Latin Prose Panegyrics." In *Empire and Aftermath: Silver Latin II*, ed. T. A. Dorey, 143-205. London: Routledge & Kegan, 1975.

MacDowell, Douglas. "The Meaning of ἀλαζών." In *'Owls to Athens': Essays on Classical Subjects Presented to Sir Kenneth Dover*, ed. E. M. Clark, 287-92. Oxford University Press, 1990.

MacMullen, Ramsay. *Roman Social Relations: 50 B.C. to A.D. 284*. New Haven: Yale University Press, 1974.

———. "Personal Power in the Roman Empire." *AJP* 107 (1986): 512-24.

Malherbe, Abraham J. "Through the Eye of the Needle: Simplicity or Singleness?" *Restoration Quarterly* 5 (1961): 119-129.

———. "'Gentle as a Nurse:' The Cynic Background to I Thess ii." *NovT* 12 (1970): 203-17. Reprinted in *Paul and the Popular Philosophers*, 35-48. Minneapolis: Fortress Press, 1989.

———. "Pseudo-Heraclitus, Epistle 4: The Divinization of the Wise Man." *JAC* 21 (1978): 54-58.

———. "Self-Definition among Epicureans and Cynics." In *Self-Definition in the Greco-Roman World*, vol. 3: *Jewish and Christian Self-Definition*, eds. Ben F. Meyer and E. P. Sanders, 46-59. Philadelphia: Fortress Press, 1982.

———. "Antisthenes and Odysseus, and Paul at War." *HTR* 76 (1983): 143-173. Reprinted in *Paul and the Popular Philosophers*, 91-119. Minneapolis: Fortress Press, 1989.

———. *Paul and the Thessalonians*. Philadelphia: Fortress Press, 1987.

———. "Herakles." *RAC* 14 (1988): 559-83.

———. *Paul and the Popular Philosophers*. Philadelphia: Fortress Press, 1989.

———. *The Letters to the Thessalonians*. Anchor Bible 32B. New York: Doubleday, 2000.

Marastoni, Aldo. "La biografia Suetoniana di Tito e il discorso sulla regalità." In *Atti del Congresso Internazionale di Studi Flaviani, Rieti, settembre 1981*, ed. Benedetto Riposati, 2: 105-23. 2 vols. Rieti: Centro di Studi Varroniani, 1983.

Marguerat, D. "2 Corinthiens 10–13: Paul et expérience de Dieu." *ÉTR* 63 (1988): 497-519.

Marino, A. di. "L'epikeia cristiana." *Divus Thomas* 55 / 3d series, 39 (1952): 396-424.

Marshall, I. Howard. *1 and 2 Thessalonians*. NCB. Grand Rapids: Eerdmans, 1983.

Marshall, Peter. "A Metaphor of Social Shame: THRIAMBEUEIN in 2 Cor 2:14." *NovT* 25 (1983): 302-17.

———. "Invective: Paul and his Enemies in Corinth." In *Perspectives on Language and Text: Essays in Honor of Francis I. Andersen*, eds. Edgar W. Conrad and Edward G. Newing, 359-373. Winona Lake, IN: Eisenbrauns, 1987.

———. *Enmity in Corinth: Social Conventions in Paul's Relations with the Corinthians*. WUNT 2.23. Tübingen: J. C. B. Mohr (Paul Siebeck), 1987.

Martin, Dale. *Slavery as Salvation: The Metaphor of Slavery in Pauline Christianity*. New Haven, CT: Yale University Press, 1990.

Martin, Hubert, Jr. "The Concept of πραΰτης in Plutarch's Lives." *GRBS* 3 (1960): 65-73.

Martin, Ralph P. *Carmen Christi: Philippians ii.5-11 in Recent Interpretation and in the Setting of Early Christian Worship*. Rev. Grand Rapids: Eerdmans, 1983.

Martz, Louis L., and Aubrey Williams, eds. *The Author in His Work: Essays on a Problem in Criticism*. Introduction by Patricia Meyer Spacks. New Haven: Yale University Press, 1978.

Mattingly, Harold, and R. A. G. Carson, eds. *Coins of the Roman Empire in the British Museum*. London: Trustees of the British Museum, 1923–.

May, James M. *Trials of Character: The Eloquence of Ciceronian Ethos.* Chapel Hill: University of North Carolina Press, 1988.

──────. "Patron and Client, Father and Son in Cicero's *Pro Caelio*." *CJ* 90 (1995): 433-41.

McCabe, Mary Magaret. "Arguments in Context: Aristotle's Defense of Rhetoric." In *Aristotle's "Rhetoric": Philosophical Essays*, eds. David J. Furley and Alexander Nehamas, 129-65. Princeton University Press, 1994.

McCant, Jerry W. "Paul's Thorn of Rejected Apostleship." *NTS* 34 (October 1988): 550-572.

McCloskey, J. "The Weakness Gospel." *Bible Today* 28 (1990): 235-241.

Mearns, Chris. "The Identity of Paul's Opponents at Philippi." *NTS* 33 (1987): 194-204.

Meeks, Wayne. "Moses as God and King." In *Religions in Antiquity: Essays in Memory of Erwin Ramsdell Goodenough*, ed. Jacob Neusner, 354-71. Studies in the History of Religions 14. Leiden: E. J. Brill, 1968.

Meiggs, R., and D. M. Lewis. *A Selection of Greek Historical Inscriptions.* Oxford University Press, 1969.

Mendels, Doron. "'On Kingship' in the 'Temple Scroll' and the Ideological Vorlage of the Seven Banquets in the 'Letter of Aristeas to Philocrates.'" *Aegyptus* 59 (1979): 127-36.

Merritt, Benjamin Dean, ed. *Corinth 8.1: Greek Inscriptions, 1896-1927.* Cambridge: Harvard University Press (for the American School of Classical Studies at Athens), 1931.

Merritt, H. Wayne. *In Word and Deed: Moral Integrity in Paul.* Emory Studies in Early Christianity 1. New York: Lang, 1993.

Mesk, Josef. "Quellenanalyse des Plinianischen Panegyricus." *Wiener Studien* 33 (1911): 71-100.

Metzger, Bruce M. *Text of the New Testament: Its Transmission, Corruption, and Restoration.* 2d ed. Oxford University Press, 1968.

──────, ed. *A Textual Commentary on the Greek New Testament.* Corrected ed. New York: United Bible Societies, 1975.

Mikalson, Jon D. *Honor Thy Gods: Popular Religion in Greek Tragedy.* Chapel Hill: University of North Carolina Press, 1991.

Millar, Fergus. *A Study of Cassius Dio.* Oxford University Press, 1964.

──────. *The Emperor in the Roman World.* London: Duckworth, 1977.

──────. "State and Subject: The Impact of Monarchy." In *Caesar Augustus: Seven Aspects*, eds. Fergus Millar and Erich Segal, 37-60. Oxford University Press, 1984.

Misch, Georg. *A History of Autobiography in Antiquity.* 2 vols. Trans. by the author and E. W. Dickes. Cambridge, MA: Harvard University Press, 1951.

Mitchell, Margaret M. *Paul and the Rhetoric of Reconciliation: An Exegetical Investigation of the Language and Composition of 1 Corinthians.* Louisville: Westminster/John Knox Press, 1991.

──────. "Rhetorical Shorthand in Pauline Argumentation: The Functions of 'the Gospel' in the Corinthian Correspondence." In *Gospel in Paul: Studies on Corinthians, Galatians and Romans for Richard N. Longenecker*, eds. L. Ann Jervis and Peter Richardson, 63-88. JSNTSS 108. Sheffield Academic Press, 1994.

Mitchell, Stephen. "Galatia under Tiberius." *Chiron* 16 (1986): 17-33.

_____. "Imperial Building in the Eastern Provinces." *HSCP* 91 (1987): 333-65.

_____. *Anatolia: Land, Men, and Gods in Asia Minor*. 2 vols. Oxford University Press, 1993.

_____, and M. Waelkens. *Pisidian Antioch: The Site and its Monuments*. London: Duckworth with the Classical Press of Wales, 1998.

Moles, John. "The Date and Purpose of the Fourth Kingship Oration of Dio Chrysostom." *Classical Antiquity* 2 (1983): 251-78.

_____. "The Addressee of the Third Kingship Oration of Dio Chrysostom." *Prometheus* 10 (1984): 65-69.

_____. "The Kingship Orations of Dio Chrysostom." *Papers of the Leeds International Latin Seminar* 6 (1990): 297-375.

Mommsen, Th., et al., eds. *Corpus Inscriptionum Latinarum I-XVI*. Berlin, 1862ff.

Montague, Holly W. "Advocacy and Politics: The Paradox of Cicero's *Pro Ligario*." *AJP* 113 (1992): 559-74.

Mooren, Leon. "The Nature of the Hellenistic Monarchy." In *Egypt and the Hellenistic World: Proceedings of the International Colloquium, Leuven — 24-26 May 1982*, eds. E. Van 't Dack, P. Van Dessel, and W. Van Grucht, 205-40. Studia Hellenistica 27. Louvain, 1983.

Morawiecki, Leslaw. *Political Propaganda in the Coinage of the Late Roman Republic (44-43 B.C.)*. Trans. John Edwards and Dorota Paluch. Polskie towarzystwo archaeologiczne i numizmatycane. Wroclaw: Wydawnictwo, 1983.

Morray-Jones, C. R. A. "Paradise Revisited (2 Cor 12:1-12): The Jewish Mystical Background of Paul's Apostolate: Part 1: The Jewish Sources." *HTR* 86 (1993): 177-217.

_____. "Paradise Revisited (2 Cor 12:1-12): The Jewish Mystical Background of Paul's Apostolate: Part 2: Paul's Heavenly Ascent and its Significance." *HTR* 86 (1993): 265-92.

Morris, Leon. *1 and 2 Thessalonians*. Rev. TNTC. Grand Rapids: Eerdmans, 1984.

_____. *The First and Second Epistles to the Thessalonians*. Rev. NICNT. Grand Rapids: Eerdmans, 1991.

Mortureux, B. *Recherches sur le 'De Clementia' de Sénèque*. Collection Latomus 128. Brussels: Latomus, 1973.

Mossé, Claude. *La tyrannie dans la Grèce antique*. Paris: Presses Universitaires de France, 1969, ²1989.

Motto, Anna Lydia, and John R. Clark. "Seneca and Ulysses." *CB* 67 (1991): 27-32.

Moule, C. F. D. "Further Reflexions on Philippians 2:5-11." In *Apostolic History and the Gospel: Biblical and Historical Essays Presented to F. F. Bruce on His 60th Birthday*, eds. W. Ward Gasque and Ralph P. Martin, 264-76. Grand Rapids: Eerdmans, 1970.

_____. *The Origin of Christology*. Cambridge University Press, 1977.

Moulton, James Hope, and George Milligan. *The Vocabulary of the Greek Testament: Illustrated from the Papyri and Other Non-literary Sources*. Grand Rapids: Eerdmans, 1930.

Muecke, Douglas C. *The Compass of Irony*. London: Methuen & Co., 1969.

———. *Irony and the Ironic.* 2d ed. The Critical Idiom 13. London: Methuen & Co., 1982.

Müller, P. -G. "Die Fortschreibung der Christologie durch Paulus." *Bibel und Kirche* 43 (1988): 54-65.

Murnaghan, Sheila. *Disguise and Recognition in the Odyssey.* Princeton University Press, 1987.

Murphy-O'Connor, Jerome. "Pneumatikoi in 2 Corinthians." *Proceedings of the Irish Biblical Association* 11 (1988): 59-66.

———. "Another Jesus (2 Cor 11:4)." *RB* 97 (1990): 238-251.

———. "The Date of 2 Corinthians 10-13." *ABR* 39 (1991): 31-43.

Murray, Oswyn. "Philodemus on the Good King according to Homer." *JRS* 55 (1965): 161-82.

———. "Aristeas and Ptolemaic Kingship." *JTS* 18 (1967): 337-71.

———. "Hecataeus of Abdera and Pharaonic Kingship." *Journal of Egyptian Archaeology* 56 (1970): 141-71.

———. "*Peri Basileias*: Studies in the Justification of Monarchic Power in the Hellenistic World." Ph. D. diss., Oxford, 1971.

———. "The Letter of Aristeas." In *Studi Ellenistici 2*, ed. Biagio Virgilio, 15-19. Biblioteca di studi antichi 54. Pisa: Giardini, 1987.

Nagy, Gregory. *The Best of the Achaeans: Concepts of the Hero in Ancient Greek Poetry.* Baltimore, MD: Johns Hopkins University Press, 1979.

Neirynck, Frans. "Paul and the Sayings of Jesus." In *L'Apôtre Paul. Personnalité, style et conception du ministère*, ed. A. Vanhoye, 265-321. BETL 73. Leuven University Press, 1986.

Newman, Robert. "A Dialogue of Power in the Coinage of Antony and Octavian [44-30 B.C.]." *American Journal of Numismatics*, 2d series, 2 (1990): 37-63.

Neusner, Jacob, William Scott Green, and Ernest S. Fredrichs, eds., *Judaisms and Their Messiahs at the Turn of the Christian Era.* Cambridge University Press, 1987.

Neyrey, Jerome. *Paul in Other Words: A Cultural Reading of His Letters.* Louisville: Westminster/John Knox Press, 1990.

Nida, Eugene A., Johannes P. Louw, and Ronald B. Smith. *Greek-English Lexicon of the New Testament: Based on Semantic Domains.* 2 vols. New York: United Bible Societies, 1988.

Niederwimmer, Kurt. "Ecclesia sponsa Christi. Erwägungen zu 2 Kor 11,2f und Eph 5,31f." In *Veritas et communicatio. Ökumenische Theologie auf der Suche nach einem verbindlichen Zeugnis. Festschrift zum 60. Geburtstag von Ulrich Kühn*, eds. Heiko Franke et al. Göttingen: Vandenhoeck & Ruprecht, 1992.

Nightingale, Andrea Wilson. "The Folly of Praise: Plato's Critique of Encomiastic Discourse in the *Lysis* and *Symposium*." *CQ* 43 (1993): 112-30.

Norman, Austin. "Odysseus/ Ulysses: The Protean Myth." In *The Odyssey and Ancient Art*, eds. D. Buitron and B. Cohen, 201-7. Annandale-on-Hudson, NY: The Edith C. Blum Art Institute, Bard College, 1992.

Nutton, V. "The Beneficial Ideology." In *Imperialism in the Ancient World*, eds. P. D. A. Garnsey and C. R. Whittaker, 209-21. Cambridge University Press, 1978.

O'Brien, Michael J. *The Socratic Paradoxes and the Greek Mind.* Chapel Hill: University of North Carolina Press, 1967.
O'Brien, Peter T. *The Epistle to the Philippians.* NIGTC. Grand Rapids: Eerdmans, 1991.
O'Collins, Gerard G. "Power Made Perfect in Weakness: 2 Cor 12:9-10." *CBQ* 33 (1971): 528-537.
Oliver, James H. *Greek Constitutions of Early Roman Emperors from Inscriptions and Papyri.* Philadelphia: American Philosophical Society, 1989.
Olney, James. "Autos-Bios-Graphein: The Study of Autobiographical Literature." *South Atlantic Quarterly* 77 (1978): 113-23.
_____, ed. *Studies in Autobiography.* Oxford University Press, 1988.
Oostendorp, D. W. *Another Jesus: A Gospel of Jewish Christian Superiority in II Corinthians.* Kampen: Kok, 1967.

Padel, Ruth. *Whom Gods Destroy: Elements of Greek and Tragic Madness.* Princeton University Press, 1995.
Padilla, Mark. "The Heraclean Dionysus: Theatrical and Social Renewal in Aristophanes's *Frogs.*" *Arethusa* 25 (1992): 359-84.
Palagia, Olga. "Imitation of Herakles in Ruler Portraiture: A Survey, from Alexander to Maximinus Daza." *Boreas* 9 (1986): 137-51.
Parca, Maryline. *Ptocheia or Odysseus in Disguise at Troy (P. Köln VI 245).* American Studies in Papyrology 31. Atlanta: Scholars Press, 1991.
Park, David M. "Paul's σκόλοψ τῇ σαρκί: Thorn or Stake? (2 Cor XII.7)." *NovT* 22 (1980): 179-183.
Parsons, P.J., ed. *The Oxyrhynchus Papyri* 42. Graeco-Roman Memoirs 58. London: Egypt Exploration Society, 1974.
Pascal, Roy. *Design and Truth in Autobiography.* Cambridge, MA: Harvard University Press, 1960.
Patterson, Stephen J. "Paul and the Jesus Tradition: It is Time for Another Look." *HTR* 84 (1991): 23-41.
Pavlovskis, Zoja. "Aristotle, Horace, and the Ironic Man." *CP* 63 (1968): 22-41.
Pearleman, S. "Panhellenism, the Polis and Imperialism." *Historia* 15 (1976): 1-30.
Pernot, Laurent. *La rhétorique de l'éloge dans le monde gréco-romain.* 2 vols. Collection des études augustiniennes. Série antiquité 137-38. Paris: Institut d'études augustiniennes, 1993.
Pesch, R. *Paulus kämpft um sein Apostolat. Drei weitere Briefe an die Gemeinde Gottes in Korinth. Paulus — neu gesehen.* Herderbücherei 1382. Freiburg: Herder, 1987.
Peterson, Erik. *Heis theos. Epigraphische, formgeschichtliche und religionsgeschichtliche Untersuchungen.* FRLANT 24. Göttingen: Vandenhoeck & Ruprecht, 1926.
_____. "Die Einholung des Kyrios." *ZST* 7 (1929-30): 682-702.
_____. "ἀπάντησις." In *Theologisches Wörterbuch zum Neuen Testament*, eds. Gerhard Kittel and Gerhard Friedrich, 1: 380-81. 10 vols. Stuttgart: W. Kohlhammer, 1933-73. English: *TDNT*, trans. and ed. Geoffrey W. Bromiley, 6: 645-51. 10 vols. Grand Rapids: Eerdmans, 1964-76.

Pignoń, Jakub. "The Emperor Galba and the Four Virtus: A Note on Tac. Hist 1, 49, 3-4." *RhM* (1990): 370-74.

Plank, K. A. *Paul and the Irony of Affliction*. SBLSS. Atlanta: Scholars Press, 1987.

Plevnik, Joseph. "The Taking Up of the Faithful and the Resurrection of the Dead in 1 Thessalonians 4, 13-18." *CBQ* 46 (1984): 274-83.

Pogoloff, Stephen M. *Logos and Sophia: The Rhetorical Situation of 1 Corinthians*. SBLDS 134. Atlanta: Scholars Press, 1992.

Poulakos, John. *Sophistical Rhetoric in Classical Greece*. Studies in Rhetoric/Communication. Columbia, SC: University of South Carolina Press, 1995.

Poulakos, Takis. "Continuities and Discontinuities in the History of Rhetoric: A Brief History of Classical Funeral Orations." *Western Journal of Speech* 54 (1990): 172-88.

Préaux, Claire. "L'Image du roi de l'époque hellénistique." In *Images of Man in Ancient and Medieval Thought: Studia Gerardo Verbeke ab Amicis et Collegis Dicata*, eds. F. Bossier et al., 53-75. Symbolae Facultatis Litterarum et Philosophiae Lovaniensis A/1. Leuven University Press, 1976.

Préchac, François. *Sénèque. De la clémence*. Collection des Universités de France. Paris: Les Belles Lettres, 1921.

Preisker, Herbert. "ἐπιείκεια, ἐπιεικής." In *Theologisches Wörterbuch zum Neuen Testament*, ed. Gerhard Kittel and Gerhard Friedrich, 2: 585-87. 10 vols. Stuttgart: W. Kohlhammer, 1933-73. English: *Theological Dictionary of the New Testament*, trans. and ed. Geoffrey W. Bromiley, 2: 588-90. 10 vols. Grand Rapids: Eerdmans, 1964-76.

Price, Simon R. F. "Between Man and God: Sacrifice in the Roman Imperial Cult." *JRS* 70 (1980): 20-43.

_____. *Rituals and Power: The Roman Imperial Cult in Asia Minor*. Cambridge University Press, 1984.

Prill, Paul. "Cicero in Theory and Practice: The Securing of Good Will in the Exordia of Five Forensic Speeches." *Rhetorica* 2 (1986): 93-109.

Raaflaub, Kurt A., and Mark Toher, eds. *Between Republic and Empire: Interpretations of Augustus and His Principate*. Berkeley: University of California Press, 1990.

Ramage, Edwin S. "Denigration of Predecessor under Claudius, Galba and Vespasian." *Historia* 32 (1983): 204-14.

_____. *The Nature and Purpose of Augustus' 'Res Gestae.'* Historia, Einzelschriften 54. Stuttgart: Franz Steiner, 1987.

_____. "Sulla's Propaganda." *Klio* 73 (1991): 93-121.

Ramsey, Ian T. "Paradox in Religion I." *Proceedings of the Aristotelian Society*, Suppl. 33, 195-218. London: Harrison & Sons, 1959.

Rawson, Elizabeth. "Roman Rulers and the Philosophic Advisor." In *Philosophia Togata: Essays on Philosophy and Roman Society*, eds. Miriam T. Griffin and Jonathan Barnes, 233-57. Oxford University Press, 1989.

Rea, J. R., et al. *The Oxyrhynchus Papyri* 43. Graeco-Roman Memoirs 60. London: Egypt Exploration Society, 1975.

Regner, R. *"Paulus und Jesus" im 19. Jahrhundert. Beiträge zur Geschichte des Themas "Paulus und Jesus" in der neutestamentlichen Theologie.* Studien zur Theologie und Geistesgeschichte des Neunzehnten Jahrhunderts 30. Göttingen: Vandenhoeck & Ruprecht, 1977.

Resch, Alfred. *Ausercanonische Paralleltexte zu den Evangelien.* Vol. 1, *Textkritische und Quellenkritische Grundlegungen. Paralleltexte zu Matthäus und Marcus.* Texte und Untersuchungen zur Geschichte der altchristlichen Literatur 10. Leipzig: J. C. Hinrichs, 1893-94.

―――. *Der Paulinismus und die Logia Jesu in ihrem gegenseitigen Verhältnis untersucht.* Texte und Untersuchungen zur Geschichte der altchristlichen Literatur 27. Leipzig: J. C. Hinrichs, 1904.

Reynolds, Joyce M. "New Evidence for the Imperial Cult in Julio-Claudian Aphrodisias." *ZPE* 43 (1981): 317-27.

―――. *Aphrodisias and Rome.* Journal of Roman Studies Monographs 1. London: Society for the Promotion of Roman Studies, 1982.

Rich, John W. *Cassius Dio: The Augustan Settlement (Roman History 53-55.9).* Classical Texts. Warminster: Aris & Phillips, 1990.

Richard, Earl J. *First and Second Thessalonians.* Sacra Pagina 11. Collegeville, MN: Liturgical Press, 1995.

Rigaux, Béda. *Les Épitres aux Thessalonieiens.* Paris: Gabalda, 1956.

Robinson, Arthur. "Cicero's References to His Banishment." *CW* 87 (1994): 475-80.

Rodríguez Adrados, Francisco. *Historia de la fábula greco-latina.* 3 vols. Madrid: Editorial de la Universidad Complutense, [1979-1987].

―――. "Sociolingüistica y griego antiguo." *Revista española de lingüistica* 11 (1981): 311-29.

―――, ed. *La fable.* Entretiens sur l'Antiquité Classique 30. Vandoeuvres-Genève: Fondation Hardt, 1984.

Roetzel, Calvin J. "'As Dying, and Behold We Live': Death and Resurrection in Paul's Theology." *Int* 46 (1992): 5-18.

Rolland, Philippe. "La structure littéraire de la Deuxième Épître aux Corinthiens." *Biblica* 71 (1990): 73-84.

Romano, Alba Claudia. *Irony in Juvenal.* Altertumswissenschaftliche Texte und Studien 7. New York: Georg Olms, 1979.

Romilly, Jacqueline de. "Eunoia in Isocrates or the Political Importance of Creating Good Will." *JHS* 78 (1958): 92-101.

―――. "Fairness and Kindness in Thucydides." *Phoenix* 28 (1974): 95-100.

―――. *The Rise and Fall of States according to Greek Authors.* Jerome Lectures 11. Ann Arbor: University of Michigan Press, 1977.

―――. *La douceur dans la pensée grecque.* Collection d'études anciennes. Paris: Société d'édition «Les Belles Letters», 1979.

Rosen, Stanley. *The Quarrel Between Philosophy and Poetry: Studies in Ancient Thought.* New York: Routledge, 1988.

Rosenstock, Bruce. "Socrates as Revenant: A Reading of the *Menexenus*." *Phoenix* 48 (1994): 331-47.

Rothwell, Kenneth S., Jr. "Aristophanes' *Wasps* and the Sociopolitics of Aesop's Fables." *CJ* 90 (1995): 233-54.

Roueché, Charlotte. "Acclamations in the Later Roman Empire: New Evidence from Aphrodisias." *JRS* 74 (1984): 181-99.

Ruiz, Guillermo. "Ma puissance se déploie dans la faiblesse (II Cor 12, 9): une interprétation d'Irénée de Lyon." In *Recherches et tradition. Mélanges partistiques offerts à Henri Crouzel, S. J.*, ed. André Dupleix, 259-69. Théologie historique 88. Paris: Beauchesne, 1992.

Russell, D. A. *Plutarch.* London: Duckworth, 1973.

———. "Classicizing Rhetoric and Criticism: The Pseudo-Dionysian Exetasis and Mistakes in Declamation." In *Le classicisme a Rome. Aux I^{ers} siècles avant et après J.-C.*, ed. Helmut Flashar, 113-34. Entretiens sur l'antiquité classique 25. Genève: Fondation Hardt, 1979.

———. *Greek Declamation.* Cambridge University Press, 1983.

———. "Ēthos in Oratory and Rhetoric." In *Characterization and Individuality in Greek Literature*, ed. Christopher Pelling, 197-212. Oxford University Press, 1990.

Rutherford, R. B. "The Philosophy of the *Odyssey.*" *JHS* 106 (1986): 145-62.

Ryberg, Inez Scott. *Rites of the State Religion in Roman Art.* Memoirs of the American Academy in Rome 22. American Academy in Rome, 1955.

———. "Clipeus Virtutis." In *The Classical Tradition: Literary and Historical Studies in Honor of Harry Caplan*, ed. Luitpold Wallach 232-38. Ithaca, NY: Cornell University Press, 1966.

Saller, Richard. "*Patria potestas* and the Stereotype of the Roman Family." *Continuity and Change* 1 (1986): 7-22.

———. "Corporal Punishment, Authority, and Obedience in the Roman Household." In *Marriage, Divorce, and Children in Ancient Rome*, ed. Beryl Rawson. Canberra: Humanities Research Centre. Oxford: Clarendon Press, 1991.

———. *Patriarchy, Property and Death in the Roman Family.* Cambridge University Press, 1994.

Sampley, J. Paul. "Paul, His Opponents in 2 Corinthians 10–13, and the Rhetorical Handbooks." In *The Social World of Formative Christianity and Judaism: Essays in honor of Howard C. Kee*, eds. Jacob Neusner, Ernest S. Frerichs, Peder Borger, and Richard Horsley, 162-77. Philadelphia: Fortress Press, 1988.

Samuel, Alan E. *The Shifting Sands of History: Interpretations of Ptolemaic Egypt.* Publications of the Association of Ancient Historians 2. Lanham, MD: University Press of America, 1989.

———. "The Ptolemies and the Ideology of Kingship." In *Hellenistic History and Culture*, ed. Peter Green. Hellenistic Culture and Society 9. Berkeley: University of California Press, 1993.

Sanders, J. A. "Dissenting Deities and Philippians 2:1-11." *JBL* 28 (1969): 279-90.

Santirocco, Matthew. *Unity and Design in Horace's Odes.* Chapel Hill: University of North Carolina Press, 1986.

Schauer, Markus, and Stefan Merkle. "Äsop und Sokrates." In *Äsop-Roman. Motivesgeschichte und Erzählstruktur*, ed. Niklas Holzberg, 85-96. Classica Monacensia 6. Tübingen: Gunter Narr, 1992.

Schefold, K., and F. Jung. *Die Urkönige, Perseus, Bellerophon, Herakles und Theseus in der klassischen und hellenistischen Kunst.* Munich: Hirmer, 1988.

Schiefer Ferrari, Markus. *Die Sprache des Leids in den paulinischen Peristasenkatalogen.* Stuttgarter biblische Beiträge 23. Stuttgart: Katholisches Bibelwerk, 1991.

Schlatter, Adolf. *Paulus, der Bote Jesu. Eine Deutung seiner Briefe an die Korinther.* 4th ed. Stuttgart: Calwer, 1969.

Schmidt, Johanna. "Paradoxa." *RE* 18.3 (1949): 1134-37.

Schoon-Janssen, Johannes. *Umstrittene 'Apologien' in den Paulusbriefen. Studien zur rhetorischen Situation des 1. Thessalonicherbriefes, des Galaterbriefes und des Philipperbriefes.* Göttinger theologische Arbeiten 45. Göttingen: Vandenhoeck & Ruprecht, 1991.

Schreiner, Josef. "Jeremia 9,22.23 als Hintergrund des paulinischen 'Sich-Rühmens.'" In *Neues Testament und Kirche. Festschrift für Rudolf Schnackenburg,* ed. J. Gnilka, 530-542. Freiburg: Herder, 1974.

Schubart, W. "Das Königsbild des Hellenismus." *Die Antike* 13 (1937): 272-88.

———. "Das hellenistische Königsideal nach Inschriften und Papyri." *Archiv für Papyrusforschung* 12 (1937): 1-26.

Schubert, Werner. "Zur Sage von Hercules und Cacus bei Vergil [*Aen.* 8, 184-279] und Ovid [*Fast.* 1, 543-586]." *JAC* 6 (1991): 37-60.

Schürer, Emil. *The History of the Jewish People in the Age of Jesus Christ.* Rev. and ed. Geza Vermes, Fergus Millar, Martin Goodman, Matthew Black, and Pamela Vermes. 3 vols. Edinburgh: T. & T. Clark, 1973-87.

Schütrumpf, Eckart. "Some Observations on the Introduction to Aristotle's *Rhetoric.*" In *Aristotle's "Rhetoric": Philosophical Essays,* eds. David J. Furley and Alexander Nehamas, 99-116. Princeton University Press, 1994.

———. "Non-Logical Means of Persuasion in Aristotle's *Rhetoric* and Cicero's *De oratore.*" In *Peripatetic Rhetoric after Aristotle,* eds. William W. Fortenbaugh and David C. Mirhady, 95-110. Rutgers University Studies in Classical Humanities 6. New Brunswick: Transaction Publishers, 1994.

Schütz, John H. *Paul and the Anatomy of Apostolic Authority.* SNTSMS 26. Cambridge: University Press, 1975.

Schweizer, Eduard. "Slaves of the Elements and Worshipers of Angels: Gal 4:3, 9 and Col 2:8, 18, 20." *JBL* 107 (1988): 455-68.

Schrage, Wolfgang. "Leid, Kreuz und Eschaton. Die Peristasenkataloge als Merkmale paulinischer theologia crucis und Eschatologie." *Evangelische Theologie* 34 (1974): 141-175.

Scroggs, Robin. *The Last Adam.* Oxford: Blackwells, 1966.

Seeley, David. *The Noble Death: Graeco-Roman Martyrology and Paul's Concept of Salvation.* JSNTSS 28. Sheffield: JSOT Press, 1990.

Seeskin, Kenneth. "Is the *Apology* of Socrates a Parody?" *Philosophy and Literature* 6 (1982): 94-105.

Segal, Alan F. "Heavenly Ascent in Hellenistic Judaism, Early Christianity and their Environment." *ANRW* 2.23.2 (1980): 1333-1394.

———. *Paul the Convert: The Apostolate and Apostasy of Saul the Pharisee.* New Haven: Yale University Press, 1990.

Sherk, Robert K. *Roman Documents from the Greek East*. Baltimore, 1969.

———. *Rome and the Greek East to the Death of Augustus*. Translated Documents of Greece and Rome 4. Cambridge University Press, 1984.

———. *The Roman Empire: Augustus to Hadrian*. Cambridge: Cambridge University Press, 1988.

Sherwin-White, A. N. *The Letters of Pliny: A Historical and Social Commentary*. Oxford University Press, 1966.

Sherwin-White, Susan and Amélie Kuhrt. *From Samarkhand to Sardis: An New Approach to the Seleucid Empire*. Hellenistic Culture and Society 13. Berkeley: University of California Press, 1993.

Simon, Erika. *Augustus. Kunst und Leben in Rom um die Zeitenwende*. Munich: Hirmer, 1986.

Smallwood, Mary E. *Documents Illustrating the Principates of Gaius, Claudius and Nero*. Cambridge University Press, 1967.

Smart, Ninian. "Paradox in Religion II." *Proceedings of the Aristotelian Society*, Suppl. 33, 219-32. London: Harrison & Sons, 1959.

Smith, Morton. "What is Implied by the Variety of Messianic Figures?" *JBL* 78 (1959): 66-72.

Smith, R. R. R. "The Imperial Reliefs from the Sebasteion at Aphrodisias." *JRS* 77 (1987): 88-138.

Spaeth, Barbette Stanley. "The Goddess Ceres in the Ara Pacis Augustae and the Carthage Relief." *AJA* 98 (1994): 65-100.

Spencer, Aida Besançon. "The Wise Fool (and the Foolish Wise): A Study of Irony in Paul." *NovT* 23 (1981): 349-360.

Spicq, Ceslas. "Bénignité, mansuétude, douceur, clémence." *RB* 54 (1947): 321-339.

———. "Le visage sans ride de l'amour dans l'Église chrétienne." Appendix 9 in *Théologie morale du Nouveau Testament*, 2: 781-815. 2 vols. Paris: Librairie Lecoffre, 1965.

———. "ἐπιείκεια, ἐπιεικής." In *Notes de lexicographie néo-testamentaire*, 1: 263-67. Orbis biblicus et orientalis 22. 3 vols. Fribourg/Suisse: Editions universitaires, 1978-82. English: *TLNT*, trans. James D. Ernest, 2: 36-37. 3 vols. Peabody, MA: Hendrickson, 1994.

———. "Πραϋπάθεια, πραΰς, πραΰτης." In *Notes de lexicographie néo-testamentaire*, 3: 570-82. Orbis biblicus et orientalis 22. 3 vols. Fribourg/Suisse: Éditions Universitaires, 1978-82. English: *TLNT*, trans. James D. Ernest, 2: 160-71. 3 vols. Peabody, MA: Hendrickson, 1994.

Stadter, Philip A. "Paradoxical Paradigms: Lysander and Sulla." In *Plutarch and the Historical Tradition*, ed. Philip A. Stadter, 41-55. New York: Routledge, 1992.

Stanford, William B. *The Ulysses Theme: A Study in the Adaptability of a Traditional Hero*. Oxford: Basil Blackwell, 1954.

Stanton, G. N. *Jesus of Nazareth in the New Testament Preaching*. Cambridge University Press, 1974.

Stowers, Stanley K. "Paul on the Use and Abuse of Reason." In *Greeks, Romans, and Christians: Essays in Honor of Abraham J. Malherbe*, eds. David L. Balch, Everett Ferguson, and Wayne A. Meeks, 253-317. Minneapolis: Fortress Press, 1990.

Strange, James F. "2 Cor 10:13-16 Illuminated by a Recently Published Inscription." *Biblical Archaeologist* 46 (1983): 167-168.

Strasburger, Hermann. "Poseidonius on Problems of the Roman Empire." *JRS* 55 (1965): 40-53.

Strecker, Georg. "εὐαγγέλιον." *EDNT*, 2: 70-74.

_____. "Die Legitimität des paulinischen Apostolates nach 2 Korinther 10–13." *NTS* 38 (1992): 566-86. Reprinted in *Verteidigung und Begründung des apostolischen Amtes (2 Kor 10–13)*, ed. Eduard Lohse, 107-28. Biblisch-ökumenische Abteilung 11. Rome: Abtei St. Paul vor den Mauern, 1992.

Sumney, Jerry L. *Identifying Paul's Opponents: The Question of Method in 2 Corinthians*. JSNTSS 40. Sheffield: JSOT Press, 1990.

Süss, W. *Ethos. Studien zu ältern griechischen Rhetorik*. Leipzig: Teubner, 1910.

Sutherland, C. H. V. "Two 'Virtues' of Tiberius: A Numismatic Contribution to the History of His Reign." *JRS* 28 (1938): 129-40.

_____. *Coinage in Roman Imperial Policy*. London: Methuen & Co., 1951.

_____. "The Intelligibility of Roman Coin Types." *JRS* 49 (1959): 46-55.

_____. *The Emperor and the Coinage: Julio-Claudian Studies*. London: Spink and Son, 1976.

_____. "The Purpose of Roman Imperial Coin Types." *Revue numismatique*, 6th series, 25 (1983): 73-82.

_____. *Roman History and Coinage 44 BC - AD 69: Fifty Points of Relation from Julius Caesar to Vespasian*. Oxford University Press, 1987.

Sutherland, C. H. V., and R. A. G. Carson. *The Roman Imperial Coinage*. Rev. London: Spink and Son, 1984–.

Sutton, Dana F. *Ancient Comedy: The War of the Generations*. Studies in Literary Themes and Genres. New York: Twayne Publishers, 1993.

Sydenham, Edward. *The Coinage of the Roman Republic*. London: Spink & Son, 1952.

Syme, Ronald. *The Roman Revolution*. Oxford University Press, 1939.

_____. *Tacitus*. Oxford University Press, 1958.

Tatum, W. Jeffrey. "The Regal Image in Plutarch's Lives." *JHS* 116 (1996): 135-51.

Taylor, Justin. "The Ethnarch of King Aretas at Damascus: A Note on 2 Cor 11:32-33." *RB* 99 (1992): 719-28.

Taylor, N. H. "The Composition and Chronology of Second Corinthians." *JSNT* 44 (1991): 67-87.

Tcherikover, V. A. "The Ideology of the Letter of Aristeas." *HTR* 51 (1958): 59-85.

Teodorsson, Sven-Tage. "Theocritus the Sophist, Antigonus the One-eyed, and the Limits of Clemency." *Hermes* 118 (1990): 380-82.

Thacker, A. "Paul's Thorn in the Flesh." *Epworth Review* 18 (1991): 67-69.

Theissen, Gerd. *The Social Setting of Pauline Christianity: Essays on Corinth*. Ed. and trans. John H. Schütz. Philadelphia: Fortress Press, 1982.

Theobald, Michael. "'Dem Juden zuerst und auch dem Heiden.' Die paulinische Auslegung der Glaubensformel Röm 1,3f." In *Kontinuität und Einheit. Für Franz Mußner*, eds. Paul-Gerhard Müller and Werner Stenger, 376-92. Freiburg: Herder, 1981.

Thesleff, Holger. *An Introduction to the Pythagorean Writings of the Hellenistic Period.* Acta Academiae Aboensis. Humaniora 24.3. Åbo, 1961.

Thompson, Michael B. *Clothed with Christ: The Example and Teaching of Jesus in Romans 12:1–15:13.* JSNTSS 59. Sheffield Academic Press, 1991.

Tietze, Victoria. "The *Hercules Oetaeus* and the Picture of the *sapiens* in Senecan Prose." *Phoenix* 45 (1991): 39-49.

Toit, Andries B. du. "Romans 1,3-4 and the Gospel Tradition: A Reassessment of the Phrase κατὰ πνεῦμα ἁγιωσύνης." In *The Four Gospels 1992: Festschrift Frans Neirynck,* eds. F. Van Segbroeck et al., 1: 249-56. 3 vols. BETL 100. Leuven University Press/Peeters, 1992.

Toynbee, Jocelyn M. C. "Dictators and Philosophers in the First Century A.D." *G & R* 13 (1944): 43-58.

Travis, S.H. "Paul's Boasting in 2 Corinthians 10–12." In *Studia Evangelica,* ed. E. A. Livingstone, 6: 527-532. Texte und Untersuchungen 112. Berlin: Akademie-Verlag, 1973.

Trocmé, Etienne. "Le Rempart de Damas: Un faux pas de Paul?" *RHPR* 69 (1989): 475-479.

Uhlenbrock, Jaimee Pugliese, ed. *Herakles: Passage of the Hero through 1000 Years of Classical Art.* Edith C. Blum Art Institute, Bard College, March-May 1986. New Rochelle, NY: Aristide D. Caratzas, 1986.

Vasaly, Ann. "The Masks of Power: Cicero's *Pro Roscio Amerino.*" *Rhetorica* 3 (1985): 1-20.

_____. *Representations: Images of the World in Ciceronian Oratory.* Berkeley: University of California Press, 1993.

Vatai, Frank Leslie. *Intellectuals in Politics in the Greek World: From Early Times to the Hellenistic Age.* London: Croom Helm, 1984.

Vermeule, Cornelius C. *Roman Imperial Art in Greece and Asia Minor.* Cambridge: Harvard University Press, 1968.

Versnel, H. S. *Triumphus: An Inquiry into the Origin, Development and Meaning of the Roman Triumph.* Leiden: E. J. Brill, 1970.

Vlastos, Gregory. *Socrates: Ironist and Moral Philosopher.* Ithaca, NY: Cornell University Press, 1991.

Vollenweider, Samuel. "Der 'Raub' der Gottgleichheit: Ein religionsgeschichtlicher Vorschlag zu Phil 2.6(-11)." *NTS* 45 (1999): 413-33.

_____. "Die Methamorphose des Gottessohns." In *Das Urchristentum in seiner literarischen Geschichte. Festschrift für Jürgen Becker zum 65. Geburtstag,* eds. U. Mell und U. B. Müller, 107-131. Beihefte zur Zeitschrift für die neutestamentliche Wissenschaft und die Kunde der älteren Kirche 100. Berlin: de Gruyter, 1999.

Vollkommer, Rainer. *Herakles in the Art of Classical Greece.* Oxford Committee for Archaeology Monograph 25. Oxford University Committee for Archaeology, 1988.

Walbank, F. W. *The Hellenistic World.* Cambridge, MA: Harvard University Press, 1982.

_____. "Monarchies and Monarchic Ideas." In *Cambridge Ancient History*, eds. F. W. Walbank, A. E. Astin, et al., 7.1: 62-100. Cambridge University Press, 1984.

Walcot, P. "Odysseus and the Art of Lying." *Ancient Society* 8 (1977): 1-19.

Walker, Susan, and Andrew Burnett. *The Image of Augustus.* London: British Museum Publications, 1981.

Wallace-Hadrill, Andrew. "Galba's Aequitas." *Numismatic Chronicle* 141 (1981): 20-39.

_____. "The Emperor and his Virtues." *Historia* 30 (1981): 298-323.

_____. "Civilis Princeps: Between Citizen and King." *JRS* 72 (1982): 32-48.

_____. "Image and Authority in the Coinage of Augustus." *JRS* 76 (1986): 66-87.

Wallisch, E. "Name und Herkunft des römischen Triumphes." *Philologus* 99 (1954-55): 245-58.

Walter, Nikolaus. "Paulus und die urchristliche Jesustradition." *NTS* 31 (1985): 498-522.

Wanamaker, Charles A. "Philippians 2.6-11: Son of God or Adamic Christology?" *NTS* 33 (1987): 179-193.

_____. *The Epistles to the Thessalonians.* NIGTC. Grand Rapids: Eerdmans, 1990.

Wankel, Hermann, et al. *Die Inschriften von Ephesos.* 8 vols. Inschriften griechischer Städte aus Kleinasien 11.1-17.4. Bonn: Rudolf Habelt, 1979-84.

Ward, Richard F. "Pauline Voice and Presence as Strategic Communication." In *1990 Society of Biblical Literature Seminar Papers*, ed. D. Lull. Atlanta, GA: Scholars Press, 1990.

Watson, F. "2 Cor. X-XIII and Paul's Painful Letter to the Corinthians." *JTS* 35 (October 1984): 324-346.

Way, David. *The Lordship of Christ: Ernst Käsemann's Interpretation of Paul's Theology.* Oxford University Press, 1991.

Weber, Valentin. "Erklärung von 2 Kor 10,1-6." *BZ* 1 (1903): 64-78.

Webster, T. B. L. *Monuments Illustrating New Comedy.* 2d ed. Bulletin of the Institute for Classical Studies, Suppl. 24. London 1969.

Wedderburn, A. J. M. "Paul and Jesus: The Problem of Continuity." *Scottish Journal of Theology* 38 (1985): 189-203.

_____, ed. *Paul and Jesus: Collected Essays.* JSNTSS 37. Sheffield Academic Press, 1989.

Weinstock, Stefan. *Divus Julius.* Oxford University Press, 1971.

Welborn, L. L. "Georgi's Gegner: Reflections on the Occasion of Its Translation." *JR* 68 (1988): 566-74.

_____. "The Identification of 2 Corinthians 10–13 with the 'Letter of Tears.'" *NovT* 37 (1995): 138-53.

Welles, C. Bradford. *Royal Correspondence in the Hellenistic Period: A Study in Greek Epigraphy.* New Haven: Yale University Press, 1934.

Wellesley, Kenneth. *The Long Year: A.D. 69.* Boulder, CO: Westview Press, 1976.

West, Allen Brown. *Corinth 8.2: Latin Inscriptions, 1896-1926.* Cambridge: Harvard University Press (for the American School of Classical Studies at Athens), 1931.

West, Martin L. "The Ascription of Fables to Aesop in Archaic and Classical Greece." In *La Fable*, ed. Francisco Rodríguez Adrados. Entretiens sur l'antiquité classique 30. Genève: Fondation Hardt, 1984.

Wheeler, Everett L. *Stratagem and the Vocabulary of Military Trickery.* Mnemosyne, Supplementum 10. Leiden: E. J. Brill, 1988.

Whitman, Cedric H. *The Heroic Paradox.* Ithaca, NY: Cornell University Press, 1982.

Whitsett, Christopher G. "Son of God, Seed of David: Paul's Messianic Exegesis in Romans 2 [sic]:3-4." *JBL* 119/4 (2000): 661-81.

Wickert, Lothar. "Princeps." *RE* 22.2 (1954): 1998-2296.

Wiedemann, Thomas. *Greek and Roman Slavery.* London: Croom Helm, 1981.

Wilson, Stephen G. "From Jesus to Paul: The Contours and Consequences of a Debate." In *From Jesus to Paul: Studies in Honor of Francis Wright Beare*, eds. P. Richardson and J. C. Hurd, 1-21. Waterloo, ON: Wilfrid Laurier University Press, 1984.

Wirszubski, C. *Libertas as a Political Idea at Rome during the Late Republic and Early Principate.* Cambridge University Press, 1950.

Wisse, Jakob. *Ethos and Pathos: From Aristotle to Cicero.* Amsterdam: Adolf M. Hakkert, 1989.

Woods, Laurie. "Opposition to a Man and His Message: Paul's 'Thorn in the Flesh' (2 Cor 12:7)." *ABR* 39 (1991): 44-53.

Worthington, Ian. *A Historical Commentary on Dinarchus: Rhetoric and Conspiracy in Late Fourth-Century Athens.* Ann Arbor: University of Michigan Press, 1992.

Wright, N. T. "ἁρπαγμός and the Meaning of Philippians 2:5-11." *JTS* 37 (1986): 321-52.

_____. *The Climax of the Covenant: Christ and the Law in Pauline Theology.* Minneapolis: Fortress Press, 1992.

_____. "Gospel and Theology in Galatians." In *Gospel in Paul: Studies on Corinthians, Galatians, and Romans for Richard N. Longenecker*, eds. L. Ann Jervis and Peter Richardson, 222-39. JSNTSS 108. Sheffield Academic Press, 1994.

Yavetz, Zwi. *Julius Caesar and His Public Image.* Ithaca, NY: Cornell University Press, 1983.

_____. "The Res Gestae and Augustus' Public Image." In *Caesar Augustus: Seven Aspects*, eds. Fergus Millar and Erich Segal, 1-36. Oxford University Press, 1984.

Zanker, Graham. "Sophocles' *Ajax* and the Heroic Values of the *Iliad*." *CQ* 42 (1992): 20-25.

Zanker, Paul. *The Power of Images in the Age of Augustus.* Trans. Alan Shapiro. Jerome Lectures 16. Ann Arbor: University of Michigan Press, 1988.

Zeitz, H. "Der Aesoproman und seine Geschichte." *Aegyptus* 16 (1936): 225-55.

Zmijewski, Josef. "Kontextbezug und Deutung von 2 Kor 12,7a. Stilistische und strukturale Erwägungen zur Lösung eines alten Problems." *BZ* 21 (1977): 265-272.

———. *Der Stil der paulinischen "Narrenrede." Analyse der Sprachgestaltung in 2 Kor 11,1–12,10 als Beitrag zur Methodik von Stiluntersuchungen neutestamentlicher Texte*. BBB 52. Köln-Bonn: Peter Hanstein, 1978.

Index of Ancient Sources

1. Jewish Writings

A. Old Testament

Psalms
2	171
2:7	171
8:7	150, 166, 175
44:5 LXX	85
89:10 LXX	85
110:1	149, 166

Isaiah
11:10	172
45:23	148

Jeremiah
9:22-23	320

Daniel
7	162, 175

Joel
4:11 LXX	337

Zechariah
9:9	18, 188

B. Apocrypha

Add Esther
3:13b	73, 86
5:1	85
8:12i	86, 235

Wisdom of Solomon, 26
2:11	26
2:19	13, 20, 22, 29, 32, 86, 258
12:8-10	238
12:16	26

Sirach
4:8	85

2 Maccabees
9	240
9:27	85, 240
10:4	237

3 Maccabees
3:12-29	201
3:15	86
7:6	86

C. Pseudepigrapha, 162

Aristeas *Letter to Philocrates*, 99, 201
208	233

4 Ezra, 162

Joseph and Aseneth
11.225	376
15.8	73, 74

Psalms of Solomon
17	162

Pseudo-Philo
18:8-9	175

Sibylline Oracles
3.652-56	211
5	162

Similitudes of Enoch 162, 174

Testament of Moses
6	99

D. Dead Sea Scrolls, 162, 165

War Scroll 174

2. Christian Writings

A. New Testament

Matthew
2:16-18	116
5:5	17
11:29	10, 11, 13, 18, 22, 27, 29, 31, 33, 187
21:5	188
21:9	153
22:15-22	116

Mark
11:9-10	153
12:13-17	116

Luke
3:19	117
19:37	154
20:20-26	116

John
12:12-19	156
12:13	153

Acts
2:29-36	171
12:23	117
13:33-35	171
19:34	153
24:4	15, 31
25:11	116

Romans
1:3	165, 172
1:3-4	167-174, 181
2:2-16	148
2:17–3:26	305
2:4	150, 256
3:5-6	148
3:25-26	150
4:6-8	150
5–8	180
5:3-4	319
5:10-11	150
5:12-21	175-176
5:17	305
5:18	150
8:1	150
8:14-15	173
8:16-18	318
8:17	174
8:23	173
8:28-29	318
8:29-30	174
8:31-39	149
8:34	166, 174
8:35-39	152
9:4-5	305
9:5	163, 164
11:21-22	150
11:26	174
13:4	186
14:9	148, 161
14:10-12	148
14:17	161
15:3	151
15:8	163
15:7-8	164
15:7-12	165, 172
15:12	167, 172-173, 174
15:13	174

1 Corinthians
1–4	283, 378
1:30	150
4:8	159, 174
4:14-21	231
4:19	160, 174
4:21	17, 250-251, 252, 255
5:1-5	253
5:4	160
6:2-3	160, 174
6:1-8	276, 279
10:4	166
10:23	268
11:4	374
15:21-28	182
15:23-28	145-146
15:24-25	161, 175

15:25	150, 166, 174	10:12-16	273, 307
15:27	166	10:12-18	269-271
15:27-28	150	10:13	269, 304, 322
		11:1	300, 309, 315
2 Corinthians		11:2-4	276, 319, 321
1:15-17	266	11:4	319, 323
1:21	163, 164	11:5	300-301, 309, 315-316
1:23	84		
1:23-24	255	11:6	276, 296, 309, 315
2:1	252	11:7	301-302
2:3-4	84	11:7-10	302
2:4	268	11:8	301
2:5	266	11:9	275
2:5-11	279	11:11	301
2:6	84	11:12	304
2:9	84	11:13	304, 322
2:10	84	11:16	275, 309
2:17	321	11:16-18	302
3:1	266	11:17	301
3:1-2	276	11:18	302, 310
4:1	321	11:19	302
4:7	321	11:19-21	301-302
4:7-15	324	11:20	254, 271, 275, 304
4:11	321	11:21	310
5:10	321	11:21b–12:10	294
5:16	310, 319	11:22	305
6:4-5	321	11:23	310
6:10	321	11:23-29	293, 294, 304
7:9-10	84	11:27	294
7:11	84	11:29	275
7:12	84, 252, 279	11:30	310
7:15	84	11:32-33	304
8:9	151, 184	12:1	310
10–13	251-256, 326, 378	12:1-6	304
10:1	275, 295, 316, 317, 321, 324, 326	12:5	310
		12:6	310
10:1-6	254, 328, 329	12:7-10	304
10:3	322	12:9	306, 311, 316, 321, 324
10:3-6	297		
10:4-5	271	12:9-10	267, 311, 312
10:4-6	83, 326	12:10	316
10:5	311, 321, 322, 323, 324	12:11	295, 303, 306, 316
10:6	83, 84	12:12	279, 306
10:7	321	12:12-13	311
10:8	83, 253, 256, 268, 269, 275	12:13	303
		12:14-15	303
10:10	252, 267, 279, 305, 307	12:14-18	303
10:12	300, 307, 308, 322	12:16	271, 303-304
10:12-13	276	12:17-18	304

12:19	256, 276, 279, 296	*1 Timothy*	
12:20	252, 253	3:3	15, 31
12:20-21	323		
12:20–13:2	252	*2 Timothy*	
12:21	83, 252, 323	2:25	24
13:1	254		
13:2	82, 84, 252	*Titus*	
13:3-4	82, 321, 324	3:2	11, 32
13:4	267, 316		
13:9	83	*Hebrews*	
13:10	82, 83, 253, 254, 256	1:5	171
		1:6-13	171
Galatians			
1:4	150	*James*	
1:8-9	248	1:21	340
1:15-16	319	2:12	340
2:20	174	3:13-14	18
3:3	248	3:17	15, 32
3:11	248		
3:16	165	*1 Peter*	
4:5	150	2:18	31
4:16	248	3:4	17
4:17	248		
4:19	318		
5:12	248		
6:1	18, 246-250		

B. Early Christian Literature

6:1-5	247
6:12-13	248

Chrysostomus, Joannes
In epist. II ad Cor. Homil.
21   38

In Gen. Hom.
52.2   44

Philippians	
1:27-30	318
2:6-11	146-148, 161, 181, 182
2:8	324
2:9-11	163
2:10-11	153
3:5	305
3:9	305
3:10	318
3:20	182, 187
3:21	150
4:5	15, 32

1 Clement
13.1	86, 87, 89
13.2	87
30.8	86, 87
56.1	86
58.2	86
62.2	86

Epistle of Diognetus, 20
7.2	88
7.3	88
7.4	22
7.4-6	89

1 Thessalonians	
1:10	173
2:1-12	243-245
2:7	243-245
3:3-4	318
4:6	166
4:13-18	154, 181

Ignatius
Ephesians, 88

3. Greek and Latin Writings

Aelius Aristides, 282
Behr 2: 23.1-7   282
Behr 2: 34.15.17 345

Aeschines, 287
Κατὰ Τιμάρχου, 278

Aeschylus, 114

Aesop, 7
Fabulae
12   363
110   363
113   363

Proverbia, 86
37   332

Antiphon
Oratio
1   281
3.2   281

Second Tetralogy
2.1   282
2.2   282

Aphthonios *Progymnasmata*, 114

Appian, 40
Basilica
1.5   67-68, 72
1.6   103

Bellum civile, 50
3.43-44   209
4.16.123   80

Parthians
19   80, 83

Syriaca
57   122

Archytus of Tarentum Περὶ νόμου καὶ δικαιοσύνης, 99

Aristides, Aelius, 61

Aristophanes, 287
Aves
350-351   344
1541   130

Aristotle, 41-42, 54-55, 96, 192, 287, 273, 274
Ethica Nicomachea
1125b-26b   192
1137a-38a   192
1143a   192
1160b   98
1161a   98
2.7.12   289
4.7.2   289
4.7.16   286

Metaphysics
2.3.995a   358

Politica
1312a   240

Rhetorica
1.1-1.2   261
1.2.4   273
1.13.13   41
1.13.15-19 41-42
2.1-17   261
2.2.24   306
3.18.7   286, 305

Arrian, 293
Alexandri anabasis, 97
7.28.1-30.3   202
7.28.3   130

Athenaeus, 63, 98
Deipnosophistai
12.72/549d   70-71, 103

Augustus *Res gestae*, 101, 113, 210, 211, 212

Aulus Gellius
Noctes Atticae
14.4.4   193

Braund, 112, 119, 126, 127, 131, 220, 233

Burstein, 206, 207, 232

Callimachus *Hymni*
1.79-90	98
4.165ff.	124
4.165-170	98

Calpurnius Siculus *Eclogue*, 101

Cicero, 79, 101, 119, 122, 207, 289, 296
Ad Atticus, Epistulae
5.1	230
7.2.7.1	208
8.13	209
8.16.2.1	209
9.4	114
9.7.1.1	209
10.4	209, 229
10.21.4	209

Ad Brutum, Epistulae
1.15.10	199
5.5	209

Ad familiari, Epistulae
6.6.8	209

Brutus
292	286, 287

Catilinam, In
1.5	276

De lege agr.
2.32-35	135

De inventione
1.24	329
1.25	328-329
2.144	114

De officiis
1.88	137, 242
1.108	344
1.113	344
1.137	238, 280
3.97	342

De oratore, 372
2.182-184	280
2.212	281
2.270	287
2.341	95, 101

De re publica
1.12	269
6.13	269

Philippicae
2.116	235

Pro lege Manilia, 101

Pro Murena
62	193
64	197
66	194

Pro Publio Quinctio, 281, 282

Quintus fratrem, Epistulae
1.1.19-21	210
1.1.23	96
1.1.25	227
1.1.38-40	227

Tusculanarum disputationum
5.63	126

Demosthenes, 278
De corona
96-100	191-192
112	307
274	191-192
299	307

Exordia
13	276

Oratio
27.1-2	275
44.1-4	275
46.1	275
48.1-4	278
52.1	275
55.2	275

Diehls-Kranz, 275

Dinarchus
In Demosthenem
1   284

Dio Cassius *Historiae Romanae*, 63
42.27.3   138-139
48.3   24, 209
51.2   210
51.19.6-7   213
52.34.6   334
52.39.2   138
53.4.1   235
53.6.1   68-69
53.7.2   68, 210
53.37.6   212
55.12   24
55.14-21   202-3
55.17.7   232
55.19.6   240
55.20.2   231
55.21.3   238
56.35-41   97
58.5.4   242
59.16.1-7   219
69.6.3   138

Dio Chrysostom *Orationes*, 46, 76, 103, 115, 120
1.7   43
1.64-84   349
2.77   238
3.1-2   353
3.26-41   354
3.34   354
3.47   73
4   291
4.26-45   372-373
7   367
7.103   371
8   372
8.30   349
8.35   350
9   372
9.1   369
12.1-8   368
12.9   374

12.10   368
12.14   354, 368
12.14-16   355
12.16   275
12.43   358
13.10   374, 376
13.13   369
13.14-28   354
14.22   345
18.3   355
18.5-7   265
32.18   238
32.39   275
32.69   60
41.9-10   78
43.8-12   354
47.4   350
47.5   350
47.8   275
51.16.3   210
52.5-6   344
52.42.8   210
53.1.1   210
53.12   132
54.3   353
55.7-8   354
55.9   354
65.7   271
70.7-8   320
70.10   374
72   373-374
72.13   357
74.7   60
77/78   374-375
77/78.34-37 320
77/78.37-39 249

Diodorus Siculus, 97
Bibliotheca historica
1.54.2   236
13.20-32   43
19.85.3   73
27.6.2   247
31.3.3   247
32.2   202
32.4   202
33.3   204

Diogenes Laertius, 39, 46
Vitae philosophorum, 93, 94
1.69	361
4.5	96
4.12	197
6.71	349
6.72	372
6.96	372
6.103	373
6.104	372
7.123	193
10:10	228
10.24	197

Dionysius of Halicarnassus, 274
Ars Rhetorica, 102, 262

Isaeus
10-11	280
116	280

Lysias
8	273
19	273
24	274-275

Diotogenes Περὶ βασιλείας, 94, 138

Ecphantus Περὶ βασιλείας, 94

EJ
98	113

Epictetus, 295
Dissertationes
1.4.23-25	353
1.9.1	353
1.17.10-12	358
1.21.4	308
2.2.6-10	354
2.2.15	353
2.2.17	354
2.2.18	354
2.11.1	369-370
2.11.13	369
2.11.18	308, 370
2.14.22	376
2.18.20-22	353
3.5.14-18	353
3.5.18	353
3.20.9-11	88
3.22.26	353
3.23.17-32	353
3.24.64	197
4.1.167-169	353
4.4.19-23	353
4.6.23-24	370
4.8.30	308

Enchiridion
43	233

Euphorion
frg. 174	124

Euripides, 114
Cyclops, 342

Hecuba
239-241	344

Favorinus Περὶ φυγῆς, 345

Galen
De placitis Hippocratis et Platonis
5.6.35	134

Heliodorus
Aethiopica
7.6-7	345

Hermogenes Περὶ ἰδεῶν λόγου, 273-281, 285, 290
322	280
326	280
327	309
329	280
345	41, 274
345-352	273-281
347	274
352	279
365	290
372	278

Herodotus *Historiae*, 346
2.134	356
3.80	138
5.66	283

Index of Ancient Sources

Homer, 39, 40, 45
Iliad
2.24-25	132
12.267	249

Odyssey
4.244-258	344
8	346
11.620-622	350

Horace, 286
Epistulae
1.2.1-26	345
2.1.1-4	131

Ode
3.1-6	213-214
4.5	130
4.15	130

Satirae
1.3.76-142	193
2.4	305

Iamblichus *Letter to Agrippa*, 99

Isaeus
Oratio
10.1	275

Isocrates, 43, 96, 139, 191, 310
Ad Demonicum
15	309

Ad Nicoclem
34	133

Antidosis
26-27	275
122	236
278	262

De pace
69	239

Epistulae
7.8	136

Helenae encomium
7-10	371

In Callimachum, 276
29-32	241

In Lochitem, 276

Panegyricus
9	276
35	239
81	239
102	235

Phillippus
81	276
109	348
114	348
116	232

Josephus, Flavius, 76, 80, 83, 84, 92, 93
Antiquities
3.322	99
6.262-268	100
7.391	131
8.356	43
11.216	79
12.122	221
13.245	204
13.294	201
15.289-90	224
15.315	225
15.326	224
15.354	224
15.356	223, 224
15.365-69	224
15.365	225
15.375	224
15.376	224
15.381	115
16.62-64	115
16.65	225
17.307-8	224
18.116-119	117
19.246	219
19.328-34	78-79
19.332-34	238-39

19.347	117		Demonax	
20.178	238		7-11	197-98
20.199	201			
			Gallus	
Apionem, Contra			23	44
2.158-160	99			
			Herakles	
Bellum Judaicum, 221			8	345
1.238	223			
2.205	219		Imagines	
2.208	219		11	51
2.604	376			
5.126-29	221		Nigrinus	
5.367	136		4	371, 376
6.414-20	201			
6.415-18	221		Peregrini, De morte	
6.420	221		33	350

Vita Josephi
163-78   201

Julian
Εὐσεβίας τῆς βασιλίδος ἐγκώμιον
106a   71-72

Libanius
Epistulae
1150.2   73

Orationes
44.5   74

Declamationes
5.27   73

Livy
3.2.5   238
37.6.6   208
37.32.12   210
43.1.2   234

Lucian, 295
Alexander
61   52, 66-67

De parasito
10   344

Phalaris, 202
1.1-13   80-81

Rhetorum praeceptor
15   52
Somnium sive vita Luciani, 51
10   65-66

Verae historiae
2.35   365

Vitarum auctio
10   51

Lysias, 277
Oratio
3   276, 278
8   276, 281
10.1-3   276
12.2   281
12.20-22   281
12.86   281
32.1   276

MAMA
8: no. 524   73

Marcus Aurelius Antoninus
Τὰ εἰς ἑαυτόν
11.18   55

Maximus of Tyre, 367

Menander, 114, 229

Menander Rhetor
βασιλικὸς λόγος, 121

Περὶ ἐπιδεικτικῶν, 102

Musonius Rufus 60, 100, 196, 370

Oliver, 211

Ovid
Fasti
2.126-144   214

Paterculus, Velleius
2.126   101

Philo Judaeus, 85
De agricultura
47   240

De Iosepho, 99

De legatio ad Gaium
119   218
141-142   99
143-158   99
352   218

De opificio mundi
103   63, 69

De praemiis et poenis
166   43, 237
167   230

De specialibus legibus
2.90-91   228
2.93   228, 233
2.92-96   48-49
2.104   49
2.110   49, 233
4.22-24   49

De vita Mosis, 99, 122
1.158   128

Quod deterius potiori insidiari soleat
146   77

Philodemus
Περὶ τοῦ καθ' Ὅμηρον ἀγαθοῦ
βασιλέως, 94, 103, 197, 343

Περὶ παρρησίας, 249

Philostratus, Flavius
Vita Apollonii
5.27   100

Vitae sophistarum
481   138
487   60
488   345
506   371
522   372
535   265
555-556   264-265
556   265
569   266
572   265
578   271
597   371

Phoenicides
frg. 4.4-21   371

Pindar *Pythia*
1.94-98   98

Plato, 282, 287, 295
Apologia, 355
17   275

Hippias maior
283a-b   351
366a   343

Leges
6.757e   41

Phaedo
60b-c   364

Politicus
294	192

Republic, 96
10	372

Symposium
215b	364
216d-e	356
221e	365

Theaetetus
174a-175e	355

Plautus
Mostellaria, 229

Pseudolus, 363

Truculentus, 364

Pliny the Elder
Naturalis historia
7.147-50	210

Pliny the Younger, 119, 120, 228
Epistulae
3.14	229
8.22	194, 233
10.96	238
10.97	238

Panegyricus, 102, 103, 114, 133
4.7	122

Plutarch, 66, 70, 100, 203, 207, 293
Alexander
2.2-3	123
27.5-28.6	128
671b	236

Aristides
332e	236

Artaxerxes
1013a/4.4	55

Caesar
15.4	70, 72

48.4	209
54.4	79
57.3	64, 71

Cato major
20.2	230
20.3	73
339a	193
340e	139

Cato minor
66.2	199
785d	208

Cicero
19.4	79
761d	193
870b	241
871a	236

Eumenes
595f	137

Flamininus
378c	236

Gracchus, Tiberius et Gaius
824f	74
825b	74

Moralia
13d	60
14e	362
16b-c	362
36f-37a	114
52c	344-345
55e	242
59a-74e	249
60c	132-133
69c	249
70a	96
73d	76-77, 238
80b	65
90e	43, 77
91d	70
141d	351
148d	284
154b-c	362
218b	242

456a	74	Pseudo-Diogenes *Epistulae*	
458c	189	5	377
483b	43	7.1	376-377
528f	241	7.2	377
529a	242	19	377
540c-541e	277	26	377
542c-d	257	34	345, 377
542e-543a	270		
544c-d	277	Pseudo-Heraclitus *Epistulae*	
545a	136	4	371
729e	70-71	5.3	198
807b	43		
808b	233	Pseudo-Plato *Definitiones*	
824d	77	412b	43
959f	70	412d	54
1104b	74	415b	132

Pericles
39.1   63-64

Pericles and Fabius
3.1   70

Pompey
636f   208
640f   208
663a   208

Sertorius
25.4   64

Theseus
6-7   349

Polybius *Historiae*, 39
5.9-12   204
5.10.1-5   203
30.17.4   234
30.31.15   239

Pseudo-Anacharsis *Epistulae*
7   197, 228

Pseudo-Aristides
Εἰς βασιλέα   61

Pseudo-Crates *Epistulae*
16   377

Pseudo-Plutarch
De liberis educandis
13d-e   230

Regum et imperatorum apophthegmata, 98

Pseudo-Seneca *Octavia*, 101, 199
442-445   200

Quintilian *Institutio Oratoria*, 122, 277, 296, 301, 372
1.2.6-8   230
4.1.33   329
5.11.19-20 362
6.2.4   268
6.2.9-17   286, 287
9.2.47-53   286
10.1.68-70 265
11.1.19-20 275
11.1.21   289
11.1.22   277
11.1.23   270
11.1.33   354
11.1.33-34 297

Rhetorica ad Alexandrum
1420a   98
1434a   279

Rhetorica ad Herennium, 122
2.25   233
1423a   234

Sallust *Catilinae, Bellum*
9-10   198
18-19   227
51   232, 235
54   193

Scriptores historiae Augustae, 102

Seneca, 114, 211
Apocolocyntosis, 101
5.2-3   123
14   220

De clementia, 101, 115, 199
1.2.2   241
1.5.1   237
1.9-10   124
1.10.1   210
1.14.1-2   230
1.18.1   228
1.24.1   236
1.26.2   235
1.26.5   237
1.137   238

De consolatione ad Polybium
13   219

De constantia sapientis
2.1   345
18.5   372

De ira, 199
1.6.2-4   237
2.5.5   139
2.21.3   230
2.21.4-6   230
3.19.5   219

De vita beata
20.5   196

Epistulae
11.9-10   193
47   228

62.3   371
80.7   114
90.5   98, 138, 239
114.7   241

Hercules furens, 349

Hercules Oetaeus, 349

Thyestes, 101

Seneca the Elder
Controversiae, 114

Sherk
no. 36a   113

Sherk 1984
no. 40   136

Smallwood, 230, 233

Sopatros *Letter to his Brother*, 99

Sophocles, 114, 346
Ajax, 342

Philoctetes, 342

Statius *Thebaid*, 99, 101

Sthenidas Περὶ βασιλείας

Stobaeus *Anthologium*, 94, 1146
4.1.132-138   99
4.5-8   99
4.5.50   193
4.5.51-60   99
4.5.55   230
4.5.76-77   99
4.7.62   138

SVF
3.632   55

Suetonius, 104
Augustus
13-15   210
94   124

Claudius
1	124-125
2	123
14	220
35	134

Gaius
51	134

Iulius
75	208
77	136

Nero
30	123

Tacitus
Agricula
20	201

Annals
2.73	122, 201
11.12	219
12.37	219
13.11	220
13.50	220
13.52	220
14.48-49	195
16.2	115
16.17-20	366

Terence *Adelphoe*, 229
64-77	230

Theophrastus *Characteres*, 286, 287
1.3	60

Theocritus *Idyllia*, 96
17	125

Thucydides *Historiae*, 202
1.76	42
3.36-49	191
3.40	233, 236
3.44	234
3.46	234, 236
3.48	42-43
3.58	232
3.66	42, 232
4.19	42, 235

Valerius Maximus, 230
Factorum ac dictorum memorabilium
5.1.5	199
5.7.1	229

Virgil
Aeneid, 101, 213-214, 348
6.852-853	199
8	346

Georgics
1.24-42	101

Vitae Aesopi, 357-367

Xenocrates Περὶ βασιλείας, 197

Xenophon, 57, 97, 191, 202, 287, 355
Agesilaus, 96
1.22	235
7.3	251

Anabasis
1.9	96

Cyropaedia
4.44.5-8	234

Hieron, 98

Memorabilia
2.1.21-34	349
2.3.9	60
2.3.16	60

Oeconomicus
15.4	55
17	60

Symposium
2.19	364
5.6	364

Index of Greek Words

ἀγάπη 28, 152
ἀγεννής 66
ἁγιωσύνης 168-169
ἀγριότης 46-47, 49, 51, 58, 81
ἀδικία 41, 77, 81, 84, 196, 238, 276, 279, 302
ἄεθλοι 346
αἰδώς 51, 52, 66, 331
αἰκία 49
αἰσχρός 374, 377
ἀκαταλλάκτης
ἀλαζονεία/ἀλαζών 286, 320, 375
ἀλήθεια 320
ἁμαρτία 41, 64, 77, 79, 196, 235
ἀμέλεια 139
ἀναίδεια 366, 370
ἄνανδρος 80
ἀνδραγαθία 134
ἀνδρεία 43, 81, 120, 132, 134, 141, 202, 295, 373, 375
ἀνεξικακία 56, 77, 336
ἀνιστάμενος 172
ἄνοξή 150
ἀνυπεύθυνος 135
ἀοργησία 54, 192
ἀπάθεια 295, 336
ἀπάντησις 154-156
ἁπλότης 77
ἀπολογεῖσθαι 296
ἀποτομία 46, 58, 78, 82, 150, 226
ἀπραγμοσύνη 68, 338
ἀρετή 43, 51, 52, 53, 131, 191, 261, 331, 351, 375
ἁρπαγμός 147, 151
ἀρχή 55, 81, 132, 140, 149, 166, 177
ἀσθένεια 21, 29, 48, 59, 295, 310, 371
ἄσκησις 370
αὐθάδεια 58, 87, 140, 141
αὐτάρκεια 43, 370
ἀφιλότιμον 59
ἄφρων 309

βακτερία/βάκτρον 320, 374
βαρύτης 46-47, 58, 83, 140, 142, 204, 245, 271, 290
βάσανος 49
βασιλεία/βασιλεύς 43, 57, 138, 143-152, 159-160, 161, 174-177, 180-181, 188, 258, 326, 349
βία 46-47, 49, 58, 67, 77, 80, 89, 139-141, 145, 151, 228, 235, 343

γνῶθι σαυτόν 296
γνῶσις 309, 311, 319
γόης/γοητεία 66, 375
γυμνιτεύειν

δειλία 48
δεινότης 58, 278, 280
δεσπότης 47, 57
δημοτικός 80, 141, 283, 284
δημαγωγός 284
διάκονος 293, 310
διαλλαγή/διαλλάσσειν 47, 55, 57, 79, 81, 142, 191
δικαιοσύνη 43, 51, 56, 65, 131-136, 143, 150, 203, 219, 224, 227
δοκεῖν 308
δοκιμή 319, 322
δόξα 149, 308, 345, 369, 370, 373, 376, 377
δοῦλος
δύναμις 21, 47, 57, 63, 78, 82, 83, 149, 167-170, 177, 251, 252, 272, 306, 319

ἐγκράτεια 43, 132, 134, 351
εἰρήνη 80, 144, 340
εἰρωνεία/εἴρων 286, 288, 289, 356, 375 (see Irony)
ἐκδίκησις 83, 84
ἔλεος 45, 57, 340

ἐλευθερία 198, 249, 320, 358, 375, 376, 377
ἐξουσία 35, 43, 47, 57, 63, 79, 82, 83, 86, 87, 90, 140, 141, 142, 166, 177, 185, 255, 258, 259, 268, 269, 272, 275, 277, 278, 285, 291, 299, 312, 320, 325
ἐπανόρθωσις 47, 57, 77, 238
ἐπιμέλεια 81, 118, 119, 132, 224, 225
ἐπιστήμη 141
ἐπιτιμία 84, 204
ἐπιφανής 128
εὐαγγέλιον 160-161, 181
εὐδιαλλακτός 79, 142
εὐεργεσία 78, 79, 138, 196, 226
εὐεργέτης 78, 127, 130, 133
εὐκολία 56
εὐμένεια 55, 63, 77, 142
εὔνοια 47, 77, 79, 139, 141, 145, 225, 226, 261, 275, 348
εὐσέβεια 51, 65, 132, 134, 141
εὐτελής 65, 320

ἡγεμονία/ἡγεμών 47
ἡδονή
ἠθοποιία 7, 260, 265, 273, 300, 312, 328
ἦθος 7, 63, 67, 259, 260-266, 268-272, 272-285, 285-291, 299, 304, 306, 311, 317, 318, 325, 327, 328
ἡμερότης 40, 44, 49, 56, 60, 64, 81, 88, 137, 196, 196, 198
ἠπιότης 16, 18, 45, 56, 198, 224
ἡσυχία 27, 40, 57, 87

θαρρεῖν 46-47, 58, 87, 316
θεός 129, 147, 149
θεραπεύειν 58
θηριώδης 47, 49, 52, 58
θλῖψις 319
θριαμβεύειν 157-159
θύμος 46, 56, 58, 62, 63, 78, 226, 336

ἰδιώτης 275, 276, 279, 284, 296, 297, 298, 317, 341
ἵλαος 45, 57
ἱμάτιον 320, 374

καθαίρεσις 57, 80, 83, 269, 271
καλοκἀγαθία 52, 56, 144, 273, 331
καρτερία 43, 51, 65, 134

κατάβασις 346
καταλλαγή 47
κατάρτισις 83, 246, 254
κόλασις 47, 55, 57, 64, 68, 77, 81, 232, 374
κόλαξ 320, 375
κύριος 147-149, 152-154, 160, 161, 177, 181, 182-183, 197, 301, 322
κωλύειν 57

λογισμός 311, 322
λόγος 54, 82, 273, 296, 319, 344

μακροθυμία 87, 150
μαλακία 48, 59, 80
μεγαλοφροσύνη 77, 78, 203, 373
μεγαλοψυχία 56, 136, 141, 373
μετάνοια 47, 58, 83, 84, 88, 142, 150, 238
μετριότης 23, 40, 45, 51, 52, 56, 64, 80, 141, 143, 191, 204, 219, 228, 273, 278, 307, 331
μικρολογία 271
μορφή 147, 148

νήπιοι 244, 245
νικητήρ 128
νόμος 27-28, 56, 135, 136, 141, 177, 235, 366, 370
νόμος ἔμψυχος 135
νουθετεῖν 58, 197

οἰκοδομή 83, 268, 284
οἴκτιρμος 45
ὁμιλία 332
ὀνειδίζειν 197, 249
ὀργή 46, 53, 55, 59, 60, 62, 64, 77-80, 88, 139, 192, 226, 336
οὐδέν εἰμι 284, 295, 306, 316, 341
ὀχύτης 58

παιδεία 51, 57, 66, 69, 237, 331, 366, 367, 373
πάθος 59
πανουργία 304
παράλειψις 279
παράνομος 139
παρουσία 154, 155, 166, 179, 244

παρρησία 77, 197, 198, 249, 254, 320, 366, 370, 375
οἱ πεπαιδευμένοι 51, 66, 74, 298, 331, 358, 375
Περὶ βασιλείας 92-95
πήρα 320, 374
πικρῶς 64, 79, 81
πίστις 152, 337
πλεονεξία 49, 151, 152, 160, 271, 304
πνεῦμα 167-170, 246, 247, 319
πολίτευμα 187
οἱ πολλοί 274, 275, 276, 284, 285, 341, 362, 378
πόνος 132, 349, 375
προκοπή 65, 69
πρόνοια 119, 133

ῥάβδος 374
ῥήτωρ 284

σάρξ 167-169, 310, 319, 322
σκαιότης 46, 49, 58, 79, 80, 140
σκληρός 58
σκυθρωπός 198, 374
στολή 374, 376
συγγνώμη 40, 43, 45, 49, 54, 57, 61, 78, 142, 196
σύγκρισις 307, 375
σύλη 207
συμφέρειν 268, 310, 375
συναλλαγή
σύνεσις 51, 56, 65, 202
συνίστημι 309
σχῆμα 295, 297, 299, 320, 356, 373, 377
σωτήρ 127, 150
σωτηρία 48, 58, 84, 89, 151, 160, 161, 199
σωφροσύνη 43, 51, 65, 131, 132, 131, 141, 269, 270, 272, 320, 351, 375

ταπεινότης 5, 10, 12, 18, 21, 24, 27, 29, 48, 51, 59, 65, 90, 258, 259, 275, 276, 277, 284, 285, 290, 291, 294, 295, 298, 299, 301, 312, 316, 317, 320, 324, 327, 328, 337, 341, 371, 374, 375, 376, 378
ταπεινοφροσύνη 12, 14, 27, 28, 86, 87, 88
τιμή 120
τιμωρία 43, 47, 54, 57, 64, 77, 78, 144, 219, 226, 232

τόλμα 46-47, 49, 58, 66, 80, 87, 235, 276, 281
τραχέως 58
τρίβων 320, 374
τρυφή 320
τυραννίς/τύραννος 47, 57, 81, 204

ὕβρις 17, 28, 46, 49, 58, 64, 67, 71, 80, 138, 249, 269, 270, 271, 272, 332
υἱὸς θεοῦ 128, 172, 171
ὑπακοή 80, 323
ὑπερηφανία 46, 58, 78, 79, 139, 140-142, 151, 271, 272, 307
ὑπομονή 294, 295, 306, 319, 373
ὑποτάξαι αὐτῷ τὰ πάντα 150

φαιδρός 142, 198
φείδεσθαι 46, 49, 57, 64, 70, 77, 79, 81, 82, 84, 197, 219, 228
φιλάδελφος 128
φιλάνθρωπα 205-207, 224
φιλανθρωπία 23, 40, 45, 49, 50, 51, 56, 60, 61, 67, 68, 78, 81, 130-132, 136-137, 141-145, 151, 152, 191, 196, 197, 201, 202, 207, 209, 218, 226, 235, 238, 240, 284, 348, 375
φιλόνεικος 58
φιλοπάτωρ 128
φιλοπόλεμος 58
φιλοτιμία 203
φιλοφροσύνη 56
φόβος 142, 202, 219, 236
φρόνησις 63, 77, 134, 143, 261, 302, 320, 344, 373, 374
φροντίζειν 119, 132
φύσις 366, 370, 371, 374, 377

χαλεπότης 46, 49, 55, 58, 67, 78, 142, 204, 211
χάρις 23, 46, 57, 90, 137, 177, 191, 193, 199, 225, 234, 302, 319, 324
χιτών 374
χρηστότης 16-17, 23, 40, 43, 45, 49, 56, 61, 66, 76, 77, 78, 81, 131, 150, 196, 230, 242, 273

Χριστός 161-166, 181, 182

ὠμότης 46, 49, 58, 66, 80, 81, 139, 204, 219, 226

Index of Authors

Adkins, A., 270
Allison, D. C., 13
Anderson, G., 298
Anderson, W., 364
Andrews, S. B., 294
Asmis, E., 372
Auvray-Assyas, C., 348

BAGD, 38, 40-41, 54, 68
Bajoni, M.G., 222
Barrett, C. K., 35
Bauder, W., 22, 87
Bauer, W., 40-41, 65, 69
Bell, H. I., 207
Betz, H. D., 1, 6, 13, 246, 247, 260, 267, 275, 276, 280, 281-282, 295-296, 297, 298, 299, 304, 305
Beker, J. C., 178-179
Blank, D. L., 351
Bornkamm, G., 1
Bosworth, A. B., 202
Brunt, P. A., 210
Büchner, W., 288
Bultmann, R., 6
Burkert, W., 356

Cairns, D. L., 270
Caizzi, F. D., 373
Carey, C., 262, 266
Chantraine, P., 39, 53-54
Charlesworth, C. H., 162-163
Charlesworth, M. P., 214, 216
Classen, C. J., 214, 215
Collins, J. J., 162-163
Crafton, J. A., 321

D'Agostino, F., 25-30, 34, 235
Dahl, N. A., 163-164
Danker, F., 334-335, 339-340
Davies, W. D., 13
Des Essarts, E., 347-349

DiCicco, M., 7
Döring, K., 352, 353
Duchatelez, K., 30-32, 34
Dudley, 349, 370, 374

Ebner, M., 293, 294
Eisner, R., 352
Enos, R. L., 263
Eskola, T., 167
Eyben, E., 229

Farber, J. J., 192
Farquharson, 55
Fears, J. R., 216, 218, 221
Finkelberg, M., 342, 346, 351
Fischer, T., 240
Fisher, N. R. E., 270, 271
Fitzgerald, J. T., 6, 34-35, 36, 254, 293, 294, 298
Forbes, C., 267
Fortenbaugh, W. W., 262
Frankemölle, H., 33, 34
Friedrich, R., 342
Frish, H., 53
Furnish, V. P., 3, 13, 301, 317

Galinsky, G. K., 347, 348, 349-350
Garnsey, P., 229
Gaventa, B. R., 245
Georgi, D., 304
Gesche, H., 217
Giannantoni, G., 344
Giesen, H., 32-34
Gleason, M. W., 271
Goldstein, J., 240
Goulet-Cazé, M.-O., 370
Griffin, J., 342-343
Griffin, M. T., 195, 201
Grimal, P., 200, 207, 208
Guilhamet, L., 288

Hagedorn, D., 273
Hannestad, N., 217
Harnack, A. von, 10-14, 19, 20, 28, 31, 33-34, 64, 86, 87
Harrill, J. A., 283
Hauck, F., 16
Hausrath, A., 1
Hodgson, R., 293
Holland, G. S., 302
Hooker, M. D., 176

Jewett, R., 167
Judge, E. A., 310

Käsemann, E., 177-178
Kennedy, J. H., 1
King, K. C., 342-343
Koester, H., 244
Kolenkow, A. B., 294

Ladd, G. E., 184-185
Lefèvre, E., 314
Lenger, M.-T., 205-206
Levick, B. M., 217, 220
Leivestad, R., 5, 14, 19-22, 33-34, 74, 76, 82, 84, 87, 90, 185
Lichocka, B., 218
Liddell, H. G., 39-40, 41, 53
Locke, J., 9, 37
Long, A. A., 348, 353
Lonsdale, S., 346
López López, M., 350
Loraux, N., 355
Lutz, C., 60

MacMullen, R., 227, 241
Malherbe, A., 6, 197, 243, 244, 245, 247, 249, 254, 260, 297, 298, 299, 376
Marshall, P., 270, 272, 301, 303
May, J., 263, 282, 285
McCabe, M. M., 262
Metzger, B. M., 244
Mikalson, J. D., 270
Millar, F., 203
Mitchell, M. M., 251, 255
Motto, A. L., 345
Murnaghan, S., 342

Nagy, G., 342-343
Nightingale, A. W., 355
Nordheider, 39

Padel, R., 308
Padilla, M., 349
Parca, M., 344
Pavlovskis, Z., 287, 288
Perry, B. E., 356
Plank, K. A., 313
Pogoloff, S. M., 275
Préchac, F., 203
Preisker, H., 14-16, 20, 33-34, 36

Ramage, E. S., 200, 211
Resch, A., 10, 13
Rich, J. W., 210
Rodríguez Adrados, F., 360, 366
Romilly, J. de, 39, 44, 45, 61, 69, 191-192, 203, 233, 234
Rothwell, K. S., 362
Russell, D. A., 265, 266
Rutherford, R. B., 342
Ryberg, I. S., 214

Saller, R., 229, 230
Samuel, A. E., 206
Santirocco, M., 214
Schauer, M., 364, 365
Schubart, W., 206
Schubert, W., 348
Schulz, S., 16
Schütrumpf, E., 262
Seeskin, K., 282
Spencer, A. B., 300, 303
Spicq, C., 14, 16-19, 22-25, 33-34, 246
Sprute, J., 262
Stanford, W. B., 341, 346
Sutherland, C. H. V., 213, 216, 218
Sutton, D. F., 229
Syme, R., 200, 211, 240

Teodorsson, S.-T., 204
Thrall, M., 34
Tietze, V., 349
Toit, A. B. du, 171
Trench, 63, 90

Vasaly, A., 367
Vlastos, G., 288

Walcot, P., 343
Wallace-Hadrill, A., 214, 215, 216
Watson, F., 1
Way, D., 177-178
Welborn, L. L., 1, 283
West, M. L., 360

Wettstein, 62
Wheeler, E. L., 343
Wilson, Stephen G., 13
Windisch, H., 6, 63, 296, 297
Wooten, C. W., 274
Wright, N. T., 175-176

Zanker, P., 213
Zeitz, H., 366

Index of Subjects

Acclamation 125, 147, 149, 153-155, 180
Adam 161, 173, 175-176, 180, 182
Adfectus 264
Aesop 7, 291, 292, 298, 327, 356-368, 369
Agrippa 78-79, 226
Alexander the Great 95, 97, 122, 123, 130, 291, 293, 349
Antiencomiastic 259, 292, 293, 298, 299, 313, 317, 327
Antiochus IV, 204, 240
Antisophistic 6, 7, 259, 280, 281, 282, 285, 292, 296, 297, 299, 304
Antisthenes 93-94, 260, 297
Aphrodisias 111-112, 119
Aphrodite 112, 125, 129
Apocalypticism 156, 161, 166, 177-181
Apollo 110, 117, 124
Apotheosis 161, 171, 172, 182
Ares 125
Asylum 112, 120, 135
Augustus 46, 68-69, 83, 98, 99, 101, 102, 104-106, 108-113, 115, 123, 124, 125, 129, 130, 203, 207, 210, 212, 213, 215-218, 223-226, 231, 235, 236, 241, 248 (see Octavian)
Autonomy 112, 130, 140

Boasting 21, 247, 260, 265, 267, 275, 277, 279, 287, 289, 299, 300-302, 305, 307, 309-312, 315, 317, 321, 322, 325, 353, 358

Caesar 65-66, 69, 71, 73, 81, 85, 94, 101, 113, 171, 172, 199, 208-209, 210, 232, 235, 236, 240, 284
Caligula 109, 123, 124
Callimachus 288
Cameo 104-106, 123
Canonical or cardinal virtues 43, 132, 134

Charlatans, 243
Children 229
Chrysippus 94, 192
Civilitas 133
Claudius 111, 123, 125, 128, 132, 134, 200-201, 219, 220
Cleanthes 93, 94, 134
Clementia 101, 104, 105, 108, 113, 115, 137, 190, 191, 194, 195, 198, 199, 200, 203, 207, 211-218, 220-224, 227, 232, 236, 239, 242, 284
Clipeus virtutis, 211-214, 221
Coins 106-110
Comitas 133
Convention(-al) 43-44, 52, 55, 232-233, 239, 260, 291, 299, 305, 325, 341, 346, 350, 351, 353, 354, 368, 370, 373, 376, 378
Corona civica 212, 213
Countercultural 259, 293, 294, 299, 305, 308, 318, 321, 327, 341, 368, 373, 378
Cowardice 241
Cynic 6, 51, 93-94, 100, 191, 197, 198, 243, 245, 249, 259, 260, 286, 291, 292, 293, 295, 296, 297, 299, 309, 310, 314, 316, 345, 346, 349, 351, 352, 360-378

David 99, 131, 149, 162, 168-172, 175
Delphi 269, 296, 358, 360, 361, 365, 376
Demagogue 283-284
Dignitas 263
Diogenes 197, 291-292, 315, 293, 349, 351, 355, 357, 366, 368, 370, 372, 374, 377

Dionysos 125, 128, 158
Dissimulation (*dissimulatio*) 286, 289, 290, 300, 313, 317, 327, 355

Encomia 7, 95, 96, 102, 103, 114-115, 120-127, 131, 136, 192, 266, 291-299, 310, 325, 355, 357, 363, 367, 370, 373
Epicurus 94, 197, 228, 294, 372
Epicureans 197, 287, 352, 372
Ethos, see ἦθος

Father, 50, 51, 60, 76, 83, 98, 124, 128, 129, 132,133, 137, 142, 147, 152, 163, 183, 200, 229, 230, 231, 238, 243, 246, 251, 268, 272
Fides 208
Flattery 244
Fool / foolishness 54, 260, 292, 299-312, 314, 315, 317, 322, 359, 369
Fool's Speech 260, 300, 312, 314, 328, 341
Friends 128

Gloria 263
Golden shield, see *Clipeus virtutis*
Gratiarum actio 103

Herakles 7, 123, 140, 161, 181, 182, 213, 291, 292, 293, 294, 298, 320, 327, 333, 345, 346, 347, 348-351, 352, 363, 367, 368, 369, 373, 377
Herod Agrippa 115
Herod Antipas 115, 226
Herod the Great 78-79, 110, 115, 116, 117, 155, 223-225, 226, 248
Humanitas 227

Irony 5, 7, 8, 192, 218, 219, 259, 260, 280, 281, 285-291, 299-304, 306, 307, 309, 312-318, 325, 327, 328, 359, 376, 377 (see εἰρωνεία/εἴρων)
Integritas 208
Isis 232, 357
Iustitia 121, 208, 211, 213, 218, 223, 224

Jeremiah 320
John the Baptist 117
Joseph 100
Julia 115

Lamps 106
Law 40-44, 46, 48-50, 52, 56, 59, 61, 68, 71, 79, 130, 134-136, 138, 140, 141, 142, 143, 150-151, 161, 173, 179, 192, 193, 197, 204, 205, 218, 223, 224, 228, 231, 233, 238, 239, 278
Lenitas 190, 208, 229
Letter of Reconciliation 84, 252, 255, 269
Letter of Tears 1, 84, 252
Livia 105, 202, 218, 231
Luxury 139

Mansuetudo 227, 242
Messianism 163-176
Misanthropy 244
Moderatio 133, 216-217
Modesty 7, 8, 17, 18, 20, 31, 34, 51, 52, 69, 259, 260-266, 272, 274-285, 285-291, 292, 296, 299, 300, 306, 307, 309, 312, 316, 317, 321, 325
Monuments 110-112
Moses 99, 122, 128, 166, 227, 233, 254
Mytilenian Debate 42-43, 191, 234

Nero 101, 109, 111, 117, 118, 123, 124, 129, 199-200, 211, 220, 352
Nicholaus of Damascus 310

Octavian 68-69, 112, 123, 128, 135, 209-210, 212 (see Augustus)
Odysseus 7, 73, 291, 292, 293, 297, 298, 327, 341-347, 350, 351, 365, 367, 368, 369, 376, 377
Oracles 124

Paradox 7, 21, 259, 299, 312-318, 325, 328, 351, 366
Parody 299, 300, 304-306, 307, 312, 313, 328, 358
Pater patriae 131, 229
Peace (see εἰρήνη) 139, 153
Peregrinus 350
Peripatetics 196-197, 287

Index of Subjects

Philosophical rhetoric 6, 7, 292, 297, 298, 308, 314, 320-321
Pietas 105, 109, 119, 200, 211-214, 216, 221, 223
Populist, 1, 3, 7, 8, 62, 64, 69, 78, 143, 144, 145, 161, 188, 259, 284, 295, 321, 327, 338, 369
Posidonias 202, 239
Providentia 129,133, 200, 215
Psychagogy 247
Pythagoras, 70, 71, 81, 373

Ruler cult 116

Sarcasm 193, 281, 302, 303, 312, 359
Saul 99-100
Severitas 195, 229, 230, 231, 242, 255, 256
Shepherd 98, 128, 129, 133, 135
Slavery 228
Socrates, 6, 7, 73, 189, 198, 230, 233, 259, 276, 282, 285-291, 291-299, 300, 313-315, 317, 325, 346, 351-356, 357, 362-368, 368-377, 378
Socratic 6, 7, 8, 259, 260, 285, 289, 290, 291-299, 300, 306, 308, 313, 314, 317, 318, 325, 327, 328, 353, 355, 367, 368, 370, 372, 377
Solomon 100
Sophist(-ic) 80, 97, 138, 269, 271, 275, 281, 282, 283, 285, 292, 295-298, 304
Stoics, 6, 31, 41, 55, 93-94, 100, 192-197, 198, 240, 259, 260, 287, 292, 297, 298, 314, 345, 347, 349, 351, 352, 366, 369, 373, 378

Tarquinius 141-144
Taxes 141
Thucydides, 70
Tiberius, 74, 97, 99, 101, 104, 105, 109, 111, 112, 113, 115, 129, 130, 132, 133, 159, 217, 218, 219, 220, 232
Titus 102, 111, 156, 202, 221, 222, 236, 255
Topos, 27, 92-103, 103-120, 121-140, 140-145, 368
– ancestry 124-125
– athletic prowess 372, 377
– beast, wild/uncivilized 60
– birth, noble, 304, 357, 371, 372, 377, 378
– body 187
– education 125-126, 357, 360, 372, 377, 378
– eloquence, lack of, 275
– humbling the proud, 361
– hunting 97, 126, 134
– kingship 92-103, 103-120, 121-140
– litigation avoidance 275-276
– low-born 66, 357
– medical care 227, 237, 250
– modesty 272-285
– money/wealth 131-132, 371, 357, 371, 377, 378
– offices and titles 127-129
– philosophy mocked 363
– physical qualities 122-124, 357
– reins of a horse 227, 230
– rustic virtue 367
– slave, clever, 363
– slave, promiscuous, 366
– sophists and true wisdom 296
Titles 129-130
Two roads 349
Trajan 95, 103, 122, 124, 128, 133, 135, 215, 216, 238
Tullius 141-144
Tyrant 68, 69, 71, 72, 80, 81, 88, 91, 96, 97, 98, 100, 101, 114, 126, 135, 138-140, 141-145, 171

Venus 59, 125
Vespasian 59, 125, 131, 200, 218, 352
Virtus 104, 109, 126, 208, 211-212, 214, 218, 223, 345

War 137, 139
Weakness 41, 48, 59, 87, 241, 246, 247, 253, 254, 255, 256, 260, 295, 299, 302, 313, 324, 325

Zeno 94, 314, 359, 375
Zeus 110, 125, 128, 181, 182, 232, 342, 358, 361, 377

Wissenschaftliche Untersuchungen zum Neuen Testament
Alphabetical Index of the First and Second Series

Ådna, Jostein: Jesu Stellung zum Tempel. 2000. *Volume II/119.*

Ådna, Jostein and *Kvalbein, Hans* (Ed.): The Mission of the Early Church to Jews and Gentiles. 2000. *Volume 127.*

Alkier, Stefan: Wunder und Wirklichkeit in den Briefen des Apostels Paulus. 2001. *Volume 134.*

Anderson, Paul N.: The Christology of the Fourth Gospel. 1996. *Volume II/78.*

Appold, Mark L.: The Oneness Motif in the Fourth Gospel. 1976. *Volume II/1.*

Arnold, Clinton E.: The Colossian Syncretism. 1995. *Volume II/77.*

Asiedu-Peprah, Martin: Johannine Sabbath Conflicts As Juridical Controversy. 2001. *Volume II/132.*

Avemarie, Friedrich: Die Tauferzählungen der Apostelgeschichte. 2002. *Volume 139.*

Avemarie, Friedrich and *Hermann Lichtenberger* (Ed.): Auferstehung – Ressurection. 2001. *Volume 135.*

Avemarie, Friedrich and *Hermann Lichtenberger* (Ed.): Bund und Tora. 1996. *Volume 92.*

Bachmann, Michael: Sünder oder Übertreter. 1992. *Volume 59.*

Back, Frances: Verwandlung durch Offenbarung bei Paulus. 2002. *Volume II/153.*

Baker, William R.: Personal Speech-Ethics in the Epistle of James. 1995. *Volume II/68.*

Bakke, Odd Magne: 'Concord and Peace'. 2001. *Volume II/143.*

Balla, Peter: Challenges to New Testament Theology. 1997. *Volume II/95.*

Bammel, Ernst: Judaica. Volume I 1986. *Volume 37*
– Volume II 1997. *Volume 91.*

Bash, Anthony: Ambassadors for Christ. 1997. *Volume II/92.*

Bauernfeind, Otto: Kommentar und Studien zur Apostelgeschichte. 1980. *Volume 22.*

Baum, Armin Daniel: Pseudepigraphie und literarische Fälschung im frühen Christentum. 2001. *Volume II/138.*

Bayer, Hans Friedrich: Jesus' Predictions of Vindication and Resurrection. 1986. *Volume II/20.*

Becker, Michael: Wunder und Wundertäter im früh-rabbinischen Judentum. 2002. *Volume II/144.*

Bell, Richard H.: Provoked to Jealousy. 1994. *Volume II/63.*
– No One Seeks for God. 1998. *Volume 106.*

Bennema, Cornelis: The Power of Saving Wisdom. 2002. *Volume II/148.*

Bergman, Jan: see *Kieffer, René*

Bergmeier, Roland: Das Gesetz im Römerbrief und andere Studien zum Neuen Testament. 2000. *Volume 121.*

Betz, Otto: Jesus, der Messias Israels. 1987. *Volume 42.*
– Jesus, der Herr der Kirche. 1990. *Volume 52.*

Beyschlag, Karlmann: Simon Magus und die christliche Gnosis. 1974. *Volume 16.*

Bittner, Wolfgang J.: Jesu Zeichen im Johannesevangelium. 1987. *Volume II/26.*

Bjerkelund, Carl J.: Tauta Egeneto. 1987. *Volume 40.*

Blackburn, Barry Lee: Theios Anēr and the Markan Miracle Traditions. 1991. *Volume II/40.*

Bock, Darrell L.: Blasphemy and Exaltation in Judaism and the Final Examination of Jesus. 1998. *Volume II/106.*

Bockmuehl, Markus N.A.: Revelation and Mystery in Ancient Judaism and Pauline Christianity. 1990. *Volume II/36.*

Bøe, Sverre: Gog and Magog. 2001. *Volume II/135.*

Böhlig, Alexander: Gnosis und Synkretismus. Teil 1 1989. *Volume 47* – Teil 2 1989. *Volume 48.*

Böhm, Martina: Samarien und die Samaritai bei Lukas. 1999. *Volume II/111.*

Böttrich, Christfried: Weltweisheit – Menschheitsethik – Urkult. 1992. *Volume II/50.*

Bolyki, János: Jesu Tischgemeinschaften. 1997. *Volume II/96.*

Brocke, Christoph vom: Thessaloniki – Stadt des Kassander und Gemeinde des Paulus. 2001. *Volume II//125*

Büchli, Jörg: Der Poimandres – ein paganisiertes Evangelium. 1987. *Volume II/27.*

Bühner, Jan A.: Der Gesandte und sein Weg im 4. Evangelium. 1977. *Volume II/2.*

Burchard, Christoph: Untersuchungen zu Joseph und Aseneth. 1965. *Volume 8.*
– Studien zur Theologie, Sprache und Umwelt des Neuen Testaments. Ed. von D. Sänger. 1998. *Volume 107.*

Burnett, Richard: Karl Barth's Theological Exegesis. 2001. *Volume II/145.*
Byrskog, Samuel: Story as History – History as Story. 2000. *Volume 123.*
Cancik, Hubert (Ed.): Markus-Philologie. 1984. *Volume 33.*
Capes, David B.: Old Testament Yaweh Texts in Paul's Christology. 1992. *Volume II/47.*
Caragounis, Chrys C.: The Son of Man. 1986. *Volume 38.*
– see *Fridrichsen, Anton.*
Carleton Paget, James: The Epistle of Barnabas. 1994. *Volume II/64.*
Carson, D.A., O'Brien, Peter T. and *Mark Seifrid* (Ed.): Justification and Variegated Nomism: A Fresh Appraisal of Paul and Second Temple Judaism. Volume 1: The Complexities of Second Temple Judaism. *Volume II/140.*
Ciampa, Roy E.: The Presence and Function of Scripture in Galatians 1 and 2. 1998. *Volume II/102.*
Classen, Carl Joachim: Rhetorical Criticsm of the New Testament. 2000. *Volume 128.*
Crump, David: Jesus the Intercessor. 1992. *Volume II/49.*
Dahl, Nils Alstrup: Studies in Ephesians. 2000. *Volume 131.*
Deines, Roland: Jüdische Steingefäße und pharisäische Frömmigkeit. 1993. *Volume II/52.*
– Die Pharisäer. 1997. *Volume 101.*
Dettwiler, Andreas and *Jean Zumstein (Ed.):* Kreuzestheologie im Neuen Testament. 2002. *Volume 151.*
Dietzfelbinger, Christian: Der Abschied des Kommenden. 1997. *Volume 95.*
Dobbeler, Axel von: Glaube als Teilhabe. 1987. *Volume II/22.*
Du Toit, David S.: Theios Anthropos. 1997. *Volume II/91*
Dunn , James D.G. (Ed.): Jews and Christians. 1992. *Volume 66.*
– Paul and the Mosaic Law. 1996. *Volume 89.*
Dunn, James D.G., Hans Klein, Ulrich Luz and *Vasile Mihoc* (Ed.): Auslegung der Bibel in orthodoxer und westlicher Perspektive. 2000. *Volume 130.*
Ebertz, Michael N.: Das Charisma des Gekreuzigten. 1987. *Volume 45.*
Eckstein, Hans-Joachim: Der Begriff Syneidesis bei Paulus. 1983. *Volume II/10.*
– Verheißung und Gesetz. 1996. *Volume 86.*
Ego, Beate: Im Himmel wie auf Erden. 1989. *Volume II/34*
Ego, Beate and *Lange, Armin* with *Pilhofer, Peter (Ed.):* Gemeinde ohne Tempel – Community without Temple. 1999. *Volume 118.*

Eisen, Ute E.: see *Paulsen, Henning.*
Ellis, E. Earle: Prophecy and Hermeneutic in Early Christianity. 1978. *Volume 18.*
– The Old Testament in Early Christianity. 1991. *Volume 54.*
Endo, Masanobu: Creation and Christology. 2002. *Volume 149.*
Ennulat, Andreas: Die 'Minor Agreements'. 1994. *Volume II/62.*
Ensor, Peter W.: Jesus and His 'Works'. 1996. *Volume II/85.*
Eskola, Timo: Messiah and the Throne. 2001. *Volume II/142.*
– Theodicy and Predestination in Pauline Soteriology. 1998. *Volume II/100.*
Fatehi, Mehrdad: The Spirit's Relation to the Risen Lord in Paul. 2000. *Volume II/128.*
Feldmeier, Reinhard: Die Krisis des Gottessohnes. 1987. *Volume II/21.*
– Die Christen als Fremde. 1992. *Volume 64.*
Feldmeier, Reinhard and *Ulrich Heckel* (Ed.): Die Heiden. 1994. *Volume 70.*
Fletcher-Louis, Crispin H.T.: Luke-Acts: Angels, Christology and Soteriology. 1997. *Volume II/94.*
Förster, Niclas: Marcus Magus. 1999. *Volume 114.*
Forbes, Christopher Brian: Prophecy and Inspired Speech in Early Christianity and its Hellenistic Environment. 1995. *Volume II/75.*
Fornberg, Tord: see *Fridrichsen, Anton.*
Fossum, Jarl E.: The Name of God and the Angel of the Lord. 1985. *Volume 36.*
Frenschkowski, Marco: Offenbarung und Epiphanie. Volume 1 1995. *Volume II/79* – Volume 2 1997. *Volume II/80.*
Frey, Jörg: Eugen Drewermann und die biblische Exegese. 1995. *Volume II/71.*
– Die johanneische Eschatologie. Volume I. 1997. *Volume 96.* – Volume II. 1998. *Volume 110.*
– Volume III. 2000. *Volume 117.*
Freyne, Sean: Galilee and Gospel. 2000. *Volume 125.*
Fridrichsen, Anton: Exegetical Writings. Edited by C.C. Caragounis and T. Fornberg. 1994. *Volume 76.*
Garlington, Don B.: 'The Obedience of Faith'. 1991. *Volume II/38.*
– Faith, Obedience, and Perseverance. 1994. *Volume 79.*
Garnet, Paul: Salvation and Atonement in the Qumran Scrolls. 1977. *Volume II/3.*
Gese, Michael: Das Vermächtnis des Apostels. 1997. *Volume II/99.*
Gräbe, Petrus J.: The Power of God in Paul's Letters. 2000. *Volume II/123.*

Gräßer, Erich: Der Alte Bund im Neuen. 1985. *Volume 35.*
- Forschungen zur Apostelgeschichte. 2001. *Volume 137.*

Green, Joel B.: The Death of Jesus. 1988. *Volume II/33.*

Gundry Volf, Judith M.: Paul and Perseverance. 1990. *Volume II/37.*

Hafemann, Scott J.: Suffering and the Spirit. 1986. *Volume II/19.*
- Paul, Moses, and the History of Israel. 1995. *Volume 81.*

Hahn, Johannes (Ed.): Zerstörungen des Jerusalemer Tempels. 2002. *Volume 147.*

Hannah, Darrel D.: Michael and Christ. 1999. *Volume II/109.*

Hamid-Khani, Saeed: Relevation and Concealment of Christ. 2000. *Volume II/120.*

Hartman, Lars: Text-Centered New Testament Studies. Ed. von D. Hellholm. 1997. *Volume 102.*

Hartog, Paul: Polycarp and the New Testament. 2001. *Volume II/134.*

Heckel, Theo K.: Der Innere Mensch. 1993. *Volume II/53.*
- Vom Evangelium des Markus zum viergestaltigen Evangelium. 1999. *Volume 120.*

Heckel, Ulrich: Kraft in Schwachheit. 1993. *Volume II/56.*
- Der Segen im Neuen Testament. 2002. *Volume 150.*
- see *Feldmeier, Reinhard.*
- see *Hengel, Martin.*

Heiligenthal, Roman: Werke als Zeichen. 1983. *Volume II/9.*

Hellholm, D.: see *Hartman, Lars.*

Hemer, Colin J.: The Book of Acts in the Setting of Hellenistic History. 1989. *Volume 49.*

Hengel, Martin: Judentum und Hellenismus. 1969, ³1988. *Volume 10.*
- Die johanneische Frage. 1993. *Volume 67.*
- Judaica et Hellenistica. Kleine Schriften I. 1996. *Volume 90.*
- Judaica, Hellenistica et Christiana. Kleine Schriften II. 1999. *Volume 109.*
- Paulus und Jakobus. Kleine Schriften III. 2002. *Volume 141.*

Hengel, Martin and *Ulrich Heckel* (Ed.): Paulus und das antike Judentum. 1991. *Volume 58.*

Hengel, Martin and *Hermut Löhr* (Ed.): Schriftauslegung im antiken Judentum und im Urchristentum. 1994. *Volume 73.*

Hengel, Martin and *Anna Maria Schwemer:* Paulus zwischen Damaskus und Antiochien. 1998. *Volume 108.*
- Der messianische Anspruch Jesu und die Anfänge der Christologie. 2001. *Volume 138.*

Hengel, Martin and *Anna Maria Schwemer* (Ed.): Königsherrschaft Gottes und himmlischer Kult. 1991. *Volume 55.*
- Die Septuaginta. 1994. *Volume 72.*

Hengel, Martin; Siegfried Mittmann and *Anna Maria Schwemer* (Ed.): La Cité de Dieu / Die Stadt Gottes. 2000. *Volume 129.*

Herrenbrück, Fritz: Jesus und die Zöllner. 1990. *Volume II/41.*

Herzer, Jens: Paulus oder Petrus? 1998. *Volume 103.*

Hoegen-Rohls, Christina: Der nachösterliche Johannes. 1996. *Volume II/84.*

Hofius, Otfried: Katapausis. 1970. *Volume 11.*
- Der Vorhang vor dem Thron Gottes. 1972. *Volume 14.*
- Der Christushymnus Philipper 2,6-11. 1976, ²1991. *Volume 17.*
- Paulusstudien. 1989, ²1994. *Volume 51.*
- Neutestamentliche Studien. 2000. *Volume 132.*
- Paulusstudien II. 2002. *Volume 143.*

Hofius, Otfried and *Hans-Christian Kammler:* Johannesstudien. 1996. *Volume 88.*

Holtz, Traugott: Geschichte und Theologie des Urchristentums. 1991. *Volume 57.*

Hommel, Hildebrecht: Sebasmata. Volume 1 1983. *Volume 31* – Volume 2 1984. *Volume 32.*

Hvalvik, Reidar: The Struggle for Scripture and Covenant. 1996. *Volume II/82.*

Joubert, Stephan: Paul as Benefactor. 2000. *Volume II/124.*

Jungbauer, Harry: „Ehre Vater und Mutter". 2002. *Volume II/146.*

Kähler, Christoph: Jesu Gleichnisse als Poesie und Therapie. 1995. *Volume 78.*

Kamlah, Ehrhard: Die Form der katalogischen Paränese im Neuen Testament. 1964. *Volume 7.*

Kammler, Hans-Christian: Christologie und Eschatologie. 2000. *Volume 126.*
- see *Hofius, Otfried.*

Kelhoffer, James A.: Miracle and Mission. 1999. *Volume II/112.*

Kieffer, René and *Jan Bergman (Ed.):* La Main de Dieu / Die Hand Gottes. 1997. *Volume 94.*

Kim, Seyoon: The Origin of Paul's Gospel. 1981, ²1984. *Volume II/4.*
- "The 'Son of Man'" as the Son of God. 1983. *Volume 30.*

Klein, Hans: see *Dunn, James D.G..*

Kleinknecht, Karl Th.: Der leidende Gerechtfertigte. 1984, ²1988. *Volume II/13.*

Klinghardt, Matthias: Gesetz und Volk Gottes. 1988. *Volume II/32.*

Köhler, Wolf-Dietrich: Rezeption des Matthäusevangeliums in der Zeit vor Irenäus. 1987. *Volume II/24.*

Korn, Manfred: Die Geschichte Jesu in veränderter Zeit. 1993. *Volume II/51.*
Koskenniemi, Erkki: Apollonios von Tyana in der neutestamentlichen Exegese. 1994. *Volume II/61.*
Kraus, Thomas J.: Sprache, Stil und historischer Ort des zweiten Petrusbriefes. 2001. *Volume II/136.*
Kraus, Wolfgang: Das Volk Gottes. 1996. *Volume 85.*
– see *Walter, Nikolaus.*
Kreplin, Matthias: Das Selbstverständnis Jesu. 2001. *Volume II/141.*
Kuhn, Karl G.: Achtzehngebet und Vaterunser und der Reim. 1950. *Volume 1.*
Kvalbein, Hans: see *Ådna, Jostein.*
Laansma, Jon: I Will Give You Rest. 1997. *Volume II/98.*
Labahn, Michael: Offenbarung in Zeichen und Wort. 2000. *Volume II/117.*
Lange, Armin: see *Ego, Beate.*
Lampe, Peter: Die stadtrömischen Christen in den ersten beiden Jahrhunderten. 1987, ²1989. *Volume II/18.*
Landmesser, Christof: Wahrheit als Grundbegriff neutestamentlicher Wissenschaft. 1999. *Volume 113.*
– Jüngerberufung und Zuwendung zu Gott. 2000. *Volume 133.*
Lau, Andrew: Manifest in Flesh. 1996. *Volume II/86.*
Lee, Pilchan: The New Jerusalem in the Book of Relevation. 2000. *Volume II/129.*
Lichtenberger, Hermann: see *Avemarie, Friedrich.*
Lieu, Samuel N.C.: Manichaeism in the Later Roman Empire and Medieval China. ²1992. *Volume 63.*
Loader, William R.G.: Jesus' Attitude Towards the Law. 1997. *Volume II/97.*
Löhr, Gebhard: Verherrlichung Gottes durch Philosophie. 1997. *Volume 97.*
Löhr, Hermut: see *Hengel, Martin.*
Löhr, Winrich Alfried: Basilides und seine Schule. 1995. *Volume 83.*
Luomanen, Petri: Entering the Kingdom of Heaven. 1998. *Volume II/101.*
Luz, Ulrich: see *Dunn, James D.G..*
Maier, Gerhard: Mensch und freier Wille. 1971. *Volume 12.*
– Die Johannesoffenbarung und die Kirche. 1981. *Volume 25.*
Markschies, Christoph: Valentinus Gnosticus? 1992. *Volume 65.*
Marshall, Peter: Enmity in Corinth: Social Conventions in Paul's Relations with the Corinthians. 1987. *Volume II/23.*

Mayer, Annemarie: Sprache der Einheit im Epheserbrief und in der Ökumene. 2002. *Volume II/150.*
McDonough, Sean M.: YHWH at Patmos: Rev. 1:4 in its Hellenistic and Early Jewish Setting. 1999. *Volume II/107.*
McGlynn, Moyna: Divine Judgement and Divine Benevolence in the Book of Wisdom. 2001. *Volume II/139.*
Meade, David G.: Pseudonymity and Canon. 1986. *Volume 39.*
Meadors, Edward P.: Jesus the Messianic Herald of Salvation. 1995. *Volume II/72.*
Meißner, Stefan: Die Heimholung des Ketzers. 1996. *Volume II/87.*
Mell, Ulrich: Die „anderen" Winzer. 1994. *Volume 77.*
Mengel, Berthold: Studien zum Philipperbrief. 1982. *Volume II/8.*
Merkel, Helmut: Die Widersprüche zwischen den Evangelien. 1971. *Volume 13.*
Merklein, Helmut: Studien zu Jesus und Paulus. Volume 1 1987. *Volume 43.* – Volume 2 1998. *Volume 105.*
Metzler, Karin: Der griechische Begriff des Verzeihens. 1991. *Volume II/44.*
Metzner, Rainer: Die Rezeption des Matthäusevangeliums im 1. Petrusbrief. 1995. *Volume II/74.*
– Das Verständnis der Sünde im Johannesevangelium. 2000. *Volume 122.*
Mihoc, Vasile: see *Dunn, James D.G..*
Mittmann, Siegfried: see *Hengel, Martin.*
Mittmann-Richert, Ulrike: Magnifikat und Benediktus. *1996. Volume II/90.*
Mußner, Franz: Jesus von Nazareth im Umfeld Israels und der Urkirche. Ed. von M. Theobald. 1998. *Volume 111.*
Niebuhr, Karl-Wilhelm: Gesetz und Paränese. 1987. *Volume II/28.*
– Heidenapostel aus Israel. 1992. *Volume 62.*
Nielsen, Anders E.: "Until it is Fullfilled". 2000. *Volume II/126.*
Nissen, Andreas: Gott und der Nächste im antiken Judentum. 1974. *Volume 15.*
Noack, Christian: Gottesbewußtsein. 2000. *Volume II/116.*
Noormann, Rolf: Irenäus als Paulusinterpret. 1994. *Volume II/66.*
Obermann, Andreas: Die christologische Erfüllung der Schrift im Johannesevangelium. 1996. *Volume II/83.*
Okure, Teresa: The Johannine Approach to Mission. 1988. *Volume II/31.*
Oropeza, B. J.: Paul and Apostasy. 2000. *Volume II/115.*

Ostmeyer, Karl-Heinrich: Taufe und Typos. 2000. *Volume II/118.*
Paulsen, Henning: Studien zur Literatur und Geschichte des frühen Christentums. Ed. von Ute E. Eisen. 1997. *Volume 99.*
Pao, David W.: Acts and the Isaianic New Exodus. 2000. *Volume II/130.*
Park, Eung Chun: The Mission Discourse in Matthew's Interpretation. 1995. *Volume II/81.*
Park, Joseph S.: Conceptions of Afterlife in Jewish Insriptions. 2000. *Volume II/121.*
Pate, C. Marvin: The Reverse of the Curse. 2000. *Volume II/114.*
Philonenko, Marc (Ed.): Le Trône de Dieu. 1993. *Volume 69.*
Pilhofer, Peter: Presbyteron Kreitton. 1990. *Volume II/39.*
– Philippi. Volume 1 1995. *Volume 87.* – Volume 2 2000. *Volume 119.*
– Die frühen Christen und ihre Welt. 2002. *Volume 145.*
– see *Ego, Beate.*
Pöhlmann, Wolfgang: Der Verlorene Sohn und das Haus. 1993. *Volume 68.*
Pokorný, Petr and *Josef B. Souček:* Bibelauslegung als Theologie. 1997. *Volume 100.*
Pokorný, Petr (Hrsg.): Philosophical Hermeneutics and Biblical Exegesis. 2002. *Volume 153.*
Porter, Stanley E.: The Paul of Acts. 1999. *Volume 115.*
Prieur, Alexander: Die Verkündigung der Gottesherrschaft. 1996. *Volume II/89.*
Probst, Hermann: Paulus und der Brief. 1991. *Volume II/45.*
Räisänen, Heikki: Paul and the Law. 1983, [2]1987. *Volume 29.*
Rehkopf, Friedrich: Die lukanische Sonderquelle. 1959. *Volume 5.*
Rein, Matthias: Die Heilung des Blindgeborenen (Joh 9). 1995. *Volume II/73.*
Reinmuth, Eckart: Pseudo-Philo und Lukas. 1994. *Volume 74.*
Reiser, Marius: Syntax und Stil des Markusevangeliums. 1984. *Volume II/11.*
Richards, E. Randolph: The Secretary in the Letters of Paul. 1991. *Volume II/42.*
Riesner, Rainer: Jesus als Lehrer. 1981, [3]1988. *Volume II/7.*
– Die Frühzeit des Apostels Paulus. 1994. *Volume 71.*
Rissi, Mathias: Die Theologie des Hebräerbriefs. 1987. *Volume 41.*
Röhser, Günter: Metaphorik und Personifikation der Sünde. 1987. *Volume II/25.*
Rose, Christian: Die Wolke der Zeugen. 1994. *Volume II/60.*

Rüegger, Hans-Ulrich: Verstehen, was Markus erzählt. 2002. *Volume II/155.*
Rüger, Hans Peter: Die Weisheitsschrift aus der Kairoer Geniza. 1991. *Volume 53.*
Sänger, Dieter: Antikes Judentum und die Mysterien. 1980. *Volume II/5.*
– Die Verkündigung des Gekreuzigten und Israel. 1994. *Volume 75.*
– see *Burchard, Christoph*
Salzmann, Jorg Christian: Lehren und Ermahnen. 1994. *Volume II/59.*
Sandnes, Karl Olav: Paul – One of the Prophets? 1991. *Volume II/43.*
Sato, Migaku: Q und Prophetie. 1988. *Volume II/29.*
Schaper, Joachim: Eschatology in the Greek Psalter. 1995. *Volume II/76.*
Schimanowski, Gottfried: Die himmlische Liturgie in der Apokalypse des Johannes. 2002. *Volume II/154.*
– Weisheit und Messias. 1985. *Volume II/17.*
Schlichting, Günter: Ein jüdisches Leben Jesu. 1982. *Volume 24.*
Schnabel, Eckhard J.: Law and Wisdom from Ben Sira to Paul. 1985. *Volume II/16.*
Schutter, William L.: Hermeneutic and Composition in I Peter. 1989. *Volume II/30.*
Schwartz, Daniel R.: Studies in the Jewish Background of Christianity. 1992. *Volume 60.*
Schwemer, Anna Maria: see *Hengel, Martin*
Scott, James M.: Adoption as Sons of God. 1992. *Volume II/48.*
– Paul and the Nations. 1995. *Volume 84.*
Shum, Shiu-Lun: Paul's Use of Isaiah in Romans. 2002. *Volume II/156.*
Siegert, Folker: Drei hellenistisch-jüdische Predigten. Teil I 1980. *Volume 20* – Teil II 1992. *Volume 61.*
– Nag-Hammadi-Register. 1982. *Volume 26.*
– Argumentation bei Paulus. 1985. *Volume 34.*
– Philon von Alexandrien. 1988. *Volume 46.*
Simon, Marcel: Le christianisme antique et son contexte religieux I/II. 1981. *Volume 23.*
Snodgrass, Klyne: The Parable of the Wicked Tenants. 1983. *Volume 27.*
Söding, Thomas: Das Wort vom Kreuz. 1997. *Volume 93.*
– see *Thüsing, Wilhelm.*
Sommer, Urs: Die Passionsgeschichte des Markusevangeliums. 1993. *Volume II/58.*
Souček, Josef B.: see *Pokorný, Petr.*
Spangenberg, Volker: Herrlichkeit des Neuen Bundes. 1993. *Volume II/55.*
Spanje, T.E. van: Inconsistency in Paul? 1999. *Volume II/110.*

Speyer, Wolfgang: Frühes Christentum im antiken Strahlungsfeld. Volume I: 1989. *Volume 50.*
- Volume II: 1999. *Volume 116.*
Stadelmann, Helge: Ben Sira als Schriftgelehrter. 1980. *Volume II/6.*
Stenschke, Christoph W.: Luke's Portrait of Gentiles Prior to Their Coming to Faith. *Volume II/108.*
Stettler, Christian: Der Kolosserhymnus. 2000. *Volume II/131.*
Stettler, Hanna: Die Christologie der Pastoralbriefe. 1998. *Volume II/105.*
Strobel, August: Die Stunde der Wahrheit. 1980. *Volume 21.*
Stroumsa, Guy G.: Barbarian Philosophy. 1999. *Volume 112.*
Stuckenbruck, Loren T.: Angel Veneration and Christology. 1995. *Volume II/70.*
Stuhlmacher, Peter (Ed.): Das Evangelium und die Evangelien. 1983. *Volume 28.*
- Biblische Theologie und Evangelium. 2002. *Volume 146.*
Sung, Chong-Hyon: Vergebung der Sünden. 1993. *Volume II/57.*
Tajra, Harry W.: The Trial of St. Paul. 1989. *Volume II/35.*
- The Martyrdom of St.Paul. 1994. *Volume II/67.*
Theißen, Gerd: Studien zur Soziologie des Urchristentums. 1979, ³1989. *Volume 19.*
Theobald, Michael: Studien zum Römerbrief. 2001. *Volume 136.*
Theobald, Michael: see *Mußner, Franz.*
Thornton, Claus-Jürgen: Der Zeuge des Zeugen. 1991. *Volume 56.*
Thüsing, Wilhelm: Studien zur neutestamentlichen Theologie. Ed. von Thomas Söding. 1995. *Volume 82.*
Thurén, Lauri: Derhethorizing Paul. 2000. *Volume 124.*
Treloar, Geoffrey R.: Lightfoot the Historian. 1998. *Volume II/103.*
Tsuji, Manabu: Glaube zwischen Vollkommenheit und Verweltlichung. 1997. *Volume II/93*
Twelftree, Graham H.: Jesus the Exorcist. 1993. *Volume II/54.*

Urban, Christina: Das Menschenbild nach dem Johannesevangelium. 2001. *Volume II/137.*
Visotzky, Burton L.: Fathers of the World. 1995. *Volume 80.*
Vollenweider, Samuel: Horizonte neutestamentlicher Christologie. 2002. *Volume 144.*
Vos, Johan S.: Die Kunst der Argumentation bei Paulus. 2002. *Volume 149.*
Wagener, Ulrike: Die Ordnung des „Hauses Gottes". 1994. *Volume II/65.*
Walker, Donald D.: Paul's Offer of Leniency (2 Cor 10:1). 2002. *Volume II/152.*
Walter, Nikolaus: Praeparatio Evangelica. Ed. von Wolfgang Kraus und Florian Wilk. 1997. *Volume 98.*
Wander, Bernd: Gottesfürchtige und Sympathisanten. 1998. *Volume 104.*
Watts, Rikki: Isaiah's New Exodus and Mark. 1997. *Volume II/88.*
Wedderburn, A.J.M.: Baptism and Resurrection. 1987. *Volume 44.*
Wegner, Uwe: Der Hauptmann von Kafarnaum. 1985. *Volume II/14.*
Welck, Christian: Erzählte ‚Zeichen'. 1994. *Volume II/69.*
Wiarda, Timothy: Peter in the Gospels . 2000. *Volume II/127.*
Wilk, Florian: see *Walter, Nikolaus.*
Williams, Catrin H.: I am He. 2000. *Volume II/113.*
Wilson, Walter T.: Love without Pretense. 1991. *Volume II/46.*
Wisdom, Jeffrey: Blessing for the Nations and the Curse of the Law. 2001. *Volume II/133.*
Wucherpfennig, Ansgar: Heracleon Philologus. 2002. *Volume 142.*
Yeung, Maureen: Faith in Jesus and Paul. 2002. *Volume II/147.*
Zimmermann, Alfred E.: Die urchristlichen Lehrer. 1984, ²1988. *Volume II/12.*
Zimmermann, Johannes: Messianische Texte aus Qumran. 1998. *Volume II/104.*
Zimmermann, Ruben: Geschlechtermetaphorik und Geschlechterverhältnis. 2000. *Volume II/122.*
Zumstein, Jean: see *Dettwiler, Andreas*

For a complete catalogue please write to the publisher
Mohr Siebeck • P.O. Box 2030 • D–72010 Tübingen/Germany
Up-to-date information on the internet at www.mohr.de